NESTOR MAKHNO
Anarchy's Cossack

The Struggle for Free Soviets in the Ukraine 1917-1921

Publications by Alexandre Skirda

Kronstadt 1921. Prolétariat contre bolchevisme (Kronstadt 1921. Proletariat versus Bolshevism) E. De la Tête de Feuilles, 1972

Les Anarchistes dans la révolution russe (The Anarchists in the Russian Revolution), Ed. de la Tête de feuilles,1973; second edition: *Les Anarchistes Russes, les Soviets et la revolution de 1917,* Ed. de Paris, 2000. Russian edition: *Volnaya Rus',* Gromada, Paris, 2003

J.W.Makhaiski: le socialisme des intetlectuels (J.W. Machajski: the socialism of the intellectuals), Ed. du Seuil, 1979: introduction and translation of texts; second edition: Edition de Paris, 2001. Russian edition: Alexandre Skirda. *Sotsialism intellectualov,* Gromada, Paris, 2004 *Autonomie individuelle et force collective. Les anarchistes et l'organisation, de Proudhon à nos jours.* Ed AS. Paris, 1987; English edition: *Facing the Enemy,* AK Press, 2002; Russian edition *Individualnaja avtonomija i kollektivnaja sila,* Gromada, Paris, 2002:

Nestor Makhno, le cosaque de l'Anarchie. La lutte pour les Soviets libres en Ukraine 1917–1921. Ed. A.S. 1982; second edition: *Les Cosaques de la liberté. Nestor Makhno et la guerre civile en Russie,* Ed. JC Lattes, Paris, 1985; third edition: *Nestor Makhno, le cosaque libertaire.* Ed. de Paris, 1999. Russian edition: *Nestor Mahno, kazak svobody,* Gromada, Paris. 2001.

Nestor Makhno. La lutte contre l'Etat et autres écrits. Paris, 1984. introduction and translation. English edition: *The Struggle Against the State and Other Essays,* AK Press, 1996; Russian edition: *Nestor Mahno. Na tchusbinjé, zapiski i stat'i: 1923–1934.* Gromada, Paris, 2004.

All Russian editions are available at www.makhno.ru & www.novsvet.narod.ru.

NESTOR MAKHNO
Anarchy's Cossack

The Struggle for Free Soviets in the Ukraine 1917-1921

Alexandre Skirda
Translated by Paul Sharkey

PRESS
EDINBURGH · OAKLAND · WEST VIRGINIA

© 2004, Text and Photos: A. Skirda
© 2004, English Edition: AK Press
© 2004, Translation: Paul Sharkey

Nestor Makhno — Anarchy's Cossack
The Struggle for Free Soviets in the Ukraine 1917–1921

ISBN 1 902593 68 5

Library of Congress Cataloging-in-Publication Data
A catalog record for this title is available from the Library of Congress.

Library of Congress Control Number: 2003114611

British Library Cataloguing-in-Publication Data
A catalogue record for this title is available from the British Library.

The English translation of Alexandre Skirda, *Nestor Makhno — Le Cosaque de
l'Anarchie: La Lutte pour les soviets libres en Ukraine 1917–1921*. Paris, 1982,
3rd edition, 1999, and 4th edition, 2003.

Published by:

AK Press	AK Press	Kate Sharpley Library
P.O. Box 12766	674-A 23rd Street	BM Hurricane
Edinburgh, Scotland	Oakland, CA	London, England
EH8 9YE	94612	WC1 3XX

Translated from French by Paul Sharkey.
Design and layout work donated by Freddie Baer.
Typesetting assistance by Jeff Rector and Laura Quilter.

Cover illustration by Flavio Costantini, from the *Art of Anarchy,*
Cienfuegos Press, 1975. Used with permission of Cienfuegos Press.

Contents

List of Maps

Foreword
History Bites Back

The spectacular collapse of the so-called communist system of the former USSR has exposed the vacuousness of the regime's historians' official theses and highlighted the intellectual complacency of their western counterparts — with only a few rare exceptions. For decades, their slavish pens have peddled a single lane version of historical truth, celebrating the supposed "triumphant march of actually existing socialism." They find themselves all at sea now that their phony certainties have evaporated. However, their writings remain and endure and these carry the stamp of their aberrations. Verifying this is the easiest thing in the world: one need only take a semantic key to certain definitions or expressions.

Let me cite but a few examples: "bourgeois revolution" is used to designate the real Russian revolution of February 1917 which overthrew the tsarist autocracy: "Great October 1917 Socialist Revolution," or "October Revolution"[1] for short, refers to what virtually every Russian and indeed French socialist ever since then has described as the "Bolshevik coup d'état," and which radical revolutionaries indeed have described as the "Bolshevik counter-revolution": "dictatorship of the proletariat" means the dictatorship of a tiny caste of intellectuals "actually" exercised over the urban and rural proletariat: "war communism" means the 1918–1921 period and in fact the systematic pillaging of the peasantry and wholesale take-over of day-to-day life by the Party-State,[2] all of it dependent upon the most bloodthirsty terror. Let us also de-mystify the expression "soviet" which, properly rendered, simply means "council," but then we would have to explain to folk why, say, France, a country covered from top to bottom by "councils" — from municipal councils to the council of ministers — is still not wrapped in the "exotic and oh so revolutionary" whiff of "soviet"! We could go on decoding many another term or expression, but for the time being let us close with "Bolshevik," which simply means "majority," when the Russian party of that name never achieved a majority in any election in Russia, except for two obscure internal votes within the Russian Social Democratic and Labor Party at its 1903 congress, which resulted in a split. A circumstance upon which Lenin seized in order to so dub his sectarian grouplet.

This mismatch between the sign and the signified has shaped the fates of tens of millions of human beings and led ultimately to an impasse. If we are to get out of that impasse, we must return to the primary resource and re-examine everything. This is the school of thought currently in the ascendant in Russia and the Ukraine. And it is apparent in the ongoing determination to recover historical memory and fill in the many gaps from the past.

Since 1989 and especially since 1991, there has been some highly intensive publishing activity in this regard: first, we have the reprinting of all the books which had appeared in Russian in the West from surviving actors in the civil war — White Army generals (now eulogized by some!) — separatist Cossack leaders, Social Revolutionaries and even, of especial interest to us here, Nestor Makhno's *Memoirs* and Arshinov's *History of the Makhnovist Movement,* which have so far run to several editions. Indeed we are witnessing a real infatuation with the person of Nestor Makhno: over the past decade a good fifteen books on the subject have appeared, the six most recent in a little over one year. He has become a popular hero in the eyes of many, a symbol of the struggle against Red and White alike on behalf of the people's freedom and the defense of revolutionary gains. True, most of these books lack rigor and are of limited interest to anyone already conversant with the subject, but the point is that for many people he represents the only bright shining light in the dark history of the civil war of his time. Allow us, however, to highlight the *Memoirs* of Viktor Belash[3] who was chief of staff of the Makhnovist insurgent movement for over a year and succeeded Makhno at the head of the movement after the seriously wounded Nestor Makhno was evacuated to Romania. Captured by the Reds, Belash's life was spared on condition that he write his memoirs so that the Red Army's strategists could finally grasp why the partisan movement in question could have held out for so long and so successfully against all its enemies. He was then released, only to be caught up in the Stalinist repression in 1937 and shot. His son rediscovered the manuscript in the archives of the Ukraine, carried out protracted, complementary personal research between 1966 and 1990 and had it published in Kiev in 1992 before his unfortunate death the following year. The whole thing represents an outstanding primary source, happily complementing Nestor Makhno's own *Memoirs* and the Arshinov book. It is essential to a fuller understanding of the organizational and military operation of the movement: it teems with telling information and undeniably illuminates the crucial part that Makhnovist insurgents played in defeating the Whites. We shall rehearse its main contributions in the bibliographical afterword to this present volume.

Let us quote one extract that perfectly illustrates what we have been saying: it is a reproduction of the uncanny address that Nestor Makhno gave at the meeting at which he bade the movement farewell on July 17, 1921 before leaving for Romania:

"The communism to which we aspire assumes that there is individual freedom, equality, self-management, initiative, creativity and plenty. We have spelled out our thoughts in our 'Declarations.' We have had the chance and we have striven to build a society on the libertarian principles of non-violence, but the Bolsheviks have not allowed us to proceed with this. They have turned the clash of ideas into a struggle against men. Not only has the entire State apparatus, despised by the people, with its functionaries and its prisons and so on, not been liquidated, but it has simply been re-cast. The Bolsheviks have proclaimed might as their only right.

The foundations of the society that the Bolshevik-Communists have laid, after eliminating all other parties and rivals, have nothing to do with communism. They amount to a closed, semi-military sect of 'soldiers of Marx,' blindly disciplined and with pretensions to infallibility, rejecting any quibbles and in hot pursuit of the goal of a totalitarian State which grants neither freedoms nor rights to its citizens and which peddles a novel brand of ideological racism. It breaks the people up into 'their own' and 'the rest.' In many respects, it is an absurdity. They deprive the toilers of all their dreams of a better life and they are building the most wretched, most unfair police society from which the joys of labor, creativity and the spirit of enterprise are to be banished.

Their experiments will be pointless and they will co-opt folk of the same outlook, authority will be extended through the conjuring up of unanswerable demagogues and dictators. They will rule and, by means of prisons and coercion, they will compel the toilers to work themselves to death for a glass of buttermilk … They will tear everything down and eliminate all who are not to the Party's taste or ideologically in tune with it … They will devise an astronomical schedule of punishments … People's sole preoccupation will be with survival in such frighteningly oppressive conditions. But it cannot continue forever. The strengthening of authority will inevitably lead to a complete psychological and ideological breakdown between those in charge and the toilers. Comrades! Be vigilant and do not cast aside your weapons for they will soon serve you again! Do not trust the Bolsheviks! We part with the feeling that we have done our revolutionary duty. Long live solidarity and unity of the toilers! Long live the third social revolution! My thanks to all of you for everything!"[4]

The account of this speech notes that right after it "bugles sounded assembly and the farewells were very dramatic, with some shedding of tears, no one knowing whether they would ever see one another again." Allow us to remark here that

Nestor Makhno and the insurgents knew the real import of words, that being what they were fighting and dying for. The Bolshevik leaders also knew that but could not tolerate their existence. Viktor Belash cites the case of the Makhnovist expeditionary force which, having just played a crucial part in defeating Wrangel's Whites in the Crimea in November 1920, was treacherously attacked by the Reds: the 700 survivors, short of ammunition and forced into surrender, were promptly mown down with machine-guns!

Not that Makhnovists could have expected anything better of the Whites. We might quote the recently published (in Paris) memoirs of a young officer cadet from the Volunteer Army, who was assigned to the artillery. The author, Serge Mamontov, reveals an utter ignorance of Makhno who "called himself an anarchist but was only an out-and-out highwayman. He lived the high life, drank heavily and for that very reason was popular with the peasants who were all for him and took a hand in the fighting."[5] At the beginning of 1919, Mamontov's unit tackled a Makhnovist detachment in the environs of Gulyai-Polye, catching it and mowing it down. His comment is as follows:

> "The wounded were finished off and prisoners shot. In a civil war there are rarely prisoners on either side. At first sight this seems awfully cruel [...] What were we to do with prisoners? We had neither prisons nor the wherewithal for their maintenance. Set them free? But they would take up arms again! Shooting them was the simplest policy."

Permit me to highlight the lack of humanity in the application of such a rationale to people who, when all is said and done, were merely defending themselves against conquerors and trying to protect their possessions and their families from exactions. That thought does not even cross the mind of the thuggish Mamontov.

By contrast let us look at the different rationale of the Makhnovists who did discriminate between enemy prisoners: officer personnel were shot but ordinary troops were set free once the beliefs of the insurgents had been explained to them. Austro-German soldiers were even dispatched homewards with provisions for the journey!

In fact the plight of the Makhnovist movement, shared by all who fought for their freedom or independence — be they peasants, Cossacks or national minorities — was that it was caught between two seemingly opposing forces which in point of fact were kin to each other in terms of their messianic imperialism: the Reds' Party-State and the Whites' Greater Russia, One and Indivisible. Moscow as the Red Mecca or as the Third Rome! Choice of side was determined by the supply of arms and munitions. Just add the disconnected, uncoordinated nature of their actions and there we have the explanation of their lack of success. This has been brilliantly demonstrated in his posthumously published book, *The Tragedy of Peasant Uprisings in Russia, 1918–1921*[6] by Mikhail Fremkin, a soviet historian who later emigrated to Israel. The age old yearning for "Land and Liberty" foundered upon the hegemony of the city-State. Sooner or later, though, Nature has the final word and sets the whole thing in motion again: a community of free human beings is still the order of the day.

— Alexandre Skirda
Paris, April 1999.

Notes to Foreword: History Bites Back

1. See, for instance, the academic *Dictionnaire de culture générale des noms propres* (Le Petit Robert, 1993) pp.1517–1518 and the decidedly worse history textbooks in use in schools.
2. Remember here that folk were freezing from the cold and starving to death in Petrograd at this time when they were forbidden to lay a hand on wood from the forests and to fish from the banks of the Neva river, on pain of being shot for trespass against State assets! See Marcel Body's testimony in *Un piano en bouleau de Carélie* (Paris 1981).
3. A.V. and V.F. Belash, (in Russian) *Nestor Makhno's Footsteps* (Kiev 1992), p. 592.
4. Op. cit. p. 570
5. Serge Mamontov, (in Russian) *Campaigns and Horses,* (Paris 1981) translated into French as *Carnets de route d'un artilleur à cheval 1917–1920* (Paris, L'Harmattan, 1998), p. 141.
6. Published (in Russian) by his widow Emma Fremkin in Jerusalem 1987, 251 pages.

1. From the Legend to the History

To anyone with any interest in the Russian Revolution, Nestor Ivanovitch Makhno, Ukrainian anarchist associated with an attempted social revolution, is a familiar figure. The experiment in which he was an active participant took place during the crucial years from 1917 to 1921 and involved millions of the inhabitants of the southern Ukraine. Moreover, Makhno and his companions were obliged to mount an armed defense of their social gains: thus it is primarily as the architects of a vast insurgent movement that they have been known thus far, especially as their fight was critical to the fate of the Russian revolution and, by extension, for the course of the century.

Having played a decisive part in that movement, Makhno has to this very day been variously perceived: to some — his adversaries — he is a sort of bogey-man, a high-born brigand whose banner of Anarchy ill disguised the simple lust for pillage and systematic destruction of the State — in any format — and of its representatives; to others — his fans — he was an exceptional libertarian militant who sought to implement the teachings of Bakunin and Kropotkin, the Russian theorists and founding fathers of libertarian communism.

※

By way of affording a glimpse of these different approaches, let us review some of the adjectives, epithets and labels employed about him: Denikin, the commander-in-chief of the White Army saw in him "… a sainted leader of an-archism, a daring and highly popular brigand, a gifted partisan [. . .] all decked out in theoretical anarchism"[1]; certain Ukrainian nationalists looked upon him as "Cossack *ataman* [leader]," a "Ukrainian Napoleon," a "national hero"[2]; Anatole de Monzie, a French political writer has him as a "gentleman anarchist."[3] While some of his Bolshevik adversaries label him "bandit president," the "uncrownable king of the partisans"[4]; as for Victor Serge, he portrays him as a "boozer, uneducated, idealistic, a born strategist quite without peer"[5]; in the estimation of the writer and historian Daniel Guérin what one has here is an "anarchist guerrillero" and a "Robin Hood."[6] Some anarchist admirers present him as a "second Bakunin."[7] Finally, the libertarian propagandist Sébastien Faure praises his "… sturdy, loyal, modest, dauntless, incorruptible figure."[8] Let us add, for good measure, to these evaluations selected hither and thither, that Makhno's brothers in arms, by way of paying tribute to his physical panache and firmness of mind yoked to his name the Cossack title *Batko*[9] and also dubbed him the "first among equals." Not because he was a little more equal than the rest, as some might sneer, but in the sense of "team leader," in that he was always to be found in the front rank of the charges of his famous horse-soldiery and that he was also in the forefront in dissemination of the ideas of libertarian communism. The legend of his military invincibility derives from the fact that, literally death-defying, he survived more than 200 attacks and engagements although gravely wounded on several occasions. Complementary to this diversity of appreciations, let us note that Soviet historians, like their leaders of the day, often talk of the "kingdom" or "republic" of "Makhnovia," when referring to the region that came under the direct influence of the Makhnovist movement. That territory covered the provinces of Ekaterinoslav and the Northern Tavrida as well as the eastern part of the province of Kherson and the southern portions of those of Poltava and Kharkov — which is to say a rectangle measuring 300 kilometers by 250 — and inhabited at the time by about seven-and-a-half-million people.

This mass movement has been dubbed the "Makhnovschina" from the name of its initiator and the suffix appended to that name can be half-pejorative in Russian. Let us point out finally that — acme of a personality cult in reverse! — Makhno's little home town, the movement's capital as it were, Gulyai-Polye, has often been dubbed "Makhnograd" by his Bolshevik enemies![10]

In the biographical entry given for him in the latest edition of the *Great Soviet Encyclopedia*, encapsulating the regime's last word on history, we may read the following.

"Makhno, Nestor Ivanovitch, one of the leaders of the petit-bourgeois counter-revolution in the Ukraine in 1918–1921, during the civil war. Born into a peasant family, he was educated at the parish school. During the 1905–1907 revolution, he joined an anarchist group, participating in acts of terrorism and 'expropriations.' In 1909 for the murder of a police superintendent, he was sentenced to death, this being commuted on account of his tender years to ten years' penal servitude. While serving his sentence in the Butyrki prison in Moscow, he completed his grounding in anarchist theory. Freed by the revolution in February 1917, he set off for Gulyai-Polye and founded an anarchist detachment in April 1918. This detachment embarked upon a partisan war against the Austro-German occupiers and the power of the hetman Skoropadsky. In this way he earned great popularity among the peasants. Makhno distinguished himself by his bravery and his savagery. In 1919–1920, he waged war on the White Guards and the Petliurists[11] as well as on the Red Army. Three times he allied himself with the Soviet authorities and three times he broke off this alliance by rebelling. In 1921 Makhno's detachments turned once and for all into gangs of looters and criminals. On August

26, 1921, he fled into Romania: he crossed into Poland in 1922 and wound up in France in 1923 where he worked as a shoe mender and printworker."[12]

Contrary to the usual hotchpotch served up by modern Soviet historiography — as we shall have occasion to appreciate — which consists of blending lie and truth, with the accent solidly on the former, this summary, aside from a few inexactitudes — which we shall set straight anon — and the customary abuse — "petit-bourgeois," "looters," "criminals" — appears essentially correct. In the same work, the entry under "Makhnovschina" rounds off the official version: it is stated there that the movement's social base comprised of the well-to-do peasantry, or "kulaks,"[13] that it was not merely a local movement, for it stretched from the Dniepr to the Don, that it was made up of volunteers, that its armaments were exclusively seized from the enemy and finally that its ideology was encapsulated in the watchwords "libertarian State" (sic!) and "free Soviets," which, according to the authors, boiled down to fighting against the proletarian State.

It is very interesting to compare that evaluation with the one contained in the lengthy obituary notice carried in the columns of the (generally well informed) newspaper *Le Temps* — the forerunner of *Le Monde* — under the byline of its Moscow correspondent, Pierre Berland:

> "*Le Temps* has registered the premature death of the famed Makhno, who died in Paris on July 27, 1934 of tuberculosis and was cremated at the Père Lachaise cemetery. Soviet newspapers have not found room the space for an obituary of the anarchist leader, nor as much as a single line at the foot of page 6 to record his demise…. This Nestor Makhno was nonetheless a very curious figure and no conspiracy of silence will succeed in erasing the memory of the important role that the popular 'Batko' played during the Russian revolution, particularly in the struggle against Denikin. Though his ephemeral Bolshevist allies, who wasted no time in getting rid of him once victory over the Whites had been secured, may not, historians of the future will reserve him the place that he deserves among the architects of the revolution.
>
> […] His political program? An anarchist, he sought to give land to the peasants, factories to the workers intact and advised them to organize themselves into federations of free communes. Which is to say that in the White generals who wanted a return of the "pomies-chikis"[14] he saw enemies. […] On several occasions he allied himself with the Bolsheviks upon whom he looked at the time as the lesser of two evils […] Acts of looting, terror or anti-Semitism were severely punished by Makhno and his lieutenants. He managed to maintain his power in the southern Ukraine and attempted to make reality of some of his 'utopias' — the elimination of prisons, the organization

of communal life, 'free communes,' 'workers' soviets' from which no stratum of society was excluded. Under his short-lived government, there was complete press freedom, and he allowed publication of Right Social Revolutionary and Left Social Revolutionary newspapers, as well as Bolshevik organs, alongside anarchist news-sheets. But it was during 1919 and Denikin's offensive, that the role of Makhno and his bands of partisans proved crucial.

[...] Against Wrangel, Makhno dispatched several detachments of his partisans, and it was his cavalry that crossed the marshes and seized the Perekop Isthmus. [...] There can be no question but that Denikin's defeat can be accounted for by the peasant uprisings that hoisted Makhno's black flag, rather than by the successes of Trotsky's regular army. The partisan bands of the 'Batko' tipped the scales in favor of the Reds, and if Moscow today prefers to forget that, impartial history will take it into the account."[15]

Berland ascribed the disagreement between Makhno and the Bolsheviks to the latters' aversion to anarchist propaganda in favor of a regime without central authority, and in favor of a federation of "free soviets," in short, for everything at odds with the "Marxist notion of the dictatorship of the proletariat, exercised in the name of the masses by the Communist Party."

This latter appreciation acts as a counter-balance to the first and enables one to restore the true measure in the historical perspective of the actions of Makhno and his people. Nevertheless, intervening between these two most believable official versions there is a teeming host of others which are mixed up and inaccurate, ranging from misapprehensions to blatant calumnies both petty and huge and all helping to cloud the issue seriously.

That a lie piously repeated can sometimes achieve the standing of a half-truth in some minds, we know: this is the case with several charges that are at once crude and serious: the charges of anti-Semitism, banditry and "military" anarchism. Be that as it may the procedure is a familiar one: one besmirches the leader or leaders and thereby belittles the movement, and the advantage is that this offers justification for the most atrocious massacres and repressions — as witness the treatment doled out to the rebels of June 1848 and the Communards of 1871.

Be that as it may, we shall return at some length to all these charges and with the assistance of manifest, obstinate facts we shall establish the truth of the matter.

However, we would do well to correct, straight-away, several habitual errors including the one that automatically identifies the person of Makhno with the movement to which he lent his name. Although, to be sure, the two are interconnected, they are not one and the same, and one cannot ascribe to Makhno alone responsibility for certain vital or disastrous decisions, for instance, the decision to enter into alliance on two occasions with the Red Army and the Kremlin authorities. Those decisions were taken collectively on each occasion after long and bitter discussions concluding in a vote. On the contrary, certain decisions were made by Makhno alone. Moreover, the movement's political complexion was not confined to the black of Anarchy but also took in the whole spectrum of the far left of the day: Left Social Revolutionaries, Maximalists, Bolsheviks at odds with the party and even "non-party," all united on a basis of free soviets. Here let us stipulate further that the Makhnovist movement was only the most important — by reason of its strength and duration — and the most remarkable — by virtue of its social achievements and internal structure — of the dozens of partisan movements that burgeoned from the Ukraine to Central Russia and Siberia, most of them similarly attached to free soviets and stamped out by the Leninist regime only with great difficulty over the years 1920–1924. Finally, if Makhno was the symbol of his movement, the Gulyai-Polye libertarian communist group was its soul. It is within that overall framework that our study is situated, although Makhno's destiny and individual actions may serve as the guidelines of our work.

❧

In support of our narrative, we shall be making use of the writings of the chief protagonists, most of them in Russian and hitherto unpublished: to it we shall add certain characteristic documents by way of appendices.

Regarding the latter part of Nestor Makhno's life — his stay in Paris — we have collected several testimonies and interviews from individuals who knew or associated with him and to whom we owe thanks here. For a start, there is the 96-year-old doyen: Grisha Bartanovsky (d. 1986), known as Barta, who first met Makhno in 1907 in Ekaterinoslav when they worked together in a factory and frequented the same nocturnal haunts, before meeting up again in exile in Paris. Then let us mention the Bulgarian libertarians who were very close to Makhno at that time: Kiro Radeff (d. 1979), Erevan (d. 1976), Nikola Tchorbadjieff (Jossif Sintov, d. 1994), and Iossif Sintov (d. 1994). Ida Mett (née Gilman, d. 1973), Makhno's secretary from 1925 to 1927, enlightened us about certain of his character traits and his living conditions during those years. Let us also salute the *grande dame* of the French libertarian movement, May Picqueray (d. 1983) who took Makhno, his wife and family in upon their arrival in Paris. Finally Nicolas Faucier and René Boucher, militants very active at that time, have briefed us on his dealings with the French anarchists.

To that gamut of sources — built up since 1964 — let us add those from the family circle of the present writer, several members of my family having been variously mixed up in the events described,[16] a circumstance not unconnected with the reasons that have prompted me to pursue my laborious researches, but which involve not so much indulgence, apology, or — who knows? — denigration, but maybe shall we say a greater readiness to show understanding of our subject.[17]

Notes to Chapter 1: From the Legend to the History

1. General A.I. Denikin, *Ocerki russkoj Smuty* (in Russian), Berlin, 1926, Tome V, p. 134.

2. V. Doubrovsky, *Batko Makhno: A Ukrainian National Hero* (in Ukrainian), Hensfeld, 1945.

3. A. de. Monzie, *Petit Manuel de la Russie nouvelle*, Paris, 1931, p. 124.

4. E. A. Chtchadenko, *The Civil War* (Russian), Moscow, 1928, Tome 1, p. 91: and V.M. Primakov *Etapy bolshovo puti* (Russian) Moscow, 1963, p. 194.

5. V. Serge, *Mémoires d'un révolutionnaire*, Paris, 1951, p. 134.

6. D. Guérin *L'Anarchisme*, Paris, 1965, p. 115. We would rather have said "Robin of the Steppes," that being truer to the local topography.

7. Quoted by Marc Mratchny in the Russian anarcho-syndicalist periodical *Rabotchij Puts* (Russian) No. 5, Berlin, 1923.

8. Sébastien Faure in his foreword to P. Arshinov *Histoire du mouvement makhnoviste (1918–1921)*. Paris 1924, p. 44.

9. The literal translation, "little father" does not quite capture the meaning that the word had in the Ukrainian; ever since the days of the Zaporog Cossack warrior communities it had implied an elected and revocable military leader. At the same time when he was being so called, Makhno was only 29 years old and thus had nothing about him that was paternal or venerable; anyway, there were other "Batkos" even in the Makhnovist movement and throughout the region.

10. S. Rosen, in *Letopis revoliutsii* (Russian), the Ukrainian C.P.'s historical review, Kharkov, 1926, 2(23), p. 121.

11. Supporters of Simon Petliura, the Ukrainian nationalist leader.

12. See the *Great Soviet Encyclopedia* (Russian), Tome XV, 1975, pp. 524–526.

13. Broadly, this term indicated well-to-do peasants but in Lenino-Stalinist mythology, it acquired a broader meaning embracing any peasant who owned his means of production (i.e., at least one cart and one horse) and not working directly for the Bolshevik State and thus a potential enemy. This semantic difficulty was resolved following the forcible collectivization of 1929–1930 (with at least 13 million deaths) for, thereafter there were only "Kolkhozians" or State-paid farm laborers.

14. The big landowners.

15. *Le Temps* August 28, 1934. This article was included in the anthology *Georges Luciani* (Pierre Berland): *Six ans à Moscou*, 1937, Paris, under the title, "Anarchists and Bolsheviks: Makhno," pp. 26–29.

16. The product of a Ukrainian father who lived through the civil war and for whom Makhno "… fought the Whites to get them to turn red and the reds to turn them white!" and a Russian mother, the author has no direct connection with the Skirda who commanded a Makhnovist detachment, as mentioned by Kubanin, the official Soviet historian of the *Makhnovschina*, Moscow, 1927. p. 111. Although some distant relationship cannot

be ruled out, it is probable that we share a name, Skirda, literally "rick," a name rather commonplace among the peasants and Zaporog Cossacks of this part of the Ukraine.

17. All translations from the Russian, Ukrainian and English have been made by the author.

2. In the Land of the Zaporog Cossacks

Before we proceed, it might be useful to provide some geographical, ethnographic and historical details of the territory that is to be the theater of operations for Makhno and his movement: the Ukraine and more especially its eastern portion, the left bank of the River Dniepr.

The Ukraine is the name of a land that extends from the foothills of the Urals and the Caucasus to the foothills of the Carpathians, more precisely between the two great rivers, Dniestr and Don, then between the River Pripet and its tributaries the Bug and the Desna, to the Black Sea and the Sea of Azov. An area slightly larger than France, it is almost entirely covered by steppes that are the natural extensions of the Asiatic steppes: which explains how this territory was for centuries on the main access route for countless invasions of peoples who gradually occupied Europe and made cousins of most of the inhabitants of the old continent. The most recent of these invaders before and shortly after the Christian Era, the Scythians and Sarmatians — Aryans — lived there in their turn, before the Khazars and Turkomens drove them out, only to be dislodged themselves by nomads, the Pechenegs and Polovtsians. The Slavs appeared there around from the fifth century, later in the ninth century under the designation of Russians; they regrouped around Kiev, a flourishing city which, having become a rival of Byzantium, is described as the mother of Russian cities. Converted to Christianity in the tenth century, they represented Europe's bulwark against Asiatic invasions, until the countless hordes of Genghis Khan overwhelmed them and laid the whole land waste in the thirteenth century. It was at that point that the land of the northern Slavs, Moscovia, adopted the name (retained to this day) of Russia, while the former Russia was henceforth to be known as the Ukraine, meaning "border land" and the "outlying land" of the civilized world.

After the Tartar domination, a real calamity, that was to persist for two-and-a-half centuries, the country came under the control of the Lithuanians, the Poles and then, from 1654 on, of Moscow and thereafter, its eastern part belonged to the Empire of all the Russias, first under the name of New Russia and then as Little Russia.

Nevertheless, the Ukrainians have always been distinct from the Russians — despite claims to the contrary from Muscovite patriots — in physical, linguistic, political and social terms. They are much more homogeneously Slavs than the Russians who intermingled with the Finns from the Northwest as well. This is evident in the physical make-up: the vast majority of Ukrainians are dark-eyed brunettes whereas among the Russians the blond or brown-haired type with light-colored eyes predominates.

Although both emerged from a common Slavic root, the two languages are as different as, say French and Italian. Customs and dress habits differ also. Ukrainian peasants wore an embroidered blouse tucked into their *charavary* or baggy trousers, wore leather boots, and the *papakha,* a large fur hat and the *armiak,* a homespun cloak. The Russian peasants or *muzhiks* (little men) wore their great blouse or *kosovorotka* outside their trousers, tucked into a broad belt and wore on the feet *valinki* (felt boots) or *laptis* (braided booties), dressed in a caftan or *poddiovka,* a wrap-around greatcoat, and on their heads wore a *chapka* (fur bonnet) and, once married, sported bushy beards whereas their Ukrainian counterparts let only flowing mustaches sprout. The counterpart of the Russian *isba* (log cabin) was the Ukrainian *khata,* with its wooden or mortar walls, whitewashed and topped with a thatched roof and surrounded by a tiny garden.

To conclude our rapid schedule of the differences between the two peoples, let us note that there has always been a certain animosity between them, as is often the case between Northerners and Southerners, and this has led them to give each other rather pejorative names like *Katsapy* (Russians) and sometimes *Moscaly* (Muscovites), and *Khakly* (Ukrainians).

The only common bonds between the two countries were originally dynastic alone, through the Scandinavian Rurik who established himself as prince of Kiev in the ninth century.

꙲꙲꙲

Whenever the Ukraine placed itself under the protection of Moscow's Tsar in 1654 on account of their shared religion, Orthodox Christianity, it was, paradoxically, in order to safeguard its independence, recently regained following a long and exhausting national liberation struggle against Pole and Turk. Not that that prevented Moscow from turning her into a vassal and from gradually reducing her population of peasants and Cossacks, holding the land collectively on the basis of egalitarian democracy to the status of an enslaved mass dispossessed of its lands; this by means of direct colonization by the tsars and their prebendaries, courtesans and favorites of every hue. This factor, added to internal social differentiation (privileges for the Cossack hierarchy), led to the emergence of Ukrainian feudal potentates. Despite revolts and sullen resistance from the peasant mass, this process was enshrined by Catherine II who formally introduced serfdom in 1781, which is to say, a century and a half after its introduction in Russia.

The better to bring its new colony to heel, Moscow encouraged intensive settlements of foreign colonists. In Ekaterinoslav province in 1751–1755, lands were awarded to Orthodox Slavs who had escaped the Turks: Serbs, Vlachs, Moldavians,

The Borders of the Ukraine in 1919

Bulgars and Montenegrins were settled in the Slavianoserbsk district. In 1779, Greeks, Georgians, Poles and Gypsies, as well as Turkish and Tartar captives were also planted in the Ukraine. An enormous land distribution was made between 1775 and 1782: five million hectares were awarded to seigneurs in good standing at the court of Catherine II, the enlightened despot so celebrated by French philosophers. Nor did she overlook her German compatriots whom she had pour in great numbers on to the richest lands, the famed "black lands" (*chernozyom*) whose fertility derived from the rapid sprouting of grass upon the loose steppe soil and the decomposition of layer upon layer of vegetation. The proverbial excellence of the land had made the region, since time immemorial, the granary of Byzantium and Europe and, as such, it had always invited the covetousness of its more powerful neighbors.

Catherine II's successors continued her pernicious policy; in 1803, some 1000 hectares were assigned to every retired officer, and 500 to every non-commissioned officer in the same circumstances. To work all this land, almost 100,000 peasants from middle Russia — serfs of course — were imported. In 1846–1850, on an experimental basis, the State settled Jewish farming colonies in the Alexandrovsk and Mariupol districts. Since before the Christian era, Jews had come along with the settlement of Greek traders around the shores of the Sea of Azov. This ancient presence had been given a massive boost under Polish rule, especially in the western Ukraine as the Polish lords found it to their benefit to use Poland's many Jews as commissariat and administrative agents. These Jews subsequently made up a significant national minority, especially in the great cities of that part of the Ukraine.

As a result of this plantation of foreigners, by 1917 the Ukrainians accounted for only two thirds of their country's population. After them, in descending order, came the Russians, the Jews, the Germans, the Bulgars, the Tartars, the Greeks, and in insignificant numbers, the representatives of other nations — Serbs, Armenians, Georgians, etc.

Let us note, further, that in this land of settlers there were 100 men for every 93 women. Finally there were four million Ukrainians serving in the Tsarist Russian army in 1914.

***

At the time of the general abolition of serfdom in the Russian Empire, most of the Ukrainian peasantry were awarded only quite tiny parcels of land — three hectares on average — and these they had in any case to buy back from their former seigneurs on many occasions. Just like their Russian brethren, among whom communal ownership of the land (*Obschina*) subsisted, they continued to govern themselves by means of the communal assembly, the *Gromada* (corresponding to the Russian *mir*). In both cases, they were all denied the best lands which were set aside for the tsar (Crown lands), the *pomieschikis* (nobles) and the clergy, i.e., the famous trilogy of "Holy Russia." Thus in 1891 to take the province of Ekaterinoslav (the figures being essentially valid for the whole of the Ukraine), the nobles who accounted for 0.9 percent of the population held 31.06 percent of the arable lands; the Ukrainian peasants, 70 percent of the population, farmed only 37.55 percent of the land; the German planters, some four percent of the population, had 9.46 percent of the land (and generally the best land); as for the Greek two percent of the population, they had 6.62 percent of the cultivable land (usually not very good land at that). The Jewish farming colonies accounted for only an insignificant figure — some 0.34 percent of the land.[1]

※※※

Agriculture was the main economic activity and occupied three quarters of the population. Agricultural production was made up of grains, beets, tobacco and sundry vegetables. Livestock were numerous, and there was on average one horse for every five inhabitants.

Nearly ten percent of people depended on the industry and mines of the Donetz coal basin or the iron mines of Krivoi Rog. Five percent of the population made a living out of trade while the remainder was made up of officials and public service employees.

The Sea of Azov ports of Berdyansk (47,000 inhabitants) and Mariupol (45,000), very active all year round, were linked by rail to Ekaterinoslav (220,000 inhabitants in 1917), the capital of the southern Ukraine, itself connected via the important rail junction at Sinelnikovo with the Crimea, via Alexandrovsk (population 52,000) and Melitopol (population 18,000).

Contrary to prejudices widespread in the West, the population did not wallow in crass ignorance; in 1923 for instance, out of those of school age in 1914, the numbers who could read and write in the Ukraine stood at 90 percent in the towns and 73 percent in the countryside (for Russia, the figures were, respectively, 82 percent and 57 percent).

Another feature of the province of Ekaterinoslav, cradle of the Makhnovschina, is that it had been the historical heartland of the Zaporog Cossacks, warrior communities of free men who over the centuries had fought ferociously to cling on to their independence. This is rather more than a coincidence, and we might do well to dwell upon it a little.

※※※

The origins of the Cossacks go back to the Middle Ages, in particular to the resistance against Tartar oppression, when a section of the Slav population opted to stand its ground and fight. The term "Cossack" is itself of Tartar origin and means at once shepherd, horseman, free warrior, vagabond and sometimes bandit. The people so called began by establishing a sort of confraternity situated along a river. At the origin of all those that followed there were two: the Don and the Dniepr confraternities formed at around the same time — in the 15th and 16th centuries. The first formation, the Don group, was made up of Russians drawn from the democratic towns of Novgorod, Pskov and Riazan, driven out by the awful persecutions visited upon them by Moscow's autocratic tsars. Taking refuge in the eastern Ukraine and the northern Caucasus, they clung to their republican traditions, what was known as "Cossack freedoms," namely, the practice of settling all their problems in general assembly, the *Krug*, (equivalent to Novgorod's democratic assembly, the *Vetchey*), and of appointing their own ataman, an elected and revocable military leader.

The second band established itself in the Ukraine along the banks of the Dniepr and, to begin with, comprised exclusively of Ukrainians. Both bands maintained close ties of friendship and cooperation with each other; it was said that the "two armies of the Don and the Dniepr are as brother and sister." It was only towards the end of the 16th century that, in the face of the Turkish threat, one of them threw in its lot with the Muscovite tsar and the other with the kingdom of Poland, all save the Cossacks from the lower Dniepr — the Zaporog Cossacks — who remained independent.

Given the crucial role played by the descendants of these two Cossacks bands in the Russian civil war of 1917–1921 and thus in our narrative, we shall take a closer look at the main features of their evolution.

From their earliest days the Don Cossacks swarmed over the adjoining regions — the Volga, the Urals, Astrakhan, etc. — thus it was one of their people who had become a Volga Cossack, Ermack, who in the 1580s conquered virtually the whole of Siberia for the Tsar. They played a vital role for Moscow and indeed for the whole of Europe by repulsing and then subjugating all the nomadic peoples of central Asia and of Siberia, who hitherto had been wont to invade and ravage northeastern Europe.

The linking of the Don territory to Moscow in 1570 was merely federative: thus, when the Tsar openly trespassed against their rights, they first displayed some agitation and then exploded in open revolts, the best known of which were the revolts of Stenka Razin in 1670, of Bulavin in 1708 and of the Ural Cossack Pugachev in 1775. These uprisings were harshly put down, (especially that of Bulavin) by Peter the Great who had a large number of Cossacks from every part executed. Those who survived these decimations were then scattered to the extremities of the empire. Turned into border guards, they formed regular troops called *Voiskos* (armies) after the rivers and regions to which they were assigned: in 1914 in order of importance these were as follows: the Don, Kuban, Terek, Ural, Orenburg, Astrakhan, Transbaikalia, Semirechinsk, Amur and Ussuri. Meanwhile they lost their Russian ethnic homogeneity either by mixing with women carried off or by absorbing adjacent local peoples: Kalmucks, Buryats, Chechens, Cherkesses, or through the arrival of exiled Ukrainians and Zaporogs.

The eleven *Voiskos* appointed after that formed staunch soldiers of the empire, coddled and privileged as such by those in power. They distinguished themselves in the campaigns and wars of imperial Russia especially when they smashed Napoleon's hitherto undefeated cavalry in 1812–1814 and watered their mounts at the fountains of the Champs Elysées in Paris.

Having become pillars of the empire, the Cossacks were not content to wage war and "carry Russia's borders on their saddles": they were also deployed for internal security. They were required to regularly dispatch *sotnias* (150-man squadrons) and regiments for service as police either garrisoning the leading towns and settlements in the country, or for use in the Tsar's personal guard. It was as the regime's praetorian guards that they cruelly put down the 19th century Polish uprisings and the great revolutionary upheaval of 1905. Their *nagaika* (leather whip) henceforth was of sinister reputation among the unbroken population.

৽৽৽

In peacetime the Cossacks could supply nearly 70,000 men and almost three times that number in times of war and when the 1914 war broke out they formed numerous units: 162 horse regiments, 171 independent cavalry *sotnias*, 24 battalions of infantry including the *plastunes* — shock commandos — from the Kuban, as well as numerous artillery batteries, in all around 450,000 troops.

Their order of battle was novel compared with the open file formations of the Russian regular cavalry, the forager's charge of French regulations and the single line of attack of the German cavalry. Among Cossacks the charge — the lava-flow — consisted of fighting in a dispersed way such as to facilitate to the utmost the individual action of each fighting-man and officers of every rank in taking whatever initiatives were best suited to the circumstances. The interval between the attackers made it possible for them to advance at speed across any terrain, and it made their actions particularly devastating. Their usual armaments comprised, of course, the saber without which the Cossack is inconceivable, the lance, the rifle, the dagger and sometimes a hand-gun. Their pugnaciousness and daring made them formidable warriors.

In 1917 the most numerous were the Don and Kuban Cossacks who alone accounted for nearly three quarters of the Russian army's Cossack complement. Come the civil war, they were to account for a similar fraction of General Denikin's anti-Bolshevik forces.

In addition, tremendous social differentiation prevailed among the populace of the Cossack lands: there were many Russian immigrants, looked upon as non-Cossack intruders and who worked as share-croppers on the lands of wealthy Cossacks. Among the Cossack masses, there were some indigents for, although each Cossack was automatically entitled to a parcel of land, the size of the holding varied according to rank. In the case, say, of the Kuban, in 1870 the hitherto collectively-held lands were divided up as follows: a general got 1,500 hectares, a colonel 400 hectares, an *essaul* (commander) 200, and a mere Cossack only 30 hectares. Moreover in the Kuban there was gulf between the Littoral Cossacks who were of Zaporog origin, and those of the interior who were of Russian extraction and clashes and rivalry between them were not unknown.

These different characteristics explain why many poor or even medium Cossacks as well as some non-Cossack inhabitants of their lands were to opt during the civil war, in the beginning at any rate, for the Bolsheviks who seemed to them to offer assurances of greater social justice.

The Dniepr Cossacks, Ukrainians, were, in spite of various adventures and revolt, brought into subjection to the power of the Polish lords — the *pans* — and were gradually absorbed into the general population under Polish control; those under Russian rule, who were also subjected to repression by Peter the Great, nonetheless supplied some regiments which, subsequently, in the wars of the empire also came to pitch their tents in Paris in 1814 and then melted into the population. In 1918 their descendants rallied in large numbers to the yellow and blue Ukrainian nationalist colors of Petliura's troops.

Finally, and of greater interest to us here, there were the Zaporog Cossacks, whose name derives from the fact that the first of them sought refuge on islands amid the inaccessible rapids of the lower Dniepr (their name means literally "beyond the cataracts"), from where they organized raids against the Tartars and Turks. They drew victuals from the wild fastness of what was termed Little Tartary, today's southern Ukraine, where a prodigal nature offered an abundance of game, fish, wild honey and natural shelter.

The Zaporogs were free men or men whose ambition was to be such, and above all, men who aimed to remain such. As such, on condition that they were of the Orthodox faith, they welcomed many outsiders to their ranks: Russians fleeing their despotic rulers or serfdom, retainers, peasants, townsfolk, vagabonds of various origins fleeing taxation, constraint and all manner of servitude and lured by the Zaporogs' manner and free way of life — their *Volnitza*.[3] They could stay permanently or just sample Cossack life for a spell. In principle, every free Ukrainian was a Cossack, while retaining his land and could be mobilized at a moment's notice.

The Zaporogs were a military and political force that played a crucial role in the 16th and 17th centuries in that part of the continent. They allied themselves with the Swedes and with Cromwell in their struggle against the Poles and Muscovites; sturdy sailors as well as valiant warriors, they could field an army of 40,000 men, a considerable figure for that time. Their forces, scattered right across the Ukraine, were divided into *polks* or regiments, and into *sotnias* or squadrons. As their military, administrative and religious capital they had the *Sitch*, a wooden stockaded stronghold on an island in the Dniepr, first at Khortitsa and then on two other islands further downriver. Women and children were not admitted to the *Sitch*; it was divided into 38 *Kurens* or working and living communities, each one bearing the name of the area of origin of its 150 men who garrisoned there, making in all nearly 6,000 Zaporogs permanently available.

Organization was democratic and egalitarian, with the elective principle in operation at all echelons of command and of civilian office; they were all directly elected for a one-year term. They could be confirmed in or recalled from office at any time by a general assembly — the *Kosh* — and any mere Cossack could accede to any post. Elections normally were held in the month of October; they determined the atamans of the *Kurens*, the hetman or ataman of all the *Kurens* as well as his staff (secretary, attendant, judge, etc.). At the same time, all territories administered by the *Sitch* were reassigned by means of the drawing of equal lots. Aside from filling those lots, the Zaporogs went in for hunting, fishing — they had a significant fleet — and, naturally, given the historical circumstances of the day, for warfare. Following Pugachev's revolt, the *Sitch* was destroyed in 1775 by order of Catherine II; Khortitsa became the site of a German settlement and the Zaporogs were either enslaved or forced into exile in the Kuban, the Crimea, Siberia or even Turkey.

Thus after many vicissitudes, the lands and liberties of the Zaporogs were whittled away and confiscated by local feudatories and agents of the Muscovite tsars; however, the memory of that era of autonomy and freedom represented by the *Volnitza* stayed lively among the region's population (the region was called *Zaporozhye*), and it is striking to note that the Makhnovist movement merely and naturally adopted the Zaporogs' traditions of an embryonic libertarian communism.

Consequently, throughout the evolution of tsarism we witness a double phenomenon: the Cossacks, libertarian-minded warrior-peasants have been either courted, dragooned then domesticated or persecuted, decimated and suppressed for that very reason. So it may be argued, paradoxically, that the true Cossacks have gone, while leaving their achievements alive, and that the people called by that name are no longer anything more than a warrior caste in the service of an autocratic authority that is the very antithesis of their initial ideal. In which case the 1917 revolution triggered a formidable reversion.

Notes to Chapter 2: In the Land of the Zaporog Cossacks

1. Statistics supplied by the *Encyclopedic Dictionary* (Russian), St. Petersburg, 1893, Tome XI, pp. 582–586 and by the *Great Encyclopedia* (Russian) St. Petersburg, 1902, Tome IX, pp. 167–172.
2. After 1926 the town was renamed Dniepropetrovsk.
3. The *Volnitza* has always been the *bête noire* of all succeeding authorities in the Russian empire, and its remembrance today is equally out of favor with the historiographers and ideologues of the Lenino-Stalinist regime.

3. A Rebellious Youth

Nestor Makhno was born on October 27, 1888 in Gulyai-Polye, a sizable town crossed by the Gaichur River and belonging to the Alexandrovsk district of the Ekaterinoslav province. Gulyai-Polye means "fair green, walking green" and the name derives from the fact that, from time immemorial fairs frequent and of high repute in the region have been held there. Some Zaporog Cossacks had settled there over two centuries before, which accounts for the town's being divided up along military lines into rotas or centuries. When Catherine II had ordered the destruction of the Sitch, many Zaporogs, rather than submit, had gone into exile; those who had not had the opportunity or time to do so had been enslaved. The ones from Gulyai-Polye had been awarded to one Shabelsky on the whim of some favorite of the empress.

At the beginning of the 20th century, Gulyai-Polye boasted nearly 10,000 inhabitants and by 1917 the figure was nearly 25,000[1]: a cantonal capital and the residence of the cantonal police superintendent, the communal magistrate and the rural agent, it possessed two orthodox churches, a synagogue, three schools, a rural first-aid post and a posts and telegraph office. Two factories, Krieger and Kerner, churned out farm implements and employed cheap local labor. There were also two steam mills, several artisan workshops and some small undertakings. The bulk of the land belonged to the big landlords while the peasants owned only 45 percent of the arable land; the poorest of them — the *batrakis* — worked for the big landlords who also hired seasonal workers who poured in from the provinces of Poltava and Chernigov at harvest times. Seven kilometers away lay the town's railway station, located on the Sinelnikovo-Chaplino–Berdiansk railway connection. Heavy traffic passed along the road that linked Gulyai-Polye to the station where there were convoys delivering loads of wheat and flour, farm machinery and from where coke and ore for various local firms were brought back.

❦

Nestor was the fifth son of Ivan Makhno and Evdokia Makhno née Perederi. His parents had been serfs of the Seigneur Shabelsky prior to their being given their freedom when Tsar Alexander II abolished serfdom in 1861. Their plot of land being insufficient to feed their family, the father went on working at his former master's place as a stable boy. When Nestor was born, his father was taken on as a coachman by a wealthy Jewish industrialist, Kerner, who owned a farm-machinery plant, a steam-driven mill, a large store and 500 hectares of land leased out to some German settlers. A short time later, with Nestor scarcely eleven months old, his father died leaving his widow utterly unprovided for and with five young boys to care for.

In these circumstances, Nestor's early childhood was marked by great poverty and by an absence of the games and gaiety that befit such tender years. His mother was reduced to entrusting him to a couple of well-to-do but childless peasants who intended to adopt him. She took him back after several weeks at the insistence of his older brothers because he was unhappy with the couple. At the age of eight, he entered the secular municipal school. To begin with he was a good pupil, then he began to play truant spending his days along with about a hundred urchins of his own age "studying" skating and all sorts of games. These "parallel classes" continued for weeks at a time until one fine day the ice gave way and Nestor was only just saved from drowning in the icy waters. This incident must have been at the root of the weakness in his lungs which subsequently proved fatal to him, for this soaking froze his clothing, and he stayed like that for a time, before seeking the shelter of his uncle's home and getting help.

His mother "tended" him by means of a memorable thrashing. He went back to school where he again became a good pupil until the summer arrived; then he had himself taken on as the handler of a team of oxen on the land of a comfortably off peasant, Janssen, at the daily wage of 25 kopecks. His greatest delight was to race the seven kilometers to his maternal home to hand over his daily pay to his mother. It was only with that thought in mind that he was able to hold out all summer, despite two lashes from a whip doled out for some minor offense by the under-manager, a brute. In all this work brought the nine-year-old Nestor some 20 rubles, and these first earnings were handed over in their entirety to his mother to whom he was at all times to display the greatest attachment.

His brothers also worked as farmhands, and they helped their mother who was in dire need. If one is to credit the memoirs of Anatol Gak, a Gulyai-Polye peasant who subsequently fled to Canada, Makhno's house on the edge of the town's fairground was extremely poor; neither pig nor any of the usual amenities of a Ukrainian *khata* were to be seen in their courtyard or farmyard, he stipulates.

❦❦❦

Nestor went back to school that autumn and was revealed as a good pupil in arithmetic and especially in reading, the first inkling of his future gifts as an orator. Unfortunately, that was the sum total of his studies for, at the end of the school year, his family's circumstance became so straitened that he had to carry on working throughout the year, although only ten years old. This sad circumstance aroused in him a "sort of rage, resentment, even hatred for the wealthy property-owner" on whose holding he worked, and above all for his progeny: "For these young idlers who often passed close by him, all fresh and neat, with full bellies and in cleanest clothes, reeking of perfume while he, filthy and in rags, barefooted and stinking of dung, scattered bedding for the calves."[2]

It was at this point that he began to awaken to social injustice although he still thought like a resigned slave, reckoning that "that is how things are": the landlord and his were the "masters," whereas he was paid for the unpleasantness of "reeking of dung."

The years passed. Nestor moved on from calves to horses, accepting his fate willy-nilly until one day he witnessed a scene that was to leave its indelible mark upon him. The landlord's sons, the manager and his under-manager were wont to give the stable lads a drubbing for the slightest peccadillo. The "dark recesses of his mind" made Nestor accept this craven spectacle and ". . . like a real slave, he strove just like the others about him to avert his eyes and pretend he saw and heard not a thing." However, his mother had told him how, under serfdom, corporal punishment was quite commonplace and how she herself as a child had on two occasions been birched, merely because, quite within her rights she had refused to perform the corvée. She had had to present herself on the steps of the seigneur's big house to receive 15 strokes of the birch in the presence of the "master."

His mother had also told him of the epic struggles of their Zaporog Cossack forebears against enemies on every side in order to safeguard their freedom.

Thus, one summer's day in 1902 the young Nestor, thirteen years old, was present at a run-of-the-mill scene: the landlord's sons, his manager and his assistant set about insulting then raining blows on the second stable boy in the presence of all the other stable hands … "half dead from fear at the wrath of their masters." Nestor could take no more and off he ran to alert the head stable boy, Batko Ivan, who was busy in a cowshed trimming the horses' tails. Learning of what was afoot, Batko Ivan, an elemental force, burst, like a man possessed, into the room where the "chastisement" was underway, pitched into the "young nobles" and their acolytes and sent them rolling in the dirt with swathing punches and kicks. The attackers, attacked, fled in disarray, some through the window, some through the nearest doorway. This was the signal for revolt; all of the day laborers and stable boys were outraged and went off in a body to demand an explanation. The old landlord took fright and in conciliatory tone besought them to forgive the "idiocy of his young heirs," to remain in his service and even undertook to see that nothing of the sort would ever happen again.

Batko Ivan related the episode to young Nestor, treating him to the first words of rebellion he had ever heard in his life: "… No one here should countenance the disgrace of being beaten … and as for you, little Nestor, if one of your masters should ever strike you, pick up the first pitchfork you lay hands on and let him have it.…" This advice, at once poetic and brutal, left a terrible mark upon Nestor's young soul and awakened him to his dignity. Henceforth he would keep a fork or some other tool within reach, meaning to put it to good use.

One year later, Nestor quit his job as a stable boy and, at the prompting of his older brothers, had himself taken on at a local foundry as an apprentice. There he learned the "art of casting harvester wheels."

Meanwhile the family's situation had changed considerably. His three elder brothers, Karp, Savva and Emilian, after marrying set up homes of their own. That left only Nestor and his younger brother Grigori in their mother's care. After a time, Nestor left the foundry and worked as a sales assistant for a wine merchant. Nauseated by his job, he gave it up after three months. Perhaps it was in the wake of this experience that he was to retain an aversion for wine and alcohol; that aversion was very real, despite all the fairy tales peddled latter about his alleged inebriate tendencies.

Then he tended his mother's four hectares of land, which he worked with their lone horse. He worked by fits and starts, especially to lend a helping hand to his brothers; for instance, he signed on with a painting and decorating firm, for just long enough to pay for the cart needed to transport his brothers' wheat.

In 1904, one of them, Savva, was called up and set off for the Russo-Japanese front. Along came the 1905 revolution. He was enthused by events, and it induced him to read some clandestine political literature. At first he fell under the spell of the Social Democrats, won over by their "socialist phraseology and their phony revolutionary ardor." He distributed their tracts in massive numbers. However, at the beginning of 1906, he made the acquaintance of anarchist peasants from Gulyai-Polye and soon became a sympathizer of their group. This group had been organized by Voldemar (Vladimir) Antoni and Prokop Semenyuta. Antoni, the son of immigrant Czech workers and a lathe operator himself, exercised a decisive influence over Nestor by "… ridding his soul once and for all of the lingering remnants of the slightest spirit of servility and submission to any authority."

Gulyai-Polye's peasant libertarian communist group operated in difficult circumstances for the Tsarist repression was at its height; a state of siege had been proclaimed nationwide, the court martial was taking a heavy toll and military expeditions were gunning down "alleged" troublemakers. A detachment of Don Cossacks stationed in Gulyai-Polye to counter any eventuality set about gratuitous bullying of peaceable inhabitants. Anatol Gak describes one scene when he saw a teacher dragged along by two Don Cossacks with sabers at the ready, while a third beat him with rifle butt, shrieking with each blow: "Take that, you wastrel, for your revolution!"[3]

Despite this oppressive atmosphere, the town's anarchist group met regularly at least once each week and sometimes more often, with its 10-to-15 members. A melancholy Makhno recalled those meetings: "For me such nights (we most often would gather to meet by night) were filled with light and joy. We peasants, with our meager learning, would assemble in winter at the home of one of us, in summer in the fields, near a pond, on the green grass, or, from time to time, in the broad daylight like young folks out for a stroll. We would meet to debate the issues that move us."

From then on, Nestor threw himself wholeheartedly into the struggle for social revolution.

Notes to Chapter 3: A Rebellious Youth

1. According to the 1897 census there were 9,497 inhabitants, 1,173 of them Jews.

2. All quotes in quotation marks incorporated into our narrative have been borrowed from the memoirs of his youth, published by Makhno, partly in Russian, in the magazine *Anarkhicheski Vestnik*, Berlin, 1923–1924, No. 1–3, and in French in *Le Libertaire* in 1926.

3. Anatol Gak, in *Suchasnist,* Ukrainian review, autumn 1972, 9(14), Munich. The author supplies interesting information on Gulyai-Polye life before 1917 and especially on the local anarchist group. In the descriptions of the scene quoted, it is notable that Gak wonders if these were real Don Cossacks or people in disguise (it happened sometimes) so much have Cossacks to Ukrainians (from wherever they may come) always symbolized freedom, and not comprehend how they could possibly have turned into police henchmen of the autocracy.

4. From Militant to Terrorist

Nestor first completed a six-month term in the anarchist study circle, and it was only once he had fully digested the ideals and goals of libertarian communism that he became a full-fledged member of the Gulyai-Polye group. At the time he was working as a foundry worker at the Kerner plant. With a degree of success, the group disseminated libertarian ideas among the nation's peasants, publishing and distributing tracts, but it also took care to reply with direct action to the governmental terror after the fashion of other anarchists from the Russian Empire who had decreed "Black Terror" against tsarism.

In order to equip itself with the wherewithal for its various operations, the group decided to carry out "expropriations"[1] against the local bourgeois and in the surrounding areas. The indictment drawn up by the prosecution of the Odessa field court martial when the Gulyai-Polye libertarian communist group appeared before it enumerates the following:

- On September 5, 1906 in Gulyai-Polye, an attack upon the home of the businessman Pleschiner by three individuals armed with revolvers and with faces blackened.
- On October 10, a fresh attack in Gulyai-Polye upon another businessman, Bruk, by four individuals, faces concealed by paper masks, who, brandishing revolvers and bombs, demanded 500 rubles for the "starving."
- A little later, a third attack upon a wealthy local industrialist, Kerner, by four individuals, with three more acting as lookouts.
- In August 1907 in the nearby village of Gaichur, a fourth attack upon yet another businessman, Gurevitch, by four individuals wearing sunglasses.
- On October 19, 1907, attack upon the mail coach; a gendarme and postman were killed.
- In 1908, three further attacks, again upon businessmen.[2]

The moneys thus accumulated were used to develop propaganda and for the procurement, through Voldemar Antoni, of weapons and bombs in Vienna. The group also had contacts with the Ekaterinoslav group and certain others in Moscow.

Another aspect of the "Black Terror" consisted of torching the properties and goods of the region's big landowners by way of replying to the so-called Stolypin reform designed to abolish the communal assembly, the *gromada*, in order to foster the emergence of a new stratum of well-to-do peasants — the *kulaks* — who, it was anticipated, would furnish fresh support for the regime.

All of these actions lit a fire under the region's cops. The local "Sherlock Holmes" (*dixit* Novopolin), police superintendent Kariachentsev, tipped off by informers and acting on information gleaned from "rough and ready questioning" of suspects, managed to identify certain individuals as responsible for attacks, although for lack of evidence, he could not arrest them on the spot. In September 1907, Nestor was apprehended in very specific circumstances: a Social Revolutionary friend by the name of Makovsky borrowed his revolver, allegedly to take revenge on a gendarme officer who had recently "put him through the mill." In fact, Makovsky used the gun to settle an affair of the heart with his fiancée; he fired two bullets into her and pumped the remainder into himself! Makhno, who was on hand, did not have the time to prevent this unexpected turn of events and rushed to the aid of the wounded. That solicitude was his undoing, for he was apprehended on the spot by the police. Some days later, Antoni, who was trying to communicate with him through an intermediary among the guard, was likewise arrested.

In vain did they "grill" Makhno and Antoni; nothing doing, they could not get the slightest admission out of them. Kariachentsev told the local post commander on this score.

> "I have never before seen men of this mettle. I have plenty of evidence on which to state that they are dangerous anarchists.... But although I have put their flesh through a little suffering, I have extracted nothing from them. Makhno seems like a peasant dolt when one looks at him, but I have very conclusive evidence for claiming that it was he who shot at the gendarmes on August 26, 1907. Well now, I have done all I was able to extract admissions but to no effect. On the contrary, he supplied me with facts — which I have checked out and which I have been forced to acknowledge as correct — demonstrating that he was not even in Gulyai-Polye on that day.... As for the other one, Antoni, when I interrogated him, having him beaten at will, he dared declare to me... 'You, dead meat, you'll never get anything out of me!' And yet I gave him a good taste of the 'swing'...."

Despite the flimsiness of the charges against them, Antoni was released only after a month and Makhno only after ten months; it was with that lengthy stay that Nestor, at the age of 18, began his lengthy acquaintance with prisons.

Paradoxically it was a Gulyai-Polye industrialist, one Vitchlinsky, who secured his release by posting bail of 2,000 rubles. All of the rest of the group's militants being outlawed, it was decided that Makhno would adopt a "line of behavior" i.e., that he should remain within the law. He then found himself employment with a decorating firm but continued to be an activist by founding an anarchist study group made up of 25 young peasants from Botchani, a village near Gulyai-Polye. At its weekly get-together, he would peruse and discuss with them sundry basic texts of anarchist doctrine.

The militant group uncovered two names who had infiltrated their ranks — Gura and Kushnir — and promptly executed them, then decided to hold a general meeting to wind up the episode, for one of its members, Ivan Levadny, was suspected of being in touch with the police. The suspicions were confirmed when, as the meeting was breaking up, the house in which it was being held was cordoned off by a squadron of Don Cossacks and members of the local Okhrana.[3] Levadny suggested that they give themselves up, his treachery being so patent, but they all determined to tough it out and fight. In a daring sortie, abetted by the darkness, they managed to carve a path for themselves by firing their revolvers, cutting down Lepetchenko, the second-in-command of the local police, some Cossacks and detectives.

In the course of the operation, Prokop Semenyuta, who had founded the group along with Antoni, was wounded in one leg; his brother, Alexander, carried him piggy-back, but, seeing their pursuers gain on them, Prokop determined to stay behind to slow them up. Down to his last bullet, he blew his own brains out.

To avenge his brother's death, Alexander Semenyuta, accompanied by Makhno and Filip Onichenko, made up his mind to execute no less a figure than the province's governor, who was due to pay a personal visit to Gulyai-Polye to look into the whole hullabaloo. This sensational scheme was aborted, for young people were banned from getting anywhere near the governor, the latter being desirous of addressing only heads of households and of sharing with them his outrage at the presence of terrorists in the town.

Undeterred, Makhno proposed to dynamite the local Okhrana Station, using two devices weighing nine and fourteen pounds respectively and originally meant for the governor. The conspirators were ready to give their own lives. An incident prevented them from carrying out their plan; they bumped into a patrol of Cossacks who made to search them. Again they managed to shoot their way out. However, Onichenko was arrested at his home, and Makhno himself was picked up a little later. That arrest probably saved his life, for he had firmly intended to go back a few hours later to give the assassination plan a second try.

It transpired that every last member of the group had been given away, first by the careless gossip of Nazar Zuichenko, a close friend of Nestor's, with a "nark," one Jacques Brin, jailed along with him in Ekaterinoslav and secondly by the "statements" of Levadny and Althausen. Interrogated briskly by Kariachentsev, Zuichenko corroborated his admissions with details galore and claimed that what he and the group had done had been prompted purely by political objectives set by the ideas of the "people's freedom."[4] In all, 16 members of the group were rounded up. Only Antoni and Alexander Semenyuta escaped the dragnet and fled first to France and on to Belgium.

❧

According to Levadny, Makhno was deemed "one of the most dangerous terrorist members of the group, after the brothers Prokop and Alexander Semenyuta." A start was made by accusing him of several expropriations and killings of gendarmes; however, for want of evidence and confessions, only some of these charges could be proceeded with.

All of the accused were removed to a prison in Alexandrovsk. Preparation of the case lasted over a year. Meanwhile, Alexander Semenyuta, who kept in touch with his people, sent a letter of personal greetings to Kariachentsev.

> "**To Gulyai-Polye, to Kariachentsev, poxy devil**: Mr. Superintendent, I have heard it said that you have been searching for me high and low and dearly wish to meet with me. If this be the case, I then beseech you to come to Belgium. Here, freedom of speech is unrestricted, and we will be able to chat at leisure. Signed: **Alexander Semenyuta, Gulyai-Polye anarchist.**"[5]

In so doing, Semenyuta was laying a false trail, for he returned to the Ukraine intent upon arranging the escape of Makhno and his comrades. Above all, he made up his mind to settle accounts with Kariachentsev, the "Sherlock Holmes" who had been behind the rounding-up of the whole group. The policeman was very fond of the theater, and, all unsuspecting in the belief that Semenyuta was a thousand leagues away, he blithely went along to see a play very highly rated in the Ukraine one autumn evening in 1909, along with his mistress. Semenyuta watched for him, took a seat three rows behind him, his pockets heavy with two loaded revolvers, but he hesitated to fire, fearing that innocent spectators might be hit. He positioned himself then at the theater exit, behind a tree, surprised Kariachentsev and pumped three bullets into him. Alexander Semenyuta had executed yet another gendarmerie officer, one who had especially distinguished himself in the repression. Then he turned his attention to planning Makhno's escape.

It was prepared for January 5, 1910 and the removal of the prisoners from Alexandrovsk to Ekaterinoslav. Along with anarchists from the region still at large, Semenyuta positioned himself in Alexandrovsk railway station, disguised as a peasant, dressed in an enormous sheepskin cloak and wearing a papakha; some comrades waited nearby and some sleighs were ready for the off. Everything seemed to be proceeding smoothly when it was learned that the train had been caught in a blizzard and was running late. Semenyuta was thus obliged to step into the waiting room and there, in spite of his disguise, Althausen, the member of the group who had turned informer, recognized him and in the belief that he himself was the target, alerted the guards. This put paid to the planned escape but the intrepid Semenyuta again managed to extricate himself at gun point.

When the authorities learned of his return to the Ukraine, they had no doubt but that he was behind several recent, sensational outrages, and they posted a substantial reward for his capture, dead or alive, as he had been decreed public enemy number one. Over several months, he thwarted all plans to search him out but nonetheless met a tragic end, one might say on account of nostalgia for the land of his birth. Indeed, in the company of a young libertarian by the name of Martha Pivel, he arrived back in Gulyai-Polye for May 1, 1910. One of Makhno's brothers offered to put him up while he himself went off to sleep at his mother's house.

Semenyuta's presence was immediately reported to the police — as was to come to light following the seizure of police archives in 1917 — by one Piotr Sharovsky who was eager for the reward money. The police surrounded him, laid siege to the house and stormed it. They found Semenyuta dead, he having kept his last bullet for himself; his female companion was gravely wounded.

That such a daring militant so fanatically devoted to the cause of Anarchy could have exercised such influence over the teen-aged Makhno (already quite resolute himself), who was to remember him with such emotion all his life, can readily be understood.[6]

❧

The direct actions carried out by the Gulyai-Polye anarchist group were not at all out of the ordinary for the years 1906–1909, for the Tsarist repression was in full swing and the firing squads and hangmen were busy. The timid reforms granted at the start by Nicholas II, who was very conscious of his station, were quickly annulled and the mailed fist took over. Also, every revolutionary in the Russian Empire was resorting to the same sort of activities. At the time, a number of militants like Makhno or Semenyuta met their deaths either in combat or on the scaffold or were deported to Siberia or consigned to penal servitude. The few who survived this heroic struggle were not to forget the sacrifice of their comrades and were to pledge themselves to avenge them promptly in 1917 against the police and other goons of the autocracy.

As a rule, the membership of the Gulyai-Polye libertarian communist group was quite young, the older members being 25 years of age while Makhno was the youngest. The indictment drawn up against the group charged the sixteen proceeded against, first of all, with "illegal subversive association" and then with sundry criminal activities — expropriations and armed struggle against the authorities. Fourteen individuals were implicated: Nestor Makhno, the brothers Anton and Egor Bondarenko, Klim Kirichenko, Filip Cherniavsky, the brothers Filip and Piotr Onichenko, Ivan Shevchenko (tried and hanged before the main case was heard), Martynova and Zablodsky (Ukrainians), plus Efim Orlov (a Russian) — all of them peasants — Naum Althausen, Leiba Gorelik (Jews) and Kasimir Lisovsky (a Pole) — town dwellers.

Let us note in passing the differing national origins of the group's membership (as noted for each person named); it represented rather well the diversity of the local population and even endowed the group's activities with a quite internationalist cachet.

Obviously, the group's membership had been even larger; the others were either on the run or had not been charged in that there was no evidence against them.

The accused whose names did not feature on the charge sheet were Levadny (Ukrainian), who officially died of typhus in the prison infirmary but who, according to Makhno, was strangled for his treachery by an anarchist hospitalized with him there, and another militant of the group, who had been very close to Makhno, one Kshiva (a Jew) who was accused of having murdered the agent provocateur Kushnir and was hanged on June 17, 1909.

Nazar Zuichenko (Ukrainian) whose "loose talk" had led to the discovery of the group, contracted an acute form of typhus and could not stand trial alongside the others (this was undoubtedly a sort of ruse by the authorities who were unwilling to compromise their informant).

Voldemar Antoni, having fled to Belgium, emigrated shortly after that to South America where he spent many a long year working hard before turning into a "soviet patriot," returning with his family to the Soviet Union (to Kazakhstan, specifically) in the 1960s. In 1967 he even made a trip back to Gulyai-Polye for the 50th anniversary celebrations of October 1917, but his anarchist beliefs had been lost. The other members of the group who made good their escape continued to carry out propaganda and organizing activities in the Gulyai-Polye region, thereby clinging to the progress made by the activities of their vanished or imprisoned comrades. These activities were thus not to be in vain and were to pave the way for the burgeoning of libertarianism come 1917.

Notes to Chapter 4: From Militant to Terrorist

1. At this time "exies" were the common currency of all revolutionary groups, whether Social Revolutionary (SR), Maximalists (a breakaway from the SRs, who espoused a "maximal" program), Bolsheviks, Polish nationalist socialists and sundry other organizations. They consisted of "expropriating the expropriators" (robbing the robbers); nowadays we would call them hold-ups.

2. Quoted in G. Novopolin's excellent study, "Makhno and the Gulyai-Polye anarchist group" in the magazine *Katorga i ssylka* (Imprisonment and Exile), Moscow, 1927, pp. 70–77.

3. The Tsarist political police, highly effective and the model for the Cheka.

4. It seems that Makhno was not aware of Zuichenko's treachery, for in 1917 he was to come across him without calling him to account but speaks of him in a warm friendly way in his memoirs.

5. G. Novopolin, op. cit.

6. At the time of publication of the first volume of his *Memoirs,* Makhno regretted not being able to include a photograph of the Gulyai-Polye anarchist group. We are pleased to make good the deficiency by reproducing the photograph taken of the group in 1907.

5. Penal Servitude

The trial of the Gulyai-Polye anarchist group took place in March 1910 in Ekaterinoslav. The court was ringed by a mass of gendarmes and troops, such was the fear, despite such prolific precautions, of an armed move by Alexander Semenyuta (then still alive) and his comrades, aimed at freeing Makhno and his jailed confederates. The guards were under orders to kill the accused on the spot at the slightest sign of external attack.

A local bigwig who arrived to visit the accused in prison had Makhno presented to him, looked him over and then declared to the chief warder: "To look at him, this Makhno seems harmless enough…. Yet they say he is very dangerous."

After five days' proceedings, the verdict was delivered on March 26, 1910: Martynova, Lisovsky and Zablodsky were sentenced to six years penal servitude; Kirichenko, Egor Bondarenko, Orlov, Althausen and Makhno were first sentenced to fifteen years hard labor for "criminal association" and then to death by hanging for terrorist offenses and "expropriations."

Counsel suggested to the condemned that they seek leave to appeal; aside from Althausen, they scornfully refused. Makhno announced to his defense lawyer: "We have no intention of asking anything of this good-for-nothing tsar…. these rascals have sentenced us to death, so let them hang us!"

Nestor and his companions were locked up in a special condemned cell, the walls of which were covered by inscriptions from all who had preceded them into that antechamber of death. This dramatic circumstance drew a few pathetic lines from Makhno in his memoirs:

> "Once inside these cells, one half feels that one has climbed down into the grave. One has the feeling that only one's straining fingertips are clinging to the surface of the earth … One then thinks of all who, being yet at large, cling to their belief and their hopes, intent upon doing something good and useful in the struggle for a better life.
>
> Having sacrificed oneself for this future, one feels flooded by a quite profound and very heartfelt love for one's comrades in the struggle. They seem so near, so dear! One wholeheartedly hopes that they may

hold on to their faith and their hopes to the very end and take their love of the oppressed and their hatred of their oppressors further."

The twelve condemned men in the cell had as their sole and exclusive preoccupation the obsessive thought of their imminent execution and tried to prepare for it with courage.

Egor Bondarenko, one of his closest comrades, predicted a most active revolutionary future for Makhno:

> "Listen, Nestor! There's a chance that your sentence may be commuted to hard labor. Then the revolution will come along and set you free. It is my profound conviction that, once freed, you will hoist again the black flag of Anarchy that our enemies have snatched from us.… You will wrest it from them and raise it proudly on high.… I have that premonition, for I have seen you in action, Nestor, and you do not tremble before torturers."

Bondarenko wanted to get him to promise to shoulder that responsibility, but Nestor, supported by two other comrades, Orlov and Kirichenko, protested that he was too much of a weakling physically as well as having intellectual shortcomings. To which Bondarenko replied that to hold on to one's faith and inner strength, what was needed was not great physical might or exceptional intellectual gifts but evidence of great determination and profound commitment to the cause.

❧

One night they came to collect Kirichenko and Bondarenko for hanging; the former took his own life with strychnine while the second, before going to meet the hangman, and realizing that Makhno would indeed escape the gallows, said these short farewells. "… Nestor, my brother, you are to live … I shall surely die.… I know that you will regain your freedom." They embraced one another as brothers and Egor Bondarenko strode firmly toward his executioners; as if there was any need of that, his pre-death prediction invested Makhno even more with the will and determination he needed to keep his promise.

After a 52-day numbing delay, Makhno was indeed informed that his sentence and that of his comrade Orlov were to be commuted to hard labor for life,[1] in view of their youth at the time of the offenses in question and, in Makhno's case, probably also on account of his steadfast behavior throughout the preliminary investigation, during which he had systematically denied all the accusations leveled against him.

❧

After this emotional strain, Makhno greatly weakened physically, fell ill and contracted typhoid fever. He spent two months in the hospital, was several days in a coma, written off by the doctors and moved to a terminal ward. Even so he managed to come through this bad patch and summoned up enough strength to object to the treatment meted out by the doctors. Let us make it clear that at this time inside prison and during penal servitude every convict deemed dangerous was shackled hand and foot and, in principle, around the clock, but certain inmates adept in the art of forcing locks abetted their fellow-prisoners to get relief at times. He was to wear his chains right through his prison term, or for upwards of eight years, so that it was some time after his release before he was able to walk normally without losing his balance!

He was then transferred to the prison in Lugansk where he was held for almost a year in extremely harsh conditions; some inmates could not bear them and took their own lives while others managed to keep going only on the hope of escape or of an imminent revolution that would set them free. He received visits from his mother and brother Grigori who bore news from home and briefed him on the death of Alexander Semenyuta.

After a further five-and-a-half month stay in Ekaterinoslav prison, he was dispatched on August 2, 1911 to Moscow's central prison, the ill-famed Butyrki. His dossier, which followed, drew a remark full of promise from the officer in charge of the convict section. "Here your dreams of escape are ended!", a reference to all the escape bids he had planned with his fellow inmates in earlier prisons, only to see them all frustrated. To drive home this threat, they replaced his handcuffs with riveted irons then placed him in quarantine for eight days. Then he got to familiarize himself with his new abode.

Most political prisoners, of any and every persuasion and assessed as being among the most dangerous or significant, were housed in this penitentiary; all in all, nearly 3,000 inmates were watched over by several hundred jailers or "two-legged curs" as Makhno described them. On the other hand, and this was a real windfall for him, there was an exceptional collective library amassed by the convicts. Thanks to that, he was going to be able to round out his knowledge of history and literature; he devoured it all with gluttonous appetite; Klyuchevsky's Russian history course, the works of Bielinski, Lermontov and even Leon Shestov. He also familiarized himself with the basic texts and programs of the various revolutionary groups — the Social Revolutionaries, Social Democrats, and their sundry tendencies, etc. He also read anarchist literature and was thunderstruck by Kropotkin's *Mutual Aid*, which never left his side thereafter.

His bridling at the provocations of the turnkeys earned him lengthy stays in the solitary confinement cell, and he fell seriously ill, laid low by a bad pneumonia. He was hospitalized, but, after three months, a tubercular lung was the diagnosis. He spent eight months in the hospital, and — thanks to the well-organized assistance to political prisoners — he made a good recovery; however, during his detention, he was to spend two or three months a year thereafter in the hospital ward.

It was there in Butyrki that he came upon another famous anarchist activist, Piotr Arshinov (Marin) with whom he was going to be bound with the ties of a solid friendship for nearly twenty years. Also he noticed the difference in treatment doled out by the administration in its dealings with intellectual and political "bigwigs" on the one hand and to mere workers and peasants on the other and likewise the attitude of the former lot of inmates towards the latter. Whereas the latter were frequently beaten, the intellectuals had no hesitation in shaking the hands of those responsible for such maltreatment; likewise, they had no problem in securing the privilege of not being obliged to carry their irons with them all the time. They worked in the workshops that were interesting and above all monitored the inmates' internal administration very closely, which meant that all help from the outside passed through their hands and that they shared out this booty as they saw fit. In this way Makhno grasped once and for all that "... such is the psychology of these intellectuals who seek from the socialist idea and from their militancy only the means of ensconcing themselves as masters and governors. These gentlemen wind up unable to understand anymore that the offering of handshakes and the making of gifts in kind or in cash to torturers who, pocketing these gifts, go off to beat up the co-religionists of the very people who have just greeted them so amicably is intolerable." So much so that from then on Makhno lost all respect for "eminent political figures" of every persuasion and thereafter he called their role into question.

❧

The years passed, swallowed up by escape schemes that came to naught and by long, heated political discussions and wide-ranging reading. Cut off from the world, Nestor was carried away with and devised fanciful schemes for combating the State; thus it was that he came to draft his first piece of writing in 1912, a violent, inflammatory revolutionary poem calling upon the exploited to revolt against their exploiters, against the authorities, against all oppressors!

"Summons.
Let us rise in revolt, brethren, and with us the people
Beneath the black flag of Anarchy will revolt.
We will surge boldly forward, under the fire
of enemy bullets in the battle
for faith in libertarian communism,
Our just regime.
We shall cast down all thrones and
bring low the power of Capital.
We will seize the gold and purple scepter
And pay no more honor to anything.
Through savage struggle
We shall rid ourselves of the State and its laws.
We have suffered long under the yoke
Of chains, prisons and teeming gangs of executioners.
The time has come to rise in rebellion and close ranks.
Forward beneath the black flag of Anarchy, on to the great struggle!

Enough of serving tyrants as their tools,
That is the source of all their might.
Insurrection, brethren, laboring people!
We will sweep away all carrion.
That's the way we shall reply to the lies of tyrants,
We free workers, armed with our determination.
Long live freedom, brethren. Long live the free commune.
Death to all tyrants and their jailers!
Let us rise, brethren, on the agreed signal,
Beneath the black flag of Anarchy, against every one of them,
the tyrants.
Let us destroy all authorities and their cowardly restraints,
that push us into bloody battle!"[2]

This vibrant summons to insurrection is a good expression of Makhno's intractable character at the age of 23 years and which he was subsequently not to renege upon. Imprisonment, torture, penal servitude; nothing succeeded in breaking the young rebel's white-hot determination. He was bolstered in his beliefs by remembrance of the stories with which his mother had fed his childhood, tales of the life of free communities of Zaporog Cossacks in bygone times. He did not have any inkling that a "…day will come soon when he will feel himself their direct descendent and draw his inspiration from them in order to contribute to the free re-birth of his country!"

Although he remained hostile to any national separatism, he did take an interest in the ideas of his Ukrainian compatriots. The 1914 war split the inmates into two camps: patriots versus internationalists. Makhno naturally gravitated to the latter despite Kropotkin's having come out in favor of the Entente western powers. Increasingly he was alive to the noxiousness of every State system and the political and chauvinistic aberrations that this involved.

The revolution of March 1917, so long awaited, erupted at last and opened the gates of the prisons, though not readily, for certain of the people newly in charge wanted to conduct a sort of triage and to make a specious distinction between "common" and "political" prisoners. Makhno, delivered of his irons, after eight years of getting used to them, wobbled on his legs sometimes, having lost his sense of balance. He registered at Moscow city hall then, equipped with identity papers in order, was put up in a former hospital. He was advised to take himself off to the Crimea to have his lungs, in a terrible state, looked after. However, he had an "… intuition that only the tempest will be enough to cure him" and his sole concern was to hurl himself wholly into the whirlwind of revolution. He linked up with the anarchist militants of Moscow and participated with them in the Pan-Russian workers' demonstration.

At first he planned to settle permanently in Moscow, and it was only on the prompting of his mother and comrades from the Gulyai-Polye libertarian communist group who bombarded him with telegrams that he decided to go home. His reluctance to return to the place of his birth, paradoxical though it may appear, can be explained by the fact that decisive events were expected in Moscow. Be that as it may, he took the train and, after two days journey, was again in the bosom of his family.

Notes to Chapter 5: Penal Servitude

1. Nestor's mother had interceded with the governor of the province, but it is doubtful whether her intervention could have had any influence in the clemency shown her son; it was indubitably his tender years that suggested the possibility of redemption; moreover, his case was not unique, for that very reason, in those post-repression times.
2. The "Summons" appeared in the Russian libertarian magazine *Probuzdeniye*, published in Detroit, Michigan, USA, No. 50-51, in September–October 1934.

6. Social Revolution in Gulyai-Polye

After nine years' absence, Makhno was understandably moved when he came to breathe again the air of home. Now aged twenty-seven-and-a-half years, the best years of his youth had been spent in the jails and dungeon recesses of a despised Tsarism. He had vengeance to take against life, but he was a militant of repute and only action could slake his thirst for social achievement.

He went first to the home of his seventy-year-old mother who struck him as greatly aged and stooped by the years. He saw again his older brothers Savva and Emilian; his other brothers who had set up homes of their own while he was away were still serving at the front.

He came upon the surviving members of the Gulyai-Polye libertarian communist group, discovered what had become of this one and that, and made the acquaintances of the new young members of the group whose main activity consisted of surreptitiously distributing leaflets. Many peasants, male and female, showed up to greet this "man back from the dead," as they called him, and this gave him a chance to gauge how receptive they were to libertarian ideas. This sampling of opinions set him at his ease, and he cobbled together a meeting with his comrades from the group. To them he spelled out his analysis of the situation; without waiting for the libertarian movement nationwide to recover its strength and start to organize itself, anarchists ought to be in the vanguard of mass revolutionary action. His activism clashed with the opposition from certain traditional anarchist militants who were calling for a propaganda drive to target the workers and designed solely to familiarize them with libertarian ideas. He and his friends found themselves outnumbered in the group. Not that that mattered for on no account could he make do with such a passive approach and the urge to act, suppressed over so many years, was seething inside him. From the moment he arrived back, he took the initiative by suggesting that local peasants appoint delegates and establish a Gulyai-Polye Peasants' Union. Some days later, on March 29, 1917, they did precisely that: the union represented most of the commune's peasants and in the ensuing days was to embrace the peasants from the district and then of the whole region. Hot on the heels of this, the metalworkers and woodworkers organized committees of their own; a contingency fund was also set up. Infected by Makhno's radical enthusiastic speechifying, they all elected him as their chairman, ignoring his wishes!

Although this amounted to a relative infringement of the anarchist teaching that forbade acceptance of any formal authority, Makhno accepted all the posts that they sought to confer upon him and was everywhere at once, in the committees and at the anarchist group; he also toured the surrounding militants, he even undertook to ransack the archives of the local police; thus it was that he discovered that an erstwhile group member, Piotr Sharovsky, had denounced Alexander Semenyuta for the 2,000 ruble reward posted for his capture; not that his greed had been fully satisfied, for, according to the very same archives, only 500 rubles had been paid out to him! Nestor in this way came to realize just why this old friend had been nowhere to be found since his return.[1]

Whenever he was further elected as chairman of the communal committee, Makhno refused the appointment, for, on the one hand, he still did not know how anarchists stood nationally with regard to such elections, and anyway, if he had accepted the chairmanships of other committees, it had only been in order to reduce the authority of those committees and forestall the election of party political representatives in his place. If the latter were to succeed in gaining the upper hand over the wishes of the workers, he reckoned that they "...would inevitably kill any creative initiative in the revolutionary movement."[2] So if he did take up these various responsibilities, it was temporarily only, in order to be better informed about the actions of the formal authorities and to get the workers used to doing without "tutors" and to learn to shift for themselves.

He was also dabbling here and there and indeed, once the operation of these committees had been well "run-in," he handed them over to a thoroughly reliable comrade, while keeping "one eye on business."

His tireless activity led to his being delegated to the Alexandrovsk regional peasant congress. There he pushed through a vote to have the estates of the big landowners handed back to the peasant communes, without payment of compensation, to the great displeasure of the Social Democrats and Cadets[3] who advocated a buy-back policy.

His calls for collectivization of the land, factories and workshops had a tremendous resonance throughout the region, and many a person traveled for a great distance to consult him and take a lead from him. So much so that even the anarchists from the big cities of Alexandrovsk and Ekaterinoslav, learning of his successes, called upon him to come and take up a place in their organization or lend them a hand in their undertakings.

But Gulyai-Polye was his priority, and there, constantly on call, he never shirked. We might cite the case of the strike by the commune's workers, of whom he had been elected trade union chairman. Begged by the workers to assume leadership of the strike, he agreed, for one thing because it was incumbent upon him by virtue of his office, and for another, because he hoped to win the most pugnacious of the workers over to the libertarian communist group.

Before launching their strike, the workers, gathered together in a general assembly, called upon him to draft and present their demands to the bosses. After lengthy common discussion, he summoned the bosses and demanded of them an 80-to-100 percent wage increase under threat of an immediate and complete stoppage. The furious employers refused; he gave them one day to mull it over; the following day they showed up with proposals for a 35-to-40 percent raise. He "deemed that offer an outright insult" and urged them to take another day to think it over. Meanwhile, he arranged with the factory committees and workshop representatives to have the strike declared simultaneously throughout, should the bosses again refuse to meet their conditions. He even proposed to the workers that they proceed immediately with seizure of all capital assets whether on company premises or in the Gulyai-Polye bank, with an eye to utterly disarming the local bourgeoisie and to forestall possible steps by the authorities against strikers, pending their taking effective control of the firms upon themselves. The workers decided to leave this latter move until a later date, for they reckoned that they were ill-prepared for it, and they preferred to have the expropriations of the firms contemporaneous with the wresting of the estates from the big landowners.

The next day, the employers came back and, after two hours of quibbling, came up with an increased offer but one that was still less than had been asked for, hoping to hold out for a compromise. Whereupon Makhno told them that the negotiations were over and that he was winding up the talks. At this point, Kerner, the richest of the businessmen and one-time employer of Nestor as well as of his father Ivan, — an old fox sensing that things were taking a turn for the worse — hurriedly told him: "Nestor Ivanovitch, you were too hasty in winding up the meeting. I reckon that the workers' demands are justified. They are entitled to have us meet them, and I for my part am going to sign right away."

Willy-nilly the other bosses followed the example of their most prominent colleague and the protocol of agreement was signed. "Henceforth, the workers of Gulyai-Polye and surrounding area take all firms under their control, examine the economic and administrative implications of the affair and make ready to take over effective management."

Incidentally, Makhno and his comrades disarmed the local militia and re-scinded their powers of arrest and search and reduced them to the role of town criers. Then they assembled the pomieschikis, confiscated title deeds and on that basis, conducted a precise inventory of all these land holdings. It was at this point that the region's peasants refused to pay the usual farm rents to these landlords, hoping to recover the land from them once the harvest was in, without "bandying words either with them or with the authorities which looked after them, and then to share the land out among all, peasant or worker, desirous of working it."

❧

In view of all these moves and of the positive results that flowed from them, Makhno was startled by the smallness of the anarchist movement in the Ukraine and in Russia, whose militants were quite numerous at several tens of thousands but ultimately rather passive compared with the left-wing political parties when not swept along in their wake. Indeed, the majority of anarchists were content to peddle libertarian ideas and notions among the working population and simultaneously to organize communities and clubs. Makhno found all this very regrettable and he deplored their failure to organize themselves into a powerful all-Russian movement capable of espousing a shared tactic and strategy so as to play an active part in the movement of the revolutionary masses, thereby shaping events and linking up life and activity in towns with those in the countryside. Only thus, he reckoned, would it be possible to keep the social movement on course for libertarian communism.

All his life, Makhno was to regret the chronic disorganization of anarchists and its baneful impact, for all their numbers and good qualities, their inability to work to make hard and fast reality of their schemes of emancipation. He was even to attribute the failure of the Russian revolution and of the libertarian movement to this grave shortcoming.

૨૭૪

For his part, Makhno feared nothing in that year of 1917 and carried away by the sort of faith that moves mountains he contributed to the most radical, most daring ventures. On August 29, 1917, General Kornilov's thrust towards Petrograd, intent upon overthrowing the provisional government of the socialist Kerensky and establishing a strong authority, accelerated events. A committee for defense of the revolution was hastily set up in Gulyai-Polye; chairmanship of it was entrusted to Makhno. As he was simultaneously chairman of the Peasants' Union which had now become a "soviet," he had to divide his time between the two tasks. To counter the attempted counter-revolution, he suggested "…disarming the entire local bourgeoisie and abolishing its rights over the people's assets: estates, factories, workshops, printing works, theaters, cinemas, and other public enterprises," which would henceforth be placed under the collective control of the workers. The defense committee accepted his proposal; however, as Kerensky had managed to cling to power, the balance of forces did not make it possible to implement every decision made. For the time being, the peasants made do with withholding rents from the landlords and with assuming control of the land, livestock and machinery. Only several huge estates were collectivized; some farming communes, made up of landless families and small like-minded groups settled on them. Each commune numbered about 200 individuals. There was a huge number of communes dotted around the whole region. Let us look more closely at the ones that Makhno personally organized in the former German settlements of Neifeld and Klassen.

These libertarian communes were founded upon the principle of equality and fellowship among all their members, male and female. Cooking and dining facilities were shared although any individual could see to his own meals provided proper notice was given. Everyone rose early and set to work right after breakfast. In the event of absenteeism, the commune member would let his neighbor know so that a replacement could be found. The work program was arranged by common consent at general assemblies. Farming was not the sole activity; there was also craft production and even a machine shop.[4]

As a member of one of these communes, Makhno helped out with the work on two days a week; come the planting in the spring, he helped with the harrowing and sowing; the rest of the time, he busied himself about the farm or even lent a helping hand to the mechanic at the electricity station. At this point he was living with a companion, Nastia.

All of the participants looked upon this free communal lifestyle as the "highest form of social justice." Certain landowners came around to that way of thinking and set about working the land for themselves. Indeed, it was left up to the former landowners to choose whether to take an equal share in the commune's lifestyle and work.

From Victor Kravchenko, the future sensational defector, we have a description of yet another libertarian commune set up in the same area, near Korbino on the Dniepr.[5] Kravchenko's father was one of the promoters of this commune which was named "Nabat" (The Tocsin). It was comprised of about 100 worker families from Ekaterinoslav who had settled on the central portion of an old estate, comprising 200 hectares of wheat land and some orchards, as well as the seigneurial home and its outbuildings. Victor Kravchenko's father had refused to join the Communist Party for he "… had no taste for dictatorship and terror, he bluntly confessed, even if these were wrapped in the folds of a red flag" and so he wanted "…to remain free and to struggle on alone for a better world."[6] The settlement proceeded with the agreement of the local peasants who had divided up the remainder of the estate:

> "The local Soviet, endorsing the initiative, had divided up the estates; it had also provided the provisions and livestock needed to complement what was left of the assets of the former owners.
>
> In the towns, industry had ground to a virtual standstill due to lack of raw materials and food rationing was so strict that people were all but dead of hunger. So the flight to the land, which held the promise of well-being for everybody, had been well-received. The wish to appease certain intellectual urges had also prompted many to throw in their lot with us. Many men, in fact, burned with the desire to put into effect, within the narrow parameters of a cooperative farm, some of the theories that had been the stuff of their dreams over years of revolutionary fervor. The Tocsin, they told themselves, would ring out as a constant reminder of the ideal of brotherhood that seemed to have been forgotten completely in the tumult of the fratricidal war in which the communists, with their Cheka, were carrying out mass arrests and wrongly shooting folk on the most absurd pretexts.
>
> [...] To the farm workers the urban workers brought the energy of despair. Of course, above all else, they wanted to be able to feed their

loved ones, but they also sought to justify the sacrifices they had made in the past for their Cause. The local peasants made fun of these city workers-turned-farmers: We shall see, they used to say with a wink of the eye, how these 'communists' shall work our land!

At bottom such teasing was without malice; it was, rather, symptomatic of friendly interest. Many peasants hastened to advise us and to help us every occasion that they had the chance. Far from resenting our experiment, they looked upon it like good neighbors, with sympathetic interest. More than once, when we were overloaded with work, they supplied us with precious assistance, and it was they who made a success of our first year."[7]

Later this commune was to fold, a victim of events. The idyllic dream of "cooperative enterprise" was to dissolve in discord and bitterness, or even in "dismal despair," with commune workers quitting one after another.

The work of the Gulyai-Polye soviet's procurement section was remarkable also. It established contacts with the textile factories in Moscow and elsewhere, with an eye to arranging direct barter with them. Despite hindrance from the "new powers that be" at the center – Bolsheviks and Left SRs[8] in coalition, die-hard statists to a man — who could not tolerate barter between the towns and the countryside unless channeled through State agencies, two trade-offs were arranged; several wagon loads of wheat and flour, against wagon loads of cloth ordered by the soviet's procurement section. It was not a question of simple barter of goods of equivalent value, i.e., of circuitous commercial dealings, no; This was an exchange of goods in quantities that varied and determined only by the stated needs of both parties.

❧

It is also interesting to learn how dealings between the commune's different committees and the delegates whom they appointed were handled. These delegates, did they not become bureaucrats jealous of their prerogatives, uncontrollable and thus unaccountable, as has often been the case in history? The "Leon Schneider" case is a perfect illustration of the control that the committees sought to exercise over their elected or appointed officers. Schneider was a militant of a local anarchist group, delegated by the metalworkers' and woodworkers' committee as their representative to the Ekaterinoslav departmental soviet of peasants, workers and soldier deputies. His task was to oversee the supply of iron, cast iron, coal and other vital raw materials to the factories and mills of Gulyai-Polye. Schneider, contaminated by the "bureaucratic" atmosphere, neglected his duties and when called to account over the tardiness or absence of supplies, his answer was that he had no time to bother with that any more, that the departmental soviet had assigned him another duty, and he invited the Gulyai-Polye committee to appoint someone else in his place. He then received a telegram hinting that he should return to Gulyai-Polye forthwith to render an account of his stewardship; otherwise, two comrades would be dispatched to bring him back.

Suddenly more solicitous of his rank and file, he went back, delivered his report and was sent back to his workbench in the Kerner plant. Mortified he was to seize the earliest opportunity to avenge himself, as we shall see.

As for Makhno's role, at this time it is hard to get the precise measure of it; for all his offices and intense activities, he was regarded only as a sort of number one advisor, which is to say his advice and opinion were forever being sought but were not automatically adopted, far from it, either in the anarchist group — where he was often challenged, especially by the younger members — or in the soviet or indeed on the committee for defense of the revolution. In short, his responsibilities were enormous but his power small. In that he was indeed the consistent libertarian militant.

᪷᪷

However, dark clouds were gathering in the blue skies of revolution; first of all, there was the Bolshevik coup d'état in October, with which the Left SRs threw in their lot, the aim being to monopolize power, supposedly on the soviet's behalf; then along came the anti-Bolshevik rebellion by Kaledin, the ataman of the Don Cossacks, and that of the Ukrainian nationalists who aimed to drive out the *Katsapy* (Russians) and above all challenge all of the social changes made by the revolutionary peasants.

Faced with this situation, the Gulyai-Polye soviet decided to come to the aid of Alexandrovsk which was threatened by the troops of the Central *Rada* (Council), the government set up by the Ukrainian nationalists. That decision faced the local anarchists with a problem, for it had them support governmental forces here which, even if they were of the "left," were nonetheless potential enemies of the masses' autonomy. Makhno reckoned at the time that "…as anarchists we must, paradox or no paradox, make up our minds to form a united front with the governmental forces. Keeping faith with anarchist principles, we will find a way to rise above all these contradictions and, once the dark forces of reaction have been smashed, we will broaden and deepen the course of the revolution for the greater good of an enslaved humanity."

On January 4, 1918, a detachment of some 800-to-900 men was formed, some 300 of whom were members of the Gulyai-Polye anarchist group. Nestor's older brother, Savva Makhno, assumed command and off they went by train to Alexandrovsk to join up with Red Guards commanded by Bogdanov. Then Nestor was appointed a member of the city's revolutionary committee. He was placed in charge of the commission of inquiry into imprisoned officers accused of conspiring against the revolution: generals, colonels, militia commanders.… He was startled to discover among them the former prosecutor who had handled his case in 1909 and who had had him placed in the "hole" for complaining about his conditions of imprisonment. Makhno in turn had him placed in the very cell that he had occupied in those days, prescribing identical conditions for this ex-prosecutor. The wheel had turned; an irony of history that should still give all who bear the responsibility for repression good pause for thought.

᪷᪷

Nestor availed of his position to secure the release of workers and peasants still imprisoned under Kerensky and whom the Bolsheviks had refused to set free for fear that they might revolt against them too!

It was at this point that Nestor underwent his baptism of fire by confronting several Cossack regiments from the Don who were returning from the front to link up with Kaledin. In view of the lively resistance that they encountered, they surrendered; their weapons were taken from them and then they were sent home. That operation over, the Gulyai-Polye detachment made for home, though not without ferrying away some additional weaponry.

Makhno ran up against the thorny problem of finding funds for the activities of the soviet and commune. To be sure, he could have obtained any sum from the Alexandrovsk revolutionary committee, but in that case he would have acknowledged its authority and thus that of the Lenin government; Makhno would have none of that at any price. So he suggested to the soviet that it commandeer 250,000 rubles from the local bank. His suggestion was unanimously accepted. The money was seized from the bank in the name of the revolution to meet the needs of the soviet; delivered within a few days, it was shared, at Makhno's instigation, between a home for war orphans set up in the residence of the former superintendent of police, and the soviet's procurement branch; the remainder was to meet the needs of the revolutionary committee.

So it was that in the space of a year the Gulyai-Polye libertarian communist group, at the instigation of the compulsive Nestor with his multifaceted activities inside agencies representative of the working class, managed to contrive the winning of new social rights and, thanks to that, awaken a radical revolutionary consciousness in the region.

Notes to Chapter 6: Social Revolution in Gulyai-Polye

1. Not to be confused with his relation Vassili Sharovsky, a fervent libertarian who was to play a significant role in the Makhnovist movement.
2. All quotations in this chapter have been lifted from N. Makhno's memoirs *La Révolution Russe en Ukraine*, Paris 1927 (republished by Editions Belfond in 1970).
3. Constitutional Democrats, a liberal bourgeois party known by the initials KD or as the Cadets.
4. Yuri Magalevsky, a Ukrainian nationalist from Alexandrovsk, has plentiful details of this whole period of Nestor Makhno's life in his article, "Batko Makhno," which appeared in the *Dniepr Calendar* (in Ukrainian), Lvov, 1930, pp. 60–70.
5. V.A. Kravchenko *J'ai choisi la liberté*, Paris 1947.
6. Ibid. p. 45.
7. Ibid. pp. 44–45.
8. Social Revolutionaries, in short, SRs, who split with the bulk of the party to form a so-called Left fraction.

7. Ebb and Flow in the 1917 Revolution

Thus far we have followed events as they occurred in the southern Ukraine; the better to understand the narrative which follows we would do well at this point to recapitulate in brief the general situation in the erstwhile Russian Empire.

The days of rioting in February 1917 — known under the name of the February revolution[1] — put paid to the Romanov dynasty which was incapable of resolving the problems posed the modernization of the country and its assumption of its place among the most advanced nations. The world war of 1914 cruelly exposed this impotence. Commanded by generals whose sole concern was for their own personal advancement — often proportionate with the number of their troops killed — poorly armed and haphazardly equipped, the Russian army had suffered colossal losses — upwards of nine million dead and wounded, including the Poles — and had no precise notion of why it was fighting. Officially the goals were the capture of Constantinople and the independence of a reunified Poland; in fact, the backstairs intrigues of French and British imperialism against the German could hardly but leave the Russian peasant masses cold as they profoundly yearned for peace. To that basic aspiration were added the claims of the Empire's numerous nationalities and above all, the pressure for the agrarian reform urgently desired by the peasantry which accounted for almost 85 percent of the total population.

The provisional revolutionary government that succeeded the Tsar felt itself obliged to honor the alliance agreement with the Western allies and continued the war, which was increasingly unpopular in the land. As for the urgent nationalist and land questions, it put these off until after the election of a Constituent Assembly — the old dream of Russian democracy — which, equipped with full powers, would resolve all these thorny issues for the best. This political foot-dragging and legislative formalism sparked off an initial left-wing revolt by the Kronstadt sailors, limply supported by the Bolsheviks in July 1917 and then there was an attempted military putsch from the right in August 1917, by General Kornilov, the army's supreme commander, seeking to restore discipline and prosecute the war to victory; both threats were contained without much problem and they merely bolstered the power of Kerensky, an incorrigible chatter-box and "cardboard Robespierre."[2] Kerensky continued to play for time and lost all credibility to the advantage of

Lenin whose influence was ceaselessly growing in that he was promising the masses so much and then some.

Identical causes produce identical effects, and Kerensky's "house of cards" was collapsed in turn by an uprising of several thousand workers and Baltic sailors. Lenin capitalized upon this windfall, picked up the power "lying in the street" and cobbled together a new government, this time of "people's commissars."

The Bolshevik coup d'état was generally well-received by working people. Indeed, the watchwords on behalf of which it had been mounted … "All power to the soviets!", "Land to the peasants, factory to the workers", "Immediate peace" and "national autonomy for the different peoples of the Empire" could not have been better attuned to the aspirations of the populace. However, the "shrewd Lenin" (*dixit* Makhno) had merely played upon these aspirations for the sole purpose of ensconcing himself in power; once at the controls, he was to devote himself primarily to consolidation of his tenuous authority for it seemed the soviets and other factory committees or soldiers' committees were there for appearances' sake only, all decisions being made without any consultation with them, through decrees handed down and railroaded through by the "new worker and peasant government."

A de facto armistice was arranged with the Central empires; the soldiers' committees were overseen by Bolsheviks who wasted no time in getting rid of hostile officers and generals.

However, Lenin and his cohorts did not dare prevent the elections for the Constituent Assembly scheduled for late November, or over a month after their coup d'état. The elections — the only free elections in Russia's entire history — provided the Social Revolutionaries with a very substantial majority; almost sixty percent of the votes, whereas the Bolsheviks, even by stuffing the ballot boxes in the big cities which they controlled, picked up only a quarter of the votes.[3] This was a resounding repudiation. In principle, the new assembly, due to meet on January 5, 1918, was to assume the reins in the country and form a government representative of the generality of the citizenry. The Bolsheviks, though, continued to act as if nothing had happened and indulged themselves with a "temporary" ban on hostile liberal newspapers, set up the Cheka at the beginning of December 1917 and set about winning over the so-called Left faction of the Social Revolutionaries by offering them some portfolios and junior positions in the government. They succeeded in this latter undertaking by adopting wholesale the agrarian program of their allies and immediately declaring the land socialized, without compensation or conditions, thereby usurping the General Assembly that was to have pronounced upon this. The measure was favorably received by the peasant masses for it often sanctioned a *fait accompli.*

Hence the dissolution of the Constituent Assembly on the day following its opening session on January 6, 1918 triggered no great or immediate upset in the country. The Social Revolutionaries and their Social Democrat allies — the Mensheviks — the big losers in the episode, were convinced that in the end their legitimacy would win through, and they omitted to conduct a military operation (for which they did not in any case have the wherewithal) against these usurpers, having no wish to see even "… a single drop of Russian blood spilled" (Chernov, the Social Revolutionary speaker of the Constituent Assembly) this sort of squeamishness was to lead to an unprecedented bloodbath (the blood being shed was not just Russian but all types).

Confronted with this confused situation, several nations of the erstwhile Empire realized their ambitions: Finland, Poland, Georgia, and the Ukraine seceded and set themselves up as independent countries. The Don, Kuban and Terek Cossacks too wished to become autonomous and to set up a Cossack federation.

The Austro-German armies, hitherto observing a watching brief, capitalized upon the situation to unleash a mighty offensive in February 1918. They forged irresistibly ahead, for the Russian army had been demobilized and there were only Red Guards, who more readily fired on unarmed civilians than tackled real soldiers[4], to stop them. The Germans got to within 150 kilometers of Petrograd, passing through the Baltic lands, signed a separate peace treaty with the Central Rada, the government of independent Ukraine, and threatened the Bolshevik regime with complete collapse. Lenin insistently sued for negotiations, first of all without annexations or tribute, and then, with his back to the wall, agreed without further ado to all conditions imposed by the people who, in April 1917, had allowed him to return to Russia aboard the famed "sealed train"! He had the treaty hastily ratified by his party's central committee and the agreement was signed on March 3, 1918 at Brest-Litovsk. It provided for dismemberment of the former Russian empire, i.e., formal recognition of the independence of Finland, Poland, the Baltic states and the Ukraine, which is to say of territories covering an area of 780,000 square kilometers and a population of 56 million, all of them placed under the protection of the Austro-Germans.

Paradoxically, this situation worked to Lenin's advantage, and the operation proved a boon to him; he had had his power recognized by the central Empires, and he had no control over the ceded territories anyway; on the other hand, this capitulation afforded him some respite during which to better consolidate his shaky authority.

❧❧❧

For Ukrainian revolutionaries it was a real stab in the back. Their units had to let themselves be disarmed or evacuate the country and be disarmed anyway by Red Guards under Moscow's orders.

The Austro-Germans swooped on the Ukraine, guided by their local allies and bringing in their wake all the former great estate owners thrown out the year before by the revolutionary peasantry. Almost a million Austro-German troops occupied the territories ceded by Brest-Litovsk. The exactions and repression of the occupiers and of the Ukrainian oligarchy quickly triggered a popular resistance movement; dozens of local insurgent detachments sprang up to harry enemy troops, engaging in a savage war of national liberation.

This was the context in which Makhno found himself. At first, he thought of resisting the invasion of the German and Austro-Hungarian troops, in all several hundred thousands of well-equipped and organized soldiers — Makhno sets the figure for the Ukraine at 600,000. To this end, he proposed in Gulyai-Polye the formation of several battalions and companies, totaling nearly 1,500 volunteers. With this detachment he meant to join up with Red Guards and partisan groups that looked likely to stand up to the invaders. He managed to secure arms from the Ukrainian Red Guard command and received several carriage loads, containing 3,000 rifles, some cartridges and six cannon complete with shells. The city of Alexandrovsk asked the volunteers of Gulyai-Polye to come to its aid. A battalion of peasants plus the cavalry detachment made up of the members of Gulyai-Polye's libertarian communist group made for Alexandrovsk. As for Makhno, he was drafted on to the staff of Yegorov, the commander of the front. While trying vainly to get there, the rout having worsened, Makhno found himself stuck in a railroad marshaling yard. It was there that he got the stunning news that Gulyai-Polye had been occupied by German troops.

In fact, a handful of Ukrainian nationalists from the town, capitalizing upon Makhno's absence and that of the region's most dependable units, had managed to bribe the company formed by the town's Jewish community and abetted by them had arrested the available members of the soviet, the revolutionary committee and the anarchist group on April 15 and 16. Their treachery complete, these conspirators had then called in the Germans.

Among these Ukrainian nationalists were some landowners keen to recover estates confiscated for the use of the farming communes, which is scarcely surprising, but there was also Vassili Sharovsky, the artillery chief, who had been led astray. The worst thing was the part which the town's armed Jewish company had played; its leader, Taranovsky (who later on was also to be the last chief of staff of the Makhnovist movement) had refused to get involved in the plot; his adjutant, Leimonsky, had jumped at the chance to replace him and with the backing of the company membership — shopkeepers afraid of libertarian collectivism, their children and other young folk misled by the demagogic speechifying of the Ukrainian nationalists — had carried out arrests of local revolutionaries, as well as tricking into disarming the anarchist detachment just back from the front.

To make matters worse, Leon Schneider, the delegate called to order by those who had mandated him, had played an extremely active role, sacking the premises of the libertarian communist group and going so far as to trample upon portraits of Bakunin, Kropotkin and Alexander Semenyuta.

❧

Makhno was flabbergasted by the news; he was devastated that such a tiny number of conspirators — a few dozen — should have been able to undo so rapidly the achievements built up at the cost of so much effort over a year. He was immediately worried about the dangers of anti-Semitism that might be evoked in the peasants by the conduct of the Jewish company under arms. He wanted to get home but was talked out of it, for the Austro-Germans were already in control of the commune, and he would have been shot out of hand. He then thought up a title for an appeal that he set about drafting: "The traitor's soil and tyrant's conscience are as black as a winter's night." Yet the enemy troops' advance was lightning fast, and, in order to avoid encirclement, the partisan groups to which he was attached fell back to Taganrog, a port and railroad junction on the Sea of Azov. Towards the end of April, a conference drew together all the anarchists from Gulyai-Polye and its environs who had managed to reach Taganrog. The situation was reviewed, and it was decided that some of them should make a tour of revolutionary Russia in order to gauge the difficulties that she faced. Others were to remain behind to work on clandestine organization of revolutionaries. A rendezvous was set for late June — early July, a time that it was reckoned would be favorable for a return to Gulyai-Polye, and the initiation of a general uprising against the occupiers and their allies.

Notes to Chapter 7: Ebb and Flow in the 1917 Revolution

1. The Russian (Julian) calendar was then 13 days behind the calendar observed in other countries, so the February revolution is sometimes called the "March revolution" just as the October coup d'état has since been commemorated on November 7.
2. He collected titles: prime minister, justice minister, minister of commerce, and he styled himself "revolutionary generalissimo," commander of the army, to boot!
3. Out of 36,262,560 electors, the Social Revolutionaries and the Mensheviks took a total of 22,600,000 and 270 seats; the Ukrainian SRs and the Ukrainian Mensheviks took 41, the national minorities 33, the Cadets 15 and the Bolsheviks 161. The last-named, however, took nearly half of the votes in Petrograd and Moscow and a large percentage also from the army.
4. As they did against the peaceful demonstration in Petrograd in favor of the Constituent Assembly on January 6, 1918.

8. Wanderings

Makhno then embarked upon his tour from town to town, moving in a northerly direction, for he was due to visit Moscow and Petrograd. In Rostov-on-Don he was struck by the disarray of the revolutionaries, anarchists included.

In Tsaritsyn[1] he came upon his fellow communards from Gulyai-Polye who had had time to escape the vengeance of the estate owners. He saw again his companion, Nastia, pregnant and near to giving birth, but, with a heavy heart, he had to leave her to continue his travels.

Along the route he witnessed disturbing scenes: "revolutionary" authorities arbitrarily and systematically disarming all autonomous partisan units on threat of shooting any who refused to abide by their *ukases*. In particular he was an eyewitness to a confrontation between the partisan groups of Petrenko, an active but non-aligned revolutionary, and Cheka units. The latter had been routed and Petrenko could have taken control of the situation and "cleaned house," but he magnanimously declined.[2] Whereupon the authorities sued for negotiations during which they treacherously had him arrested before disarming his unit. Petrenko was shot a short time later on some trumped-up charge. At this same time the attack upon anarchist associations all over Russia was mounted in a concerted way; their premises were wrecked, their publications banned or tolerated only on specific Draconian conditions; the recusant were either jailed or shot on a variety of pretexts. The Bolsheviks and their Left SR allies rid themselves of their "troublesome" companions and indeed of all who might challenge their arrogation of power.

Everywhere, Makhno came to appreciate the revolutionary faith and commitment that motivated workers but also their lack of clear-sightedness regarding the ever increasing "prerogatives" of "revolutionary government." He saw at work certain so-called revolutionary elements made up of artisans, shopkeepers and déclassé workers, many of them Jewish, and who, for all their belonging to revolutionary groups of every hue, anarchist ones included, were wheelers and dealers in the circles of power. They were going to wind up as a breeding ground ready to tackle all manner of dirty work assigned to them: as Chekists, members of requisition detachments dispatched against the peasants, bureaucrats of every kind, etc.

These sad revelations led Makhno to wonder if "… the revolution is not destined to perish by the very hand of revolutionaries; in the way of its development stands an executioner sprung from the revolutionaries' very own ranks, the government of two revolutionary parties which, for all their titanic endeavors, cannot confine the whole of the broad, deep life of the workers within the narrow compass of their teachers."[3] He saw what these "institutional" revolutionaries were made of, who placed themselves athwart the road to liberation of the masses in revolution.

Makhno continued his journey aboard an armored train, with a company of Red Guards in tow. He saved them from capture by the Don Cossacks; at a halt, the Cossacks surrounded the train and prepared to swoop gently upon the passengers. Nestor ingeniously advised the unit's commander to fake a sudden artillery exercise so as to hold back the crowd and seize the chance to extricate the train. His ingenuity was to extricate him thus many a time from worse jams. He stopped over in Saratov in the Volga estuary for a few days before moving on to Astrakhan, albeit not without some difficulty as his only travel pass was his credentials as delegate from the Gulyai-Polye revolutionary committee. In the end, he completed the first stage of his trip by arriving in Moscow, which had been made the regime's new capital because Lenin thought that Petrograd was too exposed.

All of the personalities of the new regime and the officially-approved revolutionary groups were there. Makhno, who strove right away to make contact with the anarchists, noted how the new regime had the libertarian movement under surveillance, and it was only with difficulty that he managed a meeting with its most active militants. Attending rallies, he listened to the Menshevik Martov, to Trotsky, the commissar for War, and to the anarchist Alexei Borovoy who fired him with enthusiasm. He met up again with his prison buddy Arshinov who, for want of something better to do, busied himself with the League for the Propagation of Libertarian Ideas, publishing the classical works of Bakunin and Kropotkin.

Moscow struck him as the heartland of a "paper revolution" that attracted all — socialists or anarchists — who were enthused by one and the same thing "…Lots of talk, writing and from time to time a condescending offer of advice to the masses, but at a distance, from afar…."[4]

He met Kropotkin, on the eve of his moving house to Dimitrovka on the outskirts of the capital. The apostle of Anarchy made him affectionately welcome, answered his questions satisfactorily, and talked to him at length about the peasants of the Ukraine; but whenever he sought his advice about what he intended to do upon his return home, Kropotkin categorically refused to offer the slightest advice… "This matter is bound up with a very great risk to your life, comrade, and you alone can give it a proper answer."[5]

At their leave-taking, the old anarchist told him that "… struggle is incompatible with sentimentality. Self-sacrifice, tough mindedness and determination triumph over all on the road to the goal that you have set yourself."[6] The theoretician of libertarian communism had assuredly discerned Nestor's strong personality and noted his tendency to get a little carried away; otherwise there is no accounting for the author of *Ethics* having so bizarrely vetoed sentiment from the revolutionary struggle. It was probably a recommendation that Makhno not let himself be distracted from his goals. In any event, it made its mark upon the one-time terrorist and convict who was to bear it in mind at all times thereafter. A short time later, Kropotkin sent him a message urging him to "…take good care of himself, for men like him are all too rare in Russia," which just goes to show the regard he had inspired in his venerable elder, as well as the perspicacity of the latter.

Notes to Chapter 8: Wanderings

1. Later it became "Stalingrad," and after Khruschev's de-Stalinization drive, "Volgograd."
2. Such "magnanimity" (very much in the "Russian mentality") towards the Bolsheviks was to prove very damaging for the latter always strove to steer clear of all such "sentimentality."
3. N. Makhno *Under the Blows of Counter-revolution* (in Russian), Paris, 1936, p. 41.
4. Ibid. p. 101.
5. Ibid. p. 107.
6. Ibid. p. 107.

9. Interview with Lenin

Makhno went on frequenting Moscow's revolutionary haunts and paid a visit to the peasant branch of the central Pan-Russian executive committee of Soviets. In short he briefed himself so well that he had no further need to continue his tour as far as Petrograd, and he decided to make back to the Ukraine. However, he needed some phony identity papers if he was to cross the border established between Russia and the occupied Ukraine. He made up his mind to apply to the "bureaucratic center" — the holy of holies — in the Kremlin. Passed from bureaucrat to bureaucrat, he eventually wound up before Sverdlov, the chairman of the central-executive committee of Soviets, with whom he engaged in a discussion of the overall situation in the country and the Ukraine. Sverdlov found his views of such interest that he suggested an interview with Lenin himself for the following day. An appointment was made. By contrast, Sverdlov proved incapable of obtaining a room for Makhno who was without lodgings. So, the boss of the "blotting paper revolutionaries" could arrange for him to meet the "supreme guide" but was utterly powerless in the matter of his lodgings! What a disparity of powers!

Nestor was taken in by a friend he had met inside the Butyrki, and back he came the next day, brandishing all his passes. Lenin welcomed him "paternally"; he took him by the arm, placing a hand on his shoulder and had him sit in a comfortable armchair. Then he set about questioning him minutely: from where did he come? How had the peasants of the region understood the slogan "all powers to the local Soviets?" How had they reacted to those who were against this watchword, especially the Ukrainian nationalists?

Makhno answered that the peasants had understood the watchword as the expression of the consciousness and will of the workers themselves, that the village, district or regional soviets were merely the units of a revolutionary ralliement and of a self-managing economy serving the struggle against the bourgeoisie. Lenin came back to this matter three times, asking him if he regarded that interpretation as correct: when Nestor answered in the affirmative, Lenin then stated that the region had been contaminated by anarchism, and that that influence would not last.

Sverdlov joined in the conversation and asked Makhno if anarchism should be fomented among the peasantry. Whereupon Lenin pronounced that that would be to usher in counter-revolution and lead the proletariat to perdition. Makhno then lost his cool and protested that it would be nothing of the sort; Lenin set about rephrasing his comment; in his eyes, anarchists, having no large-scale organization of any substance, could not organize the proletariat and poor peasantry and thereby safeguard the revolution's gains.

The conversation moved on to the activities of the Red Guards for whom Lenin had a high regard. Pulling no punches, Makhno gave him an eye-opener by explaining that unlike the partisans who fought deep in the countryside, the Red Guards preferred to hold the railway lines, staying aboard their armored trains and raking their heels at the first sign of danger; that was why the populace, never having laid eyes on them, could not lend them their support. Lenin concluded from this — oddly enough — that the creation of a Red Army was the best solution and then he launched into a diatribe against the idealism of anarchists which would lead them to neglect the present for the sake of the future: "The anarchists are always full of self-denial and ready for every sacrifice but as fanatics and long-sighted, they see only the distant future and ignore the present."[1] Yet Lenin begged Makhno not to think he was applying this thought to him, for he looked upon him as a "man with a grasp of realities and the necessities of our age"; if only Russia could boast of one "third of anarchists of his ilk" the communists would be ready, under certain conditions, to march alongside them and cooperate for the sake of free organization of producers.

Soothed by these fine words, Makhno felt welling up within him a feeling of profound regard for his interlocutor, of whose acrobatics, chicanery and opportunist U-turns he as yet knew nothing. As for anarchists' alleged concern with the future at the expense of the present, he raised the example of the Ukraine — correcting Lenin, who, like many Russians of every persuasion, had used the expression "south of Russia" or "southern Russia" — where most of the partisan groups that had fought against the reactionaries were led by anarchists. Moreover, nearly all the communes or associations had been set up at their instigation. In quoting these tangible examples, he showed that it was clear that anarchists stood foursquare in the "present," where they looked to what might bring them closer to the future to which they gave, to be sure, every consideration. As he finished speaking, Makhno looked Sverdlov directly in the eye; Sverdlov's face clouded, and he blushed slightly but went on smiling at him. As for Lenin, he opened his arms and declared: "Perhaps I am mistaken...."[2]

Had he known at that precise moment that, a few years on, Makhno would be giving him sleepless nights and that he would be making him the quarry for his pack of Chekists and special units of the Red Army, Lenin would have realized that he was indeed mistaken. And without any doubt at all he would promptly have repaired his error, for all his ingratiating manner and sweet words, by having his enemy-to-be cast into the dungeons of the Cheka.

The conversation limped along a little while longer, but, the essentials having been covered, Lenin, again in his "fatherly" mode, asked Makhno's requirements in respect of identity papers and promised to do the needful for him. Some days later, towards the end of June, kitted out with these papers, essential if he was to get through the various checkpoints, Makhno took the train bound for Orel.

❧

His month-and-a-half long tour, which had taken him across the country, had enabled him to "take the temperature of the revolution," gauge the weakness of the anarchist movement, a weakness both organizational and due to the depredations of the Bolshevik authorities, observe the "leading" echelons, meet with the most influential personages ... in short, to formulate an exact idea of what had been done and of all that remained to be done in order to keep the revolution on the right course.

Notes to Chapter 9: Interview with Lenin

1. N. Makhno, *Under the Blows of Counter-revolution* (in Russian), Paris, 1936, p. 131. That interview, taken from the Memoirs, appears in Daniel Guérin, *No Gods, No Masters* (AK Press, 1998) Book Two, pp. 130–137.
2. Ibid. p. 133.

10. Back Home Again

Upon arriving in Orel, a border town, Makhno was imprudent enough to climb down from the train and was unable to board again, for the carriages were swamped by passengers. He managed to get across the border even so, disguised as a Ukrainian reserve officer. He came upon some Jewish friends from Gulyai-Polye who briefed him on developments locally, including among other things the death of his older brother Emilian, a war invalid, who had been mistaken for Nestor and shot by the Germans. His other brother, Savva, had been arrested, his mother's house destroyed and his mother taken in by neighbors; finally, there were the shootings and torture directed against many anarchists and revolutionaries from Gulyai-Polye.

Although devastated by these initial reports, Nestor steeled himself; he was among his own, the peasants of the Zaporozhiye, loyal to their age-old yearnings for emancipation, far removed from the decrees and other pious pronouncements of Moscow, capital of "paper revolution." Here he was now at the heart of the real problem and only upon himself and those of his comrades from the Gulyai-Polye anarchist group who had got away could he rely for a resolution.

The closer he drew to the land of his birth, the more people he met who knew him; he was obliged to trade his Ukrainian officer's uniform for civilian clothes. At one stop, he was warned by his friend Kogan from Gulyai-Polye that the German police had boarded the train to search for him; he hurriedly left his carriage and covered on foot the twenty-seven kilometers to his destination, the village of Rozhdevstvenskoye, some twenty-one kilometers from Gulyai-Polye.

At the border, Makhno had spotted some notices in German: "Deutsches Vaterland" (German territory) — the Ukraine had become an integral part of the German and the Austro-Hungarian empire! More devastating still, since Brest-Litovsk, an expeditionary corps had been in occupation, enforcing German order.

The Central empires, delighted with the assistance rendered by Lenin and his government, hoped to draw from the Ukraine's rich natural resources the wherewithal for a second wind in their war in the west against France, Britain and the United States.

The Ukrainian national assembly — the Rada — being regarded as insufficiently compliant, had been removed from power on March 29, 1918; the occupation had replaced it with the hetman[1] Pavlo Skoropadsky whose forefather had been the last hetman of a free Ukraine prior to its annexation by Russia in the eighteenth century. A mere puppet on a string, the hetman had formed a national guard — the *Varta* — an auxiliary for the Austro-German governors of the country.

The Ukrainian bourgeoisie and feudalists had wasted no time in rallying around the new regime, for in that way they might use occupation forces to counter recalcitrant peasants before reclaiming the estates and assets of which the peasantry had collectively dispossessed them. The vengeance of these "lords" was savage: thousands of peasants were flogged, imprisoned, shot or hanged. The whole country was ransacked; all food, consumer goods and material were shipped off to Germany with the blessing of the hetman and the local squire-archy. Let us look at the testimony of one John Xydias, a Russified Greek living in Odessa, a dyed-in-the-wool capitalist, and, liberal as he was, scarcely to be suspected of subversive views:

> "German and Austrian troops having entered the Ukraine, their command had to decide upon the attitude it would adopt regarding the revolutionary distraint upon the estates of the pomieschikis. As the main concern of the central powers was to siphon off the Ukraine's reserves for their own benefit, whereas the establishment of an equitable social peace left them wholly indifferent, they opted to side with the bourgeoisie and above all the big estate owners.
>
> [...] Not only did the German occupation authorities show themselves conciliatory and well-intentioned towards the pomieschikis, bringing none of the weight of their rule to bear upon them, but they even went out of their way to do anything in their power to be agreeable to them. Above all else, the estate owners were to be restored in the property rights which revolution had stripped from them. This was one of the most shameful episodes in the entire history of the civil war. Let it be stated frankly: their conduct towards the peasants ensured that the infiltration of revolution, which had been interrupted for a time, came back with a vengeance once German troops evacuated Russian soil. Many landlords did not bother to re-install themselves on their former estates but, abetted by German and Austrian troops, set about divesting the peasants of their lands and their assets. In cruelty and cynicism, their reprisal raids outdid the famous expeditions of Tsarist times, especially as the Austrian and German officers who commanded these detachments claimed a percentage of the booty. Thus a detachment would arrive in a village; on the instructions of the *pomieschik*, a collective note was presented to the peasants, demanding the return of

given quantities of livestock, tools, chattels, etc.; the raid complete, the German or Austrian officer would pocket ten percent to twenty percent of the value of the 'restored' assets. It goes without saying that the German military, educated to the most profound contempt for the Russian people, were very appreciative of these sources of income and shrank from no measure, no matter how brutal, likely to generate them.

[...] The reprisal expeditions were marked by hangings and shootings. Executions dispensed with any sort of proceedings; the venom of the landlords cared not a jot for it, and the German officers gladly washed their hands of any show of a trial. They shot and hanged without any pretense of trial, often not even bothering to check the identity of the 'defendant.' The landowner or his agent had merely to declare that such and such a peasant had been involved in confiscation of his estates for the 'culprit' to be summarily executed.

One can readily appreciate the rancor that built up in the souls of Ukrainian peasants, and what hatred and revenge such barbarous executions engendered against landowners. Powerless against the armed might at the disposal of their oppressors, the peasants knuckled under and suffered, as they awaited their revenge."[2]

As an active revolutionary center, Gulyai-Polye merited special treatment; the members of the soviet, revolutionary committee and libertarian communist group were denounced by Ukrainian nationalists and the local bourgeois. Once arrested, they were tortured and shot, excepting those who had successfully gone to ground and who were living a clandestine existence. Among the anarchists to fall victim to this "White Terror" was the group's first secretary, Moshe Kalinichenko; shot but still alive after the opening salvo, he continued to berate his executioners before being finished off. Lioba Gorelik, a very active libertarian from the town's Jewish community, was beaten to death; Stefan Shepel and Korostelev (known as Khudai), courageous militants, also perished. Nestor's older brother, Emilian, almost blind following a wound sustained during the Russo-Japanese war in 1904, was shot in front of his wife and their five young children. Others were jailed in Alexandrovsk to await the same fate: Alexander Kalashnikov and Nestor's other brother, Savva.

Such was the picture of devastation uncovered by Makhno upon arrival here where, for nearly a year, he had made an intense contribution to the founding of a free community based on social justice. He reestablished contact with those close to him, his relatives and several members of the anarchist group, returned, like him, from Russia, as agreed at the Taganrog conference. Every one of them advised against showing his face again in Gulyai-Polye, for he would be instantly denounced by some nark in the pay of the occupation, arrested and speedily executed.

For some weeks, he hid in a neighboring village; then, unable to stand it any longer, he returned to his native town one night to seek out some reliable peasants there. With them he evaluated the situation and briefed them on his travel experiences. The letters that he had written them had been reproduced for circulation in the area. In them he had advocated autonomous and organized action by the peasants and counseled against terrorist acts that would draw down foreseeable repression and hamper the overall organization of the insurrection. Above all, he was against acts of vengeance against members of the Jewish company who, intimidated or bamboozled by the Ukrainian nationalists' threats or promises, had assisted the arrest of Gulyai-Polye's revolutionaries. Such acts might be misinterpreted and give rise to a display of anti-Semitism, thereby compromising the region's revolutionary reputation. However, he was unable to prevent sentence being passed on Leon Schneider, the group's renegade, although Schneider had completely vanished. He also managed to set aside the cases of Vassili Sharovsky and Taranovsky who, caught up in the conspiracy in spite of themselves, had promptly dissociated themselves from it and had since bitterly regretted their passivity in not opposing it.[3]

Makhno reckoned that the political preparation of minds was the priority; he zealously peddled the idea of a general uprising against foreign and native-born oppressors. He did not rest from holding get-togethers and small meetings at which he advocated, in the light of this idea, mobilization of local detachments of insurgents.

His presence was reported to the authorities, and he was obliged to quit Gulyai-Polye. However, now that it was known that he was around and trying to organize armed bands, they did not dare execute the anarchists jailed in Alexandrovsk for fear of reprisals. A substantial price was placed on his head. The dragnets and searches were stepped up; he narrowly escaped one enemy patrol simply because, caught in the act of explaining the operation of some Colt and Mauser revolvers to some peasant friends, he was able to offer an immediate practical demonstration and thus extricate himself!

The first detachment calling itself Makhnovist was formed in a village near Gulyai-Polye, Voskressenska, and it mounted raids against the squires and the enemy's detachments.

Makhno also began to lead the same sort of attacks along with peasants from Ternovka village, but he nonetheless felt that the lead should come from Gulyai-Polye which enjoyed huge popularity throughout that part of the Ukraine. So he went back there and, with the agreement of his comrades, decided to blow up the Austro-German district command center in the township. Dressed as a woman, a comrade from the group, Isidor Lyuty, alias Petya, who was never far from Makhno's side and served as his bodyguard, went off to reconnoiter. As for Nestor, he dressed up as a young woman, making up his face and equipped with some powerful bombs, set off with Petya to carry out their mission. Only the presence of some women and children in the room where the targeted officers were altered their plans, but Nestor had trouble getting Petya to accept this. Indeed, it was at all times as a conscientious militant that he evaluated their operations and their consequences, and he was very well aware that this instance, which would inevitably have cost the lives of innocents, would have been very badly received by the population.

Notes to Chapter 10: Back Home Again

1. The word "hetman" is a contraction of the German word *hauptmann*. It is characteristic to note that originally there were no Slav words to designate "chiefs" and that all terms employed since in Russian or in Ukrainian have been borrowed from a foreign language, e.g., tsar, from the Latin *caesar*, kniaz (prince) from the German *Koenig*, ataman (Cossack chief) from the Turkish word for a troop leader. We must therefore take it that the Slavs originally knew nothing of hierarchy and governed themselves by means of a direct democracy.
2. J. Xydias *L'Intervention française en Russie, 1918–1919*, Paris, 1927, pp. 56–59.
3. V. Sharovsky had nonetheless sabotaged weapons surrendered to the Germans and conveyed his support to Makhno. He was later to become responsible for all of the Makhnovist movement's artillery.

11. The Beginnings of Partisan Warfare

Having peddled the idea of a general insurrection throughout the district, Makhno and his companions resolved to strike and to make the first move by occupying Gulyai-Polye which they had designated as the insurgent center. On September 22, 1918, Nestor and his fellow members of the Gulyai-Polye anarchist group — Alexei Marchenko, Semyon Karetnik, Petya Lyuty, Andrei Semenyuta (the last brother of Prokop and Alexander, the founders of the group) and one Foma Riabko, from elsewhere — began their odyssey along with seven peasants from the villages of Ternovka and Vassilevka.

The group was some 90 kilometers from Gulyai-Polye and reckoned to cover that distance in nine hours. Nestor, disguised as a captain of the Varta, stood on a *tatchanka*,[1] atop which a Maxim gun had been mounted; his companions followed on horseback, armed with rifles. They quickly encountered a genuine Varta unit. Taken in by his splendid uniform, the hetman's guards let them get within 30 meters; whereupon Makhno stood up on the tatchanka and called upon them to drop their weapons; they made as if to rally but a burst of fire from the Maxim gun, aimed above their heads, forced them to reconsider.

Nestor proceeded to question them, passing himself off as a captain specially dispatched by the hetman to track down revolutionaries in the district. Reassured, the commander of the Varta detachment supplied him with full intelligence concerning Austro-German forces in the area, their quarters and their strength; moreover, he boasted of his own exploits in the repression against the recalcitrant peasants of the region.

Dropping the pretense, Makhno then disclosed his true identity, to the amazement of the hetman's soldiery. They fell on their knees before him to beg his mercy and tried to bribe him with promises of hefty sums of money. Having no proof of their misdeeds, Makhno decided merely to tie them up and to dump them out of sight like that off the road, until they might be freed by shepherds or might free themselves, this lest they give away his presence too soon. In so doing he revealed one of the characteristic features of his personality; outside of combat, he was always to abhor bloodshed and was to resort to it only when pushed to the limits by the atrocities of the enemy. But the Varta guards, panicking, took to their heels. Whereupon the Makhnovists were obliged to cut them down. Not far from there they came upon a local police chief who called them to explain the meaning of the shots he had heard; in view of his insistence in citing the authority of the hetman, Makhno had him hanged from the highest cross in the nearby cemetery, displaying a placard bearing the inscription: "One should fight for the emancipation of the workers and not for executioners and oppressors."

This episode can serve as an archetype of all that were to ensue: Makhno and his companions were often to show up disguised as regular soldiers and, capitalizing upon the element of surprise in the stratagem, disarm and punish their enemies.

The next night, pressing on with its ride, Makhno's detachment passed without mishap through villages lying on the route to Gulyai-Polye, thanks to the uniforms they were wearing. They arrived in Gulyai-Polye in the early morning and at the last minute just avoided running smack into numerous German troops, having just enough time to scurry away and hold up in a nearby forest. There they came upon some shepherds who informed them that the German authorities and their native-born allies were everywhere spreading a rumor that Makhno had retreated to Moscow, after having robbed the peasants of Gulyai-Polye; he had supposedly bought himself a luxury home and was living high there. He was even shown a leaflet written in Russian and Ukrainian with words to that effect. The bigger the lie the better it works, professional liars sometimes tell themselves; this was the source of the Makhno "rumor" that was to spread just as the Makhnovists' struggle assumed larger dimensions.

A little later, when they were in Marfopol, a village adjacent to Gulyai-Polye, Makhno and his band encountered an Austrian detachment accompanied by a squadron of the hetman's police. Makhno threw them off the scent by starting to flee from the village; he did so the better to expose his pursuers, then cut them down with the machine gun. Among the survivors from the enemy band, the Gulyai-Polye police chief who had distinguished himself in the repression against the peasants was instantly executed. Among the other prisoners were two Ukrainians conscripted against their will into the Austrian army. Makhno dictated a letter to them for translation into German for distribution among the troops. He urged them to disobey their officers and cease all participation in the repression of the Ukrainian working people and to go home and carry out their own revolution. If they persisted in following their officers, they would then have to face the vengeance of insurgents who would make no distinction between them and the butchers of peasants. He released these soldiers with that message then — there being limits to his trust — he made off with his group first in one direction, and then, once out of sight, swung around and stopped in a nearby village, Shanzhorovka, some 17 kilometers from Gulyai-Polye.

The next day, the Austro-Germans took severe reprisals against the Marfopol peasants. The day after that, seizing upon the absence of the bulk of the enemy forces, Makhno entered Gulyai-Polye, scattered nearly all his men through the district, charging them to raise the peasants and stayed behind in the town with just seven men. A local assembly was held the following night with 400 inhabitants attending. Discussion centered on the best way of launching the insurrection, where and how to direct it, how to seize hold of the bulk of the enemy troops and disarm all occupiers. The whole program was worked out for the next night. Meanwhile, Makhno wrote two proclamations for distribution just as soon as Gulyai-Polye would be under the complete control of the insurgents.

As scheduled, the following night the insurgents seized control of the area with great ease and no casualties on their side. They were in control of the post office, telephone exchange, railway station and the access routes to the town. Makhno's two appeals were printed — 7,000 and 20,000 copies respectively — and quickly distributed and followed up by insurrectionary acts throughout the whole region. A revolutionary committee was appointed forthwith and a telegram written by Makhno was dispatched all over the Ukraine:

> "To everyone, everyone, everyone! The Gulyai-Polye district revo-
> lutionary committee announces the seizure of Gulyai-Polye by the
> insurgents: there the power of the soviets has been re-established. We
> declare a general insurrection of the workers and peasants against the
> butchers and stranglers of the Ukrainian revolution, the Austro-Ger-
> mans and the hetman's guards."

The Austro-Germans recovered a few days later and marshaled significant forces around Gulyai-Polye. Makhno and his companions decided against digging in there and resolved to evacuate the town, letting it be believed that the populace had complied without actually supporting them, this in order to forestall reprisals such as had occurred at Marfopol. It was for this reason that the local assembly had been held at night and had attracted only the most dependable inhabitants, so as to avoid possible denunciations should the insurrection fail. Makhno handled things intelligently and with prudence, but not without mishap, for his suggestions were one by one challenged by other members of the group – who formed, as it were, the general staff of the movement. The facts, though, proved Makhno correct on several occasions and so his companions abided more and more scrupulously by his directives. He displayed remarkable gifts as a leader of men, gifts that never failed him thereafter.

On September 29, enemy troops attacked from all sides: the insurgents repulsed them and then, towards evening, when they saw the threat of encirclement looming, they peeled off in the direction of Mariupol, a port on the Sea of Azov.

En route, capitalizing upon the darkness and the suddenness of their appear-ance, they disarmed some squires and their guards, changed horses and recovered a machine-gun. Just as they had done before, they followed a false trail in order to shake off possible pursuers, and stopped over in the town of Bolshe-Mikhailovka (or Dibrivka) on the edge of the Dibrivka forest some thirty-six kilometers from Gulyai-Polye. The next day, they met up with the sixty strong detachment of Fedor Shchuss, an anarchist sailor who had taken part in the Taganrog conference and since waged a bitter struggle against the occupation. Shchuss was content to harry, successfully it should be said, the occupation troops and the punitive expeditions of the squires and the Varta. Makhno suggested to him that they should join forces in order to conduct open, rather than guerrilla warfare. The amalgamation went ahead and a joint meeting was held in the town; at it Makhno delivered a long address that scared his friends, for he issued a summons to the struggle against all enemies, present and future, in the shape of the Russian White Guards who were beginning to invade the region. The populace rallied to his proposals and within two days there were nearly 1,500 volunteers, only one in four of them armed.

On the strength of mistaken intelligence, the insurgents took inadequate precautions in the belief that the enemy was not in the vicinity. Thus, one night they were taken by surprise and, knowing nothing of the exact strength of their assailants, Makhno ordered a withdrawal. Many insurgents had not had time to join him and were penned in Dibrivka while an ambush cut off the retreat of a small group of fugitives in the direction of the forest. It was at this point that Makhno revealed an extraordinary military talent; he, who had never done any soldiering, had his men move forward at right angles, skirting the enemy position and ensuring access to the forest. Shchuss intended to retreat into the impregnable blockhouse that he had built himself inside the forest and there await the enemy's evacuation of the region, so as to be able to tend his wounded and avert reprisals against the town.

Makhno's priority was to establish the numbers of enemy troops; they proved to be far superior numerically and in terms of armaments. Even so, Makhno proposed to attack; Shchuss resisted this for a long time on the grounds that it was madness to attack such superior forces. Whereupon Makhno gave a speech that enthused all present, and this was the occasion on which the Dibrivka peasants awarded him the title of Batko: "Henceforth, you are our Ukrainian Batko, and we shall perish together with you if need be. Lead us into town against the enemy!"[2]

In his memoirs, Makhno remarks that he really must have been an anarchist revolutionary not to succumb to this honor awarded in all naiveté by the mass of peasant toilers who had faith in him. He justifies this confidence by commenting: "It would appear that I was that revolutionary for all my subsequent actions have confirmed it."[3]

That night, September 30, 1918, saw the first great feat by arms of the insurgents. Indeed, Shchuss, Makhno, Semyon Karetnik and Marchenko, Lyuty and Petrenko (the latter a local insurgent of great promise) selected the most daring and determined of the partisans, split into two groups, one with Shchuss's men armed with a Maxim and the other under Nestor's personal command, equipped with a Lewis submachine gun; in all about 30 men, attacking a battalion of the Austrian regular army — almost 500 soldiers — about 100 well-armed squires and 80 Varta guards, which is to say, odds of 25-to-one!

The enemy was bivouacked on the square in front of the town's church, awaiting reinforcements before moving out at dawn to pursue the insurgents into the forest. Well-briefed on the disposition of the enemy, Makhno and his companions skipped into the town and proceeded through the streets and the courtyards of the *khatas*. Before attacking and while waiting for Shchuss to get in position, Nestor spoke these last fiery words: "This is it, we are in the arms of death. So, friends, let us be dauntless to the point of madness, as our cause demands!"4

One final incident almost betrayed their presence; the local mistress of the commander of the Varta guards had made up her mind at all costs to warn her loved ones of any insurgent attack, and it was only on a tip-off from a peasant woman of the town that the insurgents managed to intercept the traitor at the last moment.

At a signal arranged with Shchuss, Makhno directed heavy and accurate gunfire at the enemy, sowing panic among the troops who had been calmly bivouacked with weapons stacked; a surprise attack was the furthest thing from their minds.

To hasten the enemy's rout, Makhno hurled himself into the attack. The soldiers and enemy guards fled for all they were worth, their officers setting the example while the Dibrivka peasants, brandishing pitchforks, clubs and axes, pursued them, adding to their panic. Makhno had great difficulty in extricating twenty-five Austrian soldiers from the hands of peasants eager to lynch them. The trophies of battle were great: four machine guns, two munitions trucks and eighty prisoners, mostly ordinary soldiers and Varta guards, the officer having scarpered or perished in the fighting.

The Varta members and members of the band of landowners were shot out of hand for, despite warnings, they had persisted in their repressive activities. As for the Austrian soldiers, they were fed then released on promising to fight no more against the revolutionary peasants; they were issued with provisions and a bottle of vodka but stripped of their kepis — this symbolic act indicated their "demilitarization."

᪥

From that day on, all his companions displayed great affection towards and every confidence in Nestor, his tactics and operational strategies. His renown, boosted by tales of his military prowess, grew without cease; he became "Batko Makhno," the people's avenger; reluctantly to begin with, then with his agreement once he realized that he was a rallying point.

He had occasion to wreak people's vengeance a short time later during an incident that was to remain the most famous of all. A band of insurgents had been smashed and several dozen prisoners treated cruelly and hanged near a village by the name of Mikhailovo-Lukashevo. A Varta captain by the name of Mazukhin had especially distinguished himself in this repression. One evening, after having laid waste to an enemy German settlement, Makhno and his detachment ran across this same Mazukhin, along with a small escort. As ever, Makhno seized the initiative by calling out imperiously: "Halt!...Who are you? Where are you coming from?" He heard, by way of an answer: "Who commands your detachment? I am staff captain Mazukhin, Varta commander for the Alexandrovsk district." At this point the insurgents surrounded him and took him prisoner. This savage pacifier then begged them in vain to spare his life. From a letter found on him, it was discovered that he had been en route to a soirée organized by a local squire called Mirgorodsky. Makhno and Shchuss donned the clothing of Mazukhin and his adjutant before showing up in their place at Mirgorodsky's fortified farm. They announced themselves as Mazukhin's aides and outriders. They were made welcome to cries of "Hurrah for the Russian officers!" The company there was select: a retired general, a colonel, three Austrian officers and two local squires, as well as their womenfolk.

The assembly toasted their host, the renaissance of Russia, the landlords and the salvation of the Russian church from anarchists. When a fresh toast was offered to the success of the hunt for Makhno, Makhno drew a bomb from his pocket and hurled it towards his fellow guests, disclosing his true identity, before dashing outside with Shchuss! Frozen in their tracks with fright, the revelers did not have time to escape and perished in the explosion. It ought to be said that there was no quarter given on either side; during the entire period of the Austro-German occupation of the Ukraine almost 80,000 peasants paid with their lives for their resistance to oppression.

In this climate, a dramatic incident played a capital role in the movement's birth; this was the matter of reprisals taken by the Austro-Germans and the local squires (especially German settlers) against the township of Dibrivka. They put 608 khatas to the torch and beat, tortured and murdered the peasants, raping the women. All these actions left the peasants of the region thoroughly outraged. Makhno and his detachment acted as the executive arm of this thirst for vengeance, and they showed no pity this time in laying waste the homes of the squires.

But here again, it fell to Makhno to display his tactical intelligence; he opposed systematic massacre of all the squires and bourgeois in the region and did not want some blind *jacquerie* but rather a social war waged with discrimination. He preferred to hurt the privileged in their pockets, at least provided they had no criminal acts to answer for, and he exacted from them substantial fines in money, arms and material. He also sought to stoke up the social inferno in the whole region to a maximum. The slow patient preparation over weeks paid dividends; bands of insurgents were organized throughout the region, and they harried the occupiers and their allies.

This vast game of cat and mouse was to drag on for several weeks with the insurgents and their enemies taking the roles in turns; while the latter gave chase, the former would show up in their rear and smash their isolated units.

Let us note that Nestor Makhno had learnt well from Alexander Semenyuta when he used to carry out his daring acts of terrorism, but in addition, he displayed great organizational and military talents. He was methodical to the point of mania, a thoroughness without which he obviously could not have survived hundreds of battles and preserved the essential core of the movement. Whenever he occupied an area, he immediately set up outposts on every side, day and night, and this ensured that he would not be surprised and be in a position to react as he chose, according to enemy numbers and to stand and fight or slip away. Then he would lay false trails as to which direction he was taking, by frequently changing his course; he moved, preferably under the cover of night, into areas where no detail of the topography was unknown to him and while keeping himself permanently informed as to enemy movements. Finally, he missed no opportunity to address the peasants, whipping them up with his fiery, spirited diatribes against the oppressors, so much so that they soon came to consider him their natural defender. It was for this reason that they all loved to call him "Batko" and avidly told of his exploits. To these gifts, Makhno added the qualities of rare sangfroid and presence of mind; he scarcely ever was ruffled, would sum up the situation in a flash and devised the best possible solution, which would allow him to extricate himself yet again from the hornet's nest.

&&&

Yet at the beginning, this self-mastery was not always apparent; on one occasion, his negligence even had disastrous consequences for his detachment. Billited in the village of Temirovka on November 15, 1918, some insurgents picked up a suspect, a local kulak by the name of Tsapko. This Tsapko, although quite well known as an informer for the occupiers, claimed to have come to seek permission for a relative's bridal procession to pass through the village at dawn. Against the advice of his comrades, Makhno set Tsapko free, refused to vacate the area and took no special precautionary measures. A half hour later, the camp was violently attacked by a Hungarian detachment well briefed, thanks to Tsapko, regarding the disposition of the insurgents. A shambles ensued; Makhno quickly reacted, placing a Lewis automatic rifle on Petya Lyuty's shoulder and sweeping the attackers with gunfire, bringing their advance to a stop. Marchenko attempted a counterattack with a group of horsemen but to no avail and sustained heavy losses. The insurgents fell back and found themselves in the open; the Hungarian snipers seized the chance to pick them off one by one with accurate fire. Shchuss was hit by a bullet that pierced both his legs. Pinned down by Hungarian fire, the insurgents were decimated. At one point, Podgorny, an insurgent, attempted to salvage the situation by taking the assailants from the rear with a machine gun and about fifteen partisans. The Hungarians received reinforcements, and the situation became hopeless for Makhno and his companions, who were in any case hampered by their wounded whom they doggedly refused to abandon. Semyon Karetnik was hit also. Out of ten men around Makhno, soon only two were left and one of these, losing control of his nerves, took his own life with a bullet to the head. The unarmed Makhno dashed forward to retrieve the revolver from the suicide and found himself suddenly hemmed in by silhouettes whom he thought enemies; rather than let himself be captured, he too prepared to blow his own brains out when he realized that in fact these were companions coming to his aid: Lyuty, Marchenko and Piotr Petrenko. They saved him by carrying him off at a gallop while he squatted on two rifles, crossed one over the other. Once safe, Makhno realized that he had been wounded in one hand and that the tops of his overcoat and of his papakha had been shot through in several places. The detachment managed to slip away, but its losses were dramatic — nearly half of its 350 fighters — although the Hungarians too had taken considerable casualties.

۞

The lesson was a severe one; henceforth nothing would ever be left to chance, and they would be wary of the suspect. Despite this serious reverse, the insurgents went on ravaging the fortified farms of the German colonists and the squires of the region; not without difficulty, for they were quite numerous in that *chernozyom* country and quite well-armed. Be that as it may, the insurgents were now chastened and highly motivated; in the space of a few weeks, the whole area surrounding Gulyai-Polye had been cleared of nests, units and punitive detachments of Germans, Austro-Hungarians, German colonists and the Varta.

The whole left bank of the Dniepr was aflame, as the general uprising spread like a trail of gunpowder. Towards the close of 1918, this initial front had been solidly established in the Alexandrovsk region and at its heart was Gulyai-Polye. Makhno then dispatched a menacing telegram to the German high command in Alexandrovsk; in it he insisted upon release of imprisoned members of the Gulyai-Polye anarchist group and held the German authorities answerable for their safety. This threat gave pause for thought; the reply from the German commander in Alexandrovsk to the insurgent high command was conciliatory and guaranteed the lives of the prisoners. The insurgent movement had become a viable and intimidating interlocutor.

An extraordinary conference drew all the delegates from all of the region's insurgent groups. At it Makhno blithely proposed opening up four fronts; against the hetman, the Germans and Austro-Hungarians, against the Don Cossacks of the ataman Krasnov, against the White Guard detachments of Colonel Drozdov which crisscrossed the Berdyansk district and against the White general Tillo and the detachments of Germans moving up from the Crimea to "pacify" the region.

His comrades thought he had taken leave of his senses, for they reckoned they did not have sufficient forces to hold such an extensive broad front. He countered by arguing that henceforth they had to move into a higher phase of the struggle and, to that end, had to turn their detachments into mixed battalions of cavalry, infantry mounted on machine gun carrying tatchankas, plus an artillery section. Moreover, he wanted to capitalize on the fear that insurgents had struck into their enemies and give an added boost to the resolution of the peasants of the region. He ended up securing the backing of those present, who then proceeded to elect people to take charge of the fronts; Piotr Petrenko got the one stretching from Chaplino to Grishino; Tykhenko the younger and the sailor Kraskovsky got the one between Pologui and Tsarekonstantinovka. A third front around Orekhovo would be formed under the supervision of Batko Pravda, a highly pugnacious legless cripple and anarchist. From the assembly, these overseers received the following instruction:

> "Every discretion is given them in order to introduce the revolution
> — any discipline that might abet the organization of the combat sector
> and the fielding of a single contingent of fighters — with the consent
> of the masses of the insurgents concerned, obviously. In operational
> terms, they are completely subordinate to the main high command of
> the insurgent units bearing the name of 'Batko Makhno' and directly
> answerable to the Batko himself."[5]

This federative organization rendered possible a unity of action that was essential for operations on a large scale. Makhno, then, amassed the functions of general commander-in-chief and chief of the central command which included his two aides Shchuss and Petya Lyuty, as well as Semyon Karetnik and Alexei Marchenko. Furthermore, an intelligence source was established, made up essentially of peasant women volunteers whose task it was to keep the command *au fait* with all of the enemy's movements and dispositions.

Yet there was still a huge gulf between intentions and realities and the insurgents had to go through many engagements, with varying fortunes, against all their enemies. Makhno, the movement's command staff and his escort came within an ace of annihilation in an engagement near Sinelnikovo. They were encircled by German and Austrian troops, sustained heavy losses and were only rescued in extremis by the providential arrival of several detachments of partisans summoned to the rescue by the local population.

Among the reinforcements, the detachment from Ulyanovsk, made up exclusively of 250 peasant ex-soldiers, distinguished itself by successfully, and despite a hail of gunfire, putting the enemy to flight and pursuing him over a distance of more than ten kilometers.

⁂

Little by little, Makhno and his main detachment managed to structure all of the local groups to the extent where accesses to and exits from the region were locked up tight and all passage denied to German trains.

On November 20, 1918, during a routine check on a train, Makhno and the younger of the Karetnik brothers, Pantelei, were gravely negligent; they departed from the usual practice of stationing dynamiters in front of the train and of positioning barricades in front of and behind the checkpoint. Now this was an armored train in the hands of White Guards; these White Guards let fly with murderous gunfire at Makhno and his companions before making good their escape. Several elite outriders from Makhno's detachment, experienced former border guards, were killed. Seeing the grief of the insurgents, the White Guards reckoned they must have killed Makhno. The report of his death immediately swept the country to the great rejoicing of the Austro-Germans and the landowners. The White officers in charge of the raid were even decorated in Alexandrovsk and feted as heroes in the local press. Rumor had it that the Makhnovists were on the run everywhere; the squires and their guards who had sought refuge in the town began to drift back to their estates.

Now, Makhno stepped up his raids and took it upon himself to give the lie to the rumors of his death. If they showed any resistance, the squires were wiped out; otherwise, the insurgents made do with seizing all their weapons, horses and any equipment that might prove useful.

❦❦❦

Meanwhile in Kiev, a coup d'état ousted hetman Skoropadsky and a new Ukrainian nationalist government seized power under the name of the Directory; the strong man in it was Simon Petliura, whence the name Petliurists given to its supporters. This new government sought to be independent of the Germans and Austrians who, in any event, no longer had any reason for fighting since the November 11, 1918 armistice concluded with the Western allies. The new authorities freed all political detainees; thus did the anarchists from Gulyai-Polye return home. Among them were Savva Makhno, Alexander Kalashnikov and Filip Krat.

A period of wait-and-see ensued; for several weeks a truce with the Directory held. The Directory had an interest in courting the insurgents, for it hoped to be able to deploy them in its nationalist cause while at the same time it was on the best of terms with the Russian White Guards and encouraged the formation of regiments destined to join up with the White general Denikin.

❦❦❦

In a little over two-and-a-half months, Makhno and his anarchist comrades had succeeded in the gamble of liberating the greater part of the Eastern Ukraine from the grip of the German and Austro-Hungarian armies of occupation and of their local allies. The tiny detachment of a dozen men which had set out from Ternovka for Gulyai-Polye on September 22, 1918, had turned into an insurgent army manning several fronts connected by a central command. Henceforth, Makhno and his companions were battle-hardened, at the cost of heavy losses, it is true. They had become conversant with the strategy and tactics of partisan warfare, knew how to avoid the pitfalls of classic positional warfare, chose the time and place for their engagements and always popped up where least expected. They knew how to dynamite and take over an armored train or a fortified farm. They knew too that above all they had to rely on their own devices in the defense of their interests and their freedom.

Their enemies had changed too; no longer were they occupation troops, demoralized by their defeat in the West and who thought of nothing else but getting home as peaceably as possible. A much more dangerous enemy loomed on the horizon: regiments of Cossack officers and troops, commanded by General Denikin.

Notes to Chapter 11: The Beginnings of Partisan Warfare

1. Tatchanka: a two-wheeled or four-wheeled open-backed *barouche* which Makhno put to ingenious use by installing a machine gun, machine gunner and assistant in the rear, with a driver and another fighter in the front of this horse-drawn vehicle, with its team of two or four horses. This innovation was to play a great part in the Makhnovists' military successes and was then to be taken up by every other army in the Ukraine.
2. N. Makhno, *The Ukrainian revolution* (in Russian), Paris, 1937, p. 84.
3. Ibid., p. 85.
4. Ibid., p. 86.
5. Ibid., p. 143.

12. The Civil War in Russia

Towards the close of 1918 the civil war in Russia crystallized on several fronts. For a start, in the south, in the Cossack territories of the Don, the Kuban and the Terek, several armies were making headway under the unified command of General Denikin. Let us briefly review the origins of this movement.

Nationalistic officers could not have remained indifferent in the face of the evolution of the country which they found catastrophic. Already under Kerensky, General Kornilov, appointed generalissimo (commander of the entire Russian army), had rebelled against the authorities, citing the absence of the necessary order and discipline required in his view to bring the war to a victorious conclusion. Contrary to what has often been claimed, Kornilov was a patriotic officer who had risen through the ranks, the son of a mere Cossack, with a Sart (Mongolian) for a mother, and while no inflammatory revolutionary, it had nonetheless been he who had ordered the arrest of the Tsar and his family; so he was no reactionary but was solidly anti-monarchy and wont to say to any who would listen that he would emigrate to the United States should the monarchy be restored in Russia. After the failure of his coup de force, he was placed under arrest under the supervision of his friend and successor, the generalissimo Alexeyev and of the latter's chief of staff, General Denikin. Following the Bolshevik coup d'état of October 1917, Kornilov and Alexeyev hurriedly decamped for the Don, which area they had assessed as suited to their patriotic activity. Word circulated among nationalistic officers and a tiny contingent of volunteers was formed in Novocherkassk, the capital of the Don Cossacks.

The Volunteer army came formally into existence on December 25, 1917, under the military command of Kornilov and the administrative command of Alexeyev; its objective was to raise an "…armed force capable resisting the growing anarchy and the occupation, whether Bolshevik or German; an armed force whose duty it will be to afford Russian citizens a free choice of the government of their homeland through the summoning of the Constituent Assembly." This last item was further confirmed by the dissolution of the said Assembly by Lenin some days later. A small front was established on the basis of the three main Don cities: Taganrog, Novocherkassk and Rostov. The Volunteers wore a small white ribbon to distinguish themselves from their enemies — their uniforms being for the most part similar — and it was this that ensured that they were henceforth known as the "Whites."

❧❧❧

Routed by the Red Guards, they were obliged to fall back in the direction of Ekaterinodar, capital of the Kuban. The Don Cossack's ataman, Kaledin, strove in vain to raise his Cossacks against the Bolsheviks in the name of the territory's autonomy, but he went unheeded and committed suicide out of despair on January 29, 1918. The contingent of 4,000 Whites began its march on February 9th, in the depths of winter (for which reason this march is known as the "ice campaign") and battled its way across 400 kilometers before collapsing outside Ekaterinodar at the beginning of April 1918. Kornilov, killed by a stray shell on March 31st — which suited the reactionaries in his camp just fine — was replaced by Denikin who was also of very modest origins (a father who had been born a serf before rising through the ranks as an officer) and whose mother and wife were Poles; this Denikin was a fanatical advocate of a "Russia one and indivisible."

Despite early reverses, the band of Whites grew, boosted first of all by some officers who had managed to join up with it and then by the Cossacks of the Don and the Kuban. At first neutral, the latter had quickly been persuaded by events of the danger inherent in the Bolsheviks who abruptly abolished their traditional rights and, moreover, brutally commandeered their foodstuffs and belongings. Three White armies were formed; the army of the Volunteers, the army of the Don Cossacks commanded by the ataman Krasnov, and the army of the Kuban commanded by Colonel Pokrovsky who was subsequently promoted general by the *Rada* (government) of the Kuban. It was only several months on that they were to be brought under Denikin's overall command and not without friction.

These three armies had their work cut out with a Red Army of some 100,000 Cossacks and troops. In the end they occupied Ekaterinodar in August 1918 and then the northern Caucasus, barring the road from Moscow to their adversaries; then they cleansed the whole of the Caucasus of enemy units; finally, they occupied the Don territory and set themselves the goal of seizing the rich mining basin of the Donetz and the southern Ukraine to the southwest and Tsaritsyn to the north, thereby carving a path towards Moscow.

❧❧❧

Conscious of the fact that their power was going to remain fragile unless they had solid armed backing to call upon, Lenin and Trotsky founded a new army, dubbed the "Red Army of workers and peasants" and this replaced the Red Guards and the partisan detachments which were deemed too independent. It was more than just a change of name; a complete change of outlook was involved here; this was no longer workers under arms, but a compliant armed force in the service, the *exclusive* service of the authorities.

However, this army was not created out of whole cloth; the former Red Guards and soldiers from the erstwhile Russian army were paid a wage and were led by former Tsarist officers in the guise of *military experts* and the latter were themselves shadowed by political commissars — Bolshevik militants — charged with monitoring their loyalty to the new regime.[1] Entire regiments of Latvians from the old Russian army, with officers at their head, were absorbed whole into the Red Army. "Internationalist" regiments and battalions were made up by Poles, Chinese and Hungarian ex-POWs and their Serbian and German counterparts: While awaiting hypothetical repatriation, the latter became "fighting hostages." All of these "mercenaries" did not waste much time in proving themselves. As for the Russian soldiery, they either signed on or were forcibly enlisted and, in the event of insubordination or desertion, they were liable to the death penalty. Trotsky, a lover of fine phrases, spelled out their alternative thus: "Probable death while advancing, certain death in retreat."

In this way the strength of the Red Army reached 600,000 men by November 1918, rising to a million by February 1919. On March 12, 1918, Trotsky was appointed people's commissar and president of the military council, which had been set up at his suggestion.

The most startling thing was the recruitment en masse of ex-tsarist officers, hitherto so much denounced. Most of them joined in all good faith, in the belief that they were placing themselves at the disposal of a "Russian" government intent upon the welfare of the people. The most ambitious of them spotted the chance of rapid advancement in a new army; others were forced into it, with their families held hostage against desertion on their part. These recruits included such bigwigs as Brussilov, erstwhile commander of the Front, plus instructors from the military academy, well-known ex-generals like Bonch-Bruevich and Sitin, a one-time minister of war like Polivanov and tens of thousands of officers and NCOs like Tukhachevsky, Shaposhnikov, Zhukov, Blucher, Sergei Kamenev, etc.

This being so, the Bolsheviks were to be ill-placed to take their White adversaries to task for being Tsarist ex-officers for they themselves had as many of those in their ranks as their adversaries did (some 30,000 in 1918 and more later). Of course, this whole new army and its composition represented grave injury to Lenin's theorizing as spelled out in *The State and Revolution*, but as in religion, accommodations sit easy with doctrine, provided they be made in the name of the sacrosanct cause.

❦

The presence of numerous foreigners in the contending military units — there were some 250,000 foreign combatants in the Russian civil war, and it may be said that the part they played was crucial to the course it took — was at its most spectacular in the case of the Czech Legion. Under compulsion and constraint, the Czechs had served with the Austrian troops against their fellow Slavs. At the first opportunity they had surrendered en masse to the Russian army. Having agreed, at the request of the Allies, to take up arms again against their former masters, they had been organized into an autonomous army corps some three divisions strong, led by Russian officers — a force of about 45,000 men. They had distinguished themselves in the offensive ordered by Kerensky in June 1917 and which had come to an abrupt end. In light of the turn taken by developments in Russia, it had been decided that they would be evacuated to Siberia for re-deployment on the Western front alongside the Allies. They had taken the train for Vladivostok, when, en route, in Chelyabinsk, certain incidents brought them into conflict with local Bolsheviks. Trotsky attempted to ride roughshod over them by issuing an order for them to be disarmed and that they be incorporated into the Red Army, with any who refused dispatched to concentration camps. The upshot of this mishandling of the situation was not long in coming; the Czechs went on the offensive and at the end of May 1918 they seized the main stations on the Trans-Siberian railroad, coming formally into conflict with the Bolshevik authorities. In the whole of Siberia, this important armed force, well-equipped and officered, was to play the role of arbiter for upwards of two years.

❦

The members of the Constituent Assembly dissolved by Lenin had not given up. They rose in revolt, and abetted by the Czechs, they seized Samara on the Volga and in June 1918 they formed a "Committee for the Constituent Assembly" (the *Komuch*) and then a provisional government initially made up exclusively of so-called center or right Social Revolutionaries. This government immediately promulgated several democratic decrees: some local organs of self-management — the peasant and urban committees — had their functions restored, the death penalty was abolished (even for Bolsheviks), restrictions on revictualling were rescinded, the eight-hour working day was introduced, the ban on strikes lifted, a ban placed on the lock-out, and fresh elections were to be held to the soviets, etc. The Mensheviks then joined this government which controlled a sizable part of central Russia and a population of some twelve million. At first it appealed to the inhabitants to enlist voluntarily in a Russian democratic army, but when the 10,000 volunteers proved inadequate, it ordered conscription of younger ones, which, to be sure, resulted in an army some 40,000 strong, but one badly led by officers of reactionary persuasions. The Committee for the Constituent Assembly enjoyed the support of the Czechs, all of them of democratic persuasions, who handed over to it the huge gold reserves captured from the Bolsheviks in Kazan. However, some ill-advised "bourgeois" measures were to alienate the bulk of the population from the committee; the banks and industry were de-nationalized and compensation had to be paid to landlords for properties seized from them by the peasants. Also, it was to meet with increasingly open hostility from the "Omsk bloc," the Siberian government set up with the support of the bourgeoisie and all the monarchist reactionaries who had fled there — many of them officers disinclined to forget the treatment that the Social Revolutionaries had meted out to them at the front in 1917. The latter schemed every bit as much and more in order to secure the exclusive backing of the Czechs and the Allies, and they also intended very obviously to seize the gold reserves, a substantial consideration in any diplomatic maneuvering.

The Committee for the Constituent Assembly found itself bolstered by the worker uprising in Izhevsk and Voltkinsk. Nearly 35,000 workers from the arms factories situated there rebelled against the Bolsheviks, drove them out and formed regular regiments which threw in their lot with the Russian democratic army.[2]

Samara's Social Revolutionaries found themselves between the Devil and the deep blue sea: the Bolsheviks and Omsk's reactionaries. Under pressure from the Allies, a gathering of 23 different Siberian governments and groupings — cooperative associations, political organizations, etc. — was held in Ufa in September 1918, and its protracted negotiations ended with the establishment of a common Directory made up of five members, including Admiral Kolchak (backed by the British) as Minister of War. The seat of the new government was switched to Omsk (and the gold shipped there also), Samara being, it was reckoned, too close to the front. In principle, the Constituent Assembly remained sovereign, but a new national assembly was due to be elected on February 1, 1919. In spite of everything and because of the Social Revolutionaries' presence, the Directory enjoyed the backing of the populace and the mobilization that it decreed is telling on this point; some 200,000 conscripts reported for induction. The big bourgeoisie and the toppled aristocrats could not bear, however, to be elbowed out of the direction of operations; so, with the support of the soldiery, they mounted a coup d'état on November 18, 1918 with the blessing of the British and hoisted Admiral Kolchak into power. Eliminated, the democrats found themselves hunted down, shot out of hand or treated as enemies; at first this drew from them resistance and protests, but those were followed by direct uprisings against those who had usurped popular legitimacy.

Urged on by the Allies, Denikin acknowledged Kolchak's suzerainty and both were openly abetted by the Anglo-French in terms of arms, munitions and equipment. These Allies placed formal conditions upon their support; Kolchak and Denikin had to acknowledge the authority of a future Russian government formed following the summoning of a freely elected constituent assembly, as well as the regulation of conflict caused by the prescription of the country's borders through the League of Nations to which the new Russia would be obliged to affiliate.

❦

The whole business was complicated further by the direct intervention of the Allies. Up until the Brest-Litovsk treaty, they had been lost in speculation about the intentions of Lenin's government. But confronted with a fait accompli and discovering its perilous consequences in the shape of German offensives on the French front, Paris, London and Washington were forced to make a stand; however, they had not given up hope of turning the Russian situation around, for they knew that many leaders, including the Bolsheviks' allies the Left SRs hoped for a resumption of hostilities against the central empires. The assassination of Count Mirbach,

Germany's ambassador in Moscow, and the ensuing uprising of the Left SRs which met with some initial success before meeting defeat in the hands of the Letts and Hungarians in Lenin's service, dispelled their lingering hopes and then induced them to side openly with enemies of the Bolsheviks. The principle of a "barbed wire curtain," subsequently referred to as a "cordon sanitaire" was espoused with an eye to isolating Red Russia as an objective confederate of Germany. Henceforth, all anti-Bolshevik forces were given help in the shape of arms and munitions, the Czechs were encouraged to keep control of the 7,000 kilometer-long Trans-Siberian railroad, and French, British, American, Italian and Japanese troops landed in Vladivostok in August 1918.

The entry into the war of the U.S., with its vast potential, alongside the Anglo-French, tipped the scales once and for all in the latter's favor; moreover, disorders broke out in the German army, exhausted by upwards of four years of stressful combat; confronted with this threat of disintegration at home, the central empires' general staff concluded an armistice with the Allies. The implications for this situation inside Russia were enormous; first of all, the Bolshevik leaders *ipso facto* tore up the humiliating treaty of Brest-Litovsk and gained some elbow room in areas hitherto occupied by the Austro-Germans. Moreover, the Allies were no longer bothered about intervening and directly abetting the anti-Bolshevik movements. The most serious impact was felt by the 600,000 Austro-Germans tied down in the Ukraine and now caught in a trap. Those of them who found themselves furthest to the west still managed to quit the Ukraine without too much difficulty and to return home; the rest found themselves continually harassed by partisan detachments keen to avenge 80,000 peasant fatalities caused by the occupation. Frequently Austro-German evacuation convoys had to do battle in order to force a passage for themselves, and they did not always come off best; in which case their officers paid with their lives for their collective crimes and the ordinary soldiers were freed without further harm. Obviously, the loot and arms of intercepted units were confiscated and used to equip local insurgents. Another repercussion was that Poland and the Baltic countries — Latvia, Estonia and Lithuania — regained their independence completely.

***

The withdrawal of Austro-German troops left the arena open for all movements possessed of enough men and weapons to assert themselves. In the east, in Siberia, Admiral Kolchak's 130,000-strong army began to push towards Moscow from January 1919 on; one by one it seized the stations on the Trans-Siberian route and established itself on four fronts:

- the most important front was the central front — called the Western front — established in the Kazan area. The Kolchakists were commanded by two Czech generals, Jan Syrovy and Gajda. There were 42,000 Russians and 20,000 Czechs there, well-armed and with 182 cannon at their disposal;

- the southwestern front stretched from Samara to Orenburg; essentially it was manned by Cossacks from the Orenburg, commanded by the ataman Dutov; about 28,000 men and 54 cannon;
- the Ural front, further to the south, was held by the Ural Cossacks led by General Akutin; about 5,500 averagely armed men; and,
- the northwestern front, which was to cover the vast regions lying to the north of the central deployment, was commanded by General Ivanov-Rinov who could call upon 36,000 poorly-equipped men.

Against these fronts, the Red Army, divided up into six armies commanded by Tsarist ex-generals, also numbered 130,000 men able to call upon 300 cannon. Conscripts under force have little stomach for fighting; so they were stiffened by the more readily manageable Hungarian, Latvian and Chinese units.

To these fronts let us add the front of the ataman Semenov in central Siberia; backed by the Japanese, he had at his disposal several thousand Buryats, Mongols and Ussuri Cossacks.

❦

In the far north in Arkhangelsk an expeditionary corps of 15,000 British had been landed; a supreme government was founded up there under the leadership of the old populist socialist Tchaikovsky. A little later, in January 1918, the Russian general Miller was appointed governor of the province and had at his disposal an army of 7,000, against some 20,000 Red soldiers.

In the southwest, in December 1918, the French fleet anchored off Odessa. The troops of General Franchet d'Espérey (who subsequently became Marshal of France) were due to be deployed in a possible operation in the Ukraine to back up the oversight of central Europe. The French were joined by a contingent of Greeks and an inter-allied expeditionary force 50,000 strong and commanded by General Anselme was deployed between Odessa and its region, from Tiraspol to Kherson and Nikolayev, as well as in the Crimea where the French occupied Sebastopol and Simferopol. Their arrival encouraged the growth of groups of White officers answering to General Denikin.

Further west, the Poles benefited from French military assistance and were active on the borders of their huge northern neighbor. The Ukrainian nationalists at last held much of the Ukraine, but they were poorly-equipped and had to make a stand on every front, for they were recognized by no one; the Allies looked upon them as in cahoots with the Germans, the Poles disputed with them for Galicia, Denikin denied their right of secession, Moscow simply ignored them and only with Makhno (and then only initially) was a de facto neutrality feasible.

❦

Thus towards the beginning of 1919 Lenin's Russia was encircled by several important fronts. It did, however, have at its disposal the vastness of the interior of the country — all these fronts being on the periphery — where the arms factories and the bulk of the population were located; in addition, it was able to deploy the huge arms reserves of Tsarist Russia. All of these trump cards were far from insignificant; however, Lenin lacked the chief asset, popular support, for his regime was ill-served by its agrarian, and indeed its labor policy. On some it imposed massive requisition of foodstuffs and goods; in its dealings with the others it divested of all power the factory and workshop committees that they had elected.

Not that this occurred without popular resistance and popular revolts; according to the very statistics of the Bolshevik's people's commissariat for Internal Affairs, between July and the end of 1918, 129 anti-Bolshevik revolts erupted in just the sixteen provinces of European Russia[3]; in particular, 27 armed uprisings occurred in just the two provinces of Tambov and Voronezh over the same period. According to the same source, the chief cause of uprisings was the requisitioning of wheat and forcible recruitment of conscripts. Most were the handiwork of Social Revolutionaries, but often they were spontaneous. These clashes were bloody if one is to judge by the fact that in the months of July, August and September 1918 some 15,000 Bolsheviks and the like perished in some 22 provinces of European Russia.[4] It is true that the backlash from the Leninist authorities must have been even more terrible.

It may readily be appreciated that peasants and workers mobilized under coercion had no stomach for the fight and had a tendency to surrender quickly when confronted by a determined enemy, even if it meant swelling his ranks instead.

Notes to Chapter 12: The Civil War in Russia

1. Soldier's pay was 150 rubles per month while officers and political commissars received some 3,000 rubles, or nearly 20 times as much! By comparison, the single rate of pay for all ranks in the democratic army of the Committee for the Constituent Assembly was to stand at 15 rubles as of July 1918.
2. L.M. Spirin *Classes and Parties During the Civil War in Russia* (in Russian), Moscow, 1968, pp. 261–266. The author indicates that during the two months of their insurrection, these two plants were to turn out 65,000 rifles as well as 50,000 cartridges and 500 shrapnel grenades per day! That despite the mobilization of the bulk of the workforce in the battle against the Bolsheviks. The author is obliged to comment upon this "social anomaly" by explaining that in history there have been comparable precedents where peasants and workers fought against their own interests; he cites the example of the peasants of the Vendée who fought against the French republic, and the workers in the armies of Cavaignac and Gallifet who crushed revolutionary movements. His argumentation is quite poor if one places these examples in their historical context, in no way comparable with that of 1917.
3. Ibid. p. 180.
4. Ibid. p. 185.

13. The Birth of the Makhnovist Insurgent Army

From November 1918, Makhnovist partisans were manning a front on the edge of the Don territory and the Donetz basin. They confined to that area the movements of the Don Cossack army of the ataman Krasnov and the detachments of General Mai-Maievsky's Volunteer army. Given the length of the front, it looked as if it would be hard for them to establish another one to the west, in their rear, against the Petliurists. When the Petliurists allowed the formation of White Guard detachments on their territory, relations became strained; they became openly hostile when the Directory came out in favor of the petite and medium bourgeoisie, and they were virtually at war once it announced a general mobilization throughout the length and breadth of the Ukraine, including territory controlled by Makhno. Makhno did his best to obstruct it by every means; however, at a meeting in Ekaterinoslav between Korobets, the Petliurist commander in the town, and the insurgents' command led by Alexei Chubenko, a compromise was hammered out and there were even plans for a joint campaign against Denikin. Furthermore, the nationalists supplied the Makhnovists with weapons and munitions.

However, the natures of the two movements were too much at odds for any entente to last. Paradoxically, it was an incident involving a third party that brought about the split. The Petliurists broke up the workers' soviet of Ekaterinoslav, arrested six Bolsheviks and shot two Left SRs.

The members of the broken soviet and the Bolsheviks appealed to Makhno. Out of solidarity, he agreed to intervene; also because he wanted to get his hands on the enormous arsenal stored in that city.

That was the first mistake; he flew to the aid of political adversaries whom he had bitterly criticized a short time before. His second mistake was of a military nature; he overestimated the assistance promised by the Bolsheviks and Left SRs — a thousand workers and militants, when there was to be only half that number — and underestimated enemy strength (nearly 4,000 men) not counting the endlessly awaited reinforcements. It would appear that Makhno had been dragged along against his better judgment, at the insistence of his friend Alexei Marchenko.

At the head of 600 partisans, Makhno determined upon an attack on December 27, 1918, against the garrison of the regional capital. Everything started well enough, thanks to an ingenious and daring stratagem; one band of partisans, led by Kalashnikov, shipped aboard a morning train normally crammed with workers, seized the railroad station without firing a shot while the remainder of the Makhnovists neutralized guard posts on the approaches. The booty was not to be dismissed: 20 machine guns, four cannon and ammunition. But the Petliurists dug in in the city where the street fighting, to which the partisans were hardly used, was to drag on for several days.

During the battle, the Bolsheviks "played politics" and passed to Makhno a dispatch from Lenin reminding him of their interview and confirming him as commander in chief of the "soviet" forces in Ekaterinoslav province. To which Makhno replied that there were no "soviet" forces, only the Makhnovist insurgent army. Undaunted, the Bolsheviks persisted with their rigmarole and appointed themselves to take charge of the town; as commanders of the town and the militia, as post office commissars and communications chiefs, as well as other bureaucratic officers. All this while Makhno was fighting day and night in the front lines and without rest.

When the fighting was over, all of the self-appointed bureaucrats showed up at Makhno's headquarters on the second floor of the railway station in order to take "delivery of power." As soon as he realized what was afoot, Makhno put them to flight with kicks and "slaps about the back of the head," not merely from "that story but also from the station." Driven out by the door, the Bolsheviks returned "via the windows," again approaching him to get him to back their candidacy in the town's revolutionary committee, for the Makhnovist partisans, anarchists and Left SRs had a majority on it and were unwilling to kowtow to them. Makhno paid a visit to see the location of this "politicking" and refused to have any truck with such connivance. Realizing that the situation was now beyond their control, the Bolsheviks began to shun the Makhnovists and, much more, ceased to perform the military guard duties allotted to their militants. So much so that a robust counterattack by the Petliurists, bolstered by Colonel Samokisch's riflemen, completely surprised the partisans who, to avoid being pinned down in the station and wiped out, were forced to cross the bridge over the Dniepr connecting the station with the rest of the city. The bridge was utterly unprotected, for the Bolshevik unit charged with guarding access to it had split in two; one section, panicking, had taken to its heels without waiting to be relieved, while the other turned renegade and opened fire on the Makhnovists. Their retreat thus cut off, the Makhnovists then had to scurry across the ice of the frozen river; many of them were either mown down by enemy fire or drowned in the Dniepr.[1]

The failure of the expedition was all but complete as the insurgents had been able to evacuate only part of their armaments since some Petliurist railroad workers had diverted several carriages. Once back in Gulyai-Polye, Makhno put his head together with his comrades; it was decided to convene a congress for reorganization of the Front, a task entrusted to Viktor Belash, an anarchist worker, and then a general congress of the region's peasants, workers and fighters; the convening of this latter congress was entrusted to Golovko, a peasant from Mikhailovka township.

Belash hastily toured the front to spread the word that the congress had been scheduled for January 3rd. The decision, reached one month previously, to re-deploy all detachments of partisans as regiments had not as yet been put fully into effect. Each band of partisans was always raised locally, adopting the name of the nearest town, appointing a "batko" and liaising informally with "Batko" Makhno. The supply of weapons was very inadequate; barely half of the partisans had rifles and a few cartridges, and these were mostly sawn-off hunting rifles and shotguns; the rest were armed with pikes, pitchforks and cudgels; their best weapon was still their fierce determination to liberate or defend their villages from enemies of every hue who threatened them.

The congress of the Front was held on January 3 and 4, 1919 in the railway station at Pologui, a rail depot halfway between Gulyai-Polye and Mariupol. Some 40 delegates were present on the basis of one delegate per detachment. Makhno, busy at the Front, was not present.

The opening speeches disclosed the dire need for arms and unity of command. Belash suggested that all the detachments, big and small alike, should amalgamate into regiments to which a medical unit and supply section would be assigned. A resolution on radical reorganization of the front was passed unanimously; an operational command was set up to complement Makhno's main staff. This operational staff was to enjoy discretionary authority over the Front and its rearguard; the work of amalgamating the detachments into regiments, or allocating equipment, setting up new detachments and the various staff of the Front would fall to it, as would direction of military operations. All detachments refusing to acknowledge its authority were to be disarmed and their commanders brought before a general tribunal of the insurgents.

As the congress broke up, a six-man operational command was elected; Belash was to head this. He was given wide powers to co-opt further members. He drew up an order reorganizing the Front, and this was promptly circulated among all the detachments. Along the first front, some 160-plus kilometers in length, five regiments were formed, a total of 6,200 fighters, only half of them armed. Each regiment comprised three battalions, each battalion three companies and each company three platoons. Each battalion, company and platoon commander was to be elected, and each regiment would appoint its own staff.[2]

The insurgents faced enemies who were many and well-armed; to the north-west, towards the city of Alexandrovsk, there were 2,000 Petliurists; to the west, the Eger brigade and detachments of German settlers, about 5,000 men; to the south, a detachment of 4,500 Ukrainian White Volunteers and other units under the command of General Mai-Maievsky. Included among all these troops were local peasants who had been pressed into service, and it was taken for granted that they would seize the opportunity of the first engagements to come over with weapons and baggage to the Makhnovist insurgents. That was the reason why the latter went on to the offensive on January 8th, in spite of their being outnumbered and of the inadequacy of their weaponry. Desertions gave a spectacular boost to insurgent numbers; by January 20, their southern front boasted 15,000 rifles, 1,000 horsemen, 40 machine guns and stretched over a distance of 250 kilometers. To the west, a 2,000-strong Makhnovist detachment led by Chaly tackled the Petliurists. To the north, the detachment commanded by Petrenko, assisted by anarchist, Left SR and Bolshevik partisans, numbered nearly 10,000 men. Many local partisan groups were as yet operating independently of the Front; in Gulyai-Polye and Pologui there were 5,000 men in reserve. So, not counting the autonomous local partisan bands, the insurgent Makhnovist army numbered, by January 19, 1919, nearly 29,000 front-line fighters and 20,000 men held in reserve for want of weapons. It manned a front line totaling more than 550 kilometers in length, against the Ukrainian nationalists and the Whites. The insurgent movement's strength grew on a daily basis, although the enemy offensives escalated. On January 20, at Henichesk, one of the two Crimean isthmuses, an expeditionary corps landed which had come from the Caucasus to beef up the Eger brigade and the straitened German settlers; it was made up of 2,000 infantry and 300 cavalry. On the same day, a further landing of 10,000 White infantry was made at Berdyansk. A third White contingent of 2,000 infantry and 800 cavalry, again from the Caucasus, marched on Gulyai-Polye. These were all elite troops, Don Cossacks and Chechens,[3] placed under the command of General Mai-Maievsky whose intent was to mop up the region before pressing on to Moscow.

Savage fighting ensued; the populace fled into the fields and forests, when they could, especially the menfolk, so as to avoid being shot or forcibly enlisted; for the most part they tried to make it to Gulyai-Polye, the heart of the resistance. Their womenfolk, obliged to stay behind to look after the children, were often raped by the soldiery. Irresistibly, the Whites pressed forward and captured the approaches to Gulyai-Polye. At this point, on January 23, the first regional congress of peasants, workers and fighters opened, in Bolshe-Mikhailovka. One hundred delegates represented the rural districts and partisan units. In view of the critical situation, their agenda concerned itself solely with the strengthening of the front and the overtures to be made to the Petliurist Directory to secure the return of conscripted peasants. Makhno was not present, being in action on the front. Contrary to the preceding congress, where nearly all participants had been anarchists, this one comprised — as far as the post-holders, aside from Congress chairman Golovko, were concerned — solely of Left SRs and Maximalists.

The congress members decided upon mobilization of those who had served during the 1914–1917 war and who were thus conversant with weapons handling. This call-up was not obligatory, but it was morally imperative for the revolution's defense. In addition to promising to shrink from nothing to support the Makhnovist movement, congress assigned itself the task of claiming back all those forcibly inducted into the Petliurist and White armies. To this end, a special delegation was appointed and accredited.

And this propaganda was not without impact; peasants deserted en masse from the Petliurist army once they grasped its chauvinistic, bourgeois character. So that the partisans liberated, almost without a shot's being fired, many of the places held by the Ukrainian nationalists. It was at this point that the first Red Army units arrived on the scene from Russia and ensconced themselves in the liberated or "open" villages. In Kharkov, which had been liberated by the detachment of the anarchist Cherednyak, a Ukrainian soviet government headed by the Bolshevik Christian Rakovsky was proclaimed in January 1919. Thus did Lenin secretly nullify the treaty of Brest-Litovsk.

On January 26, Ekaterinoslav, which the Petliurists had abandoned, was occupied by the Bolshevik Kronstadt sailor Pavel Dybenko at the head of a dozen armored trains and a detachment of infantry.

The Red Army's capture of Lugansk, a key port on the Black Sea, cut White expeditionary forces off from their base and forced them into withdrawing from their positions. On January 26, a joint assembly of Belash's operational staff and Makhno's main staff determined to dispatch Chubenko to meet with Dybenko and request arms and munitions. If need be, Alexei Chubenko was empowered to enter into a military agreement. Time was of the essence, for the Whites were regrouping their forces preparatory to a general onslaught. Chubenko did meet Dybenko and reached an agreement with him that he passed on by telephone to his comrades for their approval.

This purely military accord turned the insurgent army into No. 3 Dniepr Brigade bearing the name of Batko Makhno, making it an integral part of the Red Army; in return, the Red Army undertook to issue it with the requisite weaponry, supplies and funding.

The Makhnovists retained their internal structure based on the principles of volunteer service, self-discipline and election of all commanders.[4] Dybenko promised to send 10,000 rifles, 20 machine guns, cartridges, an artillery battery, some money and so on, within two days. The insurgents were itching to get their hands on all this so that they might mount an offensive and liberate their districts; they decided to send a further delegation to Kharkov to sign another agreement with Rakovsky's government and to also secure arms as speedily as possible from that source.

While this was afoot, the enemy launched his offensive; the insurgents repulsed the attackers at bayonet point and forced them to stand off. The Makhnovist counter-attack was a success beyond all expectations. The environs of Gulyai-Polye were freed once again from the Chechens. Attacks followed counter-attacks, all at bayonet point. The insurgents, galvanized by the liberation of their loved ones, managed to force the enemy right back to his former positions.

In Kharkov, the Makhnovist delegation led by Belash was received by the staff of Antonov-Ovseenko, the commander of the Ukrainian front, who reassured it concerning the agreement reached with Dybenko, whom he depicted as a formal representative of the Red Army and of the Ukrainian soviet government. It was desirable that the region should be liberated as early as possible so that it might be possible "to organize the economy and a communist society."5

Belash called at the headquarters of the anarchist Confederation of the Ukraine, the *Nabat* (Tocsin), spelled out to those present just what the Makhnovschina was and asked their assistance in the form of anarchist literature and anarchist propaganda. A first team of anarchists left immediately for Gulyai-Polye carrying in four wagons the presses of the Confederation's newspaper and some anarchist literature. A second group made ready to join them along with some other comrades from Moscow, who included Arshinov, who served time in prison with Makhno.

Notes to Chapter 13: The Birth of the Makhnovist Insurgent Army

1. N. Makhno, *The Makhnovschina and its Erstwhile Allies: the Bolsheviks* (in Russian) Paris, 1928, Makhnovist Library. All of the passages between quotation marks regarding this episode are drawn from the above publication wherein Makhno explains himself in length and refutes the Bolshevik versions of events, pp. 7–14. Although vetted and amended by Bolshevik censors, the memoirs of Viktor Belash as they appear in *Letopis revoliutsii* (Annals of the Revolution) No. 3, May–June 1928, pp. 191–229, bear out Makhno's account.

2. See memoirs of Viktor Belash, op. cit.

3. A people of the Caucasus of the Islamic faith; they fought the Russians at great length during the 19th century before becoming mercenaries in the hire of tsarism and here, of the White generals.

4. See Belash, op. cit.

5. Idem.

14. Soviet Power and the Power of the Soviets

Capitalizing upon the confusion that followed withdrawal of the Austro-German troops from the Ukraine, the Bolsheviks wasted no time in occupying the cities of Kharkov and Kiev. There they set up a Ukrainian soviet government under Christian Rakovsky, whereupon the Red Army attempted at bayonet point to push southwards. The aid requested by the Makhnovist insurgents was grist to their mill; from now on they could purport to be acting on behalf of the local masses. As yet the latter had no knowledge of the reality lurking behind the whole alluring phraseology and official slogans of the Leninists; likewise, they knew nothing of the situation in Russia and particularly of Moscow's policy as applied to the problems of the peasantry there. Anyway what did that consist of exactly?

In keeping with their old catechism, the Bolsheviks regarded as proletarians only industrial workers, the only ones truly serviceable for a social revolution; peasants were essentially conservatives, their only ambition being to become small-holders and to work their plots of land themselves and that, argued Lenin and his fellows, was the open door to petit-bourgeois capitalist production.[1] The peasants were going to be genuinely revolutionaries only if they had no land and worked as wage-earners in large-scale production, be it capitalist or state-owned. Moreover, the difficulties in keeping the cities supplied had induced nearly eight million individuals to quit the city for the countryside where they became a malleable and disposable mass due to the very fact that they had no land. It was to these rootless persons that the Bolsheviks were going to award the great landed estates that had been confiscated, and this to the detriment of the local peasantry, keen to share out those estates so as to boost their meager holdings. The "townies" — landless peasants — were to be dubbed as "poor peasants" and organized into committees — the *Kombed* — thereby representing the new power-base in the countryside; they were to be encouraged to seize the holdings and produce of "kulak" peasantry (actually, of the great bulk of the peasantry since the real "kulaks" had either been eliminated as early as 1917–1918 or reduced to more modest circumstances).

In addition, in order to ease food shortages in the towns, the authorities set up mobile requisition squads which were dispatched straight out into the countryside to issue paper — currency or receipts — against the produce seized; some blatantly pillaged the populace, if need be shooting resisters and torching their homes. As we have just seen was the case in Russia, such methods sparked off numerous peasant revolts and uprisings, drowned in blood by the regime's janissaries.

Indeed, the Leninist regime's sledgehammer argument was the argument of deliberate terror; the Cheka followed the Red Army everywhere and promptly indulged in a preventive "purge" which is to say that it shot individuals regarded as potential enemies of the authorities and did so on a grand scale. The chairman of the Kiev Cheka, Latsis, announced to his subordinates on this point:

> "Do not try to speculate whether the accused have or have not con-
> spired against the Soviet authorities, in arms or verbally. You ought to
> ask them first of all to what class they belong, of what social origin
> they are, to what degree have they been educated, and what is their
> profession. These questions should decide the fate of the suspects. That
> is the meaning and nature of Red Terror."[2]

In the Ukraine too, these methods were employed as we shall have occasion to note in the case of Ekaterinoslav which was captured for a few days by the Makhnovists, recaptured by the Ukrainian nationalists and then occupied at some length by the Red Army. One inhabitant of the city, G. Igrenyev, testifies: to begin with the Red troops made a good impression ... there were no excesses, attempts at looting by some Chinese soldiers were nipped in the bud, and some of them were even shot. Then things changed:

> "All in all, the initial days were so calm that the population was begin-
> ning to bless the Soviet regime that was bringing a troubled time to an
> end. Soon, however, they were to get acquainted with the other side
> of the coin. On the fifth day, the Cheka arrived from Kharkov and set
> zealously to work. Endless arrests and firing squads without benefit of
> trial began to become routine. All who had been one-time supporters
> of the hetman, or even of Petliura, were arrested. Many were shot out
> of hand the moment questioning began and very often mistakenly.
> Soon there was not a family left from the city's intelligentsia which had
> not had one of its members placed under arrest. No information was
> released to those anxious for their nearest and dearest; the Cheka was
> guarded by a double cordon of troops who would let no one through
> ... Cheka activity so dominated local life that it ensured that the hastily
> organized authority of the presidium of the soviet of the city's workers
> went quite unnoticed.
>
> Now, the inhabitants soon felt the impact of that authority also,
> especially where food supply was concerned. After the setting-up in
> Ekaterinoslav of a Supply Commissariat, stocks began to melt away
> discernibly. The market which hitherto had always been plentifully

stocked (even right after fighting) rapidly became deserted. Day by day prices escalated at a crazy rate. Within the space of three weeks they doubled and after that the progression was geometrical. The roots of this phenomenon were as straightforward as could be. The Supply Commissariat had vigorously campaigned against freedom of trade, after having issued the population with ration cards which, however, could not be traded for any product. Ekaterinoslav was ringed by audit detachments which ruthlessly confiscated all produce from peasants attempting to bring their produce into the city. Meanwhile, the city's huge stocks of foodstuffs were quickly bought up or purloined by all sorts of requisition detachments flooding in from cities to the north [i.e., from Russia — A.S.]. Assisted by such an arrangement, the city, hitherto so rich in food supplies thanks to the fertility of its region, was quickly turned into a starving wasteland. Given that the city had no cooperative organization of any sort, the situation became worse than it was in the north."[3]

The new authorities introduced many other reforms; not the least original was the reform of educational provision: the eighth and final year of secondary schooling was simply dropped, teachers had to seek election and, in order to do so, to spell out their "educational and political credo," all under the higher authority of a young student promoted to commissar for education. Communist cells were established in every educational site, their main object being to denounce "heretical" teachers.

Thus, this Soviet authority "imported" from Moscow fell a long way short of meeting the needs and aspirations of the populace; its bureaucratic methods soon created a situation of food shortages and complete arbitrariness in the life of society. The regime imposed its views and the Soviets worked in one direction only: as a transmission belt, from the top towards the bottom. Everything was dictated by a handful of members, higher-ups from the party's central committee.

As far as the Makhnovists were concerned, the power of the soviets was rather more than just another piece of cant; they saw them as free agencies emanating directly from the workers and expressing their wishes and aspirations without recourse to intermediaries of any sort.

The two social and political approaches were radically opposed to each other; communism built from above or from below, which is to say authoritarians versus libertarians. On this point, let us quote Piotr Arshinov, the chronicler of the Makhnovist movement:

"The Statists fear the free people. They assert that without authority, the latter will lose the anchor of sociability, will split asunder and turn wild. Naturally these are absurd arguments supported by idlers, who love power and the prospect of work for others, or by the blinkered thinkers of bourgeois society. The emancipation of the people does indeed spell degeneracy and a savage life, not for the people, though, but for those who live off power and privilege, from the toil of the workers and from their heartsblood."[4]

The peasants of the Gulyai-Polye region took it upon themselves to demonstrate the accuracy of this view. For upwards of six months between November 1918 and June 1919 and despite the state of war they lived without any political authorities and organized free soviets and libertarian communes for their work and their everyday affairs. According to one of the resolutions of a district peasant congress, it was affirmed that "... land belongs to no one, and only those who work it may use it" (this blunt rejection of the State aroused regret in the Soviet historian, Kubanin). The largest of these communes, named after Rosa Luxemburg as a tribute to that late revolutionary (tribute to *her*, not to her ideas) housed 40 families as of May 1919. By May 1st it was to boast a population of 285 (adults and children) and would have 125 hectares under crops.

Several dozens of anarchists showed up from the cities, as requested by Makhno; they included Arshinov and A. Baron who were to help get out the insurgent movement's mouthpieces *The Road to Freedom* and later the *Makhnovist Voice*.[5] The Ukrainian anarchist confederation, the Nabat, set up shop in Gulyai-Polye.

❧

In his memoirs, Viktor Belash describes Gulyai-Polye as it was then. The building housing the insurgent army's headquarters was topped by huge black banners bearing the slogans "War on the palaces, peace to the cottages," "On the side of oppressed against oppressors, always!" and "The emancipation of the workers is the affair of the workers themselves!" In the adjoining building, the premises of the district soviet of peasant deputies, worker deputies and soldier deputies, two flags flew bearing the inscriptions: "Power generates parasites. Long live Anarchy!" and "All power to the soviets right now!"

❧

As scheduled, the second regional congress of peasants, workers and fighters proceeded on February 12, 1919 in Gulyai-Polye. It drew 245 delegates representing 350 rural districts. On this occasion, Makhno was in attendance. He turned down a proposal to nominate him as chairman of the congress, as the tense situation on the front might call him away at any moment. All the same, he was elected honorary chairman. The delegation that had been dispatched to Kharkov reported on its negotiations with the secretary of the government (as it had not secured an interview with the people's commissars/ministers). That official had stated that the government had no intention of opening hostilities against the Makhnovist movement, that their agreement had been as yet unconfirmed but that it probably would be. A lively debate then took place in congress on the idea of free soviets and their incompatibility with any party political authority:

"The Ukrainian provisional government stood by, first in Moscow and then in Kursk, until the workers and peasants of the Ukraine had liberated the territory of enemies. [...] Now that the enemy is beaten ... some government appears in our midst describing itself as Bolshevik and aiming to impose its party dictatorship upon us. Is that to be countenanced? ... We are non-party insurgents, and we have revolted against all our oppressors; we will not countenance a new enslavement, no matter the quarter whence it may come!" [Speech of Chernoknizhny, delegate of the Novopavlovsk district]

And the anarchist insurgent Boino declared:

"Whatever the cost, we must set up soviets which are beyond pressure from any and every party. Only non-party soviets of workers, freely elected are capable of affording us new liberties and rescuing the laboring people from enslavement and oppression. Long life to the freely elected, anti-authoritarian soviets!"

Makhno made a contribution to the same effect. The resolution passed by the congress is thus a fine expression of the participants' defiance of the political authorities installed by the Bolsheviks.[6]

The congress finally elected a regional Military Revolutionary Soviet which became its executive organ in the interval between its sittings. Even so, this was liable to disbandment at any time by an extraordinary congress. Its powers were all-embracing, covering the military, social, economic and political aspects of the region's insurgent movement. A central supply section was established in Gulyai-Polye; it marshaled supplies and forage for subsequent distribution throughout the Front; finally, "voluntary" and "egalitarian" mobilization was confirmed, appeal being made to the conscience and goodwill of every individual; this mobilization was meant to have a measured impact upon the villages, townships and districts, so that essential agricultural tasks could continue to be assured.

Despite the influx of volunteers, many had to be sent home temporarily due to the dearth of weapons. Already what weapons were available were not being deployed along the traditional lines. Kubanin deplores this departure from tradition also; infantry mounted on tachankis and thus highly mobile could cover 60-to-100 kilometers per day; and these tachankis were fitted with machine guns when available; rifles had their barrels sawed down, rendering them more readily manageable in close quarters or hand-to-hand fighting; moreover, the latter form of combat was the insurgents' preferred form; as often as they were able, they would pop up unexpectedly in the rear or on the flanks of the enemy and mount an all-out onslaught, first with rifle and machine gun, and then with sabers, in the use of which they excelled. Nor was artillery missed out; this was commanded by Vassili Sharovsky, gunnery expert.

According to Makhno, by February–April 1919, the insurgent movement numbered almost 30,000 fighters and 70,000 men in reserve, always for want of weapons but ever ready to move to the Front if the need arose.

Let it be noted that the insurgents identified with the workers in the large cities; the peasants of Gulyai-Polye devised the watchword: "Worker, join hands with us!" and acted upon this by making contact directly. The most telling instance was the case of the 100 wagon-loads of wheat seized from the Whites in February 1919 and which a delegation shipped to Moscow. However, this independent-minded move and such spontaneous acts were deeply frowned upon by the Bolshevik potentates in Moscow and their hostility was growing without restraint.

Notes to Chapter 14: Soviet Power and the Power of the Soviets

1. This attitude was all too obvious in the regime's Constitution, adopted in July 1918, under which, in the event of elections, the vote of the city-dweller would be held to be the equivalent of the votes of five country-dwellers.

2. In the Cheka's main organ, *Krasnij terror* (Red Terror), November 1, 1918.

3. G. Igrenyev, *Memories of Ekaterinoslav*, in *Archives of the Russian Revolution* (Russian language), Berlin, 1922, Tome III, pp. 238–239.

4. P. Arshinov, *History of the Makhnovist Movement 1918–1921* (in Russian) Berlin, 1923, p. 85.

5. In Russian, *Puts' K svobodye* and *Golos makhnovtsa* respectively.

6. See the full text of the report on the congress in the appendices to this book.

15. Alliance with the Red Army

Makhno and the staff of the insurgents allied themselves with the Red Army, for one thing, because they placed the "revolution's interests above ideological differences" (Makhno) and, for another, because they were beset by a terrible shortage of arms and munitions, trophies taken from the enemy being insufficient to make up for the daily consumption of cartridges and insufficient to arm the many volunteers who showed up to fight in their ranks. As far as the Makhnovists were concerned, this was only a military and by no stretch of the imagination a political compact, for in political terms Bolsheviks were still, in their eyes, adversaries, as the second regional congress had confirmed. Moscow took a different view: from the moment that a military alliance exists, there is automatically political dependency, i.e., formal recognition of the authority of the Ukrainian Soviet government. These two very divergent outlooks were to lie at the root of a latent conflict. For the time being, the Bolsheviks had scarcely any option; they had scarcely any troops in the Ukraine and the danger of White offensives was looming.

Indeed, at the beginning of 1919 the Red Army in the Ukraine was made up almost exclusively of detachments of local partisans which had subordinated themselves for the very same reason as the Makhnovists. Such composition was not at all to the taste of the Red leadership who were preoccupied with hierarchical order and discipline. To begin with, their efforts were going to be devoted to overhauling the structure of the partisan groups and turning these into regiments, brigades and divisions. This is how Vitaly Primakov, one of the chief Bolshevik military officials of the times described this phase:

> "Towards the end of January 1919, substantial reforms were introduced in the [Red] insurgent army. Divisions were organized on the Russian model; the quality of headquarters staff was noticeably improved. Certain regimental commanders were stood down for acts of banditry. The regiments were overseen by political commissars; political sections were introduced in the divisions. Some independent regimental commanders were removed or shot. The title of 'regimental ataman' was abolished and that of 'commander' replaced it. The finest regiments were turned

into brigades. [...] Some artillery divisions were set up. Based on the Dniepr, the army proceeded all that February with this reshuffle. Then it entered into contact with the atamans Grigoriev, Makhno and others. The government was now confronted with the task of preserving its army from contagion by the Makhnovschina and the Grigorievschina; this burden fell entirely upon the army's youthful political cadres, which simultaneously conducted a political agitation campaign and Cheka work, not only educating the troops but also shooting the most inflexible atamans. This tiresome duty was performed with honor by the young political cadres."[1]

Thus the Bolsheviks' primary concern was to conduct a squalid police operation designed to turn free insurgents, revolutionary insurgents, into a slavish, obedient mass and to shoot honest revolutionaries if need be, whose only failing was their refusal to kowtow to the evangel of the Leninist State. What Primakov — who apparently played a leading part in this whole process — leaves unsaid is that during all this time the "atamans," from whom he feared contagion, held the front heroically against the White Guards.

According to the military agreement concluded, Bolshevik political commissars were to operate within the Makhnovist insurgent army ranks (this army was pompously re-christened brigade). Also the Cheka wanted to screen its members over. Both the commissars and the Cheka were chased out by the peasants or treated with contempt by the insurgents who were fighting for their land, their families and their freedom and who were well aware that these would be best guaranteed only through the success of the social revolution and who had no political lessons to learn from missionaries of the self-styled scientific socialist faith. Makhno himself, obliged to put up with them, treated them "with sarcasm," Bolshevik missionaries complained.

Moreover, the military compact was none too scrupulously observed by the Bolsheviks: aside from an initial delivery of 100,000 cartridges and 3,000 Italian special caliber rifles, each one accompanied by only a dozen shells, that was all the Makhnovists were to get, and none of the promised cannon or machine guns. Anyway, in some instances the cartridges were faulty, having been sabotaged by Denikin supporters who had infiltrated the ranks of the Red Army (some of them were later to be discovered and shot). This piecemeal delivery was deliberate, for the reasons set out by Primakov earlier and for some bizarre reason applied also to deliveries to Dybenko who, although a dyed-in-the-wool Bolshevik, was nonetheless suspected of playing along with the "atamans"; in his forces, every two fighters were entitled to a rifle between them, whereas among Grigoriev, the ratio was one between three with the worst ratio the one among four that prevailed among the Makhnovists.

The Bolsheviks also bemoaned the growing influence of anarchists over the insurgent movement, and more so, the presence of a rather sizable group of Left

SRs (who had been accepted by the insurgents only on the basis of the fight against the Whites and for the power of the free soviets). Especially since these Left SRs included Viktor Popov, a Black Sea sailor who had led the Left SR rising against Lenin in July 1918 and had come within an ace of success (he was subsequently to play a very active role in the Makhnovist movement, taking charge among other things of its intelligence branch).

Makhno was not content to quarantine the political commissars; he also arrested a detachment of Chekists who were beginning operations in Berdyansk and had them manhandled into the front lines. It was hardly surprising in these circumstances that relations became strained and that the red authorities were forever on the lookout for quibbles, inventing tales of uprisings where all that was going on was simple troop movements and units relieving one another.

❧

Josef Dybets' evidence is very revealing of these frictions and of the Bolsheviks' bad faith. To make matters worse, Dybets was a former anarcho-syndicalist of some note, having been one of the founders of *Golos Truda* (The Voice of Labor), the great Russian anarcho-syndicalist organ published in the U.S., where he had spent ten years as an immigrant. According to Dybets, the fog shrouding his thinking had lifted after he read Lenin's *The State and Revolution*, whereupon he had ardently embraced this new pope's religion of realism and efficiency. In February 1919, he was in Berdyansk. The Makhnovists occupied the port and Dybets met Makhno, which gave rise to the following laconic exchange:

"Good day, Dybets. So, it seems you're a renegade now?"

"Good day. It would appear that I am a renegade."

"Which means you are completely Bolshevik?"

"Yes, completely."

"Yes, it's true that many have sold out to the Bolsheviks. Nothing to be done about it."

"That's right, they do sell out. I too have sold out."

"Take care lest you regret it."

"I will take care."

❧

Dybets' wife, Rosa, had remained an anarchist and, what is more, had been an inmate in the same prison in Ekaterinoslav as Makhno ten years before. This was a significant point in Dybets's favor and afforded him a certain license in the tone of his conversation with Makhno. This is how their exchange went, as Dybets tells it at any rate:

[Dybets to Makhno] "What is your program?"

"To eliminate the Whites first and then the Bolsheviks."

"Well, what do you intend to do after that?"

"Afterwards, the people will govern themselves."

"And how will they be able to govern themselves? Let me have your views on that." [Makhno] spelled out, in vague fashion, the anarchist thinking about the absence of constraints upon peasant communes which would not be subordinated to the State, nor to any organizational center.

"Our activists," he said, "are confined solely to agitation and propaganda. The people themselves do everything. That is what we are doing also at the moment in military affairs. The army runs itself."

"That's absurd, Utterly absurd."

But Makhno was not to be put off.

"You will see. First we are going to rid ourselves of the Whites and then of the Bolsheviks."

෴

Dybets tackled Makhno yet again, asking him what he intended to establish as a regime. The Ukrainian libertarian's answer was: "The people's Commune. The anarchist Republic," which was hardly surprising. Dybets reckoned that he had found a crushing argument when he countered that Makhno couldn't even run a factory and was surrounded only by bandits and anarchists on the run from the bullets of the Cheka! A contemptuous Makhno brought the exchange to a close by dismissing him several times as a "renegade!"

Belated and sudden though his conversion may have been, Dybets played a significant role among local Bolsheviks; he headed a revolutionary committee in Berdyansk, a committee representing nobody but the Bolsheviks but which nonetheless arrogated certain rights to itself. Dybets thus crowed about having put one over on the Makhnovists. At a time when, according to the testimony of Antonov-Ovseenko, half of the Makhnovists were virtually barefoot and when the Gulyai-Polye Military Revolutionary Soviet urgently requested a shipment of twelve wagon-loads of leather, produced by the tanneries of Berdyansk, Dybets arranged to have the shipment rerouted to Moscow, then indignantly accused the Makhnovists of having been behind its disappearance. He smugly recalled that in so doing he had furnished himself with a decisive comment for his discussions with the Makhnovists; at the first sign of a problem, he used to say to them: "And the leather, what have you done with it?"[2]

෴

Makhno authorized the display of Bolshevik newspapers in Gulyai-Polye, Berdyansk and Mariupol. A certain Uralov, a Leninist militant, tells this tale: bearing a safe conduct pass from Makhno, he set out for Berdyansk, there to see to publication of a newspaper for his party. Right from the very first two issues, he railed violently against the Makhnovist insurgents while they at the time were busy containing a push by the enemy. Protests having had no effect, some insurgents turned up to smash the plates of the third issue of Uralov's provocative publication.[3]

෴

For their part, the insurgents kept up their side of the bargain; they sent two of their tried and tested regiments to help Dybenko combat the White Guard and German settler detachments in the Crimea. For their own part, they went on the offensive in April and got within a few kilometers of Taganrog, the headquarters of Denikin's front. For want of arms and ammunition, they were unable to capitalize upon this success. Chance brought them into Mariupol with some Frenchmen who were unloading materials and arms for the Denikinists. The Frenchmen suggested to the insurgents that they swap the weapons for some coal stacked on the dockside and which they needed urgently, but the Frenchmen met with a categorical refusal and the whole episode ended with some artillery "exchanges."

✥✥✥

The Kremlin's official mouthpiece, *Pravda*, acknowledged the merits of Makhno and wrote of him on April 3, 1919:

> "The Ukrainians say of Makhno: 'Our Batko fears neither God nor Devil, yet he is a simple man like us.' [There followed a biographical sketch of Nestor.] The peasants, despite the threat of their being shot for having protected Makhno help him in all things. He has set up a detachment and turned down a proposal of union with the Directory, declaring to a villagers' congress in Alexandrovsk that '... the Petliurist movement is only an adventure distracting the masses from the revolution.' With 600 men, he took Ekaterinoslav, investing the city via the railway station but was forced to pull back to the Dniepr [...] Being under Dybenko's command, he has been incorporated into the Red Army of which he forms a brigade. He has been assigned the task of fighting the White Volunteers and of keeping the railroad clear up as far as Berdyansk, in which he has acquitted himself brilliantly. The White's finest regiments have been smashed!"

Things livened up, nonetheless, when the Military Revolutionary Soviet appointed by the second congress of peasants and insurgents summoned the Third Regional Congress for April 10 in Gulyai-Polye. Delegates from 72 districts, representing upwards of two million inhabitants, took part. All civil and military issues were dealt "with great gusto" (Arshinov). Towards the end of the proceedings, the congress received a telegram from Dybenko in which the latter pronounced the congress counter-revolutionary and outlawed its organizers whom he threatened with "... the most rigorous repressive measures." Addressing himself to Makhno, Dybenko ordered him to ensure that there was no repetition of the episode; a copy of the telegram was forwarded to the Gulyai-Polye Soviet. The Military Revolutionary Soviet was superciliously ignored. In its reply, which has become famous, the latter made it its business to enlighten Dybenko as to the situation:

"Before pronouncing the congress counter-revolutionary, 'comrade' Dybenko did not take the trouble to establish in whose name and for what purpose it had been summoned, right? [...] So allow us, 'Your Excellency,' to inform you by whom and for what this (according to you, patently counter-revolutionary) congress has been summoned and then, maybe, it will not strike you as quite so frightening as you describe it.

The congress, as stated above, was summoned by the executive committee of the Military Revolutionary Soviet of the Gulyai-Polye (that being the central township). It has described itself as the third regional congress. It was convened in order to lay down the future policy line for activities of the Military Revolutionary Soviet (you see, 'comrade' Dybenko, there had already been two previous 'counter-revolutionary' congresses of this sort). Now to the question that you might pose yourself; whence comes the Military Revolutionary Soviet and to what end was it established? If you are not au fait, 'comrade' Dybenko, then allow us to bring you up to date.

This Soviet was established in accordance with the resolution of the second congress, which took place on February 12 in Gulyai-Polye (you see how long ago that was, for you were not even around then?), in order to organize the front and proceed to a volunteer mobilization, given that we were ringed by Whites and that the first detachments of insurgent volunteers were insufficient to hold such an extensive front. So there were no soviet troops in our region and anyway the populace did not expect much assistance, being of the mind that it was their duty to look to their own defense!"

The authors of this reply then set out how and why the Military Revolutionary Soviet with its 32 members, one delegate from each district of the provinces of Ekaterinoslav and Tavrida, had come into being. Then they harked back to the origins of the convening of the second congress which had been summoned by a five-member commission appointed by the first congress on January 23 and who had not been outlawed in that the sort of "... hero who would venture to trespass against the people's rights won in open battle at the cost of their own blood," still was not around at that time. Then they went on to explain to Dybenko, whom they held was ignorant of all this, the basic reasons behind the insurgent movement and the progress of its fight against its enemies first of all, only to return to the appointment of the impugned soviet which had only executive powers, and to the sovereign role of the third congress apropos evaluation of and formulation of policy on the events in progress. In conclusion, "comrade" Dybenko was taken seriously to task:

"There now, comrade Dybenko, you have before you a picture that should be an eye-opener for you. Collect your wits! Reconsider! Have you the right, you alone, to label as counter-revolutionaries upwards of one million workers who have, with their horny hands, cast off the shackles of slavery and henceforth look to themselves for the reshaping of their lives as they see fit.

No! If you be a genuine revolutionary, you must help them in their struggle against the oppressors and in the building of a new and free life. Can it be that laws laid down by a handful of individuals, describing themselves as revolutionaries, can afford them the right to declare outside of the law an entire people more revolutionary than themselves? (The soviet's executive committee embodies the whole mass of the people.) Is it tolerable or reasonable that laws of violence be thrust upon the lives of a people which has just rid itself of all lawmakers and all laws? Is there some law according to which a revolutionary is alleged to have the right to enforce the harshest punishment against the revolutionary mass on whose behalf he fights, and this because that same mass has secured for itself the benefits that the revolutionary promised them … freedom and equality? Can that mass remain silent when the 'revolutionary' strips it of the freedom which it has just won? Does the law of revolution require the shooting of a delegate on the grounds that he is striving to achieve in life the task entrusted to him by the revolutionary mass which appointed him? What interests should the revolutionary defend? Those of the party? Or those of the people at the cost of whose blood the revolution has been set in motion?"

This mini-anthology on the revolutionary autonomy of the workers closed with an invitation — "should Dybenko and those like him persist in their 'dirty business'" — to declare counter-revolutionary and outlaws all who had participated in the foregoing congresses and the combatants who had fought and were fighting still for the people's emancipation without seeking anybody's leave to do so. The signatories to the document, members of the soviet, finally stated that they would carry on with their tasks and had neither the right nor the duty to default upon the responsibility which the people had delegated onto their shoulders.[4]

This text was countersigned by the chairman of the Military Revolutionary Soviet, Chernoknizhnik; by the vice-chairman, Leonid Kogan; by the secretary, Karbet; and by the members Koval, Petrenko, Dotzenko and others. Makhno was not among them, not having even attended this congress, having been caught up in fighting, and in any case, he had nothing to do with the supreme organ of the movement. Thus Dybenko discovered with whom he had to deal: the mass of the people. He himself came from the mass of the people and had quite good revolutionary credentials: all he needed was the requisite finesse to distinguish between the language of revolution and that of a party which had proclaimed itself repository of the revolutionary mass's historical and political interests. In fact, he was a bumpkin who did not shrink from the most brutal and disgusting measures if they enforced respect; Dybets describes how he slew the commander of a Red Army cavalry regiment where he stood, without a word spoken, just to ensure readier obedience from the combatants. Although these were commonplace measures albeit generally used with greater discretion in that "army," Dybenko displayed great enthusiasm for them.

❦

With Antonov-Ovseenko we have a completely different kettle of fish. He was an old Bolshevik militant, one of those "professional revolutionaries" who had kept the party afloat for years. In October 1917, he had led the Petrograd military soviet which organized the storming of the Winter Palace. At this time he was in command of the Ukrainian front. He was very well aware that the Makhnovist insurgents were "… supporters of local soviets, regarded as free soviets answerable to no central authority."[5] He wanted to get a more exact notion of the whole commotion denounced by his party colleagues, and so he paid a visit to Gulyai-Polye on April 28 and has left us with a superb, objective account of the situation.

For a start he addressed a message to Makhno announcing that he would be passing through the region. By return he received a telegram from Makhno:

> "I know you to be an upright and independent revolutionary. On behalf of the revolutionary insurgent units of the 3rd Dniepr brigade and all of the revolutionary organizations of the Gulyai-Polye region which proudly bear the banner of the insurrection, I am charged to invite you to call upon us to visit our own little 'Petrograd' — free, revolutionary Gulyai-Polye."

En route, Antonov-Ovseenko reviewed all recent developments on the Front, the fine conduct of the Makhnovists and the advice of one Bolshevik leader, Sokolov, and of Hittis, commander of the southern front, to the effect that Makhno be removed from command of his brigade, which struck him as uncalled for since, as the saying goes, "one does not change horses in mid-stream."

From the railway station, a troika brought him briskly to Gulyai-Polye. He was welcomed to the strains of the "Internationale," played by an orchestra. So let us now turn to his account:

> "A group of bronzed partisans stepped forward to greet the Front commander; one man broke ranks, a man of small stature and quite youthful, with somber eyes and a high papakha perched on his head. He stopped two paces away and saluted: 'Brigade commander Batko Makhno. We are successful in holding the front. At present we are waging the battle for Mariupol. On behalf of the revolutionary insurgents of the Ekaterinoslav province, I salute the leader of the Ukraine's soviet troops.' Handshake. Makhno introduces the members of the Gulyai-Polye soviet's executive committee and of his staff. Also there

is the [Bolshevik — A.S.] political commissar of the bridge, my old acquaintance, Marussia Nikiforova.

We review the troops. The brigade's main units are on the front. Here there are only a reserve regiment undergoing training and two cavalry platoons. Dressed in a motley assortment of uniforms and clothing and brandishing all sorts of arms, the impression they give is nonetheless one full of verve and pugnaciousness. They 'devour me' with their eyes.

In silence they all listened to the front commander's speech about the import of our struggle, on the position on the different fronts, on the heavy responsibility entrusted to the Makhno Brigade, on the necessity for iron discipline, and they greeted his concluded words with 'hurrahs.'

Makhno replied to the front commander by wishing him welcome, alluded somewhat touchily to the 'unfair' charges laid against the insurgents, mentioned their successes and promised further successes '… if support in arms and equipment is forthcoming' (his voice is not very loud, there is a slight hiss to it, and his pronunciation is soft; all in all, he does not give the impression of being a great orator, but how attentively they all hear him out!). We step into the building housing the brigade's staff and quickly inspect its branches; the inspection is gratifying. One can discern the hand of a specialist [staff commander Ozerov] at work."

An exchange upon the situation of the Front ensued. The deployment of the brigade's units was reviewed; the results of the April 23rd offensive examined; while the conversation was in progress news arrived of the capture of Mariupol and of the capture of every last man of the enemy's first mixed regiment of infantry and cavalry. Makhno, though, stated that he did not have the wherewithal to follow up the offensive and that it "… would be feasible to form two whole divisions, but the arms and equipment just were not available." He added that the Red Army's 9th reserve division, deployed to the north of his brigade, was prone to panic and that its command's sympathies lay with the Whites. He cited the instance of the offensive against Taganrog when this "… 9th Division fell back abruptly, leading to the encirclement and extermination of a Makhnovist regiment which fought to the bitter end without surrendering." Then he bemoaned the shortage of armaments (in his report, Antonov-Ovseenko comments: "His complaint is well founded!"; there was "neither money nor weapons nor munitions nor equipment. Some time back Dybenko did supply 3,000 Italian rifles with a few cartridges each and now that the ammunition has run out, these rifles are useless."). The remainder of the arms and equipment was booty taken from the enemy. Half of the partisans went barefoot.

And what of the charges of banditry? Why here comes the "big bandit": Batko Pravda, the legless cripple commander of a detachment shows up and salutes Antonov-Ovseenko. He is a dyed-in-the-wool libertarian communist and a first rate fighting man; in spite of this, all sorts of rumors are peddled about him, allegedly he cuts Bolshevik throats and fights against soviet power. He has personally slain bandits. "Persecution of political commissars? Not a bit of it. But we have need of fighters, not gossips. Nobody drove them out. They buggered off themselves. Of course we do have lots who are opposed to your way of thinking and, if you wish, we can discuss." Everything that Makhno says is confirmed by the brigade's Bolshevik political commissar.

As their conversations proceed, the insurgents and their guests share a meal washed down by some reddish liqueur: Makhno tells Antonov-Ovseenko that he is not a drinker and that he has banned alcohol. The members of the Gulyai-Polye soviet congratulate themselves on their work: the town boasts three magnificently appointed secondary schools and some children's communes. Ten military hospitals house a thousand wounded but unfortunately there is no experienced doctor. Antonov-Ovseenko pays a visit to some of them, finding them to be very clean and spacious, having been set up in seigneurial homes. There is also a repair shop for artillery pieces.

Antonov-Ovseenko has a tête-à-tête discussion with Makhno about what help to afford to soviet Hungary,[6] about "… the breakthrough in Europe, the danger of an offensive by Denikin and the need to erect a united, steely front of social revolution against that."

In the end, the pair "shake hands firmly, looking each other in the eye. Makhno declares that 'as long as he leads the insurgents, there will be no anti-soviet acts and that battle without quarter will be waged against the bourgeois generals.' Without demur, he agrees to the conversion of his sector of the front into a division, under the command of one Chikvanaya, with Makhno remaining brigade commander. A great get-together brings the day to a close: everyone rallies around the watchword of … 'all out against the common foe, the bourgeois generals.'"

In 1927, in an appendix to this account, (quite startling for a Bolshevik at that time) Antonov-Ovseenko noted that, in the light of subsequent developments, his testimony might appear to "unduly idealize" the insurgents, but, he added "he had striven only to be objective"!

❧

Summarizing his impressions, Antonov-Ovseenko telegraphed the following message to Rakovsky on April 29:

"I spent the entire day with Makhno. He, his brigade and the whole region represent a great fighting force. There is no conspiracy. Makhno himself would not allow it. It is possible to organize the region well, there is excellent material there, and we must keep it on our side and not create yet another new front to fight on. If consistent work is followed through, this region will become an impregnable stronghold. The punitive measures contemplated are senseless. There must be an immediate end of the attacks against the Makhnovists that are beginning to appear in our newspapers."

Without waiting for any reply, he also telegraphed to Bubnov and to the editions of the Kharkov *Izvestia*, the official mouthpiece of the Ukrainian soviet government:

"In your edition of April 5, you carried an article entitled 'Down With The Makhnovschina'. That article is awash with mistruths and is blatantly provocative in tone. Such attacks damage our struggle against the counter-revolution. In that struggle, Makhno and his brigade have demonstrated and do demonstrate an extraordinary revolutionary valor, and are deserving, not of abuse from officials, but rather of the fraternal gratitude of all worker and peasant revolutionaries."

On May 2, he confirmed his impressions in a more considered report to Lev Kamenev. At the same time, he ordered Skatchko, the commander of the 2nd Army, to waste no time in supplying artillery, four million rubles, equipment, field kitchens, a portable telephone, cartridges for those 3,000 Italian rifles, two surgeons, two physicians, medical supplies, pharmaceutical equipment and an armored train. All as a matter of urgency. The new front line, fixed by Trotsky along the Donetz basin and under the care of the Russian command which thus stripped Makhno of the supervision of the front which was held by him, Antonov-Ovseenko also objected to. Trostky's reply was typical of him:

"Your comments, according to which the Ukrainian troops are capable of fighting only under a Ukrainian command, derive from a refusal to look truth in the face [...] The Makhnovists fall back from the Mariupol front, not because they are under the authority of Hittis and not yours, but because they faced an enemy more daunting than the Petliurists [...]. The main enemy is on the Donetz basin and it is to there that we must switch our main forces [...]. Any delay in this operation would be the most awful crime against the Republic."

Antonov-Ovseenko reacted with indignation and anger to this chastisement:

"It would not be hard to discover that (1) I had undertaken, and continue to do so, every step to convert the insurgent units into regular army; (2) neither Moscow nor the commissar for war in the Ukraine was of the slightest assistance to me in this organizational endeavor; (3) nonetheless, some excellent cadres have been formed in the Ukraine for the army of the future; the allegation regarding easy victories obtained here is a fantastic concoction by people far removed from the military work in the Ukraine. Without bothering to examine all of these arguments properly, you have condemned my whole work in extreme terms. My outrage is great."[7]

Obviously, the "Carnot" of the Russian revolution, at least as he imagined himself to be, could not countenance anyone's contradicting him in his strategic evaluations: he banked on a push by Denikin in a northerly direction, the target of which would be the Donetz basin and a link-up with Kolchak. What followed was to expose the idiocy of Trotsky's calculations. As for Antonov-Ovseenko's lobbying — that had scarcely any success: Makhno was outfitted with neither weapons nor equipment and the hostile press campaign against him carried on in the Bolshevik newspapers. In the wake of his lively retort to Trotsky's sermonizing, Antonov-Ovseenko's star seriously declined and on June 15 he was replaced by Vatsetis — a Lett and Tsarist ex-colonel — as commander of the Ukrainian front.

Intrigued by his impressions, several Soviet bigwigs paid a visit to Gulyai-Polye a week later: Lev Kamenev (a.k.a. Rosenfeld, Zinoviev's brother-in-law), Voroshilov, Mezhlauk, the commissar for war in the Ukrainian soviet government, Muranov, Zorin, Sidersky and others.

Their armored train pulled into Gulyai-Polye station on May 7, 1919, in the morning. They were greeted by Marussia Nikiforova, Mikhailov-Pavlenko and Boris Veretelnikov, who proposed to escort them into town. Half reassured, Kamenev happened to issue instructions to the commander of the train to dispatch a patrol to fetch them, should they fail to return by 6:00 P.M. Meanwhile, Makhno showed up and was introduced to the new arrivals: he escorted them and along the way pointed out a tree from which he personally had hanged a White colonel. They were welcomed to the town to the sounds of the "Internationale" and visited the movement's social achievements. They took refreshments and were introduced to a "pretty young Ukrainian," Galina Kuzmenko, Nestor Makhno's partner and secretary.[8] Everything went swimmingly, except during an interview with Makhno and his staff, when Kamenev demanded abolition of the Military Revolutionary Soviet, a creation of the regional congress. The discussions foundered, for the insurgents explained to him that the aforesaid body had been created by the masses and on no account could it be disbanded by any authority at all. The reply displeased the Red officials: even so, they bade the Makhnovists fond farewells: Kamenev even embraced Makhno and assured him that the "…Bolsheviks will always find a common language with authentic revolutionaries like the Makhnovists and that they could and always should work hand in glove."[9]

Upon arrival in Ekaterinoslav, Kamenev telegraphed Moscow to have reduced from one year to six months a conviction against Marussia Nikiforova which banned him from holding office. He also published an open letter to comrade Makhno, commander of the 3rd Brigade, wherein he stated that the rumors about separatist or anti-soviet schemes on the part of the Makhnovist insurgents were utterly without foundation. Makhno he described as an "...upright and dauntless fighter" who fought with courage against the Whites and foreign invaders. However, he recalled that the front manned by the insurgents was only a "one-thousandth part" of the overall front, and alluded to differences of opinion, which would be smoothed over "...if they deliver coal and wheat from the region, the central authorities will then send them the armaments and everything they need."[10]

Piotr Arshinov — who was present at this encounter — later wondered if Kamenev's and even Antonov-Ovseenko's attitude had been sincere, or whether they had merely provided cover for a reconnaissance operation in advance of a general Bolshevik offensive against the Makhnovists, an offensive that had been long in the preparation. He based this hypothesis on the conspiracy devised a little later by one Padalka, commander of a regiment of insurgents: bribed by the Bolsheviks, Padalka was to have seized Makhno and his staff. This scheme was only foiled at the very last minute, thanks to Makhno's unexpected return to Gulyai-Polye from Berdyansk by airplane.

This was not impossible but it strikes us more likely that the initiative had been taken here by some Chekists rather than by political leaders: and the evidence for this is supplied by the telegram that was sent to Kamenev by Lenin on May 7:

> "In that Rostov has not been taken, we need to be temporarily dip-lomatic with Makhno's army, dispatching Antonov [Ovseenko] and holding him personally accountable for Makhno's troops."[11]

So — a double-cross was intended, but postponed to a more opportune time. Also, Makhno was warned by revolutionaries working inside soviet institutions never to "... go if summoned either to Ekaterinoslav or to Kharkov, for any official summons would be cover for a trap leading to his death."[12] All of which meant that the Leninists would not on any account tolerate the autonomous activity of the region's insurgent masses and would ultimately use force to curtail it.

Some days later, a grave problem confronted the Bolsheviks: their ally, Grig-oriev, refused to go fight the Romanians by way of assisting soviet Hungary and turned against them. This Grigoriev had significant muscle at his disposal — 30,000 rifles, ten armored trains, 700 machine-guns, 50 cannon, tanks and trucks. He quickly seized a considerable portion of the western Ukraine. Fearing the worst, i.e., a revolt by the Makhnovists and their throwing in their lot with Grigoriev, which would oblige the Bolsheviks to evacuate the Ukraine, Lev Kamenev dispatched a telegram to Makhno on May 12, urging him to condemn Grigoriev's venture:

> "The traitor Grigoriev has delivered the front to the enemy. Refusing to carry out the order to fight, he has turned his guns against us. The moment of decision has come: either you will go with the workers and peasants of the whole of Russia, or you will ipso facto open the front to the enemy. There is no margin for hesitation. Report to me immediately

the disposition of your troops and issue a proclamation against Grigoriev, sending a copy to me in Kharkov. A failure to reply on your part will be deemed a declaration of war. I believe in the honor of revolutionaries: yours, and that of Arshinov, Veretelnikov and others."13

❧❧❧

Grigoriev was a one-time captain of the Tsarist army who had been promiscuous in his allegiances: starting with Kerensky, he moved on to the Ukrainian Rada, the hetman Skoropadsky, Petliura and the Directory and latterly to the Bolsheviks. Each time he had turned savagely against his erstwhile allies and masters, making a decisive contribution to their defeat. On the Bolsheviks' behalf he had fought the French and the Greeks in Odessa. He had captured that great city by routing the Allied troops and giving the French command (which was in the future to fight shy of sending infantry units on to Ukrainian soil and was henceforth to make do with occasionally shelling the revolutionaries from its ships) something to think about.

Grigoriev was a redoubtable war chief, competent and courageous and always in the thick of the action, which galvanized his men. What is more, he was a sharpshooter: once he had brought down a marauder with a revolver shot in the head at fifty paces. He was very popular among the poor peasants who accounted for the bulk of his troops, for he readily issued free the foodstuffs and goods seized from the bourgeoisie. To the great relish of his men, he had a weakness for semi-poetic, semi-Ubu-esque proclamations. In November 1918, he issued a threat to the German generals to the effect that he would "swat them like flies, with a flick of his hand," unless they quit the Ukraine within four days, taking their personal effects with them: otherwise he would send them home in their shirttails!

He had also threatened to blow out his own brains at the time of the fighting against the Greeks, if his cavalry, surrounded by Greek cavalry mounted on mules and donkeys (!) and outnumbering him three to one, managed to beat his men! Happily for him, his horse-riding cavalry had successfully overwhelmed their opponents.14 Following his entry into Odessa, he had issued Order Number One in which he declared that he had trounced the French, the Greeks, the Romanians and the White Volunteers and "thanks to one of his shells" might even have toppled Clemenceau from the presidency that he so coveted. (A claim that may not be completely devoid of substance.) When he turned against the Bolsheviks, he called upon the peasants to fight with whatever they could lay their hands on: "If you have no weapons, take up your pitchforks, axes and stakes and get stuck in!" He tried several times to link up with Makhno, but only one of his messages got through to the libertarian: "Batko! Why bother with the communists? Knock them on the head. Ataman Grigoriev."15

His strategy was that of most of the partisan groups — he stuck doggedly to his native soil and refused to go off and fight as a mercenary in Hungary. It was enough for him to hold the Bessarabian front. Let us note at this point that the

Bolsheviks had a sizable Hungarian detachment, ex-prisoners from the Austrian army who had not gone home but had been organized as a Red Army unit: they too declined to be assigned to the Southern Ukrainian front and wanted to go home and fight. In this regard, the Bolshevik tactic was systematic (and persists to this day): they always used troops who had no links with the region or country in question. Thus into the Ukraine they were to dispatch Chinese, Letts and Germans.

⁕⁕⁕

The Makhnovists did not know why Grigoriev had become a renegade, so their primary concern was to circulate a general communiqué to affirm their own loyalty to the revolution:

> "Mariupol. Campaign headquarters of the Makhnovist army. Copies to all combat sector commanders, all regimental, battalion, company and platoon commanders. Order to be read out to all Batko Makhno troop units, so-called. Copy to Kamenev the extraordinary plenipotentiary of the defense soviet.
>
> Take most vigorous steps to sustain the Front. On no grounds tolerate weakening of the revolution's external front. Revolutionary honor and dignity oblige us to keep faith with the revolution and the people; Grigoriev's squabbles with the Bolsheviks over power cannot induce us to undermine the Front which the White Guards mean to smash in order to enslave the people. Until such time as we have vanquished our common enemy in the shape of the Whites from the Don, we will not firmly and fully appreciate the freedom won by our hands and our rifles, and we shall remain on the Front, fighting for the people's freedom and not in any circumstances for power, nor for the intrigues of political charlatans.
>
> Brigade commander, Batko Makhno, Members of the Staff
> [signatures added]"16

This initial reaction meant that the insurgents were keeping clear of all intrigues and sticking to their battle against the Whites on the Front. That one was destined for their fighters: Makhno and his staff at the same time sent this even more explicit reply to Kamenev himself:

> "[…] As soon as your telegram was received, I immediately gave the order to hold the front with undiminished firmness, yielding not one inch of our positions to Denikin or to any other counter-revolutionary pack, thereby performing our revolutionary duty towards the workers and peasants of Russia and of the whole world. For your benefit, let me declare that the entire front and I will remain unshakably loyal to the worker and peasant revolution, but not to the institutions of violence in the persons of your commissars and Chekists who act

arbitrarily against the laboring population. [...] I do not know what he is doing nor what aims he pursues; for that very reason I am going to refrain from publication of a proclamation against him, until such time as I am in receipt of fuller details. As an anarchist revolutionary, let me declare that I cannot by any means support seizure of power by Grigoriev or by anyone; as hitherto, I am going to drive out, with my insurgent comrades, the bands of Denikin, while striving at the same time to let the liberated regions be networked by free unions of peasants and workers who would thus enjoy full powers in their areas. In this respect, agencies of constraint and violence such as Chekas and Commissariats, instituting a party dictatorship and exercising their violence even against the anarchist unions and their press, will find us determined adversaries.

Brigade commander, Batko Makhno, Members of the Staff [signatures appended], Chairman of the cultural section, Arshinov"[17]

❦

That answer, made in all objectivity and independence of outlook, is clear and unmistakable: the insurgents reaffirmed their loyalty to the revolutionary cause but had no wish to be the deaf, blind puppets of any party, no matter how revolutionary it professed to be. A passing swipe had been made at the Bolsheviks' repressive organs; a word to the wise is enough. Perhaps it was their excesses that had prompted Grigoriev's revolt. In order to shed some light on the matter, a panel of insurgents was set up to go and make an on-site investigation.

❦

Meanwhile, the telegram from Grigoriev, mentioned earlier, arrived. The recommendation to "knock the Bolsheviks on the head" was a touch vague, and the message went unanswered by the insurgents. Their commission of inquiry made its report: it transpired that Grigoriev was nothing more than a "war lord" but one who trailed many poor peasants in his wake. This discovery led the staff and the insurgents' Military Revolutionary Soviet to draw up a long proclamation headed "Who is Grigoriev?", exposing the adventurer, his anti-Semitic tendencies when he vented his spleen on those who "crucified Christ" and even his anti-Russian mentality when he talked about those who "came from the dregs of Moscow!" Didn't Grigoriev gladly crow that whenever he had captured Odessa — with its 630,000 inhabitants, 400,000 of them Jews — a revolutionary committee had immediately been formed, made up of 99 members, 97 Jews and two "Russian imbeciles"? The Makhnovists also denounced these contradictions when he claimed to be championing the real power of the Soviets yet simultaneously ordered everybody to "elect their commissars" and then to mobilize "carrying out his order while he would look after the rest"(!) Yet the Makhnovist proclamation made a distinction between the peasant mass that followed the ataman, a mass to be regarded not so much as counter-revolutionary as "the victim of deception," and it was to be hoped that the "healthy revolutionary intuition" of the peasants would "open their eyes and that they will leave Grigoriev and rally again to the banner of revolution." However, the causes behind his revolt also had to be sought in the Bolsheviks' coming to the Ukraine and the installation of their party dictatorship, accompanied by its sinister Chekas:

> "… of which Grigoriev has made use in his adventure. He is a traitor to the revolution and an enemy of the people, but the party of the Bolshevik communists is every bit as much the workers' enemy. Through its unaccountable dictatorship, it has created among the masses a hatred that currently benefits Grigoriev and tomorrow may benefit some other adventurer. […] Let us again remind the laboring people that its deliverance from oppression, poverty and violence will be secured only by its own efforts. No change of authority will be able to help in that. It is only through their own free organizations of peasants and workers that toilers will arrive at the threshold of social revolution, complete freedom and authentic equality."[18]

As may be seen, the Bolsheviks too were not spared and had no special grounds for congratulations on this score. The essential point, though, in their eyes was still that Makhno was not turning against them for the moment.

A huge number of copies of this proclamation was run off and these were distributed among the peasants and fighters. It was also included in the Makhnovist movement's organ, *The Road to Freedom*, and in the mouthpiece of the Ukrainian anarchist confederation, *Nabat* (Tocsin).

❦

Grigoriev became the bête noire of Moscow who dispatched against him all of the reinforcements meant for the southern front. Worse still, the First Red Cossack regiment (1,200 horsemen and eight cannon) and the assault regiment from the Crimea were pulled out of the front lines for use against him. Not everyone accepted the assignment; the Kiev-based Ninth Ukrainian Regiment refused at the beginning of May to march against him and was duly disarmed and then re-formed. Certain units fraternized with the ataman and defected to his side. He managed to capture Ekaterinoslav but was unable to hold on to it for more than two days.

On May 20, by which time Grigoriev's failure was apparent, Antonov-Ovseenko asked Dybenko to transfer his divisions forthwith to the southern front. He met with a refusal, Dybenko claiming that the ataman's revolt was still virulent and that the Red troops had taken heavy losses. This refusal frustrated Antonov-Ovseenko who was keen to marshal Dybenko's divisions plus Pokus's detachment as urgently as possible on the southern front, in order to amalgamate them with Makhno's brigade before entrusting command of the division thus formed to Chikvanaya who was under orders from the party hierarchy. In this way the Batko would have been hemmed in by dependable Bolsheviks and there would have been no further fear of a revolt from that quarter. The politico-strategic considerations of the Red Army's high command were about to confuse the situation to a singular extent and to poison relations with the Makhnovists.

Notes to Chapter 15: Alliance with the Red Army

1. V.M. Primakov "The struggle for soviet power in the Ukraine" in the anthology *Piats' Let Krasnoj armii (Five Years of the Red Army)*, Moscow 1923 pp. 171–195.
2. In Alexander Bek *Takova Doljnost*, Moscow 1973, pp. 35–140. Dybets had written his memoirs for the Civil War Memoirs Institute set up by Maxim Gorky in the 1930s: those memoirs never got beyond the manuscript stage on account of the writer's probable disappearance in the purges that followed which accounts for the belated and roundabout publication of testimony that is rather precious for our purposes.
3. *Krasnoarmeiskaya petchat'*, Moscow, February 1922, No. 3-4, pp. 8–9.
4. This reply appears in its entirety in Arshinov's book, op. cit. pp. 98–103 (Russian edition).
5. Antonov-Ovseenko *Notes of the Civil War* (in Russian), Moscow, 1924 Tome III, pp. 203–204; Tome IV, pp. 95–120 and pp. 302–308 (all of the quotations below are lifted from there).
6. At the time a council republic led by Tibor Szamuelly and Hungarian imitators of Lenin was in place in Hungary.
7. Antonov-Ovseenko op. cit. p. 105.
8. V.S. "L. B. Kamenev's expedition to ensure the provisioning of Moscow in 1919" in *Proletarian Revolution* (in Russian), Moscow No. 6 (41), 1925, p. 132 et seq.
9. Arshinov (in Russian) op. cit. p. 105.
10. See V.S. op. cit. p. 139.
11. Lenin *Oeuvres Complètes*, Tome XXXVI, p. 523.
12. Arshinov op. cit. p. 110. As we have seen this ploy was much in use for eliminating certain less-than-compliant leaders of partisan detachments (Petrenko in April 1918 in Tsaritsyn and the instances cited by Primakov).
13. Arshinov (in Russian) op. cit. p. 107.
14. Yu. Tyutyunik "The struggle against the occupiers," in *The Black Book*, an anthology by A.G. Schlichter of articles and documents on the Entente intervention in the Ukraine in 1918–1919, Ekaterinoslav, 1925 (Russian Language).
15. "The Grigoriev adventure," in *Letopis revoliutsi*, 3, 1925, pp. 152–159. Grigoriev is described there sometimes as second captain, sometimes as a Tsarist colonel and finally as an ex-Tsarist general! The editor certainly had his problems telling all the different ranks apart.
16. Arshinov op. cit. p. 109.
17. Ibidem, p. 110 and Kubanin, op. cit. p.75.
18. Arshinov op. cit. pp. 112–115.

16. The Breakdown of the Alliance and the Collapse of the Front

The whole burden of the Southern front fell upon the Makhnovists who were inadequately equipped with arms and ammunition by the Red Army in spite of the clauses of the alliance agreement. Facing them, the Whites had laid the groundwork for a big push in order to shake themselves loose of this front which threatened the left flank of their north-bound offensive. At the head of two Cossack divisions from the Kuban and the Terek, well-armed and well-appointed by the Anglo-French, General Shkuro was in charge of operations. The breach of the front came about almost fortuitously due to a gross error by the command of a red division. In his memoirs, Shkuro tells the story thus:

> "Returning to Illovaisk[1] I received a report on operations of the First Cavalry Division. It transpired that the first regiment of [White] partisans had, while advancing, clashed with a substantial force of Reds dug in on the banks of a river fordable only with difficulty. Sustaining heavy losses, the [White] partisans had begun to fall back. The Reds decided to give chase and cross the river. At this point, *essaul*[2] Solomakhin, commander of the 2nd regiment of the White partisans, using his initiative, fell upon the flanks of the Bolsheviks and drove them towards the river. Many Bolsheviks drowned there or were cut down by sabers.
>
> We took nearly 1,500 prisoners, several cannon and a quantity of machine guns and munitions. The Reds' front had been pierced. I hurled my two divisions into the breach, giving them as their objective Yuzovka, which the Caucasus division was to attack from the south and the Terek division from the north. On May 18 a division of tanks — a weapon hitherto not seen there — arrived with General Mai-Maievsky [Shkuro's superior]. I entrusted custody of them to my squadron of 'wolves.' The next day, the Kornilovites [an elite division called after General Kornilov] went on the attack with these tanks and captured Yasinovata. That same day, my division took Yuzovka, taking numerous prisoners, Reds and Makhnovists alike. After having all the communists hanged, I sent all the rest home. Wasting no more

time there, we took the railway stations at Chaplino and Volnovakha without great losses."[3]

This crucial engagement had not been taken seriously by the Red Army command and, rather than admit to incompetence, it chose instead to place the blame on Makhnovists. But for the time being, Shkuro failed to capitalize upon this breakthrough and the axis of the offensive remained fixed to the north, via Kursk and the road to Moscow. Thus it was not too late to save the southern front which played a vital role in pinning down numerous heavily armed enemy forces over a distance of more than 150 kilometers, forces that were using (for the first time in the civil war), numerous tanks and armored cars, giving them a technical superiority which accounts for Makhno's being forced back from the front.

What was afoot in the Bolshevik upper echelons at the time? The breakthrough by Shkuro was underestimated and minds were focused instead on the best way of eliminating Makhno. There was a breakdown in coordination: Skatchko, commander of the 2nd army and Makhno's direct superior, took the decision to deploy the Makhnovist brigade as a division. When Antonov-Ovseenko vigorously objected, he gave him this account of his rationale:

"The military revolutionary soviet [of the 2nd army — A.S.] is very well aware that Makhno's brigade represents a peasant mass awash with petit-bourgeois anarchist and Left SR tendencies, utterly opposed to state communism. Conflict between the Makhnovschina and communism is inevitable, sooner or later. Even at the time of the formation of Makhno's brigade, the commander of the 2nd army issued him with Italian rifles on the reckoning that if need be it would be possible to withhold cartridges from them. But the 2nd army's military revolutionary soviet is persuaded that, until such time as the common enemy of communism and of the revolutionary (albeit petit-bourgeois) peasantry, to wit, the reactionary monarchy, will be definitively beaten and until such time as the White Volunteer troops will be pushed back towards the Kuban, the Makhnovschina's leaders will not march under arms (and will not have that opportunity) against soviet power: it is for that reason that we have thus far been able to use Makhno's troops in the struggle against the Whites, while converting them internally and gradually into more regular troops better nourished with the spirit of communism. The deployment of Makhno's brigade as a division may be tremendously helpful to work within its ranks, for it affords us a pretext for dispatching a large number of our political militants and officers to it. The whole of Gulyai-Polye followed Makhno. That population supplies him with 20,000 armed partisans who make up his brigade and are now to form a division. Trotsky has interpreted the brigade's conversion into a division as an authentic deployment, but that is a mistake. It is only an organizational reshuffle that paves the way for our political militants and military specialists to penetrate the mass of Makhno's troops. An abrupt change in our policy through cancellation of this conversion into a division (endorsed by war commissar Mezhlauk for all that) will put Makhno on his guard and may well induce him to cease his activities on the front against the Whites. Obviously, such a cessation will entail an increase of White pressures upon other parts of the southern front and there will be a worsening of the situation overall. Our command will insist upon more strenuous activities from Makhno. The latter will begin to allow combat orders to go unheeded and an open breach between him and us will be opened in short order. That would be negative, for the whole 2nd Ukrainian Army at present comprises solely of Makhno's brigade. Ukrainian units from other armies, all of them drawn from insurgent detachments, will not fight Makhno. So, if he is to be liquidated, it would be essential that we are able to call upon at least two complete and well-armed divisions."[4]

The shameful secret stands exposed: the under-arming of the Makhnovists had been premeditated and had had no purpose other than to bring them to heel! Moreover, all of this whole squabble about "deployment" or "conversion" of the Makhnovist brigade into a division — which would be laughable were it not for the dramatic civil war setting — had as its common denominator the aim of reducing Makhno's influence and then of divesting him utterly of his responsibilities. A prize example of the mentality incipient at this time in these tin-pot Bolshevik Macchiavellians.

Ultimately Antonov-Ovseenko carried the day and the redeployment of Makhno's brigade as a division was revoked. The Makhnovists, who were fighting desperately to contain the push by the Whites and who were in receipt of no assistance from the Reds, grew weary of all this "scheming" and decided to recover their autonomy and then to set themselves up as an independent insurgent army headed by Makhno, retaining only operational ties with the Red Army. This they communicated to the paper generalissimos:

"To the commander of the southern front, to Front commander Antonov-Ovseenko, to the chairman of the Soviet of people's commissars Rakovsky, to commissar for war Mezhlauk, to Lenin, to the Kremlin in Moscow, to Kamenev chairman of the defense soviet in Kharkov:

The staff of the 1st Insurgent Division, having examined the communiqué from the southern front ordering the 1st Ukrainian insurgent division to revert to the status of 3rd brigade, expresses its categorical disagreement on this point. It takes profound exception to the unfair treatment meted out to the insurgents' leader, comrade Makhno, and, furthermore, anticipates that this order will have harmful consequences, perhaps involving countless catastrophes for the revolution at the front and in the rear alike. It is persuaded that it is entitled to spell out the following facts to the southern front command, and to the central authorities of the Ukraine and Russia: the insurgent movement in the Ukraine began with the desperate engagements of the peasants against exploiters of all sorts, beginning with the hetman and ending with Petliura. With time, it formed regular regiments and manned a broad front against Denikin's counter-revolution. From the earliest days of its existence, comrade Nestor Makhno has been the soul and the indefatigable moving force behind this insurgent movement: he has shown himself to be the natural commander of the brigade, and later of the Division, raised to that office by the general commander congress of insurgents. All of the eleven insurgent regiments making up the 1st Division of the Ukraine regard comrade Makhno as their closest and most natural guide, elevated to that position by all the difficulties on the long road of the revolution. It is absolutely certain that with Makhno eliminated from that position, entire brigades will not accept anyone else in his place. There can be no doubt but that that will also have a fatal impact upon the front and upon the rearguard. This is why the staff of the 1st Ukrainian Insurgent Division of the so-called 'Batko Makhno' units has determined: (1) to propose to and require of comrade Makhno that he remain in his position of responsibility, despite his attempting to quit it in the light of the situation created: (2) that all eleven infantry regiments, the two cavalry regiments, the two assault groups, the artillery brigade and the other technical units become one independent insurgent army, command thereof being entrusted to comrade Makhno. In operational matters this army will be subject to the command of the southern front, to the extent that the latter's operational orders correspond to real requirements of the revolutionary front. All operational decisions of the insurgent army are to be communicated directly to the Red Army command.

Furthermore, the attention of all central authorities of the Soviet Republics of the Ukraine and Russia is drawn to the following declaration: Comrade Makhno and we all are authentic revolutionaries, fighting for the ideals of social revolution. That is why we regard as offensive to us and intolerable on the part of a revolutionary, Dybenko's reservation-fraught words regarding comrade Makhno, as uttered in the presence of our delegation: "I've given one bandit a thrashing, one more won't be any problem," when the Grigoriev episode found in comrade Makhno a vigorous and inflexible enemy: three issues of *The Road to Freedom* and the special proclamation circulated throughout the Ukraine testify to that. Believing in the triumph of the social revolution, in absolute commitment to that from both the officers of the soviet republics in the persons of Lenin, Lunacharsky and Kamenev, as well as from comrade Makhno and his men, sons of the revolution, the command of the 1st Ukrainian Insurgent Division issues a categorical assurance that all potential misunderstandings regularly generated by false information from agents of the authorities, can and must be thoroughly dispelled by fraternal means.

The staff of the 1st Ukrainian Insurgent Division of the troops known as Batko Makhno's troops … May 29, 1919. In Gulyai-Polye."[5]

This was a clear and unambiguous stand on all the maneuvers designed to oust Makhno from his post. Apparently Makhno had wanted to step down lest the situation of the front be compromised, but the insurgents had talked him out of it. The tone of this address was still fraternal and it leaves the door open for any amicable negotiation or accommodation. Thus far the insurgents had scrupulously adhered to the military compact entered into: their view was that, even if the Bolsheviks were against their operating autonomously, this could only be at the level of ideas and that they would "discover some common language" (as Lev Kamenev had it) and that class solidarity would come into play in the contest against the Whites, the loftier interests of the social revolution being placed above the discrepancies of opinion. They were mistaken, and the "officers of the soviet republics" were about to take it upon themselves to demonstrate so. Seeing their plans frustrated, the leaders (political and military) of the southern front were first of all to threaten Makhno:

> "The military revolutionary council of the southern front signals that Makhno's activities and pronouncements are deemed criminal. Bearing responsibility for a given sector of the 2nd army's southern front, Makhno has, by his pronouncements, introduced wholesale disorganization into the administration and the command and then by allowing units to act according to their lights, he betrays the front. Makhno must be arrested and brought before the revolutionary tribunal: on these grounds the military revolutionary council of the 2nd Army hereby takes the requisite steps to forestall any possibility of Makhno avoiding the merited sanction.
>
> **V. Hittis. A. Kolegaev"**

On May 31, the Military Revolutionary Soviet of the Gulyai-Polye region, given the seriousness of the situation, resolved to convene a 4th regional congress of peasants, workers and fighters from the entire territory under Makhnovist control: 90 districts from the provinces of Ekaterinoslav, the Tavrida, Kherson, Kharkov and the Donetz basin. The Summons stipulated that "… only the toiling masses will be able to devise a way out of the situation created, and not parties or individuals." The congress was scheduled for June 15 in Gulyai-Polye. The conventional representation was one delegate per 3000 workers or peasants, one representative per insurgent unit or Red Army unit (regiment, division, etc.), two delegates for the central staff of the Batko Makhno Division and one per brigade staff: the district executive committees were to send along one delegate per faction: organizations or parties accepting the basis of the soviet regime were entitled to one delegate per district branch. Elections would take place at general assemblies. The agenda centered on the following items:

> "(a) Reports from the executive committee of the military revolutionary soviet and from delegates from the district executive committees (b) business in hand (c) purpose, meaning and tasks of the Gulyai-Polye regional soviet (d) reorganization of the regional Military Revolutionary Soviet (e) organization of military tasks in the region (f) the question of provisions (g) the agrarian issue (h) the financial question (i) the unions of peasant laborers and workers (j) public safety (k) the exercise of justice in the region (l) other business."[7]

In this way the Gulyai-Polye region's Military Revolutionary Soviet recalled that it was only the executive arm of the supreme authority of the region, namely the general congress. As was only normal for revolutionaries who believed that everything had to emanate from below, that the workers and fighters had to handle and regulate their affairs for themselves. That was not the view of Trotsky who had recently arrived in the area which he knew only through the tittle-tattle in party offices. He had already crossed swords with Antonov-Ovseenko over Makhno. He found the libertarian effervescence that prevailed in the region and the methods of direct democracy used by the insurgents deeply repugnant, he being so thoroughly imbued with omnipotence of the new State as well as being so full of himself of course. On June 2 he published this bilious diatribe against Makhno:

> "There is Soviet Russia and there is Soviet Ukraine. And alongside, there is still a known state: Gulyai-Polye. There the staff of a certain Makhno reigns. First of all he commanded a detachment of irregulars and then a brigade and then — it would seem — a division: finally, today, everything is decked out in the colors of a special rebel "White" army. Against whom have Makhno's rioters risen? That is a question to which a clear and precise answer must be given: an answer in words and an answer in deeds.
>
> Makhno and his closest confederates consider themselves anarchists and on that basis "repudiate" all governmental power. Are they in consequence enemies of soviet power? — Apparently so, since soviet power is the governmental power of the toiling workers and peasants.
>
> However, Makhno's acolytes have decided not to declare openly that they are against soviet power. They play it shrewd and avoid the

issue: they claim to acknowledge local soviet authority and repudiate only the central authorities [...] Makhno's acolytes chant: "Down with the party, down with the communists, long live the non-party soviets!" And yet this is only a pitiable lie. Makhno and his henchmen are absolutely not non-partisan. They all belong to the anarchist school and issue circulars or letters to all their co-religionists, inviting them to Gulyai-Polye, there to organize power of their own. [...] Makhno's "army" is the ugliest face of guerrilla warfare, although it does include a number of good soldiers. It is impossible to discover the merest hint of discipline or order in this "army" [...] In this "army," commanders are elected. Makhno's acolytes chant: "Down with appointed commanders!" Thus, they mistakenly mislead only the most obtuse of their own troops. Only under the bourgeois regime when tsarist functionaries or bourgeois ministers appointed as they deemed fit commanders who kept the bulk of troops in a state of subjection to the bourgeois classes could one speak of "appointed commanders." Today we have no power other than that which is elected by the whole of the working class and toiling peasantry. As a result, commanders appointed by the central soviet authorities are installed by the will of millions of workers, whereas the commanders of Makhno's bands reflect the interests of a tiny anarchist clique dependant on kulaks and obscurantism."[8]

The radical change of tone, compared with that of Antonov-Ovseenko is all too obvious: yet it was Antonov-Ovseenko who was the Bolshevik militant of long standing whereas Trotsky was but a recent convert, in 1917, after the return of Lenin in whose nostrils he had not always had the odor of sainthood: hadn't Lenin called him a "little Judas, his forehead 'branded' with the crimson of shame"? [9] Thus he felt himself compelled systematically to out-zealot the most zealous of his new party colleagues: he talked about "order and discipline," and railed against "election of commanders" by the ranks. But who was he trying to fool when he talked of Bolshevik power having been "elected by the whole of the working class and toiling peasantry"? Did he think he could erase the memory that, in the Constituent Assembly elections of November 1917, his party had taken barely a quarter of the votes? As for the "interests of a tiny clique," they were the interests of his party's central committee, a party which he defended by recourse to calumny. Even Kubanin, the official soviet historian of the Makhnovschina and not inclined to be considerate of its sensibilities, describes as ... "a typically prickly and venomous phrase" this passage from the fire-brand Trotsky: "Scratch the surface a little and one finds Grigoriev. And quite often there is no need to scratch: the rampant kulak baying for the blood of communists, or the small speculator were not long in showing their true colors."[10] The amalgamation with Grigoriev just goes to demonstrate Trotsky's utter ignorance of the situation locally but on the other hand the epithet *kulak*, a flight of fancy here used for the first time against

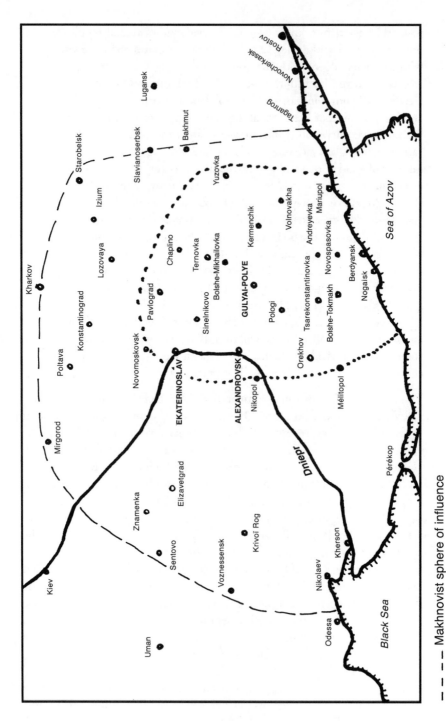

Map of "Makhnovia."

- - - - Makhnovist sphere of influence

········· "Makhnovia"

Makhno, was to enjoy a brilliant future in Bolshevik ideology. This was an original contribution by Trotsky to contemporary socio-political vocabulary.

He concluded this his first formal statement of position by stigmatizing the "atamans and straw commanders" with this menace "… It is high time to have an end of them once and for all so that none may be tempted to start up again!", and he promised a response in "… word and in deed." Two days later, on June 4, he was at it again in an interview with representatives of the press in Kharkov: he announced to them that a regeneration was crucial and that this would consist mainly of "… abolishing the independent anarchist republic of Gulyai-Polye," for "on the Donetz front rampages the brigade or army division — I do not know how one would describe it — of a certain Makhno. This 'fighting unit' currently attracts to itself all of the elements of decomposition, decadence, revolt and putrefaction [!] […] Makhno's bands are even now trying to convene a military-soviet congress of five provinces. It goes without saying that the command will neither accept nor authorize anything of the sort."[11] Meanwhile he discovered that the fourth regional congress had been summoned and he prepared his reply.

Asked by a journalist if Kharkov was not under threat from the White offensive, Trotsky expressed amazement at the posing of such a question, for he reckoned that Kharkov was no more under threat than Moscow, Tver or any other city of the Soviet Republic. He was utterly oblivious of the danger represented by Denikin and was concerned only with neutralizing Makhno!

That same day he issued his reply to the convening of the Gulyai-Polye congress, his celebrated order No. 1824: wherein he declared that this "… congress is wholly directed against soviet power in the Ukraine and against the organization of the southern front of which the Makhno brigade is a part." : its outcome could not but be the delivery of the

> "… front to the Whites, in the face of whom Makhno's brigade does nothing but retreat due to his incompetence and the criminally treacherous tendencies of his commanders.
> 1) The aforementioned congress is hereby prohibited and cannot in any event be countenanced.
> 2) The entire peasant and worker population should be cautioned orally and in writing that participation in this congress will be deemed high treason against the soviet republic and the soviet front.
> 3) All delegates to the above-mentioned congress should immediately be placed under arrest and hauled before the revolutionary court martial of 14th (formerly 2nd) Army of the Ukraine.
> 4) All who circulate the appeals of Makhno and the Gulyai-Polye executive committee should be arrested."[12]

Trotsky signed this as president of the republic's military revolutionary soviet, which gave him full powers in the Ukraine. He had recalled Antonov-Ovseenko, and it was his replacement, Vatsetis, a Latvian tsarist ex-colonel who countersigned this order as front commander. This document — which Arshinov regards as a classic, recommending that it be memorized by heart! — was followed up on June 6 by order of the day No. 107, which confirmed the foregoing order and specifically stipulated the punishment due: Firing squad. It is worth reprinting in its entirety:

> "Gathered around the irregular Makhno, a band of individuals has set out on the same road as the traitor Grigoriev and has hatched a plot against soviet power. This gang from Gulyai-Polye has dared schedule for June 15th a congress of anarchist and kulak delegates in order to struggle against the Red Army and soviet authorities.
>
> That congress is banned. Let me announce that any possible participant in this congress will be deemed a traitor, guilty of conspiring in the immediate rear of our troops and of opening the gates to the enemy. Makhno invites runaways from other armies and units to join him.
>
> **I hereby order:**
> All military authorities and blockade detachments deployed in accordance with my instructions to seize all such traitors who voluntarily quit their units to join Makhno and to produce them before the revolutionary tribunal as deserters so that they may stand trial in accordance with the laws in force in time of war.
>
> Their punishment can only be the firing squad.
>
> The Pan-Russian Central executive committee of Russia and the Ukraine has charged me to restore order on the front in the Donetz basin and in its immediate rear. I hereby proclaim that order will be restored with a mailed fist. Enemies of the workers' and peasants' Red Army, profiteers, kulaks, rioters, henchmen of Makhno or of Grigoriev are to be eliminated without quarter by staunch reliable regular units.
>
> Long live revolutionary order, discipline and struggle against the enemies of the people!
>
> Long live Soviet Union and Soviet Russia!"[13]

Here Trotsky is using the language beloved of all fans of the strong arm, of defenders of the established order: "Plot," "gangs," "punishment," "firing squad," and "mailed fist." There is, however, one novelty: This time the established order professes to be "revolutionary" and "proletarian" and addresses itself to the very people it professes to represent — the peasants and workers.

In short, it seeks to forbid them from taking their affairs into their own hands, banning revolutionaries from making revolution! An unappetizing mentality this, which unfortunately holds out the promise of an exemplary future. Here Trotsky was applying new psychological warfare methods in a revolutionary setting: Deliberate lying, misrepresentation, ideological dismissal, guilt by association — all these ingredients were henceforth to add spice to the cuisine of hegemonic power.

However, if Trotsky indulged himself in this sort of behavior and bayed at anyone daring to question his decisions, it was because he knew he had the support of Lenin who certainly had no desire to allow this region to organize itself autonomously and escape from his direct control, militarily as well as politically speaking. Otherwise, that example might prove unduly contagious.

The "answer in words" now completed, that only left the "answer in deeds" — and this was not long in coming. Three peasants, Kostin, Polunin and Dobrolyubov, taken in the very act of *discussing* the convening of the Gulyai-Polye regional congress, were hauled before the tribunal of the 14th Army and shot on the spot for just that!

And to cap it all, these famous orders were not even conveyed directly to the Makhnovist insurgents who in any case had their work cut out with the Whites.

※※※

Following the breakthrough achieved on May 17th, Shkuro returned to Debaltsevo where he had to assist the Don Cossack general, Kalinin, who had also broken through the Red front and seized Lugansk. As a result, the front facing Makhno remained stationary. According to Antonov-Ovseenko, it was because he had "…received neither the military supplies nor reinforcements [which had been dispatched against Grigoriev] that Makhno was unable to withstand the attack by Shkuro's cavalry" at Yuzovka. Even Skatchko, the 2nd Army's commander, realized on May 21st that an infantry brigade was urgently needed to repair the breach, as well as artillery and cavalry. Makhno's division was in dire need of cartridges and artillery shells. It was obvious that under the new politico-military approach introduced by Trotsky, re-supplying of the insurgents was no longer on, indeed, quite the opposite.

So what was happening with the Makhnovists? Was it perhaps in order to demonstrate their revolutionary bona fides yet again, or maybe because they underestimated their adversaries? Whatever the case may have been, they mounted a counter-attack against Yuzovka and drove out General Mai-Maievsky's troops: The general called in Shkuro, this time assigning him the task of mopping up the Makhnovist front:

> "At this point [probably the beginning of June] Makhno again went on the offensive against Mai-Maievsky's corps and forced it to quit Yuzovka. I was assigned the task of attacking the Makhnovists. Doubling back I wrested Yuzovka before marching on Mariupol which I attacked and captured along with General Vinogradov's mixed Volunteer Army detachment. Leaving the First Terek Division to support the Volunteer Army corps entrusted by Mai-Maievsky to General Kutyepov who had already captured Bakhmut and was closing on Kharkov, I — along with the First Caucasus Division — undertook an attack upon the Makhnovists' capital and repository for their booty, the township of Gulyai-Polye. This I took after bitter fighting and the remainder of

the Makhnovists were wiped out or scattered; whereupon, I put the important railway junction of Sinelnikovo to the torch."[14]

According to Arshinov, prior to Shkuro's attack, the Bolsheviks had left the stretch of the front which they were holding at Grishino, north of Makhno's front, unmanned, and it was precisely through there that Shkuro had poured in to take the whole Makhnovist division from the rear. However, several days previously the insurgents had warned the Red Army's headquarters of this weak point; also, whether due to incompetence or deliberately the Bolshevik command had failed to make good the deficiency, leading to the front's collapse. Again, according to Arshinov, Trotsky allegedly had declared that it "...was better that the whole Ukraine be surrendered to Denikin than that the Makhnovschina be allowed to develop further. Denikin's movement, being openly counter-revolutionary, will still be susceptible to decomposition from within by means of class agitation, whereas the Makhnovschina is spreading into the depths of the masses and in turn raises the masses against us."[15] Such reasoning was not at all surprising; it was a pompous variation upon Lenin's line about "whoever is not with us is against us." The military alliance had lasted for four months and had been used only in a one-sided way by Moscow. Now that the Makhnovist front had buckled, it could be abjured at the earliest opportunity, in the most profitable manner available.

Shkuro's offensive caught the insurgents by surprise and forced them to fall back 100 kilometers in a single day, abandoning Mariupol. Despite a desperate defense, Makhno even had to give up Gulyai-Polye, overwhelmed by the Cossack flood. It was at this juncture that he learned of Trotsky's orders of some days before — an outright declaration of war. He put his head together with his staff and decided to focus on the most pressing task, i.e., containing the White onslaught as best he could. Seeing that he personally was the bugbear of the Bolshevik high command, he decided to resign his posts inside his division for the sake of the overriding interests of the revolution. He reckoned that this was the only way to avert the opening of a second front and being caught in a pincer movement that the insurgents had no way of withstanding. He dispatched a telegram to Trotsky to inform him of his decision. Trotsky's reply was prompt, in the shape of an order of the day on June 8th:

> **"Have done with Makhno!**
>
> Who bears the responsibility for our latest reverses on the southern front, notably in the Donetz basin?
>
> Makhno and his gangs.
>
> In words, this clique fights the whole world and annihilates all enemies; however, when it comes to the real fight, the commanders of these troops shamelessly abandon positions entrusted to them and quite simply fall back over several dozen versts.
>
> [...] Makhno's brigade contained a number of good and faithful fighters. Even with regular organization of supplies and leadership, and

above all in the absence of internal discipline or sensible command, Makhno's units have shown themselves incapable of weathering the slightest combat; the White cavalry drove them before it like a flock of sheep.

[…] The bigwigs of Gulyai-Polye went even further. For June 15th they scheduled a congress of the military and peasant units of five regions so as to give battle openly against soviet power and the established order in the Red Army.

We can no longer tolerate our continued humiliation at the hands of this gang which has lost all following. If we leave Makhno to pursue his plans, we will be faced with a fresh rebellion along the lines of Grigoriev's, which would spring from its nest in Gulyai-Polye. This is why the central military authorities have categorically banned the congress and dispatched trustworthy and loyal units to restore order in the region where Makhno is rampant.

Today that criminal outbreak is ended. *Makhno and his adjutants have been ousted. Makhno's rebellion is in the process of liquidation.*

It is true that many profiteers and bandits professing loyalty to Makhno still remain in different units and are trying to reach to Gulyai-Polye; there is no discipline there and no obligation to fight honestly against enemies of the toiling people and thus — a paradise on earth for cowards and good-for-nothings."[16]

The balance of power being at this point tilted in his favor, Trotsky made maximum use of it; he accused Makhno and his companions of every sort of evil-doing, taking care to except "a number of good fighters," for there was always a use for cannon-fodder. After having contrived to minimize and sabotage provisions and munitions to the insurgents, he laid the blame for shortages on the absence of "regular organization of supplies and leadership," and above all of "internal discipline and sensible command" (by which is meant the absence of Chekist methods and Tsarist ex-officer military experts taken on in massive numbers by Moscow.) The resignation of Makhno and his staff was willfully misconstrued; they have been "ousted." This was the apogee of Trotsky's whole campaign against Makhno and the Gulyai-Polye region. Had these been only the bombast of the salon or of some party meeting, no great harm would have been done, but in reality the fact was that his "answer-in-deeds" turned out to be the ransacking of the "Rosa Luxemburg" libertarian commune, the arrest and execution of several dozen insurgents, sordid police operations carried out by (according to Trotsky) "trustworthy and loyal units," which is to say Chekists pressing on with the "liquidation of rebellion." And all this behind Makhnovists who were standing up to the Cossack flood of Shkuro. The most cynical and ignominious part of this declaration related to Gulyai-Polye which it dubbed "paradise on earth for cowards and good-for-nothings," when at that very moment the local peasants were hastily putting together a detachment of several dozen men, armed with axes, pitchforks and shoddy rifles. Led by Veretelnikov (a worker from the great Putilov plant in Petrograd, albeit born in Gulyai-Polye), they went off in search of the Whites. They were cut down by sabers where they stood while defending their land and liberty, while seeking to avert violation of their wives, sisters or mothers, not that that counted for much with Trotsky. But such statements of position represent an indelible blemish for their author.

✎✎✎

Skatcho was replaced as head of the Second Army — renamed the 14th – by Voroshilov, to whom was also entrusted the task of seizing Makhno and his staff. Alerted in time, Makhno sent a rather lengthy explanation to Trotsky, Lenin and Kamenev on June 9th. He repeated his request to relinquish his post to someone else; he protested against the press campaign unleashed against him and tarring him with the same brush as Grigoriev. He refuted the charges ventilated by Trotsky concerning the Makhnovists' hostile intent towards the Soviet republic; he reaffirmed his belief in the "inalienable right of workers and peasants, a right won by revolution, to themselves organize congresses to discuss and decide upon their private and general affairs. That is why the central authorities' proscription of such congresses, and the declaration pronouncing them unlawful [Order No. 1824] are a direct and shameless infringement of the workers' rights."[17] Makhno realized that he himself was the target, and, given the overall situation, rather than set up an anti-Bolshevik front he preferred to step down. It is interesting here to look at the later explanation that he was to give of this evolution in the military alliance concluded with the Red Army:

> "The Makhnovschina concluded an alliance with the Bolsheviks (in 1919) under which they were to supply it with arms and munitions; in return for which the Makhnovist movement was subordinated to the supreme command of the Red Army. That alliance was broken by the Bolsheviks on the one hand, through their police tactics towards the working population of the Makhnovist region which had set about freely constructing its social and economic life while dispensing with the oversight of the Bolshevik party and the Bolshevik state, and, on the other hand, through their sabotaging of arms and munitions supplies, which often led to Makhnovists throwing themselves into the attack against Denikin with only five cartridges per rifle, and, in the event of success against the enemy, to their seizing his munitions, or in the event of failure, to sustaining countless losses and beating a retreat, leaving behind thousands of wounded as hostages.
>
> [...]The Makhnovschina opted to combat this Bolshevik cynicism by 1) temporarily withdrawing from the high command of its armed forces, beginning with myself, and 2) placing all its armed forces back under the supreme command of the Bolsheviks, 3) painstakingly

monitoring closely and from afar all their operational activities, the object being to verify that these are compatible with the great tasks of the revolution."[18]

And so Makhno stepped down from his position of command and handed over to his successor (appointed by Trotsky) all divisional papers and documents and then, along with his closest colleagues, the ones most compromised in Bolsheviks' eyes, as well as with personal escort, he quit the front while expressing his intention of harrying the Whites in their rear.

En route, an odd incident occurred:

> "*Feldwebel*[19] Trotsky was so delighted during the first few days after my departure from the insurgent movement that he was at a loss to know what to do next. When he regained his composure, he ordered Voroshilov, commander of the 14th Army to seize Makhno, no matter what the cost, and to bring him alive to headquarters.
>
> Unfortunately for Trotsky, in the Red Army there were some divisional commanders, Bolshevik ones who, as soon as they had read this order, reported the matter to me immediately. And so Voroshilov was unable to lay hands on me. Indeed, he and his gang of Chekists came within an ace of perishing themselves. Denikinists surrounded their armed train, the 'Rudnev.' It was I who had to dispatch four machine-gunners and a squad of cavalry to them in order to rescue my would-be 'executioners,' at a time when I had already resigned my command and was en route to the front along with a small detachment. And so Voroshilov's armored train and his band of Chekists were extracted from that danger. I can remember just how happy Voroshilov was about this, and how he thanked me through my aide-de-camp. He also had delivered to me a message in which he expressed his esteem for me and insistently urged me to come and see him so that, together, we might look into a whole series of plans with an eye to the struggle ahead. My reply to him was,
>
>> 'I am aware of Trotsky's order and the part assigned to you, comrade Voroshilov, but that order is a matter for your own conscience. Which is why I regard it as impossible that I should come and examine with you what you have suggested — plans for the future struggle. Let me tell you mine: It is my intention to strike deep into Denikin's rear and cause havoc. This is extremely important now that he is engaged in a great general offensive....
>>
>> Your old friend in the struggle for the triumph of the revolution. June 15, 1919. Batko Makhno!'

The following night, this same Voroshilov issued orders for the arrest of the members of my staff, Mikhailov-Pavlenko and Burbyga, and had them shot the day after that."20

♥♥♥

Some people may find Makhno's devotion to the revolution excessive, if it led him to rescue the killer squad dispatched to capture him. In his defense, it might be said that he did not then know Voroshilov and could not but doubt that Voroshilov would be capable of having Mikhailov-Pavlenko and Burbyga put to death. As he had said, he had had dealings with honest Bolsheviks who had tipped him off about what was being hatched against him and he was not yet in a position to generalize. Also, he was not the sort to make Olympian pronouncements like Trotsky; as a simple man, he was committed body and soul to the social revolution. For him no alternative was conceivable; Denikin's hordes had to be contained. Trotsky was unscrupulous; he had Ozerov, Makhno's official chief of staff and a one-time Cossack officer and non-party revolutionary appointed by Antonov-Ovseenko, arrested. (Ozerov was to be tried before a Chekist court on July 25th with the sinister Latsis presiding and was shot on August 2, 1919). An active member of Makhno's staff, Mikhailov-Pavlenko, an engineer and close friend of Makhno had, as we have seen, been arrested and shot on June 17th. On the same day the Kharkov extraordinary court martial sentenced six Gulyai-Polye peasants — Burbyga, Olezhnik, Korobko, Kostin, Polunin and Dobrolyubov — to the same fate on charges of having sought to convene a counter-revolutionary congress. The last three named had already been executed, so the sentence merely placed a formal seal upon the *fait accompli.*

♥♥♥

Makhno's conduct had been improvised; in view of the circumstances, he had not had time to consult all insurgents. The latter, as soon as they learned of his having been outlawed and of Trotsky's attitude, insisted that their commanders take them to Makhno so that together they could determine what to do next: "To remain under the command of these 'Red' imbeciles, outright traitors to the revolution, or to wage against these criminal red cretins a struggle every whit as fierce as that against Denikin."21

Even other front-line divisions and brigades, including the "Lenin" brigade, once they learned of the outlawing of Makhno demanded in resolutions passed at general assemblies to be placed under Makhno's command, for "around them they saw naught but traitors to the revolution." Trotsky, who was charged with treachery, could devise nothing better than to openly promise impunity and reward to whoever would kill Makhno. Throughout this whole campaign against the Makhnovists, he had overlooked one essential factor: The scale of the Denikinist threat. Soon it was too late to react, as the whole of the eastern Ukraine fell into the clutches of White generals. Ekaterinoslav fell on June 12th, Kharkov two weeks later. Thus was the front, so valiantly held for over six months by Makhnovist insurgents at the cost of heroic sacrifices, sabotaged and delivered to the enemy by *Feldwebel* Trotsky and his cronies.

Notes to Chapter 16: The Breakdown of the Alliance and the Collapse of the Front

1. Town located on the edge of the Donetz basin and the Ukraine.
2. A cossack rank corresponding to commander.
3. A.G. Shkuro, *The Tales of a White Partisan* (in Russian), Buenos Aires, 1961, p. 212. There are reasons for doubting the release of Makhnovist prisoners, given the implacable hatred which the Whites bore them. V. Belash and P. Arshinov both cite several instances of Makhnovist prisoners having been roasted alive by the Whites. Moreover, Denikin had placed a price on Makhno's head, a price of a half million gold rubles.
4. This amazing document is reproduced by Antonov-Ovseenko, op. cit. Tome IV, pp. 305–306.
5. Ibid, pp. 307–308.
6. Ibid, p. 308.
7. Arshinov, op. cit. pp.117–119.
8. Trotsky, *Ecrits militaires*, L'Herne, 1967, pp. 668–671.
9. Lenin, *Oeuvres complètes*, Tome XVII, p. 39 (written 1911).
10. Trotsky, op.cit., p. 673.
11. Ibid, p. 674.
12. Reprinted by Arshinov, op. cit. (Russian edition) pp. 119–120.
13. Trotsky, op.cit., pp. 680–681. Trotsky was later to be ingenuously amazed when such methods were to be turned against him by Stalin.
14. Shkuro, op. cit. p. 213.
15. Arshinov, op. cit. p. 124.
16. Trotsky, op.cit., pp. 681–683.
17. Cf. The complete text in Arshinov, op. cit. pp. 126–127.
18. N. Makhno, *The Makhnovschina and its Erstwhile Allies: The Bolsheviks*, op. cit. pp. 53–54.
19. German for adjutant-in-chief.
20. Ibid, pp. 54–55.
21. Ibid, pp. 55–56.

17. Grigoriev, Dybets, Yakir, Slaschev and the Rest

In the small detachment accompanying Makhno were his comrades from the early days, militants from the Gulyai-Polye anarchist group and founders, along with Makhno, of the insurrection in September 1918, men who never left his side — men such as Alexei Marchenko, Semyon Karetnik, Petya Lyuty, Fedor Shchuss and Nestor's brother, Grigori Makhno. There was also the "black sotnia," sometimes called the "Kropotkin guard" or the "devil's sotnia," comprising of between 100 and 150 intrepid horsemen and some expert machine-gunners mounted on some tachankas, all of them utterly dedicated to the cause.

When they reached the outskirts of Alexandrovsk which was threatened by Denikin's outriders, the local Bolshevik boss, although au fait with the breakdown between his party and the insurgents, besought them to defend the town and the sector of the front between there and Melitopol, so as to let Dybenko's Crimean Army extricate itself from the trap and take refuge on the right bank of the Dniepr. They refused, for on the one hand, they did not have enough men, and on the other, they wanted a formal request from the Bolshevik leadership, acknowledging their own stupidity in having outlawed the Makhnovists. Their refusal earned Makhno and his companions further denunciation as outlaws and enemies of the regime.

❦❦❦

At this point Makhno's little band was joined by some groups of insurgents who had found themselves cut off following the capture of Mariupol and who had had to carve a passage for themselves across White-occupied territory. In this fashion, he put together a new insurgent contingent several thousand strong.

The Denikinists committed outrages, putting the Gulyai-Polye region to the torch and the knife, butchering recalcitrant peasants, violating the women (800 in Gulyai-Polye) and brought back the former estate owners and kulaks thirsting for revenge. Thus began the exodus of a huge number of peasants along with their families, with their meager belongings in tow. A vast cortege snaked across dozens of kilometers; runaways making towards their natural defenders, the Makhnovist insurgents.

Meanwhile, incapable of resisting the Denikinist onslaught, the Bolshevik leaders decided to give up on the Ukraine and concerned themselves solely with pulling out their troops with as much of their supplies and equipment as possible, back to the right bank of the Dniepr. They seized the chance to carry out a purge among the Red troops; they hunted down Makhnovist units, disarming them, shooting certain individuals and then reassigning the rest to more dependable units.

Faced with this situation, Makhno gave up on his initial plan to infiltrate into the enemy's rear; he decided to retreat towards the west, to the Dniepr's right bank. This brought him into the territory controlled by the ataman Grigoriev. The ataman had been sorely tried by the battles with Dybenko but still retained several thousand men and successfully conducted harrying operations against the Bolsheviks for whom he thenceforth nourished an implacable hatred. He accused them of deceiving the people, to be sure, but arguing on the basis of the many Jews belonging to soviet bodies, he systematically equated Jews and Bolsheviks. His units were credited with several pogroms (massacres) against Jews and, to a lesser extent, against Russians, especially in the Elisavetgrad (population 76,000, a third of them Jewish) where 3,000 people perished. He was careful not to make any formal statement or to criticize such killings; he stood idly by. What made the thing even more complex was the fact that there were some Jews among his troops.

The Makhnovists tried to skirt this new reef; Grigoriev enjoyed the support of the poor peasants, which is to say, of the same social class as they did. Secretly they set up a commission of inquiry into the outrages and the contacts which they suspected he had with Denikinists. In July there was a meeting between representatives of the two movements; after a day's discussions, a draft agreement was reached: The two contingents would amalgamate. Grigoriev would assume military command whereas Makhno would see to the political leadership of the new army. On July 27th, a great meeting in Sentovo drew 20,000 partisans from both camps. Grigoriev was the first to speak; he called for all-out war against the Bolsheviks and hinted at possible alliance with the Whites. Alexei Chubenko, one of the members of the Makhnovist staff, spoke next and publicly damned contacts with the Whites, for the Makhnovists had meanwhile intercepted some Denikinist emissaries and thus had the proof. Next, Chubenko accused Grigoriev of responsibility for pogroms against Jews before closing his address by violently condemning the counter-revolutionary aspect of the activities of "this war lord."

Grigoriev demanded an explanation; the two staffs withdrew to the hall of the local soviet. There Grigoriev made to draw his revolver to shoot Makhno but was beaten to it by Chubenko who gunned him down with a "pocket" revolver concealed in the palm of his hand.[1]

The Makhnovists then explained and justified what they had done before an assembly convulsed by this brutal denouement. Some of Grigoriev's partisans were recruited by Makhno. Grigoriev's death was reported by telegram to the Kremlin. Kubanin comments that with this act "…Makhno's political actions earned themselves very great prestige in the eyes of the Left Social Revolutionaries and anarchists. The revolutionary honor of Ukrainian petit-bourgeois circles was satisfied."[2] In any event, as far as the Bolsheviks were concerned, Makhno had removed a real thorn in their sides. Here again he had not had much option, for in the short term, Grigoriev would probably have betrayed him in favor of the Whites. Some of the ataman's troops were later recruited by the Red Army and were to prove implacable adversaries of the Makhnovists, exacting revenge for the death of their former leader.

As for the Bolsheviks, they persisted in keeping a judicious distance between their positions on the right bank of the Dniepr and those of the Whites. Their main preoccupation was with "disciplining" former Makhnovist units renamed the 58th Division and comprising three brigades, which is to say nearly 15,000 well-armed men in all, representing a tremendous unused fighting force. The former anarcho-syndicalist Dybets had his work cut out as political commissar, then took it into his head to enforce order on the insurgent units, although he had absolutely no experience of combat against the Whites, having been content to watch the outcome of engagements from a distance. From then on he committed himself to his neo-Bolshevik activities. Finding the Melitopol regiment unduly "independent" and rather too "Zaporog" for his taste, he spent a week looking for troops to bring them to heel and disarm them! All the other regiments in the division refused, of course, to take on their brothers in arms. Finally in Kherson, Dybets located a detachment of sailors and Spartakist Germans, in all some 700 heavily armed (machine-guns and artillery) men whom he dragged along without actually explaining the aim of the expedition to them. Once they were in place, he gave them to understand that a mutinous regiment had quit the front and was refusing to fight. Whereupon the detachment fell upon the Melitopol insurgents who were in battle readiness but in the last analysis reluctant to shoot "their own." As a result they were disarmed and redeployed, and some were shot. This "sensational action" stopped right there as far as Dybets was concerned, for the Red Army's high command decided to cut its losses on the Ukrainian front and ordered the division to fall back to Kiev and central Russia. The Kremlin opted to recall these troops for redeployment in its own defenses, for Denikin's push against Moscow was developing apace.

The ex-Makhnovists found this retreat unacceptable; they had no intention of abandoning their native districts to the Whites and indeed were itching to liberate them. According to the policy prescribed at the time when Makhno had resigned his command, several Makhnovist ex-commanders had remained at their posts — people like Kalashnikov, Dermendzhi, Budanov, Klein — and seeing that the Bolsheviks were not acting in the revolution's interests, they reasserted the freedom of their movements, arresting the Bolshevik commanders and political commissars, including Dybets, before delivering nearly the whole division to Makhno at the railway station in Pomoshnaya. En route, the punitive detachment of sailors and Spartakists was routed, thus settling that particular score.

At the end of August, Makhno's 700 horsemen and 3,000 infantry joined up with dissident units from the Red Army in Pomoshnaya. The Makhnovist insurgent army was reconstituted into three infantry brigades mounted on tatchankis, one cavalry brigade (under Shchuss's command), an artillery division, a machine-gunner regiment and Makhno's "black guard," in all, some 20,000 fighters. Many of Grigoriev's former soldiers were discharged for insubordination, for they had been infected with anti-Semitism and were bereft of any revolutionary consciousness. Dybets was sentenced to be shot by the Makhnovist staff, but Makhno, under pressure from anarchists who had joined his movement, pardoned him and sent him packing along with his wife Rosa. Among the anarchists who had thrown their lot with the insurgents were members of the Nabat Confederation, including Voline who had been taken prisoner by the Petliurists and had been rescued by a Makhnovist detachment specially dispatched for the purpose.

❧

A contingent of Whites put ashore at Odessa had put the Chekists and Bolsheviks to flight; the latter had so distinguished themselves by their sinister practices that they could expect no support from the populace. They linked up with the 45th Infantry Division commanded by Yakir who intended to fall back towards Kiev, over 500 kilometers away. However, many local insurgents joined Yakir who thus had considerable strength at his disposal: In the 45th Division's 7,500 infantry, 500 cavalry, 81 machine-guns and 34 cannon; the remnants of the 58th Division's and various units' 6,500 infantry, 48 machine-guns, 14 cannon and 400 cavalry — a total of nearly 17,500 well-armed and equipped men on the run before the 34th White Infantry Division which had just 1,500 infantry, 300 cavalry, 12 cannon and 43 machine-guns. In his memoirs, Yakir explains that he had to fight his way through, being surrounded by enemies on every side: Whites to the south and east, Petliurists to the west, and Makhno whose influence he feared might disintegrate his troops! It was primarily the proximity of Makhno that worried him, for he wanted at all costs to avoid the misadventure that had befallen the 58th Division. In fact there too most of the Red troops who came from the region could not understand this part of the Ukraine's being surrendered without a fight, and their sympathies were with Makhno. One of the Bolshevik leaders, Golubenko, called Makhno on the telephone and suggested that they fight alongside one another, but under the command of Red officers of course. Makhno answered him: "You have broken faith with the Ukraine, and more seriously, you shot my comrades in Gulyai-Polye. Your units will be defecting to me in any case, and then I will deal with all of you officials the same way that you dealt with my comrades."3 That being the situation, Bolshevik officials sought the best way of avoiding all truck with the Makhnovists, while saving themselves from their vengeance; especially since — quite apart from Chekists who had every reason to be fearful — their ranks included party militants and Red military chiefs of some renown, like Fedko, Kotovsky and Zatonsky. And there were several military "experts," tsarist ex-officers who had gone over to the

Leninist regime, like Rear-Admiral Nemitz, one-time commander of the Black Sea fleet, Kniagnitsky, Karkavy, V.V. Popov and many another. All had something to reproach themselves with in their dealings with the Makhnovist insurgents or the Whites; unable to rely upon their troops to fight Makhno, the only option left to them was flight. On Nemitz's advice, the decision was made to effect the retreat through open countryside, keeping clear of the railway tracks and usual routes. To this end, all of the divisions' armored trains were dynamited in Nikolaev and Birzula, in spite of the opposition from their crews who wanted to join Makhno. Military equipment and even spare shells were destroyed, not without difficulty as Yakir notes: "It required a campaign of explanation and agitation conducted intensively by the party organization and followed up by recourse to extreme repressive measures to ensure that every Red soldier clearly understood his task and applied all his will to the accomplishment of this duty."[4] Oddest of all was the presence within this Red Army of the 3,000-strong partisan detachment of the anarchist A.V. Mokrousov who thus blithely accepted this shameful fact when it would have taken only an arrangement with the Makhnovists to mount a powerful joint counter-offensive against the Whites and to drive them far back again. One appreciates the extent to which Bolsheviks had already identified the interests of the revolution with their party's dominant and uncontested position in the conduct of operations; then they managed to attract to them anarchists and revolutionaries of other denominations by exploiting the bogeyman of reaction in order to contrive a closing of the ranks.

We have another telling illustration of this obnoxious policy in the mutiny by the commander of the army corps of the Red Don Cossacks, Mironov, at around the same time, in August 1919. Mironov could not stomach the fluctuations and dictates of Moscow and decided to take on both Denikin and the Red Army. In an order of the day he announced to his troops that he was assuming responsibility for the welfare of the nation in the battle against the Whites, a responsibility which the Soviet authorities were not in a position to assume, and then he concluded:

> "In order to save the revolution's gains only one course remains now: Overthrow of the power of the Communist Party [...] For the causes of the country's ruination one has to look to the quite villainous actions of the government party, the party of the communists, who have aroused against them the indignation and general discontent of the toiling masses. All land to the peasants! All factories and workshops to the workers! All power to the toiling people, embodied by genuine Soviets of worker, peasant and cossack deputies! Down with the autocracy of leaders and the bureaucracy of commissars and communists!"[5]

Mironov was well aware that the Reds' military reverses were connected with their exactions against the masses of the people and could envisage no way out other than authentic representation of those masses through freely elected soviets.

His mutiny soon petered out; on the pretext of negotiations, the Cheka seized him and tossed him in jail, but the authorities freed him under an amnesty because of his military capability and deployed him against the Whites, eventually having him shot after Wrangel was defeated.

Yakir's retreat began in mid-August and was to last for 21 days before his army linked up with the 44th Red Division near Kiev. Along the way it fought some engagements against Petliura, against whom those regiments reputedly favorably disposed towards Makhno were deployed, while Chekist and other more dependable troops faced Makhno. Aside from a skirmish in Pomoshnaya, there was no armed clash with the Makhnovists. Mokrousov saved the expedition by capturing the entire staff of the strongest Petliurist division.

This flight by Bolshevik troops left the field to three adversaries: Makhno, Petliura and the Whites. The Whites, in view of the ease with which they had advanced thus far, made a gross strategical mistake: Instead of digging in along the line of the Odessa-Nikolaev-Elisavetgrad front thereby protecting the vast territories they had occupied in the eastern Ukraine, they took it into their heads to tackle Makhno and Petliura simultaneously. Yet they had only 15,000 men at their disposal, well-armed and equipped men constantly resupplied from their bases in the rear to be sure, but not enough, even so for a mission on this scale. The bulk of their forces — 150,000 men — were engaged around Kursk in the main thrust against Moscow. To begin with, the Petliurists ran from a fight, hoping to come to some accommodation on the basis of independence for the Ukraine; also, all the White Guard units converged on the Voznessensk-Elisavetgrad area held by Makhnovists. The Denikinist staff was inclined to be dismissive of the latter, given the collapse suffered by their Mariupol-Yuzovka front in May and June, the real reasons for which had thus far escaped the Whites. This is how General Slaschev, in charge of operations, was later to sum up the situation:

> "Petliura was playing it cool and sitting on the fence. That left just one typical [sic!] bandit — Makhno — who kowtowed to no power and fought them all in turns. The only thing that could be said in his credit was his ability quickly to raise and to keep his troops well under control, even enforcing a quite severe discipline on them. It was for this reason that engagements against him always took a serious turn; his mobility, his energy, and his flair in mounting operations brought him a whole series of victories over the armies he confronted.
>
> This expertise in conducting operations did not reflect the education that he had received, and it was for this reason that a legend was created about a colonel of the German general staff, who even had a name, Kleist, who helped him and directed operations; according to

this tale, Makhno complemented Kleist's military expertise with his indomitable will and his perfect knowledge of the local population. It is hard to tell to what extent any of this is true, but the incontrovertible fact is that Makhno did know how to run operations, displayed uncommon organizational capabilities, and was able to influence a significant portion of the local population which backed him and enlisted in his ranks. As a result, Makhno appeared as a very redoubtable adversary and was deserving of quite special attention on the part of the Whites, especially if one considers their comparatively small numbers and the scale of the tasks facing them.

The White staffs, however, regarded his liquidation as a secondary matter in spite of all indications from leaders of the units directly engaged against him, and at first they devoted all of their attention only to Petliura. This blind spot on the part of the main staff in Taganrog and the one in Odessa was cruelly endorsed several times over."[6]

For the record we may note this legend of the "German colonel Kleist" which goes to show just how incapable graduates of the military academy, caught up in their "military art," were of suspecting that such gifts could be discovered in a mere peasant — and one devoid of army training at that. All the same, let us take note of the especial regard in which he was held by a brilliant staff general like Slaschev who subsequently defected to the Reds and became an instructor at the Red Army's higher military academy!

৵৽

The first engagement came on August 20 in the vicinity of the Pomoshnaya railway station, when the Fifth Infantry Division sent in pursuit of Yakir's contingent which had decamped at all speed, ran into Makhno. For the Whites this meant an initial disagreeable surprise: They were beaten back with serious losses, losing a number of armored trains including the famous "Invincible." Over the days that followed the front line settled across a distance of about 80 kilometers, ranging from Elisavetgrad to the outskirts of Pomoshnaya. Frequent incursions by Makhnovist cavalry wrought havoc in the enemy rear. The Whites regrouped their forces; the Fifth Division, put to the test and demoralized, dug in around Elisavetgrad along with the Fourth Division and the 34th Division's mixed brigade, or a total of 5,000 men, 2,000 of them cavalry, with 50 cannon and numerous machine-guns at their disposal. Slaschev planned to bypass Makhno on his left flank at Olviopol so as to cut off possible supplies of munitions from Petliura, and then on his right flank in order to break the cordon around Elisavetgrad, head off any breach in the front through there and drive Makhno back towards the north and west. As his spearhead he used the officers' regiments from Simferopol and Labinsk.

The Whites' push began on September 5th; they occupied Arbuzinka and Konstantinovka (see Figure One for Operational Plan) without a shot being fired.

Makhno recaptured them in a counter-offensive. In the days that followed the Whites ensconced themselves in Arbuzinka again and took 300 prisoners. The Makhnovists surrendered when they ran out of bullets, rightly despairing for they knew to expect no mercy from their conquerors; the general rule at the time was not to encumber oneself with prisoners. The dearth of ammunition and shells in these engagements accounts for the success of the Whites, for they were assured of a continual flow of supplies from their base in Voznessensk. Arshinov writes that at this time two out of every three Makhnovist attacks were mounted for the purpose of capturing enemy munitions. This was all too obvious on September 6th when Makhnovist infantry attacked Pomoshnaya with the support of several armored trains, while Makhno himself at the head of his cavalry attacked the Whites in their rear at Nikolaevka and carried off their ammunition wagons. The Whites dug in at Pomoshnaya. In the days that followed the Makhnovist cavalry repeated its incursions behind enemy lines and inflicted considerable losses. In this way, it pinned them down to their positions, threatening to cut them off from their rear at every attack; it was during these clashes that Petya Lyuty and Nestor's brother, Grigori Makhno, lost their lives.

❦

Then the fighting shifted eastwards; the other Makhnovist contingent attacked and scattered the Fifth Division, taking prisoners and carrying off artillery. The White staff then appointed Slaschev to assume sole command of all troops engaged against Makhno and ordered him to hold Elisavetgrad at any price. Simultaneously, he launched a two pronged offensive against the rear of the second Makhnovist contingent, thereby rescuing what remained of the Fifth Division and against the first contingent at Novoukrainka. There a Makhnovist counter attack pushed the Whites back as far as their starting positions in Pomoshnaya; the battle cost 300 dead and wounded, all Whites. Slaschev writes that at this point the

> "…Makhnovists' incursions behind White lines were being mounted with increasing frequency and were sowing panic. The situation became such that attack was extremely onerous; however, the slightest delay in attacking might be fatal, for then Makhno would have attacked himself and the White troops, put to the test, would not have been able to hold with the partisans' cavalry in their rear […] We had either to fall back immediately in order to capture the Makhnovists' forces by night, and thus regain complete freedom of maneuver, or else attack at daybreak."[7]

It was the latter solution that carried the day. Indeed, had the Whites fallen back, Makhno would have taken Elisavetgrad and in so doing would have opened up the route back to the left bank of the Dniepr. The next day the Whites attacked at daybreak, their officers leading the way. The startled Makhnovists fell back, losing 400 prisoners and three cannon, still short of ammunition. Cognizant of the

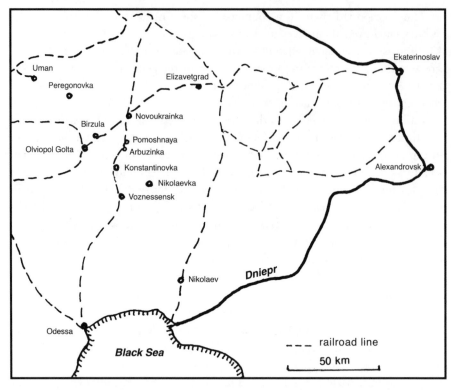

1. Engagements with the Whites in August-September 1919

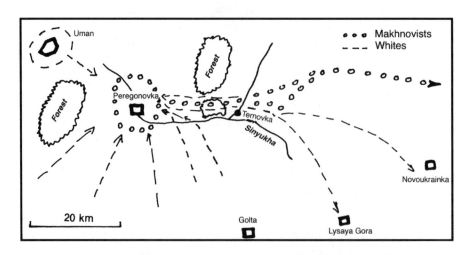

*2. The battle of Peregonovka on September 26, 1919
and the Makhnovist break-through.*

seriousness of the situation, the Makhnovists decided to fall back towards Uman, to the west, and had their armored trains dynamited.

For their brilliant service, men of the First Simferopol Officers' Regiment received 109 St. George crosses and seven military medals; their commanding officer, Colonel Gvosdakov, was promoted to major-general. Makhno himself acknowledged the courage of his White enemies:

> "The Denikinist cavalry was a real cavalry, well deserving of the name. The very numerous cavalry of the Red Army was cavalry in name only. It has never been capable of fighting at close quarters and went into action only when the enemy had been broken up by cannon fire and machine-guns. Throughout the civil war, the Red cavalry did not once accept an engagement at saber point against the Makhnovist cavalry, although it outnumbered it at all times. Denikin's Caucasian cavalry regiments and Cossacks were quite a different matter. They were always ready for a saber fight and always swooped hell for leather upon the enemy, not waiting for cannon fire and machine-gunfire to scatter them first."[8]

About this assessment, Arshinov comments: "Nevertheless, that cavalry came a cropper more than once in its battles against the Makhnovists. In their notebooks, captured by the Makhnovists, the leaders of the Denikinist regiments repeatedly noted that the war against the cavalry and artillery of the Makhnovists was the most horrific and daunting of their whole campaign."[9] According to Arshinov, Makhno was particularly impressed by the bravado and contempt for death displayed by the Simferopol and Labinsk officers' regiments, who fought hardest against him.

The Makhnovists' retreat continued for nearly two weeks; step by step they staggered back, hampered by 8,000 wounded and sick, amid a daily round of fierce fighting. They arrived in the vicinity of the town of Uman, which was held by Petliurists who had hitherto remained neutral towards both belligerents. The Makhnovists were caught in the middle; so it was with relief that they welcomed the Ukrainian nationalists' offer of neutrality. They evacuated 3,000 of their wounded to Uman, turned away small partisan groups that lacked any or a sufficiency of weapons, and then dug in in an area 12 kilometers long by 10 kilometers deep, some 30 kilometers outside Uman. By now the contingent was down to no more than 8,000 men. In order to avoid any equivocation, the Makhnovists' Military Revolutionary Soviet issued an appeal entitled *Who is Petliura?* Meant for Petliurist troops and denouncing the nationalist leader as a champion of the bourgeois classes. The Petliurists, who knew of what had befallen Grigoriev, took care not to allow their troops to mix with the insurgents.

The Whites had stalked the insurgents and resolved to finish them off; they marched on Uman and denied access to the Makhnovists. Thus the latter found themselves hemmed in on three sides, caught in a formidable noose; their retreat had lasted four months and taken them 600 kilometers from their Gulyai-Polye base. This was a critical moment; they were worn down by the incessant battles fought for over a month, were severely short of ammunition, and were outnumbered by a well-armed and supplied enemy who boasted elite troops full of self confidence and just itching to annihilate them. It was at this point that Makhno yet again displayed the measure of his extraordinary gifts as a leader of men; he announced to the insurgents that the retreat carried out thus far had been only a necessary stratagem and that it was now up to them to call the tune. This announcement was a great fillip to the insurgents' lust for battle.

❧

On September 22nd, hostilities resumed. Slaschev used his best troops, including the Simferopol officers' regiment, as a battering ram to force the in-surgents towards Uman where he intended to crush them once and for all. This time he was under formal instructions to prosecute the annihilation operation to the finish, no matter the cost. He played all his trump cards, for he was assured of no interference from Petliura; he knew too that Makhno was seriously low on ammunition and had been obliged to turn men away for that very reason. He moved in for the kill, urging his troops to set about the enemy with vigor. Over several days there had been skirmishing around Peregonovka (see Figure Two, p. 132) on the very fringes of the Makhnovists. The village was taken and retaken by both sides. Makhno must have made a thorough study of the battlefield for he had deployed his units in the woods and on the heights around Peregonovka which itself served, as it were, as bait; he waited until the Whites had committed themselves before routing them from behind. The topography lent itself readily to his design; in this part of the Ukraine, the steppe is corrugated by rather deep ravines not visible at a distance.

❧

The final battle began on the morning of September 26th: Waves of Makh-novist infantry attacked enemy positions to the east, while insurgent cavalry destroyed the Litovsk regiment to the west, before tackling the First Simferopol officers' regiment from behind, as planned, routing it.[10]

Arshinov, an eyewitness and party to the scene, relates how the battle peaked at 8 A.M. in a veritable hail of gunfire; Makhnovist foot soldiers began to give ground and fell back as far as Peregonovka, pursued by the Whites who poured in from everywhere. Every member of the insurgent staff, the cultural section and the women from the medical services, took up rifles and began to shoot their way through the village streets; it looked like the end. Suddenly there was a falling-off of the enemy gunfire and charges before they petered out altogether. What was going on? It was as if the enemy had been swept away by a hurricane.

It was Makhno and his black sotnia who had vanished at nightfall the previous day, outflanked the enemy positions, and, just at the crucial moment, had thrown themselves into an irresistible charge. "The Batko is in front! ... Batko wielding his saber!" cried the insurgents, hurling themselves upon the enemy with the energy of ten times their numbers. This was close quarter combat of incredible violence, a "hacking" as the Makhnovists would say. The Whites were stunned, made an orderly retreat for some minutes and then broke up in disarray, setting the pattern for other regiments and units. Panicking, they all took to their heels — hunters suddenly become quarry — as they tried to reach the river Sinyukha some 15 kilometers from Peregonovka. The regimental commander, the recently promoted Major General Gvosdakov, and the staff of the Simferopol regiment plus one company were the first to reach the river, and they raced on without looking back as if stricken with terror, so that by evening they were in Lyshaya Gora, some 40 kilometers away, but without the rest of the regiment. One of the escapees, Colonel Almendinger, second in command of the regiment's Second Battalion, testifies:

> "The regimental staff, the Second Company, some of the regiment's machine-gunners and the battery set out ahead and managed to ford the river at Ternovka, but the regiment's commander did not await the arrival of other companies, but rather made off again with all haste and that evening was in Lyshaya Gora minus his regiment. The other companies retreated under heavy pressure from the Makhnovist infantry coming from the right and from straight ahead and from incessant cavalry attacks upon the left flank. As we entered the woods, we signaled our people to come to our aid, but there was no response. It was learned subsequently that the regimental commander had indeed seen the signals but had nonetheless decided to move on from the ford without waiting for his companies. The latter marched to their deaths, for they all knew that no quarter would be given. We stuck to the ploughed fields, avoiding the paths. The sun was beginning to grow warm. The Makhnovist infantry was hot on our heels but was not shooting at us because, apparently, they had no cartridges left as we immediately sensed. We too had exhausted our cartridge reserves. The enemy cavalry assailed us on our flanks, attempting to panic us with a hail of grenades prior to employing cold steel. We continually had to stop and fire shots behind us in order to fend him off. Some of us fell, wounded and they put a bullet into their own brains lest they be taken alive by the enemy. The lightly wounded strove to march with the able-bodied. We reached the Sinyukha River but did not know the whereabouts of the ford. The river was deep and quite broad. In the end, some of our number threw themselves into the water; some drowned, others made it back to the bank. The Makhnovist infantry halted quite near to us. Still sniping at the cavalry, we went on walk-

ing along the river bank, in the hope of discovering a ford. Luckily some inhabitants indicated a spot where it was feasible to swim across. We crossed. Out of our six companies, no more than 100 men were left. Columns came to meet us, we thinking that they were our side; suddenly they fanned out and began to bombard us. The wounded hoisted themselves on to farm teams and fled into the distance in the direction of Novoukrainka where they arrived late in the night. The last 60 men, under the command of Captain Gattenberger, commandant of the Second Battalion, formed a line and tried to reach the nearby forest. It was said that they would not make it. With their last cartridges they again repulsed the cavalry but were mown down by enemy machine-gun fire. The last survivors were sabered. The captain shot himself. No prisoners were taken."[11]

Almendinger's account corresponds pretty much with Makhno's, entitled "The Crushing of the Denikinists," as it appeared in the fourth issue of *The Road to Freedom* on October 30, except that other regiments apart from his were sabered; hundreds of corpses littered the road for kilometers, as Voline describes. Voline also passed this world-weary remark: "That is what would have become of us by this time, had they won. Fate? Chance? Justice?"[12]

Makhno made maximum capital out of the situation; hunter now and no longer quarry, he sent his entire cavalry and artillery at full gallop in pursuit of the Whites, then raced off himself along with his black sotnia along some shortcuts in pursuit of the Denikinists, managing to capture the divisional staff and a reserve regiment. Only a few hundred Whites managed to get away.

The captured booty was enormous: Twenty-three cannon, over 100 machine-guns, 120 officers and 500 soldiers taken prisoner. Many of the Denikinist generals and officers opted for suicide rather than be taken alive by the insurgents. The fields were blanketed in epaulettes and braid, the owners of which had fled into the woods. The farmers were to be startled by this mighty odd crop the next day.[13] The Denikinist expeditionary corps had been routed.

❧❧❧

The outcome of the battle of Peregonovka was beyond reckoning; in point of fact, it determined the outcome of the civil war. That was appreciated by another Denikinist who got away, the officer Sakovitch; he was quite near to the battlefield, but his unit did not intervene, clinging to the belief that the Makhnovists were still on their way east where the trap laid by Slaschev awaited. For a moment, he heard intense cannon fire, followed by silence; he sensed that something crucial had just occurred:

"In a sky blanketed in autumn cloud, the last puffs of artillery smoke exploded then ... all was silent. All of us ranking officers sensed that something tragic had just occurred although nobody could have had any inkling of the enormity of the disaster which had struck. None of us knew that at that precise moment nationalist Russia had lost the war. 'It's over,' I said, I know not why, to Lieutenant Rozov who was standing alongside me. 'It's over,' he confirmed somberly."[14]

Why was it over? How could fighting that pitted two dozen thousands of men against one another have any influence over a war involving hundreds of thousands?

To be sure, Makhno had smashed the best troops of Slaschev, who nonetheless had taken 1,000 Makhnovists prisoner — wounded and stragglers — but the White general was in no position any longer to organize a pursuit of the insurgents and was to make do with warring against Petliura's yellows and blues. Now, Makhno did not rest upon his laurels; he dispatched the 7,000 men remaining to him in three directions simultaneously: One group headed off towards their homeland on the left bank of the Dniepr; the main contingent of 3,500 galloped off to the most strategic points, while he himself at the head of his black sotnia was over 100 kilometers away by the morrow of his startling victory. Capitalizing upon the element of surprise, with lightning speed, insurgents occupied all the settlements and towns in their path, defended only by insignificant garrisons, with the exception of Nikopol where they crushed three regiments from Kornilov's divisions, taking 300 prisoners. Within ten days, a huge swath of territory that included the cities of Krivoi Rog, Elisavetgrad, Nikopol, Melitopol, Alexandrovsk, Gulyai-Polye, Berdyansk and Mariupol had been liberated at a gallop.

On October 20th, an outrider detachment occupied Ekaterinoslav for the first time only to be dislodged before Makhno arrived in person with more substantial units to take the capital of the southern Ukraine. Even more serious for the Whites was the Makhnovist control of the region's entire rail network, with the important rail junctions at Pologui, Sinelnikovo and Losovo, as well as their grip upon the ports of Mariupol and Berdyansk where the Anglo-French had been putting ashore material needed by Denikin. All of the nerve centers of Denikin's thrust against Moscow foundered under the hammer blows of the Makhnovists. The Whites were cut off from their food and provision bases. The insurgents even reached the very gates of Taganrog, headquarters for Denikin's staff and were only just contained. As a matter of urgency, Denikin was forced to recall his best Cossack troops — led by Shkuro and Mamontov — who had been making ready to take Moscow. Indeed, the Red Army was in grave disarray, the spearhead of the Denikinist offensive lying just then only 200 kilometers outside Moscow, with White generals disputing the honors of being the first to enter the city. As for Lenin and the leadership of the Bolsheviks, they had been on the point of cutting and running for Finland, congratulating themselves for having held out longer than the Paris Commune. Thus Makhno had broken the back of the great Denikinist offensive that the Red Army had failed to halt. Seen in this light, the battle of Peregonovka had been the crucial feat of arms in the civil war. The Makhnovschina's own chronicler thus asserts with some reason that:

> "...keeping to the historical facts, the honor of having smashed the Denikinist counter-revolution in the autumn of 1919 belongs mainly to the Makhnovists. Had the latter not made their breakthrough at Uman and followed up with the destruction, behind the lines, of the Denikinists' artillery and supply bases, the Whites would probably have entered Moscow around the month of December 1919."[15]

Notes to Chapter 17: Grigoriev, Dybets, Yakir, Slaschev and the Rest

1. Kubanin, op. cit. pp. 82–83 quotes the description of the scene by Chubenko himself in a memorandum drawn up when he was a prisoner of the Cheka.

2. Ibid. p. 83.

3. A. Krivosheyev, *Everyday Life in the Red Army: Memoirs of the XIIth Army,* in *The Civil War* (Russian language publication), Moscow, 1923, Tome II, p. 197.

4. Yakir, *On the History of the 45th Division* (Russian), Kiev, 1929, pp. 234–236.

5. D. Kin, "The peasantry and the civil war," in the magazine *Na agrarom fronté (On the Agrarian Front)*, Moscow, No. 11–12, 1925, p. 123.

6. Slaschev, "The operations of the Whites, Petliura and Makhno in the southern Ukraine in 1919" (in Russian), in the Red Army review *The Military Messenger*, Moscow, 9–10, 1922, pp. 38–43.

7. Idem.

8. Quoted by Arshinov, op.cit. p.136.

9. Idem.

10. The Seventh Company of this officers' regiment was made up wholly of German settlers especially keen to get in grips with their sworn enemies, the "land-grabbing" Makhnovists.

11. Almendinger, *Short History of the First Simferopol Officers' Regiment* (in Russian) Los Angeles, 1963, pp. 16–24.

12. Voline, *La révolution inconnue*, Paris, 1947, p. 588.

13. *The Road to Freedom* No. 4, October 3, 1919, as quoted by Kubanin, op. cit. p. 86.

14. Sakovitch, "Makhno's breakthrough," in *Pereklitchka*, Munich, 1961, No. 116, pp. 11–14.

15. Arshinov, op. cit. p. 144.

18. The Whites' Failures

Autumn 1919 was the apogee of the anti-Bolshevik offensives. Increasingly the territory under Bolshevik control was shrinking until it covered little more than the borders of the former Grand Duchy of Muscovy in the 16th century. Moscow was the primary target of the Whites, for seizure of this rail center would enable them to control the whole of European Russia.

In the West, from the Baltic lands General Yudenich's 25,000-strong army was on the march against Petrograd, sweeping aside the Seventh Red Army to reach the outskirts of the city by October 2nd. The former capital was directly threatened; the Bolshevik loss of nerve was at its worst, and Lenin was talking about abandoning Petrograd. Trotsky salvaged the situation by resolving to hold it at all costs. On October 16, Yudenich captured the Tsar's former residence at Tsarskoye-Selo and then Gachina, and his troops could see the "gilded dome of St. Isaac's cathedral" on the banks of the Neva, right in the center of the city. Trotsky hastily assembled some loyal units and issued appeals to the workers, sailors, women and the *Kursantys* — Red officer cadets. Barricades and trenches were made ready; fighting broke out in the city suburbs. For several days, it could have gone either way. In this way Trotksy had gained a crucial respite, for the Red Army now had time to approach and tackle Yudenich from behind, obliging him to retreat.

Yudenich had lacked two elements: The help promised by the British squadron lying off the coast and reinforcements from Bermont-Avalov's army corps and from the German army corps — caught up, paradoxically, in fighting the troops of an independent, bourgeois Latvia. Yudenich was obliged to withdraw to Estonia where his army was disarmed.

To the north, the British ran up against the same problems as the French had encountered in Odessa, and they called off their support of General Miller and brought their troops back on board on September 26, 1919. So, left to their own devices and bereft of logistical support, the White supporters were defeated after several months with Archangelsk being captured in March 1920.

To the east, Kolchak — acknowledged as supreme commander by all the White generals — had begun his march on Moscow at the start of the year. Essentially his advance proceeded along the railroad lines. In terms of numbers, this was the strongest White offensive; the mobilization had produced unexpected results and 200,000 young recruits (preferred over the experienced soldiery of 1914–1917, having in the eyes of the White generals the advantage of never having sampled the disintegration of the revolutionary army) came forward; officers regained their omnipotent status and their old "patriarchal" methods surfaced once more.

Admiral Kolchak, "supreme regent of Russia," was, according to his entourage, "a constantly simmering cauldron in which the stew is never cooked!" He had at his disposal a staff of some 900 officers, 58 of whom dealt with censorship alone! His provisional capital, Omsk, had become a great hive of shirkers; 5,000 other officers there indulged themselves in the most unbridled debauchery and blithely held down lucrative quarter-master positions. All of this wheeling and dealing and corrupt practice worked against his under-equipped troops who were obliged to conduct operations in the height of a winter with the temperature 45 degrees below, leading to many soldiers' suffering frostbitten limbs and amputations.

Luckily for Kolchak there was the Czech Legion, placed under the (national) command of the French general Janin; thanks to it, the offensive spread in March 1919 beyond Ufa and Orenburg across a 300 kilometer front. Towards the end of April, its most advanced point was in Kazan or nearly 600 kilometers from Moscow. In May the tables turned completely; three regiments mutinied, killing 200 officers and defecting to the Reds. Other mass desertions followed. The front line troops were worn out and suffering from supply shortages, for the simple reason that supplies were at all times prey to grasping corrupt practices behind the lines. The democratically-minded Czechs had nothing but distaste for Kolchak's soldiery which had distinguished itself at the time of the admiral's *coup d'état* by butchering several thousand Social Revolutionary supporters of the "Committee for the Constituent Assembly." Their many atrocities against the populace inspired countless partisan detachments that continually harassed Kolchak's army's trains and bases. The Czechs refused to pursue the offensive any further and concentrated exclusively on the smooth running of the Trans-Siberian railroad.

The upshot of all this ineptitude, incompetence and intrigue was not long in making itself known; the initial offensive turned into a complete debacle. Staffs deserted their units which themselves defected to the enemy or else vanished into the countryside. Soon, by October 1919, the Siberian army that was to have liberated Moscow and Russia was no more than a memory. According to General Janin, this "melting away of the army has been largely due to progressive alienation of the populace from Kolchak's government, an alienation triggered by its police methods following the murders of the Constituent's supporters in Ufa in December 1918."[1] So much so that the Bolsheviks who had themselves blithely murdered thousands a short time before in Siberia were now welcomed there as liberators.

The Red Army, itself prone to serious internal disagreements and blatant under-equipment, was unable however to draw the fullest benefit from the Whites' Siberian debacle; it made do with following the enemy's retreat at a distance, capitalizing upon its disintegration and regarding the slightest consolidation as a counter-offensive. The lead in the fighting was taken primarily by the tens of thousands of Siberian partisans, most of them Social Revolutionaries who bore the brunt of the fighting and hastened the Admiral's downfall.

Having started off pompously, the adventure of the "savior of the homeland" came to a Shakespearean grief: for several weeks he wandered around the Trans-Siberian railway, escorted by a train laden with gold captured from the supporters of the Constituent Assembly in Samara. Shunned by one and all, he was finally taken prisoner by the Social Revolutionaries of Irkutsk, brought to trial and shot on February 7, 1920.

∾∾∾

The most powerful, most dangerous of the White offensives against the Bolsheviks was incontrovertibly that of General Denikin who rallied to his cause the Cossack armies of the Don, the Kuban and the Terek. Henceforth known as the Armed Forces of Southern Russia, Denikin's new army was made up of 150,000 experienced and combat-ready men and seized the whole of the Caucasus and Don territory before marching on Tsaritsyn and Astrakhan, the two key cities of the lower Volga, intent upon joining up with Kolchak. In June 1919, General Baron Wrangel forced Tsaritsyn's defenses and ousted the Red Army commanded by one-time sergeant Voroshilov who was himself attended by political commissar Josef Djugashvili (subsequently better known under the name of Stalin). The captured booty was immense: Two armored trains, 131 locomotives, 10,000 carriages — 2,085 of them laden with munitions — 70 cannon, 300 machine-guns, and 40,000 prisoners taken. To be sure, the losses sustained by the Don Cossacks and the Caucasian cavalry corps were enormous, but the officers were no longer the opera bouffe generals of Kolchak; here they had to march at the head of their troops and often perished in the fighting.

∾∾∾

To the west, as we have seen, the Ukrainian front held by Makhno had buckled in June; also on June 20th, Denikin set himself the ultimate goal of capturing Moscow. The offensive was to be mounted from three separate directions: The army commanded by Wrangel was to march on Saratov and then via Nizhny-Novgorod upon the capital; the army of the Don Cossacks, commanded by General Sidorin, was to take the Voronezh-Riazan route while the Volunteer Army under Mai-Maievsky's command was to close in via Kharkov, Kursk, Orel and Tula — all in all, a front some 800 kilometers wide. This was a grievous strategical error made in expectation of easy victories albeit ones that would be politically and militarily insignificant. Wrangel made a report on military matters to Denikin, wherein he pointed to the:

> "…[P]erils of extending the front overmuch in the absence of the necessary reserves and a well-organized rearguard. [He suggested] digging in for the moment on the Tsaritsyn-Ekaterinoslav front with our flanks protected by the Volga and the Dniepr, and then levying the necessary troops for operations in the southeast, in the vicinity of Astrakhan, while

simultaneously marshalling at our center three or four cavalry corps in the environs of Kharkov. These troops, when the time comes, might strike in the direction of Moscow. At the same time the rearguard needed organizing, as did the building-up of regimental numbers, enlargement of the reserve, and the establishment of operational bases."

The only reaction this drew from General Denikin was a derisory comment of: "I see, you wish to be the first to enter Moscow!"[2] For an "honest subordinate, born second-rater become standard-bearer" like Denikin,[3] the suggestions from the general — a cavalryman who had won his spurs earlier during the Russo-German war — could not but appear far-fetched, being at once too bold and too cautious, when he came down on the side of the view that such a wide front could not be held militarily by only 150,000 men. Moreover, a direct thrust towards the capital by an important cavalry corps might indeed have brought about the collapse of the Red Armies. The best demonstration of that was provided by the raid by General Mamontov, a one-time hussar turned Don Cossack.

Charged with easing enemy pressure on the army of the Don, Mamontov thrust deep behind Red Army lines on July 22 with a contingent of 6,000 Cossacks, 3,000 infantry, three tanks and seven armored trains. Within six weeks he had mounted a fabulous incursion some 2,200 kilometers deep, sweeping aside all infantry and cavalry divisions dispatched to head him off. During this raid, which was reminiscent of the confederate General Lee's raid at the time of the war of secession in the United States, the communications and supply lines of several Red Army corps were destroyed. Several tens of thousands of troops in the process of being forcibly mobilized by the Red Army were sent home again; important cities like Tambov, Kozlov and Tula — the latter lying only 200 kilometers from Moscow — were captured. The Soviet high command had this to say about the raid: "The enemy has seized upon the absence from our camp of an adequate number of cavalry and the poor quality of communications to move with absolute impunity throughout our entire rear, seizing numerous troops, destroying railroad lines everywhere, shooting all our officials who fall into his clutches, arming the population and urging it to wage a partisan war against us."

In the course of his raid, Mamontov — at all times in the front rank of his men — distributed all foodstuffs at no charge to the populace, armed volunteers and brought back with him a division made up of the inhabitants of Tula, which was promptly incorporated into the White army. He also brought back nearly all his men but only half their mounts, which had been decimated by the daily sorties of 60 to 70 kilometers. His cavalry formed a column some eight-to-ten kilometers long, with a seven-to-eight kilometer long convoy of 2,300 cartloads of booty in tow. Several Red divisions sought to cut off his route home; he feigned a breakthrough at one point, waited until enemy troops had concentrated there and then mounted an attack further away, wreaking havoc behind the lines of another Red Army corps. He turned up on the other side of the front lines so unexpectedly that Shkuro's Cossack army corps, taken unawares itself, made ready to engage him before they realized their mistake.

Not wanting to be idle, General Shkuro in turn forced a passage through enemy lines and seized Voronezh; finding himself now no more than 350 kilometers from Moscow, he sought permission to launch a thrust designed to capture the capital. Such a venture was formally forbidden to him, on pain of court martial. The White staff was so confident of the imminence of victory that it steadfastly opposed the kudos of victory's going to Cossacks rather than to some unit of Volunteer officers. This crass blunder was to prove fatal to the offensive, for several factors, negligible in the short term but consequential over a longer period, were to overturn the situation completely.

At a time when they had all but been able to hear "the Kremlin bells ringing," the White Generals were to be induced to beat a speedy retreat. Wrangel had had a foreboding of this situation, against the run of general enthusiasm prevailing in the White camp, which at that point ruled over a considerable area — 820,000 square kilometers with a population of 42 million inhabitants:

> "General Denikin's armies continued to march with giant strides towards Moscow. Kiev, Kursk, and Orel were captured. Our cavalry was at the gates of Voronezh. The whole of South Russia, rich in provisions of every sort, was in the hands of General Denikin, and every day brought us news of fresh successes. But to me it had been long clear as I did not conceal from the general-in-chief, that we were building upon sand, that we were taking on too much so as to be able to seize everything. Our opponent, however, adhered firmly to the principles of strategy. After I fell back to Tsaritsyn, my army weakened by three months of bloody fighting, the Red command realized that it would be a long time before I could take the offensive again, and it marshaled its forces at the point where the Volunteer army and the army of the Don met. The general-in-chief had nothing to deploy against this new enemy force."[4]

The Red Army had indeed been overhauled, well-supplied, and endlessly reinforced by fresh recruits (its total numbers rose at this time to three million); little by little it turned back the Don army and that of Wrangel. In charge of directing its operations was a former Tsarist staff colonel, Sergei Kamenev. The Red Cossack Budyenny's cavalry corps began to show its mettle and played a crucial role. But it was behind the Whites' lines and on their flanks that the difficulties were greatest; to turn again to Wrangel's comments:

> "Revolts erupted behind the lines; insurgents under the command of the bandit Makhno wrecked cities and looted trains and quartermaster depots. In the countryside, disorder was rampant. The local authorities were unable to command respect. Abuses of power were the order of the day. The agrarian issue was as confused as ever. The very govern-

ment was none-to-clear about what its intentions were on this score. Its poorly paid agents were all too often not honest."[5]

Concerned with a situation that he assessed as grave, Wrangel traveled to Rostov to the Whites' main headquarters. There he met with Denikin; according to Denikin, "everything was going for the best" and "the capture of Moscow can only be a question of time," as "…the enemy, utterly demoralized and weakened, cannot resist us." Wrangel strove to call Denikin's attention to the "bandit Makhno's insurgent movement which threatens our rear" only to come up against the general-in-chief's complete thoughtlessness: "It is not serious. We shall have done with him with a flick of the wrist."[6] In political matters too, Denikin was equally a cipher; he did not "want to yield one inch of Russian territory" to the Poles and Georgians. What was immediately more serious was that he took the same line towards the Kuban Cossacks who were eager to recover their autonomy. The Rada (government) of the Kuban was in fact becoming increasingly hostile to the Whites; its chairman, P. L. Makarenko, even became a target for the White officers because he sympathized with the Makhnovist movement. According to the Soviet historian, Kubanin, Cossacks generally sought to set up democratic, autonomous, and independent republics in the Don, Kuban, and Terek, and these would be linked federatively to Petliura's national Ukraine, to Menshevist Georgia, and later, once the Bolsheviks had been overthrown, to a democratic Russia. Kubanin readily acknowledges that the Cossacks were certainly not in favor of restoration of the monarchy; only a handful of Cossack bigwigs had that in mind, but under pressure from the mass, they had had to drop the idea.[7]

Denikin opted for strong-arm methods and ordered the hanging of Kalabukhov, a leader of the Rada; this led to alienation of and increasing desertions by the Kuban Cossacks. By this action he had also shown that he was fighting, not against Bolshevism but against every one of the gains of democracy in every single area of social life and aspired only to plain and simple restoration of tsarism and the absolute rule of the landowners, clergy, and police. And that despite his promise that the Constituent Assembly — which became increasingly hypothetical as his successes grew — would settle the land question, the land was meanwhile restored to its former owners or, at best, the peasants who worked it were compelled to hand over one-third of the harvest to the landowners.

Now, even if they indicated the best will in the world, White officers, helpless because of their reverence for hierarchy, proved powerless to alter the course of events. One of them, one of the bravest servicemen in the Russo-German war, Andrei Grigorievitch Shkuro, did indeed try to moderate the ruthless, anti-democratic conduct of his superiors. Shkuro was a small, stocky man with a raucous voice, and some of his rivals had nicknamed him "Max Linder in general's epaulettes." In fact, he had begun to fight the Bolsheviks as early as the beginning of 1918, having tasted their summary methods of justice (only the similarity between his name and another's had saved him from the firing squad); then, along with his detachment of partisans, he had joined the Volunteer armies. From the beginning of 1919, when the order of the pomieschikis was restored, his wife was pessimistic about subsequent events, and her views probably reflected those of her husband. He was outraged by the mass executions of Pokrovsky; indeed the latter was nicknamed "the Hangman," a nickname amply justified when he had hundreds of peasants hanged for the simple reason that they wore no Orthodox crucifix about their necks. Shkuro interceded with Pokrovsky, his superior in rank, to get him to spare the life of the anarchist Alexander Ge, in Kislodovsk, but to no effect. On another occasion, though, he did manage at the last minute to rescue a Jew arbitrarily sentenced to be hanged.[8] Again to no avail, he tried to snatch Kalabukhov, the leader from the Kuban, from the clutches of Pokrovsky, Pokrovsky being decidedly the doer of Denikin's dirty work. All of these interventions only succeeded in putting him in bad odor with the Denikinist staff; a shadow that he made up for with brilliant feats of service. Before carrying out his incursion through the front against Makhno, he had tried to come to an accommodation with Makhno by sending emissaries to put proposals for a joint struggle against the Bolsheviks. Being himself of Zaporog descent, he wanted to be near his distant cousins from the left bank of the Dniepr who according to him, were proud of their "Cossack" name and hoped to re-establish a Zaporog republic. He acknowledged that the sympathies of most of them lay with Batko Makhno: "He does not want pomieschikis and nor do we," they used to say, "for the land is ours; let each one take what he needs, that suits us."[9] However, Shkuro had mistakenly believed that Makhno was fighting the Bolsheviks and the Jews, and it was on that basis that he had suggested a joint fight. When Makhno declined, Shkuro had launched his lightning offensive of June 1919 against him. He relates how, at the time of this offensive, his men were initially welcomed when they reached Ekterinoslav:

> "Battered by the horrors of Bolshevism, the populace begged us not to hand the town over to the Reds (the Whites' vanguard had occupied it almost fortuitously, and their high command regarded this occupation as premature); the high command then allowed us to hold on to the town. I will never forget my entry into the city. People were on their knees singing 'Christ is risen' and were blessing us and weeping. The Cossacks and their mounts were blanketed in flowers. Dressed in their finest priestly garments, the clergy were celebrating 'Te Deums' everywhere. The workers resolved to work as hard as they could for the (White) Volunteer Army. They repaired trains and armored platforms, cannon and rifles. The inhabitants enlisted en masse in our forces. Their enthusiasm was tremendous. How come that all changed later, once gentlemen of the caliber of the governor Schetin[10] had done their work? […] The joy of the early days after the region's liberation from the Bolsheviks gave way to incredulity or even hate when the arrival of the White administration and the return of the pack of landlords thirsting for revenge made them-

selves felt. Certain White volunteers said that at first they were greeted with the greatest goodwill only to meet with curses later."[11]

He also noted the unbelievable vacuousness of the Denikinist movement:

"Mobilized by force, the workers and peasants were primarily interested in the Volunteer Army's program. The masses of the people who had had firsthand experience of the crass falsehood of Bolshevik promises and who had woken up politically, wished to see in the Volunteer Army a progressive anti-Bolshevik force rather than a counter-revolutionary one. Kornilov's program was clear and readily understood; as the successes of the Volunteer Army grew, so its program became increasingly vague and hazy. The notion of the people's rights of self-direction was whittled away to nothing. Even we commanding officers could not now answer the question: What were the essential lines of the Volunteer Army's program? What was to be said, for instance, regarding the details of that program, in answer to the questions put frequently by the Donetz miners: How did the leaders of the Volunteer army see the labor question? It is amusing to say so, but we had to *seek the White ideology in the conversations and table talk of General Denikin*[12] on this or that occasion; mere comparison of two or three of those "sources" could persuade one of the instability of the political notions of their author who, by his subsequent skepticism and caution, progressively whittled his initial promises down to nothing. There were no draft laws; rumors were current about plans drafted in shadowy offices, but no one ever asked us, who were operating on the ground and constantly confronted with the populace's puzzlement and its disappointments, and they even flew into a rage with us if we raised such issues."[13]

How implausible! The ideology of the Whites, of those who would have freed the Russian people of the Bolshevik yoke, depended upon the stomach ulcers or whims of their supreme leader, the son of one-time serfs, Denikin! One can appreciate why Trotsky feared Makhno more than he did the Whites.

❧

To return to matters military: When Shkuro was in Voronezh and making ready, in defiance of the prohibition placed on him, to swoop upon Moscow, his superior, Staff general Plyuschevsky-Plyuschik warned him that the "possibility of just such a move on your part has already been examined at headquarters, and in that event, you will be immediately proclaimed a traitor to the State and then, even in the event of complete success, produced before a field court martial."[14] Shkuro comments that he had had to submit to this, but that if he had not, maybe then Russia's history might have been different. He adds that, regardless of the many voices which alleged so thereafter, he refused to credit that the general staff had mistrusted the Cossacks and had not wanted the essential role in the liberation of Moscow to fall to Cossack troops.

Subsequently the intervention of Budyenny's cavalry and the Makhnovist threat behind the lines compromised any further advance by the Whites once and for all and preempted any fresh advance on Moscow. Let us note too that it was one of the best regiments in Shkuro's army corps, the Labinsk regiment, which the Makhnovists had crushed at Pomoshnaya and Uman; thereafter, a savage fight to the death set these Zaparog "cousins" against one another.

༄

Another typical view of the Whites, this time held by some engineers from Alexandrovsk, is reported by V. Pavlov, Lieutenant-colonel of the elite Markov Division. Asked for what the Volunteer Army fought, the interrogated officer replied:

> "'For Russia, one, great and indivisible.'
> 'That is a cliché without meaning,' protested the engineers. The Bolsheviks are fighting for the same. Except that at the same time they resolve, one way or another, political, social and economic issues in order to better the people's existence. So how would the Volunteer Army resolve those issues say?
> The officer was stuck for a reply. He could have voiced his own view, but of the Volunteer Army's policies he knew nothing. He had to extricate himself from his difficulty with some trite and quite offhand formula, but one that could not satisfy anyone:
> 'We wage war in order to free Russia. All the rest is none of our concern. The army is above politics!'
> The engineers smiled indulgently, and the conversation moved on to something else."

༄

Later, Pavlov cites the case of an officer serving in the Denikinist propaganda branch, who was called upon to explain to the peasants and workers that it was all the fault of a Masonic conspiracy and of the "Protocols of the Elders of Zion." As Pavlov himself concedes,[15] such a justification of the White's army struggle was nonetheless a scanty explanation of the origins of Bolshevism.

His Russian nationalist mysticism impelled Denikin to open hostilities against Petliura's Ukrainian nationalists who wanted nothing better than to come to some accommodation with him on the basis of recognition of their independence. He dismissed Petliura as a "bandit," threatened to hang him and ipso facto yet another front was opened up. The commander of the Volunteer Army, General Mai-Maievsky, even banned the teaching of the Ukrainian language in July 1919, in parts of the Ukraine under occupation of his troops.

༄

Another aspect of the power of the Whites did them a disservice as far as the populace was concerned: This was the looting and the atrocities carried out by officers endowed with full powers and representing a caste above all suspicion, one whose criminal activities escaped punishment — in which regard they were the worthy successors of the Chekist butchers. We have already seen as much in Gulyai-Polye in June 1919, but it was repeated elsewhere in the region too. Here we have the testimony of the Soviet dissident, General Grigorenko, a native of Borissovka, a township in the vicinity of Mariupol. Grigorenko — whose older brother was in fact a Makhnovist — tells how the municipal soviet of Nogaisk (another small town in the region), made up of peaceable notables elected after February 1917, was labeled "red" and then all its members shot by White Guards on the basis of that "charge" alone. Worse still, a certain Novitsky who escaped this execution, donned his uniform of an ex-captain of the Tsarist army, pinned on his highest military decorations and set off in search of the local commanding officer to demand an explanation for this act of barbarism. He received, by way of a reply, this: "Bolshevik swine — I'll teach you by what right!" Dragged outside, he was dispatched with a shot to the back of his head.[16] One officer from Shkuro's corps made a name for himself with his savage repression and boasted of having had 4,000 completely unarmed Makhnovist captives executed when Mariupol was taken in June 1919. Another White officer had an intellectual tortured just because the latter had absentmindedly called him "comrade." The unfortunate wretch was garroted in the head; the rope was increasingly tightened with the aid of a rod until his skull exploded. A young girl stepped up to the officer and spat in his face; he slew her on the spot with his saber. The crowd was obliged to remain there to contemplate the spectacle under the threat of the knout*. [17]

Shkuro himself, for all his democratic impulses, recommended his men (according to the British journalist Williams) systematically to rape the insurgents' women-folk[18] and Jewish women (a thousand of the latter were raped thus in Ekaterinoslav), something that had not been seen in the region since the Polovtsian invasions of the middle ages.

Such excesses went hand in hand with looting of the "liberated regions." General Mai-Maievsky set the pattern by turning his residence in Kharkov into a sale room for costly furniture and precious objects, and later earned a name for his orgies. Wrangel was well aware of all such peculation, excesses and abuses of this power; he drew up a blunt report for Denikin's eyes on December 9, 1919:

> "[The troops] had to find what was needed, distribute it and turn the tide of war to use. The war was becoming a way of enriching oneself and living off the land degenerated into pillage and speculation.
>
> Each unit strove to grab as much as it could for itself. Everything was taken; what could not be put to use on the spot was dispatched to the rear for sale and conversion into cash. The troops' baggage reached

---

* a whip used for flogging

exorbitant proportions; there were some regiments towing 200 wagons behind them. A considerable number of troops served behind the lines. Lots of officers were away on prolonged missions, concerned with the sale and barter of war booty. The army became demoralized and turned into a ragbag of hawkers and profiteers. All who were involved in 'living off the land' — and that was virtually all officers — found themselves in possession of vast sums of money: The upshot of this was debauchery, gambling, orgies. Unfortunately, some officers themselves set a dismal example by their revelries, spending money recklessly while the whole army looked on. […] The populace — which on its arrival had greeted our army with transport of enthusiasm, after having suffered so much at Bolshevik hands and wishing now only to live in peace — was soon to know again the horrors of looting, violence and arbitrary acts.

Outcome: Disarray at the front and revolts behind our lines."[19]

For himself, Wrangel did try to clamp down and had a captain shot who had committed exactions, and he did restore a semblance of discipline in his army — to no avail, for it was already too late.

Denikin, who had meanwhile been appointed successor by Kolchak, tried to reverse the trend by dismissing Mai-Maievsky and then by publishing a program on December 15, 1919:

"1. Russia, one and indivisible. Protection of religion. Restoration of order. Reconstruction of the country's productive forces and of the national economy. Improvement of labor productivity.
2. A fight to the death against Bolshevism.
3. Military dictatorship. The government will ignore the demands of all political parties. All resistance to authority — whether from right or left — is to be smashed. Only thereafter can the form of government be chosen. The people itself will determine it. We must march in step with the people.
4. Foreign policy is to be national and above all Russian. Despite prevarication among the Allies, we must continue to march with them. Any other collusion is morally objectionable and impracticable. Slav solidarity. In return for aid, not an inch of Russian soil."[20]

In this vague, ambiguous hotchpotch of patriotism, there was not a single concrete proposal, nor any response to the aspirations of the toiling masses. How kind of him still to be inclined to "continue to march" with the Allies, when it was the Anglo-French who were keeping the White troops up in arms and equipment! As for hostility towards Georgia, Armenia and Daghestan — Transcaucasia — it denied the Whites assistance, or a fallback area which they were soon to need … and how!

A paper government was established on December 17; its ministers were named "managers" but were puppets of the general staff. Denikin had fallen into the same bad habits as Kolchak as a French diplomat then on secondment in Russia concluded; Fernand Grenard states:

"What goes for Kolchak goes many times over for Denikin around whom the generals, officers, civil servants and landowners most attached to the old regime had gathered. In this entourage, Denikin was suspected of liberalism, and himself looked upon the "Political Center," a gathering of the most respectable props of a moribund society as a revolutionary. Just as Kolchak had the Czechoslovaks, so he alienated the Cossacks, his essential resource, closed down their Rada and executed one of their deputies. On both sides the most absolute arbitrariness, unknown under the tsars, reigned supreme. Rights and freedom were no more. Disturbances and revolts erupted all over. Repression struck out blindly; people known to all as enemies of the Bolsheviks were hunted down, arrested, banished. There was burning, hanging, shooting, looting. Not only was the agrarian question left unresolved, but landlords trailed in the wake of the advancing armies, snatched back their belongings *manu militari* and wrought vengeance on "their" peasants. Small wonder that the populace, in occupied areas and in areas yet to be retaken, turned against those who sought to deliver them and who taught them to see in the Bolsheviks the only true defenders of the cherished gains of the revolution."[21]

Noting everywhere they showed up the unpopularity which the Bolsheviks had left behind, the Whites had a tendency to believe that the road to success would lead them right to Moscow; on the one hand, they did not even bother to synchronize their offensives, and on the other, they promptly set about settling old scores with democracy and reviving a bygone age — the return of which was sought by none among the population. An underlying democratic tendency was attested by John Xydias, an objective witness if ever there was one:

"Neither Kolchak's entourage nor Denikin's included representatives from democratic circles, nor from the socialist parties, however moderate. Now, although a resolute opponent of socialism, I am nonetheless obliged to concede that in 1918–1919, when the Russian people were still under the spell of revolutionary maxims, no government desirous of speaking, not in the name of some caste but rather on behalf of the whole nation, could dispense with the contribution of the socialists, in that the latter still enjoyed — rightly or wrongly — the confidence of the populace who feared, above all else, the return of the ancient regime and the social counter-revolution.

Now, as we said, Kolchak's and Denikin's entourage comprised precisely only of people to whom one French general who had spent some time in Russia vocally applied the old Napoleonic saying: 'They have learned nothing and forgotten nothing.'"[22]

So, in a sense, the Whites had counted their chickens before they were hatched, having prepared everything for the succession to Lenin, everything that is, except the people's support for their cause. Therein lay the essential cause of their defeat.

Thus the Bolsheviks were to triumph, not so much on their own merits as due to the shortcomings of their White opponents. Also, it was this widespread popular resistance and the countless bands of partisans — the Greens[23] — who, like Makhno (whose crucial role is universally acknowledged) were to harry and ravage the rear of all White offensives, thereby rescuing Lenin and his party. A large proportion of these partisans were to be incorporated into the Red Army, for whom, all in all, the Whites were to prove the best recruiting sergeants.

Notes to Chapter 18: The Whites' Failures

1. General Janin, *Ma mission en Síberie 1918–1920*, Paris, 1933, p. 173.

2. *Mémoires du général Wrangel*, Paris, 1930, pp. 94–95.

3. A. de Monzie, op. cit. p. 131.

4. Wrangel, op. cit. pp. 104–105.

5. Idem.

6. Ibid. p. 107.

7. M. Kubanin, "The anti-soviet peasant movement during the civil war years (war communism)" in *On the Agrarian Front* (in Russian), No. 1, January 1926, pp. 84–94.

8. Ivan Kahnin, *Russia's Vendée* (in Russian), Moscow, 1926, p. 114.

9. Shkuro, op. cit. p. 220.

10. An especially obtuse and reactionary individual.

11. Shkuro, op. cit. p. 215 and 231.

12. Our emphasis — translator's (A.S) note.

13. Shkuro, op. cit. pp. 209–210.

14. Ibid. p. 223.

15. V.E. Pavlov, *The Markov Division* (in Russian), Paris, 1964, Tome II, pp. 83 and 203.

16. Piotr Grigonenko, *Mémoires,* Paris, 1980, pp. 70–71.

17. G. Williams, *The Defeated* in *The Archives of the Revolution* (in Russian), Berlin, 1922, Tome VII, pp. 229–230.

18. Idem.

19. Wrangel, op. cit. pp. 119–120.

20. Ibid. pp. 127–128.

21. F. Grenard *La révolution Russe,* Paris, 1933, p. 328.

22. J. Xydias, op. cit. p. 110.

23. Greens, so called after their usual place of residence — in the forests and woods.

19. The Fortunes and Misfortunes of Freedom Regained

In the wake of the June 1919 buckling of the Front, the eastern Ukraine had thus found itself for four months under the jackboots of the White soldiery and in strict subjection to all the stalwarts of the old established order who returned to reclaim their properties and station: the medium and big landowners — kulaks and pomieschiki — the squires, police, magistrates and other officials from Tsarist days. All of these, snugly ensconced and believing that their privileges had been restored permanently, had taken pitiless revenge on the peasants and other miscreants for the trials and tribulations through which they themselves had been put at the time of the revolutionary upheavals that had followed the withdrawal of the Austro-German troops.

Now the shoe was on the other foot. Like a whirlwind, the Makhnovists swept aside all resistance, punishing those behind repression (informers and judges) and destroying all remnants and symbols of slavery: prisons, police and gendarmerie posts were blown up with dynamite or put to the torch. The social heat was turned up again; the peasants rallied en masse to Makhno who by October had a reconstituted insurgent army of some 28,000 infantry and cavalry, with 200 machine-guns and 50 cannons. These insurgents crushed several enemy regiments, completely blockading Volnovakha, the main railway junction servicing the Denikinist front, obliging White headquarters to recall the best Cossack troops from the front against the Bolsheviks as a matter of urgency. These troops — the Don Cossack brigade led by Mamontov, the Terek division, Chechens and other assault regiments, in all about 25,000 men — were to be sorely missed when Budyenny's Red cavalry in turn fell upon Voronezh and drove the Whites back. These substantial White reinforcements obliged the Makhnovists by the end of October to give up the shores of the Sea of Azov — the ports of Berdyansk and Mariupol among others — as well as the Gulyai-Polye region. Instead they captured Pavlograd, Sinelnikovo, Chaplino and above all Ekaterinoslav, while retaining control of the lower Dniepr (Melitopol, Nikopol and Alexandrovsk).

In every district, town-land or city taken over by insurgents, the local residents recovered all social and political rights; they were invited to proceed with the election of delegates from their trade associations and local Soviets and then to call a regional congress to determine what policy to follow in the business in hand. And that without interference from the insurgents.

On the eve of the occupation of Alexandrovsk and Berdyansk, the central organ of the Makhnovist insurgent army, the Military Revolutionary Soviet, issued an appeal addressed to all insurgents and specifying their role in great detail:

> "Comrade insurgents! Day by day the insurgent army expands the theater of its revolutionary actions. Soon we shall go liberate such and such a city from Denikin. It will be a **city** liberated from all authority by the Makhnovist insurgents. It will be a city where free life ought to begin to bubble under the protection of revolutionary insurgents and the free organization of workers built up in full-blooded union with the peasants and insurgents!"

This appeal stressed that there should be no "violence or looting, nor questionable searches," for the whole success of the building of free communes essentially depended on the Makhnovists: "The matter of how we conduct ourselves in the areas that we shall occupy is a life or death issue for our movement as a whole."[1]

The insurgents made do with appointing one of their own to command of the town, albeit without any civil or military authority, and for the sole purpose of liaising between themselves and the agencies freely elected by the working population. The contrast between the backward-looking conduct of the Whites could not have been starker. Yet the Bolsheviks did not take this view. Thus, scarcely had Alexandrovsk and Ekaterinoslav been liberated than they created ready-made "revolutionary committees" — comprised exclusively of their own supporters, whom they tried to pass off as representative of everybody — then sought out Makhno and proposed to him a carving-up of spheres of activity; he would look to the purely military while they would see to the administration and running of the cities. Even then, in their befuddled mentality, they mistook him for the movement as a whole, and, what is more, coldly proposed that he be, as it were, the arms of a body of which they would furnish the head. This was a complete repetition of what had gone before. This time his response was even more violent against these "parasites upon the workers' lives"; he forcibly ejected them and forbade them to commit any authoritarian act vis-à-vis the working population, on pain of being shot, and he strenuously recommended that they "take up a more honest trade."[2]

Two workers' conferences were held in Alexandrovsk; these elected representatives for the regional congress that met on October 27–November 2, 1919. It drew nearly 300 participants, 180 of them peasant delegates (in the proportion of one delegate per 3000 peasants), about 20 worker delegates, and the rest were delegates from left-wing revolutionary organizations and insurgent units. The agenda included the following items: 1) Organization of the insurgent army; 2) reorganization of supply arrangements; 3) organization of a commission to convene a subsequent congress and conferences on the questions of social and economic construction; and, 4) business in hand.

The congress took the most urgent military steps; it determined upon "voluntary" mobilization of 20 classes — between the ages of 19 and 39 — with those under 25 to be dispatched directly to the front while the rest would take care of local self-defense.

This call for a "voluntary" mobilization seems contradictory, and Soviet historians have not been slow to stress that; in fact, it meant that an appeal was issued to the revolutionary consciences of all concerned so that they might defend their rights and freedom by force of arms, without their being obliged to do so, as was the systematic practice among the Bolsheviks, Whites and Petliurists.

The congress also decided that provisioning of the insurgent army was to be ensured on the basis of war booty, requisitions from the bourgeoisie, and, above all, through contributions from the peasants, for the insurgent army was still an essentially peasant army. A panel of peasants, workers and insurgents was appointed to prepare further conferences and congresses bearing on the region's social and economic reconstruction. That left, finally, any other business the delegates wished to raise. Everything went swimmingly up until November 30th when the anarchist Voline — who chaired the congress — expatiated upon the Makhnovists' theses regarding free soviets, as drafted jointly by Makhno and the movement's cultural branch at a general congress of insurgents. On October 20th, these theses had been issued in pamphlet form and distributed throughout the liberated zone as a draft theoretic declaration by the insurgents.[3]

Makhno, who was present, took over and spelled out the theses. The assembly decided to vote on the following resolution: "To support this view by every means while calling for the universal and speediest possible creation of free local social and economic organizations in coordination with one another." At this point, several worker delegates — actually, Menshevik and Social Revolutionary militants — spoke up against this idea; in its place they cited the legitimacy of the Constituent Assembly elected in November 1917 and dissolved by the Bolsheviks in January 1918. Makhno lit into them in no uncertain terms, even labeling them counter-revolutionaries in cahoots with Denikin. Outraged, 11 delegates from the soviet of trade unions, from the union of restaurant staff, printers, bank and commercial employees walked out of the hall, and made a public protest at Makhno's charges, insisting in the name of the city's working class that these be withdrawn! The congress saw no point in replying to this, for had Makhno not spelled out to them a few home truths, then unquestionably, he reckoned, the assembly "would have done the job a day or two later."[4]

One Bolshevik official, Levko, participating in the congress also spoke out against the Makhnovist view while caricaturing it crudely:

"'You tell us' — he said — 'that the soviets can organize anarchy — the absence of authority — and that we will be able to live with such soviets, but you yourselves do not implement this (pointing to the presidium of the congress). And anyway, who are you? Are you not an authority? You preside, you call speakers, call for silence, and, if you so desire, deny some the right to speak. How will it be under Anarchy? If there is a bridge linking two villages, and it is destroyed, who will see to its repair? Given that neither village will want to do so, nobody will do it, and so we shall find ourselves bridgeless, and unable to go to town.'"5

The argument was too puerile to cut much ice, especially among peasants for whom solidarity is a natural law, but it is illustrative of this ongoing tendency among supporters of authority to take people for children incapable of assuming control of themselves without lapsing into "idiocies." By way of contrast to the lines above, Pavlov, whom we have already cited, reproduces the peasants' profession of faith: "We are not Bolsheviks. They promised us much, but already we have everything (the land). What about power? We live very well doing without it completely."6

In any event the Bolsheviks at the congress did not insist, and they even designated one of their number, Novitsky, to join the insurgents' Military Revolutionary Soviet elected by the congress. Unity was the theme of the day, and it was enough for them to follow events, well-placed and awaiting their chance to intervene.

Makhno responded to the Mensheviks' protest by specifying that his accusations were addressed solely to them and not to the workers; this he explained at some length in an open letter published by the Makhnovist organ, *The Road to Freedom:*

"Can it possibly be that the workers of Alexandrovsk and its environs, through their Menshevik and Right Social Revolutionary delegates, support the idea of the Denikinist Constituent Assembly as against any free congress of workers, peasants and insurgents? When they fled from the congress like craven vulgar thieves when confronted by the justice of my charges, is it possible that you decided to protest alongside them? Is it true that these puppets of the bourgeoisie are charged with representing you so as to hide behind your proletarian honor and call for support for the old ideal of the Constituent Assembly?

I think not, that the workers of Alexandrovsk cannot possibly have awarded full powers to these people for that purpose. These impudent individuals who betrayed your interests by addressing congress in the language of Denikin. I am certain that you will keep faith with the ideas of the proletariat and peasants, with the idea of social revolution. Death to all Constituent Assemblies and other snares of the bourgeoisie! Long live the freedom, equality and justice of the toilers!"[7]

Such a posture could not help but gratify the Bolsheviks; it was grist to their mill in their politicking against the "legitimist" Social Revolutionaries and Mensheviks. Makhno's violence of language is understandable, especially in light of the vicious battles he had just fought on behalf of his cause; nonetheless, it needs to be noted that he was mistaken in lumping the Constituent Assembly with Denikin's goals. Denikin was as far removed from that as he was from the free soviets advocated by Makhnovists, as we have just seen. Also, if the (so-called Right) Social Revolutionary and Menshevik delegates were really representative of Alexandrovsk's workers, and there is every chance that that was the case, that merely signified that the working class was less radical than the poor peasantry. Makhno grasped that well enough when he occupied Ekaterinoslav for one-and-one-half months from November 9, 1919; the railway workers had turned to him, taking him for an authority — in short, a "boss," as it were — to ask him to pay the wages that they had not had for the past two months! He answered them along the same lines as what he had published in the Makhnovist paper, *The Road to Freedom*, on this very subject a short time before:

> "With the object of restoring normal rail traffic in the region liberated by us, on the basis of the principle of the free self-organization of workers' associations and peasant unions in respect of their existence and activities, let me propose to railway worker comrades that they organize themselves vigorously and **themselves** arrange the traffic, levying a suitable sum for passengers and cargoes transported (aside from military convoys and transports) by way of payment for their labors and then organize their budget on the basis of fair principles of comradeship, and finally enter into close relations with other worker and peasant associations as well as insurgent detachments.
>
> Commander of the revolutionary insurgent army of the Ukraine, Alexandrovsk, October 15, 1919. Batko Makhno."[8]

This the region's railway workers did do, insofar as they were able in the light of the military situation. There was another characteristic incident with workers from the Berdyansk workshops; they prepared some artillery pieces captured by the Makhnovists from the Denikinists, then demanded payment for their trouble when payment was not always the practice among Reds or Whites. The insurgents were shocked at this attitude since they themselves did not shrink from sacrificing their lives for the common cause. One cannot generalize, for it is probable if not certain that with time all these frictions and misunderstandings would have been dispelled, but these examples are, all the same, illustrative of the revolutionary minimalism of certain workers. It was on these grounds and in order to avoid any mistakes that Makhno was never thereafter to cease emphasizing the fact that the insurgent movement that bore his name was essentially the emanation of the impoverished peasantry.

ക

On November 2nd, a district congress met in Nikopol. It unanimously sided with the Makhnovist movement, and it too called for "voluntary" mobilization of men aged between 18 and 25 for immediate dispatch to the front; those between 25 and 45 were to form a local self-defense regiment. The congress set up a commission to aid the families of those mobilized and then delegated three representatives to Ekaterinoslav in order to liaise with the insurgent army's staff. At that time the insurgency was at its highest point, numbering almost 80,000 fighters and controlling nearly the whole southern Ukraine.

Let us note also that at the Alexandrovsk congress a stringent resolution was passed on the question of drunkenness: Any who thus weakened or contributed to the decomposition of the army of the proletariat now risked the firing squad. By contrast the Bolshevik militant Konyevets testifies that he had heard Makhno arrange with the head of the insurgent army's intelligence branch, Lev Zadovsky-Zinkovsky to have 30 barrels of alcohol (pure alcohol) supplied to Shkuro's Cossacks for the obvious purpose of sapping their fighting spirit.[9]

The Alexandrovsk congress also passed a resolution on the sum to be levied from the bourgeoisie and banks. Alexandrovsk's bourgeoisie was hit with a levy of 50 million rubles but was to cough up only ten million; a levy of the same size was imposed on Ekaterinoslav but raised only seven million. Only 15 of the 25 million levied against Berdyansk was collected; Nikopol's contribution, set at 15 million rubles, was in fact to amount to eight million.

One hundred million rubles were seized from the Ekaterinoslav banks; of these 45 million were made available to the insurgents, three million were distributed to the needy, to combatants' families, and to ex-prisoners. All this was done through the good offices of a social assistance office which, initially, sat twice a week and then on a daily basis. According to the evidence of one city resident, published in an official soviet magazine, such assistance was starkly at odds with the behavior of the Whites, and, it is implied, of the Reds:

> "This distribution of monies to the population was fairly extensive. It was announced in advance that the poorest could apply to the headquarters of Batko Makhno's insurgent army for material assistance. All that anyone was required to bring with him was his passport so that the social situation of the applicants could be authenticated. There were lots of unemployed and needy in the town, and despite the comparatively moderate cost of living (a pound of white bread then cost five or six rubles, compared with three or four under the Whites), thousands waited every morning outside the headquarters. Applicants filed one at

a time into the social assistance office. There, one of the members of the Military Revolutionary Soviet, an anarchist intellectual (apparently a school teacher), scrutinized the applicant's passport, put a few questions to him to establish the measure of need, prescribed the amount of aid, and entered this and the name of the beneficiary in a ledger. A cashier seated at another table dipped into bags strewn on the ground for bills and handed over the money without asking for a receipt. Sometimes, if the applicant (male or female, in the latter case only the wives or widows of working men) made a convincing case, the amount allocated could add up to a considerable sum for those days, up to thousands of rubles which could keep a whole family in comfort for upwards of a month. This distribution of help to the poorest of the population was kept up by the Makhnovists right up until their very last day there. Help was similarly afforded to the town's children's homes; nearly one million rubles were allotted to them, plus many products: flour, lard and sausage. One has to give credit to the Makhnovists; the children's homes were kept supplied for over a month.... However, while handing over money for the children's homes, the Military Revolutionary Soviet declared that the insurgent army was not a charitable organization, and that it would give out no more money. 'We're only an insurgent army,' said the Military Revolutionary Soviet's secretary, the anarchist intellectual, to the agent of the children's homes, 'We only came to defend you against violence from any authorities, be they Bolshevik or Denikinist. The rest is up to yourselves, up to your own actions. Organize yourselves as you wish!'

The Military Revolutionary Soviet expressed the same viewpoint in an appeal to the populace to summon a conference that would take charge of the running of the city. A conference that would assemble the working personnel of the city, excluding their exploiters."10

❧

This practice on the part of the insurgents is a good illustration of their approach; they took the lead in eliminating state power used by Whites, Reds or any other hegemony-seeking faction, before inviting workers to get on with self-organization. To begin with, using money levied from the bourgeoisie, they made do with getting the machinery of solidarity underway before stepping back into their purely defensive military function. They handed over another million rubles to the city's hospital which had not been able to function up until then for lack of funds. In fact, the financial issue was secondary for them; they had a clear preference for a natural economy, i.e., direct exchange of goods and services between different worker and peasant associations, insofar as their needs allowed. That said, the townsfolk were not yet up to that; as far as they were concerned, they had to get hold of some money. Here too the Makhnovists found a very simple solution; all currencies were — to the great annoyance of Soviet historians — taken as equally valid, whether they were nikolaevkis (rubles from the days of Nicholas II), kerenkis (rubles issued under Kerensky), Petliura's "Karbovantsy" or any other coupons or vouchers — all were welcome!

Another remarkable achievement of their occupation of Ekaterinoslav: Complete freedom of association and expression for leftist organizations and mouthpieces. The Makhnovists announced this the moment they arrived in the city:

> "1. Complete freedom to express their beliefs, ideas, teachings, and opinions, both orally and in writing, is offered to all socialist political organizations without exception. No restriction on social freedom of speech or publication can be tolerated, and no persecution along such lines should have any place in the life of the city.

> *Note*: Communications of a military nature may only be published provided they have been supplied by the editors of the revolutionary insurgents' main organ, *The Road to Freedom*.

> 2. In offering total freedom of expression to political parties and organizations, the army of the Makhnovist insurgents warns them at the same time that the cultivation, organization, and erection by constraints on their part of any political authority hostile to the laboring people — which has nothing to do with freedom in expression of ideas — will in no ways be tolerated by the revolutionary insurgents.

> The Military Revolutionary Soviet of the Army of the Makhnovist Insurgents. Ekaterinoslav, November 5, 1919."[11]

And so, for the first time since February 1917, great freedom of speech, association, and press were introduced in the capital of the eastern Ukraine. During the Makhnovists' six week sojourn, the following publications appeared, unmolested: The (so-called Right) Social Revolutionaries' *People's Power;* the Left Social Revolutionaries' *Banner of Revolt;* the Bolshevik *Star;* the Mensheviks' bulletin; the anarchist confederation of the Ukraine's *Nabat;* and the two editions (in Russian and in Ukrainian) of the Makhnovist insurgents' organ, *The Road to Freedom.*

In their publications the insurgents spelled out the meaning of all these achievements: "The meaning of the events in progress fits in with the third great insurgent revolution, bringing to the toiling masses emancipation from the yoke of all power in all its forms and manifestations," *Nabat* wrote in its December 1, 1919 edition. On October 16th, *The Road to Freedom* asserted that:

> "...the difference between Bolsheviks' economic policy and the economic construction proposed by the new course lies in the fact that

the Bolsheviks, like all authorities, connect that building closely with the policy of state power, adapting it to the existing battery of State machinery [...] for its part, the new course, which rejects all State power calls for free organization of this economic construction by anti-authoritarian groups of peasants and workers, unaided."[12]

It should be stressed that this new life was trying to establish itself against a backdrop of continual war. The city was under constant bombardment from Denikinists dug in on the opposite bank of the Dniepr, a factor that accounts for certain restrictions on the rights on the local bourgeoisie. Likewise, the whole region was prey to raids by Mamontov's and Shkuro's Cossacks, whose invasion undid nearly all of the decisions and resolutions reached in Alexandrovsk; delegates had barely returned to their villages and townships before these were reoccupied by White troops.

The situation became even more tense in Ekaterinoslav when a Bolshevik plot was uncovered. For several months past a number of Bolsheviks had been sharing in the Makhnovists' struggle; some of them had capitalized on this in order to establish clandestine liaison with one another and to pack the command positions of given regiments. Then they decided to act, which is to say mount a *coup d'Etat* against the insurgent staff; to that end, their primary aim was to do away with Makhno. On some pretext, they invited him to a *soirée*, where the plan was to offer him a poisoned drink. Tipped off by one of its members, the Makhnovist intelligence service quickly seized the plotters (the informant had wormed his way into the clandestine Bolshevik liaison), arrested them, and after a speedy trial, had the five main conspirators shot on December 5. These five were Polonsky, commander of insurgents' "Iron" regiment; his second-in-command, Semchenko; his mistress — an actress who was to have "played" the role of poisoner; Vainer, a former president of a Red Army court martial of sinister repute; plus another confederate.

Another regimental commander, Lashkevitch, who had been later the first man to enter Ekaterinoslav, was also shot for embezzlement and that in spite of his tremendous popularity among the insurgents. Some Denikinist agents, most of them ex-officers, met the same fate.

On December 22, Ekaterinoslav was attacked by Slaschev at the head of fresh and heavily armed troops. After several days of bitter fighting in an effort to cover the evacuation of several thousand sick and wounded insurgents left behind in the city, the Makhnovists were finally obliged to give the place up. As a result, the fourth regional congress scheduled to be held in Ekaterinoslav at the end of December 1919 was unable to proceed.

There was a single and principal reason for the weakening of the insurgent army: an epidemic of typhus, an enemy worse than any faced thus far.[13] The whole force and gains of the insurgent movement's struggle were thus to evaporate in just a few weeks. By late October many Makhnovists had succumbed; on December 11, the insurgent army was already down to 25,000 men, with more than 10,000 wounded or sick. Many were sent home in order to reduce risks of infection; others were hospitalized and perished by the thousands for want of appropriate treatment. Makhno and several members of his staff also contracted this ghastly disease. By the end of December, only about 10,000 insurgents were left, and these had fallen back in the direction of the Gulyai-Polye, Melitopol, and Nikopol area. It was at this juncture that the third party, the Red Army, showed up to reap the benefits of the Makhnovists' successes. Especially as the Whites too had been decimated by typhus and, following the failure of their push against Moscow, the Whites were beating a slow retreat towards their bases in the Caucasus.

Notes to Chapter 19: The Fortunes and Misfortunes of Freedom Regained

1. Kubanin, op. cit. pp. 88–89.
2. Arshinov, op. cit. p. 151.
3. Reprinted in full as an appendix to this book.
4. B. Kolesnikov, *The Trades Movement and the Counter-revolution* (in Russian), Kharkov, 1923, p. 320.
5. Kubanin, op. cit. p. 94.
6. Pavlov, op. cit. p.75.
7. B. Kolesnikov, op. cit. p. 321.
8. *The Road to Freedom* No. 9, quoted by V. Miroshevsky in "Free Ekaterinoslav" in *The Proletarian Revolution*, (in Russian), Moscow, 1922, No. 9, p. 203.
9. Konyevets (Grishuta) in *Letopis revoliutsii* op. cit. No. 4 (13), 1925, p. 83.
10. M. Gutman "Under the power of the anarchists: Ekaterinoslav in 1919" in *Russkoye proshlozhe*, St. Petersburg, No. 5, 1923, pp. 65–66.
11. Arshinov, op. cit. pp. 151–152.
12. Quoted by V. Miroshevsky, op. cit. pp. 202–203.
13. The lice that carried this awful disease were dubbed the "tanks of death."

20. The New Enemy: The Bolshevik Party-State

The disintegration of Denikin's rear beneath the concerted blows of Makhno and the Greens singularly simplified the Red Army's task; it made do with shadowing the Whites as they retreated step by step in an orderly withdrawal under the command of Wrangel and Shkuro. The latter "beat all records for slowness" as he retreated the 80 kilometers from Voronezh to Kastornaya over a three week period.[1] On the other hand the Red Army made all haste in occupying the terrain cleared by local partisans and in establishing "Soviet" authority there. Thus came true the allegation by the Makhnovists (as reported by Dybets) to the effect that: "When there is fighting to be done, the Bolsheviks are nowhere around, and there is no point in looking for them on the front, but as soon as a town is taken by partisans, up they pop and immediately proclaim themselves the new authorities. Their sole aim is to ride to power on the backs of the insurgents."[2]

Despite the widespread typhus epidemic and its heavy losses on the field of battle, the Red Army's numbers had constantly grown; by autumn 1919 they had reached the considerable figure of three million men. These were reinforced even further by incorporation of partisan bands and White captives. To be sure, only a tiny number of these troops, about one in ten, actually saw front-line service and that on different fronts. Confronting Denikin it had only 150,000 troops, regularly relieved as the casualty rate or falling morale of the fighters dictated. Indeed, the whole army represented a rather flabby military potential, the men having been forcibly conscripted; also the Red Army's command had been concerned above all with training them and with "grooming" them ideologically, then held them in reserve or else used them as occupation troops in the less dependable areas of the country in order to stabilize the Bolshevik order there.

The Makhnovists made the serious mistake of underestimating this new peril. According to Arshinov, the movement ought to have been strengthened militarily and every area of the Ukraine — as far as Orel and Poltava — liberated by insurgents under Makhnovist influence ought to have been directly occupied in order to forestall the Bolsheviks' intentions. Instead, it was insurgent detachments (like those of Bibik and Ogarkin which occupied Poltava and Orel) that sought out the Makhnovists as the Red Army forced them into retreat. Arshinov accounts for this oversight by citing on the one hand ravages caused by typhus, and on the other, the exaggeratedly optimistic outlook of the Makhnovists, convinced that the Red Army would never dare come and lay down the law to them, in view of their crucial contribution to Denikin's defeat.

The insurgents reckoned that as they had borne the brunt of the fighting and liberated the whole of the Ukraine by their own unaided efforts, Moscow simply had to take that into account. The Makhnovist high command had given consideration to whether priority should be given to military reinforcement of the region or to the positive ventures in social and economic construction by the workers. It had come out in favor of the second option, on the basis that through their revolutionary work, the toiling masses would easily see of any attempted interference by any party. There was another consideration also; the Makhnovists had no wish to end up as the new authorities but wished to leave things up to the self-organizational ability and foresight of the workers themselves, and were content merely to let them know how the Makhnovists saw things. The following handbill which was circulated at this time is a good encapsulation of this intention:

"Declaration of the insurgent revolutionary army of the Ukraine (Makhnovist).

To all Peasants and Workers of the Ukraine!

For transmission by telegraph, telephone or courier to all villages, all rural districts, all cantons and provinces of the Ukraine. For reading at all gatherings of peasants and workers of factory and workshops.

Brother toilers! The revolutionary insurgent army of the Ukraine (Makhnovist) was set up as a reaction against the oppression of workers and peasants by the power of the bourgeoisie and of big estate owners and by the Communist-Bolshevik dictatorship.

Setting itself the goal of fighting for the utter emancipation of the toilers of the Ukraine from the yoke of those two powers and the creation of a genuinely socialist soviet order, the army of the Makhnovist insurgents has fought doggedly on several fronts to achieve that objective. At this very moment it is bringing to a victorious conclusion its fight against Denikin's army, liberating region after region and eliminating all power and all organization rooted in violence.

Many peasants and workers ask the question: What is to be done now and how? What attitude should we adopt vis-à-vis dispositions taken by the authorities which have been eliminated? — and so on. The Pan-Ukrainian congress of workers and peasants will furnish a precise and full answer to these questions, a congress that will have to meet immediately just as soon as it is feasible for the workers and peasants to get together. That congress will indicate and resolve all the fundamental questions of the life of workers and peasants.

But given that this congress will not be able to proceed for some time, the army of Makhnovist insurgents regards it as indispensable that the following statement be made on the fundamental issues of the life of workers and peasants:

1. All dispositions taken by Denikinist authorities are rescinded. Dispositions of the communist authorities which conflicted with the interests of the workers and peasants are likewise rescinded.

Note: As regards those dispositions of the communist authorities injurious to the workers, it is incumbent upon the latter themselves to identify these and to take decisions at peasants' and workers' assemblies in villages and factories.

2. All the landholdings of great estate owners, monasteries, kulaks and all other enemies of the toilers pass, along with all their livestock, into the hands of peasants who work for their living. This whole transfer should be effected in an organized fashion, by decision of general assemblies of peasants who should be cognizant not only of their personal interest but also keep in mind the general interests of the entire toiling and oppressed peasantry.

3. The workshops, factories, coal and mineral mines as well as other instruments and means of production become the property of the entire working class as a whole which, through its trades unions, takes all enterprises in hand in a concerted way, organizes production there, and moves towards uniting the whole industry of the country into one all-embracing organism.

4. It is proposed to all peasant and worker organizations that they make a start on construction of free soviets of workers and peasants. Only workers participating in work vital to the people's economy should be elected on to these soviets. The representatives of political organizations have no place in the soviets of workers and peasants, given that their participation in a soviet could turn it into a soviet of party political deputies, thereby leading the soviet order to perdition.

5. The existence of Chekas, party political revolutionary committees, and other institutions of constraint, power, or discipline will not be tolerated among free peasants and workers.

6. Freedom of speech, press, association, organization, etc., is the inalienable right of every worker and all limitations upon that right would appear as a counter-revolutionary act.

7. The State's police (guards, police, militia) are abolished. In their place the population will organize its self-defense. This self-defense cannot be organized other than by the workers and toilers themselves.

8. The workers' and peasants' soviets, the self-defense of the workers and peasants, as well as each individual peasant and worker,

will not allow any counter-revolutionary action by the bourgeoisie and officers.

9. Soviet and Ukrainian currencies are to have the same value as other currencies. Those who violate this disposition are to be liable to revolutionary sanction.

10. The exchange of the products of labor and trade remains free until such time as the workers' and peasants' organizations shall take charge of that themselves. But it is proposed at the same time that the exchange of the products of labor take place only between toilers.

11. All who shall intentionally obstruct circulation of the present declaration are to be regarded as counter-revolutionaries.

January 7, 1920
The Military Revolutionary Soviet and Staff of the Insurgent
Revolutionary Army of the Ukraine (Makhnovist)."[3]

This proclamation is of high revolutionary tenor but is suggestive of an over-estimation of the potential of a population at that time bled dry and bereft of everything. And the only language that Bolsheviks understood was the language of the balance of military might. Just as they had done a year earlier, they entered the Ukraine from the north, and in the absence of power, at least as they saw it, for a free and spontaneous organizing of workers through their grassroots organs — free soviets federated from the bottom up — could not in their estimation be deemed a power worthy of the name, they imposed their own. At the close of a meeting held in Ekaterinoslav on January 1, 1920 following their occupation of the city, they pushed through a resolution that was eloquent and closed with these words: "Long live the worldwide Bolshevik Communist Party! Long live the Third International! Down with anarchy!"[4]

The first encounter between units from the two camps, at the beginning of January 1920, was amicable if not fraternal. Kubanin, the Soviet historian of the Makhnovschina reckons that: "…for the Red Army, Makhnovists seemed like allies who had conducted a ferocious struggle behind the lines of the common foe, helping to disorganize him and thereby hastening the shared victory. It went without saying that Makhnovist units had to subordinate themselves to the overall command of the Red Army."[5] And so the Red Army began to conduct itself as the master thereabouts, intercepting bands of Makhnovists then absorbing them into its ranks while dispersing them through its regiments or disarming them and dispatching them home to their hearths.

For the reasons indicated earlier, Makhno and his staff had fallen back to-wards the Gulyai-Polye region and Alexandrovsk; i.e., they had in fact abdicated all control over the region. Makhno, beset by an acute form of exanthematic typhus, was at that moment deep in a coma and would not emerge from that for a good ten days.

This was the moment chosen by the 14th Red Army's command to order the Makhnovists on January 8th to surrender on the Polish front where the Bolsheviks were preparing to launch a war of conquest with the aim of achieving a common frontier with Germany — the fatherland of proletarian revolution, according to Lenin — prior to "bolshevizing" the whole of Europe. Kubanin notes this order while explaining that it was "dictated by the need to oust the Makhnovist insurgent army from its [home] territory and thus convert it into a regular army unit."[6] What Kubanin did not know when he came to pen those lines was that the object of the order was to contrive a rift with Makhno. Indeed, in an article published some months after Kubanin's work, Levenson, a Ukrainian Bolshevik military official, offered a quite different explanation of the order by reporting the conversation between Uborevitch, commander of the 14th Red Army, and Yakir, commanding the 45th Division. Uborevitch stated that "Makhno's attitude towards that order will furnish us with definite grounds for our subsequent treatment of him…" while Yakir replied that: "Knowing Makhno personally, I know that there is no way he will accept it." Uborevitch acquiesced and concluded: "This order is quite patently a political gambit and only that. We do not even expect a positive response from Makhno."[7] Further to this individual's cynicism, let us note that several days previously on January 4th, he had issued a top secret instruction: "for all steps to be taken to disarm the population and wipe out Makhno's bands."[8]

The most sizable Makhnovist detachment, some six regiments strong — that is, about 9000 infantry and cavalry — and stationed in Alexandrovsk at first objected indignantly that there was no way that it was answerable to the Red Army and that it had not needed it to liberate the Ukraine and then that Makhno and most of their fighting men were still bed-ridden typhus victims, and finally that it did not feel that war against Poland was any of its concern. Such a response was music to Bolshevik ears in that it furnished them with an excuse to declare Makhno and the insurgents outlawed yet again on January 9, 1920 and openly to fight them. The Red Army high command sought in this way to avenge its discomfiture of August 1919 at Pomoshnaya when its troops had gone over to Makhno. The communiqué declaring Makhno outlawed developed this fallacious line of argument:

> "Decree from the Pan-Ukrainian revolutionary committee on the outlawing of Makhno and the Makhnovists. January 9, 1920.
>
> To all workers, Red soldiers and peasants of the Ukraine.
>
> Comrades! At last, after incredible losses, our valiant Red Army has been able to crush the capitalists, the pomieschikis and their confederate, Denikin.
>
> But the Ukrainian people's chief enemy — the Polish lords — have not yet been defeated. Coming to Denikin's rescue, they have occupied a whole succession of towns and districts in this country of ours and in

Russia alike. The military command is trying everything to achieve a union of all forces fighting against the common foe of the toiling people — pomieschikis and capitalists — and to that end has proposed to the Makhnovists that they join the fight against the Poles, thereby assisting the Red Army to liberate our villages and towns from the yoke of the Polish lords and spare workers the enslavement of capitalism.

Makhno has been unwilling to bow to the will of the Red Army; he has refused to fight the Poles, declaring war instead on our peasant and worker army of liberation.

In this way, Makhno and his band have sold the Ukrainian people to the Polish lords, as Petliura, Grigoriev and other traitors have done. Which is why the Pan-Ukrainian Revolutionary Committee now decrees:

Makhno and his band are hereby outlawed as deserters and traitors.

All who support and assist in the concealment of these traitors from the Ukrainian people are to be ruthlessly annihilated.

The toiling populace of the Ukraine has an obligation to support the Red Army by every means in its pursuit of the annihilation of Makhnovist traitors.

This decree is to be read compulsorily by all of the Ukraine's revolutionary committees in front of workshops, factory and mine-works assemblies and everywhere else.

The Pan-Ukrainian Revolutionary Committee:
Chairman, G.I. Petrovsky; Members: D.Z. Manuilsky, V. Zatonsky, G.
Grinko, Kachinsky, Kharkov"9

❧

Not the least startling aspect of this document is the revelation that the main enemy of the people of the Ukraine was the Polish lords absent from the area for centuries past! Furthermore, the Polish government was headed by the socialist Pilsudski! Finally, the Bolshevik satraps did not call a halt at such "trifles." Any pretext would do, just as long as it justified outlawing the Makhnovists. The Makhnovists' naiveté was all too obvious; they reckoned that they had fulfilled their role as revolutionaries so well that the Bolsheviks surely would not dare use calumny against them. But that was to reckon without the hegemonic logic of the Leninist cliques.

The decree signaled the beginning of the hunt for Makhno; he, unconscious and on the brink of death, was saved only by the devotion of the peasants of the Gulyai-Polye region who took him in and, when his hiding place was discovered, bought time for the ailing Makhno to be removed to somewhere safer. The members of the Makhnovist staff and the insurgents' main commanders managed to slip through the net and strove to contain the Reds' attacks. The insurgents' Military

Revolutionary Soviet disbanded, its members going underground or, like Voline, were picked up by the Bolsheviks.

A secret operational report from the 13th Red Army, dated January 31, 1920, notes that the "remnants" of the Makhnovists had been liquidated in the Gulyai-Polye region. The captured booty was enlightening: Thirteen cannon, eight machine-guns, 120 rifles, 300 prisoners, 60 horses, 50 saddles (!), one field telephone, four typewriters (!), 100 sabers, 50 machine-gun ammunition belts, 500 cartridges, and three sackfuls of sundry silver items.[10] In fact this operation was a surprise attack directed against the Makhnovist staff, during which Nestor's second and last brother, Saveli, a quartermaster, was shot merely for his relationship to his leader brother. When this punitive expedition was thought not to have been exemplary enough, the 13th Red Army's commander, Yegorov, ordered the commander of the Estonian Division on February 6th to crush the Makhnovists from the Gulyai-Polye region once and for all, as well as "pitilessly repressing the Makhnovists and the population harboring them." He even stipulated that "in the event of resistance in Gulyai-Polye, it will be necessary to proceed in the most severe fashion, should circumstances so require." [!][11]

It seems that not all of these efforts were crowned with success, for on February 9th, another urgent and secret operational report from the 12th, 13th, and 14th Red Armies reported the capture of the black banner of the Makhnovist staff, of three machine-guns, 38 rifles, 14 horses, and the recapture of the 42nd Division's heavy battery (seized a short time before by the Makhnovists!)[12]

For added security, the Red Army command used Latvian, Estonian, and Chinese riflemen, most of whom spoke neither Russian nor Ukrainian; having no local ties, they were easier to manipulate. What successes were registered in the Gulyai-Polye region led the Red Army command to believe that the Makhnovist movement had been, as they would say, "liquidated"; it decided thereafter to turn its attention to controlling the territory. They began by having each home painstakingly searched with a view to confiscating all weapons still at the disposal of the population which was, consequently, regarded as potentially hostile. The dissident soviet general Grigorenko, who has already offered us a description of the abuses of the Whites, this time turns his attentions to those of the Reds:

> "Thus, we hated the Whites because they had gunned down the first Soviets in 1918. That hate was well justified. Now, it was in 1920 that troikas of the Cheka began to raid villages to confiscate weapons remaining in the hands of the populace. We too earned our 'visit.' The president of the Cheka, dressed entirely in leather and armed to the teeth, addressed the village assembly; his address could not have been more laconic; he read out a list of hostages (comprising seven 'notables' from the village) and announced that they would be shot unless the population had handed over to the Cheka all weapons in their possession

by noon the next day. On the following morning, a few hunting pieces, revolvers, and daggers were found outside the premises of the village soviet. After the mid-day meal, troops from the military detachment accompanying the three Chekists conducted a search of all homes. In a vegetable garden — indeed, it seems, in the meadow beyond the vegetable garden — they 'discovered' an old blunderbuss. The hostages were shot, and the troika selected seven more."

Oddly enough, these hostages were to be spared, to the amazement of the populace, as the president of this particular 'troika' had the reputation of never shooting fewer than three batches of hostages. Grigorenko continues:

"For a long time there was a lot of curiosity and talk about the massacres that the Cheka was committing in other villages in the region. There was no end of bloodshed. In one of these villages — Novospassovka — the Chekists had even, so it was said, carried out mass shootings. Witnesses claimed to have seen the blood run in spates, forming rivulets, down the slopes of the ravine atop which the executions had been carried out.

I did not believe these tales. In 1918, Novospassovka had revolted against the Whites and had held out heroically against them for eight months until Makhno's army broke the encirclement. And the village, in an expression of gratitude to the Batko, had supplied him with two regiments of well-armed and battle-hardened infantry. I could not bring myself to believe that the revolutionary authorities could have wiped out the sort of people who had fought for them so well. Now, as I learned subsequently, those witnesses had told the truth. In Novospassovka, the Cheka had shot down one in every two able-bodied men. Men who had been capable of insurrection against the Whites might very well have rebelled some day against the Reds; that, at least, was the thinking of our leaders, and through the massacre, they had cynically preempted that possibility."[13]

This amounted to outright genocide against descendants of the Zaporogs, a genocide mounted knowingly by the Bolshevik leadership. Piotr Arshinov, chronicler of the Makhnovschina and eyewitness to this war of extermination, reckons, at the most cautious estimate, that for 1920 the number of peasants shot or mutilated by the Bolshevik authorities stood at nearly 200,000! — and a similar figure for those deported to Siberia and elsewhere. The Whites' sinister record had been beaten out of sight!

Let us also quote the testimony of an anonymous old Bolshevik, published recently, which places on record another aspect of this terror, with the Cheka abetted this time by army commander Zhloba, a Donetz miner who had become a party stalwart. Faced with resurgent Makhnovist activities in the spring of 1920, in the Sinelnikovo region, 100 hostages were taken from among the well-to-do — kulaks, priests, businessmen, etc. (of which in fact none too many could have been left by then) — and they were handed over to the Cheka:

> "After questioning, they were led out into the prison yard, and it was demanded of them that they should reveal who the band leaders were who were hiding out somewhere: In their homes, in their barns, and elsewhere? The hostages were warned that, should they refuse, 25 of them would be shot on the spot as responsible for murders and looting. The hostages said nothing. The first 25 in alphabetical order were led 20 paces away and gunned down as the others looked on. Their next of kin were immediately informed, and the corpses handed over to them."14

On the second and third days, the scene was re-enacted with the same result each time. The last 25 hostages remaining were exhorted to betray Makhnovist agents. After consideration, the hostages gave the names of Makhnovists who had wormed their way into the "organs of Soviet power and into the local party leadership. In particular, the chairman of the town soviet and the secretary of the town's party committee who had gathered around them enemies of Soviet power." These "agents" were promptly shot. The author of these *Memoirs*, though, never poses the question of how these allegedly well-to-do hostages could have been so well informed about Makhnovist infiltration of the Soviet apparatus. It is more than likely the first of them had said nothing because they knew no real Makhnovists, and that these last hostages had sought to save their lives and also to work a cruel revenge on the authorities by singling out genuine Leninist supporters whom they misrepresented for the occasion as "Makhnovists!" What bears out this thesis is the insurgents' absolute opposition to having any involvement at all in any State authority as the following address testifies:

"Address to the Peasants and Workers of the Ukraine:

Peasant and worker brethren! For upwards of three years you have been fighting against capitalism and thanks to your efforts, your staunchness and your energy, you have now all but concluded that struggle. The enemies of the revolution wore themselves out under pressure from you, and you, sensing the imminence of victory, were nearing success.

You thought that your constant and often unequal struggle against the revolution's enemies would afford you the chance to make a reality of that free soviet order to which we have all aspired. But, brethren, you can see who triumphs in our place. They are undesirable masters, these communist hangmen who triumph, they who showed up here when it was all over, treading soil liberated with your blood, by the blood of your brothers and sons who made up the revolutionary insurgent movement. These new lordlings have grabbed all of the wealth of the country. It is not you, but they who do with it what they will. And you peasants and workers have become their shield, without which they cannot call themselves a worker and peasant government, in which name they are the assassins and hangmen of the people and which allows them through their party rule to tyrannize the people. The people's name allows them all that, and it is for that alone that they have need of you workers and peasants.

In every other instance you are nothing to them, and they pay you absolutely no heed. They exploit you, draft you, command and administer you. They destroy everything about you. And you, being oppressed, patiently bear all the horrors of the repression, violence and arbitrariness perpetrated by the communist hangmen, things that can be eliminated only by your widespread protest, only by your revolutionary justice — by a revolutionary insurrection. It is to that you are summoned by your brethren, workers and peasants even as you are, who perish under the gunfire of the Red assassins who, by force of arms, carry off your wheat, livestock, and every other foodstuff for a shipment to Russia.

It is your own brothers who, taking their leave of life and of the whole radiant future to which we all aspire, call upon you to rescue the revolution, independence and freedom. Think, peasant and worker brethren, that now if you no longer feel freedom and complete independence in your hearts, you will be all the more powerless in the future to determine your fate, and you will not be the shapers of your own happiness and will not yourselves be the masters of your country's riches, of the fruits of your very own labor.

All that will be done in your stead by new masters invited in by no one — the Bolshevik-communist intruders. In order to rid themselves of these undesirable masters, every peasant and all of their best efforts have to be applied to the summoning of clandestine peasant congresses at district and regional levels, at which they should debate and decide upon all of the vital problems of the day, brought about through the unaccountability and dictatorship of these bandits. The interests of the country and of the very toilers of the Ukraine require that these new, unwanted lords and masters not be allowed to devastate the country completely; in the Ukraine there ought to be no place either for them or for their Red killers who tyrannize the people. Without wasting a single day, all peasants should organize themselves through clandestine congresses. Organize clandestine combat units in every village and township, and organize a combat agency to lead them. All peasants should once and for all deny all aid to the communist hangmen and their craven mercenaries, denying them horses and grain and crust of bread alike. The workers in turn should, in town as in countryside, refuse to join the Communist Party on the supply detachments or in the Cheka; withhold all participation from communist institutions. The people of the Ukraine should declare to the world at large and translate into action: Away with White and Red killers and hangmen! We pursue the common weal, light and truth and will not tolerate your acts of violence. Long live the international social revolution of workers and peasants! Death to all White Guards and all commissars! Death to all hangmen! Long live the regime of free soviets!

(March–April 1920)
The Staff of the Insurgent Army of the Ukraine (Makhnovist)."15

The insurgents set about putting these vengeful intentions into effect on the ground. At the end of February, the division of the Estonian "mercenaries" which had been so impudent as to ensconce itself in Gulyai-Polye no less, was suddenly attacked and crushed; all of its military and political officials were executed by firing squads; as for the ordinary soldiers, those who indicated a wish to do so were incorporated into the insurgent units, whereas the rest were stripped of their army uniforms and sent packing.

In the months that followed, there were ongoing and scattered clashes on the left bank of the Dniepr. The Red Army's strategy was to track down insurgents, encircle them and if possible, wipe them out, for it took no prisoners. It forgot that the Makhnovists were on home ground and moved like the fish in the water; well-informed as to the movements of the opposition, they wove between the different enemy units, attacking and scattering the smallest while swooping out of the blue upon the rear of the others. In short, they waged a war of harassment without let-up. A high-ranking Red official, Yefimov, in March 1921 when the fight against Makhno was still at its height, narrated his whole experience of the war against the insurgents in 1920. First of all, he explains the Red Army's failure to come up with resounding victory by reference to its social composition: Essentially peasants, the soldiers and even the officers had little heart for the fight against the Makhnovists, implicitly on grounds of class solidarity, for the Makhnovists stood for, at best, the local population's aspirations of "dispensing with all power, the State being regarded as a burden, a restrictive supervisor."16 He reckons that the insurgents had learned how to fight against a regular army thanks to Denikinist troops — which of itself speaks volumes about his ignorance of their earlier fighting against Austro-German troops — and divines an analogy of sorts between the Whites' strategy and the Reds' strategy against Makhno, even in terms of results, which is to say the lack of success by both. He makes out that the main Makhnovist detachment relied on numerous small local detachments which from time to time supplied its reserves and which enjoyed every latitude in striking at Chekists and the authorities' requisition squads. According to him the Makhnovist movement's cohesion could be put down to its "soviet" structure, provided soviet meant "free soviets" which is to say initiatives emanating from the local grassroots. According to Yefimov, all of these reasons lay behind the reverses and lack of success of the Red Army during the first half of 1920 in its dealings with Makhno.

☙❧

With the way ahead apparently open, the Bolsheviks introduced into the countryside what Lenin was emphatic in describing as "war communism." This innovation was directly inspired by the "war socialism" of the capitalist States' economies during the 1914 war when a measure of rationing and a degree of "socialization" had been introduced into the populace's consumption and into industrial production. In Lenin's case, it was concerned only with rationing of consumption; since industrial output was negligible, there could be no barter with the countryside and so it was a question of commandeering all produce and foodstuffs for the benefit, first, of the regime's new class of privileged and of the armed forces, and bottom of the list, the starving city dwellers. Of necessity everything was to be channeled through the State apparatus. The absurdity of this whole system can be grasped if one knows, say, that private individuals were forbidden to fish or hunt, for on pain of punishment, they would then have been required to surrender the product of their endeavors to the State. The same held true for wood; even if everybody was shivering in the winter cold, nobody could go out and chop wood in the forests — for the forests were State property and thus untouchable — without risking a charge of stealing State property!

In the countryside, what was euphemistically termed "requisitioning" was in fact nothing more than systematic pillaging of the peasants; they were stripped of everything — wheat, seed, pigs, livestock — and were generously issued with a receipt. If they demurred and rebelled, they were shot down and their homes put to the torch. Whole villages went up in flames. Such was the practice of communism from "above," contemptuous of the most elementary rights of peasants who were labeled "kulaks" for the occasion.

What exactly did these famous kulaks amount to in 1920? Official statistics offer the following figures for the distribution of land among the peasantry: In 1917, 71 percent of peasants worked less than four hectares, while 25 percent had between four and ten hectares, and just 3.7 percent owned more than ten hectares; by 1920, these same categories of peasants amounted respectively to 85 percent, 15 percent, and 0.5 percent of the whole.[17] So it is quite obvious that even in 1917 the number of well-off peasants — and that only comparatively and according to Bolshevik definitions — was quite small, while by 1920 it had become quite negligible. Let us bring into the picture another, even more eloquent criterion: ownership of horses. According to the selfsame source, in 1917, 29 percent of peasants owned no horse, 49 percent had one, and 17 percent had two horses while 4.8 percent used over three horses; by 1920 the respective figures stood at 27.6 percent, 63.6 percent, 7.9 percent, and 0.9 percent! To conclude, the circumstances of peasants had leveled out, and there were so to speak no more kulaks, which is to say well-to-do peasants, save in the Leninists' fertile imaginings! Also, for all their ideological baggage, the latter had always been incapable of coming up with a precise definition of what a kulak was; in fact, as far as they were concerned, the word was merely an incantation applied to any peasant independent of the Bolshevik state and thus, according to their paranoid reasoning, hostile to their all-embracing powers — an interpretation that might even be applied to nearly the whole of the peasantry.

The worst thing was that strictly speaking, this systematic looting and all of the ghastliness it involved served no purpose at all; Kubanin himself quotes instances when half of the forage collected rotted where it stood and where livestock, seized and dispatched in wagons, perished along the way for want of water and food.[18]

All the same, the regime did modify its agrarian policy a little; the number of sovkhozes hastily set up in 1919 and which, for the most part, were promptly on course for collapse, fell in 1920 from 1,185 to 640; their size shrank even more, from 1,105 thousand hectares to 341 by 1920.[19] The authorities preferred creating "clients" for themselves to redistributing these lands among their supporters. As for the diehards, their land was also seized land, wrested from the former pomieschik at great cost. Kubanin concedes that for the "bulk of the peasantry, the Soviet economy was a new and abhorrent form of rule after the fashion of the Polish lords and one which in reality had merely set the State in the place of the former big landowner."[20]

The Ukrainian peasantry did not remain passive in the face of this bloody counter-revolution; during the first nine months of 1920, upwards of 1,000 plunderers and Bolshevik agents paid with their lives for their misdeeds.[21] The Makhnovists showed them no mercy, so much so that soon there were scarcely any more volunteers ready to venture into these areas. Let us note here that out of 10,576 agents mobilized by this regime to carry out these plundering raids, there were only 323 communists, most being dubious elements, members of the criminal fraternity or other parasites attracted by the prospect of easy pickings and the lure of a few grams of power. The regime was later to have its work cut out offloading on to the latter all of the excesses committed in its name.[22] Let us also note one subtle ploy on the part of Moscow; the death penalty had supposedly been abolished on February 2, 1920 in Russia, but not in the Ukraine where the main conflicts took place. Up to now this fine distinction has escaped the bulk of Western historians of this period.

Notes to Chapter 20: The New Enemy: The Bolshevik Party-State

1. Shkuro, op. cit. p. 241.

2. Dybet, op. cit. p. 52.

3. The original of this handbill is preserved at the International Institute for Social History in Amsterdam. It has been published along with ten other Makhnovist handbills (donated by Ugo Fedeli) by the Institute's review, the *International Review of Social History*, Vol. XIII (1968), part 2. We offer our thanks to the Institute in Amsterdam.

4. *The Civil War in Ekaterinoslav Province (1918–1920), Documents and Materials*, Dniepropetrovsk, 1968, p.210.

5. Kubanin, op. cit. p. 123.

6. Idem.

7. Quoted by F. Ya. Levenson, "Against Makhno, on the Denikin front," in *Litopis revoliutsii* (in Ukrainian) Kharkov, 1929, No. 4, p. 275.

8. *The Civil War in Ukraine* (in Russian), Kiev, 1967, Tome II, p. 624.

9. *The Civil War in Ekaterinoslav Province*, op. cit. pp. 210–211.

10. *The Civil War in Ukraine*, op. cit. p. 692.

11. *The Command Directives from the Red Army Fronts (1917–1922)*, Moscow, 1978, Tome II, p. 403.

12. *The Civil War in Ukraine*, op. cit. p. 738.

13. Grigorenko, op. cit. pp. 89–91.

14. *Mémoires d'un vieux bolshévik-Léniniste*, Paris, Ed. Maspéro, 1970, p. 38.

15. International Institute for Social History, Amsterdam, op. cit.

16. Yefimov, "The operations against Makhno, from January 1920 to January 1921" in the *Collection of Works from the Military and Scientific Association in the Military Academy* (in Russian), Moscow, 1921, Book One, pp. 192–212. The quotation is from p. 195.

17. L. Kritsman, *The Heroic Period of the Great Russian Revolution (War Communism)* (in Russian), Moscow, 1926, p. 67.

18. Kubanin, op. cit. pp. 126 and 129.

19. Ibid. p. 132.

20. Ibid. pp. 133–134.

21. Ibid. p. 130.

22. Idem.

21. Between Whites and Reds

What had become of the Whites while all of this was going on? Following the failure of Denikin's great offensive against Moscow, their retreat had been made in three directions: The army corps of General Bredov and Martynov withdrew in a westerly direction; when the Romanians refused to let them cross the border, they followed the Dniestr and crossed into Poland where their troops were interned. General Slaschev's units withdrew towards the Crimea and dug in behind the Perekop and Henichesk isthmuses. But the bulk of the anti-Bolshevik forces retreated behind the Caucasus, closely pursued by the Red Cossacks of Dumenko and Budyenny. In view of the collapse of the Denikinist venture, 150 representatives of the Don, Kuban and Terek Cossacks assembled on January 2, 1920, as the Supreme *Circle* of Cossacks to draft the constitution of a federative Cossack State. So the break had finally come between the Cossack "Gironde" and the Denikinist command; the Cossacks were no longer willing to serve as cannon-fodder of the ambitions of reactionary White soldiery but were content merely to hold their territories against the Reds while hoping to agree to a de facto neutrality with them; but the Reds did not want to know and brought heavy pressure to bear on the front. The incoherence of the White high command and the increasingly blatant incompetence of Denikin who contrived to have Mamontov and Wrangel removed from their posts (they were his most able generals), plus the internal dissensions and the Cossacks unwillingness to fight, quickly turned this withdrawal into a rout. Taganrog, Rostov, and Novocherkassk, the main cities on the Don, fell to Red Cossacks. Denikin then decided to fall back into the Crimea; the army of the Volunteers and a few thousand Cossacks scurried aboard some Russian and British ships at Novorossisk in February 1920, abandoning the Cossack armies to their fate. One hundred thousand Cossacks were taken prisoner by the Reds at Novorossisk and 22,000 others at Kabardin, on the borders of Georgia, which had denied them asylum. It was a shambles; without really having been defeated militarily, the Whites — thanks above all to the Denikinist high command — had beaten themselves through insistence upon their political contradictions and their discriminatory conduct towards the Cossacks. What remained of their troops were thus in the Crimea, which became the last bastion of the White movement.

The bulk of captured Cossacks were re-deployed by the Red command on the Polish front or elsewhere in the country in order to give them the chance to make amends for what Bolsheviks saw as their "straying from the righteous path." No longer willing to be the Whites' cannon fodder, the Cossacks now found themselves between the Devil and the deep blue sea, becoming the blind instruments of Moscow's expansionist designs.

Shortly after, Denikin was forced to step down; he left pathetically for exile in Constantinople where his chief confederate and éminence grise, General Romanovsky, was murdered as soon as he arrived by a White officer. Sensing the same fate stalking him, Denikin quickly moved on to England.

On March 22, 1920, a general assembly of the White high command appointed Baron General Wrangel head of the White movement. Wrangel, a German squire of Baltic origins, "…consented to accept the position of commander-in-chief"[1] and set about the task with vigor. Although profoundly imbued with a sense of his own importance and with rather monarchistic views, he was a lot more competent and intelligent than his predecessor. He strove to break out of the isolation of the movement by attempting a *rapprochement* with the Poles, Romanians and Serbs, with some success as far as the latter were concerned. The Serbs handed over to him huge consignments of Russian arms deposited with them during the 1914 war. He renamed the Volunteer Army the Russian Army, restoring its discipline and unified command, and court-martialed General Sidorin, commander of the army of the Don, and his chief of staff, General Keltchevsky, for irredentism and banished them. Yet he had scarcely any illusions about the likelihood of his enterprise succeeding and prudently paid attention to his rear, making every provision for a speedy evacuation of his entire army from the Crimea, if need be. A sharp customer, he also appreciated that economic and political measures were necessary if his national venture was to have even the merest prospect of success. To that end he announced to press representatives in April that he was "…working on measures that will allow him who works the land to secure the largest possible tract of land as his personal property. In the future the small peasant proprietor is to be the master of Russian agriculture; landowning on a large scale has had its day. Betterment of the material well-being of the workers and satisfaction of their professional needs represent one of our prime concerns."[2] Unlike Denikin, Wrangel also grasped that one should not pursue several quarries at once; he decided to make overtures to all who were fighting against the Bolsheviks with an eye to union with them. On May 13th, he issued the following secret order to all commanders of his units:

> "Should we take the offensive along the way towards achievement of our dearest goal — the eradication of communism — we may come into contact with Makhno's insurgent bands, Ukrainian troops [i.e., Petliura's troops] and all the other anti-communist units. In the struggle against the chief foe of Holy Russia — the communists — we are on the same path as all other Russians who aspire as we do honestly to

overthrow the gang of Bolshevik aggressors who have seized power through trickery.

I hereby order all commanders in touch with all of the above-mentioned groups to coordinate their actions with those of the troops belonging to said groups, with an eye to our basic mission: To topple communism and help the Russian people rebuild its great motherland."[3]

The ulterior motive in this is clear: Come what may, the intention was to make use of all anti-Bolshevik forces. Just as the Bolsheviks on their side promised as much and more, "once the war is finished," that is, so Wrangel proposed to "drive them out and then we shall see." The populace placed little credence in blandishments from either side and when unable to take up the fight itself for its own interests, remained, insofar as it was able, indifferent and passive in the face of these "power lovers' quarrels."

For his part, Makhno was not as yet *au fait* with these speculations; as soon as he was back on his feet, he personally led an implacable fight against the Chekists while simultaneously tackling the plunderers and the Red Army units sent to track him down. Also, he adopted an approach that varied, according to whether he was dealing with officials, Red Army commanders and political commissars (these being cut down immediately) or rank and file soldiers enlisted by force. For the benefit of the latter, the Makhnovists organized meetings setting out the motives behind their struggle, before inviting them either to join their ranks or to make their way home, as we can gauge from the following handbill:

"To the Comrades from the Red Army of the Front and Rearguard.

The Ukrainian people which is oppressed by your commanders and your commissars and sometimes directly by yourselves under the direction of those commanders and commissars, protests at such oppression; you were awaited as the toiling masses' liberators from the yoke of the packs of Denikinist executioners, but after your arrival in the Ukraine, the groans, weeping and cries of the poor sounded even louder. On every side there were executions, burning of peasant homes or even of whole villages: Everywhere plunder and violence.

The people are exhausted and cannot put up any longer with the arbitrary; they exhort you all while giving you notice: Are you going to pause before this nightmare and realize whom you are shooting, whom you are tossing into the Cheka's dungeons, with whom you are filling the prisons by obeying your commanders and commissars? Are they not your brothers, fathers, sons? Apparently so!

And you subject them to all this, without noticing how the bourgeoisie stands back and rejoices, how the officers and generals of the old regime[4] manipulate your freedom and your blindness, comfortably ensconced in their armchairs as they order you to oppress poor folk. And you, comrades, without a second thought, blindly carry out those orders. Has it escaped your attention that they have you persecute poor folk whom they dub counter-revolutionaries because of their protests against the dictatorship of Trotsky's gentlemen and the pack of communists in his entourage, a dictatorship exercised in the name of the authority of a party which is strangling the revolution?

Can it be that you cannot see that the Ukrainian muzhik will not bear that yoke and, in spite of worse repressions, that he straightens his bowed back destroying every obstacle and aims to see the task of emancipation through to its term? And it is his belief that there is among you, in the very ranks of the Red Army, a majority of his brothers, themselves peasants, who are oppressed as he is oppressed and who will ultimately understand his protestations and will march with him against the common foe: Equally against the Denikinist pack on the right as against the commissarocracy decked out in the people's name on the left.

Comrades, examine for yourself what the Cheka and the punitive detachments are doing in Russia and particularly in the Ukraine. And who abets them? You Red soldiers, you and only you. Can your heart remain insensible to the complaints and wailing of your brothers, your fathers, your mothers and your children? Are you so deceived by the spectral political freedoms they have promised you as to be prevented from ridding yourself of the commissar, that new master, so as to liberate the whole people in this way, in close concert with the workers and peasants, from every yoke and all oppression? Can you possibly be blind to those in your ranks who have at the price of your blood, your lives, hoisted themselves above you and seized power and the right to tyrannize the people so disgracefully? Does your heart not contract when you go into the villages and countryside at the direction of these oppressors to repress toilers who protest against the arbitrariness and oppression to which they are subjected by your leaders? We believe that you must come to your senses and realize that your shame is in remaining silent. That you will protest against the oppression and the yoke visited upon these poor folks. That you will not let your commanders and commissars torch villages and shoot peasants who rise up in defense of their rights. Let the peasants organize themselves as they see fit, and as for you, let you continue to wipe out the Denikinist pack and, along with them, the new master, the commissar.

Do not quit the front: Carry on the fight against the wearers of gold braid and exterminate your commissars where they stand. The revolutionary peasantry and the workers will in turn wipe out, behind the lines, the parasites about their necks who exploit them. The revolutionary peasantry and workers will not forget you, and the day will come when you all close ranks together and then let all the parasites and their accomplices watch out!

Remember, comrades, that the people have seen through the falsehood of the government that you support. The people are in revolt against it, and no army will be able to contain the open-eyed insurgent masses who are fighting for their complete emancipation. Join them; they will welcome you as brothers. Remember that among the insurgents there are your peasant and worker brothers, and if you should encounter them, do not take the initiative of a bloody clash.

Let the commanders and commissars march out themselves to do battle with the insurgents. Let them cover themselves in the blood of the workers and peasants, then all of the blame will fall on them, and they will pay dearly for it.

Down with the pack of gold braid wearers! Down with those who draw their inspiration from them, the autocratic commissars! Down with artificial laws and man's power over his fellow man!

Long live the union of all workers — Red soldiers and the insurgent peasant and worker. Death to all braid wearers! Death to the commissars and hangmen!

Long live the social revolution! Long live the authentically free regime of the soviets!

May 9, 1920

The Staff of the Insurgent Army of the Ukraine (Makhnovist)."5

꘠꘠꘠

The Bolshevik press regularly carried reports of Makhno's death as well as of the "final" liquidation of the remnants of Makhnovist detachments; all the same, their readership was dumbfounded in the long run at the continual reappearance of the Makhnovist phoenix. As for the Makhnovist prisoners, their fate was settled immediately; they were shot out of hand before the assembled Red troops, probably with the intention of deterring potential defectors.

In the spring of 1920, Admiral Kolchak's venture petered out, and the foreign expeditionary forces, as well as the Czech Legion, gradually took ship from Vladivostok. With every White front smashed, Lenin decided to concentrate his best troops against Poland as the first step in a Bolshevik crusade in Europe. The Polish military commander, General Pilsudski, anticipated invasion so he launched a preemptive strike in the Ukraine himself at the end of April. He quickly scored some successes and seized Kiev. On May 14th, the Red Army under Tukhachevsky attacked from the north and drove the Poles back some 100 kilometers, whereupon the Poles brought up their reserve army, seizing back the initiative, and their former positions. The situation remained like that up until the beginning of July 1920. It is worth noting that the Ukrainian nationalists who had been driven into Poland at the end of 1919 fought on the side of the Poles.

For their part, the Makhnovists mounted some large-scale operations; there were 4,000 insurgents split into two contingents — one of 500 cavalry, 1,000 infantry on 250 tatchankis and with eight cannon; and another of 700 insurgents, i.e., 200 infantry, four cannon and a large array of machine-guns. They pressed forward in a highly mobile way, mounting two extraordinary raids through the Red Army's lines. In the first they covered over 1,200 kilometers between May 20 and July 10, setting out from and returning to Gulyai-Polye through the provinces of Kharkov and Poltava in the north of the Ukraine. The second raid lasted a month, from July 10 to August 9, and this time was launched over a distance of 1,520 kilometers, through the very same regions. The outcome was impressive; 13,400 Red soldiers taken prisoner, 26,000–30,000 rendered *hors de combat*, 2,000 of whom were political and military officials who were executed. And the booty recovered was significant too: Five cannon complete with 2,300 shells, 93 machine-guns, 2,400,000 cartridges, 3,600 rifles, 25,000 military uniforms and greatcoats, the 13th Army's field hospital, the 46th Division's entire transport, as well as a ship and an airplane where were set on fire since they could not be put to use. And to this must be added the systematic destruction of bridges, railroad lines, and two armored trains.[6]

These large-scale raids were complemented by numerous commando raids against sundry nerve centers, towns or rail junctions which were sometimes attacked several days at a time, leading to panic in Red Army ranks. For instance, on June 21, 1920, a band of 140 Makhnovist horsemen launched a surprise attack on the garrison in Gulyai-Polye and carried off 24 cartloads of cartridges. The next day, another band of 200 cavalry and mounted infantry again attacked Gulyai-Polye with the support of six artillery pieces, routing a unit of 300 Red soldiers and capturing the 46th Division's transport in its entirety. On June 24, the Makhnovists again attacked Red units in the vicinity of Gulyai-Polye. Such harrying operations took place simultaneously in different locations, often with significant impact and made the whole region insecure as far as the Red Army was concerned.[7]

By this point the Makhnovist insurgent army consisted of a core of 3,000 to 4,000 partisans, divided up into 700–800 cavalry under Shchuss's command, 1,500–2,000 infantry mounted on tatchankis, a regiment of machine-gunners under the command of Tomas Kozhin, an artillery unit commanded by the indefatigable Vladimir Sharovsky, and Makhno's black guard of some 200 elite cavalry and swordsmen along with a few virtuoso machine-gunners. There were also a hundred medical tatchankis, a doctor, and a cultural section whose task it was to publish handbills, appeals and the movement's new mouthpiece, *The Voice of the Free Insurgent* from a mobile press. This section also, when the contingent halted, laid on entertainment, conferences and meetings. At these, there would be intense propaganda in favor of free soviets. All of the property and foodstuffs seized from the Chekists' and plundering agents' depots were distributed free of charge. Flour, sugar, cloth, wire, leather, iron, furniture, and even gramophones and pianos were distributed in this way to the population.[8]

Local insurgent bands sometimes arrived to bolster the core group, but normally they appeared independently so that by September and according to a Petliurist estimate, the Makhnovist army had been able to muster upwards of 35,000 men.[9] Let us conclude this examination of the manpower by noting that the seriously wounded were left behind under the protection of the populace.

Scrupulous about explaining to Red troops just what their struggle was about, the Makhnovists circulated appeals designed for their perusal:

"Comrade Red Soldiers!

Your commanders and your commissars deceive you by persuading you that we Makhnovists kill captured Red soldiers.

Comrades! Your chiefs have invented an unspeakable lie in order to have you slavishly protect the interests of the commissars lest you surrender to us Makhnovists and discover the truth about our worker and peasant Makhnovist movement.

Comrades, we are in revolt against the yoke of all oppressors. For three years now our blood has flowed on all fronts. We have driven off the Austro-German aggressors, we have crushed the Denikinist hangmen, we have fought Petliura, and now we are fighting against the rule of the commissars' power, against the Bolshevik Communist Party's dictatorship. It holds in its steely grip the whole life of the toiling people; the peasants and workers of the Ukraine groan beneath its yoke. In the same ruthless way we shall exterminate the Polish lords who come to stifle our revolution and deny us its gains.

We fight against all power and all enslavement, regardless of the quarter whence they come.

Our most sworn enemies are the big landowners and capitalists of every land, the Denikinist generals and officers, the Polish lords and the Bolshevik commissars. We chastise them all ruthlessly, executing them as enemies of the toiling people's revolution.

But you, comrade Red soldiers, we regard as our blood-brothers with whom we should like to wage, together, the fight for real emancipation, for a genuine soviet regime free of the oversight of parties or of any authorities at all.

Those Red soldiers whom we take prisoner we release immediately to go where they will, or else we welcome them into our ranks if they indicate any such desire. Already we have freed thousands of Red soldiers whom we had taken prisoner in countless engagements, and many captured Red soldiers are currently and selflessly fighting in our ranks. So do not believe, comrade Red soldiers, the tall tales of your commissars to the effect that Makhnovists kill Red soldiers. It is a sordid falsehood.

When they dispatch you against the Makhnovists, do not, comrade Red soldiers, stain your hands with brothers' blood. When the fighting begins, kill your commanders yourselves and without turning your arms against us, come over to our side. We will receive you as our very own brothers, and together we will create for the workers and peasants a free and equitable life, and together we will fight against all who attack and oppress the toiling people.

Long live the fraternal union of the Makhnovist revolutionary insurgents with the peasants and workers, Red soldiers!

June 1920
The Makhnovist Insurgents."[10]

⁂

Such active counter-propaganda on the Makhnovists' part sometimes brought spectacular results: The 522nd Red Regiment defected to them in its entirety, which fact Kubanin disguises by speaking of their capture, for it was not seemly to acknowledge such a dismal failure of Bolshevik indoctrination. Happily, we have here irrefutable proof in the shape of the appeal issued at the time by the Red soldiers of the 522nd Regiment themselves:

"Appeal!

On June 25, 1920, we, the Red soldiers of the 522nd regiment, defected without a shot fired and with all our equipment and arms to the Makhnovist insurgents! The communists have harassed us and ascribed our defection to the Makhnovist insurgents to a brainstorm and a tendency towards banditry — all of which is merely a squalid craven lie on the part of commissars who had hitherto used us as cannon fodder. During our two years' service with the Red Army, we reached the conclusion that the whole social regime of our lives relied wholly upon the rule of commissars and that in the last analysis it would lead us to a slavery without precedent in history.

Because they conduct an implacable fight against the wealthy and the lords; because they stand for free union and soviets among the workers and peasants, without the dictatorship of any party; because they fight so that the workshops, factories, and land may pass into the hands of the workers and peasants; because the Makhnovists fight for all these goals, we also find ourselves at their side because of these very same aspirations, we, yesterday's Red soldiers and today's free revolutionaries.

Comrade Red soldiers! Follow your comrades' example! We reckon that the spirit of revolutionary struggle for the self-determination of toilers has not yet died in you. We hope that the commissars have not yet extinguished once and for all your determination to fight all plunder and oppression.

Heed us and let not your brothers' blood be shed in vain! Stand firm! Be heroes and follow our example! Our fraternal embrace awaits you.

The Red soldiers of the 522nd Regiment, now Makhnovists."[11]

❧

Other Red soldiers deserted or defected to the Makhnovists, and this created increasing anxiety among the Bolshevik leadership. The Ukrainian Cheka complained of being unable to find any more competent (!) Chekists and volunteers to serve on requisition squads or even to work in local Soviet organs; even more characteristic was a report from the Donetz Cheka which acknowledged that to the populace the Makhnovists appeared as natural defenders against "commissars and communists."[12] So much so that the supreme head of the Cheka, Dzherzinsky, arrived to supervise the campaign against "Makhnovia" personally and drafted an address in a very special tone, aimed at the peasants of Ekaterinoslav province:

"[...] Baron Wrangel makes no secret of his being an enemy of the people. Makhno is a thousand times more criminal and cowardly. He styles himself defender of the workers and peasants. This upstart has the effrontery to charge the worker-peasant government of the Ukraine with failing to adequately defend the workers and peasants and to offer himself as their sole genuine defender [...] while he lives in luxury off his booty [!], he does not hesitate to have railway bridges blown up and supply trains to the Donetz miners sabotaged. It is true that decent, conscientious peasants have long since turned away from him, but there are still some who lack conscience and let themselves be misled by him. To these we declare that he has openly allied himself with counter-revolutionaries and pomieschikis. We say that, not as a hypothesis but as a proven fact, as shown by recently seized documents."

Dzherzinsky noted Makhno's liaisons with the Petliurists, which is to say, according to him, with the "Polish lords"; from this he deduced that "Makhno is an agent of Petliura and the Polish government." This allowed him to lump Makhno with Wrangel, Pilsudski and Petliura, thus making him a supporter of restoration of the "power of the accursed pomieschikis, tsarist generals and the hetman's Varta." This sinister, deadpan comic suffered from an all too visible surfeit of information and in this regard was well behind his party colleagues who were nothing of the sort. However, he did not shrink from closing his text with an incredible call for the "tracking down and extermination of the Makhnovists like savage beasts. All assistance to these bandits is to be regarded as the greatest crime against the revolution"; any found guilty of that would deserve the severest punishment by the "worker-peasant government." These "Makhnovist bandits must be deprived of all assistance in manpower and supplies. They must be driven from the peasant khatas. The village that allows any of its residents to collaborate with Makhno is to be *leveled*[13] and will incur the severest punishment measures." This latter appeal to people to turn informer was nonetheless followed up with a promise of clemency for repentant Makhnovists who "would go and expiate their *sin*[14] against the revolution on the Polish front."[15] All the usual police ploys were there, with just a touch of religious inquisition in "expiating sin." That would be worthy of any church father of a bygone age, were it not that Dzherzinsky was the son of a Polish squire, a convert some 20 years previously to the cause of social democracy — a man whose bloodthirsty fanaticism inspired the greatest fear even in his own party colleagues. After his death in 1926 following a stroke during an angry speech, Radek, one of the stars of the party, was to declare that Dzherzinsky had "died just in time. He was a methodical sort and would not have hesitated to redden his hands with our blood."[16] Unfortunately, "methodical types" of that sort were plentiful in the Cheka and had no hesitation in "tracking down and exterminating the Makhnovists like savage beasts" or in "leveling" Makhnovist villages.

The insurgents preferred to urge the Red soldiers, used as the doers of this dirty work, to reflect upon what it signified:

"Stop! Read! Reflect!
Comrade Red soldier! You have been sent by your commissar and commander to persecute Makhnovist insurgents. At the instigation of your leaders, you are going to bring peace-loving people to ruination, to search, arrest and kill folk whom you do not know personally but who will be pointed out to you as enemies of the people. They will tell you that Makhnovists are bandits and counter-revolutionaries.

Without consultation with you, they will tell you, will order you, and will send you like a slave subject to your officers, to search and destroy. Who? Why? To what end?

Think on it, comrade Red soldier! Think on it, peasants and workers as our Red soldier brethren. We have rebelled against enslavement and constraints, and we fight for a radiant better future. Our ultimate ideal is to arrive at a non-authoritarian community of toilers, free of parasites and commissar officials.

Our immediate goal is to install a free soviet regime without the power of the Bolsheviks, without the predominance of any party.

Because of that, the government of Bolshevik-communists dispatches punitive expeditionary corps against us. It hastens to reach a reconciliation with Denikin, with the Polish lords and other White Guard scum, the better to crush the popular movement of the revolutionary insurgents who have risen up against the yoke of all authority.

We do not fear the threats of the White-Red leaders. We shall return violence for violence.

When necessary, we put any Red Army division to fight at top speed merely by applying some slight pressure; for we are free revolutionary insurgents, and the cause we defend is a just cause.

Comrades! Think, whom are you with and whom against?

Do not be a slave, be a man!

June 1920.

The Makhnovist Insurgents."[17]

This appeal did not address itself to the base instinct as Dzherzinsky did but rather to the genuine revolutionary consciousness of the individual Red soldier who had been swept willy-nilly into a fratricidal combat.

During this period of raids, in June–July 1920, a Soviet of Revolutionary Insurgents of the Ukraine (Makhnovists) saw the light of day; it was made up of seven members, elected by the partisans. This was the leadership body of the movement, and its decisions had at all times to seek endorsement from the rank and file. Essentially, it had oversight of three branches of the insurgent army: The branch in charge of "military affairs and operations, the branch in charge of organization and control, and finally the educational and cultural branch."[18]

The fight against the Bolsheviks was conducted in the name of the Third Revolution, namely the one that came after the first one (directed against tsarism) and after the second (whose target was Kerensky's bourgeois revolution) and which was now targeting the Bolshevik autocracy and party dictatorship. Henceforth, this was to be the banner that was to rally all revolutionary supporters of free soviets.

This dogged and, above all, successful struggle against the Red Army aroused Wrangel's attention. The Baron-General had himself scored some notable successes with the seizure of the northern Tavrida in June 1920; he had, in particular, literally "pulverized" the 30,000 men of Zhloba's army corps — the very same Zhloba who had been so at ease in repressing the unarmed populace.

An initial emissary, a captain, reached Makhno near Mariupol on July 9th and passed on a message bearing the signature of General Shatilov, Wrangel's chief of staff. It proposed that "Ataman Makhno" cooperate in the fight against the communists and "fight them even more energetically, ravaging behind their lines and destroying their transport so as to crush Trotsky's army once and for all." Wrangel's high command proposed, in pursuit of this goal, "to supply material, the requisite munitions and send him specialists."[19] Kubanin notes this proposition, stating that "the proof of the pudding was in the eating" and noting that the Whites based this military cooperation on a remarkable evolution in their political and economic principles which they strove to effect in territories occupied by them, while acknowledging their past errors:

"Land was transferred to the peasants without buy-back from former landlords and through the regional peasant congresses' good offices, all local self-management agencies were afforded the widest democratic autonomy, and regions of specific ethnic culture were declared autonomous of Russia, while remaining federated with her." [20]

The Makhnovists had no truck with military advice, nor with laws and decrees running their lives as they had never looked to anyone but themselves for resolution of their own affairs. Outraged, they had the unfortunate emissary shot out of hand. A little later, a second envoy from Wrangel, a colonel this time, arrived among them to repeat the offer of collaboration between their two camps. He was hanged with a placard reading: "No agreement between Makhno and White Guards has been or ever will be feasible, and all White emissaries will share this one's fate."[21] Whether because this had not been reported to him, or deliberately, Wrangel went on conducting an intensive campaign of misrepresentation, inside Russia as well as abroad, concerning his alleged alliance with the Makhnovist insurgents and the Ukrainian peasantry. Truth to tell, he was greatly abetted by the floods of calumnies gushing forth from the Bolshevik press.

For their part the Bolsheviks' leaders were conspiring at several levels; incapable of bringing the insurgents to heel, they resorted to more subterranean methods. Some anarchists (or individuals reputed to be such) and common criminals, ready to tackle anything if the price was right, infiltrated Ukrainian libertarian organizations and then, having picked out the most active militants, lured them into the clutches of the Cheka. Brandishing the threat of execution, the Cheka then did its best to force them to work for it. One of the latter, Fedya Glouschenko, a member of the insurgent movement's intelligence branch, was thus commissioned by the Kharkov Cheka to assassinate Makhno. Joining Makhno on June 20th, he repented at the last minute and aborted the assassination plan. Despite his having reneged, Glouschenko was shot the next day, along with a Chekist killer, on the grounds that "a revolutionary may not, no matter what the reasons, serve in the secret police," as was announced by the Soviet of the Revolutionary Insurgents (Makhnovists) in a tract disclosing the details of the whole affair.[22] That attempt having foundered, the Bolsheviks resorted to another "destabilization" plan; they "remotely controlled" a member of a minority in the Social Revolutionary party[23] into persuading insurgents to interrupt their struggle against the Bolsheviks and instead to join forces with them against Wrangel, who was portrayed as the greatest danger, as the minutes of the June 23, 1920 meeting between this curious delegate and the insurgents' soviet testifies:

"**Comrade Mikh** (reporting on behalf of the [minority] Social Revolutionary Party of Alexandrovsk) states that, in view of the Whites' terrifying offensive, it is crucial that all revolutionary forces unite in order to make a concerted effort to halt the Whites' progress. The [minority] Left Social Revolutionary party's committee has delegated him to Makhno, with the agreement of the Bolsheviks who suggested that he act as a go-between in arriving at a general compact against the Whites. He calls upon the assembly to cease all conflict with the Bolsheviks until such time as the enemy has been beaten. All political differences and hostilities against the Red Army must cease until victory is assured against Wrangel and the Poles, the quarter masters of a monstrous counter-revolution. In his view, a libertarian society is not practicable in the short term, and he proposes that support be given to the idea of a workers' power. He points out the differences of opinion to be found existing within the Bolshevik party and the Social Revolutionary party.

Comrade Polevoy: Responds directly and clearly to him regarding his propaganda in favor of a worker power. He states that we Makhnovists have experienced all sorts of authorities on our backs and will not let ourselves be snared by a change in the name of the authority. The nature of all authority — whether it be Wrangel or the Bolsheviks — is essentially identical. He puts two questions to comrade Mikh: 1) Is he delegated solely by his organization, or is he also delegated by the Bolsheviks who, on several grounds, are unable to send their own delegates? 2) Is he aware that the Bolsheviks who do not aim to annihilate Wrangel 'alone,' have just sent us a special delegation? One that was armed and was supposed to assassinate comrade Makhno, is he aware of that?

Comrade Mikh: Apologizes for his propaganda on behalf of a workers' power. His organization has decided to have no truck with the unlawful communists [to wit, the Cheka] who harm their party's cause. His present mission has the full endorsement of the Bolsheviks; he gives assurances that [our] [Makhnovist] delegation, sent to a general assembly involving all organizations in Alexandrovsk, would have every necessary assurance from the Bolsheviks relative to its security.

Comrade Viktor Popov: By whom and to what end comrade Mikh has been sent, I do not know. But on one point only there can be no doubt; thus far the Bolsheviks have set no traps, without quite furnishing proof of their good faith, when they have sought to use us for their purposes. Moreover, can we have anything at all in common with communists who dispatch punitive detachments into our villages and savagely gun down our parents? Of course we are going to fight Wrangel and, if need be, we will take them all on simultaneously. Alliance with the Bolsheviks would do great prejudice to the cause of revolution.

Comrade Makhno: I insist that the greatest attention be paid to comrade Mikh's mission. It has been wholly Bolshevik inspired and without question they have set him very specific objectives.

Comrade Kurilenko: Proposes that a clear and unequivocal answer by given to the delegation [i.e., to the Social Revolutionary Mikh — A.S.]. Already there are rumors circulating in the region regarding the arrival of a Bolshevik delegation, which may have serious consequences for our fronts' combat capabilities.

Comrade Belash: In spite of the talks with Bolsheviks, proposed that our fight against them be carried on.

Comrade Popov: Remember how the Bolsheviks presented an amiable face whenever they were in dire straits and what blackguards they turned into again once they had regained power. He offers to look thoroughly into the proposition and to devise a speedy answer to it.

Comrade Taranovksy: The soviet should give an answer to the Social Revolutionary party's request.

Comrade Marchenko: Comes out against any alliance with the Bolsheviks who merely seek to use us.

Comrades Dermendzhi, Belash, and Ogarkin are of the same opinion.

Comrade Budanov: We shall provide a written reply wherein we shall declare that as revolutionaries we are going to fight Wrangel but wholly independently."[24]

❧

The object of the exercise was plain; either way the Bolsheviks would come off best. In the event of a refusal, Makhnovists were to be depicted as the objective allies of the Whites and adversaries of a "sacred" revolutionary unity in the face of the reaction. In the event of an acceptance and since the proposal had not emanated directly from the Leninist authorities, the insurgents would then be presented as having sued for it, acknowledging the Bolsheviks as the rallying-point for revolutionary forces and thus as the workers' legitimate defenders. In any event, availing of the formal services of a "satellite" organization, they retained a free hand to pursue their war of extermination against insurgents. But the latter instantly grasped what this gambit was about; even so, it did manage to sow confusion in the minds of some.

Notes to Chapter 21: Between Whites and Reds

1. Wrangel, op. cit. p. 155.

2. Ibid, p. 173.

3. *The Civil War in the Ukraine*, op. cit. Tome III, pp. 115–116.

4. And now serving the Red Army [A.S.].

5. International Institute for Social History, Amsterdam, op. cit.

6. *Volnyi povstanyets* (The Free Insurgent), the Makhnovist organ, No. 44, quoted by D. Lebeds, *The Consequences and Lessons of Three Years of the Anarcho-Makhnovschina*, Kharkov, 1923, pp. 26–27.

7. Kubanin, op. cit. p. 152.

8. V. V. Rudnev, *The Makhnovschina* (in Russian), Kharkov, 1928, p. 72.

9. *The Civil War in the Ukraine*, op. cit. Tome III, p. 480.

10. International Institute for Social History, Amsterdam, op. cit.

11. A tract published in the Russian libertarian review *Volna* (The Wave) appearing in the United States, 1920–1924, Detroit, December 1921, No. 24, pp. 15–16.

12. For the revolution's defense. *On the History of the Pan-Ukrainian Cheka, 1917–1922*, an anthology of documents and materials, Kiev, 1971, p. 158.

13. and 14. The emphasis is ours.

15. *On the History of the Pan-Ukrainian Cheka, 1917–1922*, op. cit. p. 158.

16. G. Haupt and J-.J. Marie, *Les Bolchéviks par eux-mêmes*, Paris, 1969, pp. 304–306.

17. International Institute for Social History, Amsterdam, op. cit.

18. Arshinov, op. cit. p. 166.

19. Ibid, p. 168.

20. Kubanin, op. cit. p. 152.

21. Ibid, p. 151.

22. Arshinov, op. cit. pp. 163–164.

23. The Left Social Revolutionaries tendency which collaborated with the Bolsheviks [A.S.].

24. *Volna*, op. cit. pp. 16–17.

22. The Second Alliance with the Red Army

In the summer of 1920 the main focus of the Moscow leadership's attention was the position on the Polish front. On July 4, having marshaled 600,000 men — a third of them in the front line — the Red Army commander in chief on that front, Tukhachevsky, launched a fresh and powerful offensive from Russia. Attacked on their left flank, the Polish troops who had ventured into the Ukraine and far from their bases, were forced to effect a spectacular, 600 kilometer withdrawal which brought them to the banks of the Vistula within 40 days. The chancelleries of Europe became alarmed, for the professed aim of this thrust was to "export the Bolshevik revolution" to the old world. So much so that at the end of July, France dispatched a military mission headed by General Weygand, Foch's chief of staff to lend a hand to the Poles. (The membership of this mission included a certain Captain De Gaulle). Warsaw prepared for its own "battle of the Marne." The Red Army chiefs were confident of the success of their undertaking and comforted by their previous victories over Kolchak and Denikin. However, they had not properly analyzed the roots of those successes: in particular, they had neglected to take account of the decisive contribution made by Greens and local partisans, as well as of the loss of stomach for the fight on the part of the Cossacks and simple soldiery of the White armies. The Poles were a quite different kettle of fish: their country had been under the heel of Russian tsarism for over a century and a half; as far as the populace was concerned, the Red Army and the Bolsheviks were the worthy successors of tsarist expansionism and were perceived as invaders not as the liberators the Leninists, blinkered by their formal proletarian dialectic, imagined themselves to be. Quite the contrary: Poland's working people lined up with their national socialist leaders. This nationalistic factor played a crucial role.

Inferior in numbers and indeed militarily, dressed and armed in makeshift fashion, but galvanized by extraordinary patriotic zeal, 100,000 Poles with Pilsudski at their head embarked on August 16 upon a fantastic push: they drove the invaders right back and in less than 6 days covered 200 kilometers, smashing every Red division in their path. Under this tremendous battering the Red Army disintegrated, with its units fleeing in unbelievable disarray: some were decimated or wiped out, others surrendered in their tens of thousands while still others were forced to seek refuge in eastern Poland where they were relieved of their weaponry and interned. It was the greatest military disaster of these war years: 250,000 Red soldiers taken prisoner and 100,000 of those interned in Poland. The panicking Kremlin authorities scurried to open peace talks with Warsaw, regardless of conditions.

Meanwhile, Wrangel had dispatched Piotr Struve — the man who had introduced Marxism into Russia and who was now a disenchanted liberal — to Paris to sue for French backing, or, failing that, support from the British. Indeed, in view of the collapse of Kolchak and Denikin whom they had assisted on a huge scale, the British prime minister, Lloyd George, saw fit to wash his hands of the whole business, the consideration at the back of his mind assuredly being preservation of Britain's Asian possessions — India included — from possible revolutionary contagion. As for the French, what prompted them to help Wrangel was, first of all the desire to support those who had never recognized the "shameful" treaty of Brest-Litovsk and also the urge to ease pressures on the warring Poles as far as possible. The French believed themselves bound to the Poles by long-standing affinities and also by the prospect of being able to lock their sworn enemy — Germany — in a Vice of which Poland would be the other pincer. As for Struve, in a letter to prime minister Millerand on June 20, 1920, he spelled out General Wrangel's underlying motives:

"[Wrangel] is far from believing that the reestablishment of order and liberty in Russia can be secured through a merely military effort. He appreciates the necessity of a protracted pacification campaign designed above all to meet the needs of the peasants who account for the vast majority of the Russian people. That population seeks neither restoration of the old order of things, nor communist tyranny. To cater for the interests of the peasant population, to cleanse the moral life of the country, to rebuild its economic life, to unite all orderly factors, these are the goals that the commander in chief of the armed forces of Southern Russia has set himself, and which should, he reckons, lift Russia out of the condition of anarchy into which she has been plunged by the communist régime which has turned her into a test-bed for monstrous social experiments without precedent in history."[1]

Having thus received assurances regarding the Baron-General's "democratic" intent, the French government afforded de facto recognition on August 10 to the government which he had formed. This was help of a quite platonic sort, but it was useful, for it allowed Wrangel to recover the arms stocks stored in Romania and in countries under Allied influence.

Stimulated by this support, Wrangel launched a sweeping offensive along the left bank of the Dniepr that August. Despite heavy losses — every one of the officers commanding battalions and companies of the Whites' First Army Corps was rendered hors de combat — Wrangel's troops pushed the 13th Red Army back on to the right bank of the Dniepr and drove the front back as far as the Alexandrovsk-Berdyansk line. For the Reds, this was "Black August," as all their counter-offensives were smashed one by one. However, the balance of numbers was still tilted in their favor: they lined up 250,000 men, a third of them in the front line, against 125,000 Whites of whom 25,000–30,000 were in the front line. The latter made up for numerical inferiority with the courage of their fighting men and above all with the inspired deployment of some 25 aircraft, 100 tanks and the armored trains at their disposal. Their greatest problem was the question of reserves: they were desperately short of the manpower needed if they were to develop their offensive further. True, there were the thousands of captured Red troops and officers — upwards of 30,000 captured during August — who voluntarily enlisted in their ranks until, towards the end, they accounted for nearly 90 percent of the Whites' manpower[2]. But whereas they fought their former colleagues in arms with a good heart, these defectors were not sufficiently battle-hardened nor politically reliable enough in the long term, this despite Wrangel's recourse to a certain equivocation about his campaign's ultimate objectives and his adoption of a language with "democratic" overtones. Thus on July 5 in an interview with the newspaper *Velikaya Rossiya* (Great Russia) he declared:

"Why we fight.

To that question, General Wrangel declared, there can be but one answer: **we fight for freedom**. On the other side of the front, to the north, arbitrariness, oppression and slavery prevail. One may entertain the most diverse notions as to the suitability of this or that system: one may be a Republican, a Radical, a Socialist, a Marxist even — and yet recognize that the Soviet republic is merely the expression of an unspeakable, sinister despotism which is eating away at Russia and indeed its self-styled ruling class — the proletariat which is oppressed just like the rest of the population. By now this an open secret to Europe. The veil has been snatched away from soviet Russia. It is in Moscow that the reaction has its nest. It is there that tyrants who treat the people like livestock reside. As for ourselves, one would have to be blind or malicious to call us reactionaries. We are fighting to release our people from a servitude the like of which even the darkest days of their history knew not. For a long time there has been no understanding in Europe — though it seems that such understanding has begun to develop — of what we so clearly appreciate: the universal significance of our domestic struggle."[3]

Such soothing words and the socio-economic reforms introduced in the occupied territories came too late, however. The impression prevailing among the laboring population was that, in spite of everything, the Whites would sooner or later bring back the old order, at any rate in the Ukraine, for Wrangel's posturing and campaign would certainly have enjoyed greater success in Russia where the populace had not sampled the executions of the Denikinist occupation. This psycho-social-political factor is an essential one but was quite redundant after 1919, since when sides had been chosen once and for all.

❦

Wrangel's strategic plan consisted of attempting to develop his offensive in two directions: in the West, towards Poland, so as to ease the pressure from the Red Army — this at the beginning of August — and reach the 45,000 men of the Third Russian army of General Bredov in internment in Poland: and in the East, to reach the Don territory to join up with remnants of the Cossack armies of the Caucasus who were fighting on against the Bolsheviks. He also made provision for disembarkation in the Kuban of a 5000-strong Cossack contingent commanded by General Ulagai. Mounted at the start of August, this landing at first took the enemy unawares: Ulagai met with success after success as he marched towards Ekaterinodar, but made the mistake of dallying somewhat along the way, affording the Red Army time to regroup its forces and halt his offensive. Three weeks later Ulagai boarded ship again for the Crimea along with his reinforced army of 10,000, which had grown to that size despite the heavy losses sustained. On the other hand, the thrust eastwards was making headway and by September the Whites had reached Ekaterinoslav, Mariupol and the borders of the Don.

❦

White propaganda about peasant support and regarding their alleged alliance with Makhno was continually taken up by the Bolshevik press. This crossfire of misrepresentation eventually led to belief that this was indeed the case: some fell into the trap, including some insurgent detachments cut off in the region under occupation by Wrangel. Some of these did indeed join the White Army and formed a division bearing the Batko Makhno name, curiously flying a black flag bearing the Makhnovist device: "With the oppressed, always against the oppressors!" — alongside Wrangel's "For Russia one and indivisible!"

The Makhnovists tried to give the lie to this rumored alliance by going off to fight the Whites, but every time they tried to move up to the front, they were attacked from behind by Red troops. Also, they were aware of the rout inflicted on the Reds by the Poles and believed a complete collapse of the Red front against Wrangel to be imminent, and were induced to wonder about a suspension of hostilities with Moscow. A bitter argument raged inside the movement's Soviet of Revolutionary Insurgents; a narrow majority emerged in favor of a military alliance with Moscow. According to Kubanin, Kurilenko and Belash were for this, while Viktor Popov and Semyon Karetnik were against and Makhno was torn both ways. A general assembly of insurgents was called and after lengthy deliberations came out in favor of a compact. Telegrams to this effect were sent off to the Kremlin. Not that the fighting ceased, though; on August 24 and 25 there was a serious clash with the Red Army: early in September, two Red regiments of Don Cossacks were routed: the Makhnovists then captured the town of Starobelsk, north of Ekaterinoslav and not far from Kharkov. There they seized four machine guns, 40,000 cartridges, 180 horses and dispatched home some 1000 deserters who had been "confined to barracks" by the Red Army.[4]

One piquant detail is that according to an article in the Moscow *Izvestia* in 1962, the Makhnovists were allegedly indirectly responsible for the death of the journalist John Reed, the Victor Serge of America. On the return trip from Baku where he had attended an oriental congress of sympathizers with the Communist International, he was forced to fire on insurgents who attacked his train. After "the bandits had fled, he greedily drank water from a spring near an embankment [and most likely polluted], being shaken and parched. Upon arrival in Moscow, John Reed was stricken by a severe bout of typhoid fever and died on October 17."[5]

✻✻✻

Having initially feigned lack of interest in talks between the Makhnovists and its emissaries, Moscow now determined to intervene directly and on September 20 selected as plenipotentiary the one-time seminarian V. Ivanov who had embraced the new Leninist doctrine.

The military leaders were not yet au fait with the volte-face of their political "head," for the commander of the Ukrainian front, Sergei Kamenev, an ex-colonel of the tsarist army's staff who had transferred his loyalty to the new authorities, ordered his troops on September 21 to "liquidate Makhno's bands once and for all." That same day, a secret political directive from N. Gorbunov, chairman of the 13th Army's revolutionary soviet explained that:

> "... victory over Wrangel will free Red Army units presently operating in the south, for deployment in the speedy and complete eradication of the banditry of the Makhnovschina and other groups, and will install a solid revolutionary order throughout the whole Ukraine. Banditry and the Makhnovschina are extensions of the civil war and are deliberately organized by Wrangel's White Guards. Let but Wrangel vanish and Makhno will vanish along with him."[6]

For the time being such bellicose intent was put on the back burner by the political leadership. The Ukrainian Communist Party's politburo meeting on September 29, 1920 with Rakovsky, Kossior, Chubar, Ivanov, Drobnis, Yakovlev, Teplevsky and Blakitny in attendance, decided to direct the party's clandestine organization in the Wrangel-occupied zone to assist the Makhnovists while centering its intention on the strengthening among these Makhnovists of discipline and the spirit of revolutionary unity: to bring Red units into contact with the Makhnovists in operational terms if the need arose, without seeking to amalgamate with them: and finally not to oppose the release of anarchists and Makhnovists from Cheka custody.

The pact was concluded on September 30: Frunze, the new commander of the Southern front, formalized it on October 2, announcing that a cessation of hostilities had been decided at the request of the Makhnovist army, on the basis of its acknowledgment of Soviet power and of its subordination to the Red high command, whilst retaining its own internal organization.[7]

A Makhnovist delegation of Kurilenko and Popov journeyed to Kharkov to thrash out the fine print of the clauses of the agreement. This was completed, not without problems, towards the middle of October and published shortly afterwards in the Soviet press in two parts, the military and the political, with the overall implications being thus obscured from the view of the readership. This agreement was widely reproduced in Soviet works as well as by Arshinov: so, we shall quote only the essential passages:

"**I. Political Part.**

1. Immediate release and cessation of all future persecution in the territories of the Soviet Republics of all Makhnovists and anarchists, excluding those who might wage armed struggle against the soviet government.

2. Complete freedom of agitation and propaganda, both oral and written, of their ideas and conceptions for the Makhnovists and anarchists, exclusive of calls for the overthrow of the soviet government and with military censorship being observed. For their publications, the anarchists and Makhnovists, as revolutionary organizations recognized by the soviet authorities, may use the whole technical apparatus of the soviet state, while submitting to the regulations on the publishing technique.

3. Free participation in elections to the soviet, with Makhnovists and anarchists being entitled to run for election and freedom of participation in the preparations for the convening of the forthcoming Fifth Pan-Ukrainian congress of soviets due to take place in December of this year.

By order of the soviet government of the Ukraine Ya. Yakovlev. Plenipotentiaries of the soviet and command of the insurgent revolutionary army of the Ukraine (Makhnovist): Kurilenko, Popov.

II. Military Part.

1. The revolutionary insurgent army of Makhnovists becomes part of the composition of the armed forces of the Republic: as a partisan army it is subject in operational matters to the supreme command of the Red Army and retains its internal structure, free of the intrusion of the foundations and principles of the Red Army's regular units.

2. The Makhnovists' insurgent revolutionary army, in moving through soviet territory in the direction of the front and across fronts, under-

takes not to accept into its ranks any Red Army unit or any deserter from the latter [...]"8

⁂

Other, additional points concerned the obligation upon the insurgents to brief all of their supporters about this agreement so as to secure cessation of all actions hostile to soviet authorities: finally, the insurgents' families were awarded the same rights as those of Red Army troops.

This second part bore the signatures of the commander in chief of the southern front, Frunze, of the members of the front's revolutionary soviet, Bela Kun and Gusev, and of the Makhnovist plenipotentiaries themselves.

Point Four of the political part was, for the moment, left in suspension, for it related to the unhindered organization, in territories controlled by the Makhnovist army, of economic and political self-managerial agencies. While autonomous, these were to liaise with the organs of the soviet republic.

Kubanin assesses this agreement as "crucial for both sides. The regime of free Soviets could not [in his view] but be wholly unacceptable to the dictatorship of the proletariat. Thus, the accord could function only as long as a common enemy existed."9

In a report on the domestic and foreign situation which came to light only after publication in 1959, Lenin declared on October 9, 1920, that, "according to comrade Trotsky, the Makhno question has been very seriously discussed in military circles and it has emerged that there were only advantages to be expected of it. This can be explained by the fact that the elements grouped around Makhno have already sampled the Wrangel regime and what it has to offer does not satisfy them. By concluding an agreement with Makhno, we have secured a guarantee that he would not march against us."10

This declaration fairly encapsulates the Bolshevik's intention of "neutralizing" the threat that Makhno posed behind their lines, especially as, after 9 months of all-out warfare against him and despite communiqués regularly announcing its "liquidation" (actual or in prospect), the Makhnovist movement, which was still strong and active, was able, according to Yakovlev's estimates, to field a core detachment of between 10,000 and 12,000 partisans. Also, since the turn taken by the war on the Polish front, where they had been so sure of victory, the Bolsheviks no longer underestimated Wrangel's offensive: thus back-up from insurgents who were familiar with the region and had already been broken in to the fight against the Whites was very precious to them. They knew too that this agreement was going to reconcile the local populace to them and that this would have a knock-on effect upon Red Army morale which had plummeted since the Warsaw disaster. They had everything to gain from this very fortuitous windfall and agreed to nearly all the Makhnovists' conditions, granting an amnesty for past acts of war and freeing imprisoned insurgents and anarchists. At the instigation of the Makhnovists, they went so far as to carry in their newspapers a scathing refutation of all the calumnies which they themselves had been peddling up until then:

"Communiqué from the People's Commissariat for Military Affairs of the soviet republic of Russia, on the conclusion of a politico-military compact with Makhno. October 20, 1920.

As we know, the French press has often spoken of an alliance between Wrangel and Makhno. The soviet press in its turn has also published documents testifying to a formal alliance between Makhno and Wrangel. This information has now been shown to be false. Without any doubt, Makhno did, objectively, abet Wrangel and the Poles by fighting the Red Army simultaneously with them. But there was never any formal alliance between them. All of the documents recording that had been forged by Wrangel. A certain bandit from the Crimea, going under the name of Ataman Volodin, operated under orders from the White command as if he were an Ataman subordinate to Makhno, but in fact had no connections with him. This whole campaign of misrepresentation was mounted with the intention of misleading Makhno's possible protectors, the French and other foreign imperialists.

Some weeks ago, Wrangel made a genuine attempt to reach an alliance with Makhno and sent him two emissaries. As the delegates from the Red Army of the southern front were able to confirm, the Makhnovists not only did not enter into negotiations with Wrangel's agents, but had them hanged publicly a short time after their arrival at their headquarters. It was precisely this — Wrangel's attempt to court them — that showed the Makhnovists how perilous it was to fight against the soviet authorities. Shortly after, they approached the command of the southern front [with a proposal] to wage a common struggle against Wrangel. This proposal was accepted on the basis of certain conditions.

At present, the Makhnovist detachment is performing its military assignment under the immediate direction of comrade Frunze, commander of the southern front."[11]

❧❀❧

What could have brought the Makhnovists to this, with the image of the massacres and destruction carried out by the Red Army and Chekists still fresh in their memories? Hundreds, if not thousands of their colleagues had perished either in the fighting or as a result of the repression: for the most part, captured Makhnovists had been executed by the Reds: they were well aware, too, that Moscow's ambition was simply to wipe them out. In their mouthpiece *The Road to Freedom* they wrote around this time that the "Bolshevik-communist counter-revolutionaries are, objectively, a greater danger than Wrangel."[12] Furthermore, they had already had the experiences of June 1919 and January 1920, when the Red Army had declared them outlaws, disarmed some of their units and shot a number of their colleagues.

One may wonder to what extent the ploy of June 23, 1920, with the pseudo-delegate from the soviet republic as go-between, come to admonish the insurgents about their fight against the Red Army and to exhort them to join forces against Wrangel, could have inspired a belief that there were differences of opinion inside the Communist Party regarding them. In their newspaper, they scrutinized the "diplomatic" actions of the Social Revolutionaries, preceded by "talks between representatives of these latter and those of the so-called soviet power, in the shape of Zatonsky [a Ukrainian Bolshevik leader — A.S.] as well as with members of the Bolshevik-Communist Party's central committee"[13]. From this they deduced that the latter would never have allowed anybody to conduct negotiations with them unless the Communist Party had been directly involved itself." In conclusion, the insurgents stated that they stood ready to come to an accommodation "with all who place the interests of the revolution above all else. If the Communist Party's desire to reach agreement with us is this time quite sincere, in the name of the interests of the revolution, we shall meet them provided we are given serious assurances."[14] Thus, contrary to what soviet historians say, the ones who sued were not the insurgents: these in fact had only acceded to formal overtures from the Bolsheviks.

Arshinov subsequently accounted for this pact by arguing that even if the Bolsheviks were enemies of the toilers, they nonetheless had great masses of the toilers on their side:

"The communists' dictatorship is quite as hostile to labor's freedom as that of Wrangel. However, the difference between them consisted of the fact that alongside the former stood the masses who believed in the revolution. It is true that the communists cynically misled these masses and exploited the revolutionary enthusiasm of the toilers for the advantage of their own power. But the masses who opposed Wrangel believed in revolution and that counted for a lot."[15]

There are also several other possible explanations for this "unnatural" agreement. The Makhnovists must have been misinformed as to the true situation on the Polish front and the real threat posed by Wrangel. Their sources of information were quite limited: Bolshevik newspapers, the local population and the alarmists statements of the SR "delegates." They should not, for instance, have been abreast of the well-advanced negotiations that the Bolsheviks were conducting with the Poles, in the wake of which a temporary peace had been signed at Riga on October 1. Something about which the Bolshevik leaders were unable to crow due, on the one hand to the requirements of secret diplomacy and above all to the punishing conditions imposed by the Poles on the other: Lenin justified these concessions as "necessary to induce the Polish political parties and their allies to understand [his] bona fides, and to realize [that he] did not seek war."[16]

For the same reason, the Makhnovists overstated the drama of the situation in the southern Ukraine just a little: they should not have known about the failure of the disembarkation of Ulagai's contingent in the Kuban and they probably thought that the Red Army could not stand up effectively to Wrangel, like the previous year against Denikin. This time, they were convinced that it might be a lot more serious and that with the Bolsheviks collapsing those meager revolutionary gains not yet extinguished would be extinguished beyond all recovery by Wrangel. They were also greatly concerned with getting back to their home ground which was presently under occupation by the Whites, with resting up and having their wounded tended, and then with having the Red Army restock them with arms and munitions. Another far from negligible factor which may have had a part in what they did was the enormous campaign of misrepresentation jointly waged by Moscow and Wrangel concerning an alleged alliance between Wrangel and them. That rumor had not been without impact upon the morale of many isolated insurgent groups: it called seriously into question the ideal on whose behalf the insurgent army was fighting, and played into the hands of the reaction in Russia and internationally.

It is also certain that the Makhnovists hoped to win over a lot of Red troops to their way of thinking as had happened several times, by demonstrating their absolute fidelity to the revolutionary cause. The item in the agreement relating to possible deserters or Red Army soldiers desirous of joining the Makhnovists and whom the latter undertook to send back to their Red Army units, was illustrative of the scale and substance of this phenomenon. As they saw it too, showing themselves to all and sundry as the best defenders of the social and political gains of the populace would also forestall any backlash against them by the Bolsheviks in that their loyalty would have been thoroughly acknowledged. If need be, they were also probably counting upon being strong enough to successfully resist the Red Army militarily, just as they had done over the previous months. All of these considerations together prompted their decision. An editorial by Makhno in the movement's mouthpiece *The Road to Freedom* of October 13, 1920 spelled out the limits of the government:

> "Military hostilities between the Makhnovist revolutionary insurgents and the Red Army have ceased. Misunderstandings, vagueness and inaccuracies have grown up around this truce: it is said that Makhno has repented of his anti-Bolshevik acts, that he has recognized the soviet authorities, etc. How are we to understand, what construction are we to place upon this peace agreement? What is very clear already is that no intercourse of ideas, and no collaboration with the soviet authorities and no formal recognition of these has been or can

be possible. We have always been irreconcilable enemies, at the level of ideas, of the party of the Bolshevik-communists. We have never acknowledged any authorities and in the present instance we cannot acknowledge the soviet authorities. So again we remind and yet again we emphasize that, whether deliberately or through misapprehension, there must be no confusion of military intercourse in the wake of the danger threatening the revolution with any crossing-over, 'fusion' or recognition of the soviet authorities, which cannot have been and cannot ever be the case."[17]

In objective, historical terms, this agreement might have looked favorable to the Makhnovists, for it blatantly enshrined the existence of their movement: they dealt as equals: even if they were integrated into the Red Army and regarded as answerable to the soviet republic of the Ukraine, they nonetheless retained a certain autonomy. This was an unprecedented agreement and one never repeated in the whole history of the Leninist regime from its origins up to our own day. That the Bolsheviks should have conceded such conditions is ample proof of how badly they needed the Makhnovists, as well as the relationship which the latter had been able to force on them. It goes without saying that it was also a fundamental concession on the Makhnovists' part for, despite all their explanations, by this accord they were acknowledging the indubitable legitimacy of the soviet government and its Red Army. Let us say, in conclusion, that, like many members of the Bolshevik party itself, or of the Red Army, the insurgents were gambling that, once the White counter-revolution had been swept completely from the national stage, the Bolsheviks would be obliged to honor a measure of democracy and tolerate the rights of all who would have fought for the revolution, albeit not wholly sharing their own views. In a subsequent piece of writing, Makhno was to mention that this had been a "grave error."[18]

One initial and not negligible outcome was the release of Makhnovists held in Chekist jails: Piotr Gavrilenko, a gifted insurgent, Alexei Chubenko, the man behind the insurgent army's ethos, and Voline, the former chairman of the Military Revolutionary Soviet in 1919. Another positive result was that the Makhnovist movement wounded received treatment from the Red Army's medical corps: Makhno in particular, whose ankle had been torn by a dum-dum bullet, was entitled to the care of the finest physicians and surgeons sent by Moscow.

Bizarrely, the Red Army's high command, which was in the throes of marshaling 500,000 men to face Wrangel, was none too pleased with this agreement with Makhno, arguing that it was too advantageous for him:

"After the signing of the agreement, Makhno acquired citizenship rights de facto. The peasants who sympathized with him by virtue of their social class and who were afraid to say so, could now do so openly. The Makhnovists' lifestyle beguiled the Red soldier: he thought that among them there was more freedom, diversion and food and whereas hitherto the Red soldier had not joined Makhno, aware that he was the enemy of the workers and peasants, he henceforth began to have his doubts and instances of voluntary defection by Red soldiers to Makhno's side became more and more frequent."[19]

The same author adds that the presence of many women among the insurgents was a not inconsiderable factor in the Red soldiers' choice!

Notes to Chapter 22: The Second Alliance with the Red Army

1. Wrangel, op. cit. p. 212.
2. V. E. Pavolv, op. cit. p. 376.
3. Wrangel op. cit. pp. 222–223.
4. Kubanin, op. cit. p. 152.
5. *Izvestia* October 21, 1962.
6. *The Civil War in the Ukraine* op. cit. Tome II pp. 480 and 526.
7. Ibid. p. 580
8. Ibid. pp. 571–572. The text of the agreement was published at the time in the newspaper *Kommunist* No 236, October 22, 1920.
9. Kubanin, op. cit. pp. 158–159.
10. Lenin, *Oeuvres complètes,* Paris-Moscow, 1969, Tome XLII, p. 217
11. *The Civil War in the Ukraine,* op. cit. p. 642.
12. Quoted by Lebeds, op. cit. p. 37
13. Idem.
14. Idem.
15. Arshinov, op. cit. p. 170
16. Lenin, op. cit. p. 215
17. Lebeds, op. cit. p. 39
18. N. Makhno, "On the tenth anniversary of the revolutionary insurgent movement of the Ukraine: the Makhnovschina" (in Russian) in *Dyelo Truda,* Paris, 1929, No. 44-45, p. 7.
19. Yefimov, op. cit. p. 209.

The Gulyai-Polye libertarian communist group, 1907. Standing, (left to right) — Aleksandr Semenyuta, Luka Grabovoy, Ivan Shevchenko, Prokop Semenyuta, Egor Bondarenko, Ivan Levadny. Seated (left to right) — Makhno, Voldemar Antoni, Piotr Onishchenko, Nazar Zuichenko, Luka Korosteylev

The Makhnovist general staff in the spring of 1919. Third from the left — Petya Lyuty, then Nestor Makhno, Marchenko, Grigori Makhno (?) and Semyon Karetnik. Foreground, holding the sabre — Fedor Shchuss.

Staff of the Makhnovist movement in the spring of 1919.

Makhno in 1918   *Taranovsky*

*The Makhnovist general staff in October 1920: front row (left to right) —
Marchenko, Karetnik, Vassiliev and Makhno's driver, Melnik.
Second row — Kurilenko, Belash, Petrenko, Roma and Shchuss.*

Makhno in 1930–31   *Arshinov in 1926*

Group of Makhnovists

Group of Makhnovists with Fedor Shchuss (center)

Unit of Makhnovists with Fedor Shchuss (center)

General Mai-Maievsky

Baron-General Wrangel   *General Denikin*

Red Army military commanders: seated are Voroshilov (right) and Budyenny listening to reports from their subordinates.

*Cossack General Shkuro of the
Kuban Cossacks*

Chicherin, commissar for Foreign Affairs in the Lenin government

General Mamontov of the Don Cossacks.

The One-time Supreme Military Council of the USSR. Top row (left to right) Gamarnik, suicide; Tukhachevsky, shot; Yegorov, missing; Khalepski, missing; Orlov, shot; Yakir, shot Bottom row (left to right) S. Kamenev, deceased; Ordzhonikidze, poisoned; Budyenny, survivor; Alknis, shot; Mukhlevitch, missing; Eideman, shot; Uborevich, shot (from a soviet photo-montage made prior to the executions).

Galina Kuzmenko, Lucie and Nestor Makhno in 1926

*Makhno and his daughter Lucie
in Vincennes, 1928*

*Galina Kuzmenko and
Lucie Makhno in 1939*

General Kornilov

Kaledin, Ataman of the Don Cossacks

General Alexeyev

General Kutyepov

General Pokrovsky

Group of White Russian officers

Fedor Shchuss

*White officers, with General Kutyepov
on the right*

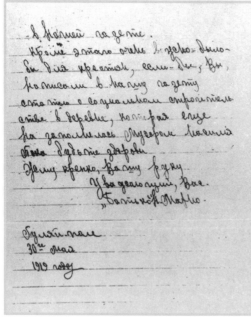

Felix Dzerzhinsky

Letter from Makhno to Kropotkin

Makhno in 1932

Makhno in 1918

Makhno in 1933

Portrait of N. Makhno by his companion
Grisha Bartanovsky in 1934 (Marquetry)

Portrait of Bakunin
by Grisha Bartanovsky

Portait of Makhno, 1922

The wounded Makhno in 1920

Group of wounded Makhnovists (left to right) Karetnik, Petrenko, Makhno, an unnamed nurse, Kurilenko

Makhnovists poring over the draft of the second alliance with the Reds, Starobelsk, September 1920.

*Series of seven stamps commemorating
the Makhnovschina, issued in Gulyai-Polye in 1993*

A tatchanka (Photo by J.P. Lagarde)

Unveiling of commemorative plaque marking the 110th anniversary of Nestor Makhno's birth on November 15, 1998, outside the house where he was born. In the center, Makhno's great grand-nephew Viktor Yalansky: behind him, the son of Leon Zadov. Foreground, a kobzar (Ukrainian minstrel) sings Makhnovist songs.

House in Gulyai-Polye used by the Makhnovists as their headquarters.

*A wing of the Tenon hospital
in Paris where Makhno died.*

N. Makhno's funeral urn in the Père Lachaise cemetery in Paris.

23. Victory over Wrangel

Following the agreement with the Red Army, relations between the Makhnovists and the Bolshevik leadership became more friendly; Bela Kun and other Red dignitaries came to visit Makhno and offered him more than 100 photographs and postcards showing the members of the Third International's executive committee! This curious gift was accompanied by a splendid declaration made out to "…fighter of the worker and peasant revolution, comrade Batko Makhno!"[1] It was a question of gaining the insurgents' confidence and convincing them of Moscow's sincerity. Bela Kun especially distinguished himself in this and upon his return to base was to brag about having really put one over on Makhno.[2] It is true that he already had a well-established reputation as a treacherous rogue and that he had not finished with exploits of this sort, for, according to Victor Serge, he had to make up for his pitiful showing at the time of the Hungarian Soviet revolution, as well as for his continual "idiocies" which led to Lenin's referring to him upwards of a dozen times at a single meeting as an "imbecile." Victor Serge's wife, who was the official stenographer there, had her work cut out to minimize this in her minutes![3]

Be that as it may, the impact of the agreement was soon being felt. The Makhnovists were assigned their own, White-occupied, home ground of Sinelnikovo, Alexandrovsk, Gulyai-Polye, and Berdyansk as their theater of operations. Once they had engaged with the enemy along that stretch of front, they had to tackle the problem of alleged or genuine Makhnovist insurgents who had gone over to Wrangel. In particular, they would be looking out for "ataman" Volodin and his 6,000 partisans who were ensconced near the waterfalls on the Dniepr, not far from Alexandrovsk. Volodin was an anarchist who had indeed been a member of the Makhnovist movement and especially been involved in the battle of Peregonovka; then, cut off from the main insurgent body and disgusted by the abuses of the Bolsheviks, he had established operational liaison with Wrangel on the basis of the notorious rumors of a joint alliance. Immediately on learning of the agreement concluded with the Red Army against Wrangel, he prepared to turn on them, but the Whites — tipped off by their "listening posts" — were one jump ahead of him and seized him and his staff, executing them and relieving his partisans of their weapons.[4]

After two attacks the Makhnovists liberated Gulyai-Polye, then forced the enemy front at Orekhov where they smashed an elite Wrangelian regiment, capturing an entire battalion. Makhno gave this account of the circumstances peculiar to this victory:

"Nikita Chaly, a Makhnovist from a poor family from the Mirgorod region, was a fine partisan and accomplished with brilliance all of the tasks allotted to him behind the White lines by the insurgent army's staff — both in Denikin's day and in Wrangel's. However, he went astray and ended up in Wrangel's camp as commander of the 10th brigade called after Batko Makhno but organized by the Wrangelian command in the wake of the provocation mounted by the Bolsheviks and by Wrangel himself regarding a supposed alliance between Makhnovists and Whites. We straightened that out, for whenever he was present at an engagement between us and White troops in October 1920, he realized his mistake and immediately came to see me, to die like a Makhnovist at the hands of another Makhnovist by way of paying for the offense that had taken him into Wrangel's camp. Well aware of the interests of the revolution and being above all else a military leader, I could not shoot him and instead assigned him the task of returning to Wrangel's people and bringing back to me every one of the officers commanding the brigade; these had been appointed by Wrangel's staff.

And so Chaly rejoined the White camp and then, on the night of October 17–18, he fetched all of the White officers to my headquarters: A colonel, some captains and some lieutenants. These were all interrogated by my aide Semyon Karetnik in front of me and in the presence of Bolshevik representatives from the Red staff of the front, Vassiliev among them. These officers briefed us on the disposition of the White forces, especially that of the "invincible" Drozdov Division and, without waiting for any joint offensive with the Red Army, I ordered the units from Petrenko's band, made up of mixed units of infantry, machine-gunners and artillery, as well as Marchenko's cavalry, to attack these famous Drozdovians who had thus far never failed to put to flight the 23rd and 42nd Red Divisions, even though outnumbered by them two to one.

The insurgents attacked this division — Wrangel's pride and joy — with the help of Chaly to guide them through the enemy deployment. They smashed this elite White unit as the Red Army had never managed to do. The Red Army command, the Drozdovians and Kutyepov and Wrangel most of all, are very well aware of this."[5]

A communiqué from Frunze dated October 24th bears out Makhno's account since it acknowledges that on October 22nd the insurgent army had smashed the enemy's flanks not far from the Dniepr and Alexandrovsk, taking 4,000 prisoners from the Drozdov division.[6]

The Makhnovists now retreated towards Gulyai-Polye in order to snatch some rest, but the Red command ordered them to carry their offensive behind the enemy's lines. Makhno requested a three-day rest period, but a second categorical order, complete with the threat to tear up the agreement, forced him to comply with this directive. He himself, wounded and unable to mount his horse, stayed in Gulyai-Polye along with his black guard; he dispatched some of his men home to rest and then marshaled a strong expeditionary corps made up of the insurgent army's finest units, namely, the famous undefeated cavalry commanded by March-enko, and the no less famed machine-gunner regiment led by Tomas Kozhin. This expeditionary force was placed under the command of Semyon Karetnik, assisted by Piotr Gavrilenko — the very same Gavrilenko just freed from Bolshevik jails — as his chief of staff.

On October 23rd, the insurgents took Alexandrovsk. On October 29th, a military dispatch for the attention of Frunze, originating with a certain Karatygin and countersigned by political commissar Andreyev, both of them on secondment to Karetnik, reported the capture of Bolshe-Tokmak. The insurgents had skirted the town on the western side, near the Heidelberg German settlement, then stormed the enemy trenches, virtually wiped out the Sixth White Infantry Regiment from Samursk and taken 200 prisoners and captured four cannon and machine-guns.[7] Then they seized the town of Melitopol and the strategically important railway station at Akimovka, again taking great booty.[8] Karetnik's detachment continued on its way — Frunze having intimated to him that he should seize the Crimean isthmuses — and smashed another enemy cavalry regiment, cutting a path as far as the Sivash, near Perekop.

Wrangel's attempt to force a passage along the right bank of Dniepr had failed, and now it was the Red Armies that crossed the Dniepr and, capitalizing on the Makhnovists' victories, stepped up the pressure on Wrangel's army, albeit extremely slowly and cautiously, for they were afraid of being lured into a trap and meeting the same fate as Zhloba's corps which the Whites had pulverized a few months before. This was the motive behind Frunze's using the Makhnovists as the spearhead of his offensive. Forced eastwards, the Whites were afraid of being cut off from their rear in the Crimea, and gradually they fell back towards the isthmuses of Perekop, Salkovo, and Henichesk which commanded access to the Crimea.

≈≋≈

The Whites had lost the decisive battle of the Northern Tavrida; they had been forced to quit all of the territory wrested from the Reds over the summer of 1920. In addition they had lost a very high number of armaments and especially wheat-carrying trains which they had been planning to sell or barter in return for weapons and munitions supplies abroad since France's aid was for the moment quite platonic. The fighting in the second fortnight of October took place in temperatures of minus 20 degrees (Celsius); the water in the reservoirs along the railroad lines had frozen and thus the trains could not be got moving in time. Wrangel gave this estimate of the booty and gains taken by the Reds:

> "Five armored trains, 18 cannon, nearly 100 wagonloads of shells, 10 million cartridges, 25 locomotives, trains loaded with food and munitions, nearly two million poods of wheat[9] in Melitopol and Henichesk. Our troops had sustained heavy losses in terms of killed, wounded and frostbitten. A huge number of prisoners and stragglers were still in enemy hands; for the most part, these were Red Army soldiers whom we had incorporated into our units in several installments. There were some instances of mass capitulations. Thus an entire battalion of the Drozdov Division surrendered to the enemy.[10] But the army as a whole had been salvaged, and our own troops had taken 15 cannon, nearly 2,000 prisoners, lots of arms and machine-guns. But if the army had been salvaged, its combat potential was no longer what it had been."[11]

Indeed, the Wrangelian Russian army's psychological buoyancy had been broken by the successive defeats; it had lost its reputation for invincibility, built up over several months!

Thus, in two weeks the Makhnovists had done what the Red Army had failed to achieve over six months! This assertion would be untenable were it not endorsed by the most official documents of the Red Army recording the engagements. Already, nearly all of the published break-downs and maps relating to the subject indicate the Makhnovist army's situation (in this instance Karetnik's expeditionary force, flanked by the 23rd and 42nd Red infantry Divisions) and testify to its being positioned in the front lines.[12] Then there are the orders and official dispatches to which we have just referred, but in addition there are the allusions to its major role. For instance, we have the editorial in the first edition of the very official Red Army review *Military Science and the Revolution* which appeared in July–August 1921 (at which point the Makhnovist movement had not yet been dismembered in the Ukraine) which reckons that Wrangel lost his campaign in the Nikopol region, which is to say, in the Makhnovists' theater of operations. Furthermore, it is specified that the "chief characteristic" of these encounters was the fact that they "…were not at all part of the projections and plans of the Red Army, which is why they had not even been anticipated by the high command."[13] In the huge work on the Russian civil war published in 1930 by a team of the most high-ranking Red Army officers from the period, namely. S. Kamenev, Bubnov, Uritsky, Eidemann and others, the article devoted to the "liquidation of Wrangel" is even more revealing. It explains first of all that the pact with Makhno was justified, self-evidently in the view of any historian, by its "operational and strategical import"; the strength of Karetnik's detachment was estimated at 4,000 infantry, 1,000 cavalry, and 1,000 machine-gunners and other fighting men, giving a total of 6,000,[14] with access to 250 machine-guns and 12 cannon, as against the Red Army's total strength of 188,771 (or more than 500,000 including the reserves and rearguard) fighting men against the Whites' 44,000. Mention is made of the crucial role played by the front around Pologui — the very place whence the Makhnovists were coming — and of the fact that Wrangel had to cut his western defenses — the ones preventing the bulk of the Red troops, positioned on the Dniepr's right bank, from crossing on to the left bank — by three divisions of Don Cossack cavalry (Wrangel's best troops, claim the authors) which were thus deployed in the direction of Pologui. What is more, the fortified town of Melitopol was regarded by the Whites as the securest possible bulwark, and we have just seen what became of it. Obviously, the authors took care not to call by its right name the mysterious unit which had overturned all the plans of the Whites; they prefer to allude vaguely to "the Red Army," the "13th Army" (to which Karetnik's detachment was seconded), or, if pressed, speak of a mixed cavalry and infantry division, avoiding further detail! One can appreciate their annoyance at having to explain how a few thousand resolute insurgents had done more to defeat Wrangel on the left bank of the Dniepr than the 500,000 Red soldiers massed in the region, whose fighting ability obviously left something to be desired. So let us re-establish the exact truth of the matter: It was the hammer-blows of the Makhnovists against Orekhov, Bolshe-Tokmak and their capture of Melitopol which forced Wrangel's troops to retreat towards the Crimea.

જૐ

On October 28, Frunze denied Karetnik a respite of four or five days' rest and reorganization, and let him know that, if he failed to abide by instructions, this would be tantamount to a refusal to participate in the liquidation of Wrangel.[15] One can appreciate that, quite logically, he was keen, on one hand, to make maximum use of such an effective unit, even at the cost of letting it be used up or destroyed in battle, while on the other hand he had to keep it ahead of him rather than behind him, and above all, as one Bolshevik leader, Kossior, has spelled out in detail,[16] it had at all costs to be kept isolated from other Red Army units lest any contamination occur! As a result, the detachment, initially seconded to the 13th Army, was suddenly placed under the command of the Fourth Army on November 4, of the Sixth Cavalry on November 5, of the Second Cavalry on November 11, and again of the Fourth Army on November 17. The detachment was either regarded as the Red Army's dogsbody or (likely) this merry-go-round is indicative of the Red high command's panicky fear at leaving the Makhnovists in contact with other Red Army units, lest these be unduly infected by their revolutionary ardor. The memory of Pomoshnaya in August 1919 must still have been haunting the Red military leaders.

On November 3, in a direct line conversation with S. Kamenev, Frunze declared that the Makhnovists had arrived by evening November 2 near the Sivash strait, which it was their mission to force in order to take the White fortifications at Perekop from behind. On November 5, he issued them with formal instructions to attack by that route. He was well aware that in so doing he was dispatching them to slaughter, for they would have to cross the open ground of the stagnant marshes of the Sivash. Also, S. Kamenev, commander-in-chief on the front, had no illusions about the outcome of this attack upon the fortified White positions. In a telegram to Lenin, he estimated that there was one chance in a hunded of capturing the Perekop isthmus![17]

The Sixth Red Army's commander, A.I. Kork, gave this account of what ensued at a military science conference on November 11, 1921:

> "The attitude of the Makhnovists to the Red Army was none too dependable, and it might have seemed inadvisable to leave Karetnik's detachment in our rear, which is why the front commander set himself the task of moving Karetnik's detachment up into the front line. As the Sivash seemed traversable, the chance arose to throw this detachment ahead to establish a bridgehead on the Litovsk peninsula. This order was passed on directly by the commander of the Sixth Army [i.e., by Kork himself — A.S.] to Karetnik who was to have carried it out on the night of the 5th–6th (November), since the launching of the general offensive was scheduled for the 7th (November). Karetnik's detachment moved forward into the Sivash, but turned back before reaching the Sivash peninsula, Karetnik declaring that there was nothing but marshes that way and that traversing the Sivash was out of the question. On the sixth (November), a further reconnaissance revealed that Karetnik's report was false and that the Sivash was quite passable. However, the ground reconnaissance had not yet been completed, and the offensive was to begin on the morning of the seventh (November) due in part to the belatedness of the 52nd Division which was scheduled to take part in the operation. [...] It was obvious that the crossing of such flat and open ground covering a distance of nearly 10 kilometers could not be made in daylight without very heavy losses; so it seemed more appropriate to make it on the night of the 7th–8th (November) after 22:00 hours. An order to this effect was issued to Karetnik's detachment and to the 15th and 52nd Divisions."[18]

Kork estimates the strength of Karetnik's detachment at this point at 1,000 infantry and 700 cavalry, with 191 machine-guns and six cannon.[19] Nevertheless, he is very discreet as to the circumstances of the Sivash crossing. In fact, some local peasants pointed out the best crossing-point. The Makhnovists led the way across under heavy fire from the Whites and sustained some losses but managed to reach the Litovsk peninsula by driving back General Fostikov's Kuban Cossacks. Whereupon they were followed up by the two divisions mentioned, one of them made up of Latvian infantrymen. This maneuver was an historical reenactment of the maneuver

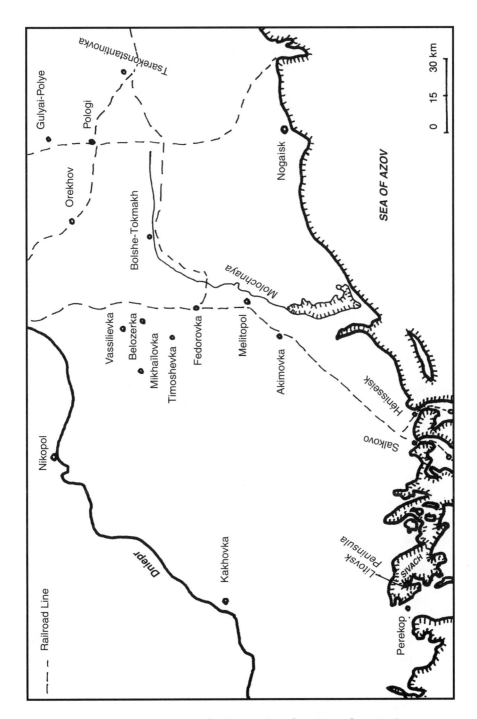

Military Operations in the Crimea (October–November 1920)

by Field Marshall Lassi of the Russian army that had also crossed the Sivash in 1737 to take the Crimean Tartars from behind. In fact, the Perekop isthmus had always been reputed impregnable; and so Kamenev's pessimism had been understandable, especially since Perekop was now defended by 750 machine-guns, 180 cannon and 48 tanks, as well as by some armored trains standing off some distance behind the lines. Also, several thousand elite White troops were dug in behind three lines of trenches and barbed wire.

Over a period of several days, some 22 attacks were mounted by Red units to no avail but incurring very heavy losses. Thus the perilous maneuver carried off by Karetnik was decisive, for it enabled a solid bridgehead to be established so that other Red troops might be brought across to tackle the White fortifications from behind. The Whites were cognizant of this danger and put up a ferocious fight to push the assailants back towards the Sivash. They managed to shove them back into the northern extremity of the peninsula by November 9th. Let us return to Kork's narrative:

> "At 15:00 hours on November 9th, on the narrow isthmus located between the Sivash and Lake Bezymianny, Barbovich's White cavalry went on to the attack. The 15th Red Division began to back up. At this point, Karetnik's detachment helped out by deploying to meet the enemy cavalry with lethal gunfire from its machine-gunner regiment. Barbovich's cavalry were hurled back. Thanks to the help supplied by the machine-gunner regiment from Karetnik's detachment, the 15th Division's left flank was quickly repaired."[20]

Another more recent soviet source provides further detail about this crucial engagement; Barbovich and his Kuban Cossack cavalry attacked the left flank of the 15th Division (Latvians) which began to scatter, and it was Karetnik's detachment which salvaged the situation. Marchenko's cavalry then counterattacked only to fan out at the last moment to leave the enemy cavalry facing the tatchankis of Tomas Kohin's machine-gunner regiment; a hail of gunfire from the latter soon dampened the ardor of Barbovich's Cossacks. The author of this description, which has been lifted from a book on the history of the Latvian infantry, stresses the major role which the Makhnovists also played in the crossing of the Sivash under enemy fire and testifies that they were the first to set foot upon the Litovsk peninsula.[21]

Another Red Army bigwig, Kakurin, a former tsarist colonel, writes in a classic work on the civil war, that "...On the night of November 8, units of the Sixth Army assigned to the capture of the Litovsk peninsula crossed the Sivash, smashed the White General Fostikov's detachment and dug in on the peninsula. Enemy counterattacks met with no success; so the 15th Infantry division and then the 52nd also arrived to dig in on the northernmost part of the peninsula. Then, come the morning, the 153rd Brigade of the 51st Division showed up, along with Krylenko's cavalry brigade."[22] Let us note the discretion about naming the Makhnovist detachment which is described only as "…units … assigned to the capture of the Litovsk peninsula," whereas every other unit is given a specific name!

Meanwhile the Red military commanders' obsession with the notorious "contamination" by Makhnovists led them, in a bizarre move, to subordinate them on November 11th to the Second Cavalry Army! They were assuredly still afraid of a comradeship of arms growing up between them and Red Army soldiers.

Caught from behind and seeing that their cause was lost, the Whites scurried in a forced march towards the Crimean ports where the Russian fleet, which Wrangel had chartered some time before against the eventuality of evacuation, took them on board in orderly fashion. On November 11, Frunze put it to them that they should surrender, and he guaranteed the lives of them all and assured them of a complete amnesty. Any who wished might stay and work in Socialist Russia; as for the others, they could leave the country if they gave their word of honor not to fight against Russia and the Soviet authorities![23] Lenin immediately amended this, reproaching Frunze for having been too generous in his concessions which could stand only if the enemy agreed that all the ships would be handed back; he ordered him to make no more such offers and to crush the Whites unmercifully if they rejected this proposition.[24] In fact, a large number of White soldiers and officers, who were above all else patriots, decided — to their great misfortune — to believe these fine promises and stayed behind.

As for the Red Army, stunned by this quick success and by the even quicker flight of the Whites and perhaps still wary of a trap, its progress was painfully slow. Again it was Makhnovists who were first to strike deep into the Crimea and who captured Simferopol on November 13. The Whites went blithely on boarding the ships, and when the first Red units reached Sebastopol, Feodosiya, Kerch, and Yalta, the Crimean ports, they found only a few stragglers and a host of distraught civilian refugees. Nearly 100,000 soldiers, 50,000 civilians (3,000 of them women and 7,000 children) had thus fled this last corner of their homeland aboard 126 Russian ships. Wrangel had successfully averted his army's being overtaken by disaster and saved its honor, but it was the end for the whole White movement right across Russia, aside from ataman Semenov and the crazed Baron Ungern-Sternberg who were to hold out for some months more in Siberia on the borders of Manchuria.

Frunze ordered Karetnik's detachment to camp at the mouth of the Kacha river, at Saki, on the western shores of the Crimea. The author of the *History of the Latvian Infantry* bluntly admits that this was in order to isolate the Makhnovists and prevent them from leaving the Crimea. To that end, they were further cordoned off by the 52nd Division, the Third Corps of cavalry and the Second Latvian Brigade.[25] On November 13, Frunze informed Kamenev by telephone that he had "…left the 42nd Division in the Gulyai-Polye area with an eye to possible complications from that quarter." Asked by Kamenev how the Makhnovists had acquitted themselves, Frunze replied that they had acquitted themselves reasonably well during the most recent fighting and had noticeably avoided missions involving the risk of heavy losses.[26] Here Frunze was displaying a touch too much presumption, probably regretting that the Makhnovists had not taken heavier losses, although it was not for want of his exposing them as much as he was able to the most perilous positions!

When they do not gloss over in silence the Makhnovists' decisive action in the operations that determined the outcome of the war against Wrangel,[27] Soviet historians acknowledge their brilliant performance. Rudnev, for instance, author of an 1928 monograph on the Makhnovschina, writes that the "…Makhnovist units took part in the Red Army's celebrated offensive on the Crimean front. They pulled off a highly important action by striking (and this was of capital importance in strategic terms) behind the lines of Wrangel's army and then, on November 13, 1920, occupied the town of Simferopol, shortly after the capture of Perekop."[28] Kork, the commander of the Sixth Red Army, also stresses the important part played by Kozhin's machine-gunner regiment at the time of Barbovich's assault. He adds that one of the consequences of this victory over Wrangel relates to the Soviet government's becoming the sole legitimate representative of Russia and able, as such, to negotiate peace and trade(!) treaties with the capitalist countries.[29]

At the time, as far as the Bolshevik leaders and their soldiery were concerned, the priority was to settle the question of the thousands, tens of thousands of White soldiers and officers who had swallowed the promise of an amnesty and surrendered to the new authorities with every confidence. Lenin's order to "crush them unmercifully" now took effect in the most barbarous fashion. Bela Kun arrived on the scene after the battle to display his expertise: "Woe to the vanquished!" the dictum goes; well, he was going to put it into full effect here. Drawing their inspiration no doubt from the French Terror of 1793, Bela Kun, the Chekists and the other doers of dirty work mowed down the prisoners — like Fouché had in Lyons — or sank barges (fully laden with officers bound hand and foot) in the Black Sea — like Carrier's drownings in Nantes. According to Victor Serge, these massacres took a toll of 13,000 victims.[30] According to Grenard, a French diplomat well informed on the question, the real figure would have been upwards of 50,000 victims![31] And this butchery was all the more horrific because the Whites who had naively stayed behind in the Crimea were probably the ones least involved in the abuses and excesses of their movement. Just as the Bolsheviks had promised them they might, they had hoped to make reparation for their offenses by taking a hand in the peaceful, socialist reconstruction of their country. Ill fortune denied them the opportunity.

❧❧❧

While all this was going on, Makhno was tending his wounded in Gulyai-Polye. Most insurgent units had been sent home to their native villages and districts, there to rest up and make up their numbers again. Other units were stationed in Melitopol, Bolshe-Tokmak, Malaya-Tokmachka and Pologui. In the belief that the agreement concluded with the Bolsheviks was a guarantee against any surprise attack, Makhno turned his attention to constructive endeavors along with the local anarchist militants. Between the first and 25th of November, the inhabitants of Gulyai-Polye came together seven times to determine the program for the reorganization of social and economic life which had been completely hobbled over the past year by the dozens of successive occupations of the town. Around mid-November, a soviet had been set up, and in concert with the insurgents' revolutionary soviet, a draft of the basic ground rules of the "free soviets of toilers" had been worked out. He had also proceeded to organize schools independent of both Church and State and involving supporters of the libertarian school founded by Francisco Ferrer. Literacy classes were laid on for illiterate adults, followed by courses in politics and economics given by insurgent peasants and workers who had some grounding in the subjects. Here it is interesting to look at their syllabus: a) Political economy, b) history, c) the theory and practice of socialism and anarchism, d) the history of the French Revolution according to Kropotkin's book, *The Great French Revolution*, e) the history of the revolutionary insurgent movement in the Russian revolution.[32]

Not that cultural activities were neglected; daily there were shows staged in the local theater. The insurgents and their womenfolk took part in these, not only as spectators and actors, but also as dramatists narrating episodes from recent local events and from the insurgents' struggle. For all too short a time, alas, a free and creative existence sprang again from the ashes of civil war!

A Polish libertarian, Casimir Teslar, who was staying in Gulyai-Polye at the time, offers this description of the place:

"The exemplary order and cleanliness which reign everywhere are striking. I have been in Gulyai-Polye in winter. The countryside and town were covered with a deep blanket of snow. In every courtyard stood the famous "tatchanka"; this was a sign that each home harbored some Makhnovist insurgents [...] Upon entering the town, I was struck by the sight of the abandoned trenches which ringed it. When I pressed on into the center, I was impressed by the horror of the war which had passed that way, leaving deep traces. The finest houses had been destroyed while others, a large number of others, were half demolished. In one such, I found the premises of the Gulyai-Polye toilers' trade union. The walls were marked with dark cracks and holes. Everywhere the traces of projectiles and fire could be seen. If you go to Gulyai-Polye, children will escort you to the spot where the Austrians burned down the little wooden house where Nestor Makhno was born and where his poor old mother was living when the Austro-German troops entered the town. They will also show you other burned-out homes, burned by the Whites or the Reds: the homes of anarcho-Makhnovist insurgents.

[…] On one of the main streets a black flag fluttered in the breeze. On it one could read: 'Staff of the Makhnovist Insurgent Army of the Ukraine.'"[33]

✳✳✳

During his stay, Teslar often saw horsemen, tatchankis and bands of insurgents gallop past, noisily making for the steppes for maneuvers and to accustom their young mounts to the noise of their weapons. He had difficulty imagining that this apparently so peaceable town was "freedom's stronghold" and that the "people under arms" lived there. He noted that the street games of the children aping battle scenes recalled recent and unfortunately all too real events.

Notes to Chapter 23: Victory over Wrangel

1. N. Makhno, "Open letter to the Russian Communist Party and to its central committee" (in Russian) in *Dyelo Truda* No. 37-38, pp. 10–12.

2. Idem.

3. Victor Serge, op. cit. pp. 154–155.

4. Pavlov, op. cit. pp. 309–311.

5. N. Makhno, *"The Mahknovschina and its erstwhile allies: The Bolsheviks"* (in Russian), op. cit. pp. 51–52.

6. *The Civil War in the Ukraine* (in Russian), op. cit. Tome III, p. 651, and *The Directives from the Command of the Fronts of the Red Army* (1917–1922) (in Russian), Moscow 1978, Tome IV, pp. 481–482.

7. *The Civil War in the Ukraine*, op. cit. p. 670.

8. Ibid. p. 697.

9. Or 327,600 quintals! A colossal amount for those famine times!

10. Wrangel refers to the Orekhov encounter when the Makhnovists took 4,000 soldiers from that division prisoner; apparently, he could not know with whom they had been dealing there; as far as he was concerned, everyone on the other side was a "red."

11. Wrangel, op. cit. p. 286.

12. *Voyna i revolyutsia*, Moscow, 1930, 8 (August), N. Gapitch, "The operations of the Fourth and 13th Armies in the Northern Tavrida in October–November 1920, pp. 81–82.

13. *Voyennazha hauka i revolyutsia*, No. 1, July–August 1921, Moscow, p. 17. Editorial signed S. Varin.

14. *The Russian Civil War* (in Russian). Editorial team headed by S. Kamenev, Bubnov, and Uritsky, Moscow, 1930, Tome III, pp. 510–541. Arshinov (op. cit.) estimates the strength of Karetnik's detachment at 2,000 fighters. See below for other estimates.

15. *The Directives from the Command of the Red Army Fronts (1917–1922)*, op. cit. p. 482.

16. *The Civil War in the Ukraine*, op. cit. p. 637.

17. *On the History of the Civil War in the USSR* (in Russian), Moscow, 1961, Tome III, p. 418.

18. A.I. Kork, "The capture of the Perekop fortifications," in *The Revolutionary Army* (in Russian) Ekaterinoslav, 1921, No. 1, pp. 17–31. The article is reprinted in *The Stages of a Great March* (in Russian) Moscow, 1963, pp. 436–454. The quotation appears on p. 443.

19. Ibid. p. 440.

20. Idem.

21. *Istoria Latyskkikh strelkov* (History of the Latvian Infantry) Riga, 1972, published under the editorship of Ya. Krastinia, pp. 668–679. The entire account is lifted from the archives of the Latvian Communist Party.

22. N. Kakurin, *Kak srazhala revoliutsia,* Moscow, 1926, Tome II, pp. 388–389.

23. *On the History of the Civil War in the USSR,* op. cit. pp. 432–433.

24. Ibid. p. 433.

25. *History of the Latvian Infantry,* op. cit. p. 678.

26. *The Directives from the Command of the Red Army Fronts (1917–1922)* op. cit. p. 513.

27. Triandafilov, author of the article, "The Red Army's Perekop Operation" in the anthology on the civil war published by Kamenev, Bubnov, Uritsky, and others (op. cit. pp. 339–356) does not, for example, shrink from avoiding all mention of the Karetnik detachment in his description of this operation. This is all the more incoherent and contradictory in that the article in the same anthology concerning "Wrangel's liquidation," which we have quoted, does mention this participation in the appropriate place. One possible explanation for this "cock-up" might be the internecine struggles raging in 1930 among the Soviet politico-military leadership and the curious revisions that ensued regarding the role of each faction during the civil war.

28. Rudnev, op. cit. p. 91.

29. Kork, op. cit. p. 454.

30. Victor Serge, op. cit. pp. 154–155.

31. F. Grenard, op cit., p. 338.

32. Arshinov, op. cit. pp. 176–179.

33. Casimir Teslar "Gulyai-Polye" in *La Revue Anarchiste,* Paris, March-April 1922, No. 15, pp. 19–20.

24. Bolshevik Treachery

Thus, there were certain signs which hinted that, in the reckoning of Lenin and others of the regime's dignitaries, the agreement concluded with the Makhnovists had been mere opportunism and could not endure beyond the time it would take to finish off Wrangel. The relative concessions granted to the insurgents had been designed only to put them at ease, in spite of the famous item four of the political part of the agreement, which in principle made provision for autonomy for "Makhnovia" (to borrow the expression of Soviet historians). This matter was left hanging and had to be worked out directly with the Kremlin. In his (it is true, posthumously published) memoirs, Trotsky is clear that Lenin and he …

> "had at one time seriously envisaged allocating certain territories to the anarchists, with the consent of the local population of course and allowing them to conduct their experiment with a stateless society there. This plan was aborted at the discussion stage though the fault was not ours. The anarchist movement failed itself when it underwent the test of the events that followed one upon another in the course of the Russian Revolution."[1]

Victor Serge also mentions such a plan by Lenin and Trotsky, but indirectly, borrowing from the text by Trotsky that we have just quoted. Victor Serge opines that … "it might have been equitable and advisable and perhaps such a broad mindedness might have spared the revolution the tragedy towards which we were all drifting."[2] It must be obvious that for Lenin and his side tolerance of any such experiment was absolutely out of the question; it would have been tantamount to admitting the shortcomings of their own ability to resolve the country's problems and that was inconceivable for anyone familiar with Lenin's trajectory ever since the break with the Mensheviks in 1903 and right through the squabbles, polemics, splits and other exercises which had carried him into power. A regime of free soviets in the eastern Ukraine! The contagion would immediately have consumed the whole country and the house of cards known as "worker-peasant government" — maintained only by bayonet and the bullet in the back of the head — would have evaporated in a trice and lingered in the memories of workers only as some ghastly nightmare.

Let us look at the explanation offered by Gusev and Yakovlev, the two signatories to the agreement on the Bolshevik side. Gusev reckoned that:

"...Makhno's proposition of an alliance with the Red Army was accepted, not in order to secure a complementary force on the front — none was needed — but in order to rid ourselves for a time of an enemy behind our lines. As soon as Wrangel was defeated, this "alliance" was quite naturally broken, for the proletarian revolution can fellow-travel with the Kulak only in the struggle against the pomieschik, but further along their paths diverge radically." [3]

One can spot the misrepresentations of the facts immediately: the "proposition" was Makhno's, the backup on the front was "not needed" and there is the utter cynicism of the explanation of the "quite natural breakdown" of the alliance; so we know what was to be expected from that quarter right from the start. In 1920, for the First Congress of the Red International of Labour Unions (to which some anarcho-syndicalists had been invited) Yakovlev, the second signatory, wrote a pamphlet simply overflowing with poisonous attacks directed against the Russian anarchists and, above all, against Makhno. He skims over his own part in the arranging of the agreement and cites Frunze's explanations regarding the breakdown which is attributed wholly to faults on the part of Makhno, on the basis of a number of acts perpetrated in various locations around the Ukraine against the Red Army. He rails against the solidarity displayed by the remainder of the anarchists towards Makhno whom he depicts as a bandit deserving of no regard.[4] Sure — wasn't he for the Whites in the Crimea? and Bolsheviks had not been great ones for the Christian virtue of forgiving trespasses against them, but even so! Thereby demonstrating that the agreement which they had initially had been, as far as they were concerned, a mere scrap of paper. This was on a par with the practices of Bismarck and other exponents of *realpolitik* and negotiated something quite new in Russian revolutionary circles. Soon it was to become the stock in trade of the State system.

As far as the Makhnovists were concerned, without harboring any illusions "... either about the durability or solidity of the agreement" (Arshinov) the view was that, in spite of everything, the agreement would hold up for three or four months, and they were counting on this interval to enable them to make the libertarian option known to the Ukraine's laboring population and to demonstrate, by contrast, the inadequacies of the Bolsheviks' options. If there was to be conflict, the insurgents at first anticipated that it would be confined to the realm of ideas.

Makhnovists also had high hopes of the general congress of anarchists due to take place at the end of November in Kharkov. It was for this reason that a part of their delegation had stayed behind in the city and availed of the opportunity to participate in meetings and debates which drew sizable audiences and at which the delegation's members — especially Victor Popov — were blunt about the necessity of power's being restored to local soviets and about implementation of the famous Item Four of the agreement, which had been shelved twice thus far. The delegation put out a newspaper, *The Makhnovist Voice,* in which they spelled out their views and their complaints regarding the Leninist authorities. In its third issue — which was also to be its last — dated November 21st, the editorial announced that having "… done their duty by the social revolution, the Makhnovists delivered a whole series of lethal blows against Wrangel. Also, of the soviet government of the Ukraine and Russia we require honest implementation of Item One of our agreement: immediate release of all Makhnovists and anarchists still languishing in the prisons and camps of the soviet republics."

According to Arshinov, Makhno's then aide-de-camp Grigori Vassilevsky, upon hearing on November 15 or 16 of Karetnik's breaching of Wrangel's defenses in Perekop, had cried out: "That's the end for the agreement! Take my word for it, within one week the Bolsheviks are going to come down on us like a ton of bricks!" [5] And, even more telling, in Gulyai-Polye and Pologui on November 23 the Makhnovists arrested nine spies from the 42nd Red Army Division which was stationed nearby. These confessed to having been sent in by their intelligence branch to discover the precise whereabouts of Makhno, members of the Staff and of the insurgents' soviet, as well as those of Makhnovist unit commanders. They were to have remained on the spot until the Red Army showed up and pointed out the domiciles or shadow the Makhnovist officials who might not be at home. According to what they claimed, an attack an Gulyai-Polye was to be expected around November 24 or 25. The insurgents promptly tackled Rakovsky and the Red Army Officials in Kharkov to press for the arrest and punishment of the officials of the 42nd Division, and then for a veto upon any Red Army units passing through the Gulyai-Polye region, so as to forestall any incidents. Kharkov replied on November 25, claiming that the whole thing was just a misunderstanding and that a joint commission would look into it. [6] In fact, finding their plot "blown," the Bolsheviks decided to unleash their onslaught the very next night.

On the morning of November 26, Piotr Rybin, secretary of the Soviet of Makhnovist Revolutionary Insurgents, telephoned Rakovksy to find out what this proposed commission was all about. Rakovksy replied that everything was going to be smoothed out peaceably along with the controversial Item Four, when in fact he knew that the attack on the Makhnovists and anarchists had been launched that very night. The entire Makhnovist delegation — Viktor Popov, Budanov and Khokhotva — was placed under arrest, shipped to Moscow and shot. Apropos of their execution, Kubanin writes that "…Moscow was not joking with the Makhnovschina and acted without losing any time."[7] In all, 346 anarchists and Makhnovists were rounded up in Kharkov in this operation. Forty were sent on to the Moscow Cheka. Among them were Sereda, one of Makhno's closest associates, Zinchenko, commander of the 2nd Cavalry Regiment, Kolesnichenko, commander of an insurgent detachment, Kuzenko, commander of one of the infantry regiments … all seized by treachery. Learning of this outrageous behavior, Rybin again telephoned Rakovksy and told him of his feelings of indignation. Thanks to this phone call, the Cheka managed to track him down, arrested him and shot him shortly afterwards. Nearly all of the membership of the Ukrainian anarchist confederation, Nabat, were also arrested and jailed: Voline, Mratchny, Baron, David Kogan, Josef Gotman, Bogush and others. Kubanin records this round-up of anarchists by noting tersely: "The Nabat was liquidated by organs of the Cheka."[8]

That very same day, the 42nd Division with its five infantry brigades and cavalry brigades attacked Gulyai-Polye. A second cordon around the town was thrown up by the 2nd Cavalry Corps, Volga Brigade and two special regiments. In spite of certain precautionary measures taken the evening before, Makhno was wrong-footed by the suddenness of the attack; in Gulyai-Polye all he had to call upon was his personal escort, the Black Guard, some 150 strong. Caught in a vice, he was encircled on every side; the end looked near when, all of a sudden, in the afternoon, one Red unit hurriedly withdrew. Fearful of a trap, Makhno hesitated and then, spotting that the way was clear, broke out of the cordon through this unexpected gap. Soviet historians ascribe this miraculous escape to treachery on the part of the commander of one of the Red units. It is likely then that once they saw what was expected of them, some of the Red troops showed solidarity with the Makhnovists and whereas the officers spoke of treachery, the fact is that some of these Red troops and especially their commanders were to pay with their lives for this gesture of revolutionary solidarity.

The 3rd Makhnovist Regiment, stationed at Malaya-Tokmachka, was less fortunate; it was almost entirely rounded up by the 126th Division brigade and a regiment of Red cavalry. Makhno counter-attacked and beat the enemy back as far as Novo-Uspenovka. Confusion set in among the many Red units; the International Cavalry Brigade which had occupied Gulyai-Polye was attacked on November 27 by other brigades from the 42nd Division who thought that they were tackling insurgents. It was only after a day's fighting that this misunderstanding was cleared up! [9] Makhno promptly regrouped various insurgent units. Some Red soldiers, sickened by the conduct of their officers, came to join him or surrendered to him at the earliest opportunity. In this way a contingent of 1,500 infantry and 1,000 cavalry was mustered. Gulyai-Polye was recaptured after a week, and the troops of the 42nd Division chased out, for now realizing the dirty work that had been entrusted to them, the Red soldiers had no stomach left for the fight or fought with very little enthusiasm. In this way — of the 6,000 Red soldiers stripped of their weapons on the day that the town captured — one in three joined the Makhnovists. Gulyai-Polye was recaptured in a few hours, too late unfortunately to save 300 local peasants who were cut down by the henchmen of Bolsheviks.

※※※

In the Crimea too, Moscow's instructions were enthusiastically implemented. As early as November 17, the strong partisan detachment of the anarchist Mokröusov, which had carried out significant harrying operations behind Wrangel's lines, had been placed under the direct command of the Fourth Army and been absorbed into regular units. On the same date, a secret order stipulated that Makhno's army, i.e. Karetnik's detachment, also be placed under the authority of the Fourth Army and that it was also to be transferred without delay to the Caucasus to take on insurgent Cossacks[10] — and that, of course, without the principals concerned being informed of what was going on. Karetnik and his staff, cut off from their detachment, were summoned on November 25 to a supposed meeting in Gulyai-Polye, arrested en route and shot out of hand. Gavrilenko, Karetnik's chief of staff, was "killed," meaning probably that he was liquidated after having defended himself. The following night, at 1:35 A.M. an attack was launched against the contingent itself. It would appear that a band of insurgents had been encircled by some Chekist units and wiped out by crossfire from several hundred machine-guns,[11] but the bulk of the contingent managed to break out of the circle shortly before this attack in circumstances related to us by Yefimov, the Red military expert on the anti-Makhnovist campaign:

> "One way or another, it became apparent to us that Makhno was building up to something and that in any event a break with him was inevitable and indispensable. On that basis, a plan was drawn up to encircle his two bands: the Crimean band and the one in the rear [the Gulyai-Polye one — A.S.]. Karetnik's band was ordered to occupy the Crimean coastline at the village of Zamruk near Saki, which it did. Then the Red Army troops were to encircle it; to this end the following units were redeployed for November 26 … three cavalry divisions, three infantry divisions of three brigades each, and one brigade of artillery. On November 27, all these divisions received the order to attack the Makhnovist contingent and wipe it out. […] Of course the encirclement plan could only have succeeded if there was the element of surprise and immediate, resolute action by the Red Army which could be ensured only after painstaking political groundwork. A good explanation needed to be devised to explain why, after an agreement had been concluded, the Red Army nonetheless had to wipe out the Makhnovists. This political groundwork reduced the element of surprise to zero which is in effect what happened. The Makhnovists were alerted several hours in advance of our attack and were partly able to avoid it. It was also obvious they knew well enough why Red units had been deploying around them. On the evening of November 26, Karetnik's band struck out for the road leading from Simferopol to Perekop. Along the way they defeated the 7th Cavalry Division. As soon as the Makhnovists' breakout had been discovered, the entire 3rd Cavalry Corps and the 52nd Division were dispatched in pursuit. However, these units acted in a half-hearted and hesitant fashion. Thus the Makhnovists were able to reach the outskirts of Perekop on the evening of the 27th; there they split into two groups, one crossing the Sivash the other traveling through the Perekop isthmus facing the 1st Infantry Division's small and nonpugnacious units. The two groups

rejoined at Stroganovka on the mainland, on the morning of November 28th. Thus were the Makhnovists able to escape from the Crimea by covering 130 kilometers in two days while fighting a rearguard action. Our own units displayed no initiative. They all waited for orders to act and would not budge unless issued with specific orders."12

Yefimov was not afraid to contradict himself in the matter of the exact date of attack; he mentions the 27th so that this fits in with the justification of the formal order from Frunze, allegedly issued on the 26th (the date mentioned in every other Soviet source), then explains that the Makhnovists took two days to cross the Crimea before arriving on the mainland on the morning of the 28th. The military precision that he was required to display was not so easily reconciled with overriding political motives. Let us also note the exceptional deployment of forces on the Bolshevik side to confront this tiny Makhnovist phalanx; this was probably indicative of the relative fear on the part of the Red leadership who still recalled the insurgents' exceptional feats against the Whites. Also, Yefimov cannot stop himself from acknowledging the Red units' lackadaisical approach to the carrying out of this sordid assignment. All of the Red soldiers were well aware with whom they were dealing and believed not one single treacherous word of their commanders' "cock-and-bull stories" about Makhno's alleged treachery and other nonsense; so it was much against their will that they had to contemplate taking on their comrades in arms now. That is why, despite the tremendous fighting abilities of the Makhnovists, it is hard to conceive of their having been able to penetrate a dense cordon of more than 200,000 Red troops between them and the Perekop isthmus unless one considers the latter's reluctance to engage them. Moreover, Yefimov acknowledges that the Makhnovists had been tipped off several hours in advance by Red soldiers about what was being plotted against them and had acted accordingly. This mentality had not gone unnoticed by the Red high command which had to act ruthlessly; as the *Red Soldier's Army Journal* reports, 2,300 Red troops had been shot in the Crimea at this time on charges of having "… undermined the just endeavors of the soviet authorities and of their valiant Red Army."13 A significant figure that, if compared with losses suffered in the capture of Perekop — 8,000 killed and 1,200 wounded. Further on, Yefimov estimates the strength of the Makhnovist contingent upon leaving the Crimea at 4,000 men — which may bear out the thesis that a thousand insurgents were massacred on the night of November 25–26, having been cut off from their comrades and not having had time to escape the Cheka's machine-guns.

By way of justifying this act of treachery, Frunze first issued an order dated November 24 and intended for the Red Army. It spoke of a communiqué of November 23 urging the Makhnovists to be assimilated into the Red Army's regular units. What is more, he drew up a veritable list of charges against them; they were accused of undermining the Red Army's rear, of distracting Red soldiers from their duties, of having committed criminal acts against Bolshevik officials or Red Army personnel, and of having refused to carry out the order given to them on November 20th to march on the Caucasus. In passing he claimed all the glory of the victory over the Whites for himself and his troops. He gave Makhnovists two days in which to comply with his instructions. What is at once disturbing and revealing and what proves that this was unquestionably a lie cobbled together after the event to meet the requirements of circumstances is that at the same time he ordered his troops "… to have done with the Makhnovschina in a trice[!] (…) All Red units must act boldly, decisively and ruthlessly. The bandit gangs must be eliminated as quickly as possible; the entire armament of the kulaks must be seized also."[14]

This crass falsehood was followed up by a second order dated November 26 and issuing from Kharkov at 1:35 A.M., alleging that the November 23 order had not been carried out by the Makhnovists and that, instead, Makhno had begun to take action against soviet authorities, as a result of which he and his units were being declared "… enemies of the revolution and of soviet power."[15] This latter order seems less of a formality than the first but was not made official on the day in question, for it was to appear in the Bolshevik press only on December 15; it had been backdated as is readily understandable. The element of surprise had to be preserved, as Yefimov admitted earlier. Not until much later and then quite by chance did the Makhnovists find out about it while reading the Bolshevik papers. Now, these ultimata with their provocative style had been drafted under the supervision of Lenin himself; the general in command of the front, Sergei Kamenev, attests to that in his memoirs.[16] Be it the anti-Wrangel compact or the order from Frunze, the whole effort had been mounted with Lenin's consent and in accordance with his directives. So the responsibility lay at the highest levels, in the highest echelons of the party and with Lenin himself. Not that that was any impediment to Frunze's breaking his word and reneging upon his signature. In his mind, these were peccadilloes, and he was above all else anxiously courting the praises of the supreme guide, preparatory to winning some medals with view to climbing up the party hierarchy. The wheel was soon to turn, and he would in turn come be ensnared by someone who out-betrayed him.

The authorities' tactics, then, consisted of shifting blame for the breakdown of the alliance onto the Makhnovist insurgents although as we have seen the latter had observed the strictest loyalty in implementation of the agreement concluded. Now, we have unpublished, first hand — and we might add, weighty evidence — its author, Marcel Ollivier, was one of the French founders of the Third International, Rosa Luxemburg's chief translator into French, and an active member of the French Communist Party for many a long year before he broke with it abruptly in the 1930s. At this time Ollivier was in Russia and had been invited, along with other French representatives including Alfred Rosmer, Jacques Sadoul and Henri Barbusse, to come to the Ukraine to witness the defeat of Wrangel. Upon arriving, he traveled on separately by truck; thus it was that at one stopover in the open countryside he saw…

"... a troop of horsemen loom all of a sudden from behind an outcrop. [They] swooped down on us so quickly that they were upon us before we could lift a finger to scramble back on board the truck and seize the rifles inside. Mounted on small, highly strung horses and armed to the teeth — carbines slung across the shoulder, saber by their side and daggers at their belts, their chests crisscrossed by leather ammunition belts, and their heads topped by enormous fur chapkas ... they had an appearance that was unsettling, I might even say unnerving."[17]

It transpired that these new arrivals were Makhnovists; Marcel Ollivier and his fellow travelers reckoned that their time had come, not knowing that a compact had been concluded between Bolsheviks and insurgents, but the latter treated them in friendly fashion and they were able to continue on their way unmolested. They reached Melitopol and at headquarters attended a soirée during which Ollivier noticed a ...

"... group of officers immersed in animated discussion. In their midst stood a fellow of about 25 years of age whom the others appeared to be besieging and who was replying with passion and ardor to the queries and arguments of his interlocutors. I asked Viktor Taratuta [who spoke fluent French — A.S.] what the discussion was all about. He explained that this officer was from the Makhno Division recently incorporated into the Red Army, and that he was defending his libertarian viewpoint against the others. As I remarked upon the impassioned tone in which he was doing so, Taratuta told me, literally: 'Once we have done with Wrangel, we will shoot him' [...] This model revolutionary [Taratuta], this 100 percent Bolshevik whom Bogdanov and Lunacharsky had accused of being an Okhrana agent — and whom Lenin himself, in conversation with Professor Rozhkov, had referred to as a 'con man' — told me that, in as many words. It will be readily understood that it came as a shock to me. But, to be honest, I did not take it seriously. A throwaway remark, I thought. Shooting a man who was fighting alongside you and with whom one had just signed an alliance open and above board, merely because his beliefs did not square with one's own, would have been an act of infamy of which I did not then think the Bolsheviks capable. In which belief, I was mistaken, as we shall see."[18]

Shortly after this, Marcel Ollivier crossed the Perekop isthmus and was amazed to see no signs of the fight which the Whites had put up in these entrenched positions which at first sight looked impregnable. It was only when he discovered that the Whites had been attacked from behind following the Makhnovists' and other Red units' crossing of the Sivash straits that he was able to comprehend, and he then found "even more scandalous the treatment to which the Makhnovists were subjected shortly after." Then he learned of the breakdown of the agreement and upon arrival in Melitopol, was informed of the fate of the young Makhnovist officer whom he had seen in discussions with Red Army officers:

> "The day before, before the garrison assembled in the square, he had found himself 1) mentioned in army dispatches for his brilliant conduct under fire and 2) sentenced to death for rebellion against the soviet authorities — sentence followed by immediate execution. So Taratuta had been farsighted — or, to be more precise — well-informed. As for the deed itself: I leave it to the reader to reach his or her own opinion of shooting a man only moments after having commended him in army dispatches for his brilliant conduct under fire. As for myself, let me say that I regard it as infamous."[19]

On the same occasion, Ollivier learned of the failure of the push against Warsaw which had been covered up for five months! This is precious testimony for Marcel Ollivier simply cannot be suspected of entertaining any sympathy at all for libertarians or Makhnovists, being at this time of rigidly orthodox views and outraged only by specific infamous methods rather than querying the very principle of the nature of power. John Xydias, from whom we have already quoted, a bourgeois liberal with little time for ideology, speaks very prosaically of an immense "thirst for power" in explaining the conduct of the Bolsheviks:

> "Power of itself, power as the goal, such was the Bolsheviks' ruling notion. Their doctrine set them free of all restraints. Morality, law, justice were so many 'bourgeois prejudices.' Hence the total indifference in the selection of means; hence the monstrous amorality of the soviet regime which shows itself in all the minutiae of Bolshevik life and Bolshevik politics; hence their recourse, during the war and before the revolution, to the most sordid methods: treachery, perfidy."[20]

Without dwelling too long at this point on possible explanations for the conduct of the Bolshevik leadership, let us recall their essential justification, namely, that they were invested with an historic social mission of capital significance to mankind's future and in order to achieve this mission "...all seemed licit to them." This formula left them free to resort to all of the methods of rule known thus far, concentrating on the best of them — which is to say the worst — in order to maintain themselves in power. However, they were not fully conversant with the mechanism for, further down the road, it was going to mangle them too just as tragically, as we shall see anon. What was at stake was neither more nor less than the basic ethical connection between the chosen end and the means used to achieve it.

Arshinov also demonstrates the undeniable premeditation behind this Bolshevik treachery; on this point he cites two assassination bids against Makhno in the months of October and November, then two handbills found on the first captured Red soldiers on November 27 headed: "Death to the Makhnovschina!" and "Forward against Makhno!" These were undated but had been issued to the troops on November 15 or 16, 1920.

Thus, to their great misfortune, the Makhnovists had yet again snatched chestnuts from the fire only to see the Bolsheviks alone reap the benefits and they were paying dearly for the lesson. Now they needed to fight desperately — in the direst of circumstances — for their very survival.

Notes to Chapter 24: Bolshevik Treachery

1. Trotsky *Stalin*, New York and London, 1941. p. 337. Oddly, this passage does not figure in the French edition of the book. It must be assumed that the publisher or the translator censored this posthumous "boldness" on the part of the master.
2. Victor Serge, op. cit. pp. 135–136.
3. S.I. Gusev, "Lessons of the Civil War" in *The Civil War and the Red Army* (in Russian) Moscow, 1958. p. 88.
4. Ya. Yakovlev, *Anarchism in the Great Russian Revolution* (in Russian), Moscow, 1921, pp. 15–36.
5. Arshinov op. cit. p. 180.
6. Ibid, p. 181.
7. Kubanin op. cit. p. 212.
8. Idem.
9. Yefimov op. cit. p. 215.
10. *The Civil War in the Ukraine* op. cit. p. 771.
11. As suggested by Alexei Nikolaev, author of three factional works on Makhno and the Makhnovschina: *Batko Makhno*, Riga, 1928; *Nestor Makhno*, Riga, 1929; and *First Among Equals*, Detroit, 1947. The author had lived in the area at the time and had also met Makhnovists and Makhno's wife, after Makhno's death. The only other reference to this alleged killing is in Rudnev, who mentions that "machine-guns were to be used" to defeat the Makhnovists in the Crimea, op. cit. p. 93.
12. Yefimov op. cit. pp. 213–214.
13. *Gazeta Krasnoarmeitsa*, quoted by G. Rimsky in *The Last Days of the Crimea*, Constantinople, 1920. p. 21.
14. M.V. Frunze *Selected Works* (in Russian), Moscow, 1957, Tome 1, pp. 427–429.
15. Ibid. p. 430.
16. *Memoirs on Vladimir Ilyich Lenin*, Tome II, p. 314 and *M.V. Frunze on the Civil War Fronts*, Moscow 1941, pp. 460 and 463.
17. Marcel Ollivier, *Un bolchévik dangereux*, typewritten manuscript, second part, pp. 142–143. We thank the author for having so kindly allowed us to publish these excerpts.
18. Ibid. p. 153.
19. Ibid. p. 160.
20. J. Xydias *French Intervention in Russia 1918–1919* op. cit. p. 74.

25. The Last Year of Fighting and the Death Throes of Libertarian Revolution in the Ukraine

The Red Army high command took it ill that Karetnik's detachment, penned up at the other end of the Crimean peninsula, managed to pierce the dense cordon and escape from the rat-trap. The troops dispatched in pursuit of him, who included Latvians, displayed little urgency about catching him up, probably because of the still fresh recollection of their brotherhood in arms; so the Red Army leaders called up troops stationed in the rear, on the continent itself. They, having played no part in the capture of Perekop did not know it was the victors over the Whites that they were now under orders to confront.

A sea of Red troops was deployed to forestall the Makhnovists' return to Gulyai-Polye. Traced to Mikhailovka, they were encircled by a division of Kursantys — Lenin's Junkers — the 42nd Infantry division, the International Cavalry Brigade, and the Fourth Red Cavalry divisions commanded by Timoshenko.[1] The Insurgents were still a daunting force: One thousand horsemen, 300 tatchankis, 250 machine-guns and six cannon. However, they were heavily outnumbered — by 20 to one! — though that was not the most serious thing: above all, they were short of ammunition, for the Red Army had taken care not to restock them after the capture of Perekop and Simferopol. On November 30, they evaded a first enemy unit and then, the following day, December 1st, in the town of Timoshevka, they engaged the 42nd Red Division all day long, inflicting heavy losses. The following night, they seized Timoshevka, capturing an enemy regiment down to the last man and stocking up on arms and ammunition again. At this point they made a grave mistake — which Makhno himself would assuredly have avoided — by not moving on immediately and allowing enemy forces to regroup and flood towards Timoshevka from every direction. In the early hours of the morning, they repulsed every enemy attack wave and even counter-attacked but — running short of ammunition — were obliged to cut and run for Mikhailovka that afternoon. There they found themselves pinned down by enemy cavalry and artillery. Six hundred insurgents died heroes' deaths while others broke up into small groups and tried to slip through the net thrown up around them. Two hundred insurgents were again intercepted and cut down by the International Cavalry Brigade's sabers (this brigade was made up of Germans, Hungarians and other ex-POWs enlisted by Moscow). Over half of this valiant body — undoubtedly the strongest fighting unit of all those which saw action in the civil war — perished in this unequal confrontation. Some escapees did manage to slip through the Reds' ring of steel in several places. The last remaining compact body of some 250–300 horsemen linked up with Makhno on December 7th in the Greek village of Kermenchik, some 80 kilometers east of Gulyai-Polye.

The meeting was a dramatic one. Marchenko and Taranovsky who were leading the contingent announced with pained irony that it was their "honor to announce the return of the Crimean army." Marchenko added: "Yes, brothers, now we know what these communists are."[2] Makhno remained somber, the sight of this tiny band of survivors from his 1,500 elite cavalry who had set off a month before having shaken him to the core. He held his tongue and strove to control his emotions. The insurgents came together in general assembly. The escapees told how Karetnik and his staff had been treacherously arrested and shot out of hand. Outraged and infuriated by this monstrous treachery, the Makhnovists were henceforth to fight spurred on by a terrible thirst for revenge.

❦

Against the insurgents, the Red Army marshaled two-thirds of the total manpower massed against Wrangel, that is, around 150,000 front line fighters drawn from five armies: The Sixth Army (59,404 men complete with staff and other services), the Fourth (81,339 men), the 13th (26,356), the First (21,089) and the Second Cavalry (15,257).[3] At this point the Red Army had a total of five-and-a-half million men in service, 130,000 of them ex-tsarist officers. On December 5th, it was decided that this sizable force would be cut by two million so as to facilitate a return to normal life, but this was a formality, for as we have seen, this army was all in all without any real appetite for battle and was only a crushing burden upon the population whose task it was to keep it supplied and billeted. It is noteworthy that, of the demobilized Latvians who had served as the regime's all-purpose troops, over half decided to make their way home to bourgeois Latvia in 1921; the rest, probably too compromised to go home, opted to remain in Leninist territory.[4]

The strategy laid down by Frunze vis-a-vis the Makhnovists tended to provide for three concentric lines of encirclement around their chief base — the Gulyai-Polye region — for pushing them towards the shores of the Sea of Azov and for wiping them out there. However, there was many a slip 'twixt cup and lip, and Frunze was forced to draft order after order, in great detail on some points, between December 5 and 15 in order to hone his maneuver further. On December 5, he "ordered a concentric offensive from the northwest, north and east, in order to beat the remnants of the Makhnovist detachments back towards the Sea of Azov and ruthlessly exterminate them"; the insurgents of the Pavlograd and Novomoskovsk region were forced back towards the Dniepr, there to be exterminated also. On December 11, all Red troops were ordered to "carry out overlapping movements" to forestall any one breakthrough by the Makhnovists and to carry out a sweep of the entire area.⁵ The order of December 6 urged careful sweeps of all occupied settlements, with anybody found in possession of weapons to be shot. On that very day the "liquidation of the Makhnovschina and of banditry in the Ukraine was acknowledged as a government target of the first importance," by the military revolutionary soviet of the soviet republic. All signs of "insubordination, questioning and foot-dragging must be ruthlessly punished."⁶ The terms "ruthless" and "annihilation" endlessly recurred in all Frunze's orders. He himself was under continual pressure from Lenin who, on December 17, issued an unequivocal resolution: "That it be demanded of Comrade Frunze in the name of the central committee that he redouble his efforts to liquidate Makhno," and shortly afterwards: "The commander in chief [S. Kamenev] and Frunze must be nagged and hounded every day into *completing* the annihilation and capture of Antonov and Makhno."⁷ "Nagged" and "hounded" in their turn, the Red Army troops did what they could but without much success — the very opposite, indeed; according to one Red Army officer, M. Rybakov, "Makhno sauntered throughout the region as the fancy took him, picking his targets and suddenly popping up wherever he chose, capturing a regiment or a whole brigade, seizing transports, munitions and artillery pieces then bursting out of the encirclement as he chose." And this, according to Rybakov, thanks to the support of the populace and his intelligence service, composed of the most unlikely looking types: "Vagabonds, Red soldiers looking to rejoin their units, miners allegedly arriving to barter coal against bread, repentant deserters, ex-members of the Communist Party even, victimized women, widows, orphans, etc."⁸ Superbly briefed on the enemy's deployment, Makhno struck where and when he wished. Brova, commanding a detachment of 600 Makhnovists operating around Pavlograd, defeated a brigade of Red hussars at Komar on December 2; on December 3 and again in Komar, Makhno himself, at the head of 4,000 insurgents, crushed a brigade of Red Kirghiz; Rybakov specifies there was:

> "…the impression that Makhno was striking everywhere, that he was irresistible, that he was beyond capture and that, with the forces at hand, a struggle against him was not feasible. The rout of the Kirghiz Brigade had so demoralized the combatants as to rob them of their absolute faith in their strength, in their expertise; so great was their fear that they did not dare wander far to carry out reconnaissance, in broad daylight, no more than a kilometer from their base and that in flat country, such was their terror of the Makhnovists' 'saber work.'"

On December 12, Makhno linked up with Vdovichenko's detachment and captured Berdyansk, where 86 Chekists and communists were sabered. On the 14th, he encountered numerous enemy troops at Andreyevka and captured two whole divisions, i.e., 20,000 men! For their benefit a meeting was laid on, the meaning of the insurgents' struggle was explained to them and any who so wished were invited to join the Makhnovist ranks; the rest were sent packing. These new recruits were not always very dependable; some wasted no time in deserting, scampering away to brief the Red command on the Makhnovist positions. Thanks to such briefings, the insurgents were more readily located and on December 16 a great battle brought the two sides together at Fedorovka. All of the Red divisions converged on Fedorovka amid the greatest confusion with some even firing upon others! The fact is that everybody, Makhnovists included, was wearing the same uniform! One Red regiment was first taken prisoner by the insurgents, then rescued in a counter-attack by their own side. The engagement — which occurred in a temperature of 17 degrees below zero — ended in a stalemate, but, since the insurgents escaped and left behind in enemy hands the black standard bearing their slogan "With the oppressed against the oppressors always!", the Red command counted the outcome as a victory for its side. Frunze sent off a telegram to this effect to Lenin on December 17: the "...contingent of 7,000 Makhnovists which had managed to breach the triple encirclement, clashed with the fourth cordon; following a lengthy engagement, its infantry has been wiped out and only Makhno and 300-to-400 horsemen managed to get away." He reckoned this a fatal blow to the Makhnovschina. [9] That was not the opinion of Rybakov who gives a detailed account of the battle and estimates Makhnovist losses at only 500 men! Frunze knowingly misrepresented the outcome in order to play down his complete failure and thereby to avoid being unduly "nagged" and "hounded" by his master.

At the start Makhno believed that by defeating a few divisions he might stop the enemy offensive in its tracks; the facts tempered his optimism, and he came to appreciate that he faced a host of Red troops whose aim was to encircle him and overwhelm him with their numbers. He was very quick to react and his strategical genius came to the rescue again; he split his contingent up into several detachments, scattering them throughout the region before setting off himself along with 2,000 partisans, in a northerly direction to begin with. He smashed some more enemy units along the way, derailing a trainload of Chekists and Bolsheviks near Alexandrovsk, before crossing the Dniepr and thrusting deep into the provinces of Kiev and Kherson, with a mob of Red divisions on his heels. Through severe frost and blizzards, the detachment covered 80 kilometers daily, swooping unexpectedly on enemy units, who had no inkling that it was so close. On every side the Makhnovists hit out at the oppression of people, coming to symbolize popular revenge: Chekists, militiamen, punitive detachments, looters on behalf of the State, Bolsheviks ... all were fair game. On December 19, the staff of the Petrograd Kursanty brigade was taken unawares and wiped out. Among the victims of this whirlwind assault, they were startled to find an ex-general of the tsarist army, Martynov, an ex-colonel, Drezhevinsky and a high-ranking officer,

Matveyev of similar background, along with several Bolshevik political commissars.[10] A prominent Bolshevik leader, A. Parkhomenko, close to Budyenny and Voroshilov, perished with his staff on January 3, 1921, when they too were taken by surprise.[11] A Red Army commander, Pavel Ashakhmanov, a survivor of the Petrograd Kursanty Brigade, while bemoaning the loss of his comrades could not disguise his admiration for Makhno and his tactics:

"The aphorism to the effect that the art of warfare is not all book-learning and that a well-made head is often to be preferred could not be more apt than when applied to the insurgent army's commander, Nestor Makhno. Of course one cannot believe that he has followed in Napoleon's footsteps who disclosed the secret of his successes by saying: 'What I do is the product only of my talent, but I have always acted in complete accord with the precepts of the great strategists.' All the same, one cannot claim he has followed Suvorov's advice and read Alexander the Great, Hannibal, Julius Caesar or Bonaparte. Here we are indubitably dealing with a well-made head and what is particularly interesting, all his 'sensible' tactical decisions have always conformed to the fundamental laws of tactics. He has quite rightly played upon the psychology of the fighter aiming to strike a lethal disorganization into our Red Army. He has tried to drive a wedge between head and heart by letting it be largely known that he amnestied simple soldiers and ruthlessly gunned down only commanders and commissars. [...] Makhno has captured the charisma of the commander superbly by throwing into the military balance his last reserve: himself. It is he personally who extricates his troops from all perilous situations. [...] Every bush, every mound, every ravine, everything has been weighed up and is a factor in the equation. Intelligence, liaison and protection are organized to perfection. He is not just very familiar with our weaknesses, but even takes the personalities of our commanders into the reckoning. [...] He strikes on the left then veers to the right, attacks Berdyansk then makes for Gulyai-Polye. He stays no longer than a day or night in any one place, lest he be seriously encircled. In the event of not succeeding, he makes off, dispersing. He does not encumber himself with prisoners; at Andreyevka he dumped 1,200 of them in our path. He is equally ready to jettison his baggage which he lays out as bait, when need be, for our cavalry while he himself makes off fast and far.

Makhno the partisan is enterprising and gallant in the extreme. The first time, he let himself be encircled in Berdyansk and thereby forced us to divert our troops southwards. This was a decoy action; we regrouped vigorously but Makhno discovered that we had not diverted our troops sufficiently towards the south and let himself be encircled once again, in Andreyevka this time. There, once our troops had been well and truly diverted, he assured himself that the road northwards was free and broke out of our circle in a flash, leaving our troops in disarray and thoroughly disappointed. Within days, he was on the far bank of the Dniepr, near Alexandrovsk; within a week, he was operating in Belgorod."[12]

In this astonishing tribute from vice to virtue, Ashakhmanov forgets only one thing: that Makhno was fighting for social revolution and freedom, whereas Ashakhmanov served only the narrow interests of the Bolshevik party-state and aspired only to a few medals to display on his breast. The difference accounts for a lot.

❧

The Red Army command entrusted the task of giving chase to Makhno to a "flying corps" under the command of Nesterovich, a corps made up of the best units from the five armies which had failed in the celebrated encirclement operation. This flying corps was charged with dogging the insurgents' footsteps, denying them all respite and facilitating the actions of the two best divisions of Red Cossacks which had been placed under the command of Primakov and Kotovsky. Makhno had to avail of all the talents that Ashakhmanov acknowledged he possessed in order to escape his terrible stalkers. Arshinov who was along on this dangerous trek describes the seriousness of the situation:

"All escape routes were blocked. The area was a veritable graveyard — nothing but rocks and sheer gorges covered by ice. Advancement was possible only with the most painful slowness, while continual fire spewed from machine-guns and artillery on every side. No one could see any way out, any salvation. However, no one wanted to disperse in disgrace. They all determined to die together, side by side.

It was unspeakably painful at this point to look upon the handful of insurgents surrounded by rocks, the vastness of the sky and enemy fire; they were motivated by the stiffest resolve to fight to the last, already convinced that all was lost. Sadness, despair and a peculiar grief gripped the soul. There was the urge to shout out to the whole world that a crime beyond expiation was in the process of commission, that all that was most heroic in the people, the best that it was capable of producing in heroic times was in the process of being done to death and perishing forever.[13]

At this point wounded, Makhno gave proof of his exceptional strength of spirit, and of the unbelievable resourcefulness of his tactical genius and still managed to give the slip to the inevitable annihilation that seemed to await the detachment. He veered as far away as the borders of Galicia before turning back towards Kiev, crossing the Dniepr again and popped up — as if by a miracle — in the province of Poltava. With the Red Cossacks still in pursuit, he veered even further north and at last succeeded in shaking off his pursuers at Belgorod towards the end of January. It had been a fantastic trek across more than 1,500 kilometers and five provinces, punctuated by daily combat and against the backdrop of a hostile Nature. To be sure, he had lost all of his baggage, his artillery and his machine-guns, not to mention half his detachment, but now he was in a position to seize the initiative himself.

Unable to defeat the insurgents on the field of battle, the Red authorities took it out on the population of their preferred theater; on December 17th, Frunze ordered all settlements to be encircled and repression of all who aroused the slightest suspicion.14

In reply other Makhnovist detachments which had remained on home ground mounted reprisals against Chekists, administrative agents, militias and the bands of plunderers commissioned to "requisition" all of the peasantry's foodstuffs. A report from victualler commissar Vladimirov, giving a catastrophic summary of the situation, left Lenin aghast. Working himself up into a frenzy, the great man conveyed his rage to Sklianski, the secretary of the regime's military soviet:

"6.11.1921.

Comrade Sklianski,

I enclose a further 'warning.'

Our military commander has failed lamentably by allowing Makhno to escape (despite huge numerical advantage and strict orders to capture him) and now he has failed even more dismally by showing himself incapable of crushing a few handfuls of bandits.

Have drawn up for me a *short* report from the commander-in-chief concerning what is going on (with a brief breakdown of the disposition of the bands and the troops).

What use is being made of our thoroughly dependable cavalry?
• the armored trains? (Are they deployed rationally? Do they not move around *haphazardly* to recover wheat?)
• armored vehicles?
• aircraft?
How are they used, and how many?

Wheat and heating fuel, all are being wasted because of these bands while we have a million men in our army. Make every effort you can to get the commander-in-chief to get a grip on himself.

Lenin"15

At the 10th Party Congress in March 1921 with the Kronstadt sailors' uprising at its height, he scathingly rebuked Frunze, reminding him of the necessity that Makhno be liquidated with all possible speed: "It is going to be an extraordinary, painful war. But we must have an end of Makhno. I wish you success."[16] During the same congress, in order to cow the internal opposition which banded together under the name of "Workers' Opposition," he equated them with the anarchosyndicalists and Makhnovists. It is true that a year earlier, he had already deployed the same arguments to confound the leader of the so-called "democratic centralist" internal faction (i.e., a faction that supported the party's actually operating internally in accordance with democratic centralism.)[17]

Lenin had good grounds for feeling uneasy, for not only were the Makhnovists stymieing the many Red units pursuing them, but they were also alerting some of their adversaries to the justice of their cause. In his memoirs, Budyenny, the one-time chief sergeant-major of the tsarist army and now commander-in-chief of the First Army of Red Cavalry whose task it was throughout this period to combat Makhno, relates that following the crushing of one of his army brigades, he had to have the brigade commander, political commissar and two regimental commanders shot in order to stiffen these units' will to win. Budyenny adds that, to the great disquiet of both himself and Voroshilov who shared command, they had had to face the face that: "none of the commanders had any inclination to complete the task of wiping out Makhno, regardless of cost and with all possible speed."[18]

Lots of Red soldiers surrendered, in the knowledge that they had nothing to fear, as the insurgents executed only officers and political commissars; some Red soldiers joined the Makhnovists, while others were released and for the most part recaptured by special commissions from the Red Army which escorted them back to their units of origin. Such generosity backfired on the insurgents, for their ex-captives rejoined the fighting and even supplied intelligence about the Makhnovists' strength and positions. The most spectacular defection was that of the commander of the First Brigade of the Fourth Red Army Cavalry Division, one G.S. Maslakov who, to the absolute consternation of his superiors, defected to Brova's Makhnovist detachment near Pavlograd on February 9, 1921, along with his whole brigade. Many other Red soldiers deserted and joined, throughout the country, the string of partisan bands fighting against the regime, on behalf of restoration of power to the people, in the format unanimously described as free soviets.

Indeed, after the defeat of the Whites, the populace had awakened to the emptiness of the Bolsheviks' promises; so it aimed to assert its rights vis-à-vis the party-state which had snatched away the gains of the 1917 revolution. Hundreds of thousands of partisans rose in revolt and turned against the regime's representatives. Soviet historians have dubbed this period the "mini-civil war," every whit as murderous as the one against the Whites, for it cost the Red Army, according to official figures, 170,000 dead in 1921 and 21,000 in the following year.

❦

The whole country was ablaze, in Byelorussia, in Russia itself, especially around Tambov where the Social Revolutionary Antonov marshaled a mighty well-organized army of 50,000 at the start of 1921; in Siberia, 60,000 partisans had revolted in one district alone [20]; in Karelia; in Central Asia, in the Caucasus and in Kronstadt, the steadfast citadel of revolution which called Lenin and his confederates to account. It was the biggest scare of the time for the Bolshevik leaders who expected to have their throats cut by rampaging "muzhiks." They wasted no time in climbing down, lifting the road-blocks and other obstacles to direct barter between town and countryside, restoring private ownership and replacing their "requisitioning/looting" with a levy in kind; in short, they made full speed astern, temporarily shelving their ideological weaponry. The essential thing, as far as they were concerned, was to cling to power and protect their position of dominance and then bide their time. This was quickly followed up by the conclusion of trade agreements (the conditions did not matter) with Britain, Germany and any other country willing to enter into them. Through the good offices of "humanitarian" organizations set up by sympathetic bourgeois, application was made to the United States for charity; other cereal-growing nations too were called upon to rescue millions of peasants from famine (wheat thus collected was of course distributed under the strictest supervision of the State machine). In parallel with this, the fight against the insurgents was stepped up; the Red Army took a back seat to special units and Chekists; they resorted to police provocations. Chekists infiltrated the insurgent groups, the better to expose and crack down on them. This strategy of the "carrot and stick" — with which all authoritarian regimes have been conversant — would nonetheless rescue the authorities and, after several years of intense fighting, contributed to the undoing of most of the insurgents.

In the Ukraine, a region prized on account of its natural resources, there were (again according to official sources) some 45,000–50,000 in revolt against Moscow by the end of 1920. In the months that followed, a secret report from the staff heading the anti-insurgent campaign listed 30 partisan detachments numbering 27,500 infantry and cavalry and with access to machine-guns and artillery pieces. The most significant of these was Makhno's; he was credited with 2,000 infantry and 600 horsemen, 80 machine-guns, 10 cannon and two armored cars with the telling names of "Death to the communist commissars!" and "Batko Makhno." For large scale operations the Makhnovists could field 12,000 men, 2,500 of those cavalry. [21]

Frunze confirmed this estimate by reckoning that he faced 15,000 Makhnovists in December 1920, 5,000 to 6,000 by January and a central core group of 2,500 infantry and cavalry, with 80-to-100 machine-guns and several cannons by March–April 1921. [22]

Adapting to the new mode of struggle, the insurgents overhauled their structures and activities. This was the first partisan war of this century and quite novel compared with all the previous forms of guerrilla warfare and fighting of that sort. For one thing, speed of movement was the priority; a speed of 80-to-100 kilometers daily at times; to this end, outriders rode ahead of detachments to pre-arranged staging posts, to arrange fresh mounts and fresh food with sympathetic local peasants and regularly they plotted the deployment of enemy forces. Secondly, given the huge numbers and concentrations of enemy forces, priority was given to small detachments of several hundreds of partisans operating in different sectors and coming together only for important operations. Certain units were permanently assigned to areas suited to rest and recuperation, and these represented bases offering fresh supplies and manpower. At the head of isolated detachments were tried and tested Makhnovist commanders like Kurilenko, Kozhin, Savonov, Brova, Ivanyuk, Shchuss, Vdovichenko, Zabudko, Parkhomenko and Khristovoy as well as new commanders firmly ensconced in their theaters of operations. Around him, Makhno kept Petrenko, Belash, Taranovsky, Zinkovsky and certain newer partisans, in order to train them in this curious strategy before they set off to implement it elsewhere once they had digested it properly. The above-mentioned secret Red Army report notes, for instance, that the chief of staff of Makhno's main detachment was one Vassiliev, the head of intelligence service was Sidorov-Pavlovich, while command of the different units was vested in three ex-sailors, Kizhko, Liachenko and Gura, and the cavalry commander was former sergeant-major Dolzhenko, almost all of them newcomers to the movement. Furthermore, nearly all Makhnovists dressed in Red Army uniform, which only added to the confusion of their opponents.

Their tactics also were very modern: all nerve points — communication lines, telegraph lines, guard and surveillance posts, sundry depots, etc. — were methodically destroyed. All agents of the authorities, whether Chekists, mobile requisition teams and administrative agents, were systematically subjected to a revolutionary hounding. And propaganda was not neglected either; the movement's *Draft Theoretical Declaration* and the *Statutes of the Free Soviets* were circulated in thousands upon thousands of copies.

The Red Army's high command had a hard time stomaching its defeats. Budyenny wrote that he and the other heads of the anti-Makhno drive "were ashamed to look at one another," and that he "was loath to go to the telephone when Frunze called. It looked like we were about to ensnare Makhno at least, but instead of news of victory, disagreeable news was received."23 Frunze and his chief strategists and lieutenants — Kork, Eideman, Voroshilov and Budyenny — pored over the reasons for their failures and made significant amendments to their strategy of straightforward encirclement. They analyzed the battle sites and the insurgents' subsequent movements, trying to anticipate and deploy strong units along the supposed itinerary and commissioned their best troops to take on Makhno there. Every modern technology was pressed into service: armored cars, aircraft, armored trains, and mobile artillery.

≈≈≈

In March 1921, during the Kronstadt sailors' revolt, Makhno dispatched Brova and Maslakov at the head of a special corps, to spread the fire of insurrection into the Don and the Kuban; Parkhomenko set off with another detachment for the Voronezh region in Russia; a third group of 1,000 insurgents under

Ivanyuk, made for Kharkov. Makhno himself criss-crossed the right bank of the Dniepr. Having been wounded in the foot, he moved around by tatchanka, but remounted his horse as soon as circumstances required it and was unfailingly and permanently to be found at the head of the detachment, personally directing all maneuvers. He returned to the left bank of the Dniepr and fell into an ambush in the vicinity of Melitopol. He gave one body of enemy troops the slip and kept up the pressure on the rest for 48 hours solid, made a forced march of 60 kilometers and overwhelmed another Red Army unit near the shores of the Sea of Azov. Then he split his men, dispatching Kurilenko to give a fillip to the insurgent movement in Berdyansk and Mariupol district, charging him especially to track down and punish a Chekist unit which had earned itself a sinister reputation by shooting the wife and suckling child of one insurgent. [24] He himself continued to criss-cross the region along with Petrenko at the head of a contingent of 1,500 horsemen and two infantry regiments, routing several enemy units including an entire kursanty regiment, and seizing munitions, weapons, artillery and horses. Two days after that, he had to tackle fresh Red troops in sizable numbers; he charged them at the head of his partisans but in a counter-attack that was "intrepid to the point of madness," he was gravely wounded in the belly. Having passed out, he was evacuated by tatchanka, regained consciousness, split his unit up into 100 or 200-man groups, sending these out in every direction and was left behind with just his celebrated black sotnia for company.

He wanted to withdraw to some quiet spot to tend to his injury but had to engage one after another, with just his tiny unit, the Ninth Red Cavalry Division and other fresh cavalry troops. A savage "saber engagement" ensued. Yet again the end seemed nigh; the insurgents were on the verge of being overwhelmed by numbers but a final square of expert machine-gunners sacrificed themselves, allowing Makhno to break out of the tightening noose. Before their engagement, their commander, Misha, a native of the Berdyansk region had announced to Makhno: "Batko, you are necessary to the cause of our peasant organization. That cause we cherish. We are all going to die shortly, but our death will spare you, as well as all who believe and protect you. Do not forget to pass that on to our parents,"[25] then hugged him and set off to sell his life dearly against the enemy. Makhno was later to recall these heroic comrades, with some emotion, thanks to whom he was able to carry on with his fight.

On March 6, 1921, the Fifth Pan-Ukrainian Congress of Soviets, organized by the Bolsheviks, ordained a drive against "banditry," which is to say against all their political enemies, as a "State task of primary importance. At the same time it declared an amnesty for all "bandits" willing to repent, an amnesty valid up until April 15th and then extended shortly afterwards by one month. According to the authorities, 10,000 insurgents availed of the chance to give themselves up, and these included certain leading Makhnovists: Staff members Zverev and Poleno, Vladimir Sharovsky (who had been in charge of the movement's artillery from the outset),

Makhno's personal runner and the man in charge of the organization's rearguard, Vdovichenko. [26] This seems unlikely and is probably a product of misinformation for the last named individual, for instance, had — according to Makhno — been seriously wounded and sent for treatment to Novospassovka. Taken prisoner, he was subjected to heavy pressure by the Chekists to get him to sign a declaration in favor of the regime. [27] In the end — one could not swear by any of this — it is very possible that a number of captured insurgents had, under threat of immediate execution, gone over to the regime. The Cheka then attempted to press some of these to dismantle the Makhnovists from within, but, as one soviet historian stipulates, they are alleged to have been shunned or executed by their former comrades-in-arms. This defeatist propaganda went hand-in-hand with a savage crackdown on wounded insurgents and their close relatives; once discovered, death was inevitable for them.

Even so, the regime strove to improve its brand image in the eyes of the populace; wide-ranging propaganda argued that the new reforms and the levy in kind would do away with the bones of contention existing hitherto; the peasants were no longer so brazenly plundered, and henceforth they were to be duly compensated or paid on the nail for requisitioned foodstuffs and horses. The authorities were keen to give the impression that they had mended their ways, were not about to repeat past mistakes and that a return to civilian life would settle all of the problems which had been pending, provided of course that all "bandits" and "wreckers" were eliminated.

In spite of all these blandishments, the insurgents pressed on with their war of partisans through April and into early May. By a quirk of fate, Budyenny and Makhno found themselves face-to-face. Cavalry had been evaluated as of little effect against the Makhnovists and had been switched to the Crimea to put down the insurgency whipped up by Brova and Maslakov. Discovering that Makhno was nearby, Budyenny decided to attempt to pull off a glorious coup: he rode ahead of his troops with a detachment of armored cars and horsemen who were supposed to be novices who would be "blooded" on this occasion. In his memoirs, Budyenny explains that he found himself cut off from his armored cars and, having to face superior forces, was obliged to make good his escape across country by car. He allegedly glimpsed Makhno and his staff watching the engagement from atop a knoll. [28] Makhno's version of events is noticeably different: Budyenny showed himself to be a comic opera Cossack and had fled without a thought for anyone but himself. "In a trice, Budyenny — who had been galloping proudly at the head of his troops — turned tail and fled like a craven coward, abandoning his men to their fate."[29] It seems that the latter were not such greenhorns nor as cowardly as their leader, for they offered ferocious resistance to the Makhnovists, such as they had rarely encountered from any Red cavalry unit before; even so, defeated they were, and this had a catastrophic impact upon the rest of the First Red Cavalry which fell apart, experiencing many desertions in the wake of its commander's shameful conduct and was in the end disbanded. This version of events seems a lot more likely than Budyenny's, for it would be odd for the commander of the Red Cavalry, a Cossack to boot, to have departed by car and to have been able to escape his pursuers across country in this manner! Also his lack of courage was well known to other Red Army chiefs and to Stalin himself who, for that very reason, spared his life during his notorious purges.

At the end of May, Makhno made up his mind to strike a major blow by attempting to take Kharkov, the political capital of the Bolshevik Ukraine. He mustered several detachments and reconstituted an insurgent army of several thousand partisans, 2,000 of those cavalry. Panicking, the Bolshevik leaders erected a veritable human wall of Red troops around Kharkov, backed up by tanks, machine-gun vehicles and substantial artillery. The insurgents were frustrated in their intentions and were forced to revert to several detachments. During one month of incessant skirmishing, they lost 1,500 of their people, suffering their heaviest defeat at the end of June in the province of Poltava. Enemy losses were even more severe, but on their side the manpower reserve was larger than on the insurgent side where new recruits could not always make up either in quantity or, above all, in quality for the loss of battle-hardened partisans. Frunze himself, who had arrived to oversee operations, was taken by surprise by a band of insurgents on June 26; his escort perished while he was wounded and he survived only due to the quality of his mount. His superiors seized upon this as a chance to remove him temporarily from operations, replacing him with Aksentievsky, a tsarist ex-officer. The commander in charge of operations on the ground, Eideman, a great expert in "minor warfare," went through a hard time. One of his adjutants was later on to write that he hovered by the telephone, very nervously awaiting the latest news of operations and, having been himself given a severe dressing-down by his superiors, he "…dealt harshly with his own subordinates and his staff, occasionally cursing them. The directives emanating from Kharkov did not consider his feelings and were increasingly laconic and imperative."30

Another brilliant Red Army chief, Blucher, was called in; he arrived to conduct an on-the-ground inquiry to discover the real reason holding up the "definitive liquidation" of Makhno. One Nikita Khrushchev — who was to make a sinister name for himself in the Ukraine in 1936–37, earning himself the nickname of the "hangman of the Ukraine" — won his spurs at this time fighting against Makhno and other insurgents: "I played my part in the bloody battle joined against the bands of Makhno, Grigoriev and Antonov."31 Was he perhaps among the Red troops that Aksentievsky ordered on July 10th to wipe out the "bands" of Ivanyuk, Semerki and Luchenko — which furnished recruits for Makhno's main detachment — within the space of two weeks?32

The fact is that the regime's whole supply policy was stymied by all these military activities and that, as soon as they learned of the approach of Makhnovist detachments, agents of the authorities scampered off as fast as they were able. The "little war" was at its height although the Reds tended to gain a certain advantage by defeating Antonov at Tambov as well as other insurgents in Karelia and Siberia. In mid-July, an official report still spoke of 18 bands of insurgents in the Donetz basin region alone, numbering 1,042 with 19 machine-guns.[33] Faced with the Makhnovist detachments, which were also still active, Red commanders decided that Makhno's core group had to be wiped out regardless of the cost; they fielded a special motorized detachment under the command of Guermanovich, with eight armored machine-gun carriers, two fortified transport lorries and two liaison motorcycles at its disposal. Having traced Makhno and 200 insurgents to near Gulyai-Polye, the motorized detachment dismounted from its train at Tsarekonstantinovka on July 12th and set off in pursuit. One of their armored cars fell into a trap laid by the Makhnovists, and its crew was captured. Makhno himself boarded it and used it until it ran out of fuel, whereupon it was burned and its crew of Chekists executed. The motorized detachment's other units managed to locate Makhno and chased him for five days, covering an amazing 520 kilometers in that short space of time! Short of ammunition yet again and with no weapons to avail them against the enemy armor, the insurgents sustained considerable losses and only with great difficulty did they manage to shake off the murderous machines. [34]

Towards the end of July, Makhno again managed to slip out of reach of the enemy's clutches to the great despair of Red Army chiefs who saw their careers increasingly compromised and certainly feared lest their failure might result in their being lined up before a firing squad. Eideman telegraphed the Kharkov military command on July 22 to insist upon the execution of Kozhine and a certain Marussia who were reserves for Makhno's core group.[35] The following day, Frunze outbid him by demanding once and for all the "definitive liquidation" of the Makhnovschina. [36]

Makhno was grieved to lose one by one his close confederates from the early days: Marchenko (who died at the beginning of 1921), Kurilenko, Shchuss, Kozhin and Zabudko during the summer of 1921. He himself was in a bad way, suffering from his many wounds and was no longer able effectively to direct operations. Even so, he pulled off two more tremendous raids into central Russia, striking out for Veronezh and the Don and then decided in consultation with all the other detachments scattered throughout the country to go abroad to have his wound tended. In his absence and up until his return, Viktor Belash was to assume command of the main core group. On August 13, he left the Don along with his wife Galina Kuzmenko and about 100 cavalry, the most loyal of loyalists, survivors of the famed black Sotnia, bound for Poland. On August 16, they crossed the Dniepr with the Reds in pursuit; on that day alone, Makhno was wounded six times, albeit only slightly. On the right bank of the Dniepr, they encountered several Makhnovist detachments who wished him well in his recovery and that he might return to "rescue" them. On August 19, they unexpectedly ran into a brigade from the Seventh Red Cavalry Division; with another cavalry regiment giving chase, they had no option but to swoop on the enemy encampment, smashing

600 enemy horsemen and carrying off 25 tatchankis with machine-guns mounted. "Recovering from their panic and realizing that they were dealing only with a handful of partisans, the entire Red cavalry galloped off in pursuit,"[37] reinforced by an armored machine-gun carrier and a rapid-firing cannon. The insurgents still defeated the 32nd Red Regiment; losing 17 men and covering 120 kilometers, the group escaped from their pursuers. On August 22, Makhno sustained his eleventh serious wound; a bullet penetrated the nape of his neck, exiting through his right cheek. On August 26, a final encounter pitted them against the Red Cavalry; in the course of this engagement, his last remaining confederates from the old days — Ivanyuk, Petrenko and Taranovksy — perished.

A scout bearing a list of intended stopovers along the way to the Polish border was captured by some Red units which consequently assumed positions along the border. Whereupon the Makhnovists switched their itinerary and headed for the Romanian frontier, bordered by the Dniestr, the Ukraine's second great waterway separating the Bolshevik Ukraine in those days from monarchist, bourgeois Romania which was hostile to Moscow and close to the Western powers. Lots of Ukrainian insurgents tried and sometimes managed to cross the river to emerge beyond reach of the Leninist authorities. The undertaking was extremely dangerous, for the whole frontier zone was closely watched by many border posts and was also continually crisscrossed by patrols. So to escape from the Bolsheviks' proletarian "paradise" was virtually impossible! Yet again Makhno devised a bold stratagem; dressed in Red Army uniforms, the insurgents galloped up to one border post. Lev Zinkovsky rudely berated the guards, wanting to know why on earth they had summoned a cavalry unit; before the guards could answer, they had been surrounded and disarmed by Makhnovists. Keen to avoid their doom or perhaps sympathetic, the guards demonstrated extreme goodwill by pointing out the best place nearby to ford the Dniestr. The insurgents acted on this advice under heavy fire from other border guards who — either because they were especially bad shots or because they had no stomach for what was required of them — missed their targets completely. On the other side of the river, the Makhnovists were intercepted by Romanian border guards, relieved of their weapons and escorted to an internment camp on August 28.[38]

During this last fabulous foray, the little band of the bravest of the brave had covered over 1,000 kilometers in the space of three weeks, cutting a path for themselves amid daily fighting, through an unbroken curtain of enemy troops who had been alerted to their coming at that!

Although Makhno's departure did not diminish the activity of the movement's various detachments, his absence did make itself felt at the level of strategy. Belash, though he had learned from the school of hard knocks along with Nestor and himself a gifted organizer, did not have his colleague's genius for partisan warfare and was unable to avoid his detachment's being taking unawares at Znamenka one day in the autumn of 1921 by sizable enemy forces and almost entirely wiped out. The ones who got away also tried to slip across the border, and a few hundred of them were to appear later in Romania or Poland. Some emigrated even further afield, to Germany, France, Canada and elsewhere. The wounded Belash was captured and hauled off to the Kharkov Cheka where he was to write his memoirs of his command before being tried and shot in 1923 along with some other Makhnovists — which just goes to show that the movement was still extant.

Lebeds, who had been officially commissioned at the end of 1921 to write an initial study of the Makhnovschina, notes that 30 commanders and 2,443 Makhnovist insurgents were to surrender during the autumn of 1921. Some of them allegedly even asked that their services against the Whites be acknowledged, Lebeds adds — half in amusement, half in indignation. [39] We may query the veracity of these figures, for a more recent official source records the elimination of a Makhnovist band in the region of Poltava in 1922 and the dismantling of a clandestine Makhnovist organization in 1923, [40] as well as the existence of 18 Ukrainian insurgent bands in 1924, only three of which were of Petliurist sympathies. Thus it is possible that Makhnovist bands may have survived as late as 1924 and beyond, for during the Second World War, some Ukrainian partisan groups were to hoist the black flag again and fight against Nazi and Stalinist alike. Perhaps one day when the regime's archives are more readily accessible, we may learn more.

Eideman, Makhno's chief adversary during 1921, was to concede that the movement had not been beaten militarily but politically:

> "It was not our military successes against anti-soviet movements but rather the strengthening of the union between the proletariat and the underlying mass of the peasantry that ensured that Makhno, Antonov, the Siberian insurgents and the Kronstadt uprising failed to live up to the hopes of the class enemies of the Soviet State." [41]

Notes to Chapter 25: The Last Year of Fighting and the Death Throes of Libertarian Revolution in the Ukraine

1. The future Soviet Marshal; see his account of the battle in *Krasniy Arkhniv*, Moscow, 1940, No. 104, pp. 101–102.
2. Arshinov, op. cit. p. 189.
3. *The Command Directives from the Red Army Fronts* op. cit. p. 222.
4. *History of the Latvian Infantry.*
5. Frunze, op. cit. pp. 431–438.
6. Ibid, p. 434.
7. Lenin, op. cit. Tome XLV, p. 37.
8. M. Rybakov, "Makhno's 1920 operations," in *Krasniya Armiya*, 1922, No. 12, pp. 11–27 (quotation from p. 12).
9. *M. V. Frunze on the Civil War Fronts*, Moscow 1941, p. 466.

10. *Voyennoye znaniye,* 1921, No. 20, p. 31.

11. He was buried in Lugansk, his biographer tells us, in the square of the revolution; on his statue(!) the following inscription has been engraved: "Here lie the ashes of Parkhomenko, a Bolshevik who died a hero's death in the fight against the Makhnovist bands," G.L.A. Tokolnikov, *Parkhomenko,* Moscow 1961. (Not to be confused with the Makhnovist detachment commander of the same name.)

12. *Voyennoye znaniye,* No. 18, October 1921, pp. 43–44.

13. Arshinov, op. cit. p. 192.

14. Frunze, op. cit. p. 442.

15. Lenin, op. cit. Tome XXXV, p. 488.

16. Quoted in *Soldiers of the Revolution,* Kishinev, 1977, p. 51.

17. Lenin, op. cit. Tome XXXII, p. 216 and XXX, p. 477.

18. Budyenny, *The Road Traveled* (in Russian), Moscow, 1973, Tome III, pp. 196 and 201.

19. I. Ya. Trifonov, *Classes and Class Struggle in the USSR at the Beginning of the NEP (1921–1923),* Leningrad, 1964, pp. 4–5.

20. Idem.

21. *Revoliutsionaya Rossiya* (Revolutionary Russia), the Social Revolutionary organ appearing in Prague, 1921, No. 11, pp. 22–25.

22. Frunze, *His Life and His Activity* (in Russian) Moscow, 1962, p. 232 et seq.

23. Budyenny, op. cit. p. 195.

24. Makhno, *The Makhnovschina and its Erstwhile Allies: The Bolsheviks,* op. cit. pp. 37–39, and his account of the operations of this period, published in Arshinov, op. cit. p. 193–200.

25. Arshinov, op. cit. p. 197.

26. Trifonov, op. cit. p. 156.

27. Arshinov, op. cit. p. 195.

28. Budyenny, op. cit. pp. 216–217.

29. Arshinov, op. cit. p. 197.

30. Varetsky, "Marshal Blucher," in *Novy Zhurnal,* New York, 1951, XXVII, pp. 260–265.

31. Khrushchev, *Souvenirs,* Paris, 1971, p. 270.

32. Trifonov, op. cit. p. 281.

33. Idem.

34. E. Esbakh, "The last days of the Makhnovschina in the Ukraine," in *Voyna i revoliutsiya,* Moscow, 1926, No. 12, pp. 40–50.

35. Trifonov, op. cit. pp. 281–282.

36. Idem.

37. Esbakh, op. cit. pp. 47–48. Esbakh had himself been directly involved in this pursuit; thus his account of events, though hardly brilliant of itself, is to be welcomed for its objectivity! In any event, it corroborates Makhno's account as given in Arshinov, op. cit. p. 200.

38. This latter episode is related by Alexei Nikolaev (*First Among Equals,* op. cit.) who must have had it direct from the lips of Makhno's wife or some Makhnovist émigrés.

39. Lebeds, op. cit. p. 41.

40. O.O. Kutcher, *The Crushing of the Internal Counter-Revolution in the Ukraine* (in Ukrainian) Kharkov, 1971, pp. 154–161.

41. R. Eideman, "The Fifth Anniversary of a Lesson," in *Voyna i revoliutsiya*, Moscow, 1926, No. 12, p. 33.

26. The Road of Exile:
Bucharest, Warsaw, Danzig, Berlin

Although formal diplomatic relations between them did not exist, Moscow contacted the Romanian Foreign Affairs ministry by radio. On September 17, Chicerin, the one-time tsarist now Bolshevik and People's Commissar for Foreign Affairs in Soviet Russia, and Rakovsky, the chairman of the Ukrainian council of people's commissars, sent a joint communiqué to the Romanian premier, General Averesco, to sue for Makhno's return:

> "On August 28 the famous bandit Makhno crossed the Bessarabian border near Monastyrievka along with his band of supporters, seeking refuge on territory which is de facto under the authority of Romania. This bandit, leader of bands of brigands, has committed numerous crimes on the territory of Russia and the Ukraine, burning and looting villages, butchering the peaceable population and extorting its property from it through torture. This is why the Russian and Ukrainian governments hereby make a formal request of the Romanian government that it hand over the leader of the brigand gangs mentioned above, along with his accomplices, as common criminals.
>
> The People's Commissar for Foreign Affairs of the RSFSR."[1]

The Leninists had no hesitation in making such diplomatic overtures to the bourgeois authorities of the kingdom of Romania; though held up to public obloquy, these same authorities now proved very useful for the stifling of the fear which the Leninists felt of Makhno. He had to be annihilated and any means would suffice. Of course Makhno could only be referred to as a common criminal, for — had he been acknowledged as a political opponent — any application for his extradition would have been doomed to failure. Let us stress that until quite recently most of the Bolsheviks themselves had been émigrés subject to extradition proceedings; now they were in power and the methods that they had deemed worthy of condemnation were thoroughly respectable. However, their first overture met with rejection on the part of Averesco whose response was passed on to them on September 27, 1921.

"I did indeed receive your radio communication of the 17th inst., and I cannot agree either with its form or with its content. If criminals really have sought refuge on the territory of the kingdom of Romania, your judicial authorities can apply for the return of these individuals and although no convention on this subject exists between our countries, the Romanian government might yet, on a basis of reciprocity, accede to such an application. But to that end one would have to act in accordance with the norms of international law, i.e., an arrest warrant would have to be forwarded, emanating from the competent judicial institution and detailing those articles of the penal code applicable to the offenders. Furthermore, the precise particulars of these offenders would have to be given. Given that the death penalty does not exist in Romania, you would, in addition, have to offer a formal assurance that the death penalty would not be applied against extradited individuals. Once those conditions have been met, the Romanian government will look into the case of the bandit Makhno and his accomplices and will determine whether there are grounds for acceding to the request for their extradition." [2]

This bourgeois general was not only pointing out that the extradition request had not been very specific, but also reminding the applicants of the conventions of international law and stressing the absence of capital punishment in his own country. In short, he gave them a lesson in good manners. Chicherin, put firmly in his place, made a further overture on October 22:

"The reply given on September 27 by the head of your government, General Averesco, to our request that the bandit Makhno and the accomplices who accompanied him be surrendered to us, is rather a statement of juridical principles than a communications of a practical nature and offers us no clarification of the real status of this affair. That statement contains no confirmation, even, of Makhno's presence in Romania. As soon as the requisite materials have been collated and the legal forms required by you have been completed, the results will be communicated to you.

However, the Russian and Ukrainian governments consider that formal procedures are only of secondary importance and that these pale into absolute insignificance before the fact that a gang of criminals that has long terrorized the peaceable population of the Ukraine has found a refuge under the wing of the Romanian government. The legal pedantry displayed in this case by the Romanian government has not always been a feature of its conduct, even when more important matters concerning, say, treaty observance, have been at issue."[3]

The Romanians were intrigued by this unaccustomed obstinacy. Their For-eign Affairs minister, Take-Ionesco, made a soothing reply in view of what was at stake — the disputed treaty awarding Bessarabia to Romania — by quite simply asking for particulars about Makhno, for he genuinely did not know if this indi-vidual was indeed "among those interned by the Romanian authorities," and he announced that inquiries had been set in motion to trace him. In spite of everything and without setting his face against the possibility of extradition, he hoped that it might proceed according to the legalities.[4] Sniffing a concession, Chicherin seized the chance to try to force a decision by somehow making the surrender of Makhno a condition of normalization between the two countries:

"[…] We await your confirmation of Makhno's arrival in Romania in order to be able to undertake further steps of a juridical nature regarding this matter. Through the good offices of their representatives in Warsaw, the Russian and Ukrainian governments stand ready to furnish the Romanian government with documentary and photographic evidence. […] It was only legalistic nit-picking by the Romanian government in the matter of the bandit Makhno which we have raised, that obliged us to embark upon an evaluation of Romania's general approach to its international commitments and to point out, among others, Romania's breach of the treaty of March 9, 1918, under which the Romanian government was required to evacuate Bessarabia within two months.

The Russian and Ukrainian governments will thus consider that the attitude assumed by the Romanian government vis-à-vis this mat-ter will be key to relations between Russia and the Ukraine on the one hand and Romania on the other. In your reply of October 29, we do not see adequate grounds for changing our viewpoint, as set out in our earlier communications, and we are still of the same opinion: that the attitude you have adopted with regard to Makhno is distinguished by such partiality as to make it impossible to discern if your relations with Russia and the Ukraine were in reality such as you describe them."[5]

The extreme importance with which Makhno was invested by Moscow, which went so far as to make his extradition contingent upon implicit acceptance of a controversial treaty, placed the Romanians in a dilemma. They had to devise some honorable solution, in terms of their interests — recognition of the disputed treaty — and also of the conventions of international law to which they had just alluded; [6] and that without loss of face. So they took advice (with regard to this famous Makhno) from the Ukrainian nationalists (Petliurists). As early as Septem-ber 2nd, the nationalists had been contacted by the anarchist from the Ukraine who asked them to place his detachment under their protection and to make it possible for him to speak with Petliura's authorized agents in Bucharest so as to examine the possibility of some concerted action aimed at delivering the Ukraine from its enemies. Makhno, his wife and two confederates had been invited to travel up to the Romanian capital for treatment and for talks with Petliurist diplomatic representatives.

The Petliurist negotiator kept notes of these conversations. These notes record that Makhno stated that it had been his intention to enter Poland, there to seek out Petliura's main headquarters, but before he could reach the frontier, one of the outriders from his detachment had fallen into enemy hands along with the addresses of the stopovers necessary before crossing the frontier; and so he had decided to veer in the direction of Romania instead. The Petliurist agent noted that Makhno and his companions were "very circumspect, do not speak openly of their strength, plans and intentions, nor above all of the reasons which forced them to leave the Ukraine." [7] He nonetheless managed to get them to tell why they sought an alliance with Petliura: They declared that they had made for the territory of the Don Cossacks and then for central Russia — Voronezh, Tambov and Kursk — in order to assess for themselves the strength of the anti-Bolshevik insurgent movements operating there and had evaluated their limitations and relative powerlessness against the many and mighty special units of the Red Army. From which they had allegedly deduced that it was only in the Ukraine that the insurgent movement stood definite chances of expansion and of throwing out the Muscovites invaders — and so they had come to the conclusion that joint action with the Petliurists was called for.

In fact, Makhno and his companions were laying a false trail; they had never collaborated with the Petliurists and were well aware that a huge gulf divided them. However, their position could not have been more delicate; they realized that of the Romanians they could expect nothing, that they were at the mercy of an extradition order and that their only hope lay in some agreement with Petliura, even if only a circumstantial and temporary one. Only at that price could they avoid being handed over to Moscow; so they accepted they would have to recognize the authority of the Ukrainian nationalist government-in-exile although hitherto, as they told their interlocutor, they had reckoned social slogans a better device for the fight against the Bolsheviks. They went on to say that they reckoned the Ukrainian nationalist government which enjoyed the support of Poland and Romania and could call upon a well-equipped army could act effectively against the Red Army by opening up an external front while they could carry on with their partisan warfare in the interior. In this case, they seemed convinced of the prospects of their insurgent movement which accurately reflected the aspirations of the Ukraine's population.

But their Petliurist interlocutor was not completely taken in by their sudden conversion; in his report he pointed out the necessity of his government's "completely liquidating this movement and its organization before absorbing it into the Ukrainian nationalist movement." [8]

❧

For neither side was the outcome of these talks very conclusive. Meanwhile, Chicherin's assistant, Karakhan, traveled specially to Warsaw to meet with Romania's diplomatic representative there and to press the demand that Makhno be extradited. But the Romanians by now knew what was what in this use of the label "bandit" to designate a political opponent. Moreover, they did not want to alienate the Ukrainian peasantry by handing Makhno over, for they knew that a future armed conflict with the Bolsheviks could not be ruled out and — should that come about — their attitude towards Makhno, if they failed to extradite him, might work in their favor.

In view of the deadlocked situation, Makhno and some of his companions decided to carry on regardless; they escaped from their internment camp and tried to cross the Polish border. They were picked up by Polish border guards who turned them back into Romania, whereupon the Romanian border guards sent them back to Poland. This game dragged on all night until they were at last accepted into Poland and shipped on April 12, 1922 to an internment camp.

The moment he arrived in Poland, Makhno besieged all of the country's official agencies — the Foreign Affairs ministry, the Polish Socialist Party, Pilsudski himself, and others — for permission to move on to Czechoslovakia or Germany. In all he wrote off a dozen letters to this effect without result. On June 30, 1922, a soviet repatriation commission visited the Scholkovo camp where he was an internee and four Makhnovists, desperate or bewildered by their predicament, asked Makhno to intercede with the Poles and Soviets on their behalf in order to have them returned to the Ukraine. The camp commander turned down this request and thereafter had Makhno and his companions closely guarded. On July 18, Galina Kuzmenko, Makhno's wife, traveled to Warsaw herself to make overtures to the ministries concerned. She was cold-shouldered; a high-ranking official at the Home Affairs ministry, one Zhelikovsky, abruptly snapped: "Wait until your case comes up, then we shall see what to do with you. We cannot let you go unpunished, for Polish citizens have suffered from your handiwork in Russia[!]"[8] For his part Pilsudski replied on August 17 that he had "passed your request to the Interior Ministry." None of these moves came to anything, for the Polish secret police — the *Défensive* — had plans of its own for Makhno. First it assigned him to a Major Szarbson to be persuaded to stay in Poland, and then it was on to Lieutenant Blonski who said to him: "Why leave Poland? The Czechs are cowards, and they will hand you over to Moscow! As for Germany, the Bolsheviks are quite at home there! Stay with us; just adopt Petliura's platform, and all will be well for you!"[10] The Poles wished to make use of him in conducting destabilizing exercises in the Ukraine, but Makhno bluntly refused all these blandishments.

❦

Not that Moscow had remained idle; having learned that Makhno was an internee, it again approached the Poles with an extradition request, and then, seeing how slim the chances of its success were, targeted the Ukrainian libertarian for a provocation. It commissioned one of its agents, Ya. Krasnovolsky, who had been keeping tabs on the Makhnovists since Romania, to suggest to Makhno that he lead an insurgent movement in eastern Galicia, a region populated by Ukrainians but arbitrarily awarded to Poland under the Treaty of Riga. Makhno responded that he "could not enter into any serious talks with the Bolsheviks until such time as all anarchists and Makhnovists imprisoned in Russia had been freed."[11] Not that Makhno's answer unduly surprised the Bolsheviks; their object was merely to compromise him in Polish eyes so that the latter would expel him to Russia. There they themselves would see that he got a hospitable welcome in the Cheka's dungeons. They arranged for their agent to fake an escape attempt on the night August 2–3, 1922 and for him to be caught in possession of documents which, he would "spontaneously" confess, had been addressed by Makhno to the Soviet diplomatic representative in Warsaw, Maximovitch. These documents were encoded using the same code that Makhno had employed in other letters sent to Makhnovists interned in Poland and Romania. In addition, they bore Makhno's signature but not in his hand. No matter, for Krasnovolsky took it upon himself to hand over the key to the code; they were plans for the insurrection in Galicia, apparently forged for that purpose by the Bolsheviks. Makhno was promptly picked up by the *Défensive*, as were his wife and two of his closest comrades, Kumara and Jacques Domashenko. All four were switched to the Paviac political prison in Warsaw and accused of subversive activities against the Polish State.

An examining magistrate by the name of Luxemburg (!) looked into the affair. They were to remain in prison for 13 months before being brought to trial. Meanwhile, Galina, Makhno's wife, gave birth on October 30 to a little girl called Lucie. Only once during his long months in custody was Nestor able to see them together.

❧

An intense press and public opinion campaign was waged in libertarian circles worldwide and especially wherever the Russian anarchist Diaspora had a presence: the United States, Canada, Argentina, France and Germany. Already, thanks to the intervention of some anarcho-syndicalists during the Profintern's Moscow congress, ten Russian anarchists (Voline among them) had been deported from Russia. For his part, Arshinov and his wife had managed to cross the border clandestinely and reach Berlin, where he hurriedly brought out a history of the Makhnovist movement in Russian, followed up soon by German, French and Spanish editions. The anarchist press worldwide carried a fair number of articles on Makhno and his role in the Russian revolution. The Russian libertarian communist weekly, *Amerikanskiye Izvestia,* published in New York, opened a subscription to help jailed Makhnovists; by November 29, 1922, $1,476 had been raised. An attempt was made to pass these funds to Makhnovists jailed or interned in Poland and Romania. However, some of these Makhnovists, unable to bear their living conditions, applied for repatriation even at the risk of being shot or, at best, deported to Siberia. As for Makhno, he had — so to speak — been "vaccinated" against imprisonment by his previous ten years of prison and penal servitude before 1917. He busied himself with drafting his memoirs which he had passed on to Arshinov; they were also published in the Berlin review of the Russian anarchist exile group, *The Russian Messenger*, (in Russian, of course). He also penned letters to émigré Don Cossacks and an open letter to the Bolshevik-Communist Party of the Ukraine and Russia. All were intercepted and seized by the examining magistrate. Just to be on the safe side, he learned Esperanto and studied German. However, harsh conditions in custody in the Mokotow prison led to a recurrence of the tuberculosis which had been gnawing at him for about ten years.

As the trial scheduled for November 17, 1923 approached, the campaign by anarchists worldwide was stepped up; libertarian papers carried a lengthy appeal "against the crime being hatched by the Polish and Russian governments," signed by German libertarian communist organizations, the French Anarchist Federation and anarchist personalities Rudolf Rocker, Sébastien Faure, Louis Lecoin, Alexander Berkman, Emma Goldman and others. The Polish libertarian, Casimir Teslar, who had been in the Ukraine with the Makhnovists and who had just been deported from Russia by the Bolsheviks was frantically active "sounding the alarm." The Warsaw anarchist youth group also issued an urgent appeal:

"Comrades!

Demonstrate outside the Polish embassies in your countries! Send them your protest resolutions. Have recourse to the most extreme measures. The revolutionary proletariat must not allow the oppression in Polish jails of brave fighters for freedom and Anarchy. Only vigorous intervention by the toilers can save Makhno."[12]

In fact everyone's fear was that Makhno would be extradited to Russia where one could easily guess the fate that awaited him. The "extreme measures" advocated by the young Polish anarchists did not fail to make an impact upon Polish opinion which had at last seen sense and was swinging now in favor of the accused. And Bulgarian anarchists openly threatened to dynamite Polish embassies and establishments worldwide.

In these conditions, the trial went favorably for Makhno and his co-accused. It transpired that Krasnovolsky had also been manipulated by the Polish secret police, the *Défensive,* and that the prosecution had insufficient evidence. Makhno spoke brilliantly and demolished the allegations; the court was obliged to acquit the accused. Freed nearly a month after his acquittal(!), Makhno was given permission to stay in the Poznan region and then to leave for Danzig (today Gdansk) which at that time was a free city, albeit under Prussian administration.

The stalking by Bolshevik agents, though, did not end. They contacted Makhno, passing themselves off as Russian foreign trade representatives, and suggested that he return to Russia with solemn guarantees from the Soviet embassy in

Germany regarding his safety and that of any who might accompany him. Makhno's answer to them was that he could make no decision without first meeting his friends Voline, Arshinov, Rocker and Berkman who were in Berlin. Whereupon it was put to him that he should go there; he agreed, thinking that this might get him to Berlin where he would be more secure. Along with a trusted friend, he set off by car along with two Bolshevik agents; shortly before they crossed the German border, his friend informed the driver that, once in Berlin, Makhno would speak only to Krestinsky, the Soviet ambassador and then only in the home of a private citizen rather than on any premises under Soviet authority. Seeing their kidnap scheme fall apart, the Bolshevik agents backtracked, only to denounce Makhno a few days later to the Prussian police. To begin with he was imprisoned; then, when his health deteriorated, he was transferred under guard to a hospital. [13] Thanks to some German anarchists, he soon escaped from there and was preoccupied with reaching Berlin, a city that, on one hand, offered greater safety and where, on the other, lots of libertarians lived. It was at this juncture that there was an incident with Voline who, on November 24, 1924, had received 75 dollars from Karpuk (an Ukrainian anarchist in the United States) to secure a phony passport for Makhno. Not a practical sort, and with a wife and five young children to support, Voline had spent the money on his personal needs; thus he was unable to secure the necessary papers. In his place he sent a German anarchist individualist from Hamburg who was on the run from the law and also in need of reaching Berlin; this very queer "go-between" had 300 gold marks on him but was imprudent enough to hand them over in advance to the seaman who had undertaken to ferry them by launch across the briny to the port of Stettin[14] in German territory. The seaman wasted no time in squandering the sum on drink the following night, then refused them the promised passage. Exasperated by such delays and having now been clandestinely in Danzig for forty days, Makhno resolved to cross into Germany on foot along with a German comrade, bringing with them the none-too-astute "go-between."[15] The plan succeeded, and Makhno at last found himself in Berlin among his Russian anarchist colleagues and other anarchists there — people like Rudolf Rocker, Ugo Fedeli, and Alexander Berkman. Even there he was scarcely at ease, for the Germans could have brought him to book for his activities against them in the Ukraine during 1918. David Poliakov, a Russian libertarian living in France, made the journey to Berlin and in April 1925 brought Nestor Makhno back with him to Paris where, in theory, the Ukrainian leader no longer had anything to fear from officialdom.

Notes to Chapter 26: The Road of Exile: Bucharest, Warsaw, Danzig, Berlin

1. *Soviet Ukraine: Four years of War and Blockade: An Anthology of Official Documents drawn from the Ukraine Red Books*, Berlin, 1922, p. 91, and *Documents on the Foreign Policy of the USSR, Moscow*, 1960, Tome IV, p. 364.
2. *Soviet Ukraine*, p. 92.
3. Ibid, pp. 96–97.
4. Ibid, pp. 98–99.
5. Ibid, pp. 101–102.
6. It is noteworthy that the countries bordering the USSR — Finland, Turkey, the Shah's Iran and of course the satellite nations — in defiance of all of the "conventions" of international law — handed back all Soviet citizens who sought asylum with them. The scruples of the Romanians at the time in question seem very old-fashioned when viewed in the light of the *realpolitik* of our own day.
7. *Soviet Ukraine*, op cit. pp. 123–123.
8. Ibid, pp. 123–125.
9. Arshinov and Voline "Makhno before the Polish Court" (in Russian), an article in the New York Russian libertarian communist weekly *Amerikanskiye Izvestia*, November 28, 1923, p. 2.
10. Idem.
11. Letter from Makhno to Jean Grave, January 11, 1927, preserved at the French Institute of Social History.
12. In *Volna*, Detroit No. 45, September 1923, pp. 45–46.
13. Letter from Makhno to Jean Grave, op cit.
14. The port was then part of East Prussia which has since been absorbed by present day Poland.
15. N. Makhno *Concerning Voline's "Explanations"* (in Russian) Paris, 1929, pp. 12–14.

27. Exile in Paris (1925–1934)

So, at the end of a long and eventful odyssey, Makhno arrived in the City of Lights. He expected to find there a little ease and that he would be beyond the reach of his many enemies: White Russians, Bolsheviks, Ukrainian nationalists and other lesser species. The better to cover his tracks, he had had a passport issued to him in Berlin in the assumed name of Mikhnienko. His wife and daughter had gone on ahead to Paris, some comrades having seen to their direct transfer from Poland. After arrival on September 18, 1924, they had at first been denied entry on December 27, probably because their papers were not in order, and then were given permission to settle in France after the socialist parliamentarian Paul Faure had intervened on their behalf. Back together again, the little family received a gracious welcome from May Picqueray who "always had a good soup a-simmering or a cafetière ready to pour" for foreign comrades in dire straits.[1] She arranged temporary lodgings for them and took Makhno off to receive the medical care he needed from some friendly physicians.

Although the language barrier made communication difficult, the French anarchists made Makhno warmly welcome; over the preceding two or three years indeed they had become conversant with the Makhnovist insurgent movement, thanks to Arshinov's book and to essays and articles carried by the libertarian press.[2]

To begin with, Makhno and his loved ones were taken in by some Russian friends at Saint-Cloud, then spent two months as Georges Friquet's guests in Romainville until Fuchs, a French libertarian, found them a little apartment at 18 Rue Jarry in Vincennes, into which they moved on June 21, 1926. For a time Nestor found work as a smelter's assistant at a foundry at No. 6 on the same street before joining Renault as a lathe operator, but the state of his health obliged him to give up both these jobs. In fact, splinters from a dumdum bullet were still lodged in the bones of his right ankle; the wound had ulcerated and gave him atrocious pain, so much so that he could not bear to stand upright and walked with a pronounced limp. An operation in 1928 failed to cure his ankle and amputation was averted only by his steadfast refusal. His wife worked for a time in a shoe factory in Paris before spending a period in a small grocery store, keeping the pot boiling

— in both senses of the phrase. A well-to-do libertarian illegalist undertook to pay Nestor a small allowance to enable him to write his *Memoirs*. He set about this task, and the first volume appeared in a French translation by Waletsky in 1927. It concerned the year 1917 in the Ukraine (and was to appear in Russian two years later). As the cover price was quite high, the book sold poorly, and this jeopardized publication of two follow-up volumes which were ready for publication by 1929 but which were to appear only after Makhno's death. [3]

Nestor's health was further assailed by a recurrence of his tuberculosis and the pains from his many wounds. The physician and libertarian feminist Lucile Pelletier who was unstinting in her treatment of him was later to say that his body was literally encased in scar tissue. For a time his wife was obliged to move out lest their little girl be infected by her father's tuberculosis.

Several Makhnovists had managed to slip through the Cheka's net and, crossing the frontiers, came to settle near Nestor. One of them, Vassili Zayats, found a life of exile so distasteful that he took his own life in despair on October 1, 1926 by shooting himself in the head, in Makhno's very room. Fortunately Piotr Arshinov, his old colleague, arrived to move into the same building along with his own wife and son. Together they were at last to make a reality of a scheme they had cherished some 15 years previously while in the cells of the Butyrki prison, by bringing out a Russian-language libertarian communist theoretical review, *Dyelo Truda*. This review, of a very high caliber, appeared bi-monthly from 1925.

In it Makhno had an article in virtually every issue over a period of more than three years. The thought processes of the magazine's leading lights crystallized in the drafting of a plan for an organizational platform for the anarchist movement in which they sought to draw lessons from anarchism's experiences in the Russian revolution: Its weaknesses they credited to what they argued was the congenital defect of the traditional libertarian current, namely incoherence and lack of cohesion. For their part they proposed to work towards a precise re-definition of the underlying principles of libertarian communism and to arrive at a practical structuring of the movement subscribing to those principles into a collective operating in close liaison with the toiling masses. This scheme was to be the focus of debate in the libertarian circles of the day throughout the world. The debate among the Russian anarchists was turbulent as detractors — spearheaded by Voline — saw the whole scheme as an attempt to "bolshevize" anarchism; this charge was rather silly when leveled against men who had engaged in armed struggle against the Leninists and paid very dearly for the experience in physical and psychological terms. [4]

A meeting was held to discuss this draft Platform at the Les Roses cinema in L'Hay-les-Roses on March 20, 1927; the premises were raided by the police who had been panicked — on the basis of "inside information" — by this gathering which drew Russian, Polish, Bulgarian, Italian and even Chinese anarchists together. French cops rounded up the participants in the belief that perhaps they had stumbled upon some vast world-wide conspiracy. Caught up in the dragnet, Makhno was sentenced to be deported from France on May 16th. Lobbying of the prefect of police, Chiappe, by the anti-militarist anarchist activist Louis Lecoin (who had good reason to know him, having been arrested by him numerous times) ensured that the deportation order was postponed for an initial period of three months by way of a trial period, from October 19, 1937, conditional upon Makhno's observing absolute political neutrality. Henri Sellier, the councilor-general and Socialist mayor of Suresnes, also stepped in and stood a guarantor for Makhno.

✿✿✿

At this point, a dramatic incident focused public attention on Nestor. On May 25, 1926, the Ukrainian national leader Petliura, also a refugee in Paris, was assassinated by Samuel Schwarzbard, a Jewish Ukrainian anarchist and an acquaintance of Makhno's to boot. Schwarzbard had lost numerous family members in anti-Jewish pogroms in the Ukraine and, holding Petliura to blame for these massacres, had gunned him down with his revolver. According to what the Bulgarian anarchist Kiro Radeff has told us, Schwarzbard had called on Makhno the evening before the assassination to consult with him and let him in on his plans. Nestor had tried to talk him out of it, telling him that anarchists fought against principles and not personalities and that, as far as he was aware, Petliura could not be held accountable for the pogroms in that he had always condemned them and had numbered Jews among his supporters and indeed even in his government (Arnold Margoline, an Ukrainian of Jewish origins, had even led the Ukrainian nationalist mission attached to the Entente). All to no avail, for Schwarzbard went ahead with his scheme. We might point out that Schwarzbard's lawyers, Henry Torrès and Bernard Lacache, made a special trip to Russia to collect documentary evidence authenticating Petliura's responsibility in the matter of the pogroms, but for all their eagerness to confound a political enemy, the Bolsheviks were unable to supply such evidence.

Capitalizing upon all this sensationalism, a rather unscrupulous author, Joseph Kessel, himself a Jew of Russian extraction, published a far-fetched novel entitled *Makhno and his Jewess,* wherein Makhno was depicted as an abominably cruel degenerate ogre and bloodthirsty butcher nonetheless touched by the beauty and love of a young Jewish woman, even to the extent of leading her up the aisle and thereby achieving his life's ambition: to marry her in church and thus convert her to the Orthodox faith! One would be hard pressed to come up with anything more dismal and shabby, but the hack Kessel, desperate to attract attention to his pathetic self, claimed that his story was true, or at least "…as true as the documentation upon which it was based" and that the "novelist, whatever his subject matter, be it imaginary or historical, reserves the right of construction, composition and direction over his story [sic!]."[5] The "documentation" to which Kessel was referring was a tale published in 1922 by a White officer by the name of Gerassimenko who was rather suspect (convicted of espionage on behalf of the Bolsheviks in Prague in 1924 and subsequently deported from Czechoslovakia).

Published in a White Russian magazine in Berlin, this "tale" had probably been intended to discredit Makhno who was interned in Poland at the time and to speed his extradition. Gerassimenko argued in it that Makhno had gone over to Wrangel and placed the following words in his mouth: "In Russia there is room only for monarchy or anarchy!" 6

Informed of the storm of indignation provoked by his "novel," Kessel corrected his aim slightly in the second edition of his text in 1927. He now wrote in his foreword that he had "invented the conflict that seemed to him most likely to throw into relief a figure and an atmosphere with which he was conversant." He also vouchsafed the information that he had discovered that Makhno was living in Paris and had allegedly "…even uttered threats against me for having dared to portray him so penetratingly and, in his estimation, falsely. " 7 Thus Kessel had supposedly displayed tremendous courage in "daring to portray penetratingly" — another publicity coup that was not allowed to go unexploited — whereas Makhno, hands tied by a threat of deportation, was denied the same facilities for expressing his opinions. As for his "text," Kessel pressed on regardless and without amending as much as a single comma of it, hinting at a further source: one Arbatov, who describes in a Russian monarchist paper the alleged "exploits" of Makhno, in much the same flavors as Gerassimenko. 8

The danger for Makhno was that Kessel might so mislead his ill-informed readership that in the emotional climate then prevailing among European Jews, some hothead — keen to imitate Schwarzbard — might select Makhno as a target. In the face of such a thinly disguised incitement to murder, Makhno was thus compelled to speak up several times on the subject of pogroms: in Le Libertaire (he did not enjoy Kessel's access to the "big circulation newspapers"), he issued an appeal "To the Jews of all Lands" to quote him specific instances of pogroms that could be laid at the door of the Makhnovist movement. All in vain, for the very good reason that there had been none, as we shall establish anon. On June 24, 1927, the Club du Faubourg organized a debate on the issue in the Hall of the Learned Societies. Makhno spoke on "the facts about the pogroms in the Ukraine" and explained how he personally had protected Jews in the region under his influence. Other Russian and Ukrainian libertarians of Jewish extraction backed him up on this point and called Kessel to order; the only excuse that Kessel, who was there, could come up with was "…the novelist's right to fictionalize." And there the "Kessel" affair stopped; the murder of Petliura and the controversy aroused concerning Makhno suited Moscow down to the ground — she had never asked so much of the country which had taken in her sworn enemies.

૨૪૨

On July 21, 1927, Makhno attended the banquet given by the Anarchist International Defense Committee to celebrate the release of the Spanish anarchists Francisco Ascaso, Durruti and Jover. He delivered a short address in Russian which was simultaneously translated for the benefit of all present. As the dinner ended, a meeting was arranged with Ascaso and Durruti. The meeting took place in Nestor's cramped quarters and went on for several hours in the presence of Jacques Dubinsky, a bilingual Russian libertarian who acted as interpreter whenever Makhno was unable to make himself understood in his poor French. The Spanish anarchists hailed Makhno as the symbol of "...all revolutionaries who have fought for the realization of anarchist ideas in Russia," and they paid "...tribute to the Ukraine's rich experience." Makhno replied that by his reckoning conditions for a "revolution of robust anarchist content" would be better in Spain than in Russia, for Spain had "...a proletariat and peasantry with revolutionary traditions, the political maturity of which is evident from their every reaction. May your revolution come in time to grant me the satisfaction of seeing alive an anarchism informed by the Russian experience. In Spain you have a sense of organization that we in Russia lacked, for it is organization that ensures the thoroughgoing success of any revolution." He hoped that they would learn from the Makhnovist experience which he spent several hours expounding to his Spanish colleagues. As he took his leave of them, he told them with an optimistic grin: "Makhno has never shirked a fight; if I am still alive when you begin yours, I will be with you."[10]

By this time Makhno was in fact ailing both psychologically and physically. He was suffering from his wounds and an aggravation of his tuberculosis. Moreover, the controversy regarding the draft Platform degenerated and relations with its adversaries, especially Voline, their spokesman, were strained. This is an important point and worth going into, for Voline was a prominent personality in the Russian anarchist movement and had also been chairman of the Makhnovists' Military Revolutionary Soviet for over two months in the autumn of 1919. He had been persecuted by the Bolsheviks and arrested in November 1920, following the breakdown of Moscow's alliance with Makhno. At the 1921 Profintern Congress, the French and Spanish anarcho-syndicalist delegates had spoken up on his behalf; after some difficulties, Lenin and Trotsky deigned to deport him along with nine other leading anarchists as well as their families. Then Voline spent some time in Berlin before moving on to settle in Paris, where he had lived prior to 1914. He was very active in publicizing the facts about the Leninist regime either on speaking tours or by drafting articles for the libertarian press worldwide, knowing several foreign languages as he did. He was a superb propagandist and above all an exceptional public speaker. During the Russian revolution he delivered upwards of a hundred talks. As a result, he felt a certain superiority over "practical types" and to some extent stood guard over the "purity" of libertarian principles although he himself was quite a newcomer to the libertarian persuasion, having been won over while an émigré before 1914 on contact with Kropotkin. Thus he was violently opposed to the Organizational Platform scheme of *Dyelo Truda* and supported instead the Anarchist Synthesis advocated by Sébastien Faure, a sort of symbiosis of the three basic strands of anarchist doctrine: the individualist, the syndicalist and the communist. Whereas Makhno, Arshinov and colleagues held that libertarian communism was built upon an all-embracing notion of class struggle, incorporating syndicalism as a means and respect for the rights of the individual as a goal. The two views were different while not mutually exclusive and, had there not been the context of the failure of the Russian revolution and the life of exile, perhaps the debate might not have been so embittered and passionate. Relations between the two men (Makhno and Voline) were embittered when Kubanin's official book on the Makhnovschina came out in 1927 and referred to the minutes of Voline's interrogation by a Chekist examining magistrate when he had been captured in December 1919. There, Voline complained of the "abuses" of the Makhnovist intelligence service — which he almost placed on a par with the Cheka — and spoke of his "clashes" with Makhno on this point.[11]

Makhno made his reply to Kubanin shortly after in a pamphlet and, in passing, dealt with the "case" of Voline. He explained how Voline had frequently turned to the Makhnovist counter-espionage service. Thus, at the time of his capture by the Red Army, on his way to Krivoi Rog — to give a talk there — he had been in the company of the leader and the finest men from the service. Then again, he had no cause to complain, for he himself took initiatives. For instance, it had been his own decision to seek Makhno out, along with a Bolshevik leader by the name of Orlov, during the occupation of Ekaterinoslav in order to secure for him a warrant for search and seizure of the goods of a Russian nobleman who had fled to join Denikin, with the benefits going to the region's Bolshevik committee. Makhno had categorically refused to oblige and had scolded Voline for his political inconsistency.[12] Things might have been left there, and the dirty linen could have been "washed" among intimates only, but there was no knowing what was eating at Voline and what induced him to publish a little pamphlet called *Explanations* over a year later, in which he reproached Makhno for "wanting to settle personal scores with him," thereby revealing certain character traits, to wit, a "hostility towards intellectuals, his suspicions and the mischievousness of his nature (sic)!" He refuted everything that Kubanin depicted him as having said, gave an account of his "capture" and announced that at the time he had not been bothered about knowing whether or not his companions were members of the Makhnovist counter-intelligence service in that he had been sick with typhus. He could no longer recall the episode with the Bolshevik Orlov either and hinted that Makhno had mixed him up with somebody else, but nonetheless acknowledged that it had fallen to him to act in conjunction with Bolsheviks who had used him as an intermediary to deal with Makhno and, anyway, dismissed this as being of secondary importance. Finally he recorded his assistance to Makhno when Makhno was caught in the "rat-trap" in Danzig in 1925 and closed by stating that all that remained of Makhno's reproaches of him was "…a dark cloud of mischief and calumny.… Whom and what can that all serve?"[13] According to Marc Mratchny, one of his own anarchist comrades from the Ukraine, Voline was regarded as a "shallow mind,"[14] but here he demonstrated singular inconsistency by pouring oil onto the fire and then asking what purpose it all served. In any case, Makhno's answer came the following month, also in the form of a pamphlet, crossing the t's and dotting the i's. Makhno explained how Voline had been specially escorted by comrade Golik and about 20 of the most reliable members of the Makhnovist counter-intelligence service and how it was because of his own "stupidity" that Voline had not only been captured but also brought about the capture of several of those with him. Apropos of his joint venture with Orlov, no, he wasn't mixing him up with somebody else, Voline was indeed the one. As for his (Makhno's) alleged "hostility towards intellectuals," he had always had high regard for "…genuine intellectuals and hates only those who are blackguards and whom he can readily distinguish from the former." Moreover, he had no scores to settle with Voline, for he "…could not do that with a comrade, which Voline had ceased to be in his view ever since he had discovered his true personality in the emigration." Finally what had him at odds with Voline was not personal considerations, although Voline's conduct had been most blameworthy at the time of his escape from the Danzig "rat-trap" and was nothing to "brag about," but rather the "falsehoods and cowardice" of the man who had for a long time been chairman of the Makhnovists' soviet.[15] Henceforth he swore undying enmity towards Voline who paid him back in his posthumous work *The Unknown Revolution* by ascribing serious personal shortcomings to him, as we shall see in the next chapter.

The squabble can be put down to the poisonous atmosphere created by the controversy surrounding the Organizational Platform of *Dyelo Truda*, or indeed to the difficulties of émigré life and the social differences, which it aggravated, between Voline the intellectual and ideologue, and the peasant-worker activist Makhno. Indeed one might speak of a clash of personalities or of misplaced sensitivities and with good reason, but there was something else as well. Makhno was very well aware that, through him, it was the whole movement and the memory of his dead comrades who were under fire from all sides, as much from those who should have been closest to them as from their avowed enemies. This was the reason why he could brook no slight against himself or his comrades in arms, of whom Voline seemed to be dismissive, forgetting that it had been they who had been in charge of watching over him, for which duty they had paid a high price. Likewise he could not accept Voline's being so offhand about his own responsibilities when it was Makhno himself who had insisted upon his being appointed chairman of the insurgents' Military Revolutionary Soviet in October 1919, something which he obviously would not have done, he now claimed, had he been aware of Voline's true character as it had been revealed to him since his emigration.

Viewed in this light, defense against all manner of attacks and criticisms became something of an obsession with him; as the gossip persisted it was up to him to explain or justify himself. Let us consider two instances which illustrate his "solicitude" on the part of "friends": On the first occasion he attended a commemoration at the hall of the (masonic) Grand Orient in the Rue Cadet in Paris, to mark the tenth anniversary of the October Revolution, under the auspices of some Russian "fellow travelers" of the Bolsheviks. Apparently he went along to heckle, yet there were some who argued that he had been invited by the Soviet embassy and was going to join the Communist Party! He found it necessary to rebut this rather cavalier interpretation of things through the columns of *Dyelo Truda*.[16] On the second occasion, he published an article on "Soviet Power: Its Present and Its Future," in the magazine *Borba* (The Struggle) run by the Ukrainian Bolshevik defector Grigory Bessedovsky; provoking criticism from Arshinov and the Russian anarchists in Chicago! He found it necessary to clarify things by saying that he was big and ugly enough to know what he should or should not do and needed "no wet-nurse; I grew out of that decades ago and acted as one myself for many a long year towards others, Arshinov included."[17]

In addition, relations between these two cooled because Arshinov tended to personalize — unduly for Makhno's taste — the debate on the Platform which they had drafted together. All the more so, in that Kubanin and some soviet authors, as well as "friendly" anarchists, had a tendency to depict both Arshinov and Voline as Makhno's spiritual "mentors." In some cases this was an effort to play down the peasants' role in the movement by making them subordinate to workers or intellectuals, and in other cases the assumption was that Makhno, being virtually "illiterate" could not possibly have thought up, much less drafted his numerous written works without the aid of a ghost-writer. This last assertion was formally refuted for us by Ida Mett, who, between 1925 and 1927, served as the secretary/typist of Makhno and the *Dyelo Truda* group. According to her, Makhno was very fussy about form, and for every occasion when he accepted suggestion and advice, there was another when he reserved the right to decide upon the merest comma in his writings.[18] Later, Marie Goldsmit, an old Kropotkinist, served him in the same capacity before she committed suicide in 1933.[19] So let us look at Makhno's "literary output" during his first years in exile.

Over the years 1926–1929, he published a whole series of articles and texts of major significance both historically and theoretically. If one also takes account of the writing of the three volumes of his *Memoirs*, one might regard these years as highly prolific, although widely underestimated. Or quite simply unknown, which is certainly unmerited. Makhno advanced a number of specific details about the movement: He ironically and categorically denied that the Makhnovschina may have flown the black pirate flag — skull and crossbones — as some claimed to be able to make out in certain photographs of the Makhnovschina.[20] Regarding the charges of anti-Semitism, he supplied rebuttals several times; he also furnished details about the character and meaning of the Makhnovist movement, etc. He especially did so in his essential answer to Kubanin, with its evocative title; *The Makhnovschina and its Erstwhile Allies: The Bolsheviks*. His theoretical contributions to libertarian communism were not negligible either: articles on the State, the national question, revolutionary discipline, the revolution's defenses and revolutionary organization. Likewise, he subjected the Bolsheviks to robust criticism, exposing their contradictions and lies, in articles like "The notion of equality and the Bolsheviks," "How the Bolsheviks lie (the truth about the anarchist sailor Zhelezniak)," "Open Letter to the Russian Communist Party and its central committee (on Bela Kun and the second alliance)," "In Memory of the Kronstadt uprising," "Great October in the Ukraine," and "The Peasantry and the Bolsheviks." He also issued appeals for solidarity with persecuted Russian anarchists in the USSR, on behalf of the Anarchist Black Cross, and on behalf of the Kropotkin Museum in Moscow. Likewise, he monitored international political developments, offering his advice in "Britain's world policy and the tasks of revolutionary toilers." All these articles appeared in Russian in the review *Dyelo Truda*; some were translated and also appeared in *Le Libertaire*.[21] In short, as far as he was concerned, the fight went on, though the pen had replaced the saber. As for the situation in France, he was obliged — having the sword of Damocles hanging over his head in the form of risk of deportation should he intervene in the slightest in internal politics — to stick to theoretical and organizational matters and to avoid appearances at public meetings and rallies.

❧

It is worth stressing this productive output for it took place in wretched circumstances: physical pain, growing psychological isolation and precarious financial circumstances. Passing through Paris, the Bulgarian anarchist doctor Baleff invited Makhno to come and settle in Kasanlik in the Valley of Roses in Southern Bulgaria. Makhno declined, for Russian Whites were solidly ensconced there, had official military units and were much to be feared. He did odd painting and decorating jobs, tried his hand at shoe-mending along with Arshinov and a few other comrades, making women's shoes, a trade very current among the Russian émigré colony in Paris until an industrialist revolutionized manufacturing techniques and rang the death-knell of handmade production.

Whereupon Makhno found himself absolutely on his uppers, financially speaking. His wife subsidized the couple's needs as best she could, but she earned only a pittance working as a domestic cleaner and laundry worker in an establishment far outside Paris, for there was the hostility of Russian émigré circles to be faced once they discovered who she was. Some French comrades, hearing of these material straits and Makhno's crumbling health, issued an appeal in the April 6, 1929 edition of *Le Libertaire* "For long-term solidarity on Makhno's behalf"[22] in the form of a regular subscription that would afford the invalid (whom vicious tongues were by then describing as the "living corpse") a small allowance. A committee was established to that end, and Nadaud was appointed secretary. Regular statements of account appeared in *Le Libertaire*. Thus, by June 20, 1929, 7,180 francs had been raised, a modest enough sum of 3,300 francs being paid out to Makhno at the rate for 250 francs weekly, just enough for him to scrape by. The committee made the gross blunder of forking out 3,880 francs on postage and stationary merely to get some circulars out! Even so, the allowance was regular for over a year up until the 1930 Congress of the Anarchist Federation, when the majority was overturned as "anti-Platformists" gained the upper hand over "pro-Platformists." Makhno, well known as an ardent "organization-ist," sent the congress an open letter that was scathing about these "anti-Platformists," whom he described as "chaotic elements": "[In many countries] the movement is disorganized within and without and finds itself in a state of decrepitude. We ought to think on that and overcome these difficulties together. In its resolutions, Congress ought to rise above the childish babbling of those who are a drag upon our movement's development."[23] Needless to say, this attitude did nothing to endear him to the new majority. From July 1930 they announced that *Le Libertaire* would no longer have anything to do with the subscription fund; any who so wished were invited to send their "mite" directly to Makhno, whose address was given (N. Mikhnienko, 146 Rue Diderot, Vincennes). In the issues of the paper after that, they carried statements of the accounts received in the interim and repeated their suggestion that monies be sent directly to the individual concerned. In June 1931, a benefit event was organized for Makhno, but organizational expenses and sundry others ensured that little money was raised. Thus, aside from some Russian, Bulgarian, Spanish and French anarchists who did not forget him, Makhno was scarcely able to rely upon solidarity from the Parisians at *Le Libertaire*. However, in the absence of his being able to go back to the Ukraine to resume the campaign he had broken off in 1921, fresh hopes were raised, for some Spanish anarchists proposed that he assume the leadership of a guerrilla campaign in Northern Spain as part of a revolutionary upheaval in 1931. So Makhno was taking an interest in matters Spanish and wrote two articles on the subject. He was insistent about the necessity:

> "...of helping toilers to establish organs of economic and social self-governance, free soviets, as well as armed detachments for defense of the revolutionary social measures that they will of necessity have to impose, after having achieved consciousness and broken all the shackles of their servile condition. It is only thus and only through these methods of overall action that revolutionary toilers will be able to act in good time against attempted subversion of the revolution by some new exploitative system. By my reckoning, the FAI and CNT ought, for this purpose, to be able to call upon minutemen groups in every village and town, and they should not be afraid to take in hand the strategical, organizational and theoretical direction of the toiler's movement. Obviously, when that time comes, they will have to avoid joining forces with political parties generally and with the Bolshevik-Communists in particular, for I assume that their Spanish counterparts are worthy imitators of their masters. They will follow in the footsteps of the Jesuit Lenin or even of Stalin, not hesitating to assert their monopoly over all the gains of the revolution [...] they will inevitably betray their allies and the very cause of revolution and turn into the worst of despots. The Russian example ought to spare us from arriving at that stage. May the Bolshevik-Communist blight not set foot on the revolutionary soil of Spain."[24]

This cautionary advice was followed up by an examination along similar lines of "…the history of the Spanish revolution of 1931 and of the role played by the socialists — of right and left — and the anarchists," in 1933.[25]

At around the same time Makhno suffered a tremendous psychological blow at the end of 1931, when his comrade and friend for over 20 years, Piotr Arshinov, went over to the Bolsheviks. This led to a stormy falling out between them. How was one to account for this unexpected U-turn by Arshinov who, up until a few months before, had been writing virulent and highly interesting articles against the Stalino-Bolshevik regime? The clarity — some might say rigidity — of the stances assumed by Arshinov in the organizational controversy had alienated the sympathies of many anarchists from him even though they had initially been attracted by the proposed overhaul of the underlying principles of libertarian communism, and he became the "black sheep" of the international anarchist movement. Some went so far as to suggest that his origins in 1904 as a member of the Bolshevik party was one explanation for his unduly "organizational" thinking. For his part, prey to continual criticism for trespasses against the Holy Fathers of Anarchy, Arshinov had become increasingly intractable regarding his detractors, even to the extent of breaking radically with traditional anarchism and advocating a highly structured and unmistakably vanguardist anarchist "party." Not that it was these options that had divided him from Makhno, who was himself a fervent "organization-ist": it was, rather, a certain sectarianism which had led him to equate his anarchist adversaries with his statist or authoritarian enemies. What is more, Arshinov had experienced a host of personal troubles, in particular deportation from France and a dramatic bust-up with his wife who, wearying of émigré life and homesick, wanted to go back to Russia along with their son. As Arshinov had formerly been on very friendly terms with Sergo Ordzhonikidze (they had shared the same cell twenty years before), the latter, who had since become a close confederate of Stalin, had offered to sponsor Arshinov's return with no old scores to be settled. Thus, more than any organizational considerations, it was these personal ones that probably explained his sudden recognition of the soviet authorities and his return to Moscow in 1933. There he was to work as a proofreader up until 1937 in which year he was executed on a charge of having sought to "…restore anarchism in Russia."

≈≋≈

Having fallen out with most of the U.S.-based Russian anarchists who were supporters of Arshinov, Makhno was left very isolated, demoralized, extremely ill and under-nourished to live in deteriorating circumstances. Only some Bulgarian anarchists and a few Makhnovists as hard-up as himself kept in touch with him and helped him insofar as their slender means allowed — although Makhno often declined financial help, out of pride. He was not inactive, though, and continued to write articles for the Russian libertarian review, *Probuzdeniye*, published in the United States. In particular, he published an "ABC of Anarchism" wherein he forcefully set out his beliefs and an essay on the "Paths of proletarian power" in which he raised pertinent questions regarding the nature and content of Bolshevik power, its relationship with the ideas of Marx and Lenin and the proletariat, a part (primarily urban) of which, he argued, had found its place in the sun under the new regime, to the detriment to the rest of its class and peasant masses. In this way he complemented the analysis of "...many anarchists who tend to think that the proletariat bears none of the responsibility for the evolution of the Russian revolution, having allegedly been duped by the intellectual social caste, which by virtue of a whole succession of historical phenomena and alterations to the role of the State, supposedly sought in the course of this process to supplant the capitalist bourgeoisie by making use of the proletariat's struggle."[26] He strenuously recommended them to painstakingly scrutinize the phases of the Russian revolution, as well as the parts played by one and all in this evolution, and this with an eye to avoiding repetition of the mistakes made and to being in a position to combat Bolshevik-Communists effectively, while offering a clear and distinct libertarian alternative. The last piece of writing from his pen was an obituary notice on his old comrade Nikolai Rogdaiev who died in Central Asia to where he had been banished by Moscow. Rogdaiev had been anarchism's trailblazer in the Ukraine and Russia at the turn of the century. He had helped set up lots of groups of militants and fighters and had fought on the barricades in Moscow himself in 1905. He had been a redoubtable "debater," confounding his Social Revolutionary and Social Democrat adversaries so well as to attract many militants from their organizations over to the anarchist camp. He had also engaged in a lengthy polemic with Lenin in Switzerland and thereafter been on friendly terms with the Bolshevik leader. During the 1917 revolution, Rogdaiev had settled in Samara and had been meaning to join the Makhnovschina in the autumn of 1919, but Voline's presence had changed his mind, for he could never forgive Voline for having been an associate of Vladimir Burtzev — the Sherlock Holmes of the Russian revolutionaries' world who had unmasked the agent provocateur Yevno Azev, among others — nor for failing to lift a finger when he, Rogdaiev, had been accused, groundlessly, of being an agent provocateur. In 1920 Lenin had summoned him to Moscow, urging him on one hand, to persuade Makhno to "subordinate himself" to the Kremlin, and on the other to take up an important post (based on his knowledge of foreign languages) on the staff of the Red Army on the Western front. Rogdaiev had unequivocally declined both suggestions, which had promptly put him in difficulties with the Samara Cheka. These were later smoothed over, as he went on to hold an educational position in Tiflis, kept in touch with *Dyelo Truda* and indeed, sent it some money. Makhno was much affected by his death and at a meeting on January 21, 1934, read a lengthy report in memory of his friend, concluding with this pathetic farewell:

> "Very dear friend, comrade and brother, sleep easy in the heavy slumber from which there is no waking. Your cause is our cause. It shall never perish. It will spring to life again in the generations to come who will

take it up again and enrich it. It will motivate the open, healthy life of the struggle of toiling humanity. Friend, you will remain with us forever! May shame and damnation rebound upon those who have besmirched your name, who have slowly and cravenly clawed at your soul and your heart right to the end."[27]

In doing so, Makhno never suspected that these very same words, right down to the curse on slanderers, might soon, very soon, be applied to himself!

In fact, he was by now absolutely destitute; only after his death was his wife to send that obituary piece off to the *Probuzdeniye*, and she was to explain that he had not been able to do so himself for want of the price of postage.[28] Due to malnutrition, his tuberculosis gained ground, gnawing away at his lungs, to the extent that less than two months later, on March 16, 1934, he was hospitalized in the tuberculosis ward of the Tenon clinic. Parisian libertarians bestirred themselves and reformed the "Makhno committee" with an eye to "…organizing vitally needed solidarity."[29] In July, Makhno was operated upon but too late to stop the downward spiral. He was placed in an oxygen tent and then, on the night of July 24–25, drifted into a sleep from which he never woke. In the early hours of July 25, he was pronounced dead. He would have been 45 years of age in another three months.

A gathering of some 500 people attended his cremation on July 28th at the Père Lachaise cemetery where his ashes joined those of the Communards of 1871. Numerous obituaries were carried in the libertarian press worldwide.

�✿�

For all the commemorative activities, one cannot help wondering about the "faltering" solidarity displayed by Paris's libertarians during his last days. We have mentioned, for instance, the worrying aspects of the accounts of the Makhno committee: A statement for the period from May 3 to August 31, 1934 records receipts of 4,131 francs in contributions from all over the world, especially from some Russian and Italian anarchists in the United States, as well as from many French libertarians, among them Jean Grave. But when one turns to the expenditure column, one is dumbfounded to discover that only 123 francs had been paid over to Makhno, another 100 to his wife and 300 for their daughter. Whereas his death mask(!) cost 310 francs, the committee's correspondence costs came to 74 francs, and insertions in *Le Libertaire* 500 francs![30] In the second statement of accounts, covering the period from August 31, 1934 to September 30, 1935, contributions were still coming in, especially from Russian anarchists in the United States, as well as from the Jewish Club in Paris, making a total of 3,467 francs. Among the expenses was an advance of 1,800 francs made out to Voline for preparation of the outstanding volumes of Makhno's memoirs, plus 650 francs for a bas-relief of Makhno(!), and sundry correspondence costs.[31] In an effort to understand this and to discover more, we inquired among the surviving members of this famous committee and put the following questions to them, among others: "In the financial statement from the Makhno committee, as it appeared in *Le Libertaire* after his death, it appears that a significant sum of money was in hand, upwards of 4,000 francs, yet between May 1934 and his death on July 25, only 123 francs had been paid out to him. How is that to be explained? Did the committee pay out anything to him between 1931 and 1934? The committee was supposed to help Makhno's wife and daughter. Did it do so?" Among the four replies we received, only Nico-las Faucier's is a complete response, but unfortunately, he was unable to offer any explanation of the committee's shortcomings, as he was not resident in Paris at the time in question.[32] The other members of the committee either sidestepped the questions asked, or — visibly ill at ease — declared they could no longer recall such ancient history to mind. So we have to take it that they found it easier to deal with a symbol — as the obituary notices described Makhno — dead rather than alive! Nicolas Faucier did tell us that there were rumors "to the effect that Makhno frequented the nearby Vincennes racetrack where … it seems he gambled what small change he had left out of whatever advances were made to him after he had paid the basic expenses of his loved ones." It was "…also said that he had taken to the drink, but that I could not confirm."[33] Quite apart from the slanderous aspect of these "rumors," those subscribers who had contributed their "mite" had certainly not intended any surveillance to be maintained on whatever use Makhno chose to make of it. The money was to have been quite simply passed on to him, leaving it to him to spend it as he saw fit, or at least that is our opinion. So we reckon these "committee men" bear a heavy responsibility, for it seems obvious to us that, had Makhno had access to more money, he would not have gone to a premature death and might have been able to participate in the Spanish libertarian revolution of 1936, for which he had prepared himself, and — who knows? — might have had a certain influence there, or even died in action as did two Makhnovists who wound up in the International Group of the Durruti Column.

As for the money paid out to Voline for "preparing" the remainder of Makhno's memoirs, let us see what use was made of that. The first volume had already come out, as we have seen, in Makhno's lifetime, in French in 1927, and in Russian in 1929. After that, the second and third volume were ready, having been typed and checked by Ida Mett and Marie Goldsmit, and all that was miss-ing was the cooperation of a publisher. Makhno had himself announced as much in 1927 in a letter to the Russian-Ukrainian worker colony in the United States, hoping that good translators could be found to see to a Ukrainian language edi-tion.[34] Meanwhile, he published a large portion of the second volume in 1932 in the U.S.-based Russian libertarian newspaper, *Rassvyet* (Dawn) under the title of *Pages of Gloom from the Russian Revolution*. Shortly before his death, sensing the imminence of the end, he had entrusted all his papers, including the manuscripts of those two volumes, to his old friend Grisha Bartanovsky — known as Barta — whom he had known in the Ukraine in 1907 and bumped into again as an émigré, asking Barta to make the best use of them. After his friend's death, Barta had sought out the doctor and libertarian activist Marc Pierrot to seek his advice. He had then decided to hand back the manuscripts of the two unpublished volumes of memoirs to Makhno's wife, Galina Kuzmenko, and to leave it to her to determine what was best. Galina passed them on to the aid committee, probably lest the monies collected be completely "frittered away" and the committee in turn commissioned Voline to "prepare" them for publication and contacted the U.S.-based Russian libertarian organizations with a view to possible publication. Other manuscripts, documents, correspondence, handbills, and newspapers Barta kept in a small case which went missing during a war-time search by the Gestapo — Barta was an anarchist and a Jew — and so have probably been lost forever.[35]

In 1936 and 1937, the second and third volumes of Makhno's memoirs came out, thanks to funds collected by Russian libertarians in the United States, under Voline's "editorship" and complete with foreword and notes by Voline. But what could this "editorship" have amounted to? We have compared the extract published in 1932 in *Rassvyet* and the version published under Voline's "editorship," and, aside from the re-deployed comma or the pruning of circumlocutions, we have found nothing extra in the Voline version. But what had Voline to say on the matter?

In his foreword, Voline "…much regrets that a personal clash with Nestor Makhno" had prevented him from "drafting" the first volume which had appeared during the author's lifetime, for he would have been able to polish up the format and avoided the "…disappointment of readers"(?). He goes on to say that "…shortly before Makhno's death, their relations had improved and that he had intended to suggest to him that the remainder of his memoirs be drafted with his "participation" and that "only Makhno's death had prevented realization of this plan."[36] This account of things is wholly false, for Kiro Radeff told us that he had tried to effect a reconciliation between the pair and had informed Makhno on his hospital bed that he had included Voline in his support committee, whereupon the Ukrainian anarchist had retorted: "You have betrayed me!"[37] Indeed, it was to misunderstand Makhno to think that he would so easily forgive Voline's past trespasses. Yet Voline states in his foreword that he had done no more than touch up the "literary form" of the text. In which case his handiwork — proofreader's work — has nothing to do with what one understands by "drafting," which would suggest that Makhno did not know how to write! However, he justifies it by mentioning that Makhno "possessed only a rudimentary education and did not have much of a grasp of literary language, though this did not prevent him from having a very characteristic style all his own."[38] Somewhat embarrassed nonetheless by his contradictions, he chooses to move on to the content of Makhno's memoirs, which he praises for their historical and documentary interest concerning the years 1917 and 1918. He does express reservations about Makhno's critical considerations regarding the passivity of certain of the Russian anarchists of the day, as well as what he considers the over-inflated evaluation of the revolutionary role of the Ukrainian peasantry and laments the fact that the memoirs stopped at the end of 1918, before the great blossoming of the Makhnovist movement. Voline promised a book that would reprint others of Makhno's writings, collecting all of the articles of his that had appeared in the Russian libertarian press, plus some unpublished manuscripts (probably the ones then in Barta's keeping). In 1945, shortly before his death, Voline was to forward all his papers and books to his closest friend Jacques Dubinsky who was to see to the publication in 1947 of Voline's overview of the Russian revolution, his book *The Unknown Revolution*. Those papers finished up later in the possession of Voline's children. We managed to get sight of a copy of them. The whole collection is made up of notes and drafts; no doubt it is this patchy condition that has thus far prevented their being published. Voline reiterates his charges against Makhno and, insofar as one can tell, the underlying cause of the rift between them can be traced to personality clashes and social tensions: Makhno "had never made the slightest move to strike up a more personal friendship with him" and had supposedly displayed a "blind trust in the peasantry and distrust of every other class in society; a degree of contempt for intellectuals, even anarchist ones."[39]

In *The Unknown Revolution*, Voline has no hesitation in stating that Makhno "…led in Paris an extremely dismal existence in material as well as in psychological terms. His life abroad was one long, lamentable agony against which he was powerless to contend. His friends helped him to bear the burden of these sad years of decline."[40] We have seen how his exile was anything but unproductive and that only the very last years were very dismal, due primarily to the actions of certain of his "friends." No question about it; Makhno who had already sampled Bolshevik "friendship" could have taken as his own the dictum: "Just preserve me from my friends, and, as for my enemies, I will see to them myself."

Notes to Chapter 27: Exile in Paris (1925–1934)

1. May Picqueray, *"May la réfractaire,* Paris 1979, pp. 186-187.
2. The Group of Russian Anarchist Exiles in Germany, *La Répression de l'anarchisme en Russie soviétique,* Paris, 1923. *Le Libertaire* in 1922: No. 163; Angel Pestaña, "The Makhno legend," No. 190; M. Ne., "Nestor Makhno," No. 193; "The Makhnovist movement and anti-Semitism," No. 194; Renato Souvarine, "Makhno in the light of anarchism," No. 198; "Against the infamies prepared by the Polish and Russian governments (For Makhno)," No. 203; Voline, "Further data on Bolshevik agents (M. in Poland)," No. 217; March 16, 1923, Teslar, "In aid of Makhno." *La Revue Anarchiste:* Teslar, "The truth about the anarcho-Makhnovist movement and on the peasant revolutionary Nestor Makhno," No. 15, 1922.
3. In his lifetime, an excerpt from the second volume was to appear in *Le Libertaire,* as "The origins of the Ukrainian insurrection and the anarchists' role," No. 224, October 5, 1929 and the two ensuing issues.
4. We intend to devote a further work to this Platform scheme and to the controversy which followed upon it.

5. Joseph Kessel, *Makhno et sa Juive*, Paris, 1926, p. 11.

6. K.V. Gerassimenko, "Makhno," in *Istorik I sovremennik*, Berlin, 1922, pp. 151–201.

7. J. Kessel, *Les Coeurs Purs*, Paris, 1927 pp. 13–17.

8. Arbatov, "Batko Makhno" in *Rul*, Berlin 1922: reprinted in *Vozrozhdeniye*, Paris, 1953, No. 29, pp. 102–115 and in *Arkhiv russkoy revolyutsii*, 1923, Vol. 12, pp. 83–148.

9. N. Makhno, "Appeal to the Jews of all lands," in *Le Libertaire* and *Dyelo Truda* 23-24, 1927, pp. 8–10; and "The Makhnovschina and anti-Semitism," in *Dyelo Truda* 30-31, 1927, pp. 15–18.

10. Conversation mentioned by Ascaso and other sources quoted by Abel Paz, *Durruti, le Peuple en armes*, Paris, 1972, pp. 117–120.

11. Kubanin, op. cit. p. 116.

12. N. Makhno, "The Makhnovschina and its erstwhile allies: The Bolsheviks" op. cit. pp. 41–43.

13. Voline, *Explanations* (in Russian), Paris 1929, pp. 3 and 12.

14. Marc Mratchny, in letter of September 7, 1970 to Roland Lewin, Grenoble.

15. N. Makhno, *Concerning Voline's Explanations* (in Russian), Paris 1929, p. 11.

16. *Dyelo Truda* No. 35, April 1928, "Reply to the questions of the American comrades."

17. *Probuzdeniye*, Detroit No. 23-27, October 1932, "N. Makhno, the Progress club of Chicago and Piotr Arshinov," p. 60.

18. Statement made to the author during several conversations in 1970–1971.

19. Marie Goldsmit, alias Marie Isidine and Maria Korn, author of many articles in the Russian and French libertarian press and, in collaboration with Professor Y. Delage, of several scientific works e.g., *Théorie de l'évolution,* 1920 and others published by Flammarion.

20. On the other hand, the Kornilov Division's White officers' regiment did wear a black badge with a skull over crossed swords.

21. We hope to be able to publish an anthology of these tests anon.

22. *Le Libertaire*, No. 198, April 6, 1929.

23. Manuscript letter, preserved in Jean Maitron's archives.

24. Letter to the Spanish Anarchists, April 29, 1931, published in the Russian anarchist review, *Probuzdeniye*, Detroit, June–October 1932.

25. *Probuzdeniye*, No. 30-31, January–February 1933.

26. *Probuzdeniye*, No. 18, 1932, pp. 45–48.

27. Ibid, No. 52-53, November-December 1934, p. 31.

28. Idem.

29. *Le Libertaire*, No. 420, July 1, 1934.

30. Ibid. No. 424, October 19, 1934.

31. Ibid. No. 475, December 20, 1935.

32. Letter to the author, November 24, 1981.

33. Letters to the author, October 8, 1979 and June 27, 1981.

34. *Dyelo Truda,* No. 29, October 1927, pp. 9–11.

35. It is to be regretted that Barta did not deposit these papers safely in a library or institute, the best guarantee of their being preserved. Also, Makhno was himself an assiduous reader at the Library of the War Museum in Vincennes (now the BDIC. in Nanterre).

36. N. Makhno, *Beneath the Blows of the Counter-Revolution*, edited by Voline, with foreword and notes by Voline, Paris, 1936, p. 3.

37. Statement made to the author in 1974 and to Michael Palij in 1975.

38. N. Makhno, *Beneath the blows* ... op. cit. p. 4.

39. For a more detailed analysis of these documents, see Bibliographical Afterword below.

40. Voline, *La Révolution Inconnue*, Paris, 1947, p. 669.

28. Nestor Makhno's Personality: Character Traits and Idiosyncrasies

Thus far and to avoid our narrative's becoming too nebulous, we have scarcely dwelt upon the personality and certain facets of the life and activities of Nestor Makhno. We now return to these and are going to attempt, with the help of sundry testimony, to reconstruct his portrait, his qualities and shortcomings which on occasion may better explain certain successes or failures of the movement as a whole.

According to the overlapping descriptions of people who met or associated with him in Paris, Makhno was rather short — standing about 1.65 meters tall — with black hair, blue-gray eyes, a high broad forehead and, by around 1927, he had a rather "hefty" look about him. This latter characteristic dated back to the years of the revolution, for ten years of imprisonment had turned the young heavy-set lad (as he appears in a photograph from 1907) into a man, a young man, to be sure, but one rather gaunt in appearance. The open air, better food and the exploits and tough encounters of the ensuing years endowed him with a more robust aspect.

The earliest portrait of him at this time upon which we can call is that by the Ukrainian nationalist Magalevsky who met Makhno in the spring of 1917. He describes him as a "…man small in stature, rather skinny wearing his hair long and with a small brown moustache"[1]; he records Makhno strolling about town for nearly an hour, listening in on the conversations and observing the behavior of all and sundry, without uttering a word himself. The anarchist Josef Gotman, known as "The Emigrant" on account of his having lived in the United States for many a long year, saw Makhno at roughly the same time as a "…man of slightly less than average height, powerfully built, with piercing steel gray eyes and a determined expression. Son of a Ukrainian peasant, in his veins flowed the blood of Zaporog Cossack ancestors renowned for their independent spirit and their fighting qualities. Although weakened by long incarceration, during which his lungs had been affected, Makhno amazed everyone with his vitality and energy."[2]

At the end of 1918 the insurgent Belash also saw him as "…not quite as tall as the average, with a lively manner, snub nose and long hair that falls to his neck and shoulders, giving him an adolescent air. Dressed in baggy pants over officer's jackboots, a dragoon's jacket with buttoned-up collar, a student cap upon his head, and a Mauser revolver slung at his shoulder."[3] A few months later, Dybets offered one of the most interesting portraits of him:

"What was he like? Well, how can I put it? He was small of stature. He wore his hair long, tumbling down his back. In winter as in summer, the only head covering he would have any truck with was the *papakha*. He was perfectly expert in the handling of all manner of weapons. He was a dab hand with the rifle and an excellent saber-man. Using the Mauser and the Nagan [revolvers — A.S.] he was a crack shot. He knew how to fire a cannon, which he required of all his entourage; the Batko himself could use a cannon […] As an anarchist, he had read the works of Kropotkin, Orgueani and probably Bakunin; there, it would appear, his intellectual baggage stopped. There was no denying his uncommon innate gifts, but one could only take him to task for failing to develop them and having failed to grasp the responsibility that he bore."[4]

In short, Dybets was carping at Makhno for not having undergone metamorphosis, as he himself had, from libertarian into Bolshevik and maybe for not having pushed his "intellectual baggage" as far as the learned works of his new masters; that said, he did acknowledge some very fine qualities in the man. These had escaped the attention of one of his party colleagues, Braznev, who met Makhno in May 1919 and noticed the "long hair hanging over his forehead," found his nose to be "long and pointed" and that he had the "long face of a seminarian"; Braznev later acknowledged that he had been tempted to pull out his Mauser and put a bullet in the back of Makhno's head while he was perusing a letter from headquarters![5]

When Lev Kamenev came to Gulyai-Polye on May 7, 1919, one of his escorts drew this thumbnail sketch of Makhno: "A thickset fellow, fair-haired [?], clean-shaven, with piercing light blue eyes, forever gazing into the distance and rarely looking his interlocutor in the eye. He listened to what one had to say with his eyes lowered and head slightly tilted, with a curious expression, as if he was about to knife us all where we stood, and walk away. He wore a *burka* [Caucasian felt overcoat — A.S.], and a *papakha* on his head, and a saber and revolver at his side. His staff commandant is a typical Zaporog."[6] The author of this portrait added that it was as if he had been transported back among the Zaporogs of the 18th century.

❦

Some months later, in August 1919, in Pomoshnaya railway station when the 58th Red Army Division joined up with Makhno, a Bolshevik by the name of S. Rosen had occasion to see him close at hand; he saw him as having blue eyes, being dressed like a hussar, resembling a "common soldier rather than the Ukrainian batko which he was made out to be," only his "wicked gray eyes hinted at extraordinary strength of will and toughness." Makhno delivered a fiery anti-Bolshevik speech, labeling Bolsheviks as usurpers and stranglers of the people's freedom and accusing them of fleeing like cowards before the Whites, abandoning the Ukraine to their mercy, whereas he pledged to smash Denikin into three short planks [a reference to a coffin? — A.S.]. Rosen stresses that Makhno shouted rather than spoke, with the consummate zeal of the agitator; the conclusion of his speech had been drowned out by cheering from the crowd of soldiers. One Bolshevik made to reply to him, but he had not allowed him to speak, and proposed that a revolutionary committee be formed forthwith.[7]

At around the same time, an Italian diplomat traveling in the area was intercepted by some Makhnovists; this was Pietro Quaroni; he offers us this picturesque description of his adventure. First of all he was confronted with "a tall, dark commander with a monumental set of moustaches and a still fresh scar running across his face. A Cossack cap sat lopsided on his head, his uniform was very vaguely reminiscent of the old Russian uniforms: Two machine-gun ammunition belts criss-crossed his chest; and lastly there was that broad leather belt with some grenades dangling from it."[8] It transpired that this was the commander of Makhno's black sotnia. Quaroni was led before Makhno in a *khata*. The batko was alone, seated in front of a crudely-hewn table. The Italian diplomat depicts him as being "short, with straight, chestnut-brown hair hanging down to his narrow adolescent's shoulders. A black cloth jacket girded by the inevitable crossed machine-gun belts; a revolver and a saber hung at his waist; on the table one could just make out his boots, gleaming." He found him to have "small dark eyes with, from time to time, a maniacal stare and the occasional flash of cold curiosity; but, throughout, the expression of an indomitable and well nigh superhuman determination." Quaroni exchanged a few words with his host and was very struck by his voice: "Such a voice as I have never heard; in tone, very high though not shrill, and abruptly modulated; one sometimes almost felt as if one was listening to a cock crow[!]." Probably an aficionado of the opera and under the influence of several glasses of vodka proffered by his host and which he did not dare decline for fear of offending Makhno, the Italian remarked a "long and strident burst of laughter" from the Batko who made an astonishing speech to him, unless, with the passage of time and his imperfect grasp of Russian, Quaroni had picked up certain words and phrases wrongly. According to him, Makhno had supposedly urged him to intercede with the Western allies to get them to support him:

> "I am the one whom the Allies should be supporting. The Whites? They no longer stand any chance, and will never get the Russian people under their yoke again. The Reds? But if they win the day, you're going to have problems putting paid to them. I, on the other hand, reckon that factory life, city living cannot but make a man unhappy; but in the countryside, once the big landlords have been done away with,

everybody will be able to live content. Look, this is marvelous soil; we shall sell you our wheat and from you we will buy the industrial products we lack and we shall all be happy; a happy, free peasant people will never seek trouble with its neighbors."9

Makhno assured him that every peasant in Russia was on his side and undertook, with the Allies' help, to rid the country of Reds and Whites alike. Although such words from Makhno's lips seem unlikely, Quaroni's version is nonetheless interesting, for he reconstructs this much more likely essential message: "It was a matter of doing away with landlords and government and of securing absolute freedom for the peasants. The old, old anarchist revolution, in short, the timeless dream of the Russian peasant — the revolution of Stenka Razin and Emilian Pugachev."10 The diplomat's short sojourn among the Makhnovists ended with a madcap race in a tatchanka, that "civil war jeep." Quaroni's recollection of the episode proved quite wistful, as he confessed, deep down, a pronounced sympathy for anarchy and recalled his interlocutor with "a twinge of regret."

One month later, shortly before the battle of Peregonovka, there were some contacts between the Makhnovists and Petliura's Ukrainian nationalists. One of the latter, a certain Vinar, portrays Makhno as a "solidly built fellow, of average height, dressed in a blue shirt tied at the waist by a green belt."11 Another Petliurist tells of Makhno's arrival at the Uman headquarters. On the eve of the scheduled rendezvous, some Makhnovist emissaries had showed up to reconnoiter the place and posted themselves in positions where they might sound the alarm at the first sign of danger. The next morning on the stroke of 10:00 A.M., about 20 horsemen arrived on the gallop, with five tatchankis mounted with machine-guns bringing up the rear; in the middle tatchanka was Makhno, dressed in a long green Cossack greatcoat; other horsemen formed a rearguard. All of this cavalry lined up in two ranks facing the Petliurist headquarters, allowing the tatchankis to pass between them. Preceded and followed by two bodyguards brandishing revolvers, Makhno dismounted and walked towards the building. Armed with two revolvers himself, he entered the staff room, briefly greeted the Petliurist commander who had risen to welcome him, then promptly sat down in an armchair in order to avoid a handshake from his host.12 There was little trust between the two sides, and the Grigoriev precedent must have been still in their minds, which accounts for the plethora of precautionary measures.

☙

In Autumn 1919, during the occupation of Ekaterinoslav, Outman, an inhabitant of the city, caught sight of Makhno and found him "...small, slight, with a face almost womanly because of the long black hair that fell to his shoulders; he inspired dread, what with his staring, maniacal [?] piercing eyes and the cruel crease at the corner of his mouth, taken together with a pallid, washed-out face. It was hard to put an age on him — perhaps 25, maybe 45. No one could rest easy under his gaze; one nurse whom he questioned for a full hour [she was suspected of harboring White officers] later had a nervous breakdown, so much so that for weeks there were fears for her sanity [!] From what she said, the hardest thing to bear had been the end of the interrogation, when Makhno became pleasant[?]."13

We have another piece of testimony to temper this chilling picture. It comes from a young student at the city's Mining Institute, who had been delegated along with some other students to approach Makhno to seek clarification of certain Makhnovist impositions upon local intellectuals, one of whom was suspected of being a Denikinist spy and had been flogged. Having arrived with some trepidation, the student and his friends had quickly been reassured by Nestor who gave them a friendly welcome, standing up, smiling and shaking hands before inviting them to be seated, offering cigarettes and asking what he might do for them. The student took in the room they were in; roomy, well-lighted, with a huge table upon which two grenades, a Colt, two field telephones with wires trailing off outside, plus a samovar had been placed. The batko was not at all like a "father" figure and the student wondered why that title had been awarded to him. Makhno was wearing a khaki tunic, held closed by strapping that passed over the shoulders. An insurgent acted as orderly and jotted down the decisions reached during the exchange. Makhno listened attentively to the grievances of his visitors, occasionally interrupting them to seek further detail, and then told them of the problems he had in preventing abuses perpetrated by bandits professing to belong to the Makhnovist movement, although he had already had a number of them hanged. He declared that certain acts were the handiwork of Bolshevik provocateurs who had "everything to gain by the intelligentsia's turning away from the Makhnovists," especially in the cases which they had mentioned, for the insurgents never used the lash on anyone. They either shot those proven guilty, or released those found innocent. His visitors noted that it pained him to see the insurgent movement thus blackened to the advantage of its enemies. He undertook to look into the matter personally, chatted amiably with the students and asked them if they did not want to throw in their lot with the anarchist movement, as their presence might bring a lot of improvements.14

෴

Towards the end of 1920, the French libertarian Mauricius (Vandamme) spent some time in the Ukraine and happened to come across an anarchist peasant whose name he discovered only later; Nestor Makhno. These were the circumstances: against a romantic backdrop — a dingy tavern in Odessa — Mauricius spoke the password: "Have you any sunflower seeds?" and was escorted up a "fire-escape" into a separate room, where he found a "thick-set peasant, with rugged features; thirty to thirty-five years old, but prematurely wrinkled, stubborn forehead, deep-set eyes as clear as spring water, with a determined, forceful manner mitigated by the timeless nostalgic dreaminess of the Slav[!]." A Social Revolutionary acted as interpreter. Makhno told him that the "Ukraine's peasants made the revolution to get rid of feudal lords who were grinding them down and exploiting them and will never agree to the return of the old regime, but they do not want to fall under the yoke of communist bureaucrats either: They want to be free. All peasants accept and like the soviet system, but [they must be] soviets freed of government influence. [...] The communist functionaries are parasites who aim to ape the tsarist lordlings and oppress the peasant; the latter is quite prepared to work, but not in order to keep these idlers in food. He will defend his freedom against usurpers. [...] The peasants want to live by their toil, not wear anybody's yoke nor oppress anyone."15 Mauricius fails to give the exact date of this encounter but places it after the breakdown of the second alliance and thus probably in 1921, when Makhno was in the Odessa region. This testimony is precious for it appeared at the beginning of 1922, at a time when the Makhnovist movement was not yet well known in France and, above all, for the first time in the West, it reproduced the full text of the second alliance between the Makhnovists and the Bolsheviks, which authenticates his gripping account beyond all doubt.

The last reference we have unearthed to Makhno's presence in the Ukraine depicts him as "...a thirty-five year old man, with the ruddy cheeks of the consumptive, long hair falling to his shoulders, a physiognomy reminiscent of the sacristan of some parish in the back of beyond."16 Now one has to take into account the many wounds he had received, as well as the extremely exacting conditions of the fight against the Red Army — which is to say, a certain physical exhaustion — further aggravated by his lengthy detention in Poland. In 1925, when Alexander Berkman finally made his acquaintance in Berlin, he was "...taken aback by his appearance": the "powerful leader of the insurgents had been reduced to a shadow of his former self. His face and body bore the scars of wounds and his shattered ankle had left him permanently infirm."17 However, his spirit and determination were intact and he expressed the desire to return to the land of his birth "to resume the struggle for freedom and social justice. He found life in exile to be unbearable, feeling wrenched away from his roots, and he pined for his beloved Ukraine." Berkman several times heard him say that he had to get back "over there, for we are needed."

❧

Nourished by his exploits, the legend surrounding him was further reinforced by the many feats, real or imagined, with which public gossip credited him. The most wide-spread gossip concerned his unexpected appearances in the most diverse disguises and appearances. In the early days and given his flowing locks and beardless face, the most commonly assumed disguise was as a woman. Wearing make-up and dressed as a peasant woman off he would go to survey enemy positions before hiding some inscription by way of registering his visit, just before disappearing. One day he did just this to check out the Bolsheviks' abuses in Gulyai-Polye and left them this blunt warning: "Came. Saw everything. Vengeance will be taken. Batko Makhno."18 Perhaps his companions employed the same procedure to ensure that he seemed to be everywhere at once and to undermine the enemy's morale? Another version has it that he arrived, in peasant garb, to sell some vegetables in a village market. Whereupon, the next day, notices pinned up on the fences announced that those who had purchased such and such a vegetable had been dealing with none other than Batko Makhno. It was also said that he had had some banknotes printed, normal on one side but bearing on the reverse this humorous inscription: "Hey, chum, stop worrying! The smart money is on Makhno!"[19] A variation on this slogan stated that "…ours are no worse than yours."[20]

Other things too attested to Makhno's ability to be everywhere and nowhere. One day the commuter train between Alexandrovsk and Melitopol was attacked by a gang of armed men. They moved through the carriages, "steaming" the passengers; when they came to one passenger who had so far been sitting quietly in his seat, they were asked: "Who are you people?" and replied "Makhnovists," whereupon the nameless passenger whipped out a revolver and gunned them down. About 50 other "passengers" meted out the same treatment to the rest of the gang. Then the "nameless" passenger reveals his identity — Nestor Makhno — and delivers a speech to the real passengers, setting out the insurgents' honest intent.[21] Another time, a peasant begs a lone horseman to help him extricate his cart from the mud; this done, he thanks him and is about to move off when two more horsemen happen by and hail the lone horseman as … Batko Makhno: Whereupon the peasant dissolves in apologies for having put him to the trouble and thanks him all the more warmly.[22]

All of these deeds, real or imagined, spread by word of mouth and they earned Makhno unparalleled popularity among the peasantry, a popularity that occasionally bordered on outright adoration. Alexander Berkman records how one day in Dibrivka he came upon an "…aged muzhik, a real patriarch, with a long white beard, who doffed his *papakha* at the very mention of Makhno's name. 'A great and good man,' he said, 'may God protect him. He passed this way two years ago, but I remember as if it were yesterday. Standing on a bench in the square, he spoke to us. We are uneducated folk and could never make head or tail of the Bolsheviks' speechifying whenever they addressed us. But Makhno speaks our language, simple and direct: "Brethren," he told us, "we have come to help you. We have driven out the landlords and their hirelings, and now we are free. Divide the land among you fairly and equitably, then work as comrades for the good of all." A holy man,' the venerable peasant concluded with conviction, going on to bring up the prophecy of Pugachev, the great 18th century rebel: "'I have only frightened you, but one day a steel broom will come and it will sweep you all away, ye tyrants over the holy ground of this Russia of ours." Well, the broom has come and it is Batko Makhno.'"[23]

The old peasant, though, had lost one of his sons in Shkuro's occupation of his village, but Makhno, tipped off, had arrived in the middle of the night with a hundred men, and, with the help of local peasants, driven out Shkuro's 3,000 Cossacks. Such personal fearlessness — Makhno always led from the front

— created fierce competition among the other insurgents, none of whom wanted to be outdone. Hardly ever wounded during the first three years of the civil war, a legend of invincibility came to surround him. Arshinov who considered this a "psychic anomaly"[24] relates that he would "…stroll around under the bullets and shrapnel as if these were raindrops." To this was added a sang-froid that was always the same, even, indeed especially, in the most threatening circumstances as at Peregonovka or the Cheka-instigated attempt on his life; as he was walking down the main street of Gulyai-Polye, a killer, lying in wait around a corner, tossed two bombs at him. Fortunately, neither exploded; without flinching, Makhno drew his revolver, shot down the Chekist, picked up the bombs and took them to the movement's headquarters, remarking that these Bolsheviks were sending him some decidedly queer presents![25]

A strategist of genius (the word is not too strong for this gift of his was universally acknowledged), Makhno exploited the lie of the land to perfection; those steppes stretching into the distance, virtually treeless and unforested but corrugated everywhere by deep ravines invisible at a distance. His familiarity with the region thus proved crucial. The tactical methods employed — trickery, the element of surprise, the lightning raid, the sham retreat and extreme mobility — made up for the insurgents' numerical and technical inferiority. It was he who invented the tatchanka with its machine-gun mounting as transport for mounted infantry. Among his stratagems, the most celebrated, was wearing the disguise of the regular soldier; one by one he became an officer of the Varta, the White Cossacks, the Denikinist army and then a Red Army NCO.

We might also mention the use of marriage or funeral processions for military purposes. Berkman quotes one instance of this sort, as related by a Bolshevik: Makhno arranged for a wedding to be held in a Denikinist-occupied village. Passing themselves off as happy revelers, the insurgents doled out generous vodka rations to the troops of the garrison. As the drinking binge reached its climax, Makhno showed up at the head of a detachment. Taken by surprise and overpowered, the 1,000 Denikinists surrendered without a fight. The conscripts among them were sent home, the others being bound for the execution stake. Yet such strokes would have come to nothing had Makhno not been permanently on the alert. In the beginnings of the movement in the autumn of 1918 he slept fully dressed on a table over a three-week period, ready for any eventuality. When it came to weapon maintenance (especially maintenance of machine-guns) and the combat training of his partisans, he was extremely meticulous, almost obsessive. He explains himself in his reply to Kubanin concerning the allegedly gratuitous machine-gunfire by his chief lieutenant, Semyon Karetnik:

> "Semyon Karetnik and all my other aides who succeeded to positions
> of responsibility adhered as if to a law to a precept which they inherited
> from myself: Upon taking up an office of responsibility, never to rely

upon anyone else in the proper running of combat units, especially prior to each operation. Always to go and check it out yourself. This rule was above all applied to machine-gun units which, during operations and marches, had to follow me at all times at the head of the entire army. In such instances it was Semyon Karetnik's duty to inspect these units, particularly in winter, when the slightest drop in temperature could freeze the machine-guns. He checked it out because he knew me well, for it was my custom to ride well ahead of the army, and he knew that, in the event of an encounter with the enemy, I would not wait for the rest of the force to arrive but would attack immediately, lest the enemy have time to organize himself, even though this might cost us many losses at the opening of the engagement, before the enemy was overwhelmed by our attack. It was on such occasions that Semyon Karetnik would test the machine-guns, usually by loosing off five or six rounds himself, in the presence of the gunners."[26]

These precautions explain the frequent successes of his surprise attacks and make absolute nonsense of Voline's allegations of alcoholism which were of course made once Makhno was dead. Had he been alive he would have rebutted them and held them up to ridicule. It is in fact inconceivable that Makhno or his close companions could have indulged in drunken binges, given the constant tension in which they lived; the slightest bingeing could have cost all their lives in an instant, for engagements erupted at the most unlikely hours of the day or night and so they had to be constantly on the alert. All servicemen know that much, and during his famous raid, for instance, the Don Cossack general Mamontov, who was extremely temperate himself and who also led his men from the front, came upon 1,000 barrels of alcohol in Frolov. He promptly ordered them smashed, in which the tearful Cossacks obliged him (we do not know whether their tears were due to the alcoholic vapors or to their regrets!). Mamontov was perfectly well aware that, had he not done so, then within the hour all his men would have become corpses.[27] Makhno did the same thing with the alcohol of the Berdyansk distillery on one of the occasions when he seized the port; the barrels were emptied onto the snow, when they might have been used to banish the chill.

An important question arises concerning the impact of "Batko" Makhno's charisma upon the movement as a whole. In the minds of many, Makhno is regarded as a chief to whom all the insurgents were subordinate. As we have seen, the supreme authority of the movement was vested in the general congress of peasants and insurgents of the region; the leadership appointed between two congresses, the Military Revolutionary Soviet, had merely executive powers. The essential decisions of the movement were always made after a general assembly of the insurgents; however, certain tactical and strategic decisions of a military character fell exclusively to

Makhno and the members of his staff. Thus, here, "Batko" Makhno meant a leader of men in military matters and military matters only. This notion was wholly in tune with the traditional usage among the Makhnovists' ancestors — the Zaporog Cossacks. In this instance, the role of Batko, equivalent then to the title of *ataman koshevoy*, had not initially had such charismatic connotations. As we may judge from a description given by Gogol. One Kirdiaga is duly elected (in his absence) as *ataman koshevoy*. A dozen Cossacks go off to fetch him and tell him:

"'Come along! You've been elected *koshevoy*!'
'For pity's sake, my lords,' he replies, 'I am unworthy of such an honor. How could I be *koshevoy*? I lack the wisdom necessary to hold such high office! Is there really no one worthier in the whole army?'

'It is as you have been told!' the Cossacks bellow.

Two of them grab him under the arms and despite his efforts to resist by bracing his legs, he is at last hauled off into the middle of the square to an accompaniment of prods, heavy claps on the back and admonishments:

'Don't by so shy, damn it! Accept the honor, you cur, since it has been offered to you!'

Whereupon the crowd is asked if it is indeed willing to have Kirdiaga as its *koshevoy*. When it replies in the affirmative, the symbolic mace is offered to the newly elected one. In accordance with ancient custom, he declines it twice before accepting: four old Cossacks then step forward from the assembly and place a handful of earth atop Kirdiaga's head, and smear his face; he remains impassive, and thanks the Cossacks for the honor they have done him."[28]

One can readily understand how, in these conditions, the title of Batko implied a limited command although he could influence certain other decisions through the power of his word or arguments. The example of the Grigoriev affair illustrates this point; after the initial contact with the ataman, Makhno and the members of his staff withdrew to consider their options. A first vote indicated that four favored an alliance, but seven were against that but for the immediate execution of this pogromist. At this point, Makhno piped up and declared that "…Whatever the cost, we must enter into an alliance with Grigoriev, for we do not know as yet what support he has and we can always shoot him later. We have to redeem those who follow him, the ones who are innocent victims and we must at all costs absorb them into our units."[29] A second poll demonstrated the impact this argument had made; now nine favored an alliance and two abstained. When the time came to make the decision — which had such tragic implications for the destinies of the movement — whether to ally yet again with the Red Army,

Makhno had been dilatory; had he set his face against it, there can be no doubt but that events would not have taken such a dismal turn. The likelihood is that he was unwilling to oppose the vast majority of the insurgents who favored such a pact. On the other hand in the case of Fedor Glouschenko, commissioned by the Cheka to assassinate him, he was unable to resist his comrades' decision to have him executed in spite of the condemned man's repentance. If Makhno clung to and made use of the title Batko, this was because he appreciated that it was a rallying point for the peasantry as a whole who looked to him. Otherwise, as a convinced anarchist, he had no truck with the honors bestowed by any authorities; he contemptuously repudiated the decorations and ranks awarded (and the substantial salaries they implied) by both the Red Army and the Whites. Let us add for the record that under Wrangel, certain White politicians had been willing to confer upon him the title of the first "Count of Gulyai-Polye," but there is no telling whether he was aware of this curious plan.[30] All of these shenanigans did not prevent his enemies from placing a considerable price on his head when the time came, in an effort to rid themselves of this symbol of people's self-rule. Thus his responsibilities did not turn his head for, as one of his obituaries had it, he "…did not know how to 'act out a part,' his pre-eminence being natural, the result merely of an exceptional strength of will."[31] And this strength was derived from his intense faith in anarchy. At the outset of the insurgent movement in 1918, he had dreamed of a life in which there was "…neither slavery, nor falsehood, nor infamy, nor despised divinities, nor chains, where love and living space will not be for sale, where there would only be men's truth and nothing else.…"[32]

As an émigré Makhno had to summon up all his strength of will just to face the adversities and the slings and arrows of exile in strange lands and often hostile surroundings. France lived up to her reputation as a land of asylum, although he was informed at the Paris prefecture of police that it was on account of him that the Allied intervention in Russia had failed, but that this was not being held against him and that he was being granted a residence permit.[33] In this light, it is all the more to his credit that he was able to engage in such intense memorialist and intellectual pursuits in the years 1925–1929, complementing on paper the fighting that he had led on the ground. Here let it be noted that his style, while not as "literary" as Voline might have wished, was quite vivid. In his writing he simultaneously described what was done and what he felt, and in some places this did not preclude a degree of pathos and undue prolixity; however, he always brings out the underlying and implicit meaning of his standpoints, sometimes with great lyricism. In his dealings with other libertarians, it was not his intention to capitalize upon his "prestige" and he was always like a brother. Kiro Radeff has told us how Makhno's personal magnetism worked with French workers and others who, knowing nothing about the man, aside from his name, Nestor, would chat very warmly with him. He had remained humble among the humble, true to his class.

Some libertarian militants from Aimargues, a small town in the Gard department — at the time it was France's most anarchist town in terms of numbers and the intensity of the libertarian activities engaged in — met him in 1929, during the short trip that he had made to deliver his daughter Lucie there to holiday with some friends. Comrades Chotand (known just as Chocho) and N. have described to us a Makhno who was anything but intimidating, with his cloth cap, steady glance, strong handshake and open, friendly manner.

જ

Honed by the misrepresentations, controversies and squabbles of the years 1927–1929, his character soured somewhat, his diffidence increased and he no longer let anything pass without a snappy reply, becoming less approachable.

What truth was there in the innuendo about his having been an habitué of the Vincennes race-track and his fondness for the demon drink? Kiro Radeff has confirmed that Makhno was wont to go along to watch the horses race, not so much to have a flutter on the outcome as to relive certain feelings at the sight of the mounts — a quite normal thing in a horseman. As for over-indulgence in wine or spirits, Bulgarian comrades who were intimate with him right to the end — Kiro Radeff, Erevan and Nikola Tchorbadjietf — have categorically denied to us that he had any such weakness. Not once did they ever see him drunk or drinking heavily; indeed, they claim that his health was such that it would not allow him to drink much. Ida Mett has something to say on this point also:

> "Was Makhno the drunkard as which Voline describes him? I think not. During three years in Paris, I never saw him drunk, and I saw him very often at that time. I had occasion to accompany him as interpreter to meals organized in his honor by some foreign anarchists. One glass, and he became intoxicated; his eyes would sparkle and he became voluble, but I never saw him really drunk. They tell me that in the last years of his life he went hungry, let himself go and maybe at that point he took to the drink; that seems to have been a possibility. But generally speaking it took only a few drops of alcohol to intoxicate his ailing and weakened body. Being ataman, he must have drunk as much as any Ukrainian peasant in his everyday life."[34]

For our part, we have not been able to uncover any first-hand evidence of Makhno's possible drunkenness; nothing to endorse the U.S. academic Paul Avrich's categorical assertion that Makhno "…found only in alcohol the means of escape from this strange world into which he had been thrown."[35]

જ

Makhno had paid a high toll to the revolution in both personal and family terms. His aged mother had been man-handled and driven from her humble abode; three of his brothers had been, respectively, killed by the Austro-Germans, the Whites and the Reds. He had split up with his first companion, Nastia, over a misunderstanding; at the time of his odyssey across Russia, she had given birth to a still-born child and then, in the belief that Nestor was dead, she had set up home with another comrade. For a time he had another sweetheart, Tina, a telephonist in Dibrivka and then, from the start of 1919 he had had a consistent relationship with the woman who was to become his life's companion, Galina Kuzmenko, a Gulyai-Polye schoolteacher. She was a highly active participant in the insurgent movement, as adroit in the handling of a rifle as of a machine-gun, and for a time she had been involved in the intelligence branch. It was undoubtedly her commitment to the cause which had brought her and Makhno together. And she had paid dearly for it. Her father who naively believed that the "Whites and the Reds are men too," had been shot by the latter in August 1919 simply for being Makhno's father-in-law. Here let us make it clear that the couple never married, contrary to some assertions which have them marrying in church(?). Galina candidly admitted this in an article on the death of her father which appeared after Makhno's death.[36] She described herself as a "Makhnovist, not an anarchist," we are told by Nikola Tchorbadjieff who describes her as a "…tall, beautiful woman, erect, candid, likeable, smiling, very dignified and a good mother." In 1921 along with Nestor she had come within an ace of death when the village where they were staying was ringed by the Red Army which knew of their presence and had searched every home with a fine-tooth comb. Standing behind a door, with revolver at the ready, Nestor and she had awaited discovery, intent upon selling their lives dear; fortunately, the troops had not been curious enough to look behind the door of the room they were searching. May Picqueray also describes Galina as … "very devoted, calm and sensible, attached to Nestor and likeable"; on the other hand, little Lucie who must have been almost three years old in 1925, struck May as a little imp, what with her climbing and jumping off the table.[37] According to certain "rumors," the couple had their ups and downs but there too we have not been able to discover anything specific; Nikola Tchorbadjieff, who had been their neighbor, denied as much to us and pointed out instead that they got along famously.

However, Ida Mett levels serious charges against Galina; she describes her as a Ukrainian nationalist, credits her with an overbearing attitude towards her companion and even accuses her of having tried to murder him in his sleep in 1924 in Poland following an affair she had had with a Petliurist officer. As evidence of this murder bid, she cites the broad scar that Makhno displayed on his cheek. We pointed out to her that it was common knowledge that the scar was the result of a bullet which had struck him in the back of the head, exiting via the cheek … to which she retorted that she had only "heard tell" of this. Ida Mett also accused Galina of having stolen her companion's private diary and of having destroyed it in concert with Voline — whose companion she allegedly became — because of scathing remarks it contained about them. Here again Ida Mett was unable to provide detail and had retreated behind a "hearsay" defense. Such allegations therefore must be taken with a large pinch of salt. Nikola Tchorbadjieff did confirm to us that Galina was on friendly terms with Voline after Nestor's death but that there was nothing to suggest more intimate relations; their dealings must have had to do with the preparation of Makhno's manuscripts and memoirs. What is not open to debate, is Galina's loyalty to the memory of her comrade, as her article in Ukrainian in *Probuzdeniye*, refuting the calumnies of Ukrainian nationalists, bears witness.[38] Also she had been jailed in a Warsaw prison for 13 months; she could not have wound up there merely for being Makhno's companion; she must have been engaged in tremendous joint activity with Nestor whose secretary and confidante she had always been. It strikes us that her part in the movement was much more important and remarkable than it seems; for instance, it was she who took on the delicate and dangerous mission of contacting the Russian-American anarchists Emma Goldman and Alexander Berkman who were at that stage well-disposed towards Lenin, in the summer of 1920. She briefed them on the real nature of the Makhnovist movement; neither Goldman nor Berkman concealed the strong impression she had made on them. Emma mentioned the risk she had run in coming to see them; Galina replied that she had "...faced danger so often that she no longer gave it a thought." The pair spent the whole night in conversation; Emma noted her "...ravishing face" and Berkman speaks of her as a "young woman of remarkable beauty." She questioned Emma Goldman about "women abroad, especially in America: What were they doing? Were they truly independent and acknowledged? How did relations between the sexes stand? And birth control?" Emma was impressed by this "urgent thirst for knowledge" and sensed her "enthusiasm quicken" in response to Galina's. It seems that for the visiting couple (Berkman and Goldman) this encounter was a watershed; hitherto, they had been starry-eyed about the Lenin regime. A meeting with Makhno was planned by means of a stratagem; Makhnovists would seize the train carrying Goldman and Berkman, thereby saving appearances in Moscow's eyes and then they could have a more detailed briefing on the Makhnovschina. But circumstances prevented realization of the plan.[39]

In exile, Makhno had patiently striven to separate his companion Galina from his activities, even claiming in one article that his wife was not politically-minded, this in the probable aim of not compromising her in the eyes of the French police and his Russian enemies. He may even have urged her, before dying, to go home and carry out a mission there among his surviving comrades. Some argue in favor of this; first there is mention of the existence of three caches of arms and valuables somewhere in the Ukraine, the whereabouts known only to these two; then we have been able to establish that, during the war, Galina and her daughter, Lucie Makhno, did set out for Berlin before trying to reach the Ukraine. According to Ida Mett, both allegedly perished in an air raid, but Kiro Radeff told us that he spotted Galina on a Paris bus after the war, though he was not sure enough to approach her. There is no question but that Galina remained loyal to the struggle waged in 1919–1921 and that she tried to carry it on by whatever means she had at her disposal.

۞

Let us move on now to the vices and various shortcomings ascribed to Makhno's personality and begin with his old comrade Piotr Arshinov who, in his *History of the Makhnovist Movement* first lists many obvious qualities before coming to his main fault; Makhno's alleged ignorance of matters historical and political, and his lack of adequate grounding in theory. Given the part that Makhno played in it, these shortcomings would have had a serious impact on the whole movement. Arshinov also mentions a "complete lack of education" and a degree of "nonchalance," especially in the autumn of 1919 when the Bolsheviks re-invaded the Ukraine.[40] He cites no other examples or specific case to back up his remarks; from which we must deduce that he took Makhno to task for not having taken sufficient precautions against Moscow and not having really opposed that second compact with the Red Army. It might have been interesting had he let us in on his own position, for it would appear that he was part of the movement at this point. In any case, as we have seen, Makhno, acting alone, never at any time arrived at any decision binding upon the movement as a whole; in which case, Arshinov's reproach applies equally to the other insurgents. Note that at the time, Bolshevism was a new phenomenon and that few were conversant with Lenin's career as a militant, his double-talk and his Jacobin-Blanquist views. Many another revolutionary, Bolsheviks included, let themselves be taken in even though they were "university graduates" or had taken "lengthy party courses" and this was true also and not least of the anarchists. Kropotkin himself had entertained illusions about the Leninist regime. Also, we do not share Arshinov's opinion of Makhno's education and his political and historical knowledge. He was not as bereft of these as all that as we have had occasion to note. Consequently, this "failing" does not stand up, unless Arshinov was willing to say more about it and focus attention, say, on the treatment meted out to the Whites' plenipotentiaries — hardly in keeping with the usual conventions — or take Makhno to task for having abdicated his responsibilities in June 1919 by deferring to Trotsky, or even for having underestimated the Ukrainian nationalist factor. That would be at once too much and not enough, so we shall stick to the single example that Arshinov does cite.

Voline repeats the fault pointed out by Arshinov and tacks on certain reproaches of his "moral qualities" and "moral duties," in which Makhno and his comrades were deficient; he looks upon this as the movement's "dark side." He has ... "heard tell that certain commanders — Kurilenko is mentioned most often — were morally better equipped than Makhno to lead and steer the movement as a whole.[44] Unfortunately, Voline did not "...know Kurilenko and could not offer any personal opinion of him," which somewhat brings his "hearsay" testimony into question. On the other hand, he puts Makhno's "carelessness" down to alcohol abuse, his "greatest failing." Curiously, this "failing" showed itself morally: "In Makhno, the inebriated state showed itself primarily in the moral domain. Physically, he was not unsteady on his feet. But under the influence of alcohol, he became perverse, over-excitable, unfair, intractable and violent." Let us leave it up to Voline to determine the difference between a "moral" and a "physical" state of intoxication and just deplore the fact that he waited until Makhno was dead before ventilating this charge, which we think unlikely for the reasons we noted earlier. Voline targets another great fault in Makhno and many of his closest associates; their "attitude towards women. Allegedly, they forced certain women to participate in 'sorts of orgies'." This very grave charge is categorically rebutted by Ida Mett; Makhno had told her "…that he could have had any woman he chose in his glory days, but that in reality he did not have the spare time to devote to a personal life. He told me this by way of refuting the legend of orgies that had allegedly been organized by and for him. Voline in his book rehearses the same claptrap. In reality, Makhno was celibate, or rather chaste. As for his relations with women, I would have said that there was in him a combination of a sort of peasant simplicity and a respect for womankind that was typical of turn of the century Russian revolutionary circles."[42]

Let us add that Isaak Teper, a *Nabat* anarchist who spent some months as a participant in the movement, cites in his study the case of the Makhnovist commander Puzanov who had raped a nurse and been brought before an insurgent tribunal. Makhno had allegedly been insistent that he should be shot and it was only on a majority vote that he was merely relieved of his command and placed in the front lines, where he was killed shortly afterwards.[43] Let us not forget, either, the presence of Galina Kuzmenko or other insurgents who would never have stood for such an attitude toward themselves or other women.

Voline also speaks of "personal caprices," or "dictatorial antics," "arbitrariness," "absurd outbursts" and "brainstorms," as well as of a "sort of military clique" — or cabal — surrounding Makhno. Here again he fails to mention many hard facts and these charges seem above all to have been prompted by personal rancor. For what reason did Voline seek to besmirch the memory of his co-religionist? To be sure he had been a participant in the insurgent movement only for four months and his opinion was valued for only that space of time, and one might discern in this personal enmity the antagonism between "talker" and "doer," in short between the gossip and the activist. For her part, Ida Mett "certifies" that not only did Makhno "…have no liking for Voline, but had no respect for him, regarding him as a worthless, characterless individual." Which probably accounts for Voline's attitude.

Ida Mett speaks of the failings that she was able to discern in the émigré Makhno, emigration being the only time she had any dealings with him. In particular she stresses his "…extreme incredulity and diffidence," even towards his closest friends who wished him well. She reckoned that his attitude was a "pathological consequence" of Nestor's military activities. She also found him to be a "cantankerous" character, and detected a "…measure of hostility towards intellectuals," towards whom he allegedly felt "a degree of envy"(?). According to her, he had also been "jealous" of the "careers" of Voroshilov and Budyenny. It would appear that she had some difficulty in translating into good French, this "resentment" on

Makhno's part towards these individuals and intellectuals whom he could see right through, ever since his days in the Butyrki prison. Magalevsky, quoted earlier, tells us that in Gulyai-Polye in 1917, he heard Makhno tell the peasants, after sitting through the speechifying of local notables and bigwigs: "Do not believe what these intellectuals tell you; they are the enemies of ordinary folk."[44] On the other hand, we saw him in Ekaterinoslav lamenting the inadequate numbers of intellectuals in the movement. In his *ABC of the Revolutionary Anarchist*, he notes that, out of every ten intellectuals who move towards the oppressed toilers, nine will seek to pull the wool over their eyes, but the tenth will be their friend and will help them to avoid deception by the others,[45] which in our view is a good general estimate. Thus he did not wholly embrace the critical theses expounded with regard to intellectuals by the Russian Pole Machaiski whom he was to encounter on his trip to Moscow in the spring of 1918.

In trying to defend Makhno's memory against Voline's charges, Ida Mett also revealed her own confusion on certain points. Indeed, among some assertions that seem well-founded, some evaluations appear very shallow:

"Was Makhno an honest man seeking the good of the people, or was he a maverick who chanced to fall from the heavens? My reckoning is that his social goodwill was sincere and above question. He was an innately gifted politician (?) and threw himself into stratagems which were often out of proportion with his limited political knowledge. However, I believe that he was perfectly at home in the role of popular avenger. As for knowing what he and his class wanted and hoped for, that was indeed the Makhnovist movement's Achilles heel; but it was a weakness shared by the whole of peasant Russia of whatever persuasion. They wanted freedom and land, but how were they to use these two things? That was more difficult to determine."

Such incomprehension of the nature and goals of the Makhnovists is the "Achilles heel" of Ida Mett herself, a young Lithuanian Jew and city dweller, a newcomer to revolutionary circles, unfamiliar with the ins and outs of the clashes in the Ukraine.

⁂

Let us just mention the rather bizarre assessment of Louis Dorlet, alias Samuel Vergine, author, in *Le Libertaire*, of a eulogistic obituary piece on Makhno; he wrote us that he had seen "…Makhno two or three times. He was a boor that believed in holding nothing back(!)."[46]

And ourselves, what might we criticize in Makhno or take him to task for? For a start, there was his serious underestimation of the Ukrainian national factor, as he later acknowledged in exile. His ignorance of the Ukrainian language and culture served him ill, although the rather Russified southern Ukraine had been more receptive to the general concerns of Russia. For instance, he made the mistake of initiating a fight against the Ukrainian nationalists without properly dissociating himself from Muscovite imperialism. A *modus vivendi* with the Petliurists could have enabled Makhnovists to devote themselves better to the fight against the White and Red invaders. As a result, a more discriminatory evaluation of the danger posed by the different enemy forces — and he patently underestimated the Bolsheviks in this context — might have wrought a complete change in the course of events. Yet these shortcomings cannot be imputed to Makhno alone, for anarchist doctrine too had neglected the national factor and the hegemonic ambitions of the Jacobin-Leninists. That leaves his excessively severe treatment of certain marauders or perpetrators of anti-social acts — he systematically had them hanged or shot. Aside from this trait, it appears to us that he acted for the best, in conjunction with the insurgent masses and the precepts of libertarian communism. Thus, Koval, a Russian anarchist who had been an active participant in the 1917 revolution, reckons that men such as Makhno are very rare and "...appear only once a century."[47] One obituary saw him as the incarnation of the struggle against all tyrannies and for "...the transformation of our servile world into a free society without masters or slaves."[48] Lipotkin, author of another obituary notice predicts that when the Russian people overthrow the Bolsheviks' dictatorship, they "...will remember with pride and love their most courageous and most authentic combatants, among whom Nestor Makhno will be well to the fore."[49]

Notes for Chapter 28: Nestor Makhno's Personality: Character Traits and Idiosyncrasies

1. Magalevsky, op. cit. p. 61.
2. Cited by Alexander Berkman *Nestor Makhno, the Man who Saved the Bolsheviks*, an English-language manuscript written shortly before his death in 1935 by this Russian-American anarchist. Our thanks to the International Institute for Social History in Amsterdam — which has it — for having authorized us to publish extracts. The text takes up and develops the "N. Makhno" chapter in Berkman's book *The Bolshevik Myth*, published in New York, 1925, pp. 182–196.
3. Belash op. cit. p. 212.
4. Dybets op. cit. p. 39 and pp. 44-45.
5. Braznev "The partisans," in *Novy Mir*, Moscow, 1925, No. 7, p. 75.
6. V. S. *L. B. Kamenev's Expedition*, op. cit. p. 136.
7. S. Rosen, op. cit. p. 125.
8. P. Quaroni *Croquis d'ambassade* (translation from the Italian), Paris, 1955, p. 4 et seq.
9. Ibid. p. 10
10. Ibid. p. 6.
11. L. Vinar "Relations between N. Makhno and the Ukrainian national army (1918–1920)" (in Ukrainian) *Rozbudova derzhavi*, Munich, 1953, 2, pp. 14–20.
12. E. Yakimov "Makhno's visit to Uman" Chernova Kalina, Lvov, 1931, pp. 78–80.
13. Gutman, op. cit. p. 67.

14. V.T., an engineer deported to Germany during the second world war before becoming a refugee in France, in *Dyelo Truda* No. 41, 1953, pp. 25–27.

15. Mauricius *Au pays des soviets. Neuf mois d'aventures*, Paris, 1922, pp. 261–267.

16. S. M. *"The Makhnovschina,"* in *Revolutionary Russia* (in Russian), Prague 1922, No. 7 p. 23.

17. A. Berkman, op. cit. p. 29.

18. A. Nikolaev *First among Equals* (in Russian), op. cit. p. 124.

19. Kalinin *Russia's Vendée* (in Russian) op. cit. p. 286.

20. A. Nikolaev *Nestor Makhno* (in Russian) op. cit. p. 95.

21. A. Nikolaev *Batko Makhno* (in Russian) op. cit. p. 17.

22. A. Nikolaev *Nestor Makhno* (in Russian) op. cit. p. 93.

23. A. Berkman, op. cit. pp. 12–13.

24. Ida Mett *Souvenirs sur Makhno*, 7 page, typewritten manuscript on deposit at the Library of Contemporary International Documentation, in Nanterre, Paris, 1948, p. 5.

25. A. Nikolaev, op. cit. p. 99.

26. N. Makhno, *The Makhnovschina and its Erstwhile Allies, the Bolsheviks* op. cit. pp. 31–32.

27. I. Kalinin, op. cit.

28. Nikolai Gogol *Taras Bulba*, Paris, 1930 pp. 84–86.

29. Kubanin, op. cit. p. 80.

30. Nazhivin *Writings on Revolution* (in Russian), Berlin, 1923 p. 314.

31. Murometz, in *Probuzdeniye* No. 52-53, November–December 1934, p. 16.

32. N. Makhno "Memoirs" (in Russian) in *Anarkhicheskiy vestnik* op. cit. no. 1, p. 28.

33. Conversation reported by Nikola Tchorbadjieff.

34. Ida Mett, op. cit.

35. Paul Avrich *Les Anarchistes Russes*, Paris, 1979 p. 275.

36. G. Kuzmenko "Memories. My father's death," in *Probuzdeniye* No. 76, 1936, pp. 14–24.

37. Author's interview with May Picqueray, September 28, 1981.

38. *Probuzdeniye* No. 50-51, September–October 1934.

39. A. Berkman, op. cit. pp. 14–22, and Emma Goldman *Epopee d'une anarchiste*, Paris, 1979, p. 263.

40. Arshinov op. cit. pp. 217–220. Note that Arshinov was himself a self-educated worker.

41. Voline *La Révolution Inconnue*, Paris, 1947, pp. 680–683.

42. Ida Mett, op. cit.

43. I. Teper, op. cit. p. 84.

44. Magalevsky, op. cit. p. 63.

45. *Probuzdeniye* No. 19, January 1932, p. 20.

46. Letter to the author, October 4, 1981.

47. F. Koval "Demand Makhno's Release," in *Amerikanskye Izvestia* January 17, 1923, p. 6.

48. "Death of N. I. Makhno," in *Probuzdeniye* No. 47-49, June–August 1934, p. 2.

49. L. Lipotkin "Nestor Makhno," in *Probuzdeniye* No. 50-51, September–October 1934, p. 16.

29. The Makhnovists

Most observers, eyewitnesses and historians of the civil war in the Ukraine are agreed in acknowledging the representative nature of the Makhnovist movement as far as the peasant population, and especially its poorest stratum, are concerned. There is in existence a rather telling breakdown of the Makhnovschina's social composition. In figures quoted by Kubanin, relating to insurgents who allegedly applied in April 1921 to take advantage of the Bolshevik authorities' amnesty (in fact, they were probably taken prisoner and forced, under threat of execution, to go over formally to the regime) we find that, of 265 Makhnovist insurgents, 117 had no land at all, either because they had been farm laborers before the revolution or because they had been workers, or because the Reds had confiscated their land; 91 insurgents worked a plot of less than four hectares — an area regarded as the minimum necessary to support a household — and only 57 owned larger tracts.[1] Such evidence invalidates the description "kulak" as applied to the movement by Trotsky and the official authorities and instead backs up Makhno's claims about the poor peasant profile of the movement. These rural proletarians — we might say "slaves bound to the soil" — were descendants of the peasants reduced to serfs by Catherine II and cheated after the abolition of serfdom in 1862,[1] when they had been forced to buy back the land which they had always worked. In addition, they had been joined by a number of workers who had been driven out of the towns by penury, chaos and arbitrary policing organized by the Leninists.

In organizational terms, the insurgent army relied upon a network of local detachments which, according to the numbers of their fighters and the extent of their activities, became regiments bearing the name of their places of origin; Kubanin for instance talks about the Sixth Ekaterinoslav Regiment. Thus these units were homogeneous, which made it hard to plant troublesome or suspect elements in them. Volunteer service was the very essence of the movement, although it earned captured Makhnovists the worst of treatment; not for them the extenuating grounds of compulsory mobilization. It goes without saying that, as volunteers, insurgents received no pay, although the Red Army — during the life spans of the two alliances — had sought to place them on a payroll. Consequently their entire upkeep was dependent upon the voluntary contributions of the local populace. Furthermore, most of the insurgents were not mobilized on a permanent basis; they had to go home to perform the requisite farm labors, provided of course that circumstances on the front allowed and that they had the agreement of their military leadership.

This status as peasant-soldiers defending their land and their liberty is reminiscent of that of their Zaporog peasant forebears; and the similarity carried over into the partisan warfare tactics that wrought such havoc among their opponents. Thus, Kubanin stresses the extreme mobility of the Makhnovist cavalry, covering an average of 60–100 kilometers a day, whereas regular cavalry covered only 40, and, on very rare occasions, 60 kilometers.[2] Such a pace was possible only with the support of the population and the painstaking organization of fresh mounts at certain agreed staging-posts; outriders, having swapped their tired mounts for fresh horses and resting up, would drop back into the rearguard. This switch-over came into play in engagements; Kubanin describes its devastating results:

> "Whenever Red troops brought severe pressure to bear on the Makhnovist army, the latter often beat a hasty retreat, striving to vanish from the enemy's field of vision, then promptly attacking his rear, having taken care to leave one unit up ahead to serve as bait for the Reds. It was through such swift, forceful, unexpected onslaughts that the Reds often found themselves beaten. Just when a Red unit thought that it had defeated the Makhnovists and went to cap its success by giving chase, it often found itself in fact under attack from the rear. If that approach failed, the Makhnovists, under constant pressure from the enemy, used to split their units into different groups, scattering in every direction, thereby completely disorienting the enemy. Sometimes these groups would split themselves up into regiments, regiments into sotnias and so on down to quite tiny tactical units. By 1921 the whole of the Ukraine teemed with such Makhnovist detachments sometimes coming together into a single force, sometimes scattering themselves throughout the countryside again and, burying their weapons, reverting into 'peaceable villagers.'"[3]

These were typically Cossack tactics and the Makhnovists may be deemed nothing short of "Anarchy's Cossacks," so reminiscent were their methods of the methods of their ancestors. Kubanin takes the line that this had more to do with "peasant cunning," both because he knew nothing or wished to know nothing of similarities with the Zaporogs, and because he confounded such fighting methods with those of the peasantry generally. Not that the insurgents scorned the latter, however; the partisan Osip Tsebry supplies us with one rather striking example; in 1918 some peasants from the Zhmerinka region (of western Ukraine) were in the habit of going out into the fields, hiding their rifles and machine-guns among their wheat; a passing patrol or small unit of Austro-Germans or Varta would suddenly find itself attacked and wiped out by the peasants who, in order to shift suspicion, wasted no time in alerting the relevant command to a detachment of origins unknown having been responsible for the raid.[4] The whole tactics of the Makhnovist detachments on campaign were based on extreme mobility, itself down to the quality of the mounts — often the horses of German settlers, which were renowned for their sturdiness — and to the courage of the individual fighter. Yefimov, a Red Army "military expert" charged with combating the Makhnovschina, quite rightly stresses the differences between the Red Army trooper and the Makhnovist insurgent. In the case of the former, the common soldier finds his idiosyncrasies and qualities leveled out by absorption into the generality which led to one of two extremes in engagements; either an infectious enthusiasm if the situation was favorable, or a general despondency and mass surrender by every unit in the event of misfortune. The Makhnovist's performance, though, was something else again:

> "By reason of his experience of partisan warfare or of the social conditions of his existence, the Makhnovist is possessed of highly developed personal qualities; he feels wholly independent everywhere. Even in combat, his favorite order of cavalry attack is the *lava* which affords every combatant maximum autonomy. His personal qualities as a fighting man ensure that he does not lose his head in the most dangerous moments, nor does he have to await specific instructions; he knows what he has to do; there is no need for him to be called to order and under constant supervision."[5]

That writer also points out that a fair number of insurgents had seen service in the Russo-German war and had emerged from it with solid experience of weapons and of coming under fire. We may add that the common effort against all the invaders and enemies of every hue was a strong bond connecting the insurgents; they called one another *bratishkis* (little brothers). Abetted in this way by social motives and its taste for independence, this "ragamuffin" army, sourcing its weapons wholly from the enemy, was able to pull off remarkable feats in defeating modern well-equipped whole armies — of Germans, Austro-Hungarians, Ukrainian nationalists, White Cossacks — and to keep the Red Army at bay for a long time.

※

Another important feature of the Makhnovist movement was the youthfulness of the insurgents, most of whom were less than 25 years of age. On this point, Kubanin quotes an interesting statistic, regarding the Fifth Ekaterinoslav Regiment towards the end of 1919; of 253 insurgents, 72 were aged 20 or less, 126 were aged between 21 and 25, 51 between 26 and 30, and only four of them were over 30 years of age. So there was a certain osmosis between the experienced fighters and the youngest volunteers. The older adults and adolescents did play their part in the movement, however, either by keeping it continually briefed on the enemy deployment or by hiding the detachments' arms and munitions, thereby representing a novel sort of "rearguard." Nor were young girls and women idle;

several thousands of them acted as couriers or intelligence agents or looked after the supply and medical services. When Ekaterinoslav was occupied in 1919, Gutman (whom we have already mentioned) was curious to find some young Amazons, dressed in black, entering the town along with the bulk of the Makhnovist troops; he described them as "intellectual anarchists."[6] Broadly speaking, Makhnovist units contained few women; it was only in 1919 when the units retreated as the Whites advanced, that many women joined their convoys either accompanying relatives or companions, or to escape violation by the oncoming Cossacks. Here, let us point out that the Russian Civil War — like all civil wars generally — was hellish for most women, a matter on which most historians are discreet to the point of silence. As far as the Whites were concerned, women were part of the booty, especially if they happened to be Jewish or related to insurgents — and here the presumption was generally enough — and were systematically raped. Where the Reds were concerned, they were generally spared this fate, but it depended on the unit commanders and whom they were forced to billet. Elsewhere in the country or in Russia, women were obliged to give themselves simply to get past Chekist checkpoints or to secure passage on a train, or to obtain a morsel of food. In view of this situation, there was a terrible upsurge in venereal diseases and rampant demoralization among the female population.[7]

The wife or sweetheart of any well-known insurgent was especially targeted. Galina Kuzmenko tells how the wife of Nestor's oldest brother, Savva Makhno, was tortured cruelly and at some length by White officers in June 1919; they beat her, stabbed her with their bayonets, cut off one of her breasts and only then did they shoot her.[8] Chekists too tormented one insurgent's wife and, in the end, shot her down with her infant in her arms; Makhno ordered Kurilenko to hunt down and punish these criminals, which he did, personally, shortly afterwards.[9]

⁂

Another thing the insurgents had in common with the Zaporog Cossacks was the unalterable principle that various command positions were elective. In its mobilization call on April 10, 1919, the Third Gulyai-Polye Congress issued a reminder about the need to elect both regimental and other unit commanders at all levels; it recommended that competent persons be appointed, preferably ones conversant with military tactics due to their service in the Russo-German war. All units had to assemble in a pre-agreed location, line up in columns and proceed with elections in strict conformity with regulations.[10] Both Yefimov and Kubanin stress the presence of former tsarist army NCOs among the Makhnovist commanders; these had "...borne all the brunt of the imperialist war"; Kubanin notes that they had "...furnished Budyenny to the Red Army and a whole series of talented commanders to Makhno." According to him, the "...Makhnovists' subtle and supple tactics required commanders in whom their detachments could have boundless confidence, commanders who were daring, wily and experienced, as the facts demonstrated their commanders to be."[11] He stresses that each detachment was a "...close-knit family, each commander dependent on it insofar as he had been elected by and was answerable to it." However, if need be, the Staff could punish commanders by reducing them to the ranks of their unit; by the same token, ranking insurgents were stripped of their mounts and their weapons.[12] According to Kubanin most of the commanders were both anarchists and peasants. Former tsarist officers whom the Bolsheviks turned into "military experts" were despised, regarded as useless and, as representatives of the hated order of the pomieschikis and bourgeois, ruthlessly exterminated.[13]

Again according to Kubanin, the "…supreme body of the insurgent army was its Military Revolutionary Soviet, elected at a general assembly of all insurgents. Neither the overall command of the army nor Makhno himself truly ran the movement; they merely reflected the aspirations of the mass, acting as its ideological and technical agents."[14] Yefimov is of much the same opinion; the detachments as a rule had every confidence in their elected commanders who, for the most part, were "…highly courageous men displaying great determination […] instigators of military operations, as well as of military and civilian strategies, in concert with the Military Revolutionary Soviet. This latter, and Makhno himself never reached any decision without consideration of the advice or position of the detachments. No decision was ever taken by just one individual. All military matters were debated in common. Usually the Military Revolutionary Soviet sat in the presence of the army's higher commanders. At every stage of the process, the Makhnovist detachment remained the driving force behind the whole movement."[15]

The highest positions of responsibility — chief of Staff, cavalry commander, commander of the special detachment and of each of the three army corps — were subject to rotation and were filled on a rota basis by the most capable and renowned of the insurgents. This stipulation regarding the collective thinking of the Makhnovists, as even official Soviet sources are forced to concede, is of the utmost importance, for certain outside observers — sometimes even anarchists, such as Voline, as we saw earlier — have misrepresented this elective hierarchy as a military "camarilla" and a "dictatorial" role played by Makhno.

※※※

Among the most prominent Makhnovist commanders, let us first of all turn to Semyon Karetnik, a comrade of Makhno's from the earliest days. A highly impoverished peasant, Karetnik had worked as an ostler before the war; during it he became an ensign and the military experience thus acquired was extremely useful to him in the struggle that he waged from the summer of 1918 on. Tall, burly, wearing a small moustache and always dressed in a leather jacket, he might be regarded as the No. 2 strategist of the movement, which owed many of its successes to him. At the time of his execution — he was captured, through treachery, by Bolsheviks who were as afraid of him as they were of Makhno — he must have been about 30 years of age. Another of the movement's leading figures, Fedor Shchuss, enjoyed among the insurgents a prestige almost equal to Makhno's.

He too was a poor peasant — the Bolsheviks labeled him a lumpen-proletarian — from Bolshe-Mikhailovka (Dibrivka). Having been a sailor during the war, he had become, in 1918, one of the most active members of the anarchist black guard of Gulyai-Polye, before fighting against the Austro-German invaders with some success. Dybets offers a highly-colored portrait of him, albeit one bereft of all sympathy for he had had a lot of trouble escaping Shchuss after his "exploits" as a Bolshevik political commissar:

> "He was a tall, strapping figure of a fellow with long black hair [this hairstyle subsequently became something of a fashion among young Makhnovists — A.S.]. His costume was eccentric; feather in his cap, velvet jacket, boots with spurs and saber by his side. During Makhno's banquets, he stayed silent and as motionless as a statue. He honestly thought that he would be immortalized in popular legends and ballads. Once he showed me some verses from some Ukrainian poet eulogizing one of the exploits of batko Shchuss when he had, unaided, rendered ten police hors de combat."

According to Dybets, he was a kick-boxing and wrestling champion, even had some expertise in jiu-jitsu and could strangle someone with a sudden grip.[16] Tremendously courageous, he was, turn and turn about, a cavalry commander, commander of the cavalry brigade of the Third Makhnovist army corps and a member of the Staff. According to the young Ekaterinoslav student mentioned earlier, Shchuss had a tendency to race off on frenzied raids which were not always justified and he had to be closely watched. Here he is described as we see him in the photographs available to us:

> "Dressed in a hussar's tunic, with sailor's cap, bearing the ship's name — St. John of the Golden Tongue — encrusted in gold letters, with a Caucasian dagger and a Colt thrust into his belt and two grenades at his side."[17]

In the rather similar account of another witness in 1919, the gold-lettered inscription on the band of his sailor's cap read "Free Russia." Oddly, his horse was "bedecked with ribbons, flowers and pearl bracelets at its feet."[18] According to A. Nikolaev who must have had it from a reliable source, Shchuss was also fancy free and took a very close interest in the prettier insurgent women.[19]

❧

Piotr Petrenko-Platonov, another native of Dibrivka was one of the most courageous insurgent commanders; an ensign during the war, he commanded an insurgent front at the end of 1918, acted as Dybenko's chief of staff for a period of two months, in May–June 1919, and then was for a long time in charge of the main Makhnovist detachment in 1921. Vassili Kurilenko was another of the movement's stalwarts. Tall, fair-haired and mustachioed he was about 28 years old in 1919, powerfully built, a born horseman of tremendous daring. He was a cobbler from Novospassovka and had been an anarchist since 1910. Dybets speaks very favorably of him, although he appears to have been oblivious of his very active work among the insurgents in that he boasts about the man's gifts as a soldier and leader of men but credits him with sympathies for the Reds which he certainly could not have entertained, given the fate reserved for residents of his home town by the Reds, as described to us by dissident general Grigorenko.

Viktor Belash, a 26 year old worker from the same area was an exceptionally talented military organizer; it was he who planned many of the operations and who was for a long time the insurgent army's chief of staff and its last commander, before capture by the Red Army. While in prison he wrote extensive memoirs (three sizable exercise books were filled) of which we have had only a very brief extract published in the Ukrainian Communist Party's historical review *Letopis Istorii*; according to Kubanin, he also wrote a treatise on the civil war. In this way he fought to the last with his pen, before being shot in 1923. We might point out that, to take revenge on the partisans, the Austrians shot his father, grandfather and cousin, before setting their home on fire.

Viktor Popov held positions of great responsibility in the movement — being the last secretary of the Insurgents' Military Revolutionary Soviet — and undeniably deserves to be rescued from oblivion. A Black Sea sailor aged about 25 in 1919, he was a member of the Left Social Revolutionaries and directed his party's revolt against the Bolsheviks in Moscow in July 1918. The rising failed, just, largely on account of the mercy shown to arrested Bolsheviks and Chekists — Dzherzinsky among them — and of the rebels' dithering over an attack upon the building containing Lenin and his party's central committee. In the forlorn hope that they might carry the day by moral pressure alone, they shrank from shedding the blood of their "brethren." A fatal error, for Bolsheviks had no such hesitation or scruples. In 1919, Viktor Popov fought against Denikinist troops alongside a detachment of his fellow party members in the Ukraine, before going over to the Makhnovists in April 1919. According to Teper, whose version is accepted by Kubanin, Popov allegedly had pledged his undying hatred of the Bolshevik-Communists and had set himself a target of 300 of them to be killed at his own hands — only two-thirds of which figure he achieved! If this is true, it would appear astonishing that he should have been the one who went with Kurilenko to negotiate the second alliance with the Red Army, and even more startling that he should have remained several weeks in Kharkov in the lions' den, before being arrested and shot by the Cheka through Moscow's treachery. Kubanin overstates his case by describing him as the most ferocious opponent of any compact with the Bolsheviks.[20] Although a bitter enemy of the Leninists, whom he could not forgive for having betrayed the revolutionary aspirations of the 1917 revolution, he must nonetheless have believed in their bona fides at the time of the second compact with the Makhnovists and was content, as many another revolutionary was, to fight them with the written and spoken word (Teper mentions meetings organized in Kharkov in October–November 1920, and refers to articles in *The Makhnovist Voice* in which Popov gave the Bolsheviks a dressing-down).

There is little material available to us on the other commanders and military leaders of the Makhnovist insurgent movement. However let us mention some figures more deserving than such heroes of the revolution as the Bolsheviks have turned into mummies; Alexander Kalashnikov — worker's son, NCO during the war, secretary in 1917 of the Gulyai-Polye libertarian communist group, he was behind the 58th Division's defection to the anti-Bolshevik cause at Pomoshnaya in August 1919; Piotr Gavrilenko whose crucial role in the defeat of Wrangel we have already stressed; Milhailov-Pavlenko, son of peasants from central Russia, a Petrograd anarchist who arrived to join the movement at the beginning of 1919 and organized and led its engineer and sapper units; Vassily Danilov, a poor peasant from Gulyai-Polye and farrier, he was in charge of keeping the artillery supplied right from the outset; Alexei Marchenko, another poor Gulyai-Polye peasant, an anarchist since 1907 and a good propagandist; Bondarets, cavalry commander; Garkusha, commander of a special detachment of insurgents; Tykhenko, in charge of provisions; Buryma, in charge of mines; and the successive commanders of the movement's main detachment ... Vdovichenko, Brova, Zabudko, Tomas Kozhin (who also commanded the famous machine-gunner regiment); Chumak, the movement's treasurer; Krat, head of the economic section; Batko Pravda (probably an alias), an odd figure, an anarchist railwayman who lost his legs in an accident — severed by a train — looked after transport and was very active, although Belash has it that he was over-fond of the drink and had little taste for collective discipline; Grigory Vassilevsky, a poor peasant from Gulyai-Polye closely associated with Makhno for whom he acted as deputy on several occasions and served for a time as chief of staff; Klein, a poor German peasant; Dermendzhi, a daring commander of Georgian extraction; Taranovsky, a member of Gulyai-Polye's Jewish community, was the movement's last chief of staff; the brothers Ivan and Alexander Lepechenko, active participants in the fight against the Austro-Germans from spring 1918 on; Alexei Chubenko, engine-driver, adjutant to Makhno and later in charge of the sappers; Sereguin, a workman, in charge of supplies for the army.

❧❧❧

All of these revolutionaries, thrown up by the masses, as best they could to combat all enemies of popular autonomy unfortunately have this in common: they all perished at Bolshevik hands, either in battle or after having been captured by treachery. Others, such as Grigori Makhno, who was the insurgent army's chief of staff for a while, or Isidor "Petya" Lyuty, a painter and decorator, or Boris Veretelnikov, a Gulyai-Polye foundry worker (who later worked at the famous Putilov plant in Petrograd), a very active propagandist and likewise chief of staff for a time, met their deaths in the fight against the Whites. Lev Zinkovsky-Zadov, commander of the special detachment, as well as Jacques Domachenko, a worker and sometime chief of staff, accompanied Makhno into Romania and thence to Poland; after which we lose track of them.[21]

One female figure in particular is deserving of attention, Maroussia Niki-forova. A working woman, born in Alexandrovsk, she was sentenced to death for terrorist acts in 1905, the sentence being commuted to imprisonment for life. Removed to Siberia, she escaped in 1910, spent some time in Japan, the USA and Western Europe and then went back to Alexandrovsk in 1917, there to set up a Black Guard of the Ukraine in conjunction with the Odessa detachments, and detachments in Ekaterinoslav, Elisavetgrad and elsewhere. These Black Guard units harried the Ukraine's bourgeoisie and big landlords. In 1919, Maroussia Nikiforova joined the Makhnovist movement; regarded by Moscow as too much of a wildcat, she was sentenced to a "ban on office-holding" (!) for one year, later cut to six months upon Kamenev's intervention at the time of his visit to Makhno, as we have seen. More sedentary tasks she found dissatisfying and so she took a hand in the fight against the Denikinists a short time later. Some claim that she was hanged by Slaschev in Simferopol in the autumn of 1919, but in the autumn of 1921 we find a certain "Maroussia" heading a detachment fighting against the Reds, though we cannot say for sure that they are the same person. An ardent libertarian, she is sometimes depicted as dressing entirely in black, and galloping on a white horse at the head of 1,500 fanatical horsemen!

We might also reveal the presence of a Frenchman, a certain "Roger," referred to simply as "The Frenchman" by Teper and by Marcel Body.[22] This Roger, it would seem, had guts and was a "hard man" who had had "…some brushes with the French courts" and had deserted from the French expeditionary corps in Russia. He had spent several months with the Makhnovist movement and could not stop singing Makhno's praises, so much so that Voline wanted to introduce him to Lenin so that he could repeat his favorable comments about the Ukrainian insurgents. By the end of spring 1919, Roger was in the Bolshevik camp and was foisted upon Podvoisky, the Ukrainian commissar for war, at Marcel Body's recommendation, as leader of a detachment of Belgian armored cars which had been lying idle since the armistice, and he took part in bitter fighting against the Whites. Subsequently, he dabbled in shadier business, in the Cheka's hire or manipulated by them, before vanishing into the maw of the system, and was never able to go home to France, because, as Marcel Body has it, he "knew too much."

⛤

In a civilian capacity, a number of teachers took part in the Makhnovist movement and in its social and economic organizational ventures. Some of them paid dearly for this; Galina Kuzmenko quotes the case of the brothers Yefim and Daniel Marutsenko, as well as Daniel's wife — all three teachers in Pestshanybrod, the town where Galina was born — who were shot by the Reds in the summer of 1919 on account of their Makhnovist beliefs.[23] Another teacher, Chernoknizhny, from the Pavlograd region, was returned as chairman of the Military Revolutionary Soviet by the Second Gulyai-Polye regional congress. After the collapse of the front in June 1919, he was outlawed and wanted by both Reds and Whites. He appears to have played a part of prime significance in defining the movement's objectives.[24] A medical team was established with the help of doctors and nurses and at the time of the occupation of Ekaterinoslav there was an attempt to train male and female nurses to render first aid.[25] Again we might mention the existence of a "Ballad of the Makhnovists" written by a Russian anarchist by the name of Ivan Kartashev and modeled on the lyrics and music of the celebrated old ballad of "Stenka Razin."[26]

So, there are several elements which help to identify the social and military character of the Makhnovist insurgent movement; the fact that it was representative of the rural proletariat, to which most of its members belonged; its self-organization and direct democracy, strongly reminiscent of Zaporog libertarian traditions, and the determination to take up arms and fight to the death in defense of its social gains. But what was its relationship with anarchism as preached at the time and what might its possible contributions to libertarian communist theory and practice have been? This is what we are now going to look at.

Notes to Chapter 29: The Makhnovists

1. Kubanin, op. cit. p. 161.
2. Ibid. p. 170.
3. Ibid. p. 169.
4. *Dyelo Truda*, New York, December 1949, No. 31 "Memoirs of a Partisan" pp. 17–18.
5. Yefimov, op. cit. pp. 220–221.
6. Gutman, op. cit. p. 62.
7. Ludovic-H. Grondijs, *La Guerre en Russie et en Sibérie*, Paris, 1922, p. 453. This is one of the best books to have been published on the years 1917–1920 in Russia, in terms of its wealth of documentation and the caliber of the observations of the author, a war correspondent for the western press.
8. Galina Kuzmenko, *Souvenirs*, op. cit. p. 16.
9. *The Makhnovschina and its Erstwhile Allies, the Bolsheviks* op. cit. p. 38.
10. Antonov-Ovseenko, op. cit. Tome IV, p. 107.
11. Kubanin op. cit. p. 175.
12. Ibid. p. 183.
13. Ibid. p. 168.
14. Ibid. pp. 167 and 226.
15. Yefimov, op. cit. p. 197.
16. Dybets, op. cit. pp. 129–130.

17. V. T. *Dyelo Truda*, op. cit. p. 26.

18. Sosinsky, *Volya Rossii*, Prague 1927, p. 41.

19. *The First among Equals*, op. cit. p. 58.

20. Teper, op. cit. p. 27, and Kubanin, op. cit. p. 175.

21. We have collated all this data from references in Arshinov and Makhno and from the various books consulted by way of reference.

22. Marcel Body, *Un piano en bouleau de Carélie mes années de Russie 1917–1927*, Paris, 1981, pp. 102–103. Body gives a gripping account of the civil war in the Ukraine in April–August 1919 (he was a participant in Yakir's retreat) pp. 99–131. We must thank him here for the additional information that he has kindly supplied us with in respect of this "Roger" and the ethos of the time.

23. Galina Kuzmenko, op. cit. p. 17.

24. See the appendices for the full text of one of his speeches on the definition of free soviets.

25. Kubanin, op. cit. p. 190.

26. A. Gorelik, "The Ballad of the Makhnovists," in *Volna* op. cit. no. 33, September 1922, p. 21. (The lyrics, none too brilliant in the Russian, would be banal in translation, so we refrain from reproducing them here.)

30. The Makhnovist Movement and Anarchism

During the years 1917–1918 the whole of the eastern Ukraine — fertile ground for the emergence of just such a movement on historical and social grounds — had been troubled by a strong libertarian current. Anatol Gorelik, the then-secretary of the Ekaterinoslav-based anarchist bureau for the Donetz basin, offers us an impressive picture of this overpowering activity. Hundreds of anarchist militants were at work inside various labor organizations and enjoyed much popularity among the masses: in Ekaterinoslav, the secretaries of the trade unions of the metalworkers, bakers, shoemakers, garment-makers, woodworkers, millers and even more were anarchists. They also had a considerable foothold in the city's factory and workshop committees. So much so that in October 1917, when the Bolshevik coup d'état was carried out, an 80,000-strong demonstration was organized, headed by the city's Anarchist Federation and the libertarian labor militants from the main local plant — the Briansk plant where Makhno had also worked in 1907; the crowd marched behind unfurled black flags. This surge of enthusiasm from the workers was unbounded for several weeks, until the Bolsheviks' freedom-stifling activities began to have their noxious effect:

> "At the time of a general regional conference, many delegates from the factory and workshop committees sought out the anarchists to ask them to help the workers to take the whole of production in hand. For three days and three nights ordinary workers sat to consider the issue. The Bolsheviks needed all of their 'influence' (denial of the necessary funding, raw materials, supplies, transportation, etc.) to bring the Ekaterinoslav workers to heel and secure recognition for the authority of statist bureaucrats. The same thing was repeated in other large cities such as Kharkov, Odessa, Kiev, Mariupol, Rostov, Petrograd, Moscow and Irkusk.
>
> [...] The masses were permeated with anarchist propaganda, through discussions, meetings and debates. So great and so imperious were the thirst for reading and the itch to understand what was going on, that in many villages, in the summer-time, at the end of a hard

day's work, the peasants would come together and spend hours at a time listening to books read aloud to them. In the province of Kiev, I happened to see some anarchist newspapers circulate through three districts, so well-thumbed that the print was now barely legible: but the young peasants read them from cover to cover nonetheless. In the Ukrainian countryside, I came upon certain peasants who had read the whole of the anarchist literature in Russian, from Stirner to Tucker, and had a grasp of theory as good as, if not better than professional politicians."[1]

In the year 1918 alone, Gorelik was in ongoing correspondence with no less than 1400 villages in the region! He reckoned that "…had anarchists wanted to recruit for an anarchist 'party' in the Donetz basin, they could have counted on members by the hundreds of thousands."[2] Yet he stresses a huge dark cloud hanging over such promise: the absence of many anarchist militants, especially the ones who had returned from exile abroad and who were looked up to as the "anarchist intelligentsia." For one thing they nearly all settled in the big cities and in the capitals of the "paper revolution" (as Makhno had it) — Petrograd and Moscow — and then again and more especially they actively collaborated with the Bolsheviks even to the extent of joining so-called soviet institutions or indeed the Bolshevik Party itself, rather than helping to create a broadly-based "specifically libertarian front":

"The lying big talk of Lenin and other Bolshevik Social Democrats turned the heads of many anarchists, especially those who were intellectuals: though continuing to be critical of the 'centralizing' Bolsheviks, the latter espoused slogans like 'In Russian the social revolution has begun — The difference between Bolsheviks and anarchists is as thin as a cigarette paper.' — 'On to anti-state socialism, on to anarchism, through the dictatorship of the proletariat!'

[…] The intellectual 'leading lights' were not conversant with the masses' state of mind. Only distant echoes from this movement reached their ears, and then mostly in a distorted form. As for them, instead of urging on the toiling masses, instead of adding to their strength and their aspirations, instead of making the necessary analyses and supplying clearly libertarian solutions; instead of building upon their libertarian consciousness, a consciousness stirring but neither solidly formed nor crystallized, instead of assisting the theoretical instruction of dynamic young militants, instead of helping to expand the libertarian movement's activities, they devoted themselves to either playing down the inevitable threat of a Bolshevik party dictatorship, or thoroughly immersing themselves in syndicalism or even peddling anarcho-Bolshevism. But nowhere did there sound a great summons to the creation of a specifically libertarian front.

Had that been done, there would have been a lot fewer casualties and the results of libertarian endeavors would have been better. In any event, the anarchists would not have found themselves under the heel of Bolsheviks, and worker and peasant organizations of libertarian outlook might have been created. But only the libertarian rank and file, more revolutionary than the anarchist leaders, were at work among the masses.

Thus, instead of making a theoretical and practical contribution to the problems of founding the country economically upon an anti-statist base: instead of being among the masses to carry on with libertarian endeavor and to answer the worried questioning from the worker and peasant masses regarding the chances of a new form of social relations and of the practices that such implied, many anarchists, especially the 'anarchist intelligentsia,' resolutely defended the Bolsheviks' 'tactic,' regarding their presence in power as inevitable."[3]

This paradoxical evolution on the part of anarchist intellectuals and militants of proven mettle was in every particular matched by that of their contemporaries in every other revolutionary organization and party — Mensheviks, Left SRs, Center SRs and Right SRs, Bundists (Jewish Social Democrats) — within the context of a socio-economic and historico-political phenomenon that we have analyzed elsewhere.[4] Gorelik speaks of "abdication and desertion by the bulk of the intellectual anarchists" and contrasts this with the obscure but dogged endeavors of the libertarian rank and file, for all its generally inadequate theoretical equipment. In part, we find this dichotomy again in the Makhnovist movement: The intellectuals placed it under the microscope to verify it was truly of the libertarian persuasion, while the rank and file unstintingly got involved in it, especially during the struggle against Denikin, when the insurgents were fighting on the same side as the Bolsheviks.

In April 1919, Arshinov arrived in Gulyai-Polye along with other anarchists come from Moscow: he promptly breathed life into the Makhnovists' cultural section and took charge of publication of their mouthpiece, *The Road to Freedom*. The following month 36 members of the Ivanovo-Voznessensk anarchist group (Ivanovo-Voznessensk being an important center of the textile industry in Russia lying east of Moscow) joined the movement, with two well-known militants at their head: Chernyakov and Makeev. Dozens of other Ukrainian and Russian militants also showed up, including some members of the Ukrainian Anarchist Confederation, the "Nabat" (Tocsin). Among these were several émigrés returned from England and the United States upon learning of the revolution: Josef Gotman, Aly-Sukhovolsky and Aron Baron (Polevoy). June 1919, when Moscow broke off the alliance with the insurgents, was a turning point. Two of the more active militants, Burbyga and Mikhailov-Pavlenko (the latter a Petrograd anarchist who had come to put his engineering skills at the disposal of the Makhnovists) were seized along with several dozen insurgents and shot by Voroshilov and the Melitopol Cheka, on Trotsky's orders.[5] Jacob Glakson, Casimir Kovalevich, Cremer and other libertarians in the Makhnovist movement or from the Ukraine pledged themselves to avenge the murder of their comrades. First of all they traveled to Kharkov, intending to execute Rakovsky, Piatakov and other Ukrainian Bolshevik leaders, before deciding to strike in Moscow against the very head of the system. They settled in the capital and surreptitiously organized themselves, contacting some Left SRs and Maximalists who were equally keen to avenge party colleagues whom the Leninists had shot. They carried out a number of "expropriations" against State banks in order to fund their schemes. They aimed to dynamite the Cheka headquarters in Moscow, followed by the Kremlin; the explosives were ready when a golden opportunity presented itself: A regional assembly was scheduled to meet on September 25, 1919 at the Moscow committee's headquarters in Leontiev Lane and the main Bolshevik leaders would be present. Lenin himself was due to attend. One of the terrorists, the left SR Cherepanov was quite conversant with the place and on his instructions Piotr Sobolev threw a high-explosive bomb just as the meeting was getting underway but before Lenin had shown up. Twelve Bolsheviks, including the secretary of the Moscow Committee, Zagursky, were killed and another 28 wounded, including Bukharin, Pokrovsky, Stieklov, Yaroslavsky, Shliapnikov, Olminsky, etc. A short time later the attack was claimed by a Pan-Russian Insurgent Committee, in the name of the *Third Social Revolution*; it stipulated that it had avenged the Makhnovists shot on June 17 and that the immediate task before it was "to wipe the regime of the commissarocracy and Chekas off the face of the earth, and establish thereafter a Pan-Russian and free federation of unions of the toilers and oppressed masses."[6] The "clandestine anarchists" published two issues of a newspaper, *Anarchy* and several handbills such as "No time to lose," "The truth about the Makhnovschina" and "Where is the way out?" There they framed a rabid criticism of the Leninist régime:

> "You are in power in Russia, but what has changed? The factories and the land are still not in the toilers' hands but in that of the boss-State. Wage slavery, the fundamental evil of the bourgeois order, is still in existence: as a result, hunger, cold and unemployment are inevitable. On account of the 'need to put up with everything' for the sake of a better future, and to 'defend' that which is already won, a huge bureaucratic machine has been set up, the right to strike abolished, and freedoms of speech, assembly and the press have been stamped out.
>
> [...] It is our belief that you, personally and subjectively, may have the best of intentions: but objectively and by nature you are rep-

resentatives of the class of bureaucrats and functionaries, of a band of unproductive intellectuals."7

Obviously such actions and declarations were of a sort to discomfit those anarchist "personalities" who had been flirting with the Bolshevik régime. And so certain indiscretions followed: Two months later, Kovalevich and Sobolev were surprised by some Chekists; they used revolvers and grenades to defend themselves before blowing themselves up with dynamite. Six other members of their organization, also pinned down in a house, blew themselves up as well. Eight others were taken into custody by the Cheka who extracted confessions before shooting them. The panicked authorities were startled to uncover tentacles of these "clandestine anarchists" even in the ranks of the Red Army and the Communist Party itself.

At the same time, the Nabat threw its whole weight solidly behind the Makhnovist movement, depicting it as the executive arm of the Third Social Revolution. The Nabat was a force to be reckoned with in the Ukraine: it had its headquarters in Ekaterinoslav, in the same building and on the same landing as the Bolsheviks. Unfortunately the fight against the Whites had absorbed nearly all of its membership, a fair number of whom never made it back from the fields of battle. Several militants of some repute nonetheless joined up with the Makhnovists but, in most cases, for no more than a few days. Makhno later referred to this intermittent presence by writing that the "…insurgent peasant masses liked and trusted those whom they saw in their ranks not just to spread the glad tidings there but also brandishing a rifle, as capable as anybody else of fighting and suffering on the cause's behalf."8 Thus he deplored the fact that many urban anarchists had often vanished just as suddenly as they had appeared, and from this he concluded that when all was said and done, the impact of these "tourists" could not have been weaker, and that all the theoretical and organizational work had been left up to the poor peasants, anarchists from Gulyai-Polye and district, among them every one of the commanders and post-holders named in the last chapter. Thus it was they who carried the whole burden of the movement. Dybets corroborates this evaluation by stating that Voline — though chairman of the Military Revolutionary Soviet at this time — had no "…real influence over Makhno who paid more heed to the lowliest commander of the tiniest band of insurgents, not to mention his Staff, at whose beck and call he was at all times and whose opinion alone counted in his eyes."9 Even so, we should specify that, in the context of the time, the military situation was the only one necessitating consultation, for one thing, and then again Makhno was very careful not to meddle in civilian issues which were left to the Military Revolutionary Soviet.

To be sure, neither the "free soviets" nor the insurgent army, with all that this implies — hierarchy (albeit elective), command, discipline, fighting and execution of enemies — were consonant with the anarchist teaching peddled hitherto, although Bakunin would probably not have disowned these methods of struggle. Following publication of Arshinov's book, several anarchist commentators were quick to seize upon those controversial or contradictory points. What line did they take? The first to open the debate was Marc Mratchny, a one-time Nabat member deported from Russia in 1922 who had spent only a day or two among the Makhnovists. In July 1923 in *Workers' Road,* the Berlin-published mouthpiece of the Russian anarcho-syndicalists, he lashed into the Makhnovschina, loosing off a few "arrows" at it. He claimed that Batko Makhno's role and that of his movement had been overrated by certain anarchists to the detriment of the role of the working class which stood accused of reformist and moderate tendencies. This, he argued, was an absurd heretical view: The revolution could not but be a workers' revolution and the handiwork of the workers themselves, especially in respect of the building of a new, rational economy. Mratchny then wanders off into Biblical quotations to demonstrate that manual and intellectual workers should expect salvation of none but themselves, and that there would be "no Caesars, nor Tribunes, nor Batko, however anarchist" (this libertarian enunciation of the obvious goes on) coming along to help out the International, "and no insurgent army, even should it be made up of folk like Bakunin and Kropotkin."[10] In a review of Arshinov's book in the same issue of the paper, Mratchny emerges from such abstract considerations to express the view that Arshinov would have done better to report what he had seen and experienced first hand, rather than writing a complete history of the movement: he singles out the attacks on intellectuals and labels the Makhnovist movement "military anarchism" whose impact upon the Russian workers' movement would ultimately have been damaging. He then asserts that "...the Makhnovschina, so mighty and victorious against the White reaction, weakened, melted away and decomposed whenever it had to deal with the Red reaction, when it sought to direct its blows against the Communist Party's dictatorship." He criticizes the execution of Gluschenko, the repentant Chekist, and of the White emissaries, then wonders in what way the insurgents' "counter-espionage" differed from that of the Cheka or the White counterpart? Likewise he stigmatizes the "dictatorial" role of the "Batko," the "anarchist authorities" of the Makhnovists, and records the privileged status of cavalry in the Makhnovist army. All in all, the Makhnovist movement for all its verbiage strikes him closer to the Left SRs than to the anarchists. With free soviets the "transitional period" was being granted citizen status and, he concludes paradoxically, "One hundred percent anarchist is not achievable immediately, especially not by some dark cavalry raid."[11]

In March 1924, V. Khudoley in a lengthy review of Arshinov's book, takes the opposite line to Mratchny: If the Bolsheviks and Italian fascists emerged victorious from their civil wars, this was only because they had annihilated their adversaries' armed forces: so anarchism will only be able to defeat the State if it in turn annihilates all statist armed forces. No trade union can accomplish this and all threats of general strikes and other bombast will in any case be nothing more than a "cardboard saber." Only an army of partisans will be able to encompass destruction of the State. Khudoley goes on at length about this military aspect in order to acknowledge the Makhnovist movement's important contribution, and he expresses the hope that some participant in the movement will manage to write a military history of the Makhnovschina. On the other hand, he is on Mratchny's side regarding free soviets, reckoning that the Left SRs there had imposed their notion of an "informal State" with diffused powers. Furthermore, he reckons that the supreme organ of the insurgents — their general congress — is only a "pale imitation of the Constituent Assembly." In his view the insurgents' theoretical *Draft Declaration* is in fact a draft of the establishment of a Makhnovist state founded upon decentralization and diffusion of power: these "free soviets." He too speaks of an "anarchist power" and wonders if anarchist society has any need of general congresses to pronounce upon anything at all. It has as its "…sole Constitution only the unfettered initiative of individuals and groups: it is set up only through the creative endeavors of the masses, groups and individuals and not through the legislative action of congresses, even should these be 'non-party.'" Finally, he welcomes only the military side of the movement, this being "quintessentially Bakuninist" and repudiates the civilian side which is stained with Left SR statism, leading on to "anarchist authorities."[12]

E. Z. Dolinin (Moravsky) also published an anarchist critique of Arshinov, taking the notion of free soviets violently to task. Indeed, he detected the birth of an army of parasitical bureaucrats through these agencies, which by his reckoning indubitably represent a sort of State, decidedly more appropriate to the "more honest of the Bolshevik marxists than to anarchists." Arshinov's reproach to the Russian anarchists, that they did not adequately participate in or support the Makhnovist movement, he turns around. "Anarchism cannot rely upon bayonets: it can only be the product of mankind's spiritual cultivation," he goes on, whilst not denying the interest of insurrections or of the Makhnovschina which may be necessary but are not sufficient for the creation of a new "human culture." By contrast, he raves indignantly against executions of unarmed folk — pomieschikis, White envoys, that repentant Chekist, an insurgent charged with having put up an anti-Semitic poster, and even ataman Grigoriev — for, he asserts, it is not with the bullet that people are to be educated or re-educated. In this regard, he considers Makhnovists no better than the Bolsheviks. Let us straightaway offer a corrective to this objection of the "angelic variety": whereas violence is not an end in itself, it seems nonetheless more pardonable in the oppressed than in the oppressor, and in the case of the Makhnovist movement, the distinction between former and latter is instantaneously discernible and so we can know what is afoot, without wondering if perhaps the other cheek should not have been turned to the blows from the Austro-Germans, Ukrainian chauvinists of the Varta, Bolsheviks, Denikinists and other aggressors against the laboring populace. Dolinin's piece closes on a crucial question: how could the Makhnovists have concluded a second alliance with the Bolsheviks, when lots of Russian anarchists had seen through these and distanced themselves from them? He regrets that the insurgents had come to their senses too late and "...had at last begun to sweep all the Bolshevik criminals and bandits from the face of the earth." And he cites this tardiness as a probable cause of the movement's failure.[13]

Naturally these criticisms and objections drew replies from Arshinov and from Makhno himself. Arshinov was to devote two lengthy articles to an item by item rebuttal of the points raised. For a start, he explained how it had been necessary to publish a documented history of the movement: the available information was too partial and too inadequate for a complete picture of the Makhnovschina to be formed. He was amazed that the criticisms, which of course were no more than was to be expected of enemies should be coming from Russian anarcho-syndicalists, Mratchny in particular, an ex-member of the Nabat now advocating a "transitional economy and political stage for the revolution." He brought up Mratchny's contradictory statements about "100 percent instantaneous anarchism," about the "transitional stage" in the shape of free soviets and his use of the term "military anarchism." And he reaffirmed the most important point:

> "The insurgent army was indeed set up by the peasants and workers themselves to defend their territory and rights against the many enemy forces aspiring to enslave them: [The] Makhnovschina has denied all statism and aspired to the building of a free society on the basis of the social independence, solidarity and self-direction of the toilers..."

claiming that most of the Left SRs and Maximalists, swept along by the libertarian current, became anarchists and that their influence upon the movement and party or faction had consequently been nil: only ignorance of the movement could explain such allegations: the argument to the effect that the Makhnovist movement had been lame in its opposition to the Bolsheviks was taking up the Bolsheviks' contentions about the insurgents' being broken up by the Red Army: but this contention did not hold water, because if, unlike the White and foreign reactionary armies, the Communist Party's Red Army had managed unaided to defeat the Makhnovschina, proletarian history would judge it all more harshly. Arshinov also took exception to Mratchy's claim about the "...decomposition of the movement..." "...up until the very last day of its existence, the movement fought with rare heroism for the basic notion of social revolution," and it was essentially for that very reason that the Bolsheviks had treacherously turned on it. How come the Makhnovschina had been defeated by Bolshevism? One might "...come up with many reasons as valid for anarchism's defeat as for those of the other socialist tendencies in the Russian Revolution." He singled out one of these, the "...dichotomy introduced between the military activity and the constructive social practice of the movement, which did not allow all organizational forces to express themselves." Another not inconsiderable factor had been:

"the demagogic fashion in which the Bolsheviks presented themselves in the face of the White counter-revolution, substituting the notion of soviet power for the idea of the social independence and self-direction of the toilers, which afforded them the chance to engage in boundless exploitation of the ideas of the social revolution and command the trust of several strata of toilers."

The Makhnovist insurgent army's counter-espionage/intelligence service had been a purely military agency: its tasks were:

"(a) not to allow agents or enemy armies to infiltrate Makhnovist ranks (b) to be fully conversant with the enemy's deployments and military plans (c) to maintain ongoing liaison between the isolated detachments of the insurgent army: in times of military operations, its members participated in engagements alongside other insurgents."

When towns were occupied, the job of the service had been to expose the hidden enemies on the ground, another purely military function — nothing to do with the police activities of the Cheka or Denikin's political counter-espionage. As for the execution of White envoys, there might be a divergence of opinions about that, but Mratchny would have been better advised at the time to join in the movement rather than hold back, only to ventilate his accusations now. And as for the 'dictatorial' role of 'batko' Makhno, his "role was that of military leader as commander of the army. However he was but one part of the whole and as subject as any other insurgent to decisions of the Military Revolutionary Soviet. Outside of the army, comrade Makhno only enjoyed a well deserved popularity, nothing more." And cavalry had enjoyed no advantages over infantry. Certain infantry regiments such as the 13th, Third Crimean and First Ekaterinoslav regiments were regarded as among the bravest and most popular insurgent army units. He makes an interesting point about the use of the word "political" to refer to the self-direction of the toilers, as mentioned in the fourth point (never activated) of the compact agreed with the Red Army in October 1920. Arshinov explains that the insurgents had used this adjective quite deliberately in that the Bolsheviks accorded a secondary and junior significance to the expression "social self-direction" in comparison with the political functions of the state. Also, the only discussion possible on the meaning of "transitional stage" consisted of asking whether a full-blooded anarchist society was to be expected overnight, or merely its groundwork and if one was not just simply mixing it up with the "outset of the construction of that society." And Arshinov closed his first reply by ascribing Mratchny's different views to the influence of Bolshevik hearsay.[14]

꧁꧂

In a further reply to critics, he readily acknowledges that the alliance reached between the Makhnovists and Bolsheviks was a compromise, a purely military compromise to be sure but a compromise for all that. He excuses point three of the agreement, relating to election of delegates to the Fifth Congress of soviets of the Ukraine, as a precaution on the insurgents' part against a surprise attack from the Bolsheviks. In any case, the military alliance agreed could not be compared, as E.Z. Dolinin had compared it, to the theoretical surrender and collaboration of some anarchists with the Leninists. Apropos of executions, Arshinov readily conceded the harshness and cruelty of such acts: however, account had to be taken of the fact that they had occurred in the context of military confrontations and that the toiler population had itself been subject to bestial treatment at the hands of its enemies — pomieschikis, police, Chekists — and that it was also often the populace itself who singled them out and reported their crimes. He also deplored the execution of the author of an anti-Semitic poster and of the Bolsheviks accused of attempting the life of Makhno (Polonsky and others) but pointed out that the military context and resultant tensions accounted for these moves which were but incidents (regrettable ones, certainly) rather than anything systematic. Nor does he deny the existence of orders, commands, and discipline in the insurgent army — things introduced at the instigation of the mass of insurgents themselves — measures which might be distasteful, but then again circumstances and the struggle against regular, well-organized, disciplined armies necessitated certain things. Then Arshinov turns to Khudoley's remarks. He is delighted to find Khudoley recognizing the need for a partisan army to defeat the armed apparatus of the State. Then he recalls that the movement had circulated and in fact implemented the idea of anti-authoritarian toilers' communes as well as the notion of free soviets, albeit not quite as ...

> "...legislative institutions, but as a sort of platform gathering together the toilers on the basis of their vital needs. Their assigned goal was to carry out the wishes already expressed and formulated by the toiling masses. Let us be clear on this: the peasants and workers of any village or township have a whole series of issues and common tasks to be resolved: provisions, self-defense, liaison between countryside and town, and many others. It behooves them to come to some agreement among themselves on all these matters and then to take decisions as a result: if these are to be put into effect, they need strength. In the minds of the Makhnovists, that strength we embodied in the free soviet of the toilers."

Arshinov points out that such agencies already existed inside the anarchist movement in the form of soviets, federations, secretariats or executive committees. So he is astonished that Khudoley should regard as anti-anarchist this means of collectively resolving practical tasks and issues, and that he should also reject congresses as supreme bodies. Arshinov thinks that Khudoley and Dolinin must have considered these free soviets as agencies empowered, not to execute but to delegate and decide, with delegates imposing their wishes upon the rank and file and not the other way around. So where are they to stand come the social revolution and what will then be their role? All these arguments are in fact superficial and infantile. The Makhnovist movement, Arshinov concludes, was open to all anarchists and it was up to them to air their disagreement with this or that feature, provided they clearly set out their reasoning and came up with another solution. Anarchism is not some "…bookish sect that might deign to take an interest from its Olympian heights in the social struggle of the toilers: quite the contrary, that struggle is its natural element."15

Pertinent or not, these criticisms, objections and reservations deserve to be known so that the free spirit of debate that prevailed among Russian libertarians may be demonstrated. On the other hand, another Nabat member, Lewandovsky who emigrated to the west, voiced graver accusations of a slanderous sort: according to him "among the Makhnovists, as among the Bolsheviks, a Cheka existed; there were shootings, mobilization, there was Makhno's dictatorship and his staff's and freedom existed only if one did not engage in propaganda against them." In particular he was critical of the execution of the Bolshevik Polonsky and reckoned that, sooner or later, Makhno and the anarchists would have found themselves at daggers drawn.16 Ugo Fedeli interviewed Makhno about Lewandovsky's accusations:

> "'To be sure,' Nestor Makhno conceded, 'the Makhnovist insurgent movement had many enemies even among the anarchists, especially now that it no longer exists. What do you expect? When we were strong and when the movement was in the ascendant on account of its size and importance, but chiefly because it had resources, well of course there was no shortage of friends or of those who, whilst not entirely favorable, sent out signals of friendship to us.'"

Concerning Lewandovsky, Makhno specifies that he had spent two days with the insurgents in October 1920, putting to them a grandiose scheme for an anarchist university in Kharkov, for which he sought the "modest" donation of 10 million rubles. At the time, Makhno, being wounded in the leg and able to get around only on crutches, was unable to leave Gulyai-Polye: so he was able to attend a meeting of the town soviet, called especially to examine this request for a subsidy, and he spoke right after Lewandovsky:

> "We occupy a region nearly 200 kilometers deep by 300 kilometers broad. We have with us millions of peasants but scarcely any schools. We are short of people willing or able to help these masses to better themselves educationally, yet you arrive here from the towns where education is already readily available. You, who could be helping us greatly in this task, come to see us only in order to ask for money towards the establishment of a new university in Kharkov. But why

there? Because it is a focal point, you will say to me. Well, no, we have no wish to go on repeating the centralist mistake made by comrades whose chief preoccupation has been to set up headquarters for their organizations in Moscow. They're all there: the anarchist federation, *Golos Truda*, etc. Yes, let your university be set up, but here among peasants in dire need of education."[17]

This line of argument struck a real chill into Lewandovsky's enthusiasm and he promptly left, without having been granted the money he sought. It was this that undoubtedly led him to proclaim to any who would listen that "…the Makhnovist movement had done a lot of harm to the anarchist movement." Makhno adds that this was not the only case: others showed up looking for "subsidies" and they included Abraham Gordin who had, however, gone over to the Bolsheviks: every time that their requests were denied, these petitioners "…became fresh enemies of the movement." In this way we get a better grasp of the roots of the resentment shown by Lewandovsky and of certain other critics whose attitude was undoubtedly, it is worth saying, less than disinterested.

≈≈≈

Although this debate may have been of great interest in establishing the nature and content of the Makhnovschina, one thing should be made clear. At no time had Makhno and his closest colleagues described the movement they led as exclusively anarchist, and that despite their being staunch libertarian communists long since put to the test. This was probably the basic reason why they shrank from calling the insurgent army "anarchist," rather than Makhnovist. Indeed, as far as they were concerned, it was a motley mass movement inside which all supporters of social revolution could co-exist. The Left SR presence — Veretelnikov, Popov (although these later became anarchists) — the Bolshevik element (one of whom, Novitsky, was even elected on to the Military Revolutionary Soviet in October 1919) and the non-party revolutionaries (Kozhin, Ozerov) testify to this plurality of tendencies. The movement's theoretical *Draft Declaration*, drawn up by Makhno and his libertarian communist comrades, was founded on the notion of free soviets as on the autonomous collective and military voice of the toilers as a whole, and not only a single class, or any single party with an appetite for hegemony, which was how the Leninists for instance thought of it. In their view the system of free soviets was only a transitional stage essential for the weaving of the social and economic ties leading on to a federation of libertarian communes, with the State thus finding itself consigned to the museum of irksome antiquities.

Nonetheless, in a later article, Makhno specifies that the *Draft*, as the name indicates, was to have been debated and possibly adopted by a general congress of the insurgents but the military situation had prevented this. He asserts that it was not a question of the "…Constitution of a Makhnovist State. It was the hurried handiwork of the Gulyai-Polye libertarian communist group."[18] As the insurgents were at loggerheads over the phrasing of certain points, they capitalized upon Voline's presence in late August 1919 to ask him to look over the draft of the text. He worked on it for a month and made do with polishing the literary style, from which Makhno concluded that the points at issue had apparently not scandalized Voline and that as a result, the *Draft* was not at odds with anarchism, especially not the Bakuninist conception of the transitional period, which would not be a "diffusion of power" but rather the elimination of the class State and economic inequalities.

A little later, Voline corroborated Mahno's version by specifying that he took Liaschenko's place as chairman of the Military Revolutionary Soviet for a two month period only at Makhno's suggestion, since he had not inserted anything of his own into the *Draft Declaration* in accordance with the express wishes of the insurgents but had made do with rephrasing certain formulations and polishing the literary style. He had not at all tried to "anarchize" the *Draft*, which he regarded as an accurate expression of the thinking of the Makhnovist insurgent movement.[19]

Bolshevik commentators for their part saw nothing very new in this text as compared with the precepts of Bakunin or Kropotkin.[20] Yefimov gives this interesting description of the Makhnovist practice of free soviets:

> "These organs of power were very primitive. There was no central organ of government: there was only the Military Revolutionary Soviet which was at once a sort of parliament and central military agency dealing with both military and civil matters. This agency had a wide range of functions, but in performing these, it presented itself only as a steering body and had no rights of its own, all power being vested in the local organs. Everything boiled down to each village and each district directing itself with complete independence. Nevertheless, the structure of this illusory power was along soviet lines: there were executive committees, soviets of deputies, where elected individuals would come together and grapple with various, though not fundamental issues." [21]

A curious admission: in their actions the insurgents implemented their anti-authoritarian preferences, realizing their age-old aspirations. Arshinov spells out the three ideas underlying this approach: "(a) the right of the toilers to complete freedom of initiative (b) the right to their economic and social self-direction and (c) the anti-statist principle in social construction." For him, the Makhnovschina showed itself to be "…an anarchist mass movement of toilers, not fully formed nor quite crystallized, but striving towards the anarchist ideal and treading a libertarian path." [22] Arshinov draws a distinction between this coherent behavior and the theoretical abdication and passivity of many intellectual anarchists, whose absence was sorely felt in the movement. Here he agrees with Anatol Gorelik's criticism and adds that, in his opinion, there are two essential reasons underlying this default: a measure of theoretical confusion, and the chronic disorganization of anarchist militants. Makhno also accepted this analysis, for it goes without saying that Anarchy was not, to him, some cherished utopia of the intellectuals who, while waiting the advent of the age of happiness, snugly occupy their cozy little niches in the existing system of alienation, but rather a practical and immediate social ideal. In exile this attitude led the two friends to devise a *Draft Organization Platform* for the anarchist movement, wherein they were to pick up and expand upon the 1919 *Draft Declaration* and then draw the lessons of the Makhnovschina experience, of the Russian revolution and of the anarchist movement's failure during that period.

✎✎✎

Be that as it may, by virtue of its peculiarities, the Makhnovist movement occupied a separate place in both the doctrine and practice of libertarian communism historically, making its own original and essential contribution. It only remains for us to look into the critical presentation of the notion of free soviets as an "anarchist" power, some sort of "anti-authoritarian authority," which is to say one restricted to a purely executive and non-decision-making role, as Yefimov diagrammatically represents it. In which case the term no longer carries the negative import of arbitrary authority or State power, the emanation of some clique or class: rather it comes to stand for the will and free choice of the community of toilers as a whole, in the ability of each to make decisions and act in harmony with all the others. Taken in that sense, the Makhnovists' Military Revolutionary Soviet was indeed an organ of power. In principle executive power but, given the circumstances, very often decision-making power as well: likewise, the aspiration of this whole revolutionary era could be encapsulated by the slogan of "…All *power* to the free soviets!" Let us note that there is here a semantic taboo for many anarchists, which has sometimes condemned them to impotence and a shirking of responsibilities, if not in fact many a time to tag along behind actual State power. By way of corroboration for our argument, let us cite the extraordinary situation that faced the Nabat anarchists meeting in Kharkov in October 1920: a delegation from several red Army units from Moscow and elsewhere sought them out to propose to them that they "take power": the delegation itself undertook to arrest Lenin and the Communist Party central committee! Voline and his colleagues blandly explained to them that anarchists did not seek power, and that the "masses" had to act for themselves and they amiably refused the offer. Anatol Gorelik also tells of this incident and adds his personal comment that had the anarchists so desired, they could have taken power in the Ukraine, so high was their revolutionary standing in the eyes of the Red soldiers and toilers.[23] Plenty of scope there for meditations upon the different interpretations of the word "power"!

Notes to Chapter 30: The Makhnovist Movement and Anarchism

1 A. Gorelik, in A. Skirda *Les Anarchistes dans la révolution russe*, Paris, 1973, p. 66 and p. 73.

2. Ibid. p. 63

3. Ibid. pp. 61–62 and p. 66.

4. J.W. Machajski, *Le Socialisme des intellectuels*, translated and with introduction by A. Skirda.

5. Gorelik was an eye-witness to the execution of 69 Makhnovist volunteers for joining up with the Red Army in Melitopol.

6. Makintsian, *The Red Book of the Cheka* (in Russian), Moscow, 1920.

7. Idem. On this affair, see Kubanin, op cit. pp. 214–222.

8. *The Makhnovschina and its Erstwhile Allies, the Bolsheviks* op. cit. p. 47.

9. Kubanin op. cit. p. 207.

10. *Rabotchy put's.* Berlin, No. 5, July 1923, pp. 1–3.

11. Ibid. pp. 15–16.

12 *Volna*, March 1924, No 51, pp. 15–20.

13. *Amerikanskiye Izvestia* No. 128, May 28, 1924, pp. 6–7, an article reprinted in E. Z. Dolinin *In the Storm of Revolution* (in Russian), Detroit, 1954, pp. 362–368.

14. P. Arshinov "Anarchism and the Makhnovschina," in *Anarkhitchesky Vestnik,* Berlin, 1923, No. 2 pp. 27–37.

15. P. Arshinov "Anarchism and the Makhnovschina," II, *Volna* No. 56, August 1924, pp. 28–34.

16. A. Lewandovsky "Outline of the anarchist movement in Russia during the revolution" in *La Revue Anarchiste* No. 29, July–August 1924, pp. 13–14.

17. Ugo Fedeli "Conversing with Nestor Makhno," in *Volontá*, II, No. 2, August 1947, pp. 44–49.

18. N. Makhno "Open Letter to Maximov," *Dyelo Truda* No. 15, August 1926, pp. 10–12.

19. Voline, *Dyelo Truda* No. 16, September 1926, pp. 15–16.

20. Kubanin op. cit. pp. 96–97, and Teper op. cit. p. 61.

21. Yefinov op. cit. p. 196.

22. Arshinov op. cit. pp. 230–231.

23. Gorelik, op. cit. p. 76, and Voline's comments as reported by Nikola Tchorbadjieff.

31. Apropos the Charges of Banditry and Anti-Semitism

The Makhnovschina, as a social movement so subversive of the established order and aspiring, in the name of Anarchy, to do away with all state power and ensure that the toilers ran their own lives, could hardly be opposed by its enemies in precisely those terms. It had at all costs to be brought somehow into disrepute and shown in the most ignominious light. Hence the charges repeatedly mooted against it, of banditry, looting and thuggery, not forgetting the allegation of anti-Semitism. Since the credibility of the charges is largely dependent on the standing of the accusers, let us have a look at whom we are dealing with here.

That the Austro-Germans should have regarded the insurgents as so many "bandits," since they were "irregulars" is only to be expected of regular troops. On the other hand, it was hard for them to bandy about adjectives such as "thieves" or "looters," when their own exploits in that regard were nothing to be proud of. Nor were the Whites of such immaculate whiteness in this respect, such was the extent (and more) to which their "warlords" had ransacked the occupied territories. As for the Reds, they were equally unqualified to pronounce such judgments, having milked the whole of the Ukraine dry by formally instituting plunder by the State. Although the true "bandits" do not appear to have been those so labeled — the facts turn the charges back against the accusers — let us nonetheless look into the Makhnovists' conduct vis à vis the populace. In order to do this, let us look to the soviet sources of the day which can scarcely be suspected of covering up: according to Yefimov, the "Makhnovists' basic precept — take nothing from the peasants was strictly adhered to. Only on the initiative of the detachment commander could it be breached."[1] Another commentator, Lebeds, took the line that: "… Makhno and the Military Revolutionary Soviet strove to preserve the army's 'popular insurgent saintliness'; insurgents were shot for looting; and it was forbidden to 'seize goods, seize flour from mills or change horses in the absence of the peasants; they exchanged several of their weary horses for one fresh mount; in his directives, Makhno issued reminders that insurgents had to be friendly and considerate towards the local population."[2] Lebeds records that in return, locals would re-supply the insurgents, tend their wounded and keep them briefed on Red

Army movements. Kubanin is even more categorical: after a scrupulous examination of the Makhnovist archives, he asserts that the command took all necessary measures to avert acts of looting or banditry, especially in 1918 and 1919 (which is to say during the time when they were not fighting the Red Army). Search and seizure warrants were "… issued only by the Military Revolutionary Soviet, the staff and the movement's supply corps"; otherwise, the detachment commander was answerable for the conduct of its members. Kubanin was forced to note that during the lengthy occupation of Ekaterinoslav at the end of 1919 there was none of the "…mass looting like under the Whites and Makhno's execution on the spot of some marauders made a great impression upon the city's population."[3] In so doing, Kubanin was formally rebutting the curious claim of his party colleague, Christian Rakovsky, to the effect that "…it was the rule among the Makhnovist army to loot for two days per month.(!) But of course the Makhnovists turned those two days into an entire month"[4] — a rebuttal very very rare, even for those days. The allegation is less queer if one knows that, on the basis of reports from Chekists and political commissars, Rakovsky had written an awful pamphlet on the situation in the Ukrainian countryside, seated all the while in his plush office as the puppet president of the Soviet Ukraine. Kubanin goes on to say that goods seized by the Makhnovist Army were distributed by the local inhabitants and the movement's supply corps. And what did these "goods" consist of? The property of the big landlords, the urban bourgeoisie, and the "depots" of the Whites and Reds, derived from systematic plundering of the laboring population.

It is, consequently, noticeable that none of the charges of banditry aired by this one or that, stands up to a serious examination of the facts. In spite of all that, how are they to be explained? Perhaps in terms of the age-old fear that the rural bourgeoisie and squire-archy felt of the dark, nameless peasant mass, these "yokels" whose wrathful vengeance they rightly feared. On the other side of the coin, one might speak of the peasant "milleniarism," of the hatred for towns as unhealthy places where the holders of power, the central administrations, the exploiters and their lackeys were ensconced. A picture that has to be refined somewhat, in that the Ukrainian countryside was strewn with large towns of 10,000–20,000 inhabitants — Gulyai-Polye for one — and hardly fitted in with Marxists' traditional notions of the peasantry; here peasants did not live a life turned in upon itself; on the contrary, they were bound by close ties, through countless yearly fairs and the incessant trade in various produce. Something else needs explaining, too; hanging the label "bandits" on individuals fighting for their autonomy — an attitude quintessentially mystifying to anyone fond of power over his neighbor — ensures that they can be unceremoniously written off; summary execution of prisoners and suspects, breach of compacts agreed to, reneging upon one's word of honor … the statist schemers shrank from nothing. So it was primarily a political argument, essential in order to dismiss one's adversary and deny him right of reply.

※

The charge of anti-Semitism is part and parcel of the same mentality. But here too let us look to the facts. The Makhnovist movement embraced without distinction representatives of the various ethnic communities of the region under its influence, to wit: a vast majority of Ukrainian peasants — nearly 90 percent of the movement, Arshinov claims — the six-to-eight percent of peasants of Russian origin, followed by members of the dozen Jewish and Greek farming communities of the region and in lesser numbers, Georgians, Armenians, Bulgars, Serbs, Montenegrins and Germans. This circumstance alone would be enough to account for the absence of chauvinist nationalistic feelings from the movement. Later, during the fight against the Red Army, some deserters, like many Don Cossacks, went over to the insurgents. Kubanin mentions the figure of 17 Jewish farming colonies in the Alexandrovsk and Mariupol districts — the heartlands of the Makhnovschina — and writes that there the Jewish peasant was a "brother" as far as peasants of other extractions were concerned, having had the same relationship as these with the pomieschik.[5]

We should specify that national identity is mentioned here only to illustrate our point, for we have yet to discover how the insurgents described themselves. For instance, Nestor Makhno did not describe himself as a Ukrainian but merely as an anarchist; his beliefs were dismissive of all national differences. He did not even speak Ukrainian — only in exile did he learn it — and expressed himself in Russian, that being the most widespread tongue in the tsarist empire. Then again, ever since his days as a teenage militant, he had had fellow-believers and fellow-activists of Jewish origin (in fact in 1905 Jews accounted for the overwhelming majority of Russian and Ukrainian anarchists) and he had never had any problems with them. When he returned to Moscow at the end of June 1918, he had been saved from certain death by his friend Moshe Kogan, himself a native of Gulyai-Polye and future president of the local soviet in 1919. Later Makhno had been ruthless with any display of anti-Semitism in the movement's sphere of influence. When bully boy tactics were employed in 1919 against some Ukrainian and Jewish peasants by persons professing to be his followers, he had issued an appeal to all peasants, raising violent objections to such conduct and even threatening suicide if his name was again to be used to cover such ignominious acts. And the population had been mightily impressed by this declaration.[6] Following a provocation by Denikinist agents, when several members of a Jewish settlement had been massacred by insurgents, Makhno had insisted upon the shooting of the culprits, rather than their being sent up to the front line as a joint Bolshevik-Makhnovist commission of inquiry had determined. He then had rifles and ammunition issued to the region's Jewish farming settlements, this at a time when there was a dire shortage of weapons among the front-line fighters, which brought him criticism from Ukrainian insurgents and peasants. In reply he had taken it upon himself to set up, with Jewish fighters exclusively, an artillery battery and support squad made up of veterans of the Russo-German war under the command of Abraham Schneider. This unit heroically defended the approaches to Gulyai-Polye against Shkuro's Cossacks and was wiped out only after it had cut down a number of the assailants.

Moreover, there were 200 Jewish infantry in one of the Gulyai-Polye regiments and a great number of others scattered through the various Makhnovist units. Several commanders, including Taranovsky, the movement's last chief of staff, and Lev Zinkovsky, commander of Makhno's personal escort at the time of his passage into Romania, were Jews. Three out of the five members of the movement's cultural section — Helen Keller, Yasha Sukhovolsky and Josef Gotman, known also as "The Émigré" (the last two were later murdered by the Cheka) — were of similar origins. Isaak Teper, editor of *The Makhnovist Voice* in Kharkov in October 1920, and other leading Nabat members, such as Mratchny, Gorelik, Aron Baron and Voline, were also of Jewish origin. There is thus no avoiding a simple commonsense realization; had the Makhnovist movement or Makhno had any anti-Semitic tendencies, not one of these insurgents and anarchists of Jewish origin would have tolerated or countenanced them and would instantly have dissociated themselves from the movement. Let us recall also the main reason why ataman Grigoriev was executed: for having ordered pogroms. Also these pogroms occurred in those Ukrainian provinces of high Jewish population, which is to say in the western parts; there were none in the Tavrida or in Ekaterinoslav province. In his book, Voline quotes the conclusions of Cherikover, a specialist investigator of persecutions and pogroms against the Jews in the Ukraine:

> "Makhno's attitude is not to be compared to that of the other armies which operated in Russia during the happenings of 1917–1921. On two points I can offer you absolutely formal assurances:
>
> 1. It cannot be gainsaid, that of all these armies, Red Army included, it was Makhno's army which behaved best towards the civilian population generally and the Jewish population in particular. I have plenty of irrefutable testimony to that. Compared with the rest, the proportion of justified complaints against the Makhnovist army is insignificant.
>
> 2. Let us not speak of pogroms supposedly organized or encouraged by Makhno himself. That is calumny or error. Nothing of the sort occurred." [7]

Cherikover specifies that on every occasion when some pogrom or some outrage was imputed to Makhnovists, he was able to verify that on that date none of their detachments could have been in the place concerned. A Jewish committee set up in Berlin in the 1920s with the participation of both Left and Right Social Revolutionaries, and members of the Bund (the Jewish social democratic labor party), Mensheviks (Aronson) and anarchists came to similar conclusions regarding such accusations leveled against the Makhnovists; on the other hand it did manage to authenticate pogroms carried out by Red Army and White army units.[8] Even more interesting: these same charges of anti-Semitism were rebutted by Soviet authors during the 1920s, even though they were on the look-out for the slightest grounds on which to discredit the movement. Lebeds states that the:

> "Makhnovist command and Military Revolutionary Soviet had declared war on anti-Semitism, unlike other atamans who sometimes played on political positions by openly using the watchword of 'Get the communists and Jews!' Makhno and his staff, in their proclamations, stressed the unacceptable nature of anti-Semitism and combated signs of it through extreme repressive measures." [9]

And Teper writes that "Makhno was as far removed from nationalism as from the anti-Semitism ascribed to him by many"; in his view, if there was anti-Semitism, it was when the Makhnovist army amalgamated with some units under Petliurist influence or simply common criminals seizing upon any excuse to indulge in looting.[10] Antonov-Ovseenko goes one better: "There was no basis for accusing Makhno of personally supporting anti-Semitic tendencies. Quite the contrary, he did all in his power to combat pogroms."[11] To back up what he says, he reproduces a lengthy appeal drafted by Makhno and Veretelnikov denouncing all acts of banditry and anti-Semitism perpetrated in the insurgents' name and proposing to punish the perpetrators as promptly and severely as possible. Kubanin is equally clear: "In 1918 and 1919, the behavior of the Makhnovist army towards the Jews displayed not the slightest hint of anti-Semitism and this is as true of the mass as of the leadership."[12] He stresses the presence of many Jews among the Makhnovist command during those years and reaffirms that "Makhno was not personally anti-Semitic"; according to him, it was only when the Makhnovists were fighting the Red Army after 1920 that they joined up with some Petliurist detachments and adopted more nationalistic attitudes denouncing "Muscovite aggressors" and calling for "the liberation of the Ukraine from the Russian yoke," but without quite turning anti-Semitic. The most recent of the monographs published on the Makhnovschina inside the USSR, Seymanov's monograph, is even more definite; it registers no inkling of Ukrainian chauvinism in the movement and argues that the "...so very widespread belief about the Makhnovschina's anti-Semitic character does not square with the facts." Semanov takes up the arguments of his predecessors, noting the presence of lots of Jews among the movement's leadership and the "complete absence of anti-Semitic statements."[13]

Makhno himself returned to these lingering misrepresentations several times in articles, written while the movement was still extant, for *The Road to Freedom*, and also while an émigré in Paris.[14] Among his fellow exiles were many anarchists of Jewish origin: David Poliakov, Ida Mett, Waletsky, Ranko, and Grisha Bartanovsky to whom he entrusted his archives before dying. All of the evidence that we have been able to amass from people who knew him in Paris bear witness to his having been a stranger to anti-Jewish prejudices which strikes us as setting the seal upon the matter.

So why this persistent rumor of Makhnovist anti-Semitism when the merest inquiry bursts that particular bubble? Several explanations are possible. On the one hand, the conduct of the Jewish armed company of Gulyai-Polye when the Austro-Germans invaded: their treachery must have left an anger among the region's population, in spite of the efforts of Makhno and his anarchist colleagues. Then again among the Ukrainian bourgeoisie degraded by the insurgents, there was also a large number of Jews, as well as among the Chekists and Bolshevik officials executed in 1920 and 1921 and so these could have been put down as casualties of popular vendetta against their co-religionists as a whole. Finally, many maverick gallows birds were ravaging the country, and it suited them to cover up their misdeeds by invoking the Makhnovist movement which enjoyed the best brand-image among the Ukrainian populace. Be that as it may, as far as their political adversaries were concerned, the argument was a weighty one enabling them to cheaply dismiss the professed aims of the movement, only to acknowledge later on, once their defeat had been finalized — as indeed the Bolsheviks did — that such charges had had no substance to them.

Notes to Chapter 31: Apropos the Charges of Banditry and Anti-Semitism

1. Yefimov op. cit. p. 196.
2. Lebeds op. cit. p. 30.
3. Kubanin op. cit. p. 185–187.
4. Rakovsky *The Struggle for Liberation of the Countryside* (in Russian), Kharkov 1921, p. 31.
5. Kubanin op. cit. p. 29.
6. N. Makhno "Memoirs," in *Anarkhitchesky Vestnik* op. cit. No. 5-6, p. 19.
7. Voline op. city. p. 675.
8. G. Maximov, "Nestor Makhno and pogroms," in *Dyelo Truda* No. 51, May–September 1956, p. 26.
9. Lebeds op. cit. p. 43.
10. Teper op. cit. pp. 50–51.
11. Antonov Ovseenko op. cit. Tome IV, p. 105.
12. Kubanin op. cit. pp. 163–165.
13. Seymanov op. cit. pp. 39–40.
14. "The Jewish question" in *Anarkhichesky vestnik* op. cit. No. 5-6, pp. 17–25; "The Makhnovschina and Anti-Semitism," in *Dyelo Truda* No. 30-31, pp. 15–18; and "To the Jews of all lands," in *Dyelo Truda* No. 23-24, pp. 8–10.

32. Historiography and Mythomania

Throughout this book we have relied upon primary sources and references, to wit, the accounts and reports of protagonists in and eyewitnesses to the events described and we have also relied upon archive materials borrowed from official soviet publications. In regard to the latter, we have been able, with only a few exceptions relating to minor details, to consult virtually every text in print. Obviously, and for all the concrete particulars that have emerged from them, we must have reservations about their use in that we cannot have direct access to the archives from which they are extracted. Among the documentation which might have rendered certain portions of our study more exhaustive, we might cite the complete collections of the three Makhnovist press organs which we have only glimpsed through a few random issues accessible here in the west. The "memoirs," or "confessions" of Viktor Belash and Alexei Chubenko, Makhnovist leaders captured by the Red Army and induced to "confess," might also have proven useful to us, for only the odd snippet quoted by Kubanin has been accessible. Likewise, Arshinov drafted his *History of the Makhnovist Movement* surreptitiously in Russia and the first four more or less complete drafts of it were lost following Cheka raids, along with the movement's fundamental documentation: personal notes from Makhno, biographical notes on the most active insurgents, a complete collection of *The Road to Freedom* (comprising 43 issues, so far as we can tell), and sundry other precious papers. In all logic, all these items should be stored in the Cheka or Red Army archives; Lebeds for instance refers to issues of *The Road to Freedom* in various formats and printed on different colored newsprint. Also the archives of the Romanian and Polish political police may hold the papers seized from Makhno; one might say the same of the little case full of papers left in the possession of Grisha Bartanovsky and seized by the Gestapo in Paris during the second world war. Perhaps someday all these materials may make it possible to complete the picture of the Makhnovist movement's deeds and feats, provided they have not been lost forever in the convolutions of police bureaucracies or fallen victim to the passage of time (and the deterioration of paper) and the destruction inherent in warfare.

We think it opportune to rehearse, briefly, the chronology of the available printed sources. "Credit where credit is due!" So we shall begin with the view of the winners, the Leninists, for whom History is their private preserve enabling them to control the present through the past and to justify all the "human sacrifices" carried out in order to build their hegemonic power. The earliest studies, at once political and military, were addressed to the party and army cadres at a time when the anti-Makhnovist campaign was still raging; the necessity of this "mini-civil war" had to be explained and the insurgents' goals and fighting methods reported. Thus it was hardly surprising that they should have been published in reviews intended for internal use, reviews of small circulation and that, at first sight, they should display a startling objectivity, except of course where the defeats and losses sustained by the Red Army are concerned, these being issues on which the greatest discretion was observed. This "objectivity" can be explained; it was necessary so that the military and political cadres might draw useful lessons from it. Oddly enough, all later soviet monographs refrain from citing them, doubtless regarding them as unduly favorable to the Makhnovists. The most remarkable of these pieces is undeniably Yefimov's — from which we have borrowed time and again — for it has the advantage of offering an overall analysis of the fight against Makhno during 1920. The other articles focus on specific clashes and these take care not to go into too much detail on the insurgents' performance.[1]

The chief military leader to whom it fell to wage the campaign against the Makhnovists, Eideman, took it upon himself to expand politically upon the reprehensible aspects of the Ukrainian "banditry" in several pamphlets and articles.[2] Another eminent Red Army strategist, the one-time tsarist colonel Kakurin, drew the lesson from this fight against "banditry" by stigmatizing it as a "specific social disease" and calling for the beefing up of the police apparatus in order to stifle it.[3]

❦

The first general official study of the Makhnovschina was written in September 1921 and appeared above the signature of D. Lebeds ... this was *Appraisals and Lessons of Three Years of Anarcho-Makhnovschina.* The author sets out his intention of making a study of this movement's "petit bourgeois and kulak banditry," though he sets out "idiosyncrasies of a revolutionary and popular nature," setting it apart from other instances of "banditry": Petliurist, or independent socialist, or populist or anarchist, or bourgeois and seigneurial counter-revolutionary, not forgetting the Cossack Volnitsa. This fruit salad acquires a curious flavor when Lebeds lumps together the Ukrainian "bedniaki" (poor peasants) and the Russian "seredniakis" (medium peasants)! And this only to deduce that the "seredniakis," Makhno's supporters, were the equivalent of the Russian kulaks and espoused the anarchist ideology as the one best suited to their fight against the soviet authorities! Makhno, "an enthusiastic practitioner of anarchist doctrine," thereby becomes "the tool of the kulaks." The contortions of this argument[4] then lead the author to say that the first alliance with Makhno simply could not have held up because his principles of "...freedom, electivity of command and his partisan warfare methods" were having an erosive effect upon the Red Army by detaching "...the least conscious groups, especially the sailors who went over to him."[5] In passing, Voline is awarded the title of Makhno's "spiritual master"; then Lebeds states that the insurgents' Fourth Congress, banned by Trotsky, had meant to sever the Makhnovist region from the remainder of the Ukraine by instituting the "...libertarian republic of Makhnovia." Further on, he corrects his aim just a touch: the Makhnovist army was not "made up solely of kulaks; authentically poor peasants also belonged to it," and the insurgents were frequently joined by entire groups of "kombeds" — the poor peasantry committees set up by the Leninists. [6] Let us pick out this interesting definition of the insurgents' ideals: "A refounding of society in such a way that everyone has an equal opportunity to enjoy life and its benefits; organization of social relationships in such a way that no group is dependent upon any other, no individual upon any other, so that every trace of power is banished from human relationships." [7] Whereas he formally rebuts the charges of an alliance between the Makhnovists and the Whites, Lebeds reckons that as a catchphrase libertarian commune failed to take account of "...the workers' and peasants' lack of preparedness for that phase of society"; he ties in the "dictatorship of the workers" with the expansion of productive forces and stresses the need for a central worker-peasant State apparatus that is well-organized if the economy is to be successfully repaired. A telling remark: Lebeds is worried about the Makhnovists' "petit bourgeois humors" infiltrating the workers' districts, into the workshops and factories, among the weary and backward (?) worker masses. [8] He notes at this point that the sailor rebels of Kronstadt had taken up the Makhnovists' catchcries of "free soviets and the third social revolution," which had attracted some Communist Party members, especially younger ones, over to their revolt. Kronstadt's proclamations had even been reprinted by the anarcho-Makhnovists who made no bones about their sympathies with that insurrection. Finally, to justify three successive alliances with the Makhnovists — who, let it be said in passing, acknowledge only two — Lebeds reckons that this was due to the "...proletarian party's underlying attitude towards the petite bourgeoisie. We may reach an understanding with it, and pass accords, but in the final analysis we have to master it." Thus he could see no "sin" in armed struggle waged against the insurgents, for this was merely a "question of tactics." [9] This convoluted reasoning avoids neither confusion nor the most blatant contradictions, and it is startlingly revealing of the regime's dilemma, unable as it was to explain its struggle against Makhnovist "banditry"; even so, it was to be the same old story with all subsequent policy statements, to which the occasional minor variations were to be added. But his book is no less precious for all that; it contains substantial extracts from the Makhnovist press and invaluable factual material drawn from sources to which we could not otherwise gain access.

❧❧❧

Three years later the account of Isaak Teper-Gordeyev, a one-time Nabat member who had probably been asked by the Cheka to make honorable amends, saw the light of day. In fact, in the guise of taking Makhno to task, Teper indulged himself in an outright tirade against his former organization. His thesis is quite bizarre: that the Nabat guided the Makhnovschina by remote control in order to seize an autonomous territory where it might indulge in a social experiment in anarchism! Teper even goes so far as to depict Aron Baron, his ex-comrade, as the "dictator" of the Makhnovist movement during a good part of 1920! Not that this hinders him from peppering his account with numerous scathing remarks about Makhnovist "kulaks" and other recantations inspired by his Chekist "supervisor of studies." His pamphlet boasts but one positive point; it supplies details of certain Makhnovists, and — above all — it reprints, for the first time in toto, the text of the agreement concluded in October 1920 between the Makhnovists and the Red Army.

In 1926 we may note Anissev's curious foreword to I. Kalinin's book (Kalinin was a White ex-reporter) on *Russia's Vendee* (the Cossacks of the Don and Kuban). Anissev takes exception to Kalinin's depiction of Makhno as a mere bandit who allegedly recruited solely on the basis of sharing plundered goods. In his view "...such an assessment of the Makhnovschina could only be acknowledged as tenable for the second quarter of 1921," in that it would be a mistake not to discern behind Makhno's banditry a general peasant uprising against the dictatorship of the big landowners and generals. This clarification gives pause for thought; on the one hand, it is out of place in the foreword, and, on the other, one needs to read Kalinin's book from cover to cover to find that he only has a few lines about Makhno anyway![10]

The following year, in a monograph on the "Denikinschina," D. Kin acknowledges that the Makhnovists were a real "nightmare for the Whites," but at the same time he asserts that "Anarchy was the flag that shrouded the aspirations of kulaks."[11] Also in 1927, a real monograph appeared on the Makhnovschina above the signature of Kubanin and under the sponsorship of Pokrovsky, the then "boss" of official historiography. Kubanin has scientific pretensions and seeks as a Marxist to comprehend "the only attempt this century to achieve libertarian communism." He painstakingly examines the movement's social and economic characteristics, the Bolsheviks' agrarian policy in the Ukraine and the various phases of the Makhnovschina. However, his approach is most convincing when he notes that the centers of the movement matched those rebel districts most active in 1905 against the pomieschikis, before going on to try to explain it away in terms of the importance of beet production! Remarkably, he cites virtually none of the earlier official studies as references, implicitly dismissing them as worthless. His reasoning is transparent; allegedly, the Makhnovist movement was made up for the most part of "seredniakis" who were supposedly led, in the period of the struggle against White counter-revolution by "bedniakis" and workers, and later, in the days of the fight against the soviet authorities, by "kulaks."[13] His conclusion is less simplistic: the Makhnovschina was on the right lines in 1918 and 1919 when it fought foreign occupation and the White backlash, but once it opposed Moscow, it became inherently counter-revolutionary! "The entire history of the Makhnovschina rests upon

the dithering of the southern steppes' seredniak between reaction and revolution."
In spite of such reductionism, his work is extremely useful — in the absence of
other sources — with regard to various aspects of the Makhnovist movement, in
terms both of the plentiful quotations, the statistical evidence and the usage (for
the first time) of the archives of the Cheka and Red Army, as well as for certain
"admissions" about the "mistakes" of Leninist agrarian policy and the approach
of the Bolshevik party-state, of which we shall give a sample. Let us open with
this "gem": "In criticizing soviet power, Makhnovists stated that in Soviet Russia
there was no freedom of speech, no press freedom, etc., which the Bolsheviks were
supposed to have promised. These petit-bourgeois revolutionaries failed to grasp
that if we enforce the dictatorship of the proletariat, we are consequently the foes
of democratic freedoms. When and where have the Bolsheviks ever talked about
liberty, equality and fraternity under the dictatorship of the proletariat?"[14] Had
Leninists dared issue such a statement in 1917, we are prepared to wager that they
would have quickly vanished into historical oblivion. But now, ten years on, they
could casually fly their true colors! Kubanin then recalls that the sovkhozes had
been "organized along the lines of nationalized industry, i.e., the produce was to be
placed at the complete disposition of the State," which caused dissatisfaction in the
petit-bourgeois producer who had taken the slogan "Factory to the worker, land to
the peasant" in a petit-bourgeois, syndicalist sense, as meaning "All of the land and
the factories would come directly under the disposition of the producer who worked
on that land and in those factories."[15] He goes on to note that many anti-soviet (or
more "precisely, anti-proletarian") seredniak peasant movements were mobilized in
the name of "soviet power."[16] Finally in a note, he draws a parallel between one of
the Makhnovist tactics — individual terror — and that employed by the kulaks in
1927, thereby acknowledging the peasantry's ongoing anti-Bolshevik struggle.[17]

In order to condemn these Makhnovist methods, Kubanin conveniently
uncovers in Eideman's archives a personal diary kept by Makhno's "wife," one
Gaenko, killed in the spring of 1921 — a diary that portrays the actions of the
insurgents in an unfavorable light. In vain was Makhno to deny any connection
with this alleged wife and to rebut with ease the deeds and dates set out in this
canard; all for nothing: to this day this "diary" remains the clinching argument
of Soviet historians and their foreign acolytes — like Aragon[18] — in denouncing
the misdeeds of the Makhnovists.

In 1928 on the occasion of a second edition of Gerassimenko's "account,"
Batko Makhno, we are rewarded with a preface and critical notes by P.E. Schegolev
previously known as an expert on the Decembrists, Pushkin and Lermontov (which
is to say on the 19th century) and also as one of the founders of the Museum of the
Revolution in Leningrad. He opens by quoting the orthodox views of Yakovlev and
Trotsky on the Makhnovschina, before going on to mention Kurilenko, Karetnik,
and Ivan Lepechenko and Viktor Belash, as if they were still alive and "...working
peaceably in the Ukraine." Too often, he says, published materials and memoirs

on this period are of "dubious quality," when not neglectful of those which could be of primary importance. Then he describes Gerassimenko as "naive" for having stated that Makhno had prevented Denikin's seizure of Moscow (which was the first time this assessment was made public in writing in the USSR). All in all, Schegolev's foreword sticks to the "official" line, but the notes less so; he derides the accounts of Boris Pilnyak and of the "young French writer Joseph Kessel" whose "novel" is "…complete fabrication!" The main novelty in this publication consists of the reprint in full, as an appendix, of directives and telegrams Makhno sent to Moscow regarding Grigoriev and his resignation from his position as Red Army divisional commander, as well as of his long letter to Arshinov concerning the final moments in 1921 of the anti-Bolshevik struggle. These documents, lifted from Arshinov's work, are brought to the attention of the Soviet public for the very first time. Schegolev himself underlines this and has no hesitation in speaking about the "colorful language" of Makhno's letter, reminiscent in his eyes "…of the finest passages of Babel's short stories on the civil war." We may wonder what led this venerable historian, who died three years later, to take such a close interest in Makhno. Doubtless it was some barely disguised sympathy.

1928 also saw the appearance of the monograph by Rudnev, a sort of popularized version of the Kubanin work, in that it contains neither notes nor references. The author tells the whole story of the movement in a much more coherent fashion than Kubanin; he is openly hostile to the Makhnovschina "…a cover for the kulak movement" but nonetheless concedes that it played a crucial role against Wrangel in 1920, notes "Makhno's efforts" to "abide loyally by the agreement concluded with the Bolsheviks" and points out that some Red units and their commanders crossed over to the Makhnovists during 1921, an allegation tantamount to sacrilege at the time. Let us take note of his conclusions: "Soviet power and the laboring peasantry were at loggerheads. The former called for the land to be taken into the hands of the State; the latter wanted it handed over in its entirety to the local community which was supposed to know better than anybody else how it should be shared out." [20] Thus this analysis registers fairly faithfully the antagonism between the respective outlooks of the insurgents and the Bolshevik party-state.

❧❧❧

In 1930 at the time of the "de-kulakization" which was proceeding apace, the Ukrainian Communist Party's history review, *Letopis Istorii*, carried Erde's analysis of the *political program of the anarcho-Makhnovschina* which in itself had nothing new to contribute, simply borrowing from all previous official studies. [21] Not until 1937, when the Stalinists clashed in Spain with Spanish anarchists, did the topic recover any immediacy. Em. Yaroslavsky published a survey of *Anarchism in Russia* (translated into several languages) repeating the most hackneyed charges against the Makhnovists, nonetheless leaving a way out for "well-meaning" Spanish anarchists for, he said, the "Makhnovist movement had not always been hostile to the revolution from its outset and throughout its existence. There were times when it helped the revolution."[22] A direct reference to the two alliances agreed with the Bolsheviks. Not that that meant that Leninists could countenance "free soviets," which provoked Yaroslavsky to anger: "The very notion of a Soviet without any power is one of the most damaging concoctions to emanate from Mensheviks and White Guards. It is a light which gives no heat[!?], a cold fire[?], senile impotence, an empty, noxious phrase." [23] It is true that the Stalin years registered a lively enrichment of the language of abuse and the author was not one to be outdone by official speeches anathematizing the "lewd vipers" and other "monsters" in the hire of the international reaction! With Yaroslavsky, one finds more social nuances than in Lebeds or Kubanin: "The Makhnovists' hatred for the poor peasants was the hatred of kulaks for the poor peasants and workers." [24] Intoxicated, he even speaks of the "Makhnovian state of Gulyai-Polye," of a "…kulak police state with its spies, executioners, prisons, irresponsible despotic commanders, its army," and of the destruction of "all press freedom, all political liberty." [25] It appears here Yaroslavsky is extrapolating and crediting to the Makhnovist movement specific features of his own party. Only those anarcho-syndicalists who went over to the Bolsheviks are spared in his view, for they "…took a tiny step forward towards a proper understanding of the revolution, its course and its tasks." Very obviously, this was pointing out to the anarcho-syndicalists of the Spanish CNT the road they too should go down. Echoing the ravings of this unsavory individual, the *Great Soviet Encyclopedia*, in its first edition in 1938 carried an entry devoted to the Makhnovschina: "Movement of kulaks, anarchists and White Guards […] carried out anti-Jewish pogroms, savage looting and murders of communists." [26]

Beginning around the same time was a succession of "Moscow trials" which captured the attention of worldwide public opinion, which was intrigued more by these intestinal struggles than by the fate of the millions of peasant victims of Stalinist collectivization in the foregoing years. An international panel of figures "on the left" was set up to look into the origins of score-settling: straight away it came to seek an explanation from Trotsky (who had been banished from the "holy of holies" some years before) of his own conduct towards the Kronstadt sailors and Makhno. The one-time "Carnot" of the Bolsheviks deigned to answer thus:

> "Makhno was a blend of fanatic and adventurer. But he became the focus of the tendencies that provoked the Kronstadt uprising. Generally, cavalry is the most reactionary category of troops. [?] The man on horseback holds the man on foot in contempt. [!?] […] Makhno's anarchist ideals (negation of the state, contempt for central authority) could not have been better matched to the mentality of this kulak cavalry. Let me add that in Makhno the hatred felt for the urban worker was complemented by a pugnacious anti-Semitism." [27]

A while later he was at it again, declaring peremptorily that "only a man with an empty mind could see in Makhno's bands or in the Kronstadt insurrection a struggle between the abstract principles of anarchism and state socialism."[28] Trotsky kept faith with himself as he had been during his offensive against the Makhnovists in June 1919; in this way he demonstrated his inability to grasp the way that the Russian revolution had degenerated from its beginnings. Failing to question at all his own contribution to this dismal evolution, indeed the very opposite, he continued to stake his claim to the Bolshevik inheritance seized by his twin Stalin, by using precisely the same arguments and anathemas. It was only a short time before he himself fell victim to methods he had so adroitly used against the revolutionary insurgents that he was to revise part of his incisive judgment of Makhno, who "had good intentions but acted damned badly."[29] The hubris that had earned Trotsky so many enemies in his own party was still casting him in the starring role of the man who knew how to act "well" or "badly."

༺༻

For nearly 20 years after that date, a leaden silence hung over the Makhnovschina; this was the heyday of the regime's "hacks writing to order." Didn't they go to the lengths of rewriting the whole history of the civil war just to uncover the hitherto well-hidden feats of that "little father of the peoples" Josef Vissarionovich Djugashvili, alias Stalin! For instance the book by one A.V. Likhovat on *The Crushing of the National Counter-revolution in the Ukraine in 1917–1922* has not a single word to say in its 651 pages about Makhno! Rehearsing such memories could well have put ideas into the heads of mischief-makers, a sort that were thick on the ground in the vast jail that the USSR had become!

In 1962, in a Ukrainian encyclopedia the Makhnovist movement was still being lumped willy-nilly with the "kulaks, Social Revolutionaries, anarchists and Petliurists," the free soviets became "soviets without communists" and so on and so on.[30] Not until 1964 and the after-effects of the Khruschev "thaw" did a study of some interest appear; within the framework of the "mini-civil war" it deals with military and political aspects of the fight against the Makhnovists. With a print-run of only 2,140 copies, Trifonov's work was meant for "students of history, secondary-school and university teachers, as well as party cadres." As the "mini-civil war" had been completely neglected during the period of the "Stalin cult," the stress was henceforth to be on "the activity of the Soviet government, with Lenin at its head, and of the local party organs, Red Army Cheka, militia and special counter-insurgency corps."[31] Trifonov takes the precaution of reporting that the campaign waged against the dictatorship of the proletariat by kulaks — led by the petit-bourgeois parties of the Social Revolutionaries, Mensheviks, anarchists and all the rest — was inspired and organized by international imperialism. This ritual incantation is still relevant, for the old, old ploy of ascribing the roots of "difficulties" at home to the handiwork of foreign foes excuses even the worst repressions. In spite of this, the book furnishes details galore, especially about military operations, all drawn from archives. But what makes it really interesting is its critical handling of all previous monographs on the Makhnovist movement.

Out of all the contradictory sources, only Arshinov's book is quoted; the writer — who is described as the "personal tutor" and "mentor" of the arch-bandit Makhno — cannot, says Trifonov, disguise a "zoological hatred of communism;" his book can be dismissed on account of its "anti-communist venom!" As for Lebeds, he is taken to task for uncritical use of sources (probably his substantial quotations from the Makhnovist press) as well as for having described the Makhnovschina as a "petit-bourgeois spirit of revolt." Teper too is accused of having raised doubts about Makhno and even for having "tried to rehabilitate him!" Kubanin is alleged to have allowed gross methodological errors regarding definition of the social na-ture and political complexion of Ukrainian banditry to slip through. Trifonov puts him straight: Makhno and his entourage represented the interests of the wealthiest village kulaks from 1918 on! Furthermore, Kubanin is alleged not to have been critical enough of the "Memoirs" of arrested Makhnovists and to have quoted too extensively from Arshinov, without the requisite authentication. Only Yaroslavsky is spared and with good reason: their loyalties are the same, with Trifonov's Stalin-ism merely dispensing with Stalin. [32]

Finally in 1968 a substantial article by Seymanov appeared. Trifonov's black and white judgments are toned down a bit; Makhno supposedly "enjoyed for a time the support of a comparatively broad stratum of the peasantry. This is why the struggle against him was so protracted, wearying and bloody." [33] Seymanov proposes to expose the "absence of positive social ideals" from the movement, a goal readily achieved in that from his sources — all of them familiar — he heeds only the most negative aspects likely to bolster his thesis. To conclude our review of the historiography, let us mention Kanev's monograph on anarchism where the author rails against the "western bourgeois counterfeiters of history who dare make revolutionaries of anarchists and Makhnovists and take Bolsheviks to task for having eradicated them."[34]

The regression since the 1920s is self-evident; compared with such liturgi-cal paeans to the role of Lenin and the Party, the studies by Yefimov, Antonov-Ovseenko and, to a lesser extent, Lebeds and Kubanin could pass for paragons of objectivity! Whereas these authors were not afraid to reprint Makhnovist texts extensively and hint at certain weaknesses and shortcomings in the Leninist regime, post-Stalinist hagiographers do not shrink from denying all voice to opponents of their Manichaean contentions.

In the West, historians were for a long time content to examine only the views of the victors, ignoring the "mini-civil war" of the years 1920–1924 virtually entirely. Over the past few years there has been a clear turn-around on this count, and some studies have been marked by a resurgence of interest in this period. In English, several works are deserving of attention, including the monographs on Makhno by Michael Palij, an American of Ukrainian extraction, and by Michael

Malet, a Scottish historian.[35] Their common intention has been, so to speak, to rehabilitate in academic circles Makhno and the Ukrainian insurgent movement which he led; a very laudable object to be sure, but one that we hold to be secondary, the most important being to make the experience of the Ukrainian libertarian communists known to a wider public and to extract from it lessons of use to the contemporary revolutionary project. Dealt with in broad outline, the actions and feats of the Makhnovists — as well as the complex of military operations connected with this — remain isolated from the context of the Russian revolution overall. Here again we come upon the classic drawbacks of academic research, which is generally content coldly to catalogue events without venturing any thoroughgoing analysis, nor, above all, describing their phases with all the detail that one might hope for. On the methodological side, certain basic sources — such as Yefimov — are omitted or inadequately used, whereas other more dubious ones are utilized and are the source of scattered inexactitudes. In spite of everything one should rejoice at publication of these excellent studies which are correctives to the mediocre Anglo-Saxon university literature tackling the subject.

In French, since the 1920s, only Arshinov's book and the first volume of Makhno's memoirs were available. 1947 saw the appearance of Voline's posthumous work *La Révolution inconnue*: Voline had promised a great work on Makhno and the Makhnovschina, but this falls far short of that, maybe on account of the war or other circumstances. Let us quote, from memory, the criticism that Ida Mett made of it at the time of its publication:

> "Far from disclosing fresh facts, the author reprints whole pages lifted from the *History of the Makhnovist Movement* written by Arshinov in 1921. On the other hand, he quotes not one word from the private *Memoirs* of Nestor Makhno despite being in possession of the original which he discovered under the pillow of Makhno's hospital deathbed. To be sure there are points of interest in his description of the Makhnovschina, but their historical value is undermined by the absence of footnotes, the turgid hectoring and a measure of distasteful self-obsession. To conclude, the author, his objectivity and impartiality overflowing, launches into descriptions of the negative personal aspects of Makhno's, and this inelegant, 'impartiality' is singularly reminiscent of personal, posthumous vengeance." [36]

Legitimate criticism, for we can discern long paraphrases of or quotations from Arshinov and from Makhno; Voline's few rudimentary anecdotes were not such as to justify his moral judgments on Makhno and his comrades, judgments out of place after such reasoning.

In 1970 the first volume of Makhno's *Memoirs* was re-published thanks to the writer Daniel Guérin. In a short preface Guérin reviews the characteristics of the movement and laments a "certain relative weakness," due to the "dearth of libertarian intellectuals in its ranks," although at least "intermittently it was helped by outsiders[?]." Guérin takes the opportunity to look forward to a "brilliant psychological profile of Makhno by an English author, Malcolm Menzies." [37] This "profile" duly appeared in 1972, in a translation from the English manuscript, and leaves our hunger unassuaged, for the author — utterly ignorant of his subject — makes do with rehashing some autobiographical writings of Makhno (available in French at that) as well as a few items of gossip, collected who knows where, since he quotes no sources and peppers the whole with psychological considerations more revealing of his own turmoil than of Makhno's. Having acted as godfather to this "own goal," Guérin does not stop there; in an anthology of anarchist texts that could not have been bettered, he describes the Makhnovist movement as a "gigantic *jacquerie* accompanied by a guerrilla war spearheaded by an avenger, a sort of Robin Hood [...] a relatively uneducated peasant [...] a guerrilla war foreshadowing the revolutionary war of the Chinese, Cubans, Algerians, and of heroic Vietnam.[!]" Undaunted by unnatural comparisons, Guérin adds that Trotsky should be "respected," ... "having been a great revolutionary," and that the "sins accumulated by the Bolshevik authorities between 1918 and 1921, the culmination of which would be Kronstadt [and Makhno?] take nothing away from the conviction and genius of the authors of the October Revolution."[38] With his contradictory evaluation, Guérin discloses his difficulties in reconciling the irreconcilable; his Lenino-Trotskyist sympathies, his neophyte zeal for peddling the curious amalgam dubbed "libertarian marxism," and the anarchism of the Makhnovists.

In 1975 Wolodymyr Holota (apparently of Ukrainian extraction) submitted a Ph.D. thesis at Strasbourg University on *The Ukrainian(?) Makhnovist Movement* and at the end of an unimaginative compilation of slim references in French and a few others in Russian and Ukrainian, arrived at an ambiguous conclusion, close to Guérin's thesis. [39]

It was on the basis of these French "sources" that Yves Ternon, a urologist and amateur historian, published a small book on Makhno in 1981. Let us skip the inaccuracies, confusions and unwarranted inclusions, to take note of the author's medico-historical diagnosis: Makhno was the "indicator, the intermediary between a people and its entry into history, the diastatic [!] factor which accelerated the reaction and acted only where the wherewithal for action was to hand[?]."[40]

Some may perhaps advance as an extenuation these authors' sympathies for Makhno. That argument carries little weight, in view of the very personality of the Ukrainian libertarian who had little taste for indulgence and would assuredly not have appreciated the means employed by such lame "defenders" in putting themselves forward.

Despite the notorious weaknesses and shortcomings of the genre, one can account for their appearance by the dearth of works on Makhno deserving of the name; it must be obvious that they would have never seen the light of day had French institutional historians tackled the subject seriously as their Anglo-Saxon counterparts Palij and Malet have done. Thus Roger Portall, who teaches Russian history at the Sorbonne, has no hesitation in a small volume issued in 1970 in talking about the Makhnovschina as a "movement of anarchist inspiration, grouping under Makhno's command, very diverse political and social elements and allying itself successively with the Bolsheviks and then with the White armies [which] complicated the situation even further. The movement was liquidated in 1921; the Red Army absorbed part of its troops." [41] And should this "uncomplicated" Sorbonne character wish to apply for the imprimatur of the Kremlin, we should point out to him that even Soviet historians have moved on from this!

Such handling of Makhno and of the Russian revolution in general deserves some clarification of what a methodology really suited to the subject should be like. For a start, let us stress the condition *sine qua non*; a perfect knowledge of Russian ought to be a prerequisite, for only in that tongue are all sources accessible. Yet that is a necessary condition but not a sufficient one, for there is no shortage of students of Russian in France; other qualities are equally desirable, if not crucial; the ability to tackle rigorously but open-mindedly the differing points of view of all parties concerned. Thus, such work implies a complete independence of mind, namely no dependency on any "thesis supervisor" nor on any "mandarin," and no concern to please/displease the established authorities or some possible "clientele." As we can see, this rules out dilettantes greedy for "acclaim" and academics preoccupied with "furtherance" of careers. Let us also consider the intense effort required to authenticate the accuracy and appropriateness of sources, the need to make things as accessible to the reader as possible — in short, the accomplishment of a thankless and wearying task from which many recoil. Yet something very important is at stake; millions of men fought and died for their beliefs, others carry on their fight. That alone is what matters and not the self-esteem nor notoriety of any side. Contrary to the Leninists' zealot axiom "only the truth is revolutionary" — we know what this one-way truth amounts to — let us adapt the adage and say that only the *quest* for the truth is revolutionary. As we see it, only with this attitude can a fruitful approach be made to the events of the years 1917–1921 — among others.

To wind up this bibliographical tour we now must look at an area where the elementary rules we have just catalogued do not apply: novelistic literature. Without dwelling too long upon it, let us quote a few snippets from these "oeuvres": Vetlouguine, a White Russian refugee in Paris, performed the opening honors with a pamphlet published in 1920; a chapter of this is given over to the "Night over the Ukraine," in fact to Makhno who is depicted in the most caricaturish light. The author puts these words into his mouth: "Free Russia needs neither posts nor telegraphs. Our ancestors wrote no letters and sent no telegrams and were none the worse for that!" [42] According to Vetlouguine, Makhno only took his political bearings every autumn! Hélène Isvolsky, daughter of the former tsarist ambassador to France, follows Vetlouguine's example. She credits Makhno with the "first exploit" of having "murdered an aristocratic marshal who was imprudent enough to arrive to look into some shady affairs." Makhno had been "dispatched to Siberia, from where he escaped several times. [...] He is feared and adored like a god[?]" and there is more of the same to follow.[43] Z. Arbatov published what purports to be a life of Makhno; he describes him as being "small of stature, arms stretching to the knees, face marked by smallpox, dark brown eyes, reminiscent of an owl blinded by a sudden light." The author claims to be the son of the household in which Makhno allegedly set up his headquarters at the time of the occupation of Ekaterinoslav; according to Arbatov the Makhnovists had supposedly and systematically sabered down in the street all who wore furs or good overcoats, amusing themselves by cutting off heads with one stroke and by other actions that need not be mentioned, for they undoubtedly testify to Arbatov's deranged mind.[44] Gerassimenko, of whom we have already spoken, depicts Makhno in similar colors; at age eleven he had allegedly been a "shoelace-seller" in Mariupol and distinguished himself by wayward behavior which had earned him a thrashing from his superior, who supposedly admitted to having "smashed 40 rods on the back and head of young Nestor in three months, to no effect," for Nestor had allegedly taken his revenge by cutting the buttons off his clothes! We have seen the use to which these "sources" were put by Joseph Kessel; however, he does not stand alone. Boris Pilnyak[45] "produced" a novel along similar lines! Both of them have been flayed by the Soviet historian Schegolev as we have seen. For the record let us note that Bagritsky, Mayakovsky and Demian Bedny all "conceived" atrocious poetry on Makhno.

❧

The "proletarian" Count Alexei Tolstoy (no relation to the illustrious author of that name), an inveterate ex-monarchist who became Stalin's sycophant, mentions Makhno and the insurgents in a novel, with equally unsavory imagination.[46] Closer to our own day, Paustovsky the "liberal" Stalinist of the 1950s offers us an excellent example of novelistic invention: one scene takes place in the railway station in Pomoshnaya where two trainloads of Makhnovists speed past the narrator, who nonetheless has time to store a mountain of details in his memory, such as the tattoos of a "broken-nosed sailor": "I did not have time to take in the details of this masterpiece. All I can remember is a hotchpotch of female legs, hearts, daggers and serpents[!]" The author obviously has problems matching the time to his fertile imaginings. He sees Makhno in a "black felt cap and unbuttoned blouse," his "expression signified laziness, smug serenity, languor. [...] A moistened fringe fell over his furrowing brow. His eyes — the mischievous yet empty eyes of a polecat or a paranoiac — glinted with a hothead's fury. [...] Lazily, Makhno raised his revolver and without a glance at anybody, without taking aim, just fired. Why? Go ask him. Can anyone guess what goes on inside the head of a rampaging monster?"[47] What is going on inside the head of this Paustovsky? No doubt serious mental storms in that he seeks to depict a scene that lasted for only a few seconds over six full pages of the most minute detail! Yet he is not the king of this particular castle. A British science fiction writer, Barrington Bayley, presents us with one "Kastor Krakhno" (sic!), leader of the "Death to life!" anarchist movement. His French publisher, fearing that the allusion might not be too obvious, takes the trouble to resolve the equation "Krakhno=Makhno," which instantly categorizes the setting and the intentions behind Bayley's novel. In his stellar kingdom, rent by civil war, Krakhno emerges to mount a spirited celebration of anarchist nihilism and "Death to life!" [48]

Finally, a study on the "Cossacks" blithely states that "Makhno was a stockily-built blond, dressed entirely in black [...] real name Afouka Bida, a Jew converted at a very early age to anarchist beliefs." [49] What can one say about all this literary garbage which certain of the aforementioned "apprentice Makhnologists" have no hesitation in utilizing as the basis for their delirious imaginings? To "literary" experts we shall leave the task of diagnosing the pathological roots of the inspirations of those scribblers whose compulsive myth-peddling and vulgarity are equaled by their incompetence.

And let us add a personal note: During a 1960s screening in Moscow of the film adaptation of Vishnievsky's play *The Optimistic Tragedy*, one scene shows Makhno carried on palanquins and holding a parasol; this sight, designed to provoke hilarity, was greeted by the hundreds of spectators by a stony silence, evidence that no one is taken in by the officially-approved travesty.

Notes to Chapter 32: Historiography and Mythomania

1. In addition to the texts and articles already mentioned, we might cite the series carried by the Red Army review *Armiia i revoliutsiia*; Likharevsky, "The Andreevka confusion" (the battle against Makhno on December 14, 1920) No. 3-4, 1921; Makusenko, "Operations against Makhno from June 9 to 16, 1921," No. 3-4; Eideman, "Makhno," No. 1-2, 1923; then N. Sergeyev, "The Poltava operation against Makhno," in *Voyna i revoliutsiia*, Moscow, No. 9, 1927; Romanchenko, "Episodes from the struggle against Makhno, Summer 1920" (in Ukrainian) in *Letopis revoliutsiia* No. 4, 1931.
2. Eideman, *The Struggle Against the Insurgent Kulaks and Banditry* (in Russian) Kharkov, 1921, and *The Stamping Grounds of the Atamans and Banditry*, Kharkov, 1921.
3. N. Kakurin, "The organization of the drive against banditry according to the Tambov and Vitebsk experience," in *Voyennaya nauka i revoliutsiia*, No. 1, 1922, Moscow p. 83.
4. Lebeds op. cit. pp. 7 and 10.
5. Ibid. p. 16.
6. Ibid. p. 25.
7. Ibid. p. 33.
8. Ibid. pp. 48 and 50.

9. Ibid. p. 53.

10. Kalinin op. cit. p. 1.

11. D. Kin *The Denikinschina* (in Russian), Moscow, 1927, pp. 190–194.

12. Kubanin op. cit. p. 226.

13. Ibid. p. 98.

14. Ibid. p. 119.

15. Ibid. p. 59.

16. Ibid. p. 63.

17. Ibid. p. 114.

18. Aragon, *Histoire de l' URSS,* Paris, 1972, Tome 1, pp. 260–261.

19. V. I. Gerassimenko *Batko Makhno* (in Russian) 2nd edition, Moscow 1928, pp. 6, 8, 38 and 107.

20. Rudnev op. cit. pp. 4, 90–91, 95–96 and 100.

21. *Litopis istorii* (in Ukrainian) Kharkov 1930, 1(40) pp. 41–63 and 2(41) pp. 28–49.

22. Em. Yaroslavsky *L'Anarchisme en Russie,* Paris, 1937 p. 68.

23. Ibid. p. 74.

24. Ibid. p. 89.

25. Ibid. p. 90.

26. Tome XXX VII, pp. 500–501.

27. Victor Serge and Leon Trotsky *La Lutte contre le Stalinisme*, Paris, 1977, pp. 175–176 (the text is from September 10, 1937).

28. Ibid. p. 198 (text published in March 1938).

29. Trotksky *Stalin*, English translation from the Russian by Ch. Malamuth, New York and London, 1941, p. 337. Let us remember that this passage and the pages following, containing interesting self-critical comments, do not appear in the French edition published by Grasset, Paris, 1948.

30. *Ukrainska radenska entsiklopedia* 1962, Tome VIII, pp. 561–562.

31. Trifonov op. cit. p. 2.

32. Ibid. pp. 7–16.

33. Semanov, op. cit p. 37.

34. S. Kanev The October Revolution and the collapse of anarchism (in Russian), Moscow, 1974 p. 348.

35. Michael Palij *The Anarchism of Nestor Makhno, 1918–1921: An Aspect of the Ukrainian Revolution*, Seattle and London, 1976; Michael Malet, *Nestor Makhno in the Russian Civil War*, London 1982.

36. *Masses: Socialism et liberté* Paris, December 1948, pp. 30–31.

37. Makhno *La Révolution Russe en Ukraine* Paris, 1970, pp. 8–10.

38. D. Guérin, *Ni Dieu ni maître*, Paris 1970, Tome III p. 134 and Tome IV pp. 5–6 and p. 53.

39. W. Holota *The Ukrainian Makhnovist Movement, 1918–1921, and the Evolution of European Anarchism through the Debate on the Platform, 1926–1934*, Strasbourg, 1975 (Roneoed).

40. Y. Ternon *Makhno, La révolte anarchiste,* Brussels, 1981, p. 161.

41. R. Portal, *Russes et Ukrainiens,* Paris, 1972, p. 75.

42. A Vetlouguine *Les Aventuriers de la guerre civile* (in Russian) Paris, 1921 pp. 148–150.

43. *La Revue de France* No. 16, November 1921, pp. 183–184.

44. Z. Arbatov "Batko Makhno" in *Vozrozhdeniye* Paris, September–October 1953 pp. 102–115; lifted from the article "Ekaterinoslav 1917–1922" in *Arkhiv Russkoy revoliutsii* XII, 1923, pp. 83–148.

45. Pilnyak "The debacle" in *Russkiy sovremennik* III, 1924.

46. A. Tolstoy *The Road of Storms* Moscow, 1962, Tomes II and III.

47. C. Paustovsky *Une Ère inconnue commence* Paris, 1964, pp. 208–214.

48. B.J. Bayley *Les Planètes meurent aussi,* Paris, 1974, blurb. (In English, *Annihilation Factor* New York 1972).

49. Y. Bréhéret *Les Cosaques,* Paris, 1972, pp. 287–289.

33. Summing Up and Lessons

Through the militant and revolutionary activities of Nestor Makhno and his comrades we have been able to trace the process initiated in the Russian Empire by the tremors of 1905, continuing through the convulsions of 1917 and concluding with the torment of the years that followed. Hindsight has made our vista even wider: these events were only harbingers of a more thoroughgoing cataclysm which was to cast its shadow over the whole century. Viewed in this light, what happened in the Ukraine takes on a tremendous significance. Let us take note of the curious repetition of history which turned the region under Makhnovist influence — the steppes of the southern Ukraine — into the main battleground of this process, just as it had been in the days of the great historical upheavals which followed the Asiatic invasions from the beginnings of the Christian era right up to the waning of the Middle Ages. Let us note too that the decisive military clashes of the Russian Civil War set Cossacks of various persuasions at one another's throats: White Cossacks, Red Cossacks, yellow-and-blue (Ukrainian nationalist) Cossacks, and Black Cossacks (Makhnovist-Zaporogs). Let us now look at the results and the lessons to be drawn.

This upheaval, intended to make an end of all alienation and violent oppression, led a people which had but recently emerged only a few decades earlier from feudal serfdom, into an enslavement to the state without parallel and precedent in history. The cost in human terms was of catastrophic proportions: by our reckoning, nearly one-and-half million people lost their lives during these ghastly years in the Makhnovist region[1] and nearly 20 times as many in the whole of Russian territory in the course of armed struggle, repressions, famines and epidemics, plus the huge losses inflicted by the Russo-German war. Gulyai-Polye, capital of "Makhnovia" saw its population fall from 25,000 of 1917 to 12,027 by 1926.[2] The Makhnovist movement had lost 90 percent of its active participants, which is to say 300,000 men, according to an estimate of March 1920.[3]

One image of this devastation: Since the construction at the beginning of the 1930s by American engineers and slave laborers from the Gulag of the Dniepro-Stroi dam near Alexandrovsk, the "Makhnovist" region has seen its topography altered, and the waterfalls and rapids on the Dniepr — features symbolic of the Zaporogs — have been submerged by flood waters.

We have managed to pick up the trails of several Makhnovists who got out to France: Kharlamov, Mazer and Zarenko settled in the Paris area near to Makhno's home. Bolshakov and Soldatenko served with the Durruti Column during the Spanish revolution and fell at Villa Mayor near Zaragoza in 1937[4]; David Poliakov, after refusing to wear the yellow star during the German occupation, was deported to — and never returned from — the Nazi camps, and it seems that two other Makhnovists may have emigrated to Canada after 1945.

The fate of other, less glorious protagonists proves equally tragic. Mai-Maievsky, the embezzling White general who commanded the army of White Volunteers in 1919 only to be replaced in 1920, died of a heart attack on the very day that Wrangel's defeated troops evacuated the peninsula. Baron-General Wrangel also died in 1929 in Brussels in mysterious circumstances. General Pokrovsky-the-Hangman was killed in Bulgaria in 1923 by his own Cossacks. Slaschev, criticized by his own in Constantinople, defected to the Reds, taught at the Higher Military Academy of the Red Army and died in Moscow in 1929, assassinated by someone who claimed to be the brother of one of his victims in the Crimea. During the second world war, Krasnov and Shkuro formed Cossack units in the service of the Germans, but the Germans grew suspicious of them and avoided deploying them against the Red Army. In 1945 the British handed them over to Stalin: he had them hanged in Moscow's Red Square in 1947 with eleven other Cossack generals as "traitors to the nation." Only Denikin died in bed, that same year, in the United States.

As for the Red generals, who distinguished themselves in the fight against the Makhnovists, and had been burdened with medals and certitudes, they in turn fell headlong into the trap. Nesterovich who had commanded the special "flying corps" in December 1920 against Makhno, never recovered from this sinister assignment: while on a mission abroad, he abruptly gave up all activity and found a job as a "factory worker." The GPU did not quite see it like that; Nesterovich was too knowledgeable about too many compromising matters. "One of his former friends invited him to dinner and poisoned him. His corpse was photographed and the negative sent to Moscow as proof of his execution."[5] Kotovsky who had been involved in Yakir's retreat and the hunting down of the Makhnovists in January 1921 was killed in 1925 in "unexplained circumstances" by one of his associates, probably on GPU instructions; his excessive popularity in the army incurred the displeasure of Stalin who was concerned to eliminate all potential Bolshevik "Bonapartes." Frunze, the commander in chief of the campaign against Makhno in 1921, replaced Trotsky as Commissar for War; he died on October 31, 1925, during a routine stomach operation. A haphazard accident can be ruled out; it had been on express orders from Stalin and the Central Committee that he had made up his mind to undergo the operation. According to one of his adjutants, he had had a premonition of its fatal outcome. Officially, he succumbed to an "overdose" of anaesthetic.[6] The celebrated Red generals Yakir, Eideman, Uborevich, Primakov, Kork and Tukhachevsky were shot on July 11, 1937 after the gravest accusations. Levenson, S.S. Kamenev, Kakurin, Rakovsky, Karakhan, Dybenko and Yakovlev (Epstein) — who signed the agreement with Makhno — disappeared when their turn came, victims of the perverse operation of the mechanism which they themselves had set in motion. Probably none of them had sufficiently pondered Saint-Just's famous phrase: "A revolution that stops half-way is digging its own grave!" Only Voroshilov and Budyenny proved spineless enough to weather every storm: they passed away peaceably in their beds.

Thus, sooner or later the "victors" shared the fate of the "vanquished" and they too were gobbled up by the "cannibalistic" revolution. Very few of them had realized that it was not enough to give the worm-eaten edifice of the Russian Empire a coat of Red paint to change its nature. The enshrined system of exaggerated state centralization, the despicable nature of the methods used, the dictatorship of the leaders and the passive obedience of the masses could only have exacerbated, not the class struggle, but the "competition for placements" and in that game, no one could be sure that he would not be out black-guarded. But that is not all — the historical responsibilities must be determined with precision: Arshinov denounces the "noxious role" of Bolshevism which "…snuffed out revolutionary initiative and the autonomous activity of the masses, thereby eradicating the greatest revolutionary opportunities that the workers had ever had in history." He reckons, however, that Bolshevism did not bear "sole responsibility for the failure of the Russian revolution. It has merely acted out what was devised decades ago by socialist science. Its every move was inspired by the general theory of scientific socialism."[7] In Arshinov's view, the working class worldwide had to hold "socialism as a whole" responsible for the deplorable situation foisted upon the Russian peasants and workers. From which he deduced of course that the proletariat has no socialist "friends" — these being in reality "enemies aspiring only to seize the product of their labor"[8] — and that they should count on nobody but themselves.

Nestor Makhno arrived at the same conclusion and recalls that it is by destroying the State once and for all — (the State of which socialists are the stalwart supporters) — that the toilers will at last be able to build the society of their dreams:

> "The final and utter liquidation of the State can only take place when the approach of the toilers' struggle is as libertarian as possible, when they themselves will work out the structures for their social action. These structures must take the form of organs of social and economic self-direction, the reform of free (anti-authoritarian) soviets. The revolutionary toilers and their vanguard — the anarchists — must analyze the nature and structure of these soviets and stipulate their revolutionary functions in advance. It is upon that that the positive

evolution and development of anarchist ideas among those who will shift for themselves in liquidating the State in order to build the free society, is dependent."9

In this regard, the exemplary struggles and achievements spearheaded by Makhno and the Ukrainian insurgents offer comfort to all who — some fine day — may seek return to these roots of the Russian and Ukrainian revolutions and this time see things through to their natural conclusion in a *genuinely* humane society.

A.S. 1982

Notes to Chapter 33: Summing Up and Lessons

1. We have used the method of cross-checking demographic statistics, taking soviet sources into account: one set of figures mentions 250,000 victims in the province of the Northern Tavrida alone (quoted by Makhnovets, "The truth about Makhno," in *Novoye Russkoye slovo*, New York, March 2, 1969, p. 8), but it goes without saying that these figures can only be approximate in that there were vast migration movements.
2. *The Great Soviet Encyclopedia*, First Edition, Moscow, Tome XIX. The third edition sets the town's population in 1970 at 16,000 inhabitants.
3. P. Arshinov, op. cit. p. 7 and A. Nikolaev *The First Among Equals*, op. cit. p. 40.
4. Louis Mercier-Vega *L'Increvable Anarchisme* Paris 1970, p. 14 and further information supplied to the author and confirmed by the Spanish Libertarian Fortera, from Montpellier.
5. Gregory Bessedovsky *Oui, j'accuse!* Paris, 1930, pp. 34–36.
6. I. K. Hambourg *The Way it Was* (In Russian), Moscow 1965, p. 182 (in 1926 Boris Pilnyak wrote a novella directly based on this affair, *The Tale of the Unextinguished Moon*, which created a sensation in its day and subsequently led to his being swallowed up by the Gulag.)
7. Arshinov op. cit. pp. 250–251.
8. Idem.
9. N. Makhno "The course of struggle against the State," in *Dyelo Truda* No. 17, October 1926, pp. 5–6.

Documents from the Makhnovists

To complement our study, we reprint in full the most telling statements of principle issued by the Makhnovist movement.

Document No. 1 is lifted from the review *Russkaya Mysl* (Russian Thought) Books I and II, published in Sofia by Piotr Struve. The document contains the essential passages from the pamphlet (32 pages in 8§) published by the Gulyai-Polye "Nabat" anarchist group in 1919 and previously inaccessible in the West.

Document No. 2 consists of the Makhnovists' *Draft Declaration* — their political charter based on a Bulgarian edition published in Sofia in 1921 (37 pages in 32§), a copy of which exists at the International Institute for Social History in Amsterdam: lengthy quotations (in Russian) appeared in Kubanin's *Theses on Free Soviets* and Kolesnikov's *The Worker Question,* so we [A.S.] have re-translated it from the Russian and Bulgarian, with Matin Zemliak's kind assistance in the case of the Bulgarian.

Document No. 3 is taken from the same Bulgarian publication Sofia.

Documents Nos. 4 to 9, originals of which are in the possession of the IISH in Amsterdam, were published in Russian in the Institute's journal, *International Review of Social History,* Vol. XIII, part 2, 1968, with a foreword by I. J. Van Rossum (pp. 246–268).

Document No. 10 was published in the review *Volna* (The Wave), Detroit, No 24, December 1921.

Document No. 11, a reconstruction of Chernoknizhny's speech, has been borrowed from A. Nikolaev's *First Among Equals,* op. cit. pp. 44–46.

Document No. 1

A minute on the February 2, 1919 Second Regional Congress in Gulyai-Polye, attended by 2245 delegates from 350 districts, soviets, unions and front-line units.

Comrade Makhno declines the proposal that he chair the congress, citing "military development on the front" and is elected honorary chairman of the congress.

The delegation which journeyed to Kharkov to make contact with the [Bolshevik — A.S.] provisional government of the Ukraine, makes its report: Comrade Lavrov relates his conversation with the deputies (the delegation had not been received by ministers or commissars): the spokesman reports that a response was forthcoming on the attitude of the provisional government of the Ukraine to Batko Makhno: as yet there has been no formal agreement, though one is anticipated and the provisional government nurtures no hostile intent towards Makhno and looks forward to doing all it can to help him in the struggle against the Counter-Revolution. During the ensuing debate, comrade Chernoknizhny (delegate from the Novapavlovsk district) points out: "The report informs us of the recent formation in the Ukraine of a Bolshevik-communist government, which is making ready to monopolize the soviets." He went on to say: "While you peasants, workers and insurgents were containing the pressure from all the counter-revolutionary forces, that government, ensconced in Moscow and then in Kursk, waited for the Ukraine's workers and peasants to liberate the territory from the enemy. Now that the enemy is beat … a government arrives among us calling itself Bolshevik and seeking to foist its party dictatorship upon us. Is that to be tolerated? We are non-party insurgents who have revolted against all our oppressors and we will not countenance fresh enslavement, no matter what party it may emanate from!"

Another delegate, the peasant Serafimov, declares: "Already a new danger looms before us — the danger of one party, the Bolsheviks, who are already forging new statist chains destined for us. The Bolshevik government does its best to convince us that it serves the interests of workers and peasants and that it brings emancipation to toilers … But why then does it aspire to **rule** over us from above, from its ministerial offices? From our Russian brethren we know what sort of revolution Bolsheviks make … We know that up there the people are not free, and that the whim of the party, Bolshevik chaos and the violence of the commissarocracy rule the roost. Should this party attempt to bring such 'freedoms' here to us in the Ukraine, we must then announce loudly that we need no such savior or master, that we have no need of dictatorships, that we can arrange our new life for ourselves."

Comrade Bozhno, an anarchist insurgent, declares: "No matter what the cost, we must set up soviets that are beyond all pressure from whatever parties.

Only toilers' soviets, non-partisan and freely elected are capable of affording us new freedoms and rescuing the toiling people from slavery and oppression. **Long live freely elected anti-authoritarian soviets!**"

The Bolshevik-communist Karpenko interrupts, but his speech is continually heckled. When he declares: "The dictatorship of the proletariat over the bourgeoisie must be introduced," one voice retorts, "At the moment all we can see is the Bolsheviks' dictatorship over the anarchists and Left SRs." Another voice heckles: "Why do they send us commissarocrats? Those we can live without. But if we must have commissars, we can always appoint some from our own ranks."

In a speech on the current situation, chairman Veretelnikov offers the following important news: "In 1905 when the atmosphere was so oppressive, an anarchist group was organized here in Gulyai-Polye: its existence was soon made known when comrade Alexander Semenyuta, whose name was familiar to few people up to that point, died in action against the police. Comrade Makhno was arrested and sent with many other revolutionaries for penal servitude, where he served ten full years. After the overthrow of the autocracy, Makhno returned to Gulyai-Polye. When the revolutionary movement here took on a serious character, I was in Sebastopol. This joyous news brought me home to the town of my birth, where a harrowing scene awaited me [the Austro-German occupation — A.S.] ... Events then moved at a dizzying pace. The 'batko' set off with one detachment, others spread out in the directions of Taganrog, Rostov, Tsaritsyn, etc."

Comrade Makhno delivers a purely revolutionary address of unmistakably anarchist tone and directed at the Bolsheviks. For openers, Makhno stated that the ... "people, starving and bereft of everything, bled white after the fratricidal war, refused to fight on the front." But in place of the bloody tsar, a new criminal had ensconced himself on the throne, in the shape of the provisional government. "At that point anarchists mounted intense propaganda and fought with every means at their disposal against the provisional government's adventure. Everywhere, in factories, workshops and barracks, anarchists explained that the fratricidal war at the front had to be prosecuted further: which led, in Petrograd, to their being arrested at their headquarters at Durnovo House and to the shooting of certain of their number." Noting that anarchists and Bolsheviks had been united then by the persecution they suffered, Makhno declares: "once power had fallen into the hands of the toiling people in the shape of freely elected soviets, things proceeded apace ... These free soviets did not long survive ... The Bolshevik party extended its monopoly over them and set about purging the revolutionary soviets and persecuting anarchists; those who, only the day before, had been hunted and persecuted with them now refused to acknowledge their fellow strugglers. Until today when we witness the Bolsheviks' brute force and oppressive violence against toiling people who can stand no more." In conclusion, comrade Makhno declares that if the Bolsheviks are coming to help their comrades he will tell them: "Welcome, dear brothers," but if they come to bring the Ukraine under their sway, we shall tell them: "Hands off!"

❧

Other speakers (Khersonsky, Chernyak) spoke to the same motion. Khersonsky declares: "No party has any right to arrogate State power to itself." Chernyak stipulates that: "all who denounce the activities of the commissars and Chekas have themselves sampled them to their cost, and have been under their yoke.... Many decent revolutionaries who knew jail, imprisonment and penal servitude during tsarism, are now once again filling Russia's prisons." He insists that the necessary steps be taken to set up economic soviets, non-party political and anti-authoritarian, on the basis of elective principles allowing for recall of representatives failing to act upon the wishes of their mandatories. "We want all vital issues resolved on the spot and not according to the decrees of some power 'on high' [we want] all workers and peasants to determine their destinies for themselves, with delegates having merely to **implement** the wishes of the toilers."

Comrade Kostin (Left SR) speaks of peasant uprisings against the Bolsheviks: "These are not the actions of individuals; rather, the peasants of many districts, marching out with their wives, children and aged parents to face the bullets of the Letts and Chinese in that they can see no other option. These are all your brothers, the same poor peasants every bit as oppressed as you are here in the Ukraine. Why do they revolt against the Bolsheviks to the cry of 'all power to the soviets. Down with the commissarocrat!'? Because the policy of those currently in power in Russia pushes them to it. For instance, the Bolsheviks have invented supply detachments. They arm workers and send them into the countryside to wrest wheat from the peasants by force, giving them nothing in return. They carry off the last reserves of wheat, often bought by the peasants themselves and they carry off the last jugful of milk, the last item of clothing, the last pair of boots; they take everything. They organize general plunder, which has become the rule. That in a few words is what Bolshevik policy is all about."

Comrade Baron (anarchist) also speaks out against the Bolsheviks: "We have what is called the 'soviet Government,' which describes itself as a worker-peasant government but which not one of us has elected. It is a government of usurpers that capitalizes on our weakness — the absence of close cohesion from our ranks — wields its usurper power over us, makes deals with foreign imperialism and again slips a noose around the necks of toiling people. The Bolsheviks, who were revolutionaries before the October coup d'etat, now shoot genuine revolutionaries whose only crime is to think differently from them." Baron concludes his speech with these words: "Insurgent comrades. Your task now consists of creating everywhere, in every single village, anti-authoritarian and freely elected soviets which will meet all your needs, and of building your economic life and defending your real interests without interference from any commissars representing the narrow interests of one party and subjecting you from above to their party's yoke. There is no way to complete emancipation from the yoke of capitalism and of all power, no way to social revolution except through economic, anti-authoritarian, free soviets, through an authentic regime of toilers' soviets. **Long live the free anti-authoritarian people which builds its life without any political authorities and tutors at all!"**

✿✿✿

Batko Makhno endorses the resolution moved by the anarchists' union, the Left SRs, the insurgents and the congress presidium. It is carried by 150 votes to 29 against, with 20 abstentions. The resolution is scathing in its assessment of Bolshevism:

> "The political commissars and others appointed by government and not elected by us monitor every move of the local soviets and ruthlessly crack down on peasant and worker comrades who make a stand to defend the people's freedom against the representatives of central government. The latter, styling itself the worker-peasant government of Russia and of the Ukraine, is blindly obedient to the party of Bolshevik-communists who, in the narrow interests of their party, persecute all other revolutionary organizations in despicable fashion. Sheltering behind the slogan 'dictatorship of the proletariat,' the Bolshevik-communists have decreed themselves a monopoly on the revolution, regarding all who do not think as they do as counter-revolutionaries. The Bolshevik authorities arrest and shoot Left SRs and anarchists, ban their newspapers, and stifle any manifestation of revolutionary discourse.
>
> To demonstrate its power and without consulting the workers and peasants, the Bolshevik government has opened negotiations with the allied imperialist governments, promising them all sorts of advantages and concessions and allowing them to bring troops into certain places in Russia which thereby come under the sway of the Allies.
>
> The Second regional congress of front line fighters, insurgents, workers and peasants from the Gulyai-Polye region calls upon comrade peasants and workers vigilantly to monitor the actions of the Soviet-Bolshevik government which, through its handiwork, represents a real threat to worker and peasant revolution. That different revolutionary organizations, freely expressing their ideas, should exist is only normal, but we will not allow any to set itself up as the only power and force others to dance to its tune. In our insurgent struggle, we need a fraternal family of workers and peasants to defend land, truth and liberty. The Second regional congress urgently calls upon worker and peasant comrades to undertake for themselves, on the spot, without any constraints or decrees and despite all oppressors and aggressors the world over, the building of a free society without lords or masters and without subject slaves, without rich or poor.

The congress salutes all the workers and peasants of Russia who struggle as we do against world imperialism.

Down with the commissarocrats and self-appointed representatives!

Down with the Cheka, the new Okhrana!

Long live the freely elected worker-peasant soviets!

Down with the exclusively Bolshevik soviets!

Down with the accords between the Russian and international bourgeoisie!

Shame on the socialist government that parleys with the imperialist allies!

Long live the worldwide Socialist Revolution!"

The congress then passes a resolution … "against anti-Jewish looting, attacks and pogroms carried out by various suspect individuals who misuse the name of decent insurgents."

Apropos of pogroms against Jews, this resolution spelled out the following stance:

"National antagonism, which in some places has taken the form of anti-Jewish pogroms, is a bequest of the autocratic régime. The tsarist government whipped up the unconscious masses of the people against the Jews, in the hope of thereby shifting responsibility for its crimes on to the poor Jewish mass, thereby distracting the attention of the toiling people away from the real causes of their misery: the yoke of Tsarist autocracy and its thugs."

The movement's internationalism finds expression in the following points from the resolution:

"The oppressed and exploited of every nationality and persuasion have revolted in solidarity with the Russian revolution and the coming worldwide social revolution. The workers and peasants of every land and all nationalities face a huge common task: the overthrow of the yoke of the bourgeoisie, the exploiter class, the overthrow of the yoke of *capital and State* with an eye to establishment of a new social order founded on liberty, fraternity and justice.

The exploited of every nationality, whether they be Russian, Polish, Latvian, Armenian, Jew or German, must come together into one huge united community of workers and peasants and then, in a mighty onslaught, deal a final decisive blow to the class of capitalist imperialists and their lackeys in order to shrug off once and for all the shackles of economic slavery and spiritual serfdom.

Down with capital and power!

Down with religious prejudices and national hatreds!
Long live the social revolution!"

On the matter of organization of the front, congress, repudiating mobilization "through constraint," came out in favor of "mandatory" mobilization: "Each peasant capable of bearing arms ought **himself** to recognize his duty to join the ranks of the insurgents and to defend the interests of the whole toiling people of the Ukraine."

On the agrarian issue, the congress passes a resolution based on the following principles:

> "The land belongs to no one and only those who work it may have the use of it. The land should pass into the hands of the Ukraine's toiling peasantry *gratis,* in accordance with an *egalitarian working arrangement,* i.e. it should ensure that the needs of each person are met according to established norms and should be worked by each individual *in person.* Until such time as the agrarian issue is radically resolved, congress wants local agrarian committees to draw up an immediate inventory of all holdings of the big landowners, the common lands and all the rest; then they can share them among the landless peasants or peasants with inadequate holdings, supplying them with the wherewithal for planting."

Document No. 2

Draft Declaration of the (Makhnovist) revolutionary insurgent army of the Ukraine adopted on October 20, 1919 at a session of the Military Revolutionary Soviet.

The toiling classes of Ukraine are today confronting events of enormous importance and historic implications. Without doubt, the significance of these events goes beyond the limits of the revolutionary insurgent army's activity. But, being in the vanguard of the fight in progress, the latter deems it its duty to spell out to the toilers of the Ukraine, Russia and the whole world the aims for which it fights, as well as its analysis of recent happenings and the current situation.

In February–March 1917, Russia and the Ukraine experienced the *First Revolution,* which led to the fall of Tsarist autocracy and brought about the advent of a State political power comprised at first of personages from the big industrial bourgeoisie and then of representatives of the small and medium bourgeoisie. Neither of those two governments proved stable. Eight months were enough for the revolutionary masses to overthrow these authorities which had nothing in common with the interests and aspirations of toilers.

As early as July 1917, the necessity of a *Second Revolution* was apparent. This took place at the end of October and paved the way for seizure of State power by the Bolshevik Social Democrat party which looked upon itself as representing the revolutionary proletariat and poor peasantry or, to put it another way, the social revolution. That party was very soon waging an ongoing campaign against all competing parties with an eye to arrogating power to itself. Since its watchwords coincided with the aspirations of the toiling masses, the latter threw their weight behind it when the crucial time came. And so this eight month period of government by the bourgeoisie in coalition and of rivalry between the differing political parties ended in the Bolshevik Party's taking power.

However it very quickly became apparent that this party and this State power — just like any party and all State power — functioned only for themselves and turned out to be utterly powerless to achieve the great objectives of the social revolution: by virtue of that very fact they were a hindrance to the free creative activity of the toiling masses who alone were capable of tackling this task. It is self-evident that in controlling the whole of economic and social life, any State power inevitably gives rise to new political and economic privileges and undermines the very foundations of social revolution.

The Bolshevik-Communist Party's inability to offer an authentic avenue of struggle for socialism quite naturally led to discontent, disappointment and bitterness among the toiling masses. The disorganized condition of economic life, the consequence of a bad agrarian policy led to serious disturbances in the countryside. The Bolshevik authorities have succeeded, however, in organizing in Russia a mighty State machine and a compliant army which it uses as its predecessors did, to stamp on any manifestation of popular discontent and resistance.

In the Ukraine the situation is otherwise.

Before making the acquaintance of the Bolshevik authorities, the Ukraine was occupied by the Austro-Germans who installed their vassal, the hetman Skoropadsky there. They were replaced by the power of Petliura. The excesses of these authorities triggered an explosion of outrage from the people and a wholesale rejection of the very idea of State power, which assumed the form of a mighty popular insurgent movement, driven by an authentically revolutionary anti-party and anti-authoritarian mentality. In a series of engagements after the departure of the Austro-Germans, revolutionary insurgents purged the Ukraine of supporters of the hetman and of Petliura: the Bolshevik-Communist authorities seized upon this to arrive and ensconce themselves in the spring of 1919, bringing disappointment very quickly in their wake. Within a few months, the discontent and hostility of the toiling masses of town and above all of countryside was made violently manifest.

Large regions, such as the provinces of Ekaterinoslav and Tavrida, began to drift more and more unmistakably towards economic and social self-organization on a basis of animosity towards parties and State power. No political activity was allowed there. Towards the end of the summer, the whole country was prey to huge peasant insurgent movements against the Communist Party's arbitrary rule. The *Third Revolution* comes to light and guides this widespread insurrection.

Meanwhile, the reaction had raised its head. The *Third Revolution* stood against the attempt to restore the old régime. In the hope of finding themselves once again masters of the situation by annihilating both their enemies — the revolutionary insurrection and the reaction — the Bolshevik authorities plotted and treacherously facilitated the crushing of the main core of the Makhnovist insurgent army. However the State machinery and armed forces of the Bolshevik-Communist authorities in turn proved incapable of putting down roots in the Ukraine and of replacing the revolutionary insurgent movement in its fight against Denikin. The revolutionary insurgents emerged from these difficult circumstances weakened but not defeated. Driven far from their home ground, they strove to survive at any price and while roaming other regions of the Ukraine they prosecuted an all-out struggle against the Denikinists, against Trotsky's deliberate misrepresentations and the dangerous set-back to the revolution.

Now the flames of peasant insurrection and the struggle against reaction are raging throughout the whole Ukraine. A new enemy of the toilers appears, in the shape of Petliura's bourgeois, republican government. A confrontation, at once inevitable and critical (only time will tell who will emerge victorious from it) pits the notion of libertarian organization as taken up by significant masses in the Ukraine against the notion of political power — be it monarchist, Bolshevik-Communist or bourgeois republican.

Such, in broad outline, has been the hard revolutionary experience that we Makhnovist insurgents have been through over these past two and a half years of revolution. It only remains for us to add that in our region and in many another more distant one, we have been witnesses to and participants in successful essays in libertarian social and economic organizing, free of interference from any government. Most of them were interrupted only following violent intervention by some authority or another.

The upshot of this difficult but enriching experience, as well as the theoretical tenets that characterize it, leads us to make the following clear and specific declaration:

The unraveling of the revolution has convinced us beyond all question that no political party and no State authority is capable of resolving the great issues of our day, or of re-launching and organizing the country's devastated economy while stimulating and meeting the needs of the toiling masses. We are persuaded that in the light of this experience, huge masses of the peasants and workers of the Ukraine have come to the same conclusion and that they will not countenance any political oppression.

Our reckoning is that in the near future all the toiling classes will arrive at the same conclusion and that they themselves will see to the organizing of their professional, economic, social and cultural lives on the basis of free principles, dispensing with the oversight, pressure and dictatorship of any personage, party or power whatever.

We declare that the popular insurgent movement presently developing in the Ukraine represents the start of the great *Third Revolution* which will once and for all free the toiling masses of all oppression by State and Capital, be it private or statist.

We declare that our Makhnovist insurgent army is merely the fighting core of this Ukrainian people's revolutionary movement, a core whose task consists everywhere of organizing insurgent forces and helping insurgent toilers in their struggle against all abuse of power and capital. The Ukraine is on the brink of a genuine peasant social revolution. That is the import of the situation. We Makhnovist insurgents are the children of that revolution, here to serve and protect it. Whenever it spreads like a mighty brushfire through the whole of the toilers' Ukraine, freeing it of all aggressors and all powers, we faithful fighters will mingle with the millions of people's insurgents. Then, shoulder to shoulder, we will partake in the free building of a new life.

As regards our thinking on the essential issues of economic and social reconstruction, we regard it as essential that the following be stressed: once toilers have the freedom required to determine their fate for themselves, they will naturally and inevitably, the vast majority of them, move towards realization of genuinely communist social principles. We reckon that only the toiling masses have the capacity to enact these principles, provided that they have access to the completest freedom of socio-economic creation. Thus we consider imposition of our ideal by force as quite irrational and out of place. We think, likewise, that it would be wrong to seek to trail the masses along in our wake, by means of leadership from **above**. We mean to restrict our role to simple theoretical and organizational assistance, in the form of proposals, advice, suggestions or guidance. Our thinking is that whereas the people should have the opportunity to listen to all opinion and advice, they alone should decide to act upon them with absolute independence and freedom, without interference from parties, dictators or governments of any sort.

We make every effort to communicate these views to the toiling masses, whilst focusing their attention upon their own autonomous role in free soviet construction.

The soviet system.

Our conception of an authentic system of free soviets we express as follows. In order to introduce a new economic and social life, the peasants and workers naturally and freely set up their social and economic organizations: village committees or soviets, cooperatives, factory and workshop committees, mine committees, railroad, Post and Telegraphs organizations and every other union and organization imaginable. In order to establish natural liaison between all these unions and associations, they set up agencies federated from the bottom up, in the shape of economic soviets whose technical task is to regulate social and economic life on a large scale. These soviets may be district soviets, town soviets, regional soviets, etc.... organized as the need arises on a basis of free principles. In no case would these be political institutions led by this or that politician or political party, who would dictate their wishes (as happens behind the mask of "soviet power"). These soviets are only the executive arms of the assemblies from which they emanate.

Such a soviet arrangement is a true reflection of the organization of the peasants and workers. If this creation is indeed the free handiwork of the peasant and worker masses themselves, if the bracing economic work of all the grassroots agencies and federative soviet organizations begins to attract more and more toilers, without any interference or arbitrary meddling by any party or authorities whatever, then, by our reckoning, it will be possible speedily to introduce an economic and social system based on the principles of social equality, justice and fraternity and thereby put paid to the existence of class differences, political parties and States, as well as the domination of one nationality over others. Gradually and naturally the backward and non-toiler strata of the population will be absorbed into this system. All "political activity" which leads inescapably to creation of privilege and a mechanism for economic and political enslavement of the toiling masses will be proved redundant in practice, and "political" organizations will tend to wither away of themselves.

Our answer to the questions that will be put regarding "official" agencies and sundry social pursuits relating to education, medicine, statistics, registration of marriages, deaths and births, etc. is that maximum scope will be afforded the priceless and prolific initiative of the individual, within the framework of the soviet. All of this will be no problem and will be best resolved by local agencies of self-governance.

Judicial and administrative machinery.

As far as the depiction of this machinery as necessity goes, we must first of all reaffirm our position in principle: we are against all rigid judicial and police machinery, against any legislative code prescribed once and for all time, for these involve gross violations of genuine justice and of the real protections of the population. These ought not to be organized but should be instead the living, free and creative act of the community. Which is why all obsolete forms of justice — court administration, revolutionary tribunals, repressive laws, police or militia, Chekas, prisons and all other sterile and useless anachronisms — must disappear of themselves or be abolished from the very first breath of the free life, right from the very first steps of the free and living organization of society and the economy.

The free organizations, associations and soviets of workers and peasants must themselves prescribe this or that form of justice. Such justice should not be enforced by specialist officials, but rather by trustees who enjoy the confidence of the local population, by arrangement with it and utterly repudiating sanctions prescribed in the past. Likewise, popular self-defense must be based on free organization, and not left to specialist militias. Not only does formal organization of justice and defense by the State not achieve its aims, but it is a betrayal of all true justice and defense.

The question of supplies.

At present this question could not be posed any more acutely. Resolution of it is of the utmost urgency, for the whole fate of the revolution hinges upon it right now. The major flaw in the previous revolution [the Bolsheviks' — A.S.] proceeded from the complete disorganization of supplies, which led to a dichotomy between town and countryside. The toilers must pay the utmost attention to it. This issue was particularly easy to resolve at the beginning of the revolution, when life was not yet in complete disarray and when food was available everywhere in more or less adequate supply. At that point, the contest between socialist parties for control of political power and then the Bolshevik party's struggle to hold on to it, monopolized the attention of the workers and peasants who left the question unresolved and failed to display sufficient vigilance. As for the Bolshevik authorities, they proved quite naturally incapable of resolving the matter.

Here too we reckon that a just resolution of this matter and restoration to order of everything relating to it can only be devised by the toilers themselves through their free organizations. None but they will be able to settle the matter viably. In this regard, the toilers must fight shy of disunity, and close unity between workers and peasants has to be achieved. This will not be hard if they dispense with political organizations and verbose politicians. Released from all political authority, the towns will convene a comprehensive congress of workers and peasants and this will establish among its priorities the supply question and the re-establishment of economic links between towns and countryside, setting in train an equitable exchange of basic necessities. It will be up to trades organizations, cooperatives and transport agencies to take this further. Suitable agencies will be set up to seek out, consolidate and relaunch industrial and agricultural production: these will introduce a system for trade and fair distribution of goods. In this context, the workers' and peasants' cooperatives and free associations will have to play a crucial role. Only in this way, we reckon, can this particularly important issue of supply be resolved.

The land question.

The process of rebuilding and rapidly improving our agrarian economy which is at present in ruins and very limited, requires reorganization of the working of the land through absolutely free and voluntary decision-making by the toiling agricultural population in its entirety (obviously help from experts can be assumed). The village traders will have to be removed from this process quickly. We are persuaded that the solution to this problem of land will emerge unaided through communist organization of the peasant economy. Everyone will quickly be persuaded that growth of output and the meeting of all needs can only be ensured by the community and not by private individuals. However, any imposition of communism through constraint or top-down administration must be rejected.

The Bolsheviks' decree regarding "nationalization of the land," which is to say the placing of all lands in the hands of the State (in fact the hands of the government, its agencies and functionaries) must be disregarded. A State take-over of land will inescapably lead, not to fair and free agricultural structures, but to the reappearance of a new exploiter and master in the shape of the State, which will have recourse — as bosses do — to wage slavery and will impose all manner of corveés, levies, etc. upon the peasantry by force, just as its pomieschiki predecessors did. The peasantry will reap no advantage from being faced by just one master — the State — even more powerful and cruel than the thousands of little bosses, masters and pomieschikis. Lands seized from great estate owners should not be at the disposal of the State but placed in the hands of those who actually work them: the peasant organizations, free communes and other unions.

The manner in which the land, equipment and very organization of the agricultural economy are to be handled should be worked out freely at peasant congresses, after discussion and passed as resolutions, without any interference by any authority whatsoever.

We consider that solution of all these matters by the peasants themselves will usher in a natural process of expansion of the social organizations of the peasant economy, beginning, say, with egalitarian and commensurate division of the land, farm equipment and livestock: with social organization of labor and of the distribution of produce on a basis of cooperation: with social usage of the land and equipment, etc.: that is to say, according to a more or less avowedly communist formula. The manual and mental exertions of experienced and capable villagers, in close concert with workers' organizations, will complement this process and speed its development. Meanwhile, private holdings will be speedily and easily whittled down. The active peasant population will readily gain the upper hand over representatives of the large proprietor class by first of all confiscating their estates for the benefit of the community and then integrating them naturally into the social organization.

Let us draw the attention of the peasant population to expanded cooperative organizations (artels) and production for distribution. Our reckoning is that cooperative organization is, as an initial phase, the most appropriate and natural step along the road to constructing the agricultural economy on new foundations.

What is called the "soviet economy," where, inevitably, wage-slavery and arbitrariness and violence from Bolshevik-Communist functionaries prevail, must be wholly eradicated. The issue of the role of capable and specialist agronomists, as well as sundry other problems can be settled through discussion, as will decisions taken by peasant organizations and peasant congresses. Wage-slavery in all its manifestations must be eradicated beyond recovery.

It is all too apparent that a fair solution and further evolution of the land question are largely and closely dependent upon an equitable solution of the labor question. It is also up to the workers' organizations to establish a number of links with the villages ... enough such links to be in a position to barter all sorts of industrially produced materials and items for agricultural produce. Only a close, brotherly union of worker and peasant in organizations for mutual aid in production and in economic exchange, will be able to devise a natural, well-planned and fair solution to the agrarian question.

The labor question.

Having witnessed many an attempt mounted by various political parties, "businessmen" or "erudite personages" to resolve the labor issue: and having scrupulously examined the idea and the results of state take-over (nationalization) of the means and instruments of worker production (the mines, communications, workshops, factories, etc.) as well as of the workers' organizations themselves (trades unions, factory and workshop committees, cooperatives, etc.), we can announce with certainty that there is one genuine and fair solution to the workers' question: the transfer of all the means, instruments and materials of labor, production and transportation, not to the complete disposal of the State — this new boss and exploiter which uses wage-slavery and is no less oppressive of the workers than private entrepreneurs — but to the workers' organizations and unions in natural and free association with one another and in liaison with peasant organizations through the good offices of their economic soviets.

It is our conviction that only such a resolution of the labor issue will release the energy and activity of the worker masses, give a fresh boost to repair of the devastated industrial economy, render exploitation and oppression impossible, and put paid to speculation and swindling and bring to an end the artificial escalation of prices and runaway rise in the cost of living.

We have come to the belief that only the workers, with the help of their free organizations and unions, will be able to secure their release from the yoke of State and Capital (private and state alike), take over the working of mineral and coal reserves, get workshops and factories back into operation, establish equitable exchanges of products between different regions, towns and countryside, get rail traffic moving again, in short, breathe life back into the moribund shell of our economic organization.

No State authorities, no party, no system for direction and supervision of workers, commissars, officials, political activists and others can, we are thoroughly persuaded, meet the target set. The organization of work, production, transportation, distribution and exchange should be the task of free workers' unions, abetted by experienced and competent individuals, in a context of free labor in factories and workshops.

In order to ensure that such organization is active and its development fruitful it is vital that, above all else, genuine worker congresses and conferences be prepared on free foundations, without pressures or dictatorship from parties or individuals. Only those free congresses and conferences will have the capacity to arrive at an effective resolution of all the urgent issues of worker life and of worker construction along necessary and purposeful lines.

Needless to say, just resolution of and further progress on the worker question are largely dependent on an equitable solution to the supply issue and the division of the land, as well as the financial question which is also closely bound up with the worker question.

෴

The housing issue is part and parcel of this and so we are offering only the essence of our position on this matter: one of the primary tasks of the free worker organizations is to see to equitable allocation of available accommodation and thereby pursue the construction of requisite housing and this is achievable only in collaboration with those in charge of housing management (the house and district committee).

The financial question.

The financial system cannot be divorced from the capitalist system. The latter will soon be replaced by free communist organization of the economy, which will incontrovertibly lead to the disappearance of the finance system and its replacement by direct exchange of produce through the social organization of production, transportation and distribution.

However this transformation will not be effected in a day. Although the monetary system today may be in complete disarray it must of necessity continue to operate for a time. For the moment, it is vital that it be organized on new foundations.

Thus it is not a matter of retaining or re-establishing it, but only of adapting it on a temporary basis to fairer ground rules. Up until the October coup d'état, the people's wealth was concentrated either in the State's hands or in those of the capitalists and their agencies. Compulsory taxation and growing exploitation were at the root of this concentration. The Bolshevik-Communist authorities set themselves above the toilers as a boss-exploiter-State. They see themselves as the rulers and organizers of the country's monetary system. In fact the Bolshevik State and its officials have sole disposition of the people's wealth. In our view, this situation has to change radically.

In keeping with the introduction and expansion of the system of free toilers' soviets, ushering in a new and free life, all compulsory taxation should be discontinued and replaced by free and voluntary contributions from toilers. In a context of free and independent construction, these contributions will undoubtedly produce the best results.

By implication, the State's centralized public treasury, in whatever form it may appear (even in the guise of "People's Bank") should be wound up and replaced by the decentralized system of genuine people's banks established along cooperative lines. The founders and depositors of these banks should be workers and peasants only, that is to say their associations, unions and organizations, on the basis of a freely agreed levy.

In the case of unavoidable outlay on this or that undertaking or service at a regional or even national level (take Posts and Telegraphs, for instance), the general congress or soviet of that agency should receive the required sum from the people's banks. These latter may be communal, soviet or social, etc. as the case may be. The amount of these voluntary contributions will be determined by reckoning social needs and outlays. Not one single kopeck of the people's money may be spent without the express permission of the organization (be it congress, commune, soviet or union). At the appointed time, the different social services and agencies submit their projected expenditure to their respective agencies which, if need be, endorse the projected budget.

Such, in broad outline, is the financial system which we think should be employed during the time when currency and money circulation are still extant. Only that sort of an arrangement is going to be fully compatible with an authentic soviet system.

As regards currency as such, at the outset there may be more of this in circulation than needed. Thus, as the new organization of labor is reinforced and develops, workers and peasants will move from the money system towards the system of simply recording social labor performed. Such recording will afford the bearer the right to draw from social stores and markets those items and articles of which he has need, and which will begin to be in plentiful supply thanks to the organization of the new need-centered economic machinery.

The day is not far off when every toiler, thanks to his labors on society's behalf (and thus on his own behalf as a member of society) will upon producing the necessary proof, be able to obtain those products and goods he cannot do without.

The national question.

Clearly, each national group has a natural and indisputable entitlement to speak its language freely, live in accordance with its customs, retain its beliefs and rituals, draw up its school books and have its own managerial establishments and agencies: in short, to maintain and develop its national culture in every sphere. It is obvious that this clear and specific stance has absolutely nothing to do with narrow nationalism of the "separatist" variety which pits nation against nation and substitutes an artificial and harmful separation for the struggle to achieve a natural social union of toilers in one shared social communion.

In our view, national aspirations of a natural, wholesome character (language, customs, culture, etc.) can achieve full and fruitful satisfaction only in the union of nationalities rather than in their antagonism. One people's struggle for liberation leads naturally to the same chauvinistic struggle on the part of other peoples and the upshot, inevitably, is isolation and animosity between the different nations. Of necessity, this appreciation of the national question, a profoundly bourgeois and negative one, leads on to absurd and bloody national conflicts.

The speedy construction of a new life on socialist foundations will ineluctably lead to development of the culture peculiar to each nationality. Whenever we Makhnovist insurgents speak of independence of the Ukraine, we ground it in the social and economic plane of the toilers. We proclaim the right of the Ukrainian people (and every other nation) to self-determination, not in the narrow, nationalist sense of a Petliura, but in the sense of the toilers' right to self-determination. We declare that the toiling folk of the Ukraine's towns and countryside have shown everyone through their heroic fight that they do not wish any longer to suffer political power and have no use for it, and that they consciously aspire to a libertarian society. We thus declare that all political power of whatever provenance, that seeks to rule and direct by means of constraint and arbitrariness, is to be regarded by the toiling Ukrainian masses as an enemy and counter-revolutionary. To the very last drop of their blood they will wage a ferocious struggle against it, in defense of their entitlement to self-organization.

Needless to say, in the society founded on truly soviet foundations, such as we have spelled them out, the question of proportional representation and other political procedures do not arise.

Culture and education.

In a free society, culture and education cannot be the monopoly of the State, nor of government. They can only be the concern of individuals and organizations freely and naturally united with one another. The living and free creation of the cultural values to which the spirit of the toiling masses will cling can only come about in those conditions.

Civil liberties.

It must be self-evident that the free organization of society affords every practical opportunity for realization of what are called "civil liberties:" freedom of speech, of the press, of conscience, of worship, of assembly, of union, of organization, etc.

The defense of society.

For as long as the free society may need to look to its defenses against outside attack, it will have to organize its self-defenses, its army. We see this as a free contingent, founded on the principle of election to positions of responsibility, and closely tied to the populace. It should be placed under the authority of the toilers' organizations of the towns and countryside, so as to protect them against any violent trespass on the part of any State or capitalist power, and to guarantee them freedom of social construction.

Relations with foreign states.

The expanded congresses that represent all the organizations from the towns and villages — which make up the free society — will appoint a commission whose task it is to maintain regular relations with foreign states. This activity ought to be public and free of ambiguousness: no "secret diplomacy" can be countenanced. Issues that the commission cannot resolve will be left for extra-ordinary congresses to debate and determine.

Such, as we see it, are the bases upon which the free, just and wholesome society for which we are fighting, should be founded.

It is not for us to impose these ideas upon the toiling populace through coercion: our reckoning is that our duty is merely to make our view known and to offer workers and peasants the chance to debate this viewpoint freely — this and others as well, so that they may have absolute freedom to opt for this or that path to the economic and social reconstruction of society.

We are convinced of it: it is only by appealing to the most comprehensive freedom of inquiry and experiment in matters of reconstruction that the toiling population will be able to devise the natural route that leads on to an authentic and wholesome socialism. This freedom of inquiry and experimentation in construction we shall maintain and defend with all our might: it will no doubt be defended in the same way by all the toilers of the Ukraine whom we call upon to take a hand in our great common fight, amending as the need arises the inevitable mistakes and shortcomings, by displaying their sympathy and bolstering it through the continual recruitment of new fighters and defenders of freedom. It is through the concerted efforts of the broader community of toilers that the shape of the new society will be freely molded, and by defending this entitlement to creative freedom with armed force that *we shall win.*

Document No. 3

To the entire working population of the city of Alexandrovsk and environs. Comrades and Citizens!

Detachments of the Revolutionary Insurgent Army of the Ukraine (Makhnovist) are at present stationed in your city. That army has broken the back of the Denikinists, defeating them between Uman and Pomoshnaya, and is hotly pursuing the remnants of the enemy as they flee eastwards.

The staff and the entire Makhnovist movement deem it their most important duty to inform you of the following:

1. Hitherto you have been told on every side that Makhnovists were bandits, brigands, and pogromists. Be informed that this is the foulest slander. The members of our insurgent army are decent revolutionary peasants and workers. In any case, let the peaceable population of the city, regardless of nationality, be assured of its safety, let it carry on blithely with its work and let it not look upon us as its enemies.

2. The Revolutionary Insurgent Army has set itself the goal of assisting the peasants and the workers in their long and demanding struggle to emancipate toilers from every form of the yoke of capital and political power, a catastrophic yoke which they can well do without. For that reason, our army appears as the friend and defender of the workers, peasants and the poor generally. It relies not only upon their sympathy and their trust but equally upon their collaboration and involvement.

Whilst not meddling in the civilian life of the population, the Insurgent Army will be taking certain essential measures aimed at the wealthy bourgeois class, as well as at Denikinists and their supporters. Measures that will be enforced in an organized way. Persons who may arrive to carry out searches and make arrests in the name of the Makhnovists should, if they fail to produce a warrant, seal and signature from the unit commander and signature of the army inspection service, be instantly placed under arrest and brought before the unit staff or that of the inspection branch.

The same procedure should be applied to looters and assailants who may face execution on the spot.

3. The Revolutionary Insurgent Army urges the toiling population of the city and its environs to embark forthwith upon independent organizational endeavor, to wit: any organization representative of local factory workers, railroad workers, posts and telegraphs employees and peasants shall convene a general conference

of representatives of all the region's toilers. That conference is to raise, discuss and resolve a whole series of social and economic issues: city defenses, organization of fair distribution of essential goods and socially useful items available in the city; it will see to relations between the city and the villages so as to organize exchange of goods and merchandise.

This assembly will lay the lasting groundwork for a free system of peasant and worker soviets. Non-authoritarian reconstruction of social and economic life should thus be initiated.

4. The Revolutionary Insurgent Army calls upon the entire toiling population of the city and its environs to embark in a general way upon autonomous activity in matters social and military alike. The insurgent army will withdraw from the city just as soon as its work has been completed. The toiling population itself is to see to the organization of its social and economic life as well as its defenses against all trespass on the part of the bourgeoisie and any authorities, and is to take upon itself the struggle for the complete success of the revolution.

> Alexandrovsk, October 7, 1919.
> The Staff of the Insurgent Army (Makhnovist)

Document No. 4

Peasant Comrades!

The toiling peasantry of the Ukraine has been struggling against its age-old enemies and oppressors for many a long year. Thousands of the finest sons of the revolution have fallen in the struggle for complete emancipation of toilers from every yoke. A mortal blow was dealt to the butcher Denikin through the heroic efforts of the insurgent army of the Ukraine. The peasant insurgents, with their guide — Batko Makhno — at their head, stayed for long months in the rear of the White Guard enemy, surrounded by an enemy outnumbering them ten to one, and decimated by the most horrific malady — typhus — which daily carried off hundreds of the finest fighters in their ranks: running low on munitions, they all swooped upon the enemy with daggers drawn, and under their mighty onslaught Denikin's best troops, the units of General Shkuro and Mamontov, took to their heels. At the cost of unbelievable effort and blood spilled by the best fighters, insurgent peasants destroyed Denikin's rear and opened up a route to brethren in the North, peasants and workers: in the wake of Denikin's hordes, Red Army comrades entered the Ukraine — workers and peasants from the north. In turn, the toiling peasantry of the Ukraine was confronted by — besides the broader issue of the fight against the White Guards — the problem of building a real soviet order, in which soviets elected by the toilers would be servants of the people, carrying out decisions that the toilers themselves would reach at a Pan-Ukrainian congress of toilers.

However, the Communist Party leaders who, in the Red Army, had created a blind and docile tool for defending the commisarocracy, set about mudslinging and peddling the worst calumnies about the best leaders of the insurgents, having determined to "grasp the nettle" and destroy the revolutionary insurgent movement which was hindering these commissar gentlemen from lording it over the toilers of the Ukraine. In the toilers, these commissarocrats wish to see only "a human weapon," as Trotsky said at one congress, only cannon fodder to be hurled at anyone one wants but who must on no account be afforded the right to dispense with the Communists' help and make their own working lives and their own order for themselves.

Peasant comrades! The insurgent army of the Ukraine (Makhnovist) is drawn from among you. Your sons, your brothers and your fathers have filled our ranks. The insurgent army is blood of your blood, flesh of your flesh. Having sacrificed tens of thousands of victims, the insurgent army has fought for the toilers' right to build their order for themselves, to determine the disposition of their goods for themselves and not for all the world to hand over to the commissars.

The insurgent army has fought and fights still for real soviets and not for the Cheka and commissarocracy. In the days of the hangman — the Hetman's day — and the Germans and Denikin, the insurgents rose up en masse against oppressors in the defense of the toiling people. Now too the insurgent army considers that it has a sacred duty to defend the interests of the toiling peasantry against attempts by these commissar gentlemen to hitch the Ukraine's toiling peasantry to their chariot. The insurgent army knows these "upstarts" only too well and well remembers these "liberator" commissars. The autocrat Trotsky has ordered the disarming of the insurgent army set up by the peasants themselves in the Ukraine, for he appreciates that as long as the peasants have their army defending their interests he will never be able to force the toiling people of the Ukraine to march under his baton. By avoiding clashes with the Red Army and abiding only by the wishes of the toilers, the insurgent army, not wishing to shed fraternal blood, will take care to protect the toilers' interests and will lay down its arms only on the instructions of a free Pan-Ukrainian toilers' congress, at which the toilers themselves will articulate their wishes. The insurgent army — the sword in the hands of the toilers — calls upon you, peasant comrades, immediately to convene your own congress of toiling muzhiks and to take into your own hands both the further pursuit of your well-being and your hard-earned wealth.

It is true that the power-hungry commissars will take every step to thwart the holding of a free congress of toilers: for that reason and in the very interests of the toilers the stifling of this congress by the commissars must not be allowed: to that end, it should be clandestine and held in a secret location.

Peasant comrades, prepare yourselves for the holding of your congress! Make haste to accomplish your task! Your enemies are not sleeping; don't you sleep either: that will ensure your victory!

Long live the free congress of the region's toilers! Down with commissarocracy! Long live the insurgent peasant army!

February 8, 1920.
The staff of the insurgent army of the Ukraine (Makhnovist).

Document No. 5

Who are the Makhnovists and for what do they fight?

1. The Makhnovists are workers and peasants who rose up back in 1918 against the oppression of the bourgeois power in the Ukraine of the Austro-Hungarian and German occupiers and of the Hetman. The Makhnovists are toilers who have raised the banner of revolt against Denikin, against any yoke, any violence and any falsehood, from wherever they may come. The Makhnovists are the very toilers whose labors enrich, fatten and sustain the bourgeoisie in general and at present the Bolshevik bourgeoisie in particular.

2. Why do we call ourselves Makhnovists?

Because in the darkest days of the reaction in the Ukraine we have seen among us through thick and thin, our friend and guide Makhno whose voice has spoken out against all oppression of toilers throughout the Ukraine, inciting struggle against all oppressors and all the marauders and political tricksters who misled us. Now this friend through thick and thin still marches in our ranks towards our ultimate objective: the emancipation of toilers from every yoke.

3. How do we see any emancipation coming to pass?

Through the overthrow of all government: monarchist, coalition, republican, Social Democrat, Bolshevik-Communist ... which must be replaced by a soviet re-gime independent of them all, and without authority or arbitrarily determined laws: for the soviet order is not the power of Bolshevik-Communist Social Democrats which currently proclaims itself the soviet power, but is instead the higher form of anti-authoritarian, anti-governmental socialism which expresses itself through the construction of a free, harmonious community independent of every power: and the social life of the toilers, wherein every individual toiler and the community in general will be able to seek a happy, prosperous life in an autonomous way accord-ing to the principles of solidarity, friendship and equality for all.

4. What is the Makhnovists' conception of the soviet regime?

The toilers themselves ought freely to choose their soviets: soviets that would carry out the wishes and decisions of these same toilers, which is to say executive soviets, not authoritarian ones.

The land, workshops, factories, mines, railways and other assets of the people should belong to the toilers who work there which is to say that these must be socialized.

5. What are the means used by the Makhnovists to attain these goals?

Revolutionary, unflinching and consistent struggle against all falsehood, all arbitrariness and all oppression, no matter whence it may come: this is a fight to the death, the struggle of free speech and true endeavor, conducted with weapons in hand. Through the elimination of all who govern, through destruction of all the foundations of their lies, whether in the political, statist or economic spheres. And it is only through destruction of the State and by means of social revolution that the realization of a truly soviet socialist regime of workers and peasants will be feasible.

> April 27, 1920.
> The Cultural Instruction Section of the (Makhnovist)
> Insurgent Army.

Document No. 6

Down with fratricidal strife!

Red soldier brethren: Nicholas's henchmen kept you in ignorance and led you into fratricidal war against the Japanese and then the Germans and many another people, simply to increase their own wealth, whereas all you had to look forward to was death at the front and complete ruination at home.

But the dark clouds and fog that blinded your eyes lifted, the sunlight broke through and touched you and you put paid to that fratricidal war. That, though, was only the calm before a fresh storm broke.

Now they send you out again to fight us "Makhnovist insurgents" on behalf of a so-called "worker-peasant" power which once again brings you shackles and slavery! The wealth and the delights go to this gang of parasite bureaucrats who suck your blood. Can you have failed to grasp this in three years of fratricidal strife?

Will you again shed your blood for the freshly resurrected bourgeoisie and for the commissars it has created who dispatch you to the slaughter like cattle!

Have you not yet understood that we "Makhnovist insurgents" are fighting for complete economic and political emancipation of the toilers, for a free life without these commissars and other agents of repression!

May the dawn rise also over your camp and show you the way that leads to eradication of fratricidal strife among the toiling masses. On that road you will find us and you will go on fighting in our ranks for a better future, for a free life. At every encounter with us and in order to avert shedding of brothers' blood, send us your delegates for talks, but if this is not possible and the commissars force you to fight us anyway, throw down your rifles and come to our fraternal embrace!

Down with the fratricidal war between toilers!

Long live the peace and fraternal union of toilers of every land and nation!

May 1920.
The Makhnovist Insurgents.

Document No. 7

To all toilers of cart and hammer!

Brothers! a new and mortal danger threatens all toilers. All the dark forces of the former lackeys of Nicholas the Bloody have come together and with the help of the Polish lords, French instructors and the traitor Petliura are bearing down on the Ukraine to restore the autocracy among us, and burden us with the estate-owners, capitalists, land agents, gendarmes and all the other executioners of the peasants and workers.

Comrades! the commissars and leaders of the Bolshevik-Communists are good warriors only when they are fighting poor folk. Their punitive detachments and Cheka are above all expert in killing workers and peasants and torching villages and countryside. But against the revolution's real enemies, against Denikin and the other bands, they shamefully take to their heels, like the despicable cowards that they are.

You, comrades, will not have forgotten how last year, the gold braid-wearers all but entered Moscow and, had they not been stopped by the insurgents, the tricolor flag of Autocracy would long since have been unfurled over revolutionary Russia.

The situation is the same now, comrade! The Red Army, sold out at every turn by its generals and cowardly commissars, quits the front in panic, ceding region after region to the Polish lords. The towns of Zhitomir, Kiev and Zhmerinka have long since been occupied by the Poles: the White Guards' front line nears Poltava and Kherson. And in the Crimea, Denikinists who have been dug in for the last four months await the opportune moment to reoccupy our native regions.

Brothers! Are you going to blithely await the arrival of the Whites without lifting a finger, are you going to yield up your wives and your children to the exactions of the generals and the Polish Lords?

No, that must not be. As of one mind, to arms and join the ranks of the insurgents!

Rise up along with all of us Makhnovists against all oppressors! In every village, organize detachments and liaise with us! Together we shall drive out the commissars and Cheka, and along with Red Soldier comrades we shall build a solid fighting front against Denikin, Petliura and the Polish Lords!

Comrades! This is not the time to delay: organize your detachments without delay. To work!

Death and ruination to all oppressors and lordlings!

Let us commit ourselves to the crucial final struggle for a true Soviet regime, in which there will be neither Lords nor serfs!

To arms, brothers!

> May 1920.
> The Cultural Instruction Section of the Revolutionary
> Insurgents (Makhnovists) of the Ukraine.

Document No. 8

To the young!

Why do you stay at home, comrade? Why are you not in our ranks? Or perhaps you await the arrival of the commissar with his punitive expedition to enlist you by force? Do not kid yourself with the thought that they will not find you, that you will be able to hide, to run away. The Bolshevik authorities have already proved that they will stop at nothing: they will arrest your family and your parents and will take hostages: when they so choose, they will have their artillery bombard the whole village and so, sooner or later, you and your chum who is still at large will be carried off by the government as soldiers.

And then they will send you, weapon in hand, to kill your own worker and peasant brothers, the revolutionary Makhnovist insurgents ...

So we Makhnovist insurgents are not stay-at-homes, although each of us has a family and parents and dear loved ones, whom we have been reluctant to leave. But we are revolutionaries. We cannot look on with indifference as the toiling people is once again reduced to serfdom, as new despots posing as socialists and revolutionaries and displaying the badge of worker-peasant power, lord it over us without control.

Three years of revolution have clearly demonstrated that all power is counter-revolutionary, whether it be the power of Nicholas the Bloody or that of the Bolshevik-Communists. We Makhnovists have raised the banner of insurrection for a complete social revolution against all power, against all oppressors and we fight for the free soviets of toilers.

Join us, comrade! Let the rogue and the coward hide behind someone's skirts at home, we have no need of those who hide behind anyone's skirts. But you, decent worker or peasant, your place is with us, with the Makhnovist insurgent revolutionaries. We press no one into service. But remember that with their savage repression the Bolshevik authorities have forced us into a struggle without quarter.

So make up your mind, comrade! Mobilized by the commissars, you will be sent against us and we will be forced to deal with you as an adversary and as an enemy of the revolution. With us or against us. The choice is yours!

> June 1920.
> The Makhnovist insurgents.

Document No. 9

The Makhnovists' address to the toiling Cossacks of the Don and Kuban.

Cossack toiler comrades! For two years you have groaned beneath the yoke of the tsarist general Denikin. For two years your sworn enemies, the big landowners and lordlings have forced you to defend their riches and the oppressors of the toiling people. For two years running, they have squeezed you in a vice. While the wealthy amassed their riches from your blood and sweat, made merry and gave themselves up to debauchery. For two years, the blood and tears of the toilers have flowed in the Kuban and on the Don. For two years, the revolution was smothered in your region, Cossack toilers.

Through your efforts, comrades, the yoke of Denikin and his gang has been shrugged off and the revolution is triumphant once again in the Kuban and on the Don.

However, scarcely had you had time, comrades, to recover from the nightmare you lived under Denikin before new oppressors arrived in your regions.

The party of the Bolshevik-Communists, having seized power, dispatched its commissars and Cheka to your villages and your stanitsas: they oppress you no less than their tsarist henchmen predecessors, Cossack toilers.

As under Denikin, the Bolshevik authorities' punitive detachments seize your wheat and livestock, and take your sons, and if you dare to protest at the violence done before your eyes, well, they will flog, imprison and indeed shoot you.

Why, then, Cossack toiler comrades, did you revolt against Denikin if it was only to place yourselves under a new yoke now in the shape of the Bolshevik-Communists? Is that what you shed your blood for, to allow the commissars and power-lovers now to lord it over you, stifle you and do violence to you?

Listen, brothers, to what we Makhnovist revolutionary peasants have to tell you. We too have been oppressed since the revolution by a whole series of powers and parties. At first the Austrian and German oppressors tried to reign over us along with the Hetman: then it was the adventurer Petliura, then the Bolshevik-Communists, and General Denikin. But we very quickly disabused them of any inclination to carry it on and, as you have certainly heard tell, as early as the summer of 1918, with the Gulyai-Polye peasant, toilers' friend, anarchist and revolutionary Nestor Makhno as our guide (he whom the tsarist authorities had locked up for more than ten years in its prisons and penitentiaries because of his love for the toiling people), we rose up and drove out the Austro-German bands and for nearly two years now we have been pressing on with our struggle against all oppressors of the toilers. We are now waging a relentless struggle against agents and commissars of the Bolshevik authorities: we execute and drive these oppressors from our regions.

The ranks of our revolutionary insurgent detachments are swelling daily. All the oppressed and humiliated join our ranks and the time is approaching when the toiling people in our region will rise up and drive out the power of charlatan Bolshevik politicians, just as they did before with Denikin.

But having driven out the Bolshevik oppressors, it is our intention to entrust power over us to nobody from now on, for we Makhnovists consider that the toiling people has long ceased to be a flock of sheep for anyone to lead as he may see fit. We find that the toilers will be able to organize a free regime of soviets along independent lines, dispensing with party, commissars and generals: a soviet regime in which those who will have been chosen as members of the soviet will not, as now they can, be able to command us and give us orders, but will instead be the instruments of what we will have determined at our assemblies and toilers' congresses.

We will make every effort to ensure that all the wealth of the country such as the land, mines, workshops, factories, railways and the rest belong not to private individuals nor to the State, but exclusively to those who work them.

We shall not put up our weapons until such time as we have eliminated economic or political servitude once and for all, until such time as genuine equality and fraternity reign on earth.

That, comrades, is what we fight for and what we summon you Cossack toilers of the Don and the Kuban to fight for.

In our insurgent army there is a goodly number of Don and Kuban Cossacks: they formed two cavalry regiments which fought bravely with us against the Denikinists. We now call upon you Cossack toilers again, to join our ranks in order to wage a common struggle against the oppressors and the Red hangmen Trotsky and Lenin. Enough of slavish submission and toleration of the yoke and the power which calls itself worker-peasant. To arms and into the ranks of the revolutionary insurgents, and then we shall quickly rid anyone and everyone of this urge to oppress and grind us down.

Do not, comrades, believe the calumnies that label us bandits or which say that we are only a gang. These are lies peddled by the Commissars for the sole purpose of misleading the peasant toilers and workers who are well aware that Makhnovists are decent toilers who, having no wish to be enslaved, have risen up to free themselves once and for all from every yoke. Do not believe the Bolsheviks' newspapers which report virtually every day that Batko Makhno has been killed and that we Makhnovists have been crushed. These are only lies. Batko Makhno lives and continues with us to defeat the regiments and punitive detachments of the power of the commissars day after day, striking mortal panic into the hearts of Red oppressors.

Rise up, Cossack toilers, against the yoke and oppression of the commissars! Do not let them set foot in your villages and stanitsas! Pay them no taxes! Deny them your wheat! Do not let them take your sons as soldiers! Organize your insurgent detachments. Execute the aggressors. Join with us. We will afford you all possible help.

Enough of slavish forbearance! Let us put an end to the vexations visited upon us!

Long live the insurrection for a genuine system of worker and peasant soviets! Long live the free Don and the free Kuban!

Long live the fraternal union of the toilers of every land and all nations!

Long live the social revolution!

> June 1920.
> The Soviet of the Revolutionary Insurgents of the Ukraine (Makhnovists).

Document No. 10

Workers, peasants, and Red soldiers!

With your own eyes you saw how the villainous bourgeoisie, with Denikin and company at its head, sought to reduce the workers and peasants to serfdom for fully a century and tried to reintroduce the feudal system of the great landowners. But they have been definitively crushed through the spirit of revolutionary revolt that is abroad among the Makhnovists.

Now again the beast bares its fangs: abetted by the western bourgeoisie of which it seems to be the final card, it hurls its hordes upon us, seeking to subject us to its power and foist its yoke upon us. We can have but one reaction: to have no truce of any sort with them, for we have set ourselves a single goal: to fight to the last drop of blood to annihilate our bourgeoisie once and for all, and with it the worldwide bourgeoisie, or perish in the attempt.

Listen to what the Bolshevik-Communists, the agents of the "worker and peasant" government, say about us. By means of craven falsehoods they accuse us in their slanderous propaganda of siding with Wrangel: which makes them the laughing-stock of workers and peasants the world over. Have they no shame? Do not they themselves represent the new counter-revolution with their authoritarian institutions like the Cheka and the power of the commissars who make up a new aristocracy like the autocracy before them?

Yes, we must record the fact that the only ones responsible for the emergence of the counter-revolution are the Bolsheviks themselves, the advocates of the "socialist State." They lead us in the direction of State capitalism, of new despots at home and they revive private capitalism, our greatest enemy.

We Makhnovists will either fall in combat or we will win and destroy the new capitalism in both its guises, and we will build a new life under a genuinely free socialism!

Down with oppressors of the toiling people, whether they come from the Right or Left!

Long live the worldwide union of towns and villages!

Long live the social revolution!

> July 1920.
> The Information Committee of the Insurgent Army of the Ukraine (Makhnovist).

Document No. 11

The Makhnovist conception of soviets

The first session of the free soviet of Gulyai-Polye was held in the great hall of the town's college. The teacher Chernoknizhny, chairman of the soviet, gave this address:

"Comrades! Let us salute the formation of Gulyai-Polye's first free soviet. On this occasion, I think it essential that a brief general account be given of the nature, organization and import of free toilers' soviets such as they have been established at the toilers' own instigation in this free region of ours.

Let it be stated first of all that the characteristic feature of social life among us takes the form of toilers' self-governance in local affairs; this going hand in glove with organization of the partisan struggle: and all of this is at odds with the Bolsheviks' conception of political soviets.

The free soviets of toilers represent a firm realization of the principles underlying such self-governance...

- Soviets free, in that they are wholly independent of any central authority whatever and are elected with complete independence to boot.
- Soviets of toilers, in that they are founded on a basis of shared labor and embrace only toilers, operate in accordance with their wishes, serve their interests alone and are wholly impervious to any and all political influence.

Each such soviet is executor of the wishes of local toilers and their organizations. Soviets elsewhere, which are to liaise closely with them, will be able to set up popular self-governance bodies, coordinating their activities insofar as their territorial remit and economic activities require.

Publication of a declaration on the principles, broad characteristics and organization of free soviets on the part of the Military Revolutionary Soviet[1] represents the prescribed constitution of these organizations.

It is interesting to note that since its inception, the idea of free soviets has begun to be favorably and instantly received by the masses, and has spread in very quick order to regions far removed from Gulyai-Polye.

Having instinctively grasped the simple system of free soviets, the peasants have striven slowly but surely to establish such organizations. Once they have accomplished this, they will indubitably become its staunchest supporters and will without the shadow of a doubt feel that this is a wholesome foundation that guarantees the construction of a shared, free existence.

Likewise appreciation of the necessity for direct union with the workers of neighboring towns is beginning to ripen and gain ever greater sway over the peasant masses.

Let us quote the example of the Gulyai-Polye peasants' appeal: "Worker, hold out your hand to the peasant," which has not gone unheeded: it spreads and is discussed and has become our region's watchword: among the urban workers whom it has reached it arouses lively interest. And neither encirclement by hostile forces from every camp, nor the expression of other schools of thought, are impediments to propagation of the notion of a rapprochement between workers and peasants.

The conception of free, toilers' soviets springs from life itself. This transitional form of self-governance leads on in practice to the non-authoritarian order of the future, founded upon principles of unrestricted freedom, complete equality and fraternity.

In other words I would say that the libertarian current will, in this way, have found its true expression, its rightful one: social action. The receptivity of the toilers is an irrefutable demonstration that love of liberty is abroad among the peasants, as is the unshakable determination to play their parts in the building of a free, independent and egalitarian life.

In a different, less troubled context, that same movement could have taken a different tack, found expression in quite different ways and would also have been quite wholesome, original and deliberate in its development. Ultimately, we must believe that it would have led to construction of the groundwork of a really free society of toilers.

But to our regret, these are at present naught but dreams, for harsh reality presents a very different face. What does this consist of, exactly?

The fact of the matter is that even now the traditional enemy of Labor and of Liberty — Authority — is making inroads in this region of ours. The essential and underlying motivation of the exploiters who invade our region (Bolsheviks and Denikinists) consists of their steadfast determination to assert their power by violently eradicating everyone else's freedom and, what is more, wholly reducing the toilers to the status of inanimate objects.

By such methods, all these statist-authoritarians will annihilate all the efforts and advances of the toilers.

In the first instance, the peasant's life and labors would be saddled with the yoke of the Cheka and the Sovnarkom [soviet of people's commissars], which is to say a gang of adventurers, expert in political chicanery: the very same people who have adroitly deceived the toilers and have turned the Russian social revolution into a vague effervescence of the masses.

In the second instance, the peasant has to look to the rule of the cosh of these privileged "gentlemen" who hide behind the gold-braided saber-draggers.

The peasantry could not and of course would not accept this prospect, once having sampled the fruits of the liberty tree. For that very reason, it has risen up as one man in defense of its derided interests. It has risen because it has once and for all rejected state exploitation of society, rejected economic plunder and political whimsy.

❦

"I call upon you," Chernoknizhny closed, "to watch over the peasantry's ideal of free, toilers' soviets, as you would over the apple of your eye, for, as I have indicated, such soviets assure the people of authentic self-governance by the toilers themselves and lead on to real freedom, genuine equality and honest fraternity."

Note to Document 11

1. A reference to the Draft Declaration: see Document No. 2.

Bibliographical Afterword (1984)

It seems opportune here to review some new publications and information that have come to light since the publication of our biographical study, itself the fruit of 18 years of research and authentication, which is to say that it was by no means improvised, which is more than can be said of most of the publications on the subject. Generally the sensational aspects of certain accusations and allegations is played up so as to overshadow the real import of the Makhnovist insurgent movement. This is true for example of the publication by Pavel Litvinov (the grandson of Stalin's Foreign Affairs minister of that name) of a samizdat text (i.e. a clandestinely self-published text) entitled *Nestor Makhno and the Jewish Question*.[1] Litvinov is at pains to show that Makhno was never an anti-Semite, quite the opposite indeed, that he "deserves to be held in high regard and have his memory honored by Jews." Quite an attractive and welcome undertaking this, were it not for the fact that it is bringing coals to Newcastle for, as we have pointed out before, even Bolshevik historical studies have always repudiated this absurd allegation of anti-Semitism on Makhno's part. What is more, Litvinov ties in this issue with the rebirth of Jewish nationhood and indeed with the attempt to create some revolutionary Jewish "Zion" in the Ukraine! What is to be welcomed though is the fact that Litvinov capitalizes upon the opportunity to retrace the main features and accomplishments of the Makhnovist movement, especially its crucial part in defeating the Whites. Let it be noted that essentially the sources that he has used have been published outside Russia: some come from Russian anarchist reviews and other works published in France and in the United States during the 1920s and 1930s: which is to say that against all the odds they have achieved their objectives even inside Russia by helping to restore the truth of events. Aside from a few mistakes — Litvinov has Makhno working in Paris as a film technician! — this essay does deserve to be more widely known, especially in Israel and among Jewish readers, given that many of these still place credence in the "rumors" about Makhno. On the other hand, it has nothing new to offer Western readers who have access to much more comprehensive texts and works on the subject: also, it is hard to fathom the sensational publicity accorded Litvinov's essay by certain French and Italian anarchists.[2] Maybe because for such a long time there was a dearth of historical and theoretical investigations and works on the subject of anarchism, this accounts for many anarchists having become "avid consumers" and applauding as soon as some academic or somebody quite removed from the movement and its beliefs, deigns to show an interest in Anarchy!

⁂

We have also come by another Russian manuscript text dealing with the life of Lev Zadov-Zinkovsky, the commander of the unit that smuggled the gravely wounded Makhno over the border into Romania in August 1921. The author of this manuscript, one Jacob Gridin, describes himself as a former member of the NKVD, (the Cheka was first renamed the GPU, then became the NKVD before becoming the KGB of today) and a recent emigrant to Israel. According to Gridin, Zadov — who had for a time been chief of the Makhnovist intelligence service — allegedly contacted the GPU while in exile in Romania and rendered it valuable services. In particular he is alleged to have lured a captain of the French counter-espionage service into an ambush in the Ukraine and to have murdered him in his sleep, all in order to prove his bona fides to the GPU and secure rehabilitation for himself as well as for his brother. This little spy story even features a grieving and pretty widow whom this Zadov allegedly took it upon himself to console! Where the shoe pinches is with the allegation that Zadov had been ordered by his Muscovite superiors to "liquidate" Makhno who, it is alleged, was then (in 1922) to be found in one of Warsaw's finest hotels (in fact, Makhno was then sampling the "delights" of a lengthy and uncomfortable stay in the city's political prison!). Zadov purportedly accomplished this task successfully and lived a life of ease up until the "nasty" Stalinist purges of 1938, whereupon he is alleged to have met his end.

As we know nothing of Zadov's true fate, it is still feasible to embroider upon what became of him: however, unlikely circumstances are rather too thick on the ground here and we should bear it in mind, first, that in Bolshevik studies, Lev Zadov and his brother are portrayed as the executors of Makhno's "dirty work" and especially as unmerciful Bolshevik-killers and, secondly, that they had been convinced anarchist activists ever since 1905, which fact had earned them several years in tsarist prisons, and thirdly, that they had repeatedly given proof of their devotion to the Makhnovist movement's cause.

All of which makes us skeptical about such unlikely claims about them, unless they have been confused with other individuals. Moreover, we should expect further revelations of the same sort from emigrating Soviet Jews, for a goodly number of them have, like Gridin, been ex-members of the GPU, or indeed privileged members of the State apparatus or other agencies of the regime, or indeed children or parents of such. Self-evidently there is no question of placing the slightest credence in this sort of misrepresentation, unless of course there is documentary or tangible evidence to substantiate their ravings.

⁂

In our book we mentioned the existence of a manuscript essay of memories of Nestor Makhno by Ida Mett, a member of the *Dyelo Truda* group from 1925 to July 1928. A small publisher has had the bright idea of bringing this out as a 28-page booklet (starting from an original of just six and one quarter pages!) augmented by a few personal remarks on the "radicality of Nestor Makhno, in which respect he emerges as determinedly modern, in that, practically and historically he steps outside anarchist ideology.... For Makhno the revolution simply cannot be the endorsement of any ideology — even the anarchist one — but rather is the destruction of all ideologies."[3] For some years now, it has been fashionable to toss the term "ideology" around, until it has become universally applicable and all-embracing, but if one takes it to signify a coherent view of life and society there is much to be gained from comparing such glib and empty assertions with the views spelled out in great profusion in Makhno's own articles. As for Ida Mett's essay, we have already spelled out its limitations. Certain of her remarks are well "over the top": she has Makhno "jealous of the Jews," but "capable of being a friend to a Jew without a second thought."(?) She also has him "jealous of intellectuals" and, more seriously, "jealous" of the careers of Red generals Budyenny and Voroshilov, so much so that his "mind was stalked willy-nilly by the idea that he too could have been a Red Army general. However, he himself never told me as much."(!) Such a "telepathic" approach greatly undermines the relevance of her opinions and might even border upon base slander and backstairs gossip: it would have been better to call a halt to it. Ida Mett, whom we knew personally deserves to be assessed on other, more pertinent of her writings.

⚒

We come now to one of the most interesting of bibliographical novelties. In our biography of Makhno we mentioned the existence of certain manuscripts by Voline which had remained unpublished to date and to which we had been unable to gain access. They had been in the possession of Rosa Dubinsky, the widow of the first publisher of Voline's posthumous book *The Unknown Revolution* before being "retrieved" forcibly by Voline's eldest son, Igor Eichenbaum who at that time subscribed to political views far removed from those of his father. On the strength of what we had been told by Rosa Dubinsky, the historian Daniel Guérin seemed to have played an ambiguous role at the time of this episode. He subsequently forwarded to us a denial wherein he stated that this "episode had taken place unbeknownst to me."[5] Duly noted.

We have also learned since that several copies of these manuscripts were in circulation: first of all in the hands of Daniel Guérin, then with the Historical Secretariat of the French Anarchist Federation and finally Leo Eichenbaum, Voline's second son, had deposited a copy with the "Banque du Son et de l'Image" founded by Roland Fornari.[6] Thanks to the kindness of the latter, we were able to consult these famous unpublished notes by Voline. And what do they contain? Well, to our great astonishment there is first and foremost the conclusion to *The Unknown Revolution*, which four successive editions of that book have thus deliberately jettisoned! And a rather substantial text it is too — 110 pages — and only the portion dealing with the meeting with Voline and Trotsky in New York, shortly before their return to Russia in 1917, was used by Daniel Guérin in the latest edition of his anthology *Ni Dieu ni maître (No Gods No Masters)*. Given that Guérin was also involved in the publication of the two latest (French) editions of *The Unknown Revolution* we asked him why they had been bereft of this "conclusion" which is part and parcel of the whole. His reply was that the decision not to use it had been made jointly with Igor Eichenbaum in that it struck them that the contents of the "conclusion" "weakened" the rest of the book. Once we read it in our turn, we reached a different opinion for it strikes us as being quite consistent with Voline's psycho-moral analyses and whereas he is mistaken in presenting events worldwide *"from 1914 up until September 1940"* as the *"destructive period of the worldwide social revolution,"* one could forgive him this error but not in any way condone censoring his posthumous book of its "conclusion," which should be making sense of the whole thing. We can only hope that the next time the book is due for republication, this amputation will be well and truly repaired.

Among Voline's unpublished papers there is also correspondence of his from towards the end of his life, and here he tackles the subject of interest to us here. In a letter from Marseilles dated November 4, 1944, to one Henri, he berates a certain Frémont for allegedly *"peddling rumors about my relations with Makhno"*: Frémont had it from *"…Makhno's own lips that since a particular moment, the latter and I have not been such good friends as once we were,"* and had supposedly leveled the *"stupid charge"* against Voline of having *"stolen some documents from Makhno."* By way of *"formal and palpable proof of the nonsensicality of this crude invention,"* Voline cites three things in his defense: (1) he had allegedly *"sacrificed two whole years of my activities in 1921–1923 to bringing out Arshinov's* History of the Makhnovist Movement*"*: he goes on to say that *"…and I mean 'sacrificed,' for I could have devoted my free time instead to literary work of my own that I was pressed to do and that interested me."* (2) He had taken a back seat to Arshinov because he himself had only been involved with the Makhnovist movement for six months whereas Arshinov had been there right to the end and was consequently better *"qualified to write its history."* Subsequently he had only made use of the latter, and made do with adding a few personal anecdotes to that portion of *The Unknown Revolution* dealing with the Makhnovist movement. This is only a banal statement of facts obvious to any reader, but it is good to see Voline making it explicit himself: (3) he alludes to his work as "literary editor" of Volumes II and III of Makhno's *Memoirs* which appeared in Russian in 1936 and 1937. Translations into French of his forewords to both volumes followed, as did part of his introductory essay on the Makhnovist movement, lifted from *The Unknown Revolution*. Voline concludes his second letter of November 11, 1944, again to Henri, by hoping that his explanations *"will satisfy the comrades' curiosity and prove to them that the yarns about my conduct are merely the consequences of a crass and stupid calumny that was predicated upon many comrades' ignorance of the true situation."* Without more detailed knowledge of the precise contents of this alleged "calumny," we can only record what Voline has to say and of which everyone may make what they will.

Let us above all note Voline's important clarification of the fate of Makhno's manuscripts: Galina Kuzmenko, Nestor's wife, is supposed to have burned the valise filled with her spouse's papers during the German occupation and to have let Voline know shortly before she left for Germany in 1942. Let us stress her lack of imagination in so doing: she would have been better advised to entrust the papers to reliable friends or to some library.

In other letters addressed to Marie-Louise (Berneri?), Voline outlines a complete history of his writings on the Russian revolution and makes them the basis for *The Unknown Revolution*. He also announces a forthcoming work on Makhno but is having trouble finding the *"way to tackle it."* He is counting upon using the notes that he had used during lectures on Makhno in 1935–1936. Tuberculosis denied him the time to complete the undertaking and he died a short while later, leaving the project at the notes and outline stage, though these by themselves amount to 236 partly typewritten pages. Let us look at their contents.

The text is entitled *Makhno, a Contribution to Studies on the Enigma of the Personality*. Drafted in 1945, it deals with generalities regarding the Russian revolution and supplies autobiographical information on Voline himself. The first item of interest for our purposes is its disclosure of Voline's influence on Arshinov's *History of the Makhnovist Movement*. It had been at Voline's insistence that Arshinov had mentioned the movement's shortcomings and those of Makhno himself, after having retorted that *"set alongside the immeasurable positive aspects of the movement what few shortcomings there may have been are truly of no significance"* (pages 31, 45 and 126). According to Voline, such an "omission" on the movement's flaws was profoundly to be regretted for they *"are, in my estimation, more important than its positive sides."* That comment encapsulates the general tone: he alternates eulogy with the most acerbic criticism in, say, this thumbnail sketch of Makhno: *"He was an extremely complicated personality, 'muddled' would be the right word: a sort of formidable 'raw' genius riddled with boorish as well as refined shortcomings as outstanding as his traces of genius...." "Incontrovertibly he belongs in the Russian revolution to that category of personalities who remain in History forever a little woolly... Enormous positive qualities coexist alongside deep-seated negative dispositions"* (page 38).

In an uncompleted chapter entitled "The Nub of the Matter," Voline berates the existence in *"Ukranian peasants as well of course as among peasants (and even among manual workers generally) everywhere, of a sentiment that is a blend of mistrust, contempt and unspoken hostility which can stretch to fits of acute hatred towards intellectuals, 'non-manual [workers]' and 'non-peasants.'"* He then complains of the *"harmful prejudice very widespread among revolutionary militants"; "concealing as much and as long as possible from the 'public' and indeed from the ordinary party militants, shortcomings, 'blemishes,' faults and failings of the movement."* For his part, he had documented with *"disheartening and piece-meal slowness,"* the *"dark sides"* of Makhno's personality: in

1938, he *"already knew a fair amount,"* but, *"by the conclusion of my work (the end of 1941) I knew a lot more...."* One could marvel at such belated intelligence, for, as he himself admits, although he had spent six months in Makhno's company in 1919–1920, he had *"known nothing of the personal and intimate life that would have afforded access to the very depths of (Makhno's) personality."* Furthermore, the latter *"had never made the slightest move to strike up a more personal friendship with me";* thus in order to divine his real personality, he was to use as his chief source confidences of Makhno's spouse Galina Kuzmenko who it seems had been challenged by certain "Makhnovist commanders" living in France (Voline unfortunately refrains from giving their names) who allegedly regarded her as "mismatched" with Makhno.

Voline draws a very eulogistic portrait of Makhno's qualities: a *"very quick and, I should say, complete grasp of the truth which he managed to unravel from life as a whole."* ... *"Just and proper attention that never diminished to all that he regarded as important in life, his own or life in general ... possession of an extremely solid and luminous master-thought, that too is a stroke of genius."* ... *"A boundless daring and rashness in the face not just of combat but of life as a whole... he sought to make life what he wished to see of it"* ... *"a specifically fighting gift, I do not mean military... he never lost his cool head, his boldness and acted with simplicity, precision and at the same time with cold clear tactics until the objective was achieved."* However, as an *"unbalanced man of genius whose excitability was also beyond the norm,"* the more that Makhno *"displayed signs of genius, the more he knew of its ups and downs"* (pages 58–63). But after these roses come the thorns. Voline notes the temperamental incompatibility between them, so much so that when Makhno had him freed from Chekist jails in October 1920, Voline hesitated before he set off to join him in the Ukraine. Furthermore, Makhno had, according to Voline, the infuriating habit of constantly toying with his revolver even to the extent of threatening his future spouse with it, perhaps to "put her character to the test" (?), as well as members of the Makhnovist movement's soviet and above all he was wont to gun down deserters from the front, or insurgents guilty of outrages where they stood. He had allegedly killed folk *"without having looked into their case and not knowing if they were innocent or guilty"* (page 138). If well founded, this charge strikes us as the most considerable of Voline's criticisms, for it seems to us, where the rest are concerned, that we are dealing with a somewhat obsessive fixation on his part, deriving probably from the frictions between them as exiles, both personal (Makhno had accused him of dishonesty) and theoretical (Voline championed the Synthesis, whereas Makhno was a fervent supporter of the Platform).

Let us also take note of some startling inaccuracies in Voline's data: he has Makhno dying a year later than in fact he did and attributes to him as his real name the pseudonym — Mikhnienko — which he had adopted upon arrival in France. These mix-ups and recriminations can perhaps be explained in terms of Voline's living conditions at the time when he drafted most of these jottings: it was under the German Occupation in Marseilles where he had everything to fear from the Gestapo and Pétainist militia and was experiencing the rigors and privations of clandestinity. Yet it seems to us that the key to the animosity between the two men lies in the contrast that we have already mentioned between the peasant activist and the moralistic intellectual disconnected from social practice.[7] Moreover, Voline seems to have nurtured this rancor for he recalls that in Berlin in 1925, upon seeing Makhno again for the first time in years he told him that he *"an intellectual, Arshinov a worker and Makhno a peasant"* made up a *"team"* and that they should remain *"inseparable."* Makhno allegedly failed to heed this[8] and had supposedly *"thrown it all away"* by *"hitting the bottle maybe even more than before."* His was *"a nature undoubtedly brilliantly gifted, capable of actively and doggedly pursuing an objective that he had set himself, a man who had marvelous expertise and at the same time could plummet from such heights into the lowest depths even to the point of becoming a 'human wreck'"*(!) (page 75). Likewise, in the Ukraine, he had been unwilling to come under Voline's *"moral sway"* (page 142) because he was under that of a *"camarilla"* of a segment of the Makhnovist commanders. In spite of all his "qualities," Makhno remained, in Voline's estimation an *"unlettered, philistine, uneducated man"* (page 60), especially as he had an aversion to *"anything that was not peasant. Being himself a peasant through and through, he had a thoroughgoing understanding of peasant life and went so far as to criticize all that was not peasant. He did not have a lot of confidence in workers because the worker, according to him, was already to some extent depraved by the crazy bad life of towns and of industry where he rubbed shoulders with the bosses. He had even less confidence in intellectuals and poked fun at them. In these conditions, it was very hard to talk to him about the flaws in his organization because he responded with all sorts of ridicule which left you nonplussed and denied you any chance of settling things one way or the other"* (page 134). Also, Voline mentions these character traits of Makhno's even more clearly: *"blind* trust *in the peasantry,* mistrust *of all other classes in society: a certain* contempt *for intellectuals, even anarchist ones"* (page 49). There is the rub and the thorn in Voline's side! He strove to act as director of Makhno's conscience in his capacity as a "morally irreproachable" intellectual, so as to steer him onto the "straight and narrow." Instead of which Makhno refused his advice, perhaps mockingly, and surrendered instead to his base "muzhik" instincts! And while an émigré in Paris, had not Voline publicly dismissed him as a "muzhik" one day (a term of abuse which must have been equivalent for him to "dreadful idiot" or something of the sort), until an anarchist honor panel had to get together to smooth out their differences![9]

In fact, of the 236 pages supposedly dealing with Makhno, only a tiny number touch upon the subject directly, the bulk being merely digressions in every direction. To back up his criticisms, Voline sets out some specific instances in which he purports to have been a witness or protagonist, whereas the rest are mere impression, hearsay and superficial confidences from Makhno's spouse who seems rather cavalier about the gravity of her accusations. Thus it seems obvious to us that the credence to be placed in this should be measured by the degree of hostility that he bore towards Makhno. He would have been better advised to offer detailed descriptions, not of a few episodes, but rather of his full term among the Makhnovist insurgents, unless he spent that "cloistered" in his cultural activities and had no desire to mingle with "muzhiks" so as to be able to address them directly and pertinently without having to make use of second hand reports. He could also have recalled the circumstances which had led to his arrival in the insurgent camp: it was Makhno himself who had sent out a detachment to rescue him from the clutches of Petliurist partisans. It was also at Makhno's suggestion that Voline had been made chairman of the insurgent movement's Revolutionary Military Soviet for several months and again it was Makhno who had made Voline's release one of the conditions for honoring the military and political agreement concluded with the Bolsheviks in 1920. Voline also omits to mention the "deposition" that he made before a Chekist examining magistrate, a "deposition" that was, moreover, critical of the Makhnovists to say the least, in that Soviet historians have since used it as a means of damning them.[10]

All in all, all these random jottings, swamped by general considerations strike us as more revealing of their author's personality than of Makhno's: which probably accounts for their having remained unpublished to date. However, in spite of their blatant exaggeration, these texts deserve to be better known, certain passages being of undoubted value for the times. As for Makhno's "true" personality, that can be sufficiently divined from all his writings — memoirs and articles — and we need not have recourse to the anarchist "grapevine" in hope of sensational disclosures.

Within the framework of this bibliographical update, let us take note of the oral testimony of a historian of Ukrainian origins, Oleg Koshchuk. His mother was interned in Poland in the same camp as Makhno and remembers that certain Petliurists wanted to assassinate the libertarian, probably on account of some clash in which they had been bested. At which point high-ranking nationalist leaders let it be known that any action against Makhno would be deemed a hostile act against the Ukrainian cause. In spite of political differences, ethnic solidarity thus came into play to bring Ukrainians from both sides of the Dniepr closer together.

A.S. 1984

Notes to the Bibliographical Afterword

1. *Dyelo Truda,* February–March 1928, No. 33-34, pp. 7–9.
2. Ibid., June–July 1928, No. 37-38, pp. 10–12.
3. Ibid., March 1927, No. 22, p. 12.
4. Ibid., July–August 1927, No. 10-12, pp. 10–12.
5. P. Litvinov *Nestor Makhno and the Jewish Question,* 20 type-written pages dated Moscow, June 18, 1982. This essay was published by the magazine *Vremya I My* (Time and Us) in Israel, No. 71, 1983.
6. *A Rivista Anarchica,* Milan, Italy, November 8, 1983.
7. Sixteen page manuscript.

8. Ida Mett, *Souvenirs sur Nestor Makhno,* Paris, 1983, pp. 25–26.
9. Letter to the author, December 27, 1982.
10. Its location is 5 rue Caplat, 75018 Paris.

Afterword

This book was drafted nearly twenty years ago on foot of research begun in 1964. In 1984 we added a bibliographical afterword when we published an anthology of articles by Nestor Makhno, in which we commented upon certain new sources, including some unpublished manuscript materials by Voline.[1] Later, in 1987, we published a lengthy examination of the "Organizational Platform of the Dyelo Truda Group" (of which N. Makhno and P. Arshinov were the main authors) and of the ensuing controversy.[2] In a way, it amounted to a historical and practical assessment of the Ukrainian insurgent experience and of the part that anarchists played in it. It only remains for us now to look at all the new information dished up since then in a range of publications in the West as well as in Russia and in the Ukraine. Let us begin in chronological order, by harking back to the book by Serge Mamontov referred to in our foreword (*Carnets de route d'un artilleur à cheval 1917–1920*), as it devotes a fair number of pages to his military meanderings through Makhnovist territory and offers us his thoughts on civil war, displaying a rare bluntness and candor:

> "Confident that they were beyond punishment, the Reds descended into utter bestiality and lost all human dignity. Not that we were angels either and often we were cruel. Every army has its share of perverse personnel: we had our share in our ranks too (…) Looting is a ghastly thing, one that does an army a lot of harm. All the world's armies pretty much loot (…) There is a rule to be observed in time of war: turn a blind eye to the blood and the tears! I have to laugh when the rules of warfare are cited. War is the most immoral of undertakings and civil war is worse still. Rules governing absence of morality? Is it supposed to be all right to kill and mutilate the able-bodied but forbidden to finish off the wounded? Where is the logic in that?
>
> Notions of chivalry are out of place in warfare. Such talk is merely propaganda for imbeciles. Criminality and murder become heroism. One tries to get the jump on the enemy, under cover of night, from the rear, by ambush, through superiority of numbers. The truth goes

untold. What nobility is there in all that? My thoughts are that an army composed exclusively of philosophers would be a very poor army and I would rather an army of criminals. Better, I reckon, to speak a cruel truth than peddle falsehoods."[3]

To this muddled thinking the author adds falsehood when he claims that Makhno had come up with the slogan: "Kill the Jews, save Russia!" Although, he remarks, Makhno himself saved no one and lived high on the hog, with no thought except for "his own pleasure"! Obviously, an adversary portrayed in such colors is good only for extermination, like some "bothersome insect."

The Whites and the Cossacks

Nicolas Ross's book, published in Germany in 1982 and dealing with the Crimea under Wrangel, contains unpublished material drawn from the archives of the White generals deposited with the Hoover Institute in Stanford, California. In particular, it records how Wrangel speculated upon the chances of military collaboration with Makhno against the Bolsheviks. In a secret order issued to his units, the Baron-General wrote that "in the name of the sacred goal: wiping out communism" he might just rub shoulders with Makhno and other anti-communist Ukrainian groups. In the fight against the principal enemy of "Holy Russia," he ordered his commanders to coordinate their operations with all "Russian folk" fighting the Bolsheviks to bring back the "Greater Fatherland"!

Yes indeed, Wrangel had understood nothing of what had been going on in recent times and he carried on denying the Ukrainian character of the insurrections in the land. This attitude is reminiscent of the old Russian saw according to which "there never have been any Ukrainians and never will be"! The specific and distinguishing features of what Muscovites used to dismiss as "Little Russians" are denied utterly. Furthermore, asking Makhno to fight for "Holy Russia" and the "Greater Fatherland" was a crackpot notion. Nicolas Ross reprints in its entirety a letter from General Shatilov, Wrangel's chief of staff, to "Batko Makhno," going on about the suffering of "Russian soil" and informing him that "the command of the Russian army is fighting only against the communists and commissars and is wholeheartedly on the side of the Russian people," its motto being "land to the people, truth to the people; the people alone must determine its own fate [...] We share a common goal." It is put to Makhno that he should coordinate his military operations and, to that end, organize his detachments into a division, which is to be furnished with arms and munitions on the same basis as other divisions of the Russian army. Makhno is confirmed in his command of that division: the Makhnovist commanders become regimental or brigade commanders: all who would defer to the Russian army are offered guarantees that both their lives and their property will be safeguarded.[4]

An emissary — a Captain Mikhailov, bearing messages from Wrangel — was dispatched to Makhno. A bad move, for this well-intentioned ambassador was recognized as the man who had captured a full company of the Novospassovka Insurgent Regiment in 1919 and who had had 70 insurgents shot and a further 50 hanged, on the grounds that they were on their way to join Makhno! [5] He himself was strung up, bearing a placard that read: "No compact between Makhno and the White Guards can or could ever be entered into, and should the White camp send us another emissary, the same fate awaits him." And that is precisely what befell that second emissary, a colonel.

Yet Wrangel's pipe-dreams managed to bamboozle several Makhnovist detachments. Cut off from the main body of insurgents, they accepted Wrangel's claims regarding alliance with Makhno at face value. This was the result of the unspeakable terror enforced by the Cheka and the Reds' punitive expeditions. The Makhnovist detachments that went over to the Whites were organized into a brigade of several thousand men and dubbed the "Batko Makhno Brigade." Even so, Wrangel's "howler" eventually backfired on him in the worst conceivable fashion: the brigade was deployed in the northern Tavrida, directly facing the offensive by the Makhnovist insurgent forces. When the Makhnovist Chaly commanding the brigade discovered that he had been gulled, he sought to redeem himself by handing over to the Makhnovist command all the White officers staffing his brigade. These disclosed the precise locations of White troop deployments. On the basis of which intelligence and with the assistance of the "Batko Makhno Brigade" (now defectors) the Makhnovists routed the enemy's divisions, thereby breaking through the White front.[6]

Wrangel's political blandness prompts us briefly to review the Whites' failures. The godfather of their movement, the prematurely deceased General Kornilov, whilst a great Russian patriot, was a democratic republican and supporter of the Constituent Assembly. He managed to come to an accommodation with the Rada, the elected sovereign assembly of the Kuban Cossacks, thanks to which he was able to register his earliest successes. The Kuban Cossacks, like the Don Cossacks after them, had only gone over to the Volunteer Army because of persecution they had endured at the hands of Red invasion forces.[7] They had no notion of conquering Russia: they wanted only their own independence under the auspices of US President Wilson's recently proclaimed right to self-determination. But neither France nor Britain nor any other Entente power was prepared to recognize them. The Entente was only prepared to furnish the Whites with weapons and munitions, the Whites being, to their mind, the heirs of its former ally of 1914, imperial Russia. Driven by the Reds into the arms of the Whites, the Cossacks persistently had to fend off overtures from the White high command which was eager to bring them to heel.

Denikin proved to be not merely a dismal military strategist but also a disaster as a politician. He had no real program other than overthrowing Bolshevism, the downfall of which he regarded as imminent and inevitable, so much so that in September 1919 he circulated commanders of the most forward Volunteer Army units with a questionnaire asking them to indicate what course they would like to see the country follow![8] He forbade the Kuban Cossack general Shkuro from capturing Moscow, on pain of court martial.[9] But he went too far when he covered up the murder of Riabovoy, the chairman of the Kuban Rada (whose father before him had been murdered by the Reds). He then had A. Kalabukhov, a priest and chairman of the Kuban's delegation to the Paris Peace Conference in June 1919, hanged and tagged with a placard that read: "Traitor to Russia"! Such was the impact upon the Cossack units embroiled in fighting in the front lines that not only did they quit the front in droves, but they went further and severed their links with the Whites.

By pulling out, these elite troops, accounting for three fourths of the forces deployed against Moscow, men who had repeatedly driven the Red armies backwards, brought about a caving-in of every one of the White fronts. Worse still, the White high command and Denikin, instead of acknowledging their own strategic and political blunders, blamed the Cossacks. So much so that they refused to see them evacuated from Novorossisk to the Crimea. General Sidorin, the commander of the army of the Don, came close to killing Denikin where he stood, such was the explosive nature of their encounter.

Bereft of all command, Shkuro was obliged to leave the country for exile, whilst General Mamontov was poisoned on the night of January 31, 1920 before the very eyes of his powerless spouse in the hospital where he was recovering from typhus. We cannot be certain who was responsible for this murder but suspicions fell on hard-liners from the Volunteer Army, members of OSVAG, the Denikinist Cheka, who had already eliminated Riabovoy.[10] It should be said that General Mamontov had, on foot of the prerogatives of the Don's sovereign assembly, the Krug, violently opposed Denikin (although he himself was only Cossack by adoption), which just goes to show his democratic leanings. Let us add that he was extremely able and very popular with the Cossacks and could, by himself, have turned the military tide against the Reds.

The dim-witted Denikin deliberately sawed away the limb upon which his entire venture rested. Rejected by his own, forced to flee far from home territory, and after his closest collaborator and friend, General Romanovsky, was cut down practically in front of him at the Russian embassy in Constantinople by an ultra nationalist officer, Denikin turned to the writing of his memoirs, or rather, to a self-serving apologia for all his plans. Many years later, in 1937, he still had learned nothing for in a little pamphlet entitled *Who Rescued Soviet Power from Perdition?* he claimed that the man responsible had been ... Pilsudski, the Polish marshal and president, who had refused in the autumn of 1919 to coordinate his operations against the Reds with Denikin's.[11] He forgot to say that he himself had at no time been willing to recognize Polish independence and intended to absorb Poland back into the Russian Empire (perhaps because his mother and his wife were Poles and he was trying to hold his family together!) In any event, he had unnecessarily made himself an irreconcilable enemy in the shape of the former socialist and rabid Polish nationalist, Pilsudski!

His successor, Wrangel, repeated the same mistakes vis à vis the Cossacks who retreated with him into the Crimea. On April 8, 1920, he had General Sidorin hauled before a court martial on charges of "Cossack separatism." Sentenced to four years' penal servitude, then "pardoned" by Wrangel but denied the right to "wear a uniform," having been discharged from the army, Sidorin emigrated to Prague.[12] Wrangel, who was equally shortsighted in military affairs, was so confident of easy victory over the Reds that he deployed only 40,000 men in the front lines, whilst retaining 300,000 in the rear. In spite of all his efforts, he therefore tasted the same disappointments as his predecessor but at least, to his credit, oversaw the evacuation of all the troops that expressed a desire to place themselves beyond the reach of the Cheka. Lenin, Trotsky and the Bolshevik leadership could scarcely have dreamt of finer nincompoops with whom to grapple.

✦✦✦

The fateful year of 1989 — when the Berlin Wall came down — witnessed the first stirrings inside the USSR of revisionism regarding Nestor Makhno. On February 8, 1989, a young investigative journalist, Vassili Golovanov, had a wide-ranging article published in *Literaturnaya Gazeta*, the influential weekly paper of the Writers' Union on *Batko Makhno, the Civil War Werewolf*.[13] It amounted to a sort of "rehabilitation" of the Ukrainian revolutionary. We immediately contacted this journalist with an eye to the chances of our publishing our works on the subject in Russian. Progress Editions in Moscow, the then specialists in works of the sort, devoted a lengthy review to this present book. Written by N. Silin, the review was rather favorable but — and this was evidence of the critic's plight at being confronted with a long-forgotten past — he scolded us over the omission of Soviet archival sources — when he himself acknowledged that these were inaccessible even to Soviet researchers (!) and for not having dwelt longer on Western sources — oral sources or Makhno's own writings — which were not available in the USSR! The upshot was that our book could never see publication in Russian unless complemented by Soviet archival materials.[14] In point of fact, this delicate refusal amounted to an acknowledgment of the ignorance and powerlessness of official Soviet historians in the face of a mass of data emanating from the West and concerned with a past history consigned to oblivion by single party rule.

The fate of Makhno's wife and daughter

Golovanov's article was the starter's flag for a whole series of sensational publications. We might focus on that from Sergei Seymanov, the last Soviet historian to have shown an interest on the topic, through a mischievous piece back in 1968.[15] Under the title *Underneath the Black Flag, the Life and Death of Nestor Makhno*, he tells of the lengthy correspondence and conversations that he had with Makhno's widow, Galina Kuzmenko, and his daughter, Lucie. He might have been better advised to publish this only in an edition with commentary in the margin, because it is of tortuous construction and endlessly intercut with personal thoughts of the most maudlin sort and the whole thing makes for a difficult read. Even so, let us draw out the substance of it. Following publication of his article, he received a letter dated April 4, 1968 from the town of Dzhambula in Kazakhstan, from Galina Kuzmenko who gave him a lengthy account of everything that she had been through, not merely as an emigré in France but also inside the USSR to where she had been deported from Germany in 1945, along with her daughter. Let us take a look at the main new information on offer: Galina offers a precise description of Nestor's last days and final hours in the Tenon hospital: she confirms that his real year of birth was 1888, a year earlier than the date shown on the official records, the purpose being to put off his being called to the colors (this being something that played a crucial role in the commuting of Makhno's death sentence to one of imprisonment for life — precisely because of his tender years). She recalls how his father's real surname had been Mikhnienko who, being nicknamed Makhno, had adopted this surname instead and registered all his children under it. Galina confirms the authenticity of her "celebrated diary," seized by the Reds in 1920, wherein she gave a day by day account of the activities of the core Makhnovist group from February 19 to March 26, 1920. Written in Ukrainian, translated into Russian, this text has been reprinted many times over since then. All in all, it has the ring of truth, except in the passages where she has Nestor — a drunken Nestor at that — dancing to his own accordion accompaniment! Remember that Makhno himself challenged this "diary," supposedly kept by his spouse, certain passages of which had been used by Soviet historians to discredit him.[16] As Vassili Golovanov wrote us, only handwriting analysis could establish its authenticity.[17] The main point to emerge is just how extremely severe Makhno and his comrades were, not shrinking from on-the-spot execution of all insurgents guilty of extorting money from or bullying the populace. They were not ones to bandy words about revolutionary ethics!

Seymanov makes a passing reference to the fate of Leon Zadov, "executioner" of many Bolsheviks, bodyguard to Makhno and the man who carried the wounded Makhno in his own arms into Romania. Of Jewish extraction (which puts paid to any charges of anti-Semitism levelled against Nestor, not to mention all of the protracted rebuttals offered Makhno himself or by others!), Zadov was later recruited by the GPU! He worked for the GPU up until 1937 when he was "purged," as were virtually all protagonists of the civil war. Seymanov notes with amazement that Zadov's son made a glittering career for himself in the Soviet navy under his father's real name of Zinkovsky before retiring with the rank of rear-admiral. Seymanov wonders — without however advancing anything to substantiate his thesis — whether Zadov might not have been "planted" inside the Makhnovist movement right from the outset by the "organs," which is to say, the Cheka. The argument may be a bit raw but Seymanov argues that the Cheka was capable of anything. Galina continues her tale: with Nestor and a dozen other insurgents she was evacuated to Romania, before moving on to Poland in the spring of 1922, where she was jailed with Nestor for fourteen months in Warsaw, charged with having fomented an armed uprising in eastern Galicia (then part of Poland). There she gave birth to her daughter Elena on October 30, 1922. On their release all three of them moved on to Danzig where they were rearrested by the German authorities on charges of having persecuted German settlers in the Ukraine. She was freed shortly after that and made her way to Paris with her daughter.[18] As for Nestor, he then made his escape "like something out of a novel": a rope made of torn blankets, bars sawn through with a file, etc. without giving her the full details, in accordance, no doubt "with the rules of revolutionary conspiracy" at that time. Among the other intriguing details offered by Galina — although Seymanov explains that she was cautious in her choice of words, this being in 1968 when she had not yet been "rehabilitated" by the regime and was therefore still "under surveillance" — we have confirmation that Swartzbard, member of a Yiddish anarchist group, was well known to Makhno in Paris. Makhno did not agree with his holding "Petliura responsible for anti-Jewish pogroms carried out in the Ukraine, because Petliura had in fact opposed them," even though "Makhno had no great liking for him." Galina stresses that Swartzbard's defence lawyer, Henry Torrès, helped Nestor and her smooth over their "difficulties with the French police" (probably to overturn proceedings to have them expelled from French soil). Their daughter Elena (pet name Lucie in French) was often taken in by French anarchist families, never learned Ukrainian and even forgot her Russian. Galina worked fitfully for a variety of Ukrainian organizations in France. Conscripted under the STO (Compulsory Labor Service) scheme, her daughter was sent to Berlin in 1943 and Galina went with her. On August 14, 1945, they were both arrested by the Soviet authorities and repatriated to Kiev. Galina was sentenced to eight years in a labor camp in Mordovia. Curiously enough, there she met the wives of Yakir — the man who persecuted the Makhnovists back in 1919 — and of General Vlassov ("turned" by the Germans during the Second World War and handed over to Stalin by the British and Americans, before being hanged in Moscow along with Shkuro, Krasnov and other generals). She must have had a hellish time there for she wound up in the "invalids'" section of the camp. She was freed on May 7, 1954 and assigned residence in Dzhambula in Kazakhstan, where her daughter was also assigned. When they met at the railway station they did not recognize each other, such were the changes in their appearances! It was only later on that they were reunited. Which leads Seymanov, "a young, unassuming citizen" in 1968, "moved" by this picture, to say that Galina was worthy of featuring in a play by Homer, Shakespeare or in *Quiet Flows the Don*.

The impression she made upon Seymanov, after their many encounters, was that of a "strong and extraordinary character"; the ordeals to which she had been subjected had not broken her nor her "dogged common sense," the "suspicion-driven caution" which, according to him, was a legacy from the ghastly times in which she had lived. Seymanov notes here that the "misfortunes she had endured had not steered Galina's spirit in the direction of God" and that she was, from her younger days through until she breathed her last, a "dyed-in-the-wool atheist" as well as a "genuine, robust revolutionary." He was not afraid that this might not quite square with his "graphological" reading of Galina's handwriting which identified "ambition, bordering even upon despotism," plus a degree of "dissimulation" discernible in the formation of the letters a, o, b and l! As we see it, the overriding impression was that she had remained true to herself, to Nestor and to the movement in which she had played a large part. Hats off! (She died in 1978.)

Seymanov also offers us information as to the fate of Lucie (Elena) Makhno. Banished to the middle of the Asian steppes, under police surveillance, she was only able to survive by turning her hand to a range of exacting manual trades: canteen worker, factory worker, piggery employee, etc. from which she was often fired once the identity of her father was discovered, and this went on for many a long year. When Seymanov met her in 1968 she was not yet married nor a mother but was living with a civil aviator. She had reluctantly agreed to the rendezvous: she was "edgy, irritated and trusted no one." To him she seemed still young and elegant with her dark eyes and dark hair and bore a stunning resemblance to her father. He found her very much the "Parisienne," as he imagined one at any rate. Her Russian was still heavily overlaid with a French accent. In her mother's presence, she declared to Seymanov that she had always despised politics, that she remembered her father well and recalled that his house had always been filled with people and newspapers. Way back then she had pledged that she would take no interest in politics or newspapers. She reckoned that she had no homeland and could not bring herself to regard either France or Russia as such [...] Many men had shown an interest in her but on learning whose daughter she was they had promptly made themselves scarce, sometimes properly, sometimes in a cruder or more craven fashion, thereby exposing their own true natures. "I never wanted children. Bring more wretches into this world? So that they might share the same fate as me? When I was in France I knew nothing of my father's part in your history. When I found myself incarcerated in Kiev, one of my fellow prisoners, discovering whose daughter I was, asked me if he was the renowned bandit? I took offence at that and slapped her."

At the end of their meeting, she asked Seymanov to send her some French newspapers as they just could not be had where she was living.

It has to be said that Seymanov in no way retracts any of the comments regarding the negative views expressed in his 1966 study of the Makhnovist movement. Quite the opposite. His text closes bizarrely with his imploring "the Lord to forgive his servants Galina and Nestor, for they knew not what they were doing," and calling upon Him to "forgive all of us poor sinners" [he probably means all Russians]. As for himself and in spite of the belated onset of compassion, he never lifted a finger to help Galina and her daughter back in 1968. What hypocrisy. Lucie (Elena) Makhno died an untimely death in 1993 at the age of 71, still confined to Dzhambula. We can only suppose that she had had to grapple with the straits caused by the break-up of the Soviet empire and visited upon the Russian and Ukrainian minorities by the Kazakh nationalist authorities.

Belash's key book

Scenting the dangers of an "historical and political" rehabilitation of Makhno, the ideologues of the Communist Party of the USSR, while they still held absolute power, urgently commissioned a negative study of the subject. One V. N. Volkovinsky published *Makhno and his Downfall* in Moscow in 1991.[19] Rehashing all the old Leninist clichés and relying upon a one-sided critical apparatus, he delivered he latest anathema upon the Ukrainian insurgents. Alas, the USSR (so-called) met its own spectacular "downfall," whereby the Party-State's right of imprimatur over historical publications evaporated. Whereupon a whole series of works much more favorably disposed towards the subject saw publication. We shall dwell upon the most significant of these, Viktor Belash's memoirs (to which we have referred earlier).

Seymanov wrote that in 1976 he had had a visit from Belash's son who had given him some information about his father: released by the Reds, he had been banished to Krasnodar in the Kuban where he worked as a mechanic in the workshops of the Hunters' Union (!). In December 1937 he was arrested and sentenced to face a firing squad. On April 29, 1976, he was posthumously rehabilitated on the basis of "insufficient evidence."

※※※

The published book contains the full text of his self-justifying memoirs, drafted in a Cheka jail and fleshed out by his son through the addition of a large number of documents. In spite of our reservations about passages in which the author claims that he was always a passionate advocate of honest alliance with the Reds and offers the occasional criticism and reproach directed at Makhno — it was this that earned him his "freedom" (one thinks here of the *Confession* that Bakunin wrote for the Tsar and which also earned him his freedom and facilitated his escape from Siberia) — the book as a whole represents an important source of information. For our purposes, we shall make do with rehearsing the main items of information from Belash which present our monograph in a new light.

Take for a start, the Gulyai-Polye anarcho-communist group in the aftermath of 1905. It had fifty active — activist — members, each of them in touch with a further four sympathizers. It was in close contact with local and regional anarchist groups, having a supply-line to libertarian literature and arms from Ekaterinoslav and Moscow, through Voldemar Antoni, the group's founder and leader. (He was of Czech origin). The group's members got together with Antoni on an almost daily basis in order to familiarize themselves with the thought of Proudhon, Stirner, Bakunin and Kropotkin. The reforms of Stolypin, the tsarist prime minister — reforms that destroyed the rural commune — were fiercely criticized (p. 13). In 1905 the group passed a resolution attacking "any trespass against the physical integrity" of any member placed under arrest by the authorities: such trespass would be answered by implacable "revenge." Let us leap forward in time to a full reprint (see pp. 73–89 of Belash's book) of the minutes of the 2nd Congress of Insurgents on February 12, 1919, which we ourselves have reprinted in part in our book (see Chapter 14 and the documentary appendices). This, a document of the greatest significance, was drawn first from the archives by Belash's son. It records the composition and affiliations of the 13 elected members of the revolutionary military soviet: three Left Social Revolutionaries, three Bolshevik-Communists, and seven anarchists (Belash, p. 88). For good measure, Belash's son also reprints (p. 96) the minutes of the 3rd All-Ukrainian Congress of Soviets controlled by the Bolsheviks. Also included is the resolution from the congress of the Makhnovist revolutionary military soviet which drew delegates from 32 districts of the region (pp. 104–105) and which issued a call for a united front of revolutionaries: it recognized the authority of freely elected soviets: it repudiated any party dictatorship: it called for the death penalty for looters, bandits and counter-revolutionaries to be closely supervised by the local revolutionary military tribunal: for immediate abolition of the Cheka: for all unit commanders to be elected: for freedom of speech, press and assembly for all left-wing organizations, without any repression whatsoever: there was an insistence that there be no national persecution within the revolutionary army: and a strict fraternal discipline rooted in awareness of revolutionary duty was introduced. This text was omitted from both Arshinov's book and my own book here. The Belashs, father and son, cite several Bolshevik memoranda and reports on frictions between the insurgents, the anarchists and Communist political commissars, offering the occasional interesting and unexpected detail — for instance, that two wagon-loads of literature and appeals meant for the inhabitants of Berdyansk and Mariupol and escorted by anarchist and Social Revolutionary agitators, were sent out in March 17, 1919, provoking the wrath of the political commissar author of the report, for they included an appeal from Makhno denouncing the parasites arriving to talk down to and order people around (p. 109). Look at the resolution from the Nabat (Tocsin) anarchist congress of the Ukraine: the one from the 3rd regional congress of insurgent soviets, held in Gulyai-Polye on April 10, 1919. Belash gives a detailed breakdown of the military deployment on each front, which affords us some idea of the part played by the Makhnovists. He reprints numerous appeals and proclamations from Makhno (pp. 196–197, 222–226, 230–231, etc.) as well as other articles or texts lifted from the insurgents' newspapers and now made available for the first time. Precisely what Makhno did not have at hand when he came to write the remainder of his movement's history (having stopped at December 1918).

A secret order (pp. 238–239) from Trotsky that "the Makhnovschina be mopped up without prevarication or hesitation and with all firmness and severity," also drawn from the archives, deserves to be publicized, as do other (hitherto unpublished) orders along the same line (pp. 238–239 et seq.). This amounts to a veritable indictment of Trotsky who stabbed the insurgents in the back and had them gunned down whilst they were trying, with scarcely any arms or munitions, to hold the line against the White offensive: Trotsky's responsibility here is exposed with plenty of supporting evidence. It is also a terrific indictment of the Bolshevik regime as a whole, which opted to surrender the front to the Whites rather than allow an autonomous popular movement to spread.

Viktor Belash drafted his memoirs on the basis of his staff notes and campaign diary. They offer us a highly detailed picture of insurgent numbers, their organization, the military operations in which they engaged and the outcome thereof.

Apropos of the crucial battle with the Whites in Peregonovka in September 1919, he cites the figure of 18,000 Whites slain — a considerable toll in terms of the numbers committed. Nearly 7,000 others were eliminated, including 2,500 Chechens, near Alexandrovsk and in the ensuing fighting, etc. At that point the Makhnovists numbered 100,000 men: 250,000, if we count the unarmed reserves in their rear! Their units completely smashed the White rearguard, cutting them off from ports, arms and munitions supply lines in the rear. Denikin was obliged to pull troops out of front line service against the Reds in order to send in his best troops to halt the Makhnovist onslaught. What we have now are detailed figures regarding what we already knew about the crucial significance of the famous encounter at Peregonovka in terms of the outcome of the civil war.

It should be stressed that Belash claims the credit for having dispatched numerous units to all four corners of the territory in order to reap maximum benefits from this victory and this contrary to the opinion of Makhno who allegedly upbraided him for weakening the insurgent army. Among other interesting items, he cites the distribution of wheat to the peasants, free of charge: a 50 percent prior deposit was paid on clothing orders placed with workshops and garment-factories, even though the insurgents were often in no position to pick up those orders on account of the fluid military situation. There are intriguing statistics regarding the social extraction of the insurgents: 25 percent were farmhands or landless peasants, 40 percent were medium-sized or poor peasants, 10 percent were well-to-do peasants owning no land of their own, 10 percent were landless peasants who earned a living from fishing, 5 percent were drovers, 7 percent industrial and transport workers and, finally, 3 percent were petit bourgeois. Broken down according to age, it transpires that 80 percent of insurgents were aged between 20 and 35. As a result, many had been participants in the 1914–1917 war.

Their geographical provenance is similarly intriguing: 50 percent were from the Ekaterinoslav province, 25 percent from the Tavrida and Kherson, 7 percent from the Don, 8 percent from Poltava province and the remaining 10 percent were drawn from several other regions (Belash, p. 346). In October 1919 the front manned by the Makhnovists covered 1,150 kilometers from end to end (when the Whites' entire front facing the Reds covered 1,760 kilometers).

Note that in the wake of the second agreement with the Red Army, nearly 8,000 partisans refused to accept this accommodation and left the main body of the army. Even so, the latter fielded 13,000 insurgents along the lines facing the Whites — where they played the telling part of which we know.

One of the most important statistics quoted by Viktor Belash relates to the movement's political persuasion: of the 40,000 partisans in the insurgent army, in November 1919 — 35,000 of whom were laid low by typhus — 70 percent were Makhnovists and sympathizers, 5 percent of whom were anarchists: 20 percent were sympathetic to the Social Revolutionaries and Petliura: and only 10 percent were former Red Army soldiers, 1 percent of them Bolshevik-Communists (Belash, p. 362).

In short, the Belashs' book represents a crucial source on the Makhnovist movement. Not merely on account of the statistics cited and the minute descriptions of operations mounted but also because of its reprinting of lots of texts lifted from the archives. It is a splendid book and we look forward to seeing it translated and published in French.

The archives and the Makhno publishing "boom"

From the use made of them by the younger Belash, it is plain that there are lots of archival materials available, especially in the Ukraine itself. The State Archives in Kiev appear to be the best equipped, but every town of any significance has its own archival collection as well. We salute the archives in Dniepropetrovsk (formerly Ekaterinoslav) which in 1993 published a pamphlet reproducing a number of documents and drawing up a detailed listing of its holdings on Makhno and the Makhnovist movement. Unfortunately, access is not easily come by for a variety of different reasons, in the immediate term at any rate. Be that as it may, there must be materials there on the basis of which a number of other facets of the Makhnovist movement can be explored further.

As we said before, lots of publications on the subject have seen the light of day. However, it is very hard to get hold of them in current circumstances, for there is no national distribution network either in the Ukraine or in Russia and it requires a good network of connections before one can lay hands on them. For instance, none of the books recently published have been able to cite Belash, due to their having been unable to get hold of a copy of his book.

⁂

We salute the 1995 republication of Arshinov's *History of the Makhnovist Movement* by Rough Country publications in Zaporozhiye (formerly Alexandrovsk): of several editions of the *Memoirs* of Makhno, including a 334-page one in Moscow in 1992 from Republic Editions (albeit that much of the 1st volume has been dropped): the 192-page anthology put together by V.F Verstyuk in Kiev in 1991 (even though it offers no details or source for the texts presented): the literary study, *Tatchankas from the South* by the journalist V. Golovanov (Moscow 1997), a joint publication by Mars and Rough Country editions containing many irksome and ambiguous personal remarks, citing numerous unpublished testimonies and heavily reliant, indeed, upon our own monograph: in Moscow and Smolensk, Olympus and Rusitch publishers produced Vadim Teylitsyn's 444-page *Nestor Makhno* (using the works published previously, albeit without acknowledgment): finally, there is Alexander Shubin's 176-page *Makhno and the Makhnovist Movement* (Moscow 1998, MIG publishers) which represents a political rehabilitation of Makhno and of the call for free soviets. Shubin cites examples to show how self-management operated in the region. He is a historian, a one-time anarcho-syndicalist and leader of the Greens in Moscow. His plentiful references to sources and archives which are not plainly identified and not reprinted as they are in the Belash book (which he ignores) hoist it into the academic register but undermine its interest as a source of documentation. Note the smallness of its print-run: 1,000 copies were printed — indicative of the publishing and distribution problems in Russia today. By comparison our own book — 10,000 copies spread over three editions — is a very respectable effort and speaks well of the French public's interest in the matter. Speaking of which, we salute Hélène Chatelain for her documentary film, *Nestor Makhno, Peasant of the Ukraine*, broadcast by the Arte television channel on February 26, 1997. Among projects in the making, there is the plan for a Russian-language edition of the anthology of Nestor Makhno's writings published by us in French in 1984 (and by AK Press in English in 1996 as *The Struggle Against the State and Other Essays*) to mark the jubilee of Makhno's death. This will prove a real find for Russian and Ukrainian readers, these essays being utterly unknown to them. This present monograph was issued in Russian in Paris in 2000. An important anthology of documents (including a contribution from ourselves) regarding Nestor Makhno and his wife Galina Kuzmenko was issued in 1999 for simultaneous publication in Russian and Ukrainian in Kiev and Gulyai-Polye. Some homecoming that will be for the prodigals to the land of their birth! Which is only right as far as a matter of this significance is concerned, because in the 20th century — an age of calamity upon calamity — the Makhnovist experiment and that by the Spanish comrades in 1936–1939 represent the only attempts to install a society wherein human liberation might be something more than mere empty rhetoric.

— A.S. Paris, 2001

Notes to the Afterword

1. See Nestor Makhno, *The Struggle Against the State and Other Essays* (AK Press, 1996).

2. Alexandre Skirda, *Facing the Enemy* (AK Press, 2002), Chapters XV and XVI.

3. Op. cit. pp. 7, 148 and 156.

4. Nicolas Ross, *Wrangel in the Crimea* (in Russian), Frankfurt-am-Main, Germany 1982, pp. 255–262.

5. Belash, op. cit. pp. 421–422.

6. Belash, op. cit., pp. 462–468, and N. Makhno, *the Makhovschina and its Erstwhile Allies, the Bolsheviks,* op. cit. pp. 50–52, as well as Chapter 23 of this book.

7. Belash quotes a directive signed by Sverdlov and Trotsky and dated January 29, 1919, which amounted to an outright call for genocide of the Don Cossacks, which could scarcely have done other than prompt them to revolt en masse.

8. *The Kornilov Shock Regiment* (in Russian), Paris, 1936, p. 142.

9. See Chapter 18 above and the author's interview with Don Cossack colonel Dubentsev in February 1986 in Courbevoie (the Cossack Museum). Dubentsev confirmed to us that Denikin had dispatched an officer from his general staff, by plane, to instruct Shkuro to turn around.

10. See the account by Mamontov's widow in the Don Cossacks' organ *Rodimoy Kraiy* (Native Region), Paris, No. 52, May-June 1964.

11. General A.I Denikin *Who Rescued Soviet Power from Perdition?* (in Russian), Paris 1937, p. 16.

12. He was an active contributor to a Cossack review and his articles were collected into an anthology under the title *The Cossacks' Tragedy* (in Russian), Paris, 1936–1938.

13. Translated in its entirety by ourselves and serialized in *Le Monde libertaire*, No. 746, April 6, 1989 to No. 748, April 20, 1989.

14. "Social thought abroad" (in Russian) in *Bulletin bibliographique critique*, No 5, May 1991, pp. 54–58.

15. See above, Chapter 32.

16. S. Seymanov, *Underneath the Black Flag*, (Moscow 1990), 70 pages.

17. Letter to the author, October 5, 1998.

18. N. Makhno, *The Makhnovschina and its Erstwhile Allies*, op. cit. p. 30.

19. V.N. Volkovinsky, *Makhno and his Downfall*, Moscow 1991, p. 246.

KATE SHARPLEY LIBRARY

Comrades and Friends —

No doubt some of you will be aware of the work of the Kate Sharpley Library and Documentation Centre, which has been in existence for the last eight years. In 1991 the Library was moved from a storage location in London to Northamptonshire, where we are now in the process of creating a database of the entire collection. At the same time, a working group has been formed to oversee the organisation and running of the Library. The catalogue of the Library material will be published by AK Press (Edinburgh).

The Library is made up of private donations from comrades, deceased and living. It comprises several thousand pamphlets, books, newspapers, journals, posters, flyers, unpublished manuscripts, monographs, essays, etc., in over 20 languages, covering the history of our movement over the last century. It contains detailed reports from the IWA (AIT/IAA), the Anarchist Federation of Britain (1945–50), the Syndicalist Workers Federation (1950–1979) and records from the anarchist publishing houses, Cienfuegos Press, ASP and others. Newspapers include near complete sets of *Black Flag, Freedom, Spain and the World, Direct Actions* (from 1945 onwards), along with countless others dating back 100 years. The Library also has a sizeable collection of libertarian socialist and council communist materials which we are keen to extend.

The Kate Sharpley Library is probably the largest collection of anarchist material in England. In order to extend and enhance the collection, we ask all anarchist groups and publications worldwide to add our name to their mailing list. We also appeal to all comrades and friends to *donate* suitable material to the Library. *All* donations are welcome and can be collected. The Kate Sharpley Library (KSL) was named in honour of Kate Sharpley, a First World War anarchist and anti-war activist — one of the countless "unknown" members of our movement so ignored by "official historians" of anarchism. The Library regularly publishes lost areas of anarchist history.

Please contact us if you would like to use our facilities. To receive details of our publications, send a stamped addressed envelope to:

KSL
BM Hurricane
London WC1N 3XX
England

Kate Sharpley Library
PMB #820
2425 Channing Way
Berkeley, CA 94704
USA
www.katesharpleylibrary.org

 THE KATE SHARPLEY LIBRARY

Ordering Information

AK Press
674-A 23rd Street,
Oakland, CA 94612-1163,
USA

Phone: (510) 208-1700
Fax: (510) 208-1701
E-mail: akpress@akpress.org
URL: www.akpress.org
Please send all payments (checks, money orders, or cash at your own risk)
in U.S. dollars. Alternatively, we take VISA and MC.

AK Press
PO Box 12766,
Edinburgh, EH8 9YE,
Scotland

Phone: (0131) 555-5165
E-mail: ak@akedin.demon.co.uk
URL: www.akuk.com
Please send all payments (cheques, money orders, or cash at your own
risk) in U.K. pounds. Alternatively, we take credit cards.

For a dollar, a pound or a few IRC's, the same addresses would be delighted to provide you with the latest complete AK catalog, featuring
several thousand books, pamphlets, zines, audio products and stylish
apparel published & distributed by AK Press. Alternatively, check out
our websites for the complete catalog, latest news and updates, events,
and secure ordering.

Also Available from AK Press

Books

MARTHA ACKELSBERG—*Free Women of Spain*

KATHY ACKER—*Pussycat Fever*

MICHAEL ALBERT—*Moving Forward: Program for a Participatory Economy*

JOEL ANDREAS—*Addicted to War: Why the U.S. Can't Kick Militarism*

ALEXANDER BERKMAN—*What is Anarchism?*

HAKIM BEY—*Immediatism*

JANET BIEHL & PETER STAUDENMAIER—*Ecofascism: Lessons From The German Experience*

BIOTIC BAKING BRIGADE—*Pie Any Means Necessary: The Biotic Baking Brigade Cookbook*

JACK BLACK—*You Can't Win*

MURRAY BOOKCHIN—*Anarchism, Marxism, and the Future of the Left*

MURRAY BOOKCHIN—*Post-Scarcity Anarchism*

MURRAY BOOKCHIN—*Social Anarchism or Lifestyle Anarchism: An Unbridgeable Chasm*

MURRAY BOOKCHIN—*Spanish Anarchists: The Heroic Years 1868–1936, The*

MURRAY BOOKCHIN—*To Remember Spain: The Anarchist and Syndicalist Revolution of 1936*

MURRAY BOOKCHIN—*Which Way for the Ecology Movement?*

DANNY BURNS—*Poll Tax Rebellion*

CHRIS CARLSSON—*Critical Mass: Bicycling's Defiant Celebration*

JAMES CARR–*Bad*

NOAM CHOMSKY—*At War With Asia*

NOAM CHOMSKY—*Language and Politics*

NOAM CHOMSKY—*Radical Priorities*

WARD CHURCHILL—*On the Justice of Roosting Chickens: Reflections on the Consequences of U.S. Imperial Arrogance and Criminality*

WARD CHURCHILL—*Speaking Truth in the Teeth of Power: Lectures on Globalization, Colonialism, and Native North America*

HARRY CLEAVER—*Reading Capital Politically*

ALEXANDER COCKBURN & JEFFREY ST. CLAIR (ed.)—*Dime's Worth of Difference*

ALEXANDER COCKBURN & JEFFREY ST. CLAIR (ed.)—*The Politics of Anti-Semitism*

ALEXANDER COCKBURN & JEFFREY ST. CLAIR (ed.)—*Serpents in the Garden*

DANIEL & GABRIEL COHN-BENDIT—*Obsolete Communism: The Left-Wing Alternative*

VOLTAIRINE DE CLEYRE—*Voltairine de Cleyre Reader, The*

EG SMITH COLLECTIVE—*Animal Ingredients A–Z (3rd edition)*

HOWARD EHRLICH—*Reinventing Anarchy, Again*

SIMON FORD—*The Realization and Suppression of the Situationist International: An Annotated Bibliography 1972–1992*

YVES FREMION & VOLNY—*Orgasms of History: 3000 Years of Spontaneous Revolt*

BERNARD GOLDSTEIN—*Five Years in the Warsaw Ghetto*

DANIEL GUERIN—*No Gods No Masters*

AGUSTIN GUILLAMON—*The Friends Of Durruti Group, 1937–1939*

ANN HANSEN—*Direct Action: Memoirs Of An Urban Guerilla*

WILLIAM HERRICK—*Jumping the Line: The Adventures and Misadventures of an American Radical*

FRED HO—*Legacy to Liberation: Politics & Culture of Revolutionary Asian/Pacific America*

STEWART HOME—*Assault on Culture*

STEWART HOME—*Neoism, Plagiarism & Praxis*

STEWART HOME—*Neoist Manifestos / The Art Strike Papers*

STEWART HOME—*No Pity*

STEWART HOME—*Red London*

STEWART HOME—*What Is Situationism? A Reader*

JAMES KELMAN—*Some Recent Attacks: Essays Cultural And Political*

KEN KNABB—*Complete Cinematic Works of Guy Debord*

KATYA KOMISARUK—*Beat the Heat: How to Handle Encounters With Law Enforcement*

NESTOR MAKHNO—*The Struggle Against The State & Other Essays*

SUBCOMANDANTE MARCOS—*¡Ya Basta!: Ten Years of the Zapatista Uprising*

G.A. MATIASZ—*End Time*

CHERIE MATRIX—*Tales From the Clit*

ALBERT MELTZER—*Anarchism: Arguments For & Against*

ALBERT MELTZER—*I Couldn't Paint Golden Angels*

RAY MURPHY—*Siege Of Gresham*

NORMAN NAWROCKI—*Rebel Moon*

HENRY NORMAL—*A Map of Heaven*

HENRY NORMAL—*Dream Ticket*

HENRY NORMAL—*Fifteenth of February*

HENRY NORMAL—*Third Person*

FIONBARRA O'DOCHARTAIGH—*Ulster's White Negroes: From Civil Rights To Insurrection*

DAN O'MAHONY—*Four Letter World*

CRAIG O'HARA—*The Philosophy Of Punk*

ANTON PANNEKOEK—*Workers' Councils*

BEN REITMAN—*Sister of the Road: the Autobiography of Boxcar Bertha*

PENNY RIMBAUD—*The Diamond Signature*

PENNY RIMBAUD—*Shibboleth: My Revolting Life*

RUDOLF ROCKER—*Anarcho-Syndicalism*

RUDOLF ROCKER—*London Years*

RON SAKOLSKY & STEPHEN DUNIFER—*Seizing the Airwaves: A Free Radio Handbook*

ROY SAN FILIPPO—*A New World In Our Hearts: 8 Years of Writings from the Love and Rage Revolutionary Anarchist Federation*

ALEXANDRE SKIRDA—*Facing the Enemy: A History Of Anarchist Organisation From Proudhon To May 1968*

ALEXANDRE SKIRDA—*Nestor Mahkno—Anarchy's Cossack*

VALERIE SOLANAS—*Scum Manifesto*

CJ STONE—*Housing Benefit Hill & Other Places*

ANTONIO TELLEZ—*Sabate: Guerilla Extraordinary*

MICHAEL TOBIAS—*Rage and Reason*

JIM TULLY—*Beggars of Life: A Hobo Autobiography*

TOM VAGUE—*Anarchy in the UK: The Angry Brigade*

TOM VAGUE—*The Great British Mistake*

TOM VAGUE—*Televisionaries*

JAN VALTIN—*Out of the Night*

RAOUL VANEIGEM—*A Cavalier History Of Surrealism*

FRANCOIS EUGENE VIDOCQ—*Memoirs of Vidocq: Master of Crime*

GEE VOUCHER—*Crass Art And Other Pre-Postmodern Monsters*

MARK J WHITE—*An Idol Killing*

JOHN YATES—*Controlled Flight Into Terrain*

JOHN YATES—*September Commando*

BENJAMIN ZEPHANIAH—*Little Book of Vegan Poems*

BENJAMIN ZEPHANIAH—*School's Out*

HELLO—*2/15: The Day The World Said NO To War*

DARK STAR COLLECTIVE—*Beneath the Paving Stones: Situationists and the Beach, May 68*

DARK STAR COLLECTIVE—*Quiet Rumours: An Anarcha-Feminist Reader*

ANONYMOUS—*Test Card F*

CLASS WAR FEDERATION—*Unfinished Business: The Politics of Class War*

CDs

THE EX—*1936: The Spanish Revolution*

MUMIA ABU JAMAL—*175 Progress Drive*

MUMIA ABU JAMAL—*All Things Censored Vol.1*

MUMIA ABU JAMAL—*Spoken Word*

FREEDOM ARCHIVES—*Chile: Promise of Freedom*

FREEDOM ARCHIVES—*Prisons on Fire: George Jackson, Attica & Black Liberation*

JUDI BARI—*Who Bombed Judi Bari?*

JELLO BIAFRA—*Become the Media*

JELLO BIAFRA—*Beyond The Valley of the Gift Police*

JELLO BIAFRA—*High Priest of Harmful Matter*

JELLO BIAFRA—*I Blow Minds For A Living*

JELLO BIAFRA—*If Evolution Is Outlawed*

JELLO BIAFRA—*Machine Gun In The Clown's Hand*

JELLO BIAFRA—*No More Cocoons*

NOAM CHOMSKY—*An American Addiction*

NOAM CHOMSKY—*Case Studies in Hypocrisy*

NOAM CHOMSKY—*Emerging Framework of World Power*

NOAM CHOMSKY—*Free Market Fantasies*

NOAM CHOMSKY—*New War On Terrorism: Fact And Fiction*

NOAM CHOMSKY—*Propaganda and Control of the Public Mind*

NOAM CHOMSKY—*Prospects for Democracy*

NOAM CHOMSKY/CHUMBAWAMBA—*For A Free Humanity: For Anarchy*

WARD CHURCHILL—*Doing Time: The Politics of Imprisonment*

WARD CHURCHILL—*In A Pig's Eye: Reflections on the Police State, Repression, and Native America*

WARD CHURCHILL—*Life in Occupied America*

WARD CHURCHILL—*Pacifism and Pathology in the American Left*

ALEXANDER COCKBURN—*Beating the Devil: The Incendiary Rants of Alexander Cockburn*

ANGELA DAVIS—*The Prison Industrial Complex*

JAMES KELMAN—*Seven Stories*

TOM LEONARD—*Nora's Place and Other Poems 1965-99*

CASEY NEILL—*Memory Against Forgetting*

CHRISTIAN PARENTI—*Taking Liberties: Policing, Prisons and Surveillance in an Age of Crisis*

UTAH PHILLIPS—*I've Got To Know*

DAVID ROVICS—*Behind the Barricades: Best of David Rovics*

ARUNDHATI ROY—*Come September*

VARIOUS—*Better Read Than Dead*

VARIOUS—*Less Rock, More Talk*

VARIOUS—*Mob Action Against the State: Collected Speeches from the Bay Area Anarchist Bookfair*

VARIOUS—*Monkeywrenching the New World Order*

VARIOUS—*Return of the Read Menace*

HOWARD ZINN—*Artists In A Time of War*

HOWARD ZINN—*Heroes and Martyrs: Emma Goldman, Sacco & Vanzetti, and the Revolutionary Struggle*

HOWARD ZINN—*A People's History of the United States: A Lecture at Reed College*

HOWARD ZINN—*People's History Project*

HOWARD ZINN—*Stories Hollywood Never Tells*

DVDs

NOAM CHOMSKY—*Distorted Morality*

ARUNDHATI ROY—*Instant-Mix Imperial Democracy*